A Century of Giants

Think not that I am come to send peace on earth:
I came not to send peace but a sword.

Jesus Christ (Matthew 10:34, King James Version)

A Century of Giants

The greatest of the century's giants, many would agree, were undeniably the three shown on the cover: Luther, Loyola, and Calvin. But there were lesser giants, no less important to the events of the 1500s, including (from left to right) Emperor Charles V, who fought to unite Catholic and Protestant Christians against the descending armies of Islam; Philipp Melanchthon, who became Martin Luther's indispensable aide and successor; Francis Xavier, who brought Christianity to the great empires of the East; John Knox, who took Calvinism to Scotland and founded what would become the Presbyterian Church; Pope Paul III, who against every conceivable obstacle forced into being the Council of Trent, which defined the theological foundation of the Catholic Church for the oncoming modern era; William the Silent, who launched and led the war that would produce the amazing Dutch Republic; Don Juan of Austria, whose naval victory at Lepanto blocked the Islamic advance into Europe through the Mediterranean; and Queen Elizabeth I of England, whose compromise religious policies prevented in her realm such bloody warfare as shattered the Netherlands and France in her own time, and would largely destroy Germany in the ensuing century. Giants all, they and many more as well will be encountered in the pages that follow.

A.D. 1500 to 1600

In an age of spiritual genius, western Christendom shatters

The .
Christians
THEIR FIRST TWO THOUSAND YEARS

Ninth Volume

CHRISTIAN HISTORY PROJECT
An Activity of SEARCH
The Society to Explore And Record Christian History

THE EDITOR:

Ted Byfield has been a journalist for sixty-three years and was a western Canadian news magazine publisher for more than twenty-five. In 1973, he founded *Alberta Report* newsmagazine and in 1988 *British Columbia Report*. A columnist for many years with Canada's *Sun* newspapers and sometime contributor to the *National Post* and *Globe and Mail*, he was a winner of the National Newspaper Award for spot news reporting while serving as a reporter for the *Winnipeg Free Press* in the 1950s. He was also one of the founders of the St. John's Anglican schools for boys, where he developed a new method of teaching history. In the 1990s he became editor and publisher of *Alberta in the Twentieth Century*, a twelve-volume history of his province of Alberta. He was the visionary behind the Christian History Project and served as general editor of the first six volumes. When the project became insolvent in 2005, he formed SEARCH—the Society to Explore and Record Christian History—which has undertaken to publish volumes 7 through 12. Byfield is president of SEARCH and continues as general editor of the series.

THE DEPUTY EDITOR:

Ric Dolphin comes from a career in journalism that has included positions at *Maclean's* magazine, the *Globe and Mail*, the *Edmonton Journal*, the *Calgary Herald*, and the *Western Standard*. He worked for Ted Byfield's *Alberta Report* newsmagazine in the 1980s, helped write and edit the *Alberta in the Twentieth Century* history series in the 1990s, and his company Keystone Press published *The Book of Ted*, a compendium of Byfield columns.

THE COVER:

Pictured on the left are Martin Luther (top) from a 1525 painting by his German friend Lucas Cranach the Elder. Below is John Calvin, by the sixteenth-century Venetian master Titian (Tiziano Vecellio). On the right is Ignatius of Loyola, founder of the Jesuits, painted in 1556 by the Florentine Mannerist Jacopino del Conte. While by no means the only giants in this turbulent century, Luther, Calvin, and Ignatius were the men most responsible for moving Christianity from the relative stability of the Middle Ages into the theological and actual battlefields that bloodied this century and the one to come.

SEARCH CANADA:

The Society to Explore And Record Christian History is incorporated under the Alberta Societies Act. It has been registered as a charity by the Canada Revenue Agency.

Directors:

Ted Byfield, Edmonton, AB, President
Douglas G. Bell, CA, Edmonton, AB, Treasurer
Murray Lytle, Calgary, AB
Richard McCallum, Edmonton, AB
Allen Schmidt, Chase, BC

SEARCH USA:

The Society to Explore And Record Christian History is incorporated under the Societies Act of the Commonwealth of Virginia.
The society has been recognized by the Internal Revenue Service as a 501(c)(3) tax exempt organization, donations to which are tax deductible.

Directors:

Jaan Holt, Alexandria, VA, Chairman
Ted Byfield, Edmonton, AB, Canada, President
Christopher Gerrard, Rockville, MD, Treasurer
Douglas G. Bell, CA, Edmonton, AB
George Kurian, Yorktown Heights, NY
Richard McCallum, Edmonton, AB
Joe Slay, Richmond, VA
Keith T. Bennett, Edmonton, AB, Canada, General Manager

A Century of Giants, A.D. 1500 to 1600, In an age of spiritual genius, western Christendom shatters
being Volume 9 of the series: The Christians: Their First Two Thousand Years

Writers: Virginia Byfield, Vincent Carroll, Ric Dolphin, Francis Fast, D'Arcy Jenish, Jared Tkachuk, Lianne Laurence, Joe Woodard
Director of Research: Francis Fast
Assistant Director of Research: Adam Macpherson
Design and Art Director: Dean Pickup
Map Research and Design: Lianne Laurence
Indexer: Adrian Mather

Academic Advisers: Dr. David Appleby, tutor in history at Thomas Aquinas College, Santa Paula, CA; Dr. Peter Engle, Dean of Education at Living Faith Bible College in Caroline AB; David J. Goa, director of the Chester Ronning Centre for the Study of Religion and Public Life, Augustana campus, University of Alberta, Camrose; Fr. Brian Hubka, priest of the Roman Catholic diocese of Calgary, AB; Dr. Eugene TeSelle, emeritus professor of church history and theology, Vanderbilt University, TN

Research Readers: Ross Amy, Mary Chadworth, Deidre Collins, Pat Cooney, Richard de Candole, Celia DeCastro, Francis Fast, Adam Macpherson, Matt McCall, Pat Ryland, Jake Schmiedicke, Jared Tkachuk, Jim Wainwright, Joe Woodard

Style Control: Pro-Noun Editorial Services
Proofreaders: P. A. Colwell, Louise Fairley

Library and Archives Canada Cataloguing in Publication

    A century of giants, A.D. 1500 to 1600 : in an age of spiritual
genius, western Christendom shatters / editor: Ted Byfield.

(The Christians : their first two thousand years ; 9)
Includes bibliographical references and index.
ISBN 978-0-9689873-9-1

    1. Europe—Church history—16th century. 2. Church
history—Modern period, 1500-. 3. Protestantism. 4. Christianity
and politics. 5. Europe—History—16th century. I. Byfield, Ted
II. Society to Explore and Record Christian History
III. Series: Christians, their first two thousand years ; 9

BR305.3.C38 2010   270.6   C2010-906114-4
PRINTED IN CANADA BY FRIESENS CORPORATION

CONTENTS

MAPS

This engraving from the mid-1500s is of a map by the Dutch cartographer Gemma Frisius depicting the known world, and including the Tropics of Cancer and Capricorn, the equator, and the prevailing winds. The map reflects the then-limited knowledge of North America— labeled "Baccaleurum"—and the complete ignorance of the existence of Australasia.

FOREWORD

The first point most readers will notice about this volume is its size. Where the eight that preceded it all ran to 288 pages, this one is more than twenty percent larger and runs to 352. It has fourteen chapters where the earlier volumes usually had ten. It also covers a much narrower time frame, a span of one hundred years, where the time frames of all the earlier volumes, except the first and third, were much longer. Enlarging the size enlarged the cost as well as lengthening the time it took to produce the book, roughly nine months against an average seven months for five of the first six.

This was predictable. Humanity records its past in even hundred-year parcels called centuries, but what actually happens inside those neat packages is by no means evenly apportioned. As with our personal lives, where some years are almost uneventful and others bursting with change and activity, so too with history. And the sixteenth is a very eventful century indeed, when change was so explosive that we are still living with the results of it.

The fact that this explosion turned into a cosmic quarrel between Christians made the job of describing it an especially formidable challenge. Our goal is not to write a Catholic history, nor a Protestant history, but a Christian history in which both sides of the quarrel are represented as fairly as possible. In doing this, we have been greatly helped by our academic consultants. True, one Catholic academic felt we were far too influenced by the Protestant view of history, and one Protestant saw us as far too uncritically admiring of individual Catholic heroes, but with the criticisms coming from both sides, we concluded that we must be doing something right. Whether our readers agree, they will judge from the pages that follow.

My own most perceptive critic, namely the one I married sixty-one years ago, who has been editing and otherwise contributing to all these volumes, remarked rather dryly that I had personally failed to conceal either my "affection for Martin Luther" or my "fascination with the Jesuit order." Both charges are probably accurate; she is almost always right.

The only hero I consciously cherished, however, was the emperor Charles V, whose story leads the volume. For it was Charles, and sometimes Charles alone, who perceived what most others did not—namely, that the greatest threat to Rome was not Protestantism, and the greatest threat to Protestantism was not Rome. Both of them arguably were about to be destroyed by the Muslim Turks, who were moving down upon them with the most technologically advanced military machine in the world. To meet this threat, Charles struggled vainly to resolve the Catholic-Protestant conflict, even to the point of fighting wars, first against the Protestants and later against the papacy (although he himself was a devout Catholic). In the end his efforts at reconciliation did not succeed, and he died a failure in his own eyes, quite possibly even foreseeing the hideous catastrophe this conflict between Christians would inflict upon Germany in the coming seventeenth century.

But against the Turks the emperor was more successful. He united Catholics and Protestants long enough to save Vienna, though in the next century the Muslims would be back again at the city's gates. Moreover, at the Battle of Lepanto on the Mediterranean, thirteen years after Charles's death, his illegitimate son, the famous Don Juan of Austria, ended for good the threat of a massive seaborne Turkish invasion of southern Europe. This did not end the threat of terrorism, however. For another two hundred years and more, Muslim pirates wrought slaughter upon the coastal towns of Christian Europe, enslaving the marketable population and killing anyone else they could.

All of which might prove instructive to Christians facing renewed Muslim terrorism of another kind in our present century. For to extract from the past what may apply to the present is one of the things that history is about.

Ted Byfield

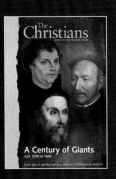

OUR THANKS GO OUT TO THE PEOPLE WHOSE FINANCIAL GIFTS TO SEARCH MADE THE PRODUCTION OF THIS VOLUME POSSIBLE

PATRONS OF THE PROJECT

L.R. Cable, Edmonton   Dr. Ernest Hodges, Edmonton   John Hokanson, Edmonton   Jack Klemke, Edmonton
Sandy Mactaggart, Edmonton   Gerald J. Maier, Calgary   Allan Markin, Calgary
Stanley A. Milner, Edmonton   Ray Nelson, Lloydminster, AB   Frank Vetsch, Calgary

THE TWELVE APOSTLES OF VOLUME 9

Due to the increased size of Volume 9, we encountered a cash shortfall as this volume went to press.
The following "Twelve Apostles of Volume 9" came to the rescue. We are most grateful.

Charles Allard, Edmonton   Richard Bird, Calgary   William L. Britton, Calgary
Margo S. Cable, Edmonton   James K. Gray, Calgary   Dan Klemke, Edmonton
Masha Krupp, Ottawa   Herman Leusink, Edmonton   Hugh MacKinnon, Toronto
Christine Peters, Tatla Lake, BC   Ed Sardachuk, Calgary   Al Stober, Kelowna

684 OTHER NORTH AMERICANS WHOSE GIFTS SAW THE VOLUME FINISHED

A-D

Jean Abt, Calgary AB; Walter Achtymichuk, Kelowna BC; Peter Adema, Acton ON; Joyce Agnew, Brandon MB; Ginny Alexander, 100 Mile House BC; Scott Allan, Fredericksburg VA; Charles Allen, Grapeland TX; Janice Allison, Veteran AB; Faye Altwasser, Yellow Grass SK; Bob & Karen Anderson, Orange MA; Maggie Anderson, Osseo MN; Virginia Andrews, Imperial MO; Harry Antonides, Dubuque IA; Brent Applegate, Calgary AB; Frances Apps, Burford ON; Gina Armstrong, Calgary AB; Kevin Armstrong, Calgary AB; Ken Ashley, Fort MacLeod AB; Art Ashton, Vancouver WA; Katherine Asleson, Moline IL; Herb Assman, Sherwood Park AB; Eckehart Augustini, Gibsons BC; Virginia Austin, Franklin NH; Leslie Avila, Germantown TN; John & Linda Bachmann, Mission BC; Owen Baker, Enderby BC; Irene Bakos, Calgary AB; Helen Balfour, West Vancouver BC; Kenneth Bannister, Edmonton AB; Casey Barendregt, Smithers BC; Marie Barkess, Delta BC; Norman Bartel, Kleefeld MB; Wilhard Barth, Waterloo ON; William Barthel, Coalhurst AB; Milton Bartos, Leask SK; Gary & Elizabeth Bartz, West Caldwell NJ; Eugene Batstone, Happy Valley Goose Bay NF; Wallace Bays, Wasilla AK; Muriel Beatty, Richmond Hill ON; Kelli Beaucage, North Battleford SK; Cornelis Beek, Cranbrook BC; Timothy Bees, Dubuque IA; Helena Bell, Saskatoon SK; Randall Belle, Coronach SK; Myfanwy Bentley-Taylor, Toronto ON; Elesa Bentsen, Duluth GA; Robert Berry, Winnipeg MB; Ronald Berry, Washington MI; Bruce Bieri, Rhodes MI; Alvin Bingaman, Seattle WA; David Bjorem, Tempe AZ; Dorothy Blaak, Abbotsford BC; E. David Blair, Calgary AB; Ken Blashill, Morinville AB; Rick Blevins, Great Falls MT; Myrna Bloch, Langley BC; Sandra Bogenholm, Los Alamos NM; Lillian Bokenfohr, St. Albert AB; Edna Bonertz, Drayton Valley AB; William Bontje, Red Deer AB; Joe Boonstra, Telkwa BC; Royce & Pietie Boskers, Ardrossan AB; Lorraine Boucon, Hart MI; Dale Bowler, Sherwood Park AB; Chris Boyle, Beausejour MB; Bill Braak, Abbotsford BC; James Bradfield, Berrien Springs MI; Stan Braim, Fairview AB; Jerry Brand, Rockville MD; Ron Braxton, Greenville NC; John Breneman, Shippensburg PA; Mark Brewster, London ON; Ralph Brinsmead, Calgary AB; Klaas Brobbel, Oakville ON; Deborah Brookfield, Calgary AB; Bill Brough, Cadwell IL; Ray & Beverley Brown, Vista MB; Hendrik Bruinsma, Brampton ON; Gene Buchanan, Walworth WI; Kristine Buchholtz, Sherwood Park AB; Michael Burgard, Bozeman MT;

John & Margaret Burnham, San Jose CA; Mary Burnie, Toronto ON; Carole Burton, Clarkes Beach NL; Graham Butcher, Stouffville ON; Carmen Bycok, Kingston ON; Sylvia Byrnes, Los Lunas NM; Sylvia Byrnes, Los Lunas NM; Tom Cadle, Peoria IL; Jill Cahoon, Tofield AB; Don Calvert, Slave Lake AB; Roy Calvert, Downers Grove IL; Howard Cameron, Manning AB; Carol Campbell, Aurora ON; Janne Campbell, Woodlawn ON; Elise Campbell, Monroe CT; Kenneth W Campbell, Calgary AB; Pat Carroll, Kamloops BC; Colin Catley, Calgary AB; Pamela Cavey, Janesville WI; Clarence & Femmie Cazemier, Red Deer AB; James Chabun, Emerald Park SK; Garfield Challoner, Norquay SK; Larry Chandler, Payette ID; Stan Chappell, Edmonton AB; Wilma Cheesman, Guelph ON; Jim Christie, Pickering ON; Dallas Christopherson, Olds AB; Andy Clark, Edmonton AB; Vivian Clark, Alliance AB; Judy Clark, Hoonah AK; David A Cline, White Rock BC; Jerry Cline, Williamsport PA; Joy Cline, Fort Myers FL; David & Sarina Cliplef, Onoway AB; Patrick Clock, Kalama WA; Robert Coleman, Everett WA; Donna Coleman, Bellingham WA; Stan Collier, Penhold AB; Shirley Colton, Calgary AB; Charles & Susan Conrad, Spartanburg SC; Mike Cooney, Edmonton AB; Dirk Cornish, Thorsby AB; Noel Corser, Hinton AB; Robert & Edith Coutts, Rolla BC; Marv Crombie, Armstrong BC; Timothy & Lori Culp, Taylor MI; Bert Dacosta, Kitimat BC; Bent Damkar, Stony Plain AB; Michael Davis, Orange Park FL; Derrick Day, Palos Verdes Estates CA; Maurice de Putter, Richmond BC; Ronali DeBock, Barrhead AB; Fred Demoskoff, Langley BC; Errol Dennison, Calgary AB; Daniel Dennison, Willowbrook IL; Marj Derochie, Claresholm AB; Gerrit & Wilma Dewit, Chilliwack BC; Michelle Dion, Bon Accord AB; James & Janice Dixon, Orchard Park NY; Mark & Adele Dolan, Hudson WI; Alice H. Doll, Smithers BC; Dan Domanski, Edmonton AB; Chris Dombroski, Edmonton AB; Mary Frances Doucedame, Newbury Park CA; Cliff Downey, Edmonton AB; Peggy Drehmel, Wausau WI; Steven Driggers, Avon IN; Robert Drinnan, Dunrobin ON; Robert Dueck, Red Deer AB; Tera Dueck, Sexsmith AB; Julia Duggan, Callander ON; Maida Duncan, Vancouver BC; Milt Duntley, Arkdale WI; Carol Dyck, Rosemary AB; John & Gisela Dyck, Brooks AB; John & Sue Dyck, Calgary AB;

E-I

Nancy Edmondson, San Anselmo CA; Bryan Elliott, Westwold BC; Lewis & Jane Elzinga, Peers AB; Peter & Michelle Englefield, Edmonton AB; Elizabeth Epp, Surrey BC; Terry Epp, St Albert AB; Lavern Erickson, Rosebud AB; Jon & Janet Erlandsen, Williston ND; Katie Everett, Windham NH; Caryl Evjen, Hampton MN; Audrey Ewanchuk, Edmonton AB; Lydia Fedor, Edmonton AB; Cornelius Fehr, Lowe Farm MB; Elsie Fehr, Barriere BC; John Fehr, Nipawin SK; Ruth Fehr, Kelowna BC; Bill Ferguson, North Pole AK; Norman & Sophie Filtz, Edmonton AB; Steven & Kristie Firme, Haxtun CO; Mark Fischer, Mokelumne Hill CA; John Fischer Jr., Inver Grove MN; Kathy Fisher, Farmersville TX; Tom & Marianne Flanagan, Calgary AB; Peter & Virginia Foley, The Woodlands TX; Marc Fontaine, Vonda SK; Keith Fowler, Edmonton AB; Jere Fox, Riverside CA; Hipolito Franco, Scarborough ON; Ron Frank, St. Albert AB; Katherine Frankos, Raleigh NC; Carol Fraser, Calgary AB; Sandra Frazier, Omaha NE; Harold Friesen, Calgary AB; Jack Friis, Lawrencetown NS; Laura Frost, Delta BC; Gwen Funk, Neville SK; Doug Gaetz, Surrey BC; Donna Gallier, Alabaster AL; Gloria Gardner, Port Carling ON; Deanna Gass, Arrowwood AB; Suzanne Gaudet, St. Louis SK; Allen Geary, Peace River AB; Jakob Geertsema, Ancaster ON; Herman Gelderman, Neerlandia AB; Therese Gervais, Morinville AB; Donald Gibson, Wall Lake IA; Bill Giebelhaus, Sherwood Park AB; Cliff Ginn, Claresholm AB; Judy Godsil, Auburn AL; Gloria Golka, St Albert AB; Edwin Good, Harrisonburg VA; Jim Goodvin, Edmonton AB; Luann Gorichanaz, Mukwonego WI; Sydney Goring, Odenton MD; Paul Gowdy, Kelowna BC; W. D. Grace, Edmonton AB; Charles Graham, Edmonton AB; William Green, Chilliwack BC; Ralph Greene, Brampton ON; Lori Griffin, Owatonna MN; Joseph Grill, Rochester MI; Norm Grinde, Wetaskiwin AB; Helen Griscowsky, Medicine Hat AB; Arie Grootenboer, Murillo ON; Maryanne Gross,

Independence MO; George Haack, Ste. Anne MB; Arnold Hagen, Camrose AB; Marguerite Hagen, Kaukauna WI; Frank Haley, Edmonton AB; Wilfred Haley, Loretto ON; Monika Halwass, Calgary AB; Harley Hammond, Tofield AB; Theresa Hango, Athabasca AB; Wayne Hansen, Sherwood Park AB; Ken Harcus, Edmonton AB; John Harder, Calgary AB; James Hargrave, Abbotsford BC; Myrna Hargrave, Cochrane AB; Kathleen Harjes, Green Isle MN; Arend Harke, St. Albert AB; Leonard Hart, Steinbach MB; Jerry Hart, Alliance OH; Fred Hauf, Edmonton AB; Arnot & Lenore Hawkins, Thunder Bay ON; Margaret Hearn, Victoria BC; Jakob Heckert, Ann Arbor MI; Gary Hedstrom, Owatonna MN; Elner & Alma Heebner, Regina SK; Henry Heinen, Picture Butte AB; Art Heinrichs, Calgary AB; John & Margaret Helder, Edmonton AB; Steve & Christine Hendrix, Tahsis BC; Owen Henry, Lapeer MI; Wayne & Gabriele Henze, Rose Prairie BC; Fred Herfst, Vancouver BC; Jorge Hernandez, West Palm Beach FL; Wayne Hertlein, Langenburg SK; Harry Hess, Edmonton AB; Brian & Barbara Hewitt, Granisle BC; Jim & Marcia Hibbert, Calgary AB; Graham Hicks, Edmonton AB; Richard Higgins, Rockville MD; Sandra Hill, Flint TX; Thomas & Catherine Hilton, Gibbons AB; Gary Hinkle, Bremen IN; Peter Hinterkopf, Waynesboro PA; Pamela Hladik, Stamford NY; Theresa Hodge, Blacksburg VA; Fremont Hodson, Temple TX; Fred Hofsink Sr., Smithers BC; Elaine Hogan, Curtice OH; Cory & Nora Holden, Finland MN; Tom Holder, Leduc AB; Chris Holmes, Comox BC; Paul & Ameda Hooley, West Liberty OH; Rosalie Howerton, Tyler TX; Brian Hubka, Calgary AB; Daniel Hudelson, Coopersville MI; Heidi Huff, Broomfield CO; Don Hughes, Edmonton AB; Bert Huizing, Abbotsford BC; Don Hurlbert, Escondido CA; Don Hurlbert, Escondido CA; Carson & Vicky Ikert, Stratton ON; David Imes, Crawford TX; Dudley Inggs, St. Helena CA;

J-M

Norman Jacobsen, Mission BC; Wallace & Pamela Jans, Medicine Hat AB; Jan Jansma, Port Alberny BC; Allen Janzen, Castlegar BC; Natalie Jerwak, Edmonton AB; Michael A Johnson, Chilersburg AL; Brad & Wendy Johnson, Red Deer AB; Connie Johnson, Warrensburg MO; Angie Johnston, Morristown TN; Oce & Max Jones, Clive AB; Robert Kalbach, Farmington NY; Ed & Linda Kalish, Brewer ME; John Katrichak, Sparwood BC; Everett & Marlo Kearley, Saskatoon SK; Maria Kemp, West Hills CA; Henry Kennedy, Calgary AB; Forrest & Jenny Kennerd, Cochrane AB; John & Donna Kennison, Jacksonville FL; Steven Keske, Lakeville MN; Nagui Khouzam,Winter Garden FL; Shirley Kiffiak, Picture Butte AB; Robert Kimball, South Lake Tahoe CA; Jitsche Kingma, Smithville ON; Donald & Jeanne Kirchner, Onomowoc WI; Lutz Klaar, Prince George BC; Stacey Kleiboer, Meskanaw SK; Thomas & Linda Knott, Baltimore MD; Earl Koch, New Hamburg ON; Alois Kolinsky, Edmonton AB; Eric Kolkman, Ardrossan AB; Dino Konstantos,Woodbridge ON; Phyllis Kopen, Edmonton AB; William Korvemaker, Dorchester ON; Cor Korver, Lethbridge AB; Barry Kossowan, Edmonton AB; Ed Kowalenko, Calgary AB; Darlene Kraft, Saskatoon SK; David Kronberg, Minneapolis MN; Maureen Krueger, Orange CA; Donna Kuhn, Spokane WA; Jim Kulchisky, Calgary AB; Virginia Kurtz, Cape Elizabeth ME; Lillian Lafrance, Longueuil QC: Michael & Rose Marie Lalor, St. Albert AB; Oakley & Ruby Lambert, Columbus MS; Thomas Landers, White Rock BC; Hazel Landgraf, Spruce Grove AB; Dorothy Lane, Athabasca AB; Janine Langan, Toronto ON; Elva Langland, Bassano AB; Judy Langner, Edmonton AB; Carl Langstaff, Calgary AB; John & Marjorie Lawrence, Calgary AB; Anthony Leenheer, Edmonton AB; Ed Lehman, Edmonton AB; Charles Lester, Tallahassee FL; Donald & Mary Lincoln, Adrian GA; Victoria Link, San Diego CA; Wil Link, Vacaville CA; Don & Lynda Lipsett, Summerland BC; Edward Littleton, Valencia CA; Louise Lobdell, Carbon AB; Betty Lockhart, Dayton NV; Joe Lorencz, San Leandroo CA; Norm Lorenz, Dunster BC; Don & Joyce Low, Vancouver BC; Dorothy Lowrie, St. Albert AB; Paul Lowrie, Anahim Lake, BC; Philip & Sandra Luchka, Lethbridge, AB; David Lunsford, Redding CA; Dale Lunty, Edmonton AB; Roy Luyendyk, Cremona AB; Maria Lyon, Indianapolis IN; Heather Maahs, Chilliwack BC; Don & Jean MacDonald, Elrose SK; Murdoch & Katherine Macleod, Calgary AB; Juanita Mahieu, Davenport IA; Emmanuel Malterre, Calgary AB; James Marchant, St. Lambert QC; Gary & Gladys Marcial, Calgary AB; Ernie Marshall, Edmonton AB; Ernie Marti, Medicine Hat AB; Allan Martin, Mount Forest ON; Erma Martin, Cochrane AB; John & Coralie Martin, Kayville SK; Chris Martin, Houston TX; Laura Matsuda, Lone Butte BC; Lilly Matzigkeit, Kelowna BC; David Maxwell, Adrian MI; Sharon Mayo, Arlington TX; Bruce McAdam, Olney MD; Neil & Nancy McAskill, Burnaby BC; Richard McCallum, Edmonton AB; Ron McCarthy, Columbia TN; Gerald McClintock, Tucson AZ; Alex & Ruth McCombie, Chesley ON; Donna McCormick, Toronto ON; Donna McCullough, Suffolk VA; John & Sharon McCune, Edmonton AB; Patrick McDonald, Lethbridge AB; William & Freda McGill, Edmonton AB; Joanne McGlinch, Lima OH; Annie McIntyre, Langley BC; Audrey McKay, Blackfalds AB; John McKean, Edmonton AB; Jim McKee, Woodville ON; Monty McKenzie, Strasbourg SK; Candis McLean, Calgary AB; Dolores Meckelborg, Calgary AB; Allan Megli, Linden AB; Patricia Mehlberg, Lawrenceville GA; Norma Melindy, Aspen Cove NF; Peter Mendes, Edmonton AB; Jessie Mercer, Calgary AB; Thomas & Beverly Mercer, Langley BC; James Merz, Sherwood Park AB; Jessie Middleton, Abbotsford BC; John Miedema, Edmonton AB; Milford Miller, Boise ID; Theryn Mills, Edmonton AB; Dave Mitchell, Vulcan AB; Jon Mitchell, Sherwood Park AB; Walter Mitchell, Lumby BC; Candace Molberg, St. Albert AB; Carol Monk, Delta BC; Celestine Montgomery, Edmonton AB; Gwendolyn Montrose, Abilene TX; Christopher Morbey, Sydney BC; Casey Moroschan, Edmonton AB; Shirley Moss, Medicine Hat AB; Sandra Mulcahy, Arlington TX; John Mulder, Coalhurst AB; Patricia Murphy, Sudbury ON; Rodger Murry, Napoleon OH; Hugh Mutlow, Siske SK; Jim Myers, Columbia Heights MN; Leslie Myram, Prince George BC; Einar Myrholm, Edmonton AB;

N-S

Thomas Nelson, Birmingham AL; Timothy Nelson, Walnut Cove NC; Floyd Neuen, Okotoks AB; Chuck & Melva Neufeld, Penticton BC; Reinhard Neufeld, Winnipeg MB; Philip Ney; Victoria BC; Don Nielsen, Red Deer AB; Kent Nielsen, Calgary AB; Doris Nikkel, Lundar MB; Erland Nord, Edmonton AB; Cathy Nordli, High River AB; Dan Odom, Valdosta GA; Betty Offerdal, Conrad MT; Agnes Olfert, Drumheller AB; David & Doreen Olson, Camrose AB; Shawn & Amy Oltz, Niles MI; Valerie Omelchuk, Stenen SK; Esther S. Ondrack, Spruce Grove AB; Gloria Opgenorth, Edmonton AB; John Opmeer, Richmond BC; Kevin & Lise O'Reilly, Mission BC; John & Trudy Paetkau, Edmonton AB; Carl Palmateer, White Post VA; Ken Palmer, Calgary AB; Neville Pearson, Moncton NB; James Peck, New Wilmington PA; Fred Pedersen, Innisfail AB; Philip Pelletier, Calgary AB; Edna Penner, Linden AB; Gloria Peronto, Ishpeming MI; Edward Peter Franck, Bangor SK; Gene Petersohn, Sheboygan WI; Donald E Peterson, Rose Prairie BC; Paul Peterson, Hazelton BC; Kenneth Petruk, Edmonton AB; Dallas Petry, Edmonton AB; Howard Pettengill, Indialantic FL; Tina Philipsen, Olds AB; Fred & Marilyn Pilon, Richmond Hill ON; Rick Plett, Linden AB; Edward Plume, Calgary AB; Paul Pollex, St. Thomas ON; Kim Poon, Markham ON; Bill Pordhowski, Calahoo AB; Graeme Postill, Airdrie AB; Nathan & Jodi Powell, Logan IA; Tom Powrie, Edmonton AB; Priscilla Poynter, Lexington KY; Eberhard Preisinger, St. Albert AB; Jake Prins, Lacombe AB; Peter & Kim Pytlik, Naples FL; Barry R. Giovanetto, Calgary AB; Bill Raap, Winnipeg MB; Joseph & Mary Radulovich, Shelbyville KY; David Rainforth, Lacombe AB; Cheryl Ranns, Victoria BC; Eugene Ratsoy, Edmonton AB; Bill Rawlins, Qualicum Beach BC; Redeemer Lutheran Church of St. Cloud, St. Cloud MN; Randy Redekop, Vauxhall AB; Faith Reece, Hazel Park MI; Holly Reed, Nepean ON; Anne Reedyk, Three Hills AB; Gordon Reid, Cremona AB; Nora Reimer, Winnipeg MB; Sidney Reiners, Grand Rapids MN; Fred & Teresa Reitsma, Smithers BC; Frank Rempel, Swift Current SK; Kathleen Reyes, San Jose CA; Linda J. Reynhout, De Smet SD; David & Deborah Reynolds, Burnsville MN; Edward Rice, New Hartford NY; Stephen & Janet Richards, Thorsby AB; Sam Richter, Calgary AB; Darrell Riemer, Pine Lake AB; Tom Rigby, Littleton CO; David Robbins, Alhambra CA; William Robertson, Ellijay GA; Ted Rodgers, Spokane WA; Miriam Roemmich, Edmonton AB; Dirk Rook, Cobden ON; Patricia Rooke, Victoria BC; John Rosevear, Knowlton, QC; Denise Roth, Saskatoon SK; David Rousseau, Haverhill MA; Clay Rowe, Gadsden AL; Doug & Geri Rozander, Okotoks AB; Rosalind Russell, Maple Ridge BC; Kathleen Rutledge, Edmonton AB; Wim Ruysch, Rolly View AB; Harold Sadler, Tofino BC; Suzie Sage, Republic WA; Diane Sandberg, Lake Elsimore CA; Helmut Sass, Winnipeg MB; Robert Saunders, Winnipeg MB; Bill Saxon, Guyton GA; Ken Schade, Kitchener ON; Mervin Schafer, Calgary AB; Hans Schaffland, Calgary AB; Richard Schalich Mesa WA; Corry Schalk, Strathroy ON; Dan Schmidt, Aurora IL; Linda Schramm, Sandusky MI; Lois Schulte, Okotoks AB; Ellis Scott, Stratford ON; Robert Scott, Redding CA; Seed Sowers Christian Books Publishing House, Jacksonville FL; Burke Seitz, Don Mills ON; Gordon Setterlund, Sherwood Park AB; Margaret Sever, Gardnerville NV; Margarida Sewell, Langley BC; Arnold & Elna Sexe, Worthington MN; William Sheehan, Pasco WA; Darrel Sheppard, Mobile AL; Janet Shostak, Kinuso AB; David Shoulders, Monument CO; Doug & Janis Siemens, Morrin AB; Gwen Silkwood, Morgan Hill CA; James Simmons, Murray KY; Gay Simpkins, Grants NM; David & Mary Skelton, Edmonton AB; Don Skolly, Woodstock ON; Harry Slagter, Calgary AB; Alma Small, Edmonton AB; Marianne Smit, Edmonton, AB; Adrian Smith, North Vancouver BC; Derrell S Smith, Innisfail AB; Jeff Smith, Fredericton NB; Oliver Smith, Fort Assiniboine AB; Walter Smith, Shreveport LA; Robert Smith, Cedar Park TX; John Snesar, Abbotsford BC; Morris & Helen Sobool, Peachland BC; Victor Sopkiw, Calgary AB; Brenda Spark, Lloydminster SK; Walter Spencer, Rochester Hills MI; Carol Stankievech, Calgary AB; Roy & Sarah Steffen, North Collins NY; Linda Stein, Toronto ON; Spencer Stevens, Calgary AB; Harold Stiansen, Calgary AB; Chris Stodola, Osoyoos BC; Lief Stolee, Edmonton AB; Don Strauch, Tucson AZ; Martin Stribrny, Edmonton AB; Donald L. Stuva, Osceola IA; Herb Styles, Calgary AB; Rebecca Sullivan, Reidsville NC; Laura Swehla, Pillager MN; Audrey Swinton, Edmonton AB; Richard Sykes, Aiken SC; Bill Szaroz, Carstairs AB;

T-Z

Marvin Tegen, Midland MI; Jim Telford, Abbotsford BC; Dick & Erlyce Tenhove, Blackfalds AB; Henry Thalheimer, Kelowna BC; Larry Theis, Shelbyville TN; Horst Thiele, Pitt Meadows BC; Caral Tholenaer, Calgary AB; William Thompson, Winston Salem NC; Bonnie Thomson, Pickering ON; Terry Thomson, High River AB; Albert & Elizabeth Tiemstra, Barrhead AB; Earl Tilleman, Crossfield AB; Will Timmer, Abbotsford BC; Gerald Toews, Grande Prairie AB; Myron & Lynn Toews, New Norway AB; Peter & Elsie Toews, Olds AB; Tim Toews, Beaverlodge AB; Jeffrey Toivonen, Barrhead AB; Ivan Tomlinson, Beaverton ON; John Tors, Toronto ON; Rose Tratch, Wetaskiwin AB; Maurice Tremblay, Port Renfrew BC; John Trueman, Quesnel BC; Dave Turner, Edmonton AB; William Turner, Kamloops BC; Judith Tyrrell, Ottawa ON; Gloria Uldrich, Hot Springs AR; Martin Ulrich, Cochrane AB; Stefan Ulrich, Claresholm AB; Christa Unger, Drayton Valley AB; Gordon Unger, St. Albert AB; Henry Unrau, Edmonton AB; Richard Updegraff, Eau Claire PA; Bob Valek, Columbus IN; Joe Van Aerden, Okotoks AB; Ernie & Helen Van Boom, Ft. Saskatchewan AB; Roy Van Boom, Leduc AB; Frans Van de Stroet, Iron Springs AB; Ary Van Es, Burdett AB; Jacob & Christa Van Gelder, Corner Brook NL; Harry & Jane Van Gurp, Belmont ON; Adriaan & Evelyn Van Hoeve, Cochrane AB; Willy Van Randen, Surrey BC; Dorothy Van Sant, Louisville KY; Jean Van Wieringen, Picture Butte AB; Arie Van Wingerden, Sunnyside WA; Oliver Vandagriff, Ormond Beach FL; Rick Vandenberg, Telkwa BC; Leonard Vanderhoeven, Woodstock ON; Martin Vanderspek, Norwich ON; Andy Vanderveen, Carman MB; Kelvin Vanderveen, Carman MB; William & Tine Vandervelde, Dorchester ON; Hans & Rita Van'tland, Coalhurst AB; Michael Veenema, Fall River NS; Bram & Joanne Vegter, Spruce Grove AB; Melvin Veldhuizen, Loveland CO; Gary Veraghen, Dearborn MI; Peter & Barbara Verhesen, Trochu AB; Steve & Luella Vetch, Valleyview AB; Hank Vissers, Qualicum Beach BC; Bonnie Vocque, Pollock LA; William Voron, Johnson City TX; Chris Voss, Mission TX; Richard & Deborah Wagner, Jackson TN; Ken Waite, Ucluelet BC; Don Wakelam, Nanton AB; Al Walker, Athabasca AB; Roger Wall, Durham NC; Tamara Wallinga, Coopersville MI; Doreen Walls, Edmonton AB; Hazel Walter, Cemesco MI; Fred Walz, London ON; Ray Ward, Mantua OH; Eldora Warkentin, San Luis Obispo CA; Reginald Watson, Sundre AB; Bill Webb, Calgary AB; Tom Webber, Tampa FL; Esther Weeks, Orion AB; Alfred Weimann, Sherwood Park AB; Doris Westoby, Brookings OR; Gerald Wheeler, Calgary AB; Edward Wiater, Toronto ON; David Wiens, Duchess AB; Melvin Wiens, Beechy SK; Harvey & Coreen Wierenga, Smithville ON; Tom & Mary Ellen Williams, Rochester AB; Dorothy Willms, Montney BC; Chris Wilson, Delta BC; Dale & Bel Wilson, Edmonton AB; Helen Wilson, Calgary AB; Eldon Wilson, Newport NY; Samuel Wilson, Fox Lake IL; John Witmer, Houston TX; Jim Wolter, Victoria BC; Don Woodbridge, Summerland BC; Rosanne Woods, Calgary AB; Charles Wootten, Matoaca VA; Henry Woudstra, Edmonton AB; Iris Wright, 150 Mile House BC; J W Wright, Rouleau SK; Lyle Wright, Kerrobert SK; Elyssa Wright, Roanoke VA; Scott Wycherley, Townsend WI; James Yoder, Bonanza OR; Sheila Ypma, Taber AB; Rodney Zabel, Elkhart Lake WI; Jacob Zekveld, Camlachie ON; Dan Zelinger, Kenosha WI; Marlys Zimbelman, Fullerton ND; Donald Zoell, Sherwood Park AB

SEARCH thanks all those hundreds of other supporters who by ordering extra copies of Volume 1 enabled us to convert some of our huge inventory into cash, all of which went into this volume's production. Donations received after Sept. 1, 2010, will be applied to the production of Volume 10 and recorded on the donors' page of that volume.

A sixteenth-century portrait by Titian depicts the emperor Charles V at the height of his problems and his power. (It may also be the most flattering ever done.) He had traveled a long, perilous road since assuming, as an unprepossessing youth of seventeen, his vast and precarious inheritance. No flashy Renaissance-style prince, Charles Habsburg was a plodder, but his strongest loyalty was to Jesus Christ and the Catholic Church.

CHAPTER 1

A divided Christendom and its young emperor face the Muslim peril

Constantinople is gone, the Balkans are fallen, the Turkish army is the world's most formidable, and Europe must depend on an unpromising youth

In about January of the year 1517, the sultan Selim I—recognized with good reason as "Selim the Grim" by his tens of thousands of Christian slaves and his untold millions of admiring Muslim subjects—resolved upon a major campaign in the West. It was time, he decided, to achieve the crowning triumph of his spectacular reign by vanquishing, finally and forever, those benighted and accursed infidels known as the Christians.

Selim's grandfather Sultan Mehmed II (the Conqueror), had made a crucial start some six decades earlier by seizing the last Christian bastion in the East, which the sultans before him had surrounded but never taken in their seemingly inexorable invasion of eastern Europe. By enslaving some fifty thousand of Constantinople's Greeks and putting to the sword all those too young or too old for the market, Mehmed transformed the Byzantine capital into a Turkish city almost overnight. The magnificent Cathedral of the Holy Wisdom, *Hagia Sophia*, became a mosque, as did nearly all the city's Christian churches.

By the time Mehmed the Conqueror died in 1481, he and his predecessors had succeeded in imposing the directives of the Koran on Greece, Albania, and most of Bulgaria along with the region that became European Turkey, requiring Christians and Jews to live as second-class subjects known as *dhimmis* in ghetto-like communities. (See p. 58.) Further, he had reduced Macedonia, Croatia, Bosnia, and Serbia to the status of vassal states, and many of their Christian inhabitants had seen fit to embrace Islam.

Mehmed's son and successor Sultan Bayezed II appears, by contrast, to have been more interested in improving the lot of his subjects than in adding to their

Sultan Selim I "the Grim" (above), ruler of millions of Muslims, master of hundreds of thousands of Christian slaves, commander of the world's largest army, and western Europe's looming threat.

number. But Bayezed's son and heir, the future Selim the Grim, held these irenic policies in such contempt that he overthrew his father and arranged to have him fatally poisoned. Then, as was becoming customary among the Turks, Selim had his own two brothers strangled, along with his nephews, to discourage future dynastic challenges.

He next campaigned eastward and demolished the army of the Shi'ite Persians, simultaneously eliminating thousands of Shi'ites in Anatolia itself, all Shi'ites being regarded by the Sunni Ottomans as odious heretics. Nor was Selim's taste for the sanguinary limited to his enemies. Senior servants lived in constant terror, and the heads of seven successive viziers ended on the chopping block. To the south, meanwhile, his armies proceeded to conquer Syria, Palestine, Egypt, and Arabia.

Altogether, Selim the Grim would triple the size of the Ottoman Empire. Moreover, when Cairo capitulated, he triumphantly induced the last Mamluk sultan to surrender to him the title of "caliph"—that is, to recognize him as successor to Muhammad himself and to pass on to him the Prophet's reputed standard, sword, and mantle. Then, after subduing western Arabia and taking control of the holy cities of Mecca and Medina, he added "Servant of the Two Holy Shrines" to his existing titles.

His logical next step was to consolidate Turkish holdings in the Balkans and clear the way for the conquest of Christian Hungary and Austria. After that, fragmented Germany could be swiftly subdued, and Islam would rule forever on the Rhine. Specifically, the Ottomans must first take three key cities on the mighty Danube: Belgrade at the mouth of its tributary the Sava, then Buda some two hundred miles northwest, and then, just 135 more miles upstream, the major prize, Vienna.

Selim had every reason for confidence. His army was the world's biggest, with an inexhaustible supply of replacement manpower from the Asian steppes. At its core were the renowned Janissaries, crack soldiers seized as youths from Christian families, circumcised, indoctrinated in Islam, and trained to devote life and limb to the sultan. Backing the army was a centralized bureaucracy, also staffed and managed by the sons of conquered Christians conscripted from their families as children and "educated" into the service of Allah. Finally, his soldiers were arguably the world's best equipped and particularly well supplied with cannon, the latest and most decisive weapon of war. In any even match, they were almost certain winners.

But the match was by no means even. Pitted against the highly centralized autocracy of the Muslim colossus was the chaotic Christian shambles known as the Holy Roman Empire, a conglomerate of some three to four hundred German duchies, counties, and petty princedoms, its emperor chosen by the seven "electors" who ruled its principal components, its army a piecemeal assembly of contributed troops whose conduct was as uncertain as their pay. The title of Holy Roman Emperor was august, ancient, and everywhere solemnly reverenced, but what powers did the emperor actually have? No one really knew. The empire officially included, for instance, a few of the wealthy little states of northern Italy, over which successive emperors, would-be emperors, popes, kings, and king-makers had been quarreling for more than four hundred years. The three rising powers of the West—France, England, and most recently Spain—jockeying constantly for alliances with or against one another, always took the empire into account, but none had managed to gain control of it.

Until, that is, the rise of the emperor Maximilian I, patriarch of the boundlessly ambitious Habsburg family. While Selim was conquering the East by means of

While Sultan Selim was conquering the East by means of war, Maximilian, patriarch of the boundlessly ambitious Habsburgs, was busily conquering the West by means of matrimony.

war, Maximilian was equally busy conquering the West by means of matrimony. By wedding his son to the daughter of Spain's joint monarchs, Ferdinand and Isabella, and his daughter to their only son, he cemented a nuptial bond connecting the Iberian Peninsula, the German principalities, the Netherlands, and Italy. This amounted to a virtual European union—except that it left the French trapped in a Habsburg pincer and determined to escape it by somehow frustrating Maximilian's vast scheme.

Fate intervened and almost saved France the trouble. Ferdinand and Isabella's son died young and childless. Maximilian's son Philip died young too—but not

Emperor Maximilian I (left) looks upon his family: his first wife, Mary of Burgundy (right); their son, Philip the Fair (center); his two grandsons, Ferdinand I (left) and Charles V (center); and his grandson-in-law, Ludwig II of Hungary (right). Maximilian found one could conquer by calculated matrimony as effectively as by war.

before his wife had borne him two sons. Upon the elder of these grandsons Maximilian now placed all the Habsburg hopes, backing him as his own successor on the imperial throne and thereby also conferring upon him the central duty of thwarting the aspirations of Selim the Grim. In 1517, as the victorious sultan turned from his conquest of Egypt and looked westward, this grandson was not yet seventeen years old.

Nor did young Charles of Burgundy present, by many accounts, very promising imperial material. He was generally described as shy, dull, unimaginative, plodding, slow of speech, and primly pious—in short, an anachronism utterly out of touch with the style, philosophy, and morality of the sixteenth-century Renaissance ethos. Even his facial appearance, despite a broad forehead and clear blue eyes, was marred by an extraordinarily prominent lower jaw (a persistent characteristic in the Habsburg line). All told, in an age when what would one day be called charisma mattered much in a ruler, poor Charles seemed to possess no charisma whatsoever.

Above, the future Charles V poses for his portrait in a suit of armor, a gift from his grandfather Maximilian. The nineteenth-century painting below, by Edouard Jean Conrad Hamman, depicts dutiful young Charles in court, listening intently to a learned lecture by the celebrated humanist scholar Erasmus of Rotterdam.

He did, however, demonstrate certain other notable qualities. He could be trusted to tell the truth, for example, and to keep his promises. Court chroniclers describe him as quietly courteous and kind, diligent, and intelligent. He was said to be physically agile and to have learned to ride a horse before he learned to talk. Furthermore, his strongest loyalty was clearly to Jesus Christ and the church, possibly due to the influence of his tutor, the deeply devout Bishop Adrian of Utrecht who (much to Charles's disadvantage) would one day be pope.

But family, too, loomed large in Charles's regard. His affection for the three sisters with whom he spent his childhood in the Netherlands—Eleanor two years his senior, Isabella a year younger than he, and Maria five years younger—would last their lifetimes, as would theirs for him. This bond may have been forged by the fact that they were raised almost as orphans. Due to the strained marriage of their playboy father, Archduke Philip of Burgundy, called *le Beau* (the Handsome), and his Castilian wife, known to history as "Mad Joan," after earliest childhood they scarcely saw their parents.

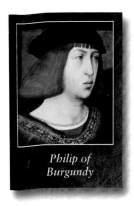

Philip of Burgundy

Ferdinand of Aragon

The family moved from Flanders to Spain in 1501, when Charles was a year old, but problems in the Netherlands soon called Philip back north. Joan, who never could bear to be away from him, soon followed and spent three unhappy years at the Flemish court, incensed by her husband's constant philandering. In April 1506, accompanied by a troop of Flemish mercenaries, they returned to Castile, where Philip quarreled bitterly with his father-in-law, King Ferdinand of Aragon, over the Spanish monarchy. This abruptly ended, however, with Philip's death that September at the age of twenty-six.

The widowed Joan sank into a paroxysm of grief, refusing to be separated from his coffin or to allow his body to be buried. The following January saw the birth of her fourth daughter, Catherine, who would be raised entirely in Spain.[1] There, too, the unhappy Joan would remain, in deepening mental distress. (A rare visit by Charles and his sister Eleanor to their closely guarded mother, some ten years later, is described in the chapter on the Spanish monarchy in vol. 8, p. 182–3.) Also raised in Spain was Ferdinand, second son of Philip and Joan, born at Alcalá de Henares in 1503 and educated at the court of his grandfather Ferdinand.

At this point, grandfather Maximilian, as Habsburg patriarch, assigned to his twice-widowed daughter Margaret the task of educating the four older children, and also appointed her duchess of Burgundy and regent of the Netherlands. The children were very fond of her, formally addressing her as "lady aunt and good mother," and she of them. She did an equally good job politically, writes the German historian Karl Brandi (*The Emperor Charles V*, 1939), who rates her "one of the greatest rulers of the sixteenth century." Thus when much of Europe would stand against her nephew, Margaret would ensure that the Low Countries remained loyal.[2]

Charles's boyhood was brief, almost nonexistent. We find him at age seven attending all meetings of the ducal council and approaching the frugal burghers of Louvain to seek an increased subsidy for his aunt's government. At eight he writes to grandfather Ferdinand in support of someone's request for a government position. At fifteen he assumes the title archduke of Burgundy and reorganizes his court. He notably asserts his authority as family head to veto a supposed "love match" that young Frederick, Count Palatine, was trying to engineer with Charles's sister Eleanor. (Charles banished Count Frederick.)

He did go through what seems very like a teenaged rebellion, inspired by his wily and ambitious chamberlain, Guillaume de Croix, lord of Chèvres. This was aimed directly at his aunt Margaret, whom Chèvres aspired to supplant as regent of the Netherlands. Acting on his own, Charles arranged for Chèvres to accompany him on his first official tour of the lands of the House of Burgundy (i.e., present Netherlands, Belgium, and parts of northern France). But Maximilian quickly vetoed this idea, and Margaret became Charles's official companion instead.

1. All four of the daughters of Philip the Handsome of Burgundy and Joan the Mad of Castile would make appropriate, if not necessarily happy, marriages: Eleanor (1498–1558) to Manuel I of Portugal and later to Francis I of France, Isabella (1501–1526) to Christian II of Denmark, Maria (1505–1558) to Louis II of Hungary and Bohemia, and Spanish-born Catherine (1507–1578) to John III of Portugal.

2. Duchess Margaret of Burgundy was a strong and decisive personality in every respect but not inclined to seek power by assuming male roles. When her father wanted her to attend a military exercise, for example, she replied that she would do so because he asked her to, "but beyond that it is not the place of a widowed woman to go about visiting armies for pleasure."

This pleasant sixteenth-century portrait by Nicolaus Alexander Mair von Landshut provides no hint that the lovely woman depicted would be known to history as "Mad Joan." Always temperamentally fragile, Joan of Castile was entirely overcome at the early death of her beloved husband. The children are Charles and his sister, Eleanor.

The following year, a new opportunity arose for him to assert personal authority when death claimed Ferdinand of Aragon. Next in line for the thrones of both Aragon and Castile was Joan. By then, however, she was deemed unfit to reign. This made her son heir to all Spain and the expanding Spanish possessions in America. In 1517 he sailed south to be recognized as such, accompanied by Chèvres and other Flemish grandees, all intent upon assuming the titles and wealth they were sure would come with the Spanish crown.

When their ship foundered in a storm, they had a harrowing landing on the rocky Iberian coast. But that was minor in comparison to the political storms they provoked after their arrival, in contending with which Charles made some of the worst mistakes of his life. With the young monarch's full approval, Chèvres and company began assigning to themselves the most powerful and lucrative offices in the realm, and Charles, as a "foreigner" who could neither speak the language nor understand the rigorous etiquette of the Spanish court, soon found himself facing multiple rebellions. Only with great difficulty did he secure the affirmation of his monarchy by Castile's *cortes*, while the cities of Toledo, Salamanca, Valencia, and Valladolid verged on outright revolt. It took nine months to affirm his claim to the crown of Aragon—and even then the Aragonese nobles required that he reign jointly with his mother.

Two years later came a development that further incensed his Spanish subjects. On January 12, 1519, the emperor Maximilian died without achieving the last and probably greatest challenge of his reign, to assure in advance the election of his chosen grandson as his successor. Charles's agents nonetheless managed to bribe the imperial electors far more lavishly than all other rival contenders, so the newly

enthroned king of Aragon and Castile soon received the joyous news that he also had been unanimously elected emperor. His Spanish subjects were not so enthusiastic. As they had predicted, it seemed that this honor guaranteed chiefly one thing, namely that their monarch would find a hundred new places, far distant from Spain, to spend the vast fortunes pouring in from their possessions in America. When Charles sailed for Germany in 1520 to receive the imperial crown, at least three Spanish cities were in open revolt.

Yet his first Spanish sojourn had been in one respect an unqualified success. He had at last made the acquaintance of his Spanish brother, Ferdinand, and they had got on very well indeed. In fact, they formed a partnership that would endure through all the pitfalls and chaos that lay ahead of them both. Ferdinand, it would ultimately be decided, would become duke of Austria and rule in the east while Charles ruled in the west, an arrangement carrying two implications probably foreseen by neither. First, it created a division between the Spanish and Austrian Habsburgs that would endure for generations. Second, it meant that Ferdinand as duke of Austria would stand squarely in the path of the oncoming Turks. Younger brother Ferdinand would have to take the hit.

Somehow, in the midst of it all, Charles grew up and grew wise. The disastrous Chèvres soon died, saving Charles the unpleasant task of firing this longtime mentor along with all his opportunistic colleagues, who, he now realized, might have cost him the Spanish crowns. Never again, he resolved, would he place non-Spaniards in positions of authority in his Spanish realm. Neither would he ever again regard any man's advice as infallible; he would think things out for himself. Finally, and without hesitation, he restored his aunt Margaret as his regent in the Netherlands.

Charles also became conscious of another reality. While at first he had disliked the Spanish, possibly as much as they disliked him, in a sense he had much in common with them. Like him, they belonged more to the old order of things than the new. They were soldiers, something he had always wanted to be. They took their Christian faith very seriously, as did he. They thought that promises, particularly marriage vows, must be kept, as did he. True, by this time Charles himself had fathered an illegitimate son, a fact so far hushed up. (This was sinful, he knew, but less so than if he had already been a married man.) Although raised in the Netherlands, Charles had definite Spanish affinities.

While at first Charles disliked the Spanish, as they disliked him, they had much in common. They were soldiers, they took the faith seriously, and they thought that promises should be kept.

En route north he stopped briefly in England to meet the bluff and portly Henry VIII, his uncle by marriage (to Catherine of Aragon, Joan's sister). As a boy Charles had been betrothed to Henry's sister, Mary Tudor, later acclaimed as the most beautiful woman in England; at age eight he had been required to write her a love letter. But this arrangement was canceled in 1514 so that Mary, then aged eighteen, could marry Louis XII of France, aged fifty-two. (Louis died less than twelve weeks later—exhausted, it was said, by his unsuccessful efforts to sire a male heir—and the widowed Mary subsequently wed the duke of Suffolk.) Two other matrimonial plans for Charles had also foundered: one to Claude, eldest daughter of Louis XII, to whom he had been engaged at the age of one; the other to Renée, Louis XII's second daughter, when he was fifteen. Now that he was emperor-elect, he could negotiate his own marriage, but he had nothing immediate in mind.

Henry VIII

3. By tradition, the Holy Roman Emperor must first be crowned king of the Romans at Aachen, Germany, and crowned again as emperor, usually by the pope. Charles's predecessor, Maximilian I, had reigned as emperor without papal coronation, however, and Charles was the last to receive it. His successors became merely "emperors-elect," and the qualifier "elect" was soon dropped. The final Holy Roman Emperor would be Francis II of Austria (1768–1835), who in 1806, after his defeat by Napoleon at the Battle of Austerlitz, would style himself simply emperor of Austria.

4. The editors apologize for following academic advice and referring to this historic assembly as the "Reichstag of Worms" rather than the "Diet of Worms," thereby depriving English-speaking history students of what has been a source of amusement for close to five hundred years.

On October 22, 1520, not yet twenty-one years old, Charles was crowned at Aachen under the ancient title "king of the Romans," becoming in effect emperor-in-waiting, for he must still be crowned by the pope as well.[3] Leaving Aachen and preparing to attend a *Reichstag* (i.e., a parliament, sometimes translated into English as a "diet") to be held at the city of Worms[4] at this time, he must have been preoccupied by three problems. Two were major or would become so; the third he likely regarded as a preposterous nuisance.

Though problem number one was the Turks, the immediate threat to Charles's empire posed by the menacing Selim the Grim seemed to be evaporating. Just before launching his conquest of Europe, Selim had decided to attend to one last matter in the south. The Knights Hospitaller still held the island of Rhodes, off the coast of Turkish Anatolia, where they could imperil commercial traffic into Turk-controlled

Alexandria, and while leading an enormous army against Rhodes, the much-feared Selim the Grim suddenly died. Officially the cause was sirpence, a skin disease acquired from livestock, although some historians suggest cancer and others that Selim was poisoned by his physician. In any case, an elated Pope Leo X assured Christendom that Süleyman, Selim's son and successor, was "a gentle lamb" and ordered a Mass of thanksgiving for this benevolent new sultan.

Problem number two, which showed no sign whatsoever of evaporating, was the new French monarch, Francis I.[5] The contrast between Charles and Francis could hardly have been greater, for Francis was the preeminent Renaissance man. He was a lavish patron of the arts, poetic, witty, socially charming, brilliant in conversation, and a sexual libertine. Indeed, he seemed to be uninhibited by any moral scruple and, therefore, boundlessly tolerant of cultural or religious nonconformity—until, that is, it directly threatened him. Francis I was, in short, everything that Charles was not. Then, too, Charles had beaten him badly in the imperial elections. For reasons of both state and personal rivalry, Francis was a dangerous enemy.

As for the third problem, it must have seemed to Charles so bizarre as to defy rational understanding. Apparently some mendicant friar in Saxony, in defiance of all ecclesiastical authority, was somehow swaying untold thousands of people into increasingly militant opposition to the papacy. Although Pope Leo X had declared him a heretic and had excommunicated him by papal bull in June of 1520, the German princes, one of them in particular, were providing him refuge. Charles might order his arrest but had been convincingly warned that this could lead to armed revolt, even civil war. So he temporized. Over the vigorous objections of the papal legate, he cordially invited the obstreperous monk to appear before the upcoming Reichstag of Worms and guaranteed him safe-conduct. The man's name: Martin Luther. ■

Charles V is crowned king of the Romans by Pope Clement VII, assisted by the archbishops of Cologne, Trier, and Mainz. This papal coronation, which took place in Rome nearly ten years after Charles's crowning as emperor at Aachen, was the last of its kind. After the Protestant Reformation the emperor was no longer crowned by a pope.

5. King Francis I of France, born in Aquitaine in 1494, inherited the French crown because none of the three wives of his predecessor, Louis XII, had managed to produce a male heir. Francis's father was Louis' first cousin, and at the age of twelve Francis was betrothed to Louis' daughter Claude, duchess of Brittany (the same who had earlier been affianced to the infant Charles of Burgundy). Francis and Claude were married in 1514 and a year later became king and queen of France.

Martin Luther's statue, standing huge and heroic in Hesse, Germany, points the way to heaven. Salvation is gained through faith alone, he proclaimed—through total surrender to the will of God—and not through so-called good works or papal injunctions. This was a message that resonated deeply with so many Germans it ignited the Protestant Reformation.

CHAPTER 2

The coarse-tongued genius who founded Protestant Christianity

Martin Luther's incendiary writing split Christendom—though he didn't intend it. Yet he spoke to men's souls as none else did, and a grasping nobility saw a bonanza

We are to imagine a meadow ringed with trees, on a sultry summer afternoon. As evening approaches, the sky darkens ominously. There is a rumbling of thunder. The wind rises. Soon rain lashes the earth. Cracks of lightning, growing louder, seem to shake the land. The wind is now fierce. Trees crash to the ground. Running through them in wild terror we perceive a young man. Suddenly lightning strikes so near that it knocks him to the ground. He grasps at the earth, gasping a prayer. Save my life, he pleads, and I will devote it to God. The date is July 2, 1505. The meadow is near the Saxon village of Stotternheim in Thuringia. The young man is Martin Luther, and in such a scene as this he would attempt thirty years later to describe the event that changed his life—a life that in turn would change the path and shape of Christianity in the West.

Luther, who came from mining country, had addressed his prayer to St. Anne, patroness of miners. His friends assured him that a promise made under such circumstances could be discounted, but he stood by his vow and fifteen days later offered himself as a novice at the Augustinian monastery in Erfurt. His father, Hans, who was working his way up from unskilled laborer to ownership of six mines and two foundries, was understandably outraged. Martin was his second son and the most promising of his nine children, and Hans had invested heavily in educating him as a lawyer. Now, at age twenty-two, with a master's degree in law, Martin proposed to spend his life as a mendicant friar! To his furious father this seemed a disaster.

A popular twenty-first-century tourist destination is the meticulously preserved Luther Room in the former monastery in Wittenberg, Germany, where Martin Luther lived and worked for almost thirty-five years, as a lecturer, theologian, and polemicist as well as a husband and father. From here he bombarded critics and dispensed stern but kindly pastoral advice. The portrait (below), painted in 1525 by Lucas Cranach the Elder (1472-1553), depicts him as a young man.

Whether or not young Luther's resolve was indeed disastrous would be debated by the Christian world for the next five centuries. Among the Augustinians he diligently applied himself to whatever work was assigned him, was ordained priest after only two years, visited Rome as part of an Augustinian mission, and actually impressed the order's vicar-general, Johann von Staupitz, as a possible successor. But one specific characteristic in young Father Martin began to gravely concern von Staupitz and others also, namely a morbid propensity to doubt his vocation. This tendency made one early and unsettling appearance, for example, while Luther was celebrating his first Mass, normally an occasion for joyful commemoration. His father, resigned now to his son's vocation, proudly attended, along with some twenty friends. But at the point in the liturgy where the priest, having lifted up the sanctified bread, intoning of "the terrible divine majesty," the neophyte celebrant seemed stricken with terror, tried to run from the church, and had to be restrained by a fellow priest. He would explain years later that the thought of holding God in his hands had horrified him.

This sense of his own unworthiness kept deepening, he wrote, until he came to dread making confession and, when he did so, might spend up to six hours in the confessional. Eventually he concluded that genuine commitment to God was impossible—the Deity was demanding conduct of which his creatures were simply incapable. In this "hellish torment of the soul" he came to hate God, and celebrating the Mass became repugnant to him. He was acutely and painfully aware of Satan and of the evil in his own heart, and was terrified of both.

Little of this seems to have been outwardly apparent. Father Martin developed into a skillful teacher and awe-evoking preacher. Physically he presented an impressive figure—swarthy and husky, with deep-set and radiant eyes (which some future enemies would describe as demonic). Socially he was humorous, boisterous, and companionable, a great beer drinker and singer, at home in any crowd. His career within the Augustinian order prospered. By 1512 he had a doctoral degree and was a theology professor in the new university that Elector Frederick III of Saxony, one of the most powerful men in the empire, had founded in his capital city of Wittenberg. Even Frederick himself seemed to fall under

Johann von Staupitz

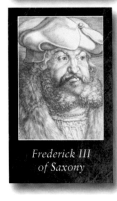

Frederick III of Saxony

the powerful spell of this new faculty member.[1]

The following year, Luther began a series of lectures on the Psalms and the Epistles to the Galatians and Romans. His students took notes and passed them round, sparking interest in the exciting new professor. Attendance at his lectures soared, as did awareness that in crucial particulars Luther's ideas were increasingly at odds with church teaching. He had discovered in the Psalms, for example, grounds for attack on the Aristotelian view that God can be explored through human reason, a theory embraced by Aquinas in the thirteenth century (see vol. 7, ch. 7) and later by the church as a whole.[2] Luther poured vehement scorn on both Aristotle and Aquinas, insisting that God can become known solely as he reveals himself through the Bible.

The "scholastic" theology

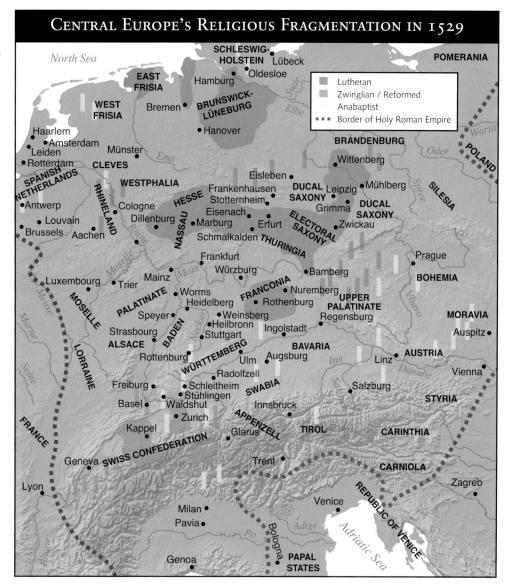

CENTRAL EUROPE'S RELIGIOUS FRAGMENTATION IN 1529

Lutheran
Zwinglian / Reformed
Anabaptist
▪▪▪ Border of Holy Roman Empire

North Sea
SCHLESWIG-HOLSTEIN   Lübeck   POMERANIA
Oldesloe
EAST FRISIA   Hamburg
WEST FRISIA   Bremen   BRUNSWICK-LÜNEBURG
Hanover
Haarlem   BRANDENBURG
Amsterdam   Münster   Wittenberg
Leiden   CLEVES
Rotterdam   Eisleben   Oder   POLAND
SPANISH NETHERLANDS   WESTPHALIA   Frankenhausen   DUCAL   Leipzig   Mühlberg   SILESIA
Antwerp   RHINELAND   HESSE   Stotternheim   SAXONY   Grimma   DUCAL SAXONY
Louvain   Cologne   Eisenach   ELECTORAL   Zwickau
Brussels   Aachen   Dillenburg   Marburg   Erfurt   SAXONY
NASSAU   Schmalkalden   THURINGIA
Frankfurt   Prague
Würzburg   Bamberg   BOHEMIA
Luxembourg   Trier   Mainz   Main   FRANCONIA
MOSELLE   Worms   Nuremberg   UPPER PALATINATE   MORAVIA
PALATINATE   Heidelberg   Rothenburg   Auspitz
Speyer   Weinsberg   Regensburg
Heilbronn   Ingolstadt   AUSTRIA
Strasbourg   BADEN   Stuttgart   BAVARIA   Linz   Vienna
ALSACE   Rottenburg   WÜRTTEMBERG   Augsburg   Inn   Danube
LORRAINE   Ulm   Radolfzell   Salzburg   STYRIA
Freiburg   Schleitheim   SWABIA   Innsbruck   CARINTHIA
Basel   Stühlingen   Waldshut   APPENZELL   TIROL
Kappel   Zurich   Glarus   CARNIOLA
Geneva   SWISS CONFEDERATION   Trent   Zagreb
FRANCE
Lyon   Venice   REPUBLIC OF VENICE
Milan   Adige   Adriatic Sea
Pavia   Po
Genoa   Bologna   PAPAL STATES

that dominated the church, he argued, had turned the Bible into an encyclopedia of irrelevant abstractions, whereas it ought to be treated as the uniquely indispensable manual of the faith, through which God communicates with humanity. Emphasis on Christ crucified, not on "dense theology," must be restored, he declared. If mind and soul are open and attentive to God, he promised, constant reading of the Gospel will pour grace upon a faithful Christian as the sun warms still water. Furthermore, matters of faith must be settled by the Bible alone, for human reason may resolve questions pertaining to this life, but not about the nature and activity of God. As for the canon law of the church, it was "an obstructive, cancerous excrescence which spelt death unless it was cut away."

This emphasis on the Bible was nicely timed. Copies of the scriptures in vernacular languages were appearing throughout western Europe in numbers hitherto unimaginable, due to the invention of moveable type and efficient printing presses (see sidebar, p. 14). Soon any literate person would be able to read scripture—a situation offering great benefit but also, from the standpoint of Christian unity, great danger. Meanwhile, Luther's confidence grew, and his challenge to traditional Christian teaching broadened accordingly. If a man could find salvation in the Bible alone, of what use were the clergy? Strictly speaking, he began to

1. By 1510 Germany had thirteen universities, fully half of them founded in the previous fifty years. This was only two fewer than Italy, birthplace of the Renaissance, and one fewer than France. Spain had just five universities in all, England two. Wittenberg, which would become Luther's lifetime headquarters, had a population of three thousand. Its chief industry was brewing beer, and it had two monastic foundations, those of the gray-clad Franciscans and black-habited Augustinians.

2. Aristotle believed in God but purely in the abstract. The notion of prayer in which we communicate with God, or God with us, was unthinkable to Aristotle—though not, of course, to Aquinas.

The man who made Luther possible

Printing's innovator was secretive, much sued, and prone to disappearing

Johann Gutenberg needed more money. In three years he had spent no less than eight hundred gulden borrowed from lawyer Johann Fust (enough to have bought several sizable farms), and now, amazingly, he wanted as much again. Even more amazing, Fust was willing to loan it—at six percent interest, of course—but only if he, too, could get in on the "business of the books." The shrewd Fust saw riches ahead, but he could not possibly have foreseen how drastically Gutenberg's enterprise would change the world. The year was 1452, the place was Mainz, Germany, and Gutenberg had just invented the printing press.

Notwithstanding Gutenberg's crucial historic role, much of his life remains a mystery. His name was Johann Gensfleisch zur Laden, Gutenberg being the family's ancestral home. His father, Friele, was an aristocrat and a businessman, probably a cloth merchant, in Mainz. No accurate portrait of Johann exists. A birth date of 1400 is an educated conjecture. He never signed nor dated his printed pieces. Details of his education and youth are negligible, and misfortune (when at pivotal periods he landed in court) is often the sole source of records of his life.

Just such a pivotal period, in Strasbourg in 1439, followed the death of one of Gutenberg's three business partners, Andreas Dritzehn. On that occasion a strange apparatus in Dritzehn's quarters allegedly was dismantled on Gutenberg's orders and other devices melted down. Dritzehn's brothers

sued to be part of his consortium, but so tight-lipped were Gutenberg and his colleagues about their project that legal documents refer to it only as the "art and adventure." Gutenberg won that case, but in 1444 he departed Strasbourg for parts unknown, leaving behind his debts and a well-stocked wine cellar. Four years later he resurfaced in Mainz, where he was so successful that by late 1454 he had completed the printing of the famed Gutenberg Bible—an estimated 180 copies, all of them sold beforehand.

Before Johann Gutenberg's marvelous innovation, books had either to be laboriously copied by hand or painstakingly produced as "block books" in which a page of text was carved in mirror-image relief on a wooden block. The image was then transferred by laying a sheet of paper on the inked block, and rubbing or "burnishing" it. Gutenberg's genius was to produce each individual letter as a single piece of moveable metal type. He cast these by pouring a soft metal alloy, mainly lead, into matrices of harder metal in which the indented form of the letters had been punched. These small metal letters could be assembled in infinitely varied combinations to produce the text, exponentially faster than carving in wood. Composed into a page, they were locked into forms and inked. Gutenberg's press then transferred the image to paper with one firm imprint—again, much quicker than rubbing.

The Gutenberg Bible, of which forty-nine copies survive, was nevertheless an immense undertaking. Consisting of two volumes, 324 and 318 pages respectively, it likely was copied from an illuminated manuscript of the Latin Vulgate. It was printed in black ink—a mixture of soot, varnish, and egg white—with its red highlights ("rubrication") and illuminations added later by hand. But Johann Gutenberg had no time to collect his profits. New partner Fust sued him for the amount of his loan plus interest, and also charged him with embezzlement, accusing him of ignoring their major enterprise—presumably the Bible—to print other jobs, notably papal indulgences and warnings against the Turks.

In November 1455 Johann Fust (who, incidentally, is cited by some as the inspiration for the Dr. Faust of German legend who sold his soul to the devil) won his lawsuit and took over the Gutenberg shop. Two years after that, Fust and a longtime employee named Peter Schoeffer published the stunning two-color *Latin Psalter*, the first dated book printed in Europe. Some see Gutenberg's own hand in the psalter's intricate designs, possible evidence for Fust's claim that he had neglected the famous Bible to work on other alluring projects. Gutenberg, deprived of his shop, meanwhile dropped from sight again. Perhaps he found another patron and resumed

Despite the major effect that Johann Gutenberg exerted upon the world, no accurate portrait exists of the man who made possible the process of printing. Even this formidable painting by William Wilke von Radierung is pure conjecture.

printing; possibly he was among the eight thousand citizens exiled after the city was sacked in 1462. But he appears once more in the records as receiving an annual pension after 1465 from Archbishop Adolph of Mainz and, when he died three years later, seems not to have been destitute.

As for the printing industry, it experienced such phenomenal growth that in 1471 a typesetters' strike is recorded in Basel. By 1500 an estimated 1,100 printing shops were operating in 240 European towns. While humanist scholars delighted in the production of Latin and Greek manuscripts, vernacular publications also multiplied. According to Stephan Füssel (*Gutenberg and the Impact of Printing*, 2003), the number of vernacular publications between 1501 and 1517 tripled in the following eight years. The watershed date was 1517, the year Martin Luther issued his Ninety-five Theses.

Luther's works, Füssel estimates, account for fully one-third of German books printed between 1500 and 1550. His 1518 sermon on indulgences was reprinted twenty-five times in two years. His 1522 German translation of the New Testament had an initial press run of three thousand, and by mid-century an estimated half-million copies were in circulation. But he was not alone in recognizing the potential of the press. Cardinal Nicholas of Cusa, for example, reform minded and a brilliant philosopher, early introduced this powerful technology in Italy.

Luther himself naturally ascribed the new art to divine inspiration and the impetus through which "God drives the objectives of the evangelists forward." Printing, he proclaimed, "is the last flame before the extinction of the world." His prophecy would not quite hold, of course. Other powerful "flames" in mass communication—radio, cinema, television, and the Internet, for example—would follow and arguably eclipse this one. But that would require another five centuries. ∎

Johann Gutenberg (below) examines the first proof from his revolutionary innovation. He died in 1468 and by the mid-sixteenth century an estimated half million copies of Luther's New Testament would be circulating. At right, his reconstructed workshop in the Gutenberg Museum, Mainz, Germany.

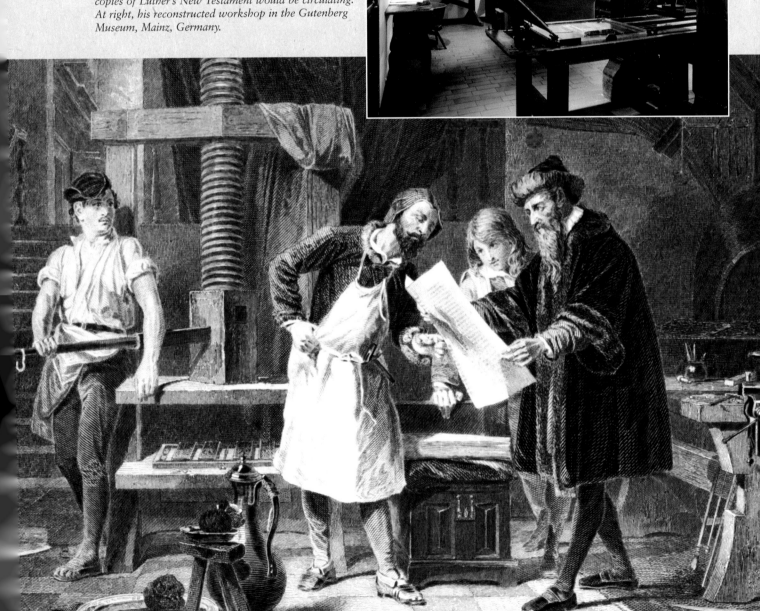

The title of a sixteenth-century woodcut says it all: The Holy Communion of the Protestants and Ride to Hell of the Catholics. *At left, Protestants diligently earn God's favor; at right, his wrath is poured upon Catholic practices.*

3. Verses 13 through 19 of the sixteenth chapter of the Gospel of St. Matthew, where Jesus asks his disciples who they think he is, have arguably occasioned more controversy than anything else in the New Testament. When Simon replies, "You are the Christ, the Son of the living God," Jesus responds: "You are Peter ["stone" in Greek], and upon this rock I will build my church, and the gates of hell shall not prevail against it. I will give you the keys of the kingdom of heaven. Whatever you bind on earth will be bound in heaven, and whatever you loose on earth will be loosed in heaven." Roman Catholics believe that this commissioned Peter as supreme head of the church and that the power of "the keys" descended to his successors as bishops of Rome. The Eastern Orthodox and some Protestant scholars hold that Peter's primacy among the apostles was a matter of first among equals and that his powers never extended beyond his western patriarchy. Many Protestants interpret the word "rock" as referring to the content of Peter's confession of faith—that is, that Jesus is the Son of God—not to Peter himself, and they cite Augustine as holding the same view. Many recent Protestant scholars, however, have accepted the contention that the assertion must surely have applied to Peter, not to his confession of faith.

claim, no intermediary whatever is needed between God and the individual soul, since every baptized Christian has direct access to the Almighty. Then what about the pope? Here Luther took the gloves right off. The notion that Jesus instituted the papacy was mere fiction, he charged, and the papacy an invention of the medieval church.[3]

At some point between 1515 and 1518, when Luther began his lectures on the Epistle to the Romans, he made the "discovery" that he said altered his entire concept of the Christian faith. The verses were Romans 1:16–17:

> I am not ashamed of the gospel, because it is the power of God for the salvation of everyone who believes: first for the Jew, then for the Gentile. For in the gospel, a righteousness from God is revealed, a righteousness that is by faith from first to last, just as it is written, "The righteous will live by faith."
>
> (New International Version)

As a "rudely demanding man," writes Luther of himself, he had for years "raged with a furious and stormy conscience." But while meditating upon this "forbidding text," he received a "great revelation." He had always assumed that the "righteousness of God" was something God did *against* sinners like himself. He now realized it is what God does *for* sinners. God's mercy is not offered as recompense for our attempted goodness. We can in no sense *win* God's approval, and therefore our salvation is not a sort of transaction but God's free gift. Christ through his death has saved us. Our individual attempts to contribute to this process are worthless—our sole function is to acknowledge our hopeless bankruptcy and receive the mercy of God.

In this light, Luther offered a different view of the Holy Communion, the Lord's Supper. In the thirteenth century, following the teaching of Aquinas, Christians in the west had embraced the doctrine of transubstantiation. Five years after Luther's death the Catholic Church at the Council of Trent, over against the emerging Protestant teachings, would endorse it as dogma (see pp. 191, 194). But this explanation suggested to Luther a mechanical process unaffected by the attitude of either celebrant priest or recipient communicant. Rather, he argued, here too the essential element must be abject surrender to God. His analogy pictured God as present in the bread and wine as fire is latent in a red hot iron. If what it touches is combustible, it will burst into flame. If not, then nothing occurs. This doctrine would come to be called *consubstantiation*.

The indignant response of Catholic Christians was led by the Dominicans, writes historian Richard Marius (*Luther: The Christian Between God and Death*, 1999), who at the time were the most ardent, and least popular, of the orders. They noted that Luther was not calling for reform of a faithless church, something the Dominicans themselves had been demanding for several centuries, nor was he targeting indolent priests, avaricious bishops, or dissolute popes. He was targeting the normal practices of devout priests, genuinely pious bishops, and all popes, good or bad—targeting, indeed, the papacy itself. Critics particularly objected to two of his contentions. First, they maintained, he must concede that the meaning of many biblical passages is elusive, even downright baffling, so who was to interpret them? Luther himself, as a kind of substitute pope? Or was every individual to provide his own answers—every man his own church, so to speak? Precisely so, was Luther's unsettling reply; that was indeed what he was advocating—a "priesthood of all believers." "If you succeed," said a papal nuncio, "you will place a pope in every heart."

Second, his critics continued, surely he was not claiming that nothing a man does—his good works or bad—can have any effect whatsoever upon God's ultimate judgment. What of the moral teaching of Jesus himself: the Sermon on the Mount, the parables, the Beatitudes? Are these not guides for Christian behavior? Must we believe that deeds count for nothing, that all we need is faith and God does the rest? By faith, Luther insisted, he did not mean mere acquiescence to a set of theological dogmas. He meant total trust in God. From this, good works would inevitably result, but the saving factor was the grace of God, received through faith, not through works.

Such were the issues raised and expanded by the treatises he poured forth from Wittenberg. Reprints and copies, spreading across Germany with alarming speed, became the talk of nobles, knights, merchants, soldiers, monks, and priests, and soon everyone was involved, literate or not. What secret enchantment, people wondered, did this fellow Luther possess? Was he moved by the Spirit of God? Or by Satan, perhaps? Or might his power simply lie in the novelty of Bible reading, combined with endemic resentment of papal exactions?

The more astute realized that Luther had somehow tapped into an urgent need in many souls. "The faith that saves," Jesuit priest John Patrick Donnelly would write 450 years later (*Reform and Renewal*, 1977), "is a casting of the whole self, naked and helpless, upon God's mercy, a clinging to Christ crucified who alone delivers man from his corruption . . . God became man, endured human pain, suffered human death, and has now risen as the first-born of the new creation. On the eve of the Reformation, Germans were God-obsessed and God-starved. Luther preached a God they could trust, who could satisfy their hunger."

A typical Reformation-style pamphlet, published in 1520, shows the devil sitting on an indulgence slip and holding a crosier and money casket. A whole tableful of clerics is crammed inside his mouth. Some of the sufferings of hell play out atop his head, while to the right, two of his demons are dragging in more souls—some wearing miters.

An oil-on-wood painting, one of several portraits by the reform leader's friend and devotee Lucas Cranach the Elder, reveals a more mature Martin Luther. He appears fiercely determined and more confident of his stance—confidence that was about to be severely tested. Although by this time he had definitively broken with Rome, he continued to be depicted wearing the same outfit—a black robe and cap—that he would have worn as an Augustinian monk.

4. In a ribald poem, Luther portrays a monk reading Matins while seated on the monastery latrine. The devil admonishes him for irreverence. "You can't read Matins here," he chides. The unrepentant monk replies: "I am cleansing my bowels and worshiping God Almighty. You deserve what descends and God what ascends."

Something else may also have endeared Luther to ordinary people. The earthiness, indeed coarseness, of his language, which abounds in scatological metaphors, was less jarring perhaps in the sixteenth century than in some later eras but notable even then. He habitually bombarded critics (as well as the devil, with whom he was seemingly in constant conflict) with words that can be adequately translated into English only by vulgarities.[4] Indeed, notes historian Heiko A. Oberman (*Luther: Man between God and the Devil*, 1982), this element in his writings has inspired some critics to attribute his intolerance of the church to the digestive afflictions that plagued him lifelong. Luther fought God, they claimed, chiefly because he was constipated.

He also dispensed down-to-earth pastoral advice, however, both stern and kindly. Avoid solitude, he writes to a young man afflicted by doubt and depression. Don't get into arguments with the devil—hold him up to ridicule, for the devil cannot bear scorn. "Whenever the devil pesters you with these thoughts," Luther continues, "at once seek out the company of men, joke and jest, or engage in some other form of merriment. Sometimes it is necessary to drink a little more, play, jest, or even commit some sin in defiance and contempt of the devil, in order not to give him opportunity to become scrupulous about trifles. We shall be overcome if we worry too much about falling into some sin."

Yet another quality in Luther's writing often cost him dearly, namely the increasing bitterness with which he assailed his adversaries, regularly consigning them to the "everlasting flames" and accusing them of being "ignorant, stupid, and impious, of committing sacrilege against the word of God," and of "wounding the whole gospel." A bishop who neglected God's word was "a wolf and an apostle of Satan." The church's universities were "synagogues of Satan." Of the early fathers he wrote, "I do not care if a thousand Augustines, a thousand Cyprians, a thousand churches of Henry [meaning England's King Henry VIII, who had formally attacked him] stand against me. God cannot err or fail. Augustine and Cyprian, like all the elect, can err, and they did err." As for the papacy, he demanded of his fellow Christians, why "do we not fling ourselves with all our weapons upon these masters of perdition, these cardinals, these popes, and all this sink of Roman sodomy that ceaselessly corrupts the church of God, and wash our hands in their blood?"

Such fulminations distressed many a friend and follower, including the highly respected biblical scholar Desiderius Erasmus. The work of Erasmus, who was widely recognized as the principal voice of Renaissance humanism in northern

Desiderius Erasmus

Europe, was an early and powerful influence upon Luther (see sidebar, p. 20). Some observers, in fact, dismissed the noisy friar as essentially a kind of "crude Erasmian." Erasmus himself, ruefully agreeing, tried to exercise a friendly and moderating influence, and he deplored among much else Luther's virulent response to any criticism.

His spectacular rages might have ended as a mere footnote to history, however, but for the arrival in neighboring Brandenburg in 1517 of a firebrand Dominican preacher named Johann Tetzel. A sixteenth-century prototype of some less savory twentieth-century televangelists, Tetzel was a super-salesman of indulgences, those papal certificates against which Luther so vehemently inveighed. In the ideal, an indulgence was something acquired by risking one's life on a crusade, paying to the church a sum of money as a sacrificial substitute for some other penance, perhaps replacing a lengthy fast. The practice was easily abused, however, and the ideal often sullied. By Luther's time one could purchase exculpation from purgatorial punishment for sins committed, sins one planned to commit, or sins committed by

Johann Tetzel

departed loved ones. Flagrant indulgence sales had been controversial throughout the fifteenth century, but the church had become dependent on the revenue. Presented as being the least one could do for a departed wife or beloved child, they sold especially well on behalf of the dead.

"As soon as the coin in the coffer rings, the soul from purgatory springs," was Tetzel's alluring pitch.[5] His mission had a specific goal. Half the proceeds were to compensate the plump, genial, and ambitious Albrecht von Hohenzollern of Brandenburg for the immense sums he had spent to purchase for himself the archiepiscopal sees of Mainz and Brandenburg. The other half would go to Pope Leo X to finance the massive new St. Peter's under construction at Rome. Wittenbergers swarmed over to nearby Brandenburg to hear the Dominican spellbinder, inspiring Luther to new heights of polemic.

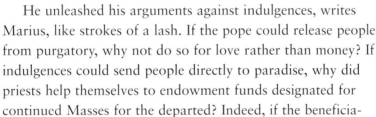

Pope Leo X

He unleashed his arguments against indulgences, writes Marius, like strokes of a lash. If the pope could release people from purgatory, why not do so for love rather than money? If indulgences could send people directly to paradise, why did priests help themselves to endowment funds designated for continued Masses for the departed? Indeed, if the beneficiaries were now safely in heaven, why not return the endowments to their families? And why did the pope demand money from poor Germans to build St. Peter's when wealth was pouring into Rome from the whole Christian world?

5. Edith Simon, a German-born English sculptor and historian, in her biography of Luther (*Luther Alive: Martin Luther and the Making of the Reformation*, 1968) portrays Tetzel echoing the cries of people in purgatory: "Pity us! Pity us! Can't you hear our screams and groans—your fathers and mothers? We bore you, fed and clothed you, brought you up and left you our worldly goods. Can you then be so callous that you won't release us, for the merest pittance?"

"As soon as the coin in the coffer rings, the soul from purgatory springs," promised the Dominican indulgence salesman Johann Tetzel, depicted below in a late-nineteenth-century oil by Carl von Haeberlin. Tetzel opened his campaign in Saxony in 1517. Half the proceeds were to go to the local prince-archbishop and the other half to help pay for the new St. Peter's at Rome. For fully a year Luther fulminated against this campaign and got no response. Then he acted.

Luther's many-sided friend and foe

Erasmus strove to unite Luther and Rome, but Rome declared both heretical, and Luther's increasingly heated declarations eventually drove them apart

Desiderius Erasmus is a hard man to pin down. Was he a hero of the faith or an opportunistic sycophant? Wise and sincere Christian or traitor to the Catholic Church? Sincere friend of Martin Luther or Luther's unscrupulous betrayer? Heroic moderate defending a hopeless cause or coward afraid to take an honest stand? Few have denied, however, that this stubborn Netherlander was arguably the greatest humanist scholar of the northern Renaissance, an early and outspoken harbinger of the Reformation, and a major influence on Martin Luther. A cynical joke at the time was that Erasmus laid the egg and Luther hatched it. Erasmus agreed, but regretfully observed that he himself would have expected a rather different bird to emerge.

Two less likely collaborators than Luther and Erasmus would, in fact, be hard to imagine. Luther was big, bombastic, and belligerent, Erasmus small, slight, and conciliatory. Luther liked to present himself as a man of the people; Erasmus had small interest in the role of crowd-pleaser. Luther was seemingly always ready for a fight; Erasmus, a determined pacifist.

But they had also had much in common. Neither was to the manor born, for example. Luther's father was a miner who rose to become a major foundry owner. Erasmus (1466–1536) was the illegitimate offspring of a bourgeois Rotterdam family that nevertheless recognized and nurtured him. Both men received a sound Christian, Latin, and classical education. Both took monastic vows and found them an unsatisfactory fit. (Luther ultimately repudiated his outright, and Erasmus was eventually relieved of his by papal dispensation.) Both men strongly condemned, as destructive and pernicious, various long-hallowed practices of the Church of Rome. Both believed that the key to reform lay in proper interpretation of the Bible, especially the New Testament. And both seem to have been motivated by genuine commitment to Jesus Christ.

Erasmus's destiny was to become a scholar, an international academic star, an academic power broker, and what a later age would call a Christian pundit. Well acquainted with many of the early players in the Protestant Reformation, he would agree with some of their ideas and reject others. But he would unswervingly back the Catholic Church as essential to the survival of Christian Europe. He would never consider leaving the church himself, would survive unscathed through the reign of four popes, and would be consulted by Europe's rulers, including Emperor Charles V.

Sent by the Augustinian order to the University of Paris, young Erasmus came to detest the scholastic theology dominant there, and to abhor what he saw as its chop-logic, hairsplitting concentration upon matters neither accessible to human minds nor relevant to a Christian life. (As with other humanist critics of scholasticism, of course, being himself a product of it, he used the rational methods it taught him to assemble arguments against it.) To support himself, he tutored private pupils while building a reputation in classical and biblical research.

His first major work was an erudite collection of Greek and Latin proverbs published in 1500, called *Adagia*, and one of his students had meanwhile introduced him to happier theological surroundings. William Blount, fourth Baron Mountjoy, later to become his patron as well, invited him to visit England, and in sojourns there over the next two decades Erasmus made other staunch friends among reform-minded English humanists like John Colet, Thomas More, and John Fisher. He even briefly taught divinity and Greek at the University of Cambridge, and he gradually became convinced that the key to sound Christian faith lay in genuine knowledge of the gospel message itself. Therefore, it was important to get it right. Aware of the philological and textual work of Renaissance scholars on Greek philosophy and Roman literature, Erasmus resolved to use these same techniques to ensure that Christian literature, particularly the New Testament, had been accurately translated from the Greek.

In this he was following the lead of pioneer linguist and grammarian Lorenzo Valla (1407–1457), who had compared the New Testament of Rome's official Bible, the Latin Vulgate, with the earliest Greek texts and discovered what he regarded as seriously misleading translations. Unearthing Valla's manuscript in a monastery library in 1504, Erasmus created a sensation by having it printed and distributed. He also collected the most authentic Greek manuscripts he could find and by 1516 was ready to publish his own New Testament translation, with Latin and Greek side by side, and marginal annotations. Many Catholic scholars approved it, Protestants welcomed it unreservedly, and Luther would use it as the basis for his own German translation (while acidly challenging some of Erasmus's annotated comments).[1]

Meanwhile, his polemical publications continued to enhance his reputation. *Manual of a Christian Knight* (1504) was part of his campaign against heedless ritual and bogus popular traditions. *In Praise of Folly*, a biting social satire that rocked Europe in 1509 and is described in the *Catholic Encyclopedia* as "a cold-blooded, deliberate attempt to discredit the church . . . not intended as a healing medicine, but as a deadly poison," went through seven printings in as many months. In 1515 Erasmus's growing fame brought him an appointment to the council of the young Habsburg archduke

Charles, which inspired *The Education of a Christian Prince* (1516) and *The Complaint of Peace* (1517).

Genuine agreement between Erasmus and Luther became at length impossible. Erasmus grounded his faith on the Christian message as preserved and interpreted by the Catholic Church, aided by human reason. Luther would ultimately declare that reason, though helpful in human affairs, must never be applied to the Divinity, and would denigrate the church and reject it out of hand. But Erasmus, who in January 1521 led a delegation of moderates at the Reichstag at Worms, still sought to calm him both by letter and through mutual friends,

He also tried to protect Luther. When the emperor-elect Charles asked him for an honest evaluation of the man, Erasmus joked that Luther was guilty of just two crimes—he had attacked "the crown of the pope and the bellies of the monks!"—then characteristically added that Luther's enemies chiefly hated sound learning. In July 1521 he again wrote to Luther urging prudence, but that September Luther unleashed his *Babylonian Captivity*, a polemic described by historian Richard Marius as "a forty-four page Latin bomb planted in the delicate midst of the Catholic sacramental system."

This bomb, moreover, seemed eminently ready for immediate detonation. By now Erasmus was vehemently disputing Luther's radical theology, and Luther was roaring back. In the Lutheran concept of salvation by faith alone, for example, with its corollary that man can contribute nothing to his own salvation but need only love God, Erasmus saw exceedingly harmful error. In that case, he contended, why should anyone try to behave decently? Luther replied that good works would naturally flow from loving God. Erasmus, who had a waspish streak, observed that few good works seemed to be flowing from Luther's followers.

What he greatly feared would flow from them, sooner or later, was an all-out war of religion, and to Erasmus war was in itself a nearly unthinkable horror—a tragic necessity at times but, nonetheless, an outrage. As A.G. Dickens and Whitney R.D. Jones observe in *Erasmus the Reformer* (1994), "What he refused to do was to swallow the specious justifications of aggression and bloodshed which masqueraded as just war, or for that matter, *pace Machiavelli*, as the ineluctable corollaries of political power." As for war between Christian monarchs, he maintained, this simply must not happen. Therefore, the church must act as guide to Christian princes and guardian of the peace of Christendom, but in this impossible task it would signally fail. Hideous battles between Christians would soon engulf Europe, even the city of Rome.

Erasmus kept on working at his home in Basel, Switzerland, until increasing religious agitation there caused him to move to nearby Freiburg, in the western Habsburg territories, in 1529. There he died seven years later, while supervising publication of his treatise on the controversial third-century theologian Origen. The effect of his efforts is little clearer now than it was then. Scholars have traced his influence on various Protestant streams, especially the

Contemporaries joked that the scholarly Desiderius Erasmus (above, in a 1523 portrait by Hans Holbein the Younger) actually laid the theological egg that Luther hatched. Possibly so, was Erasmus's wry comment, but he would have expected quite a different bird to emerge.

Lutherans and Anglicans, giving particular credit to his calm Christocentric teaching. His scholarly reputation has never faded. His books survived, and as the Catholic Reformation gained momentum, even Catholic educators began to use some of them.[2]

Hardly a spectacular triumph, but spectacle was not the style of Desiderius Erasmus. Furthermore, in view of his relentlessly controversial career in an age of increasing sectarian violence, some might consider that his death of natural causes at the age of seventy was a triumph in itself. ∎

1. The concept of an "accurate" translation of any document, biblical or otherwise, is regarded by some scholars as an impossible ideal. As the translator chooses what he believes to be the equivalent word in the other language, some bias in the translated document is inevitable. In the highly charged intellectual environment of the sixteenth century, bias naturally abounded on all sides.

2. The zealous Pope Paul IV banned Erasmus's works in 1559, along with those of numerous other Catholic writers. Paul's decree was greatly modified at the Council of Trent but renewed by Sixtus V in 1590. Some of Erasmus's works long remained on the Index of Prohibited Books (see sidebar, p. 198)—and rightly so in certain instances, according to some twentieth-century theologians.

The wooden double doors of Wittenberg's All Saints' Castle Church, to which Martin Luther famously (if not quite historically) nailed his Ninety-five Theses, were destroyed in 1760 during the Seven Years' War. They were replaced in November 1858 by commemorative bronzed doors (right) inscribed with the original Latin text of the theses.

For nearly a year Luther tried, without success, to provoke professors in other universities to formal debate. Then, having formulated all his contentions as Ninety-five Theses—propositions for debate—he took the action often designated as the launching of the Protestant Reformation.

On October 31, 1517—All Saints' Eve—he nailed this document to the door of All Saints' Castle Church of Wittenberg, inviting scholars and churchmen alike to argue out these matters.[6] No one showed up. But Luther also sent a copy to Archbishop Albrecht, who forwarded it to Rome, and had a local printer run off copies for other interested parties. Initial reactions varied. Tetzel's response was: "Within three weeks I shall have that heretic in the fire!" Pope Leo X, by contrast, made light of the matter at first, dismissing Luther as "a drunken German" who would "feel different" when he sobered up. The man had obvious talent, the pope added, doubtless making other mendicants jealous—it seemed to be just another "row" among monks.

But then Luther published his *Explanations* for the Ninety-five Theses, which far exceeded the sales of the original and put all Germany abuzz. Tetzel wrote a rebuttal and sent eight hundred copies to Wittenberg. Pressured by the Dominicans, the Augustinians summoned their incendiary brother before a council of the order at Heidelberg in April 1518, the first time Luther had had to venture outside his own territory. He traveled there on foot fearing the worst, probably excommunication and dismissal from the order.

Instead, he found his fellow Augustinians powerfully behind him, and the council became a celebratory rally for their champion against the rival Dominicans. Returning home, however, he preached a particularly inflammatory sermon in which he contended that if the pope excommunicated him on invalid grounds, the excommunication would itself be invalid—papal or not. Dominicans in the audience took notes on this sermon and dispatched them to Rome, where they triggered a heresy charge against Luther.

The case was entrusted to one Silvestro Mazzolini da Prierio, known as Prierias, a Dominican long schooled in Vatican politics. Prierias boasted that it took him just three days to compose the official accusation, in which he altogether ignored Luther's arguments, confined himself chiefly to calling him names ("son of a bitch . . . libeler . . . leper with a brain of brass and nose of iron"), and concluded by asserting that a pope could not err because he was infallible. The Vatican consequently ordered Luther to appear in Rome within sixty days on charges of heresy and defiance. Luther, mindful of the earlier fate of John Hus under similar circumstances, appealed to Frederick of Saxony.[7]

Frederick was a sorely conflicted man regarding Luther. On the one hand, the elector was a devout Catholic, and especially prized his collection of holy relics,

6. The German Catholic historian Erwin Iserloh contended in 1960 that Luther did not actually post his Ninety-five Theses on the door of the Wittenberg church, but simply had the document published and distributed. This claim has provoked heated scholarly debate because the visual image of Luther's defiant act has always been iconic among Lutherans. Iserloh, who was sympathetic to Luther, played a part in the twentieth-century movement to reconcile the Lutheran and Catholic churches.

7. Just over one hundred years earlier, the Czech priest and reformer John Hus obeyed a papal summons to face heresy charges before the Council of Constance in southwest Germany, relying on a safe-conduct from the emperor Sigismund. When Hus was arrested and imprisoned at Constance, however, Sigismund refused to honor his guarantee. John Hus was tried, convicted, and burned at the stake in July 1415 (see vol. 8, ch. 4).

Nineteenth-century artist Ferdinand Pauwels
here captures the event widely credited with
triggering the Protestant Reformation. The
young monk Martin Luther defiantly points
to the documents he has just finished nailing
to the doors of All Saints' Castle Church,
Wittenberg—his challenge to the pope and
the Catholic Church. The action was clandestine but word of it soon spread, inspiring one
bitter adversary to vow: "Within three weeks
I shall have that heretic in the fire!"

Frederick III, ruler of Electoral Saxony and a devout Catholic, was put in a quandary by Martin Luther's growing popularity but ultimately decided to protect the ex-monk from emperor and pope alike. His reasoning? Luther was the star of Wittenberg University, and the alternative might have been civil war.

8. A twentieth-century Luther biographer, Roland H. Bainton (*Here I Stand: A Life of Martin Luther*, 1950), describes Frederick as "a man of simple and sincere piety." His collection of relics included a tooth of St. Jerome, four fragments of St. Chrysostom, four of St. Augustine, and six of St. Bernard, four hairs of the Virgin Mary and three pieces of her cloak, one piece of Jesus' swaddling clothes, and 19,013 bones of other saints. Papal indulgences sold at the museum, it was claimed, reduced purgatorial time for their beneficiaries by 1,902,202 years and 270 days. For an account of Christian tradition regarding relics, see vol. 6, pp. 30 and 31.

said to be the best in Europe outside of Rome. Luther, characteristically unrestrained in his views on the "worship" of relics, had called the museum housing Frederick's collection a "whorehouse."[8] On the other hand, Luther was the star academic of Wittenberg University, attracting students from all over Europe, and Frederick was frankly impressed with many of his criticisms of the church. As long as Luther remained in Electoral Saxony, he would be safe from pope and emperor alike.

But now Rome put another Dominican on his case, a man far more formidable than the hapless Prierias. Pope Leo entrusted Cardinal Tommaso de Vio Gaetanus, widely known as "Cajetan," papal legate to the court of Emperor Maximilian, with three important assignments during the Reichstag currently scheduled at Augsburg. The first was to persuade the German princes to mount a crusade against the Turks. Here Cajetan failed; the princes had no interest in the Turks. The second was to elicit from Maximilian a denunciation of Luther as a peril to the unity of the empire, and in this he succeeded. The emperor wrote to Rome urging that the rebellious monk be excommunicated and arrested.

Cajetan's third task was to quietly thwart Maximilian's plan to have his grandson Charles elected to succeed him. If the Habsburgs, through Charles, were to gain control of Spain, Germany, and Italy, the pope feared, they would become far too powerful for Rome's safety, so Cajetan was to back the French king, Francis I. Maximilian already had six of the seven electors on side but wished young Charles's endorsement to be unanimous. Since Frederick of Saxony was the lone holdout, Cajetan began by doubly ensuring his negative vote. Frederick reassured him as requested but demanded a quid pro quo. What about this summons to Rome of his monk Luther? Why not try the man right there in Augsburg? Surely Cajetan himself could handle the case. Cajetan had to agree. The summons to Rome was canceled, and Luther reluctantly made his way to Augsburg.

The confrontation between monk and cardinal began with notable courtesy, Cajetan affecting the role of concerned spiritual father and Luther that of supplicant and sincere inquirer. But when the cardinal began questioning the infallibility of scripture and Luther the infallibility of papal bulls, the debate turned into a three-day shouting match. It ended with the cardinal roaring that he wished never again to lay eyes upon Luther and Luther fleeing by night, precariously clinging to a hard-galloping horse (reportedly his first time on horseback).

Nevertheless, writes the Jesuit theologian Jared Wicks, it is worth noting that up to the end of the year 1518, Luther considered himself and strove to be recognized as a faithful member of the Catholic Church (*Roman Reactions to Luther: The First Year*, 1983). He did not come up with his emphasis on the Bible and early fathers out of the blue. This had been part of a much broader Catholic reform movement dating to the previous century and earlier. In April of 1518, writes Wicks,

Charles V

Maximilian I

Luther submitted the Ninety-five Theses to his bishop, who authorized they be printed. In August Luther declared: "I will never be a heretic. I may err while arguing in disputation, but I do not want to assert conclusions."

Luther reached Wittenberg in safety, however, and his fate again rested entirely with Frederick the Wise. But Cajetan did one thing more. Himself a respected scholastic, he wrote a memorandum declaring that no indulgence could ever change the will of God or alter the guilt of a sinner, and this became a papal bull, which instantly put Tetzel out of business. The star indulgence preacher was ignominiously dumped by his former associates, who proceeded to accuse him (without grounds) of sexual promiscuity. The embittered Tetzel soon died in a monastery, but not before Luther had written him a sympathetic note: "Don't take it too hard. You didn't start this agitation. It had another father."

The death of Emperor Maximilian in January 1519, before he had ensured the election of his grandson as emperor, put a temporary damper on the Luther controversy as everyone focused on the intensive, and expensive, campaign of Charles's own electoral agents. Frederick, after some hesitation, flatly refused to arrest Luther, a position he maintained thereafter with unwavering resolve. But now a new papal champion appeared: Johann Eck, a professor from the University of Ingolstadt, a skilled debater particularly adept at luring opponents into making indefensible assertions. An affirmed scholastic, Eck was also almost the only German academic who had taken seriously Luther's Ninety-five Theses and formulated a reply.

With Luther himself under papal disfavor, Eck invited his Wittenberg reform supporters instead to publicly debate the theses, although (as both sides knew) the central question would inevitably come down to the validity of the papacy itself. This proposal brought into the fray Frederick's cousin and great rival, Duke George of Saxony.[9] Splendid suggestion, said the duke, but the debate should be held at his university at Leipzig, and Eck's chief adversary should be Luther himself, whose safety Duke George would unconditionally guarantee.

Thus began a seventeen-day confrontation between Martin Luther and the square-set, barrel-chested Eck, the man destined to become his most determined foe on the Catholic side. They fought it out before an impressive array of ecclesiastics, nobles, and academics, and Eck prevailed. The two official umpires, the universities of Paris and Erfurt, refused to declare a winner, but Louvain University and also Cologne, where the Dominicans predominated, declared for Eck. Cologne also denounced Luther as clearly heretical.

However, each side had made one especially telling point. Luther noted that Eck defined the true church as consisting only of those who accept the pope as the final fount of Christian truth. Then what about all those millions of Eastern Christians, whose churches dated from the apostles and who had always rejected papal authority? Were they automatically consigned to hell? Eck had no satisfactory answer to this, but Luther was similarly cornered when Eck forced him to declare that neither pope nor church council could infallibly explain the precise meaning of scripture. In that case, Eck demanded, who could? Was every Christian to be his own authority? Or was Luther claiming sole validity for his own personal view? Was he in effect establishing his own church, in his own name? By now this impasse was becoming evident to Luther himself. He had begun by wanting to change the Church of Rome, but his radical departures would in effect establish another institution altogether.

Johann Eck, professor at the University of Ingolstadt, was the first Catholic academic to give serious attention to Luther's Ninety-five Theses. While everyone else ignored or dodged the upstart's challenge, Eck accepted it, formulated a reasoned reply and engaged him in public debate. Square-set, barrel-chested and clever, he became Luther's most inexorable Catholic foe.

9. Saxony in the era of Martin Luther was divided into Electoral Saxony, ruled by Elector Frederick III from his capital of Wittenberg, and Ducal Saxony, ruled by Frederick's cousin Duke George, whose capital was Leipzig. The cousins frequently disagreed, particularly over religion. Frederick protected Luther and died a Lutheran. Duke George remained a stalwart Catholic.

Soon Eck left for Rome, where he toiled assiduously against the German reformer, and the next salvo was a papal bull condemning Luther's teaching in the strongest terms. Proclaimed by Pope Leo on June 15, 1520, *Exsurge Domine* ("Rise up, O Lord") bade God arise against "a bellowing boar from the forest that is trying to demolish thy vineyard." It commanded Luther to remain silent, ordered his books burned, and on pain of execution forbade any Catholic to read or praise anything he had written. He had sixty days to recant or be excommunicated; anyone who helped him would also be excommunicated. Johann Eck, the bull's probable author, went north to distribute it in Germany, a task that soon confirmed in his mind its extreme urgency.

At Leipzig, where barely a year earlier he had been graciously received, Eck now found himself shunned. He could scarcely find a printer there willing to make copies of his bull or anyone to distribute them. His life was threatened at least once, and he fled by night in fear of armed students. At Erfurt students pitched all his copies of the bull into the river. At Vienna the university would have nothing to do with him. When Luther finally saw the bull (his nervous followers allegedly having kept it from him), it provoked his customary bellicose response. Its purpose, he roared, was to compel men to worship Satan instead of God. Good Christians should trample it underfoot. The pope was "an unjust judge, hardened and erring," and from the evidence of his writings a "convicted heretic and schismatic." In conclusion: "Whether this bull is by Eck or the pope, it is the sum of impiety, blasphemy, ignorance,

Below, as imagined by the nineteenth-century artist Friedrich Paul Thumann, Luther and his followers in Wittenberg burn a copy of the papal bull issued by Pope Leo X in June 1520. Probably composed by Johann Eck, the bull called Luther "a bellowing boar" trying to destroy God's vineyard. It ordered his books burned, and gave him sixty days to recant. Inset is a facsimile of the bull itself.

Bulla contra Erro
res Martini Lutheri
et sequacium.

impudence, hypocrisy, and lying." In December he formally burned it at Wittenberg. With it he threw in a copy of the canon law, making a breach with Rome a virtual inevitability.

He had meanwhile unleashed a series of treatises intended to provoke rebellion against "the Antichrist," (i.e., the pope). In his *Address to the Christian Nobility of the German Nation,* he urged the princes of the empire to take the lead in church reform and condemned as unbiblical the entire concept of holy orders. This was soon out of print, but further supplies were rapidly churned out at Leipzig, Strasbourg, and Basel. Next came *The Babylonian Captivity of the Church,* repudiating all the sacraments save two—baptism and the Holy Communion—which it claimed were the only ones specifically ordained by scripture. And finally there appeared *The Freedom of a Christian,* prefaced by an open letter to the pope, urging him to resign his office and join Luther in rescuing the

In his 'Freedom of a Christian,' Luther urged the pope to quit his office and join in rescuing the church from Satan (i.e., the papacy). Some think it the finest thing Luther wrote.

church from Satan (i.e., the papacy). Historian Marius calls this treatise—minus its sarcastic preface, that is—"perhaps the finest thing Luther ever wrote."

In it he replied to opponents who argued that if all human effort at goodness is indeed worthless, as he claimed to be the case, there is clearly no point trying to live ethically. Marius sums up Luther's answer:

> A Christian is utterly free, master of all, slave to none. But a Christian is also the willing slave of all, commanded by all . . . Christians are freed from the law and freed from the tyranny of perfection, from the fear of never being good enough. Christians know that the commands of God humble mortals because no one can obey them. The commandments destroy pride, the quality that makes us put ourselves in the center of the universe and usurp the place of God. Only in humiliation do we perceive that we are not divine, and only then can we truly let God be God.

For the hopeful peacemaker Erasmus, Luther's *Babylonian Captivity* treatise and his burning of the papal bull came as two blows too many. He had tried hard to maintain that a negotiated truce was possible between Lutheran views and the papacy, but now he despaired. The divorce between extremist and moderate became complete, and in the mid-1520s, when thousands would perish in the Peasants' Revolt, Erasmus would very largely blame Luther's teachings.

Meanwhile, in June 1519 the archduke Charles had won the imperial election, with Frederick of Saxony making the vote unanimous despite his deal with Cajetan. The seven electors had also exacted a further concession in addition to their customary electoral cash payments. Charles had had to agree to a new provision in the imperial constitution—a decree that no German of rank was to be taken for trial outside Germany. Whether papal officials knew about this at the time is not clear, but nearly a year later, when the pope issued *Exsurge Domine,* they evidently did not expect it to apply to Luther.

10. Historians offer three possible explanations why Emperor Charles V changed his mind on the Luther question: 1. He feared that if Luther were turned over to Rome for certain execution without a trial in Germany, it could provoke a civil war within the empire. 2. He had adopted Erasmus's proposed policy of negotiating with the Lutherans rather than persecuting them. 3. He had discovered that Pope Leo was trying to foment a French war against the Habsburgs, making the pope an even greater danger than Luther to European unity.

Although Luther had been excommunicated by papal bull in 1520, the newly elected emperor Charles V guaranteed him a chance to defend his doctrines the following year at the Reichstag (parliament) at Worms. In this 1877 painting by Anton von Werner the condemned heretic stands a lonely figure among the princes and prelates, right hand on heart, refusing to repudiate either his banned volumes or his beliefs. His words would ring down the centuries: "I cannot and will not recant . . . Here I stand. I can do no other."

Charles was crowned king of the Romans at Aachen on October 22, 1520, taking the time-hallowed pledge to "hold fast to the Catholic faith" and to "yield due and loyal submission to the pope and Holy Roman Church." Thirteen days later he assured Elector Frederick at Cologne that Luther would not be condemned without a hearing and on November 28 proposed that he appear before the upcoming Reichstag at Worms (pronounced *Voorms*) in the Rhineland. Luther biographer Roland H. Bainton calls this "an amazing reversal of policy." Until recently the new emperor had seemed unalterably opposed to Luther and all his doings, even pausing in the Netherlands en route to Aachen to see that his heretical books were duly burned.[10]

Cardinal Girolamo Aleandro, experienced Vatican diplomat and current papal representative at Worms, protested in horror. How could this "Satan," Martin Luther, already examined and condemned by a papal court and excommunicated by papal bull, now appear at the Reichstag of the Holy Roman Empire, to be tried not by the clergy but by laymen? "How can the church be called 'the Ship of Peter,' " demanded Aleandro in an indignant letter to Emperor Charles, "if Peter is not at the helm? Has the Catholic Church been dead for a thousand years to be revived only by Martin? Has the whole world gone wrong, and Martin only has the eyes to see?" So Charles withdrew the invitation, fearing that if Luther were to come to Worms, the city might be placed under interdict.

On February 13, 1521, Cardinal Aleandro presented to the Reichstag the text of a proposed imperial edict proclaiming Luther a heretic and a revolutionary.

Unless absolved by the Reichstag, he would be imprisoned and his works destroyed. This set off a near riot. Frederick and the elector of Brandenburg came close to blows and had to be pulled apart, while the characteristically reserved Elector Palatinate was described as "bellowing like a bull." If this edict were to be adopted without giving Luther a hearing, civil war would clearly be inevitable in Germany. When tempers cooled, it was agreed that he should be brought to Worms, his safety guaranteed, "to be examined by learned men," but must only answer questions— not preach. If he would renounce his accusations against the Catholic faith, other points could be discussed. If he refused, the imperial edict would be endorsed.

Charles therefore composed an immediate invitation to "our noble, dear, and esteemed Martin," a salutation that left Aleandro aghast. This was no way to address a condemned heretic, he objected. Undeterred, the emperor continued: "We and the Reichstag have decided to ask you to come under safe-conduct to answer with regard to your books and teaching. You shall have twenty-one days in which to arrive." Luther, still conscious of the fate of Hus, wavered at first, then with memorable words decided to go: "Unless I am held back by force, or Caesar revokes his invitation, I will enter Worms under the banner of Christ against the gates of hell."[11]

Accompanied by a party of Wittenberg students and preceded by the imperial herald sent by Charles as escort, Luther embarked for Worms in a two-wheeled cart. At town after town, hundreds knelt by the roadside to receive his blessing. At Erfurt, where he had been jeered after the Leipzig debate, a great party was held for him.

11. It is noteworthy that as Luther made his way to Worms, a moderate party on the Catholic side proposed a compromise. Persuaded that his appearance at Worms would make permanent schism inevitable, they urged him to recant his attack on the sacraments, and also to demand that Rome relinquish its taxing powers on the German principalities and grant the German church the same degree of independence already conferred in France, England, and Spain. Historian Roland Bainton believes this would have prevented the breakup, but Luther turned it down cold. He was now as set on going "up to Worms," he vowed, as Christ had been set on going "up to Jerusalem."

While war became an increasing pre-occupation for Charles V, depicted here in full armor by Titian, he remained fervently invested in defense of the church. Having invited the upstart Luther to the Reichstag at Worms and heard him out, the emperor remained unconvinced. "That man will never make a heretic of me," he declared. In April 1521 Luther, equally determined, informed Charles in the above letter (inset) why he, too, could and would not alter his course.

There was an opulent reception at Frankfurt. Aleandro, fearing an armed attack on the Reichstag itself, warned the emperor that the people of Worms were "ready to destroy the clergy to the last man." Nearing the city, Luther's entourage was met by a company of mounted spearmen sent by a supportive prince. He dismissed them, saying that he had no wish to take up arms for the gospel.

He entered Worms to a fanfare of trumpets sounded from the cathedral, with people trying to touch him as they would a saint. "The whole world flocked to see him," mourned Aleandro, who had wanted Luther quietly spirited in at night and sequestered. Instead, after a lavish supper at the Hospice of St. John, Luther was again besieged by well-wishers. Aleandro and other papal officials had refused to attend his appearance before the Reichstag next day, holding it an illegal proceeding, but they had stipulated that Luther must be allowed to speak solely in response to two questions, answering only "yes" or "no"—nothing more. The first question: "Were these his writings?" The second: "Did he now reject them?"

As the lone mendicant friar stood before the assembly of bishops, princes, and imperial dignitaries in a conference room of the bishop's palace, observers noted his flashing dark eyes. Some thought them obviously satanic, while others discerned the fire of God. Aleandro wrote that he "looked like an idiot" with his grinning and laughing. Emperor Charles was also unimpressed. "That man will never make a heretic of me," he muttered. The archbishop of Trier, acting as prosecutor, indicated to Luther a display of about twenty of his books, assembled in a window well, and demanded—in Latin and then in German—whether he had written them, and whether he was prepared to renounce all or some of them.

Seemingly overawed, Luther replied in a barely audible voice that the salvation of his own and other souls might depend on his answer, and therefore "I beg you, give me time to think about it." How strange, the archbishop commented, that a scholar was not prepared to defend his own writings, and others wondered how this mumbling dolt could be the preacher who had stirred so many Germans to the brink of rebellion. All agreed, however, to give him twenty-four hours to consider his reply, a concession that Aleandro may well have regarded as another tactical error.

Such a huge crowd turned out next day that the session had to be moved to a bigger hall, delaying its opening by two hours. Luther himself, when he finally appeared in the glow of the flaming torches, seemed strangely transformed—there was no resemblance whatsoever to the shrinking, cringing creature of the previous day. Then came the crucial question: Was he ready to renounce the books whose author he had admitted himself to be? This time his reply rang out clearly. His books, he declared, were not of one sort. Some were purely theological and said many things with which he was sure all good men would agree. Others described the exploitation of Germany by papal tax collectors, with which he was sure a great many gentlemen present would agree. Still others involved criticism of individuals, and while he might retract the violence of the language, he could not retract the criticism.

The archbishop asked Luther to repudiate his works and their errors. Luther's response was to resound through the ages: 'I cannot and will not recant. Here I stand. I can do no other.'

At this point even Charles seemed to lose his accustomed imperturbability. "No!" he thundered, possibly meaning that the speaker should be silenced, but Luther had the floor. He plunged on unrestrained, likening himself to Jesus at Jerusalem, under pressure from the high priest to incriminate himself. If evidence could be brought demonstrating anything he taught as unscriptural, he said, he would of course recant—but none had. And if he was simply accused of stirring up trouble, had not Jesus himself said that he came to bring not peace but a sword? "I do not say this because I think great lords like yourselves need me to instruct you, but because I do not shirk my duty to this country."

"You have not described your works sufficiently," the archbishop indignantly responded. "Let me do it for you." Luther's earlier writings were bad, he declared, and the later ones worse. Who was Martin Luther to put himself above the great saints and thinkers of the Christian past, sealed by the blood of martyrs, confirmed by the sacred councils? And finally: "For the last time I ask you, Martin, to say without horns or teeth, do you or do you not repudiate your books and the errors they contain?"

Luther's response was to resound through the centuries: "I cannot and will not recant . . . Here I stand. I can do no other."[12] Then he raised his arms with hands outspread, the victorious gesture of the winning knight in a feudal joust.

Brief silence followed and then uproar—but the uproar of a crowd divided. "Into the fire with him!" yelled the Spaniards and Italians, but the Germans, who dominated, were plainly swept away, perhaps by Luther's undoubted courage. Many raised their arms in emulation of his triumphant gesture and swarmed after

12. Though the famous line, "Here I stand," does not appear in the trial record, it is recorded thus by the earliest printed version subsequently issued at Wittenberg. Historian Roland Bainton believes these may indeed have been his actual words at Worms. "Though not recorded on the spot, they may nevertheless be genuine, because the listeners at the moment may have been too moved to write."

After agreeing at the Reichstag at Worms that Luther was indeed a "notorious heretic," the emperor Charles afforded him safe passage to Wartburg Castle (below), high above the town of Eisenach. It was in the room pictured above, complete with cabinets, armchair, footstool and desk, that Luther managed, despite attacks of spiritual melancholy and malfunctioning intestines, to complete his translation of the New Testament into German. Arguably the first literary masterpiece in that language, his vernacular Bible was of incalculable influence.

him into the street. Next day, when passions had cooled somewhat, Emperor Charles reassembled the Reichstag and read a statement expressing his own equally irrevocable loyalties:

> You know that I am descended from the most Christian emperors of the noble German nation, the Catholic kings of Spain, the archdukes of Austria, the dukes of Burgundy, who have all been until now faithful sons of the Roman church, having been defenders of the Catholic faith, in sacred ceremonies, decrees, ordinances, and holy customs for the honor of God, the increase of the faith, and the salvation of souls according to the passage of time, in which by natural law and inheritance we have been left these sacred Catholic observances, so that we may live and die by their examples, which as true imitators of them our predecessors have by the grace of God lived until now.

For these reasons, Charles continued, he would honor Martin Luther's safe-conduct to Wittenberg but thereafter would consider him "a notorious heretic" under the ban of the empire. He then asked the Reichstag to pass his edict against Luther, and it did so, although so many delegates had already left for home that its legality would later be questioned. The encounter nevertheless appeared a victory for Rome, but skeptics took note of two discordant facts. First, nowhere in his statement did Charles specifically recognize the authority, role, or office of the pope. Second, for the following three days, imperial aides met privately with the "notorious heretic," trying to reach a compromise that might satisfy both him and the papal delegation. When this failed, Luther slipped quietly out of Worms.

Soon came the dire news, however, that on the road home he had been set upon and slain by unidentified horsemen, and his body thrown down a mineshaft. Great was the mourning for this hero of the reform movement, until word leaked out that the supposed murderers were Frederick's men. The elector proceeded to quarter Luther safely for nearly a year in Wartburg Castle, high above the town of Eisenach. There, Luther translated the New Testament into the German language—its first literary masterpiece, which still forms the basic literary standard of the High German language.

The frontispiece of the Luther Bible of 1534, by Hans Holbein the Younger. This was Germany's first vernacular edition to include both the Old and the New Testaments, Luther having completed the latter in a ten-month span while sequestered at Wartburg Castle. Theologian Philip Schaff describes this achievement as "the most important and useful work of his entire life."

Meanwhile, in all the excitement something else went almost unnoticed at Worms. The ambassador from Hungary, Hieronymus Balbus, had been allowed to address the assembly briefly to appeal for help against an impending attack on his country by the Turks. Leo X, it seemed, had been mistaken about the new sultan Süleyman, son of Selim the Grim. Apparently Süleyman was not quite the "gentle lamb" upon whose accession the pope had offered a thanksgiving Mass. Even now, the Hungarians had been reliably informed, he was preparing to pick up where his father had left off by launching an attack on Rhodes. And the Reichstag should be aware, Balbus declared, that Belgrade, Buda, Pest, and Vienna would be next.

Unimpressed, the assembly delayed its response until the Luther situation had been dealt with. Then it replied: "The holy Catholic power and seat of sacred power cannot at present promise troops or other assistance against the Turks." If the Hungarians could not defend themselves, perhaps their king should seek a truce with the sultan, "provided always that it should be one not dishonorable nor injurious to himself, to the Catholic faith, or to the commonwealth of Christendom." In other words, the imperial Reichstag had more important things to worry about. Events would soon prove it catastrophically wrong. ■

CHAPTER 3

As the Muslims strike, a divided Europe fails to save Hungary

But an embattled Charles fights the pope and the French in a quest for European unity, and with Vienna in peril Protestants join Catholics and block the Turkish attack

When Charles V, the twenty-one-year-old emperor of much of the known world, left the city of Worms and headed for the Netherlands in late April 1521, he knew that he had some major problems. He also had reason for confidence, however, that all were well on the way to solution. At Worms, for example, he had given the fractious mendicant friar Martin Luther an impartial hearing before the Reichstag of the empire—which to Charles was far more than he deserved—and had himself written the decisive imperial edict concerning him. Since Luther had been declared heretical by the pope, Charles had decreed, he must now be arrested as an enemy of the empire, his books burned, and the property of his supporters seized. What could now inhibit its enforcement?

Second, there was the French problem, perhaps more properly described as the Francis I problem. King Francis, to whom Charles's sister, Eleanor of Habsburg, would one day be married, was often described as a Renaissance man. This admiring designation seemed to signify that Francis subscribed to the pragmatic "new morality" of the times, which, so far as Charles could see, meant no morality at all. But the young emperor was confident that no truly Christian king could really sink to such a level of depravity.

Third on Charles's agenda was the Spanish problem. When he left Spain the previous year, he had appointed as regent his onetime Dutch tutor, Adrian of Utrecht, an upright and dependable man of unswerving Christian commitment. Unfortunately, Adrian had proved to be no great administrator, the Spanish nobility

The deadly Ottoman artillery, shown here at the siege of Constantinople a century earlier, became the bane of Europe under Süleyman I and his vast armies. "Resisting them is impossible," wrote Archduke Ferdinand of Austria to King Louis II of Hungary. "We are both doomed." The hapless Louis was indeed doomed, but the Turks would nevertheless be stopped—though only at the very walls of Vienna.

Francis I of France, above left in a sixteenth-century painting by Tiziano Vecelli, was notorious for shirking oaths, switching sides, and shedding Christian blood. Europe was scandalized, however, that even Francis would seek an alliance with Süleyman I (at right) against his rival Charles V, which he did in 1535. Just fourteen years earlier the sultan had led his Turks in the siege and capture of Belgrade (inset), the first stage in his thrust westward.

had been in a state of rebellion ever since, and Adrian was now the virtual prisoner of these rebel lords. So from Brussels Charles would briefly visit England to arrange a treaty with King Henry VIII against France, then proceed to Spain, where he was sure he could bring the rebels under control.

Finally, there was the Turkish problem. Having conquered most of the Balkans, the Turks were seeking vigorously to convert its Eastern Orthodox Christians to Islam. They had seized Egypt as well and were extending their control to the entire north African coast. With the new sultan Süleyman plainly emulating the aggressive policies of his father, Selim the Grim, it appeared that Catholic Hungary would be next. But Charles was confident that the Turkish threat was being exaggerated, and his solution here was in any case purely administrative. Concluding that ruling the empire was far too big a job for one man, he had decided to split it. His younger brother Ferdinand, just eighteen, would become archduke of Austria with five Austrian territories under his immediate rule; three more would later be added. With Ferdinand running imperial affairs in the East, the Turks would be his to deal with.

History was not about to vindicate Charles's optimism, however. Of his four problems he would resolve only the Spanish one; the other three would harass him for much of the rest of his life. The Francis problem would be solved only by the death of King Francis more than two decades later, in 1547. At the death of Charles himself in 1558 the Turks would be more dangerous than ever. As for his determination to reconcile Luther's followers and the Catholic Church, some 450 years would pass before much headway was made on that score. Meanwhile, Charles, champion of the Catholic cause, would sometimes find himself criticizing the pope in terms rivaling even Luther's in severity.

He met the first of his disillusionments before he even reached Brussels, discovering while en route to Wittenberg that Luther, though shielded by an imperial safe-conduct, had been kidnapped and supposedly murdered. This turned out to be incorrect—Luther was in fact being hidden by his protector, Elector Frederick the Wise of Saxony, who obviously proposed to ignore Charles's Edict of Worms. Moreover, the emperor was informed, other German princes were likely to do the same, so both Luther and his writings were still very much a problem.

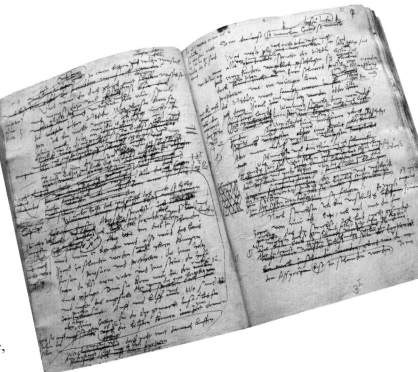

"That all may understand" was Martin Luther's avowed aim in translating the Bible into German. Seen above are pages from his translation of the Old Testament (now at the Forschungsbibliothek at Gotha, Germany), a task he completed in 1534. Due primarily to illness and his relative unfamiliarity with Hebrew, it had occupied him for much of twelve years.

Worse news followed. On April 22, the very day when Luther was standing trial at Worms, nobles allied with King Francis had begun attacking Charles on two fronts—south into Navarre and north into Luxembourg. And from the Balkans came information that an enormous Turkish army, equipped with the world's finest artillery, was again on the march to Belgrade, gateway to Hungary. May 18 brought confirmation that already it was laying siege to that all-important city.

Charles may have hoped that Belgrade's fortress would hold, just as it had under the indomitable Jan Hunyadi against Süleyman's great-grandfather six decades earlier (see vol. 8, pp. 134–37). But this time it did not. After a five-week siege the city's impossibly outnumbered defenders surrendered Belgrade under a white flag, on condition the citizenry be allowed to leave with their families and given land to settle on. Muslim records claim that Süleyman honored this condition. According to Christian accounts the Muslim troops moved in, cleared the cathedral of all Christian symbols and declared it a mosque, and then Süleyman gave the defeated citizens the land he had promised—by ordering them all killed and buried in it.

Luther, sequestered in Wartburg Castle, was meanwhile hard at work on his translation of the New Testament into German, much of it from its Greek sources, a task he is said to have accomplished in some eleven weeks. Published in September 1522, it became known as the *September Testament*. It guaranteed Luther's permanent fame, writes Luther biographer Heiko Oberman (*Luther: Man Between God and Devil*, 1982), not least because it "shaped the modern German language." On account of subsequent illnesses and his relative unfamiliarity with Hebrew, his German translation of the Old Testament took twelve years.

Biblical translation was central to Luther's view of Christianity. If only people could read the Bible, he wholly believed, they would see clearly that the papal church had departed from the vision of the apostles. Yet in some respects his efforts seemed actually to argue the Catholic case. He added introductions to the biblical texts, for example, to help people see in them what he did. Critics objected to this. But why should Luther's biblical interpretations be preferred over those made by hundreds of other Christians, faithfully examined and preserved by the church? Further, he offered opinions on the relative merit of the biblical books. The Fourth Gospel should be preferred to the first three, for instance, and the book of Revelation regarded as an appendix (an opinion he later revised). The Epistle of James must be seen as "non-apostolic" because it did not "preach Christ." The Epistle to the Hebrews could not have been written by Paul, but possibly by Paul's contemporary Apollos. But if the Bible was to be enshrined as the sole and infallible authority for Christian belief, his opponents contended, on what basis were some parts of it to be deemed more authoritative than others?

Philipp Melanchthon

Andreas Karlstadt

Meanwhile, other people were indeed reading their Bibles, developing ideas about what they found there, and acting on them with results that Luther found frankly alarming. With Luther isolated at the Wartburg, his deputy at Wittenberg was Philipp Melanchthon, a devoted disciple and a brilliant linguist who had assisted him with the New Testament translation. Melanchthon was soon sending him anxious reports concerning one Andreas Karlstadt. Formerly Luther's academic superior at Wittenberg University, and once a severe critic of the reform movement, Karlstadt was now a fervent convert and trying to take the movement over (see ch. 4). He was preaching that Luther did not go nearly far enough, insisting, for example, that clerical celibacy was not merely unnecessary but actively evil, as was anybody committed to it. Music could become a form of idolatry, Karlstadt claimed, and must be banned. Congregations should elect their pastors, and as for the Holy Communion, it was scarcely holy at all. It was a simple community meal in memory of Jesus' sacrifice on the cross. Equally disruptive were the Bible-based "Zwickau Prophets," unemployed and impoverished weavers from the nearby town of Zwickau who moved into Wittenberg late in 1521.

With all this plurality of practice, violence began to flare. Gangs of youths disrupted the Christmas Mass that year in churches that still observed it, beating up priests and smashing statues and stained glass windows. Known as *pfaffensturm* (priest-storm), such vandalism spread across Germany. In Erfurt, capital of Thuringia, for instance, rioting students destroyed sixty rectories and seven monasteries, and murdered a priest. By March 1522 Luther had to leave the Wartburg and at great personal risk return permanently to Wittenberg to restore order. With Elector Frederick's help he expelled Karlstadt, and the Zwickau Prophets departed on their own.

But both remained active, with Karlstadt publishing a denunciation of Luther as a self-appointed pope. Luther's friends urged him to respond, though they begged him to restrain his abusive language, an increasing embarrassment to them. Characteristically, Luther paid no heed to the latter request.[1] He was facing the frightening realization that Karlstadt and the Prophets were merely two instances of what could become a much bigger problem, for the movement he

1. Some Luther biographers maintain that Martin Luther's reply to Karlstadt, entitled *Against the Heavenly Prophets*, exceeds in unremitting hatred and coarse abuse everything he had previously written. Even the modern American translators and editors of this treatise, observes historian Richard Marius, "record their embarrassment at its hateful tone."

2. The grand master of the Teutonic Knights became Lutheran. His cousin the archbishop of Mainz, who had helped set off the controversy over indulgences, became partly Lutheran. He wrote Luther that he had come to see himself as an idolater—a "piece of dung in the eyes of God," as he put it—and so had canceled all relic and indulgence schemes in his archdiocese. But he could not bring himself to go the whole way. He still forbade his priests to marry, while continuing to maintain a private harem of his own. Nor would he give up his monopoly on the prostitution business in the cities under his control.

had launched was engendering ideas he could neither accept nor control. His writings were widely read, but others could write, too. Moreover, he was having problems with inconsistency. He had objected strongly, for example, to Karlstadt's congregation-appointed clergy, but had not he, Martin Luther, proposed a "priesthood of all believers?" He may not have meant that all believers are called to a public ministry of word and sacrament, but this was how it could be taken. Then again, how could any such issue be dealt with rationally when he had ruled out human reason as inapplicable to the experience of God? But surely, Luther replied, they could see that he had not ruled out human reason in questions of good order in the church. Indeed, he affirmed it.

Attendant doctrinal problems notwithstanding, the rapid spread of Luther's ideas was seemingly irresistible. With Charles absent in Spain, enforcement of the Edict of Worms was left to his brother, Archduke Ferdinand, and the German princes. Hardly had the Reichstag broken up than many of them began questioning its decision. Edict or no edict, in 1523 the free city of Frankfurt declared itself Lutheran, as did Landgrave Philip of Hesse, neighbor to Saxony, and thus also the powerful Archbishop Hermann von Wied of Cologne.

Landgrave Philip of Hesse

John the Constant

In Nuremberg, by city decree, congregations of monks and nuns were forced to accept the supervision of Lutheran ministers instead of priests, and religious orders were similarly affected. Nuns were dragged from their convents by Lutheran parents. The famous Italian preacher Peter Martyr Vermigli became Lutheran. So did the grand master of the Teutonic Knights, the order controlling the region that would become Prussia.[2] Luther's protector, Frederick the Wise, died in May 1525, after receiving Communion in two kinds. He was succeeded by his brother John (the Constant), who continued to protect Luther.

Against all this the papacy seemed powerless. The year 1522 was only nine days old when startling news arrived from Rome that Charles's old tutor, Adrian of Utrecht, was now Pope Adrian VI. (He would be the only Netherlander to gain the papacy, at any rate up to the twenty-first century, and the last non-Italian chosen until John Paul II in 1978.) By June 1522 Adrian would greatly impress Rome's citizens by arriving in their city to assume his office when some forty thousand Romans were fleeing it. The plague was raging there, and the streets were piled with bodies.

Adrian dismissed the hundreds of servants, poets, artists, and builders employed by his predecessor, Leo X. Retaining just four servants, he lived in a little house within the papal palace grounds, while personally risking his life to do what he could for the plague-stricken. But soon he also demonstrated himself the uncompromising hardliner who had previously served as Spain's inquisitor-general, and ultimately would prove no more adept as ruler of the Catholic Church than he had as Charles's regent in Spain.

Furthermore, Adrian had barely arrived in Rome when events in the East sent panic through the entire Italian peninsula. Süleyman had

Adrian VI, former tutor to Charles V and sole Netherlander ever to become pope, as portrayed by Francesco Ubertini Bacchiacca in 1525. Pope Adrian initially impressed the citizens of Rome by entering the city to assume office despite a raging plague that had littered the streets with corpses. But Adrian's austere ways ultimately turned them against him, and he proved no more capable of ruling the church than he had as Charles's regent in Spain.

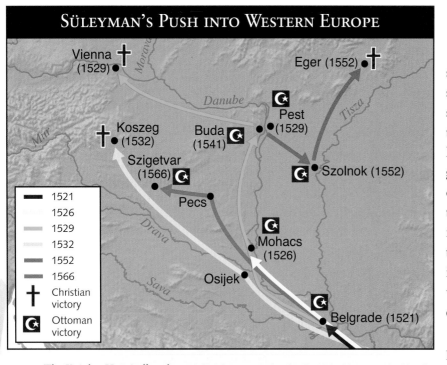

SÜLEYMAN'S PUSH INTO WESTERN EUROPE

Vienna ✝
(1529) ●

Eger (1552) ✝
●

Danube

Pest ☪
● (1529)

Koszeg ✝
● (1532)

Buda ☪
(1541)

Szigetvar
(1566) ☪ ●

Szolnok (1552) ☪ ●

Pecs ●

	1521
	1526
	1529
	1532
	1552
	1566
✝	Christian victory
☪	Ottoman victory

Drava

Mohacs ☪
(1526)

Osijek ●

Sava

Belgrade (1521) ☪ ●

The Knights Hospitaller, the Crusader military order once responsible for defense of the Holy Land, settled on the island of Rhodes after Acre fell to the forces of Islam in 1291. By 1522 they numbered no more than three hundred knights and perhaps five thousand paid troops and militia, but their fortifications (below) were considered the strongest in the entire Mediterranean.

shown up off the island of Rhodes, scene of his father's only failure, with some two hundred ships and more than one hundred thousand men. The Knights Hospitaller, who owned and governed the island, could assemble only three hundred knights, another three hundred armed servants, forty-five hundred men in the Rhodes militia, and about four hundred mercenaries from Crete. In short, the defenders were outnumbered by something like eighteen to one.

The Hospitallers were well prepared, however, and their fortress on Rhodes, to which they had retreated after the fall of Acre during the Crusades 231 years earlier, was considered the most impregnable in the entire Mediterranean theater. For the next six months Rhodes held off the Muslim horde. Though Turkish artillery reduced much of the wall to rubble, wave after wave of attackers was repelled with casualties that horrified the Muslim commanders. By one count, half the attacking force was wounded or killed. In vain Süleyman angrily berated his generals, firing one after another, and publicly thrashed his naval commander. Still the fortress held.

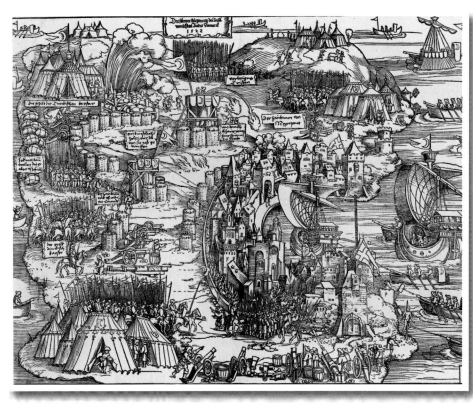

Throughout the autumn Pope Adrian pleaded with the princes of Europe to send relief to Rhodes, but they ignored him, being otherwise occupied. Finally, with more than half their number dead, the knights agreed to surrender, on condition they be allowed to vacate the island unmolested. This time Süleyman kept his word, though his Janissaries visited rape and pillage on the townspeople.

The valor of Rhodes's defense, however, could not disguise the frightening implications of its loss. For more than a century the Hospitallers had denied the Muslims unimpeded control of the eastern Mediterranean. Now Süleyman had removed Rhodes by conquest and had also neutralized Venice, his biggest naval rival, by treaty. Nearly all the Christian ports on the Mediterranean and Adriatic lay open to raids by Muslim corsairs, which would visit terror upon them for the next two to three hundred years. Meanwhile, the homeless Hospitallers asked Charles for a place to live. Eight years later, in 1530, he ceded to them the island of Malta—a decision which, though the emperor could not have known it, would save western Europe from Islam (see ch. 11).

As the knights were surrendering Rhodes, Pope Adrian was sending a legate north to an imperial Reichstag at Nuremberg to demand the arrest and execution of Luther, and to plead for a crusade against Süleyman. No sooner had the papal legate crossed the Alps than he found himself publicly jeered, and the Reichstag met his pleas and demands with torrents of abuse. What had the pope done all these years, its members angrily demanded, about the hundreds of grievances sent to the Vatican?

The legate's private instructions contained an admission that the curia itself might be the chief cause of dissension in Germany, but he could hardly say so in public. He returned to Rome chastened, having accomplished nothing. Adrian died within the year, by then hated by the Romans for his austerities.[3] His successor, the Medici pope Clement VII, would produce what the Catholic historian Warren H. Carroll calls the papacy's "greatest disaster since the Lombards devastated the country a thousand years before" (*The Cleaving of Christendom*, 2000), notably the sack of Rome by Charles's unpaid army (described in vol. 8, ch. 11). And within two years disaster of a very different kind would also befall parts of Germany—the terrible Peasants' Revolt (see sidebar, p. 44). For this many would blame not the pope but the teachings of Martin Luther, who was hailed by the unfortunate peasants, with good reason, as their prophet and leader. For example, after the Catholic loyalist Duke George of Saxony ordered copies of his Bible confiscated, Luther wrote this about the German princes:

Although the Knights Hospitaller and their militia were outnumbered by an estimated sixteen to one, half the Turkish force is believed to have perished in its initial attack. The besieged fortress (diagramed above) then held out for six months but, with no help coming from Europe, had to surrender in December 1522. Though the Hospitallers established a powerful new base on the island of Malta, most Christian ports on the Mediterranean now lay vulnerable to raids by Turkish corsairs.

3. The citizens of Rome were famous for the harsh treatment to which they subjected popes they disliked. When rumors circulated that Pope Adrian had been poisoned by his physician, the Romans began taking up a collection to build a statue—of the physician. The epitaph on Adrian's tomb, incidentally, noted that he regarded his call to the papacy as the greatest misfortune of his life.

Aye, princes, your just reward is at hand. You are recognized for what you really are: rogues and rascals. You are weighed in a just balance and found wanting. The people know you, through and through, and a terrible chastisement is encircling you closer and closer and it will not be turned aside. The people, utterly wearied of you, will no longer endure your tyranny and iniquity, nor will God. The world now is not the world as it used to be, wherein you hunted men as though they were beasts.

What could this be but a call to rebellion? Luther firmly denied any such intent, pronouncing a condemnation of the peasants that would be quoted against him for years to come. In it he exhorted the nobles to "stab, smite, throttle, and slay these mad dogs without mercy, with a good conscience to the last ounce of strength . . . Such times are these that a prince shall win heaven by bloodshed sooner than others by prayer." Nothing "can be more hurtful or devilish than a rebel," he added, seemingly unconscious of the fact that much of the Catholic world by then considered Luther himself the worst of rebels.

Viewing the whole spectacle of the revolt with horror, Luther denounced Thomas Müntzer in particular because he used the gospel to urge the peasants to "slay the godless." But he loosed an equally harsh execration on the princes for their vengeful brutality in suppressing the revolt.

Curiously, his reason for condemning the peasants was embedded in his theology. In a sense he was still a mendicant friar, who did not consider that the comforts or pains of this world should be of central concern to Christians—their focus should be on the next world. The peasants' complaints were essentially worldly, therefore religiously irrelevant. Townspeople proved to be no more pleased than the peasants with this sort of sermon. When Luther preached it in Thuringia, his listeners threw mud at him. At Eisleben, his birthplace, some listeners tried to drown him out by ringing the church bells.

Replying to the princes who blamed him for causing the revolt, he pointed out that the Wittenberg region, where his influence was greatest, remained relatively quiet. Gradually and reluctantly, however, Luther was coming to view the princes in a pragmatic light, recognizing that many of them regarded his activities primarily as a chance to benefit financially and politically at the expense of the Church of Rome. He was also beginning to believe that he never would succeed in changing the Roman church. He would have to establish a new one, and who but the princes could back it?

Something else would soon radically change, notably Luther's life. Monks and nuns continued to abandon their monasteries throughout Germany (though this was a criminal offense), and often married one another. When twelve nuns wanted to leave the Cistercian convent at Grimma, Saxony, in 1522, Luther arranged for a fish merchant to spirit them away in empty barrels, then found them husbands. But for one woman, Katherine von Bora (from a town near Hanover), he found no takers although she was attractive, intelligent, and witty. "I guess I'll have to marry Martin himself," Katherine reportedly quipped, and apparently the idea took root. Luther (age forty-two) proposed and Katherine (twenty-six) consented. Duly wed, they moved into an old Augustinian monastery donated to them by the elector, and Luther—although still occasionally beset by severe

Katherine von Bora was one of twelve nuns whom Luther helped escape from their convent. Concerned about their subsequent fate, he sought husbands for them all but reportedly could find no match for the attractive and intelligent Katherine. "I guess I'll have to marry Martin himself," said she. The marriage was by all accounts exceedingly happy.

Hans Luther, Sr.

Philip II of Spain

depression—became exceedingly happy. How wonderful it was, he later wrote, to have someone else at your table, and to awaken with two pigtails on the pillow beside you. Hans, the first of their six children, was born a year later.

Luther's imperial enemy was likewise matrimonially inclined, but marriage for Charles Habsburg necessarily hinged on strategy and state policy. Love came second if it existed at all, and since infancy he had been betrothed to at least six candidates. In 1526 he married his cousin Isabella of Portugal. He had three reasons: Spain wanted a treaty with Portugal to secure its western frontier; Isabella brought with her a handsome dowry; and she was said to be intelligent, devout, and wise.

Afterward, possibly to his own astonishment, Charles fell deeply in love with this princess who bore the name of the great Isabella, Charles's grandmother and the ancestor to whom Charles is most frequently likened (see vol. 8, ch. 8). He made his queen regent of Spain during his many absences, a job she performed most competently. They had five children, three of whom would survive—two daughters, and a son destined to become Philip II. Thirteen years later, when Isabella lay dying, Charles spent day after day kneeling in prayer by her bedside. He wore mourning garments for the remaining nineteen years of his life.

His marriage in March was followed by bad news for his empire. That summer the German princes met as a Reichstag at Speyer, on the Rhine upstream from Worms, to decide what to do about the Edict of Worms. Ferdinand, chairing the meeting, wanted the edict enforced and Luther arrested and executed. So did Charles and the pope. Though Catholic princes were dominant in numbers, the Protestant contingent had sufficient strength to make it virtually certain that an imposed decision would result in civil war. After arguing for two months, the Reichstag compromised by agreeing to refer Luther's fate to a church council. In the meantime, it decided, "every state shall so live, rule, and believe as it may hope and trust to answer before His Imperial Majesty."

Back in Spain, Charles reluctantly concluded that the Edict of Worms was indeed dead. Soon Schleswig-Holstein, Silesia, Lüneburg, East Friesland, and the cities of Hamburg, Lübeck, Bremen, Ulm, Frankfurt, Augsburg, and Nuremberg declared themselves Lutheran. Only south Germany remained in the Catholic fold. This division was on the way to becoming permanent, and Luther consequently was safe. Someone else presumably also rejoiced. As the delegates left the Reichstag of Speyer, the army of Süleyman, more massive than ever, crossed the Drava River and headed north for Buda and Pest. The enemy, their spies assured them, was still reassuringly divided.

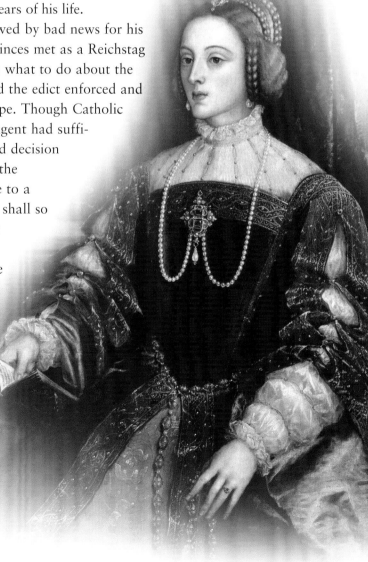

Queen Isabella of Portugal, by Titian. Betrothed in 1526 to Charles V for political reasons, she became the great love of the emperor's life. Reputedly both devout and wise, she bore her husband five children in Spain during his frequent absences. Isabella died in 1539, and Charles wore mourning for the remaining nineteen years of his life.

Luther triggers a mass slaughter

Misreading his message, peasants in their thousands slay and are slain

How could Lady Helena, countess of Lupfen, possibly have predicted the effect of her perfectly reasonable request on that August holiday in 1524? She merely asked the peasants of her estate to stop putting up hay for a while and pick fresh strawberries instead, for a dinner at Stühlingen Castle. And oh yes, she added, would they gather her some ground snails as well—their shells made such handy spools for her skeins of thread.

To her astonishment, her Lupfen peasants seemed to go berserk. Why should they forfeit a chance to stockpile vital forage for their cattle, they angrily demanded, to harvest strawberries and snails? Anyhow, why must they make these labor payments to lords and monasteries? Why should they be treated like serfs or slaves? And off they marched to carry the word to three nearby estates in the Black Forest area of the Rhine Valley.

More marchers joined along the way, and at the village of Bulgenbach they acquired a leader, Hans Müller, a veteran of the Italian wars. Müller had them make a flag featuring the imperial black, red, and yellow, under which they proceeded to a big church festival at Waldshut, where beer was flowing freely. By then their numbers had swelled to some twelve hundred, they had collected a fair amount of money, and they were sending messengers in every direction. Complaints having achieved nothing, they proclaimed, it was time for action. Through the territories of Baden, the Rhineland, and the Moselle, the word went out and the peasantry rose.

The imperial flag was significant. There was no need whatsoever for the nobility, the revolutionaries contended, or for these huge monastic estates. One central government would suffice—namely the emperor's—to levy taxes, maintain order, and terminate the ceaseless warfare among princedoms. But the emperor's representative, Archduke Ferdinand of Austria, though he might secretly cherish such an idea, knew it was a practical impossibility. He gave the peasant representatives a conciliatory audience while hurriedly assembling troops.

From its epicenter in the Black Forest and Swabia, the revolt swiftly spread to Franconia in central Germany, west to Alsace and Lorraine, east to Tirol and Salzburg, north to the Upper Rhine, and south to German Switzerland. Disaffected urban dwellers and some entire cities, including Frankfurt, Mainz, and Würzburg, also rose. The newly founded Evangelical Peasant Brotherhood formulated its revolutionary manifesto, the "Twelve Articles of the Swabian Peasants," reprinted twenty-four times within the year. Their main demand: abolition of serfdom because "the Bible proves we are free, and we want to be free." Among other things, they claimed the right of a community to choose its own pastor and in conclusion promised to abandon any request proven to be unscriptural.

Who better to judge this last than Martin Luther? He would surely understand. But Luther did not understand. He condemned the revolutionaries as "mad dogs," urging the princes to slaughter them in good conscience. Soon the rebels were giving their enemies ample reason to do so. By April 1525 an estimated three hundred thousand peasants were in armed rebellion, seizing and burning towns and castles, and gorging on food and wine along the way. If only they had refrained "from fire and bloodshed," wrote a Würzburg episcopal official, the uprising could have been called a "wine war."

It was much more than that, and much worse. Monks and nuns fled from blazing cloisters; castle after castle was ransacked and gutted. Rebels in Alsace conscripted recruits from villages "in the name of Jesus Christ our Lord," then pillaged and burned all the churches they could. In Bamberg they spent three days torching castles, wrote a chronicler, and became "so evil and unruly" after swilling purloined wine that "no one was certain of his life and goods."

The mayhem crested in Weinsberg on Easter Sunday 1525. Goaded by a vengeful innkeeper named Jäcklein Rohrbach, a mob forced its way into the church. According to Ernest Belfort Bax (*The Peasant War, Germany*, 1903), some forty lords, knights, and their men-at-arms who had sought refuge there were struck down. The rebels then forced Count Ludwig von Helfenstein to run a gauntlet of spears before fatally stabbing him in front of his wife and two-year-old son, whose face was slashed in passing. They stripped the countess and dressed her in rags; clutching her wounded toddler, she was transported by dung cart to the town of Heilbronn, itself under assault.[1] A stronghold of the wealthy Teutonic Knights, Heilbronn—and its riches—soon fell. That Easter day the city of Würzburg joined the rebellion; destruction of forty district monasteries and one hundred and twenty castles followed. Stuttgart and Erfurt fell a week later.

Meanwhile a certain Thomas Müntzer, thirty-six—much influenced, it was said, by the radical "Zwickau Prophets"—had emerged as a leader in the Thuringian rising. As his peasant gangs rampaged through Thuringia, he castigated Luther, his onetime mentor, as "Dr. Pussyfoot, the basking sycophant" of the nobility, who refused to see that poor men had no time to read the Word of God. The common people, Müntzer thundered, were God's elect, intended by the Almighty to vanquish the unholy and bring in a new order. "Strike! Strike! Strike!" he cried to his men. "Remember the command of God to Moses to destroy utterly and show no mercy!"

Mercy was arguably even less evident in mid-May 1525, when Catholic and Lutheran forces from Bavaria, Lorraine, Hesse, and Saxony marched on Müntzer and his ragtag army at Frankenhausen in

Thuringia, near the future Frederick Barbarossa monument on Kyffhäuser Mountain (see vol. 7, p. 89). A rainbow suddenly appeared, and the jubilant peasants greeted it as a sign of God's providence—it was, after all, the very symbol on their banner. But then the cannonade began, and five thousand of them soon lay dead. Thomas Müntzer was captured, tortured, and executed on May 25, 1525. A Catholic priest, he returned before death to his faith.

The duke of Lorraine meanwhile suppressed insurgents in Alsace with equal efficiency and savagery, massacring some sixteen thousand near the town of Zabern (now Saverne), leaving their corpses to rot. The troops of the Swabian League slaughtered thousands more in Württemberg, then defeated and burned Weinsberg. They captured innkeeper Rohrbach, chained him to a tree, and burned him to death. Uprisings in the Odenwald and Rothenburg were subdued in June; Stühlingen, where the revolt began, surrendered in July. The Peasants' War effectively ended in mid-July, when original leader Hans Müller, captured while besieging Radolfzell, was tortured and beheaded.

Reformer Andreas Karlstadt evaded a similar fate by sliding down Rothenburg city wall on a rope one night and seeking refuge with Martin Luther. Karlstadt, one of Luther's most virulent critics, was in a particularly anomalous position, mistrusted by the peasants for opposing violence and hunted as a rebel by the princes for his radical preaching. Despite their bitter theological differences, Luther sheltered him and his family for eight crucial weeks.

This war, in which an estimated one hundred thousand peasants died, altered the course of the Reformation. Radical groups like the Anabaptists, hitherto intent on transforming society, pacifically withdrew from the world instead, while Lutheranism became increasingly allied with established secular authority. In the immediate aftermath, the rebels continued to suffer pitiless reprisals. The margrave of Ansbach blinded sixty townsmen because they "refused to look upon him" as their master. Sixty-four rebels were executed in Würzburg; the bishop then traveled through the diocese with his executioner and dispatched 272 more. In August an imperial Reichstag mandated clemency, but the lot of most peasants grew worse under princes now incontestably entrenched.

Though the brief and brutal rebellion is known to history as the "Peasants' Revolt," there were many such uprisings in late medieval Europe. Euan Cameron's *The European Reformation* (1991) records: "These revolts grew more frequent in the years up to 1525. Only seven have been identified in the first half of the fifteenth century; six during 1450–75, eight in 1475-99, but no less than eighteen in 1500–24."

The 1525 insurrection, whatever its causes and consequences, would find admirers in a much later age. The nineteenth-century Marxist theorist Friedrich Engels would cite it as a prototypical example of class warfare, and the East German mark in 1975 would carry a portrait of Thomas Müntzer. However, in his *History of the Church* (1980), editor Hubert Jedin notes that the 1524–25 outbreak was not a uniform and centrally directed undertaking. Rather, it was a group of individual movements, all of which caught fire on the same combustible material. Neither were the rebels the poor of the villages. They were, he writes, "the prosperous and respected farmers." ∎

1. According to Bax, Countess Martha, an illegitimate daughter of Emperor Maximilian, survived the ordeal, as did her son; she later entered a convent. Count von Helfenstein had on several occasions slaughtered small bands of peasants.

The attack of a well-armed horde of peasants on the town of Weinsberg on Easter Sunday 1525, is depicted by twentieth-century artist Carl Hinrichs. In the Peasants' Revolt of 1524–1525, rebel leaders had incited the peasantry to sack and destroy towns, castles, and monasteries throughout Germany. Luther, condemning them as "mad dogs," urged the princes to destroy the revolutionaries. This they did, with much slaughter.

There followed the greatest military catastrophe in Hungarian history. In the five years since the fall of Belgrade, Hungary's repeated pleas for western military help had been consistently refused—partly because the West was preoccupied with its religious divisions but also because the Hungarian government, in the view of some observers anyway, was notoriously inept. King Louis II (*Lajos II* in Hungarian), descendant of the Polish Jagiello family, had inherited the throne at age ten in 1516. Strange stories were told of his birth—how he had been removed from his dead mother's body, for instance, and kept alive in the warm carcass of a slaughtered hog. Growing prematurely into adulthood, Louis, his many critics said, had become a gray-haired playboy by age eighteen—carousing long, hard, and nightly, sleeping until noon, and gradually bankrupting his treasury. His nobles looked on disgusted, baffled, and anxious. They knew Süleyman would soon be upon them.

Some historians offer somewhat different causes for Hungary's oncoming disaster, however. Brian Cartledge in his *The Will to Survive: A History of Hungary* (2006) blames Hungary's incessantly feuding nobility. Charles's ambassador describes them: "Everyone is seeking his own profit and, if he can, lives on the fat of public property. They have no esteem for other countries. There is no case so evil that it cannot be won by the bribing of two or three men. They are haughty and proud, unable to either command or obey, but unwilling to take advice."

The hapless King Louis II (above), a playboy at eighteen whose critics said he was inclined to carouse the night away while the Turks pressed closer, could find no support in the West despite his close Habsburg connections. He and his Hungarians faced the Turk alone in August 1526 at odds of five to one. Below, a worker scythes the grass at the memorial to their defeat on the plain of Mohacs.

Mary of Austria

When Louis called on his nobility to meet the Turk advance, says Cartledge, many barons, jealous of the Habsburgs, ignored him. Lesser nobles were unwilling to leave their estates at harvest time.

One thing, however, King Louis II had undeniably done right. Possibly through the sagacity of his Polish father he had married Mary of Austria, younger

sister of Charles V. (She would later serve for years, however, as the competent and beloved governor of Charles's possessions in the Netherlands.) Louis' marriage to Maria brought help from the West, however, even if it also made Archduke Ferdinand in neighboring Austria his brother-in-law. Ferdinand apparently saw the situation as simply hopeless. "The Turks are so powerful," he wrote the beleaguered Louis in 1523, "that resisting them is impossible. We're both doomed."

The blow fell in August 1526. Süleyman had moved north into Hungary, his army supplied by some eight hundred barges and riverboats that followed it up the Danube. The young king dithered. Should he move out what forces he had to meet the enemy in the difficult marshlands of the south? Should he meet him at the gates of Buda? Somewhere in between? Finally opting for this third possibility, he commanded his nobles to march southward. They would do no such thing, they replied—not unless King Louis went with them.

So he did. But when he rode out of Buda, Cartledge records, he headed a force of only four thousand men. Others later joined him, but by then it was too late. Thus the twenty-five-thousand-man Hungarian army, outnumbered by five to one at least, met Süleyman's massive contingents on the plain of Mohacs (pronounced *Mo*-hatch), on the right bank of the Danube about ninety miles due south of Buda. Some three thousand Hungarians died in that battle, including twenty-eight nobles, five hundred knights, and seven Catholic prelates. King Louis, fighting to the last, drowned when he fell from his horse while crossing a stream. Two thousand prisoners were decapitated, and their heads arrayed on poles stuck in the mud before the sultan's tent.

A memorial at the site near Mohacs, Hungary, where attacking Turks killed three thousand Hungarians in battle and afterward decapitated another two thousand. The sculpture depicts Sultan Süleyman I dangling some of his enemies' heads.

Queen Mary, escorted by fifty German knights, escaped to Austria as the Turks marched north from Mohacs. Süleyman's Janissaries slaughtered or enslaved the entire populace of helpless Buda and Pest before burning the two cities to the ground, and then the sultan headed homeward, cutting a wide swath of massacre, mayhem, and destruction. His victory carried another significant consequence for Hungary. King Louis having perished without heirs, Ferdinand immediately claimed the Hungarian throne for the empire, a claim the Habsburgs would assiduously pursue.[4]

Some historians have wondered about the entire absence of Charles from all this. Where was the emperor? But the answer seems clear enough—he was wholly absorbed with his second problem, Francis I. Francis's invasions of Luxembourg and Navarre had both failed, but Charles realized that Europe could not be united against the Turkish threat until this interior enemy was thoroughly vanquished. So he created an alliance against him. Charles was to attack France from Spain and Italy, while Henry VIII would attack from England (with a view to becoming king of France). The new pope,

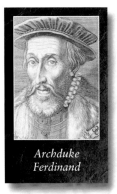

Archduke Ferdinand

Pope Clement VII

4. The Turkish invasion of Hungary inaugurated a very long period of subjugation. Süleyman set up a Muslim client king as rival claimant for Louis' crown. Archduke Ferdinand persistently asserted the imperial Habsburg claim. In the eighteenth century the Habsburgs would finally prevail, becoming in some sense Süleyman's beneficiaries. This situation would last until the end of the First World War in 1918 (which would see the end of the Ottoman Empire as well).

5. The nineteenth-century French poet and playwright Honoré de Balzac, in one of his "droll stories" (*The Continence of King Francis I*), details the agony supposedly suffered by the "lecherous" king for lack of female companionship in his Spanish prison. When his jailer, a Spanish nobleman, consults both Charles and the pope, the sympathetic emperor confers royal assent to some relief for Francis, and the pope supplies a special indulgence. But the problem remains, since no acceptable French woman is close at hand, and Francis refuses to consider a Spaniard. His distraught jailer nonetheless sends a lady to his apartments, whom the king finds eminently satisfactory. "Who was she?" he asks. "I'm sorry to confess," replies the nobleman, "it was my wife." Given Francis's reputation, the story—whether history, classical French fiction, or mere gossip—becomes believable.

6. Charles V several times challenged Francis I to settle their differences with a duel—a clear measure of the emperor's frustration with his slippery adversary. Dueling was a practice still common among the nobility, though more for settling personal grievances than for affairs of state, but among kings it was rare indeed. The very idea would occur to few but Charles, a thoroughgoing medievalist. Francis refused all his challenges, and the next pope, Paul III, forbade dueling between kings.

Clement VII, likewise anxious to see Europe united, eagerly made the papacy a party to this plan.

But then Charles had to watch his grand scheme fall apart when Henry failed to invade France, and Charles's own invasion from Italy got as far as Marseilles and stalled. Francis took the initiative, drove the emperor's force into Lombardy, and seemed on the verge of certain victory. Pope Clement, predicting an imperial defeat, quietly switched sides to ally himself with Francis. Charles in a fury condemned him as "a poltroon of a pope," adding bitterly: "I have lost money, men and friends for his sake. I could never have believed he would desert me." Perhaps someday, he mused, "Martin Luther will prove to have been a man of worth." In any event, the pope had guessed wrong. In a desperate night attack Charles's army assailed the French at Pavia, twenty-five miles south of Milan, defeated them, and took the king himself prisoner.

The Battle of Pavia on February 24, 1525, should have ended the conflict but did not, being followed by two major reversals for the emperor. The story of how his troops, unpaid and uncontrolled, rampaged south from Pavia and sacked the city of Rome, effectually making Pope Clement his prisoner, is told in vol. 8, ch. 11. The emperor, rightly or wrongly, was widely blamed for this. The second reversal was due to the severe terms set by Charles for the release of his royal captive, whom he imprisoned first in Italy, then in Spain.[5] So extreme were these terms that Francis signed them but the minute he crossed the border into France he claimed rightful cause to scornfully repudiate them. Oaths made under such duress are not binding, he declared.

Thus the war continued. Francis tried to persuade Venice, Milan, Florence, and Pope Clement to drive the imperial forces out of Italy. Failing in this, he allied himself with Henry VIII, who had again switched sides. When the French and English ambassadors confronted Charles at Burgos in northern Spain with their declaration of war, the emperor rose furiously to his feet and indignantly spurned it. King Francis, he roared, had amply demonstrated himself a liar, a coward, dishonorable, and not a gentleman, and must be allowed to shed no more Christian blood in battle. He, Emperor Charles, was thereby challenging the king of France to settle their dispute hand to hand, in personal combat. Thunderstruck, the ambassadors reported back to Francis, who toyed with the idea and then rejected it.[6]

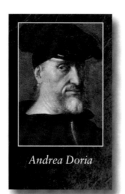

Andrea Doria

Queen Eleanor of Austria

Meanwhile Andrea Doria, the renowned Genoese admiral who was besieging the imperial forces at Naples, suddenly withdrew his fleet and declared for the emperor. You couldn't trust King Francis, he complained. At about that same time the French army in Italy was stricken by plague and disintegrated. But fighting continued, stopping briefly after Charles's aunt Margaret, then his regent in the Netherlands, brokered a treaty with Francis's mother, Louise of Savoy, in 1529. Known as "the Ladies' Peace," it also arranged a marriage between Francis and Charles's older sister Eleanor, widow of the king of Portugal, but this had no discernible influence on the French king.

The Catholic-Lutheran gulf was meanwhile widening. The Catholic princes, confronting the Lutherans at a second Reichstag of Speyer in March 1529, voted to put a brake on further expansion of Lutheranism, pending a full church council promised by the pope the following year. The Lutheran princes walked out, met separately, and published their "protest" against this decision—and it was here, according to some records, that the word "Protestant" first came into use. In October the Protestant landgrave Philip of Hesse arranged a colloquy with Luther and Swiss reformer Huldrych Zwingli, to try to resolve their differences. They failed. (See sidebar, p. 50.)

But that fall there occurred what many saw as the day of final doom, when Süleyman the Magnificent and his Turks drew up before the almost indefensible city of Vienna. With their thousands of neat white tents stretching to the horizon, the sultan issued dire warnings of the slaughter and slavery that would be the penalty for any resistance. The defenders answered with their cannon, and Süleyman ordered his men to attack. In three days, he boasted, he would be eating breakfast in St. Stephen's Cathedral.

This was bravado and he knew it. Months earlier his vast force had departed in great magnificence from Ottoman-held Bulgaria, but since then much had gone badly—particularly the weather. Interminable rain turned roads to mush, bogging down the heavy cannon. Rivers became raging torrents almost impossible to cross. At Belgrade he was a month behind schedule and at Buda had to abandon all his heavy cannon. He still had his light cannon, however, surely sufficient for Vienna's crumbling walls. But these walls had been hastily and effectively reinforced by a defense force consisting of urgently assembled Austrian militia, along with

The war with Francis I of France was going poorly for Charles V, so poorly that Pope Clement VII switched his allegiance to the French. But the battle fought in February 1525 at Pavia, Italy, changed everything. King Francis, cowering at the lower right corner of a painting by Bernard van Orley (above), was taken captive. (below) Charles V shows his chivalrous side by visiting his well-tended prisoner—magnanimity that Francis would reward by reneging on the release terms.

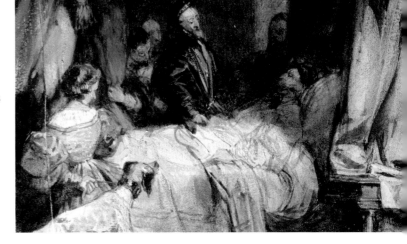

The archrivals of the new age

Zwingli fought Martin Luther for years, then wept when they couldn't agree

When Huldrych Zwingli inexplicably disappeared from Zurich in September 1529, people half believed the devil had carried him off—until his explanatory letter reached the city council. He had stolen away, the zealous pastor confessed, because he feared the councillors would oppose his going. Despised by both Catholics and Lutherans, and vulnerable to imperial arrest, Zwingli had nonetheless ventured 240 miles north to Marburg, Germany, to meet at last his longstanding rival—Martin Luther.

For years the two men had disputed theology, the nature of the Eucharist in particular, but always at a distance. Zwingli, acknowledged front-runner of the Swiss Reformation both theologically and politically, may have been jealous of his German contemporary. He (Zwingli) had been preaching the gospel of Christ, he once testily remarked, before the world ever heard of Martin Luther.

Zwingli and Luther had much in common, including a background in humanist philosophy, an admiration for the renowned Dutch scholar Desiderius Erasmus, and intense devotion to Bible study. Zwingli recalled poring over the New Testament as a young priest, seeking to

The seemingly contradictory Swiss reformer Huldrych Zwingli, "third man of the Reformation," whose theology would inform the basic confessions of the reformed churches.

"learn the meaning of the Word out of the Word itself." But his birth and education in Switzerland gave him quite a different perspective from Luther's. Ordained in 1506 at age twenty-two, he served ten years in Glarus, a canton that supplied many mercenaries for foreign wars. Zwingli accompanied them as chaplain in several pro-papal Italian campaigns, which persuaded him that mercenary service was immoral and that Switzerland's cities and its thirteen cantons must unite.

At thirty-three he left Glarus to concentrate on scholarship and in 1519 was appointed "people's priest" at the Grossmünster ("great church") in Zurich, where he became a preaching sensation. Abandoning the traditional cycle of scripture readings, Zwingli's startling technique was to read straight through the Gospels beginning with Matthew (a book he claimed "unknown to the Germans"), pausing frequently to explain the text. Within two years he was also elected a canon of the Grossmünster, which helped him persuade the Zurich council to radically reform their canton.[1]

This began in 1522 with "the affair of the sausages," when he defended Grossmünster parishioners who defied the Lenten fast by publicly slicing and serving smoked meat. (Since specifically abstaining from meat was not mentioned in the Bible, he said, fast-breaking was no sin.) Later came statue-smashing riots that enabled Zwingli to persuade the council to scour Zurich churches of images and stained glass, and exult in their "positively luminous" whitewashed walls. The reformers also converted monasteries and convents into civic hospitals and welfare institutions, and petitioned the bishop to cancel clerical celibacy.

Zwingli, who was living with a beautiful widow, Anna Reinhard, had a personal stake in this issue. (They were publicly married two years later, just before the birth of their first child.) The next item to vanish from Christian worship in Zurich was music, choral or instrumental. Zwingli himself was an accomplished musician, scorned by Catholic critics as a "guitar player and evangelist on the flute." By Easter Sunday 1525, when an austere vernacular Communion service of his own devising replaced the Mass, Zurich's reformation was essentially complete.

The process was not without violence, nor Huldrych Zwingli without a dark side. Reform's radical wing, the Anabaptists in particular, wanted the town run by the church, not the city council, and baptism became crucially divisive. With Zwingli's apparent approval, the council decreed in 1525 that parents must baptize their babies or be banished and in 1526 forbade adult rebaptism on pain of death. Three defiant Anabaptists leaders were banished; Felix Manz returned only to be executed by drowning in 1527. The sect was effectively driven from Zurich.

Meanwhile, Zwingli was provoking the ire of German reformer Martin Luther concerning the manner in which Christ is present in the Eucharist, Zwingli insisting that Holy Communion was entirely an affair of the mind—a sign or pledge, like a soldier's oath of allegiance. He doubtless drew this in part from the "sacramentarian" movement, whose roots lay in the spiritualist teachings of Desiderius Erasmus. It was largely this issue that occasioned Zwingli's 1529 journey to Marburg to meet Luther in person at a colloquy organized by Landgrave Philip of

Hesse to reconcile German and Swiss reformers.

Their historic encounter was a heated one. It climaxed with Luther furiously chalking on the conference table the words of Jesus: "This is my Body"—the Gospel underpinning his conviction that Christ's body and blood are physically present in the Eucharist (Matthew 26:26–28, Mark 14:12–25, and Luke 22:7–20).

"This passage breaks your neck!" Zwingli shot back, countering with John 6:63—"The Spirit gives life but the flesh profits nothing." Luther was unimpressed. "German necks don't break that easily," he retorted, "and this is Hesse, not Switzerland." In the end, one bystander wrote, Luther refused to shake hands, and "tears sprang to Zwingli's eyes, so that many noticed it."

The central importance of this issue was underscored nine months later when three separate documents were submitted to the Reichstag of Augsburg: the Augsburg Confession (Lutheran), the Tetrapolitan Confession, and the Zwinglian Confession.[2] Landgrave Philip's hope for an amicable alliance among German and Swiss reformers was doomed when in February 1531 Zwingli refused to join with the Lutheran-sponsored league to oppose Catholicism. He cited insuperable theological differences with the Lutherans.

His own efforts for military unity among Switzerland's reform cantons continued, however, even though these made him increasingly unpopular even in Zurich. That October he died in battle, at age forty-seven, leading Zurich's small army against the attacking Catholic forest cantons. Many councillors were slain and Zwingli wounded. Twice he refused the offices of a priest, causing an infuriated Catholic captain to spear him through as a heretic. Discovering this was the hated Zwingli, forest soldiers quartered his corpse, mixed it with dung, and burned it.

Although generally acknowledged as "the third man of the Reformation," Huldrych Zwingli left no following bearing his name. Yet he and his colleagues produced, between 1525 and 1531, the influential Swiss-German Zurich Bible (also known as the Froschauer Bible, after its Zurich printer). Moreover, Zwingli's theology is foundational for the basic confessions of reformed churches. Scholars note that Heinrich Bullinger, his immediate successor in Zurich, was quick to proclaim Zwingli as a martyr and to build upon his work. Twenty years later Bullinger was able to work out with Swiss reform leaders a unified theology of the Lord's Supper acceptable to them all.

Their agreed-upon wording, not incompatible with Zwingli's, was that "in the Lord's Supper we eat and drink the body and blood of Christ, not, however, by means of a carnal presence of Christ's human nature, which is in heaven, but by the power of the Holy Spirit and the devout elevation of our soul to heaven." Signatories to this statement, called the *Consensus Tigurinus* (Zurich Consensus), included a man who arrived in Switzerland five years after Zwingli's death. His name was John Calvin. ∎

1. Zwingli's appointment as a canon of the Grossmünster encountered opposition because he was accused of seducing a respectable maiden. He admitted to fornication but claimed the woman was neither respectable nor a maiden. Church authorities accepted this.

2. The Tetrapolitan Confession, presented as a compromise on behalf of Strasbourg and three other cities, declared that Christ's body and blood are spiritually but not corporeally present in the Eucharistic feast. Zwingli's own formulation was: "We confess that the body of Christ is present in the sacred supper not as a body nor in the nature of a body, but sacramentally (i.e., symbolically) to the mind that is upright, pure, and reverent toward God."

The historic encounter at Marburg between old foes Huldrych Zwingli, sitting chin on fist at right, and Martin Luther, lecturing from notes, was not so serene as this painting by Wilhelm von Lindenschmit the Younger might suggest. At its close, Luther refused to shake hands, and Zwingli quietly wept.

Spanish musketeers and German pikemen (many of them Lutherans) sent by the emperor. Further, before Süleyman's arrival they had removed eight hundred buildings from the area outside the city walls, to provide their own cannon with a clear field of fire.

When his first assault wave was beaten back with frightful casualties, the sultan realized that Vienna would be no Mohacs. Before he could mount a second attack, the pikemen burst from the gates, slashed into the Janissary lines, inflicted heavy losses, and were back inside the city before their enemy could muster against them. The Janissaries, they had discovered, were not invincible. A second concerted Turkish attack also failed, and the Viennese sent mocking word to the sultan that his breakfast was getting cold.

His troops were getting colder. Day after day through September, unseasonably freezing rain drenched their tents and left them sagging. Their morale sagged with them. Süleyman had to thrash his men into a third assault, and when this too failed, he began his withdrawal. Last to leave were the Janissaries, after making a huge bonfire of the remains of their camp, into which they threw their Christian prisoners, many of them women and children. All the way home the rain assailed them.

Behind them the bells of Vienna tolled in victory. Süleyman explained that he had not really intended to take the city, merely to challenge Charles, who was too cowardly to face him. He was everywhere congratulated. No one dared to state the obvious, at any rate to his face, namely that for the first time he had been truly beaten. Even so, all Christian Europe knew that Süleyman would be back, if only because he soon acquired a new supporter, namely Francis I. No longer able to find Christian allies, Francis had sent his emissaries to the "Grande Porte" at Constantinople, where they were warmly welcomed. In the Ladies' Peace he had sworn to fight the Turks, of course, but what was a small matter such as that to a Renaissance man?

The Muslim incursion into Austria alarmed Lutherans as much as Catholics, Luther himself included. Initially he had depicted the Turks as God's judgment on a corrupt Christian church—just as the Assyrians had been God's judgment on a corrupt Israel—and had mocked papal calls for a crusade as just one more means

Below, the still formidable Turkish army besieges Vienna, as interpreted by seventeenth-century artist Pieter Snayers. After Süleyman defeated Hungary, extreme cold and rain slowed his army, forced it to abandon its heaviest cannon, and seriously disheartened his soldiers. Nevertheless, by September 1529 he was at the gates of the Austrian capital, boasting that soon he would eat breakfast in its cathedral. But its Catholic and Lutheran defenders, united at last, inflicted upon him his first significant defeat.

of channeling money into Rome. As Turkish forces closed in, however, his outlook changed. The Koran became "a foul and shameful book," the Turks an empire of "murderers." By 1529 he was preaching that to fight the Turks was to fight the devil, and the emperor had a clear responsibility to stop them.

But the emperor believed that the Turks could not be stopped unless Christians would effectively unite. With his Francis problem in abeyance, Charles came north, leaving Queen Isabella as regent in Spain. He paused at Bologna to be crowned emperor by the pope according to time-honored tradition, then proceeded to a third Reichstag being held at Speyer, where this time he would preside.[7] It was now March 1530, nine years since his imperial edict had ordered Luther arrested. Because this had not happened, Charles reasoned, the religious division had vastly widened, and now the Lutherans must be either reconciled to the church or suppressed. Greatly hoping for the former, he had asked them to prepare a definitive statement of what they believed, and why.

The document they produced, which would be known as the Confession of Augsburg, has often been hailed as the Magna Carta of Protestantism. Drawn up by Luther and Melanchthon, it was presented by the latter because Luther, still technically under the ban of the empire, was forbidden to attend the Reichstag. In the first of two parts it set forth, in delicately chosen language, points upon which its originators thought both sides were sure to agree. The second part covered points they thought would need debate. The Reichstag turned the document over to a Catholic committee, which rejected it on numerous counts. Charles then declared that the reformists had until the following April to return to the church—without mentioning what he would do if they refused.

This proved an inauspicious prelude for what would eventually follow. Archduke Ferdinand was elected king of the Romans in January 1531, preparatory to his eventually succeeding Charles as emperor, and the Protestant princes boycotted his subsequent coronation. In February Philip of Hesse formed an alliance with Elector John of Saxony and other reformist princes for the military defense of Protestantism. But by March 1532, when the princes Catholic and Protestant met at the Reichstag at Regensburg, the whole mood of belligerence had vanished. There was no mystery as to why. Süleyman was preparing a bigger and better assault on Vienna. With scant debate, both sides agreed to sustain the accepted religion of Catholic and Lutheran states, and to provide troops for Vienna. For one man in particular this represented a failure. Acting on behalf of his new ally, agents of King Francis I had striven mightily to foment a Catholic-Protestant war in Germany. They failed.

With religious strife unabated, Charles V asked the Lutherans for a definitive statement of belief. One was formulated by Luther and Melanchthon, and the painting above shows its presentation to the emperor. But at the Reichstag of Augsburg in 1530, which Charles convened by imperial edict (inset), Catholic representatives definitively rejected what has been called the Magna Carta of Protestantism.

7. The tradition that the Holy Roman Emperor must be crowned by the pope came to an end with Charles V. Thereafter, with Germany legally recognizing both Lutheran and Catholic churches, the Holy Roman Emperor reigned as "emperor-elect," in effect a purely secular title.

By the time their new treaty was signed on July 23, 1532, however, Süleyman's juggernaut was already at Belgrade, moving cross-country directly for Vienna, and this time the weather was fine. But something else went wrong. At the little town of Koszeg, near the Hungarian-Austrian border fifty miles south of Vienna, he encountered the first of a series of puny little forts. The Turks expected all of them to surrender either immediately or quickly to their overwhelming force, but to their surprise and initial amusement the commander at Koszeg, a Croatian noble named Nicolas Jrischitz, refused.

The usual bombardment with light cannon followed, but the walls held, and a mass assault against them likewise failed. Unaccustomed to such impudent defiance, the infuriated Süleyman resolved that the place must be taken, so he sent an advance force of sixteen thousand men on to Vienna and spent the next twenty-five days making eleven more onslaughts on the little fortress. But still it held, and finally he had to offer its defenders safe passage to Vienna if only they would quit. They accepted this offer, and he honored it.

But Koszeg's seven hundred soldiers had cost him valuable time. Some twenty thousand well-trained troops, Catholic and Protestant, had in the interval poured into Vienna to save the city. There were more to follow, and Charles himself was

Süleyman's juggernaut was at Belgrade, moving towards Vienna. But something went wrong. At Koszeg he encountered a series of puny forts, expecting them to surrender at once. They didn't.

in command. Worse still for Süleyman, a contingent of Protestants from Saxony had maneuvered the Turks' advance force into the teeth of a major artillery battery, wiping out almost the entire sixteen thousand. By ravaging the Austrian countryside, the sultan tried to lure Charles into open country for a fight, but Charles knew better. So Vienna was saved, and Süleyman had to go home again.

Twice more, respectively twenty and thirty-four years hence, Süleyman would move against Vienna, and twice more he would fail, and for much the same reason: his attack was stalled by a Christian outpost. In 1552 he would be stopped by the strong fortress of Eger, fifty miles northeast of Buda. Its two thousand defenders (both men and women) would hold out against an eighty-thousand-man Turkish army for thirty-four days, until the Turks would simply give up. The 1566 failure would be at Szigetvar, some fifty miles northwest of Mohacs. After many days the Szigetvar garrison would be overwhelmed and slaughtered, but a major calamity would coincidentally afflict the Turkish army. Sultan Süleyman—aging, sick, bitter, and depressed—would die in his tent. All his plans were thereupon canceled.[8] But this was years ahead, and in the interim Emperor Charles would meet his Muslim adversary again, not in Austria but in the Mediterranean theater (see ch. 11).

After 1530, Luther's role in the Protestant Reformation had begun to subside. He never entirely stopped preaching, lecturing, counseling, and writing, but he was increasingly obliged to divert his central attention to the necessities of a new church. He did not welcome the thought that this church would be named for him, however. Overhearing some youths at Wittenberg referring to themselves as "Lutherites," for example, he advised them to describe themselves simply as "Christians."

8. Süleyman, writes historian Diane Moczar (*Islam at the Gates: How Christendom Defeated the Ottoman Turks*, 2008), was the greatest of the Turkish sultans. His son and successor, known as "Selim the Sot," was one of the worst—although Süleyman had ordered the strangulation of two other sons and one grandson to assure his succession.

But as Lutheran this church most assuredly would be known. It would retain many Catholic practices and much Catholic theology as well—but in both respects with very significant departures. It preserved the solemnity of Holy Communion, for example, and Luther vigorously defended and retained infant baptism and kept an ordained clergy called by the congregation or other authorized agency. But its clergymen could be married, Communion in both kinds could be instituted at the desire of the congregation, and fasting and confession were optional. Sermons were to be short (twenty to twenty-five minutes), based on scripture, and devoid of theological controversy. But in Germany Lutheranism abandoned the Catholic-Orthodox principle of the episcopacy with a succession of bishops dating back to apostolic times. And the concept of "sacrifice" in the Holy Communion was also rejected. (See sidebar, pp. 190–92.)

The Hungarian town of Eger, shown here in a National Geographic photo by Albert Moldvay, stood directly on Süleyman's path to Vienna in 1552. The fortress seemed a negligible obstacle, but its garrison of just two thousand withstood eighty thousand Turks for more than a month. The siege was ultimately called off, ensuring that Süleyman's third attempt at capturing Vienna would fail as sensationally as the first two.

Vernacular German replaced Latin in Lutheran services, but only over time. Joseph Lortz, in his *Reformation in Germany* (1968), notes that until the 1530s and '40s and even later the old chants were often sung in Latin by Protestants in almost every province of Germany. And nearly two hundred years after Luther the Lutheran composer J. S. Bach composed in Latin his imperishable *Mass in B Minor*. Latin services were held in Nuremberg, Germany, until the nineteenth century, and in North America Lutheran services in the twenty-first century can be found in German, Danish, Swedish, and Norwegian, though these are not usually the vernacular.

Apart from the joy he found in married life, Luther's later years were far from happy. His teachings, he knew, were being fervently adopted throughout northern Germany and Scandinavia. But he also knew that many of the princes who

Martin Luther died of a stroke at three o'clock in the morning of February 18, 1546, while visiting Eisleben, the town where he was born. In the estimation of some scholars, the remarkable heritage left by the great visionary was in large part due to the fact that he so insistently based his faith on his personal experience of God.

embraced them were even more fervently embracing the new revenue from expropriated church properties. Nevertheless, it was upon these princes that he must depend to protect himself and his followers against the Catholics, the emperor, and the stake.[9] More trying yet were the divisions among Protestants, which forced him to fight a two-front war—one against the Catholics, the other chiefly against the Anabaptists and the Zwinglians. Nor did religious life in the Protestant communities always appear to be as exemplary as he had hoped.

Perhaps it was in some consequent mood of despondency that Luther would publish, three years before his death, a pamphlet entitled *The Jews and Their Lies*. This paean of hatred, violence, and bigotry recommended that the synagogues of the Jews be burned, their books be seized and destroyed, and they be forbidden on pain of death to praise or thank God or in any way use the holy name "within our hearing." He repeatedly returned to this theme, and it would in fact be the subject of his last sermon, preached three days before his death. Four hundred years hence it would bring upon him great and deserved rebuke, while providing useful fodder for the Nazi regime in Germany. His defenders, while distancing themselves from such sentiments, could only protest in defense that time and again he said the same kind of thing, or worse, about the popes, about the Anabaptists, and about rebelling peasants.[10]

But for Charles V, wars and other conflicts were far from over. During the next ten years he sought desperately to bring about theological reconciliation between Lutherans and Catholics. He clashed frequently and fiercely with the new pope, Paul III, who bluntly informed him that laymen—emperors included—should stay out of theological controversy. Finally, at the Reichstag of Regensburg in 1541 Charles had to acknowledge defeat. The German princes, both Catholic and Lutheran, affirmed the policy known as *cujus regio, ejus religio* (to each realm its religion). Henceforth every prince could decide for his own territory, but this policy did not bring peace. On the contrary, it entrenched in Germany a schism destined in the next century to see tens of thousands of people killed in Europe's last great religious war. After Regensburg, writes historian Karl Brandi (*The Emperor Charles V*, 1939), Charles's view of religion changed profoundly. He was a deeply disappointed man, though he played a central role in the Catholic Council of Trent that followed (see ch. 9).

His dealings with Francis I continued chaotic. Right up to Francis's death in 1547 the French king repeatedly promised to abandon his treaty with the Turks. But each time he would renew it without warning, attacking Charles in the Netherlands, or fomenting rebellion among the German princes, or sheltering Muslim slavers in French ports and even providing them with a marketplace in Marseilles where they could sell newly captured Christian slaves. Many historians are harsh in their assessment of Francis, depicting him as ambitious, ruthless, false, devoid of moral principle, and a valuable ally for the Muslim conqueror.

As for Charles's Süleyman problem, it too remained far short of resolution. But the wily Turk merely gave up his assaults on Austria for a while in favor of attacking Christian Europe by sea, and here too Charles moved to counter him (see ch. 11). ■

9. An incident that greatly afflicted Luther in his later years concerned the marital status of the Protestant leader Philip of Hesse. Disenchanted with the wife who had borne him seven children, Philip fell hopelessly in love with seventeen-year-old Margarethe von der Saal, and he wanted a divorce. Luther, who opposed divorce, advised him to marry Margarethe secretly and bigamously instead, and in 1539 Philip did so. When the story leaked out, however, Philip was confronted with a criminal charge, and Luther's followers were scandalized that their spiritual leader would allow polygamy. They were not even mollified when he cited similar practices among the ancient Israelites. Ultimately Philip had to return to the Catholic Church to get his first marriage annulled, which meant that he also had to halt military operations against Catholic Charles.

10. Luther's defenders, while admittedly appalled by his anti-Jewish effusion, point out that his attitude to the Jews was actually somewhat ambivalent. He began by questioning how they could be blamed for rejecting Christianity when the Roman church was the way it was, and he gladly accepted Jewish converts. Unlike Calvin, he remained opposed to usury (the loaning of money at interest), the means by which many Jews supported themselves. They note, too, that in his last sermon his attitude toward the Jews has become conciliatory. In all criticism of Luther's belligerency, they add, one should keep in mind that his interests were primarily the purity of doctrine and the effect of heresy on his flock. He was also quick to forgive. They cite the case of Andreas Karlstadt, the target of one of his most fiery condemnations. Yet later, when Karlstadt became a fugitive, it was in Luther's home that he found refuge.

The fate of Islam's Christian subjects

Their sons are routinely seized and made Muslim soldiers or bureaucrats; education all but ceases, churches become mosques, culture disintegrates

1. Much of the material in this article is drawn from historical work of Bat Ye'or, which in Hebrew means "Daughter of the Nile," the pseudonym of Gisèle Littman (née Orebi), an Egyptian-born British scholar and author of eight books, mostly on the history of Christian and Jewish communities living under Islamic governments. She has provided briefings to the United Nations and U.S. Congress and lectured at Georgetown, Yale, Brown, Brandeis, and Columbia universities. She is married to the British historian and human rights advocate David Littman. Her book cited here has an introduction by the late Jacques Ellul, a Christian law professor, sociologist, and philosopher.

The Ottoman Turks, whose empire by the mid-1500s reached into three continents, are shown here besieging a Christian castle along the Mediterranean, as illustrated below by seventeenth-century artist Jan Peeters. The Ottomans took seriously the Islamic injunction to conquer the entire dar al-harb—that is, all the lands not ruled by Muslims—and to convert its inhabitants to Islam by means either voluntary or very much otherwise.

When the prophet Muhammad and his warriors began their seventh-century conquests, he offered to the defeated idol worshipers of northern Arabia just one stark choice: Accede to Islam, or die. His mandate, as subsequently revealed, was ultimately to extend the *dar al-Islam* (the lands of submission) to embrace the entire world. Until then, all non-Muslim lands were part of the *dar al-harb* (the lands of war), which must be brought under Islamic law—whether by persuasion, by subterfuge, or by jihad (holy war).

Such a mandate boded ill for the Christian churches of the Middle East, North Africa, and Spain under the ensuing Arab onslaught. Within a decade after the Prophet's death, three of the five Christian patriarchates—Jerusalem, Alexandria, and Antioch—came under Muslim domination. Similarly, eight centuries later, the Muslim Ottoman Turks had systematically subjugated nearly all the lands in Anatolia, Greece, and Eastern Europe, previously ruled by the Byzantine Empire. When Constantinople fell at last in 1453, of the original five patriarchates only Rome remained free of Muslim control.

The logical consequence of Muhammad's divine instructions should have been complete elimination of Christianity in the Middle East and Eastern Europe. Christians in their thousands died or were enslaved by the advance of those seemingly invincible Muslim armies. Many embraced Islam to escape death or gain status but in numbers that varied greatly from country to country and from century to century. In the southern Arabian province of Najran, for example, the number of Christians is believed to have plummeted from forty thousand to eight thousand in the first eight decades of Muslim rule. The Caucasian country of Georgia, by contrast, although overrun by Arab armies in the seventh century and ravaged by the Turks in the tenth, remained almost entirely Christian. In Egypt the church survived, although grievously diminished. The rest of North Africa, once solidly Christian, became entirely Muslim. Spain recovered completely from Muslim domination, but it took eight centuries to do so.

The Arab armies soon discovered in their attempts to transform the dar al-harb into the completely pure dar al-Islam, however, that wiping out entire defeated populations, even if they refused to accept Islam, was impractical. The crushing taxes levied upon Christian peasants and artisans alike were urgently required. When the Christians fled to escape those taxes, writes the historian of the Middle East Bat Ye'or (*The Decline of Eastern Christianity under Islam*, 1996), "stripped of everything, and forced to hide and flee from place to place, they became a hunted population, on whose exploitation was built the ostentation of the Abbasid [Arab] court."[1]

In the second great conquest, the Turks, likewise, soon found it was clearly preferable—often essential—to use the knowledge and expertise of the more educated and sophisticated among their defeated foes, along with the sheer labor of the ordinary folk, to support the aristocracies and armies of the conquerors. Thus, the concept of tributary

populations of Jews and Christians, as early established by the Prophet, continued through the centuries.

Because these two peoples preserved and revered the scriptures, Mohammed recognized them as "People of the Book," who could be governed as separate subject groups under temporary and stringent treaties. (The Zoroastrians of Persia would be accorded similar status.) Koran jurisconsults worked out the terms on the basis of Muhammad's treaty in 629 with the Jewish farmers of Khaybar Oasis. Previously, the Prophet had either killed or expelled Jews who refused to accept Islam, and enslaved their women and children (see vol. 5, ch. 6). But when the settlers at Khaybar, a hundred miles north of Medina, surrendered to his army, Muhammad was divinely inspired to offer them a *dhimma* (contract) instead.

As a tributary people they could continue to practice their faith and farm their land. Because no *harbi* may possess any part of the earth, however, their farms, homes, and other possessions now belonged to the Islamic community, and they must turn over half their harvest as tax. Furthermore, the dhimma was by nature temporary and could be canceled at any time by the Muslim leader. In the event, the Khaybar treaty proved to be of very short duration.[2]

This concept would determine the fate of most Christians and Jews who survived the ensuing Muslim attacks. No longer was the command "Accept Islam or die." The new ultimatum became "Accept Islam or become a dhimmi"—namely, a definitely second-class individual leading a debased and precarious life in a rigorously circumscribed tributary community. One important purpose of this arrangement, as it gradually developed, was to ensure that conquered peoples remained unmistakably subservient in every respect to the true faith and to the true believers.

Thus, dhimmis were frequently required to wear some identifying garment or symbol, for example, and live within a restricted area. They were often forbidden to ride a horse because no unbeliever must be above a Muslim either physically or metaphorically. (A mule, being smaller and more humble, was not so objectionable.) They were subject to many and onerous special taxes, which filled the dual purpose of oppressing the conquered and greatly enriching the conquerors. If they retained the use of their former possessions, it was only to devote them to the benefit of the Islamic state.

Christian churches were often converted into mosques, military establishments, warehouses, and such. One became a zoo. Only a few, located nowhere near any Muslim holy place, could be used for Christian worship,

The Seljuk Turks, conquerors of Jerusalem in 1077, roughly escort its patriarch to prison. By the fifteenth century, when the Ottoman sultan Mehmed II took Constantinople at last, its patriarch seemingly fared better because Mehmed fancied himself a successor to the caesars. But for the Orthodox Church, this was a sad delusion.

and they must exhibit no external grandeur. No church could be built or repaired without Muslim permission (rarely granted). Bell ringing and public displays such as processions were naturally forbidden. Nor could dhimmis hold public office of any kind, though some did, particularly in the early stages of a conquest. Worst of all, although theoretically these conquered populations enjoyed the protection of Islamic law, their testimony was inadmissible in an Islamic court. The word of a dhimmi, in fact, could not under any circumstances stand against that of a Muslim. If a Muslim raped a Christian woman and denied it, for example, neither she nor any other non-Muslim could

2. The dhimma that Muhammad granted the conquered Jewish farmers of Khaybar Oasis in 629, considered the precedent for all such later arrangements between Muslim rulers and their subject populations of Christians and Jews, was itself of notably short duration. The second caliph, Umar ibn al-Khattab, drove all the Jewish and Christian tributaries out of Arabia in 640. They have never been allowed back. If a non-Muslim is discovered in the holy cities of Mecca or Medina, the prescribed penalty is execution.

3. Three years before the fall of Constantinople, writes historian Diane Moczar in *Islam at the Gates: How Christendom Defeated the Ottoman Turks* (2008), the Knights Hospitaller at Rhodes received a pathetic missive. Greek Christians in Asia Minor wrote to tell them that they were "heavily vexed by the Turk . . . they take away our children and make Muslims of them . . . Let us come to your domains and live and die there as your subjects." But the knights were in no position to help them.

Every fourth year, Ottoman agents appeared in all subjugated towns and villages to seize the brightest and fittest Christian boys, age five to about fifteen, as boy tribute. Taken to Constantinople, these youngsters were converted to Islam and trained for the Ottoman army (usually the famous Janissaries), or for the sultan's court and bureaucracy. Sorrowful scenes occurred as the boys were taken, as imagined below by a twentieth-century illustrator Ippolito Caffi.

offer acceptable testimony to the contrary.

As Bat Ye'or observes, the Koran recognizes that Islamic jihad can be waged by peaceful as well as military means. That is, the faith may be spread by proselytism or propaganda, or the judicious use of rewards and gratuities designed "to win over hearts." That such factors loomed large in the intentions of the original Arab designers of what she terms "dhimmitude" seems unlikely. Daily degradation and humiliation must have provided powerful incentive, however, to simply accept Islam and be done with it. Why not just bow before Allah and become in that instant a fully privileged citizen?

Under the Ottoman Turks, conversion of conquered subjects became a fully recognized objective, by various means both involuntary and voluntary. The military success of the Ottomans had been accomplished in no small measure by means of the *devshirme* (boy tribute), which they regularly levied upon vanquished Christian populations.

At approximately four-year intervals, Muslim agents would appear at every subject town and village. Obtaining the names of the community's children, they would summon all teenaged males to be looked over. There were, as can be imagined, pitiful scenes as the brightest and fittest were chosen for the sultan, later to be circumcised, instructed in Islam, and trained as soldiers. Younger Christian boys (six to ten years old) were similarly seized to be trained as administrators in the college of pages attached to the sultan's palace.[3] Girls were not included, although an attractive daughter might occasionally be

seized for the harem of a local grandee.

In approximately three centuries "from one to two million of the flower of the Christian population must have been brought into the Ottoman nation" by means of this system, writes historian Albert Howe Lybyer in *The Government of the Ottoman Empire* (1913). The Janissary corps, the elite personal infantry initiated by Sultan Murad I in the late fourteenth century, was almost entirely supplied by boy tribute exacted from Christian families in the Balkans.

Augmented by slaves taken in battle or bought or received as gifts, it was also the source of supply for the extraordinary Turkish invention of the "ruling institution." Every member of the intricate bureaucracy that ran the Ottoman state—from page to bureaucrat to diplomat—was the personal slave of the sultan. They prospered or failed, lived or died, at his behest and whim. To be a slave of the sultan was considered an especially high honor, however, and this practice was duplicated in ruling households across the empire.

Most of these slaves were former Christians, but to the Ottomans slavery carried no particular stigma. They bestowed a great deal of trust upon their Islamized slaves and often affection as well. Besides, Lybyer writes, "conversion was a principal object of the system, and favor and promotion waited as rewards upon acceptance of the Muslim faith." As Sultan Mehmed II, the Conqueror, is said to have remarked, "Our empire is the home of Islam, and from father to son its lamp is kept burning with oil from the hearts of the infidels."

By contrast, the general population of conquered but continuing Christians was governed separately through what were called *millets*, similar to the Arabic *dhimmi* system and similarly frustrating and unpleasant for its subjects. A Christian leader, customarily a bishop responsible to the sultan, governed each millet, and for its members there could be no hope of advancement so long as they stubbornly clung to their faith. Nor could there be much traffic the other way. Death was the Koranic penalty for anyone preaching the gospel to a Muslim and for any Muslim who dared to accept it.

The inevitable consequence was the further weakening of the Greek-speaking church. When Constantinople fell, four centuries had elapsed since the Great Schism between the Latin churches of the West and the Greek churches of the East. The major doctrinal division between them at that time had concerned the filioque clause in the Nicene Creed, but their bitter ecclesiastical conflict has never been resolved.[4] What originally exacerbated it, however, was a language problem, not a theological one, because the Greeks could not speak adequate Latin, nor the Romans adequate Greek. The more serious problem was Rome's claim to jurisdictional supremacy over all. The eastern patriarchs were willing to honor the patriarch of the West as "first among equals" but not to grant him administrative jurisdiction over the eastern patriarchates. This, far more than the doctrinal question, gave rise to the schism and would maintain it.

But distinctive differences in thought and practice had also accumulated. The East was far less inclined than the West to spell out doctrines in detail, because various heresies in the West had forced more specific definitions. Doctrinally, this was not needed to the same degree in the East because there the threat came from outside the faith—that is, from Muslim overlords—not from within. So Byzantium produced no equivalent to Thomas Aquinas.

Moreover, from the earliest days of Christianity the East had rejected the concept of an entirely celibate priesthood. It had a long and honored tradition of monasticism, celibacy was a requirement for bishops (who therefore were often monks), and any priest could also choose to be celibate. But marriage was always an option for parish priests, provided they were married before they were ordained, and most were family men.

Nor had wide-ranging religious orders developed in the East. Monks were attached to individual monasteries, and groups of them would move on to launch other monasteries. But perhaps the greatest East-West difference was the relationship between

emperor and the patriarch. The emperor ruled the empire, writes historian Steven Runciman in *The Great Church in Captivity* (1968), while the patriarch, at least in principle, was viewed as the keeper of the empire's conscience. Meanwhile, in the West conflict raged for centuries over the powers of church and state.

Before Constantinople fell, its patriarch had taken refuge in Italy, but Mehmed II greatly admired things Byzantine. He wanted his rule be seen as the empire's extension and himself (among his other titles) as *Kayser i-Rum* (Caesar of Rome). A patriarch was needed for this scenario. Besides, to run his new capital, Mehmed needed the knowledge, technical skills, seamanship, and business acumen of at least some of its former Greek citizens. He set about enticing or ordering them back, and their patriarch would be the logical man to oversee the Greek millet.

As patriarch the sultan chose the monk George Scholarius, a scholar of high repute and on record as opposing union with Rome. After some difficulty locating Scholarius, who had been sold as a slave, he was enthroned in 1454 as patriarch of Constantinople, taking the name Gennadius II. Sultan Mehmed turned over to him the historic Church of the Holy Apostles, and provided funding to administer the millet and what was left of the patriarchate. (The magnificent nine-hundred-year-old Hagia Sophia cathedral was already being adapted as a mosque. Nor could Patriarch Gennadius afford to maintain the adjoining patriarchal palace. He moved to a lesser building, and his successors were eventually forced out of that.

Even so, Gennadius and Mehmed reportedly used to have long, private theological discussions so frequently as to set off rumors that the sultan was considering becoming Christian. Not so pleasant for Gennadius or successive patriarchs, however, were the Ottoman changes to church governance, placing the patriarch under the control of an elected holy synod whose diverse

A photograph from the late nineteenth century shows a Turkish woman in Islamic dress standing with her slave. Although the majority of earlier Ottoman slaves were former Christians, many Muslims were also enslaved. In any event, to the Turks, slavery seemingly carried no great stigma. To be a slave of the sultan, in fact, was considered a high honor.

Preaching the gospel to a Muslim meant death. The same applied to those accepting it.

membership would facilitate Muslim intervention. Nor would Mehmed's successors share his interest either in things Roman or in Christianity.

Thus began the long Ottoman process of Christian eradication. As the years passed, one church after another was seized in Constantinople (including the Church of the Holy Apostles) until only three preconquest Christian edifices remained in the capital. The same process occurred in provincial cities, wherever the Turks settled, and the attitude of the sultanate generally hardened. Mehmed's grandson Selim I, the Grim, wanted to force all Christians to embrace Islam, but his advisers persuaded him that this was simply impossible.

Meanwhile, the renowned intellectual capacity of the Greeks weakened as they became a servile and beaten people. Runciman writes: "As absolute power corrupted the sultans, absolute impotence corrupted the Christians." Soon almost every church office had to be obtained by bribing Muslim officials or bribing churchmen, or both, while cash payments to the sultan for appointment as patriarch reached incredible amounts. By 1726, Runciman recounts, Callinicus III bid the equivalent of fifty-six hundred pounds of gold for the patriarchal office—and next day died of a heart attack when informed that the job was indeed his.

Outside the capital, humbler Christians suffered in somewhat different ways. In 1678 Sir Paul Rycaut, an Englishman much traveled in Eastern Europe, published a book lamenting the state of Christianity under Muslim rule:

> How tragical is the subversion of the sanctuaries of Religion, the Royal Priesthood, expelled from their Churches, and these converted into Mosques; the Mysteries of the altar concealed in secret and dark places; for such I have seen in cities and villages . . . rather more like vaults and sepulchres than Churches, having their roofs almost levelled with the Superfices of the Earth, lest the most ordinary Exsurgency of Structure should be accused for Triumph of Religion, and stand in competition with the lofty spires of the Mohometan Mosque.

Churches were left derelict, historian Bat Ye'or confirms, cemeteries were desecrated, and Christians became an object of pity in the eyes of many Muslims. Their sole advantage, she adds, was that this latter attitude tended to protect them from more overt persecution.

Byzantine scholarship, which so long had preserved the classical legacy of ancient Greece and Rome, was dying out or had already fled westward. Christianity was thus reduced to "a stagnant level of superstition and spiritual death," writes Edwin Pears in *The Destruction of the Greek Empire* (1903). Only in Constantinople itself was the situation even minimally better, since the Turks permitted Christian residents who could afford it to go to Venice (once the great rival of Constantinople) to receive an education in Greek.

> The renowned intellect of the Greeks weakened as they became a servile and beaten people.

As the learning in the capital deteriorated, in the empire's former provinces it virtually ceased. Monasteries, losing appreciation for their libraries, began using ancient manuscripts for wrapping paper. Many parish clergy could barely read nor understand the liturgy. Young boys received little education and girls none.

As all this transpired, the church of the West was not entirely inactive, although the effect generally was to add to the confusion. In 1540 the Jesuits opened missions to the East but were hampered by the still smoldering old antipathy. In 1565 Patriarch Metrophanes of Constantinople made overtures to the West but seven years later was excommunicated by the holy synod. Even so, Runciman notes, by the seventeenth century Jesuit schools were appearing throughout the Ottoman Empire, and powerful pro-Catholic forces emerging in the Greek patriarchate. Pope Gregory XIII founded the College of St. Athanasius at Rome "for the education of Greeks in the proper faith." (These initiatives would bear fruit in the Western movement into Eastern Europe in the late sixteenth century and will be described in the next volume.)

Protestants, too, were taking an interest in Eastern Orthodoxy. Luther disapproved of some of its ritualistic practices and its deep commitment to monasticism but gave it credit as an early antagonist to Rome. His senior lieutenant, Philipp Melanchthon, was even more favorably disposed, although his initial exchange of letters with a Greek in Venice was disappointing. The Greek correspondent discovered altogether too many incompatibilities between Lutheran theology and Orthodoxy.

But then a man identifying himself as James Basilicus the Heraclid appeared at Luther's home base of Wittenberg in 1555, claiming he was a descendent of the kings of

5. Catholic biographers of James Basilicus Heraclid identify him as the son of a Cretan sailor in the service of the lord of Samos, who discerned great potential in the boy and provided him with an education. Young James may have been secretary to the ruler of Samos until he took service with the emperor. His claimed relationship to the patriarch of Constantinople and the princess of Moldavia is probably pure invention, however.

Epirus, and had served in the armies of Charles V for twenty-two years with such distinction that the emperor had made him count palatine.[5] Clearly well educated and from a Greek background, he had come to know several Lutheran princes and had himself become Protestant. As a cousin of the Greek patriarch at Constantinople, he said, he believed that the Greek church could be persuaded into Protestantism.

Melanchthon was thrilled and gave him letters of introduction to the king of Denmark, through whom he found his way into the court of Moldavia, a Lower Danube principality then under Turkish suzerainty. Claiming to be a cousin of the Moldavian princess, Basilicus recruited Polish Protestants and led a successful revolt against her husband, the prince. He then seized the royal palace, appointed a Lutheran archbishop, and announced that Moldavia was now Protestant. However, when he began pillaging Moldavia's Orthodox churches, seizing their property, and reforming their liturgy, the people rebelled, overthrew his government, and put him to death.

But the Lutherans did not give up. In 1574, fourteen years after Melanchthon's death, they sent an emissary to Constantinople carrying a Greek translation of Protestant doctrine as defined in the Augsburg Confession (which was, in fact, a version of the confession previously tweaked by Melanchthon himself to make it more compatible with Orthodox doctrine). Three years later they received the patriarch's response. Examining the confession point by point, it detailed where it conflicted and where it accorded with Orthodox doctrine and practice, and concluded that Orthodoxy and Lutheranism were incompatible.

He wished to maintain friendly relations nevertheless, the patriarch wrote, and this in fact did happen. For years to come, Greek students were welcomed at Lutheran universities. Calvinism would fare even better than Lutheranism in its approach to the Orthodox East. Indeed, in the next century one patriarch of Constantinople would be a Calvinist—which also will be covered in the next volume.

But the factor that would most effectively ensure the survival of Christianity in the East came neither from Protestantism nor from Catholicism but from Orthodoxy itself. In the eleventh century Constantinople had begun the conversion of the eastern Slavic peoples, known as the Rus, including those beyond the lands where the Turks themselves originated. Under Mongol domination, Orthodox Christianity had survived among these people for two centuries.

Meanwhile, Muscovy assumed hegemony

over many of the Slavic lands, and the Grand Prince of Moscow became tsar, or caesar, of "all the Russias." With the fall of Constantinople, Moscow declared itself the Third Rome, the first being the one on the Tiber and the second Constantinople (see vol. 8, ch. 7). In 1589 the patriarch of Constantinople would recognize Moscow as the "fifth patriarchate." Meanwhile, the Russian church provided Orthodoxy with a base the sultan could not control.

Moreover, despite all the power of the sultans and the seeming disintegration of Orthodox faith under their subjugation, it somehow would survive even in most of Eastern Europe's Ottoman-controlled lands as well. As the Turkish empire suffered a long and painful period of decline over the eighteenth and nineteenth centuries, the Orthodox Church would spring to life again in Greece, Macedonia, Serbia, Romania, and Bulgaria. Only in Albania would the Muslim presence prevail. History—by the end of the nineteenth century—would pronounce the Turkish endeavor to convert Eastern Europe to Islam an almost total failure. ■

An ink and gold on vellum painting, circa 1558, shows a Janissary officer assessing a batch of devshirme (boy tribute) for Sultan Süleyman I. These youngsters would be a mere handful among the one to two million of the flower of the Christian population, estimated by historian Albert Howe to have been brought into the Ottoman nation as tribute over a three-century span.

For some hundred years Anabaptists were persecuted by Catholics, Lutherans, and Calvinists alike, in orgies of execution that became regular public events. Martyrdom became a veritable Anabaptist hallmark. Pictured here is the burning of eighteen at Salzburg in 1528, who typically accept and even welcome death as the seal of true faith. The chief Anabaptist "offenses": iconoclasm, resistance to all worldly authority, and rejection of infant baptism.

CHAPTER 4

The anarchic origins of Christendom's great pietistic movements

With wild theology, violence, and eager martyrdom, the Anabaptists swept Europe and paid dearly, but they left their mark on all Protestant Christianity

During his exile in the early months of 1522, Martin Luther got the first inkling of the Pandora's box he had opened when his lieutenant, Philipp Melanchthon, wrote him alarmed letters about events back in Wittenberg, birthplace and headquarters of his movement. Three men from Zwickau, a coal-mining city in Saxony, ninety miles to the south, were proclaiming themselves to be the "Zwickau Prophets," Melanchthon reported. Claiming to be in direct communication with God, they were encouraging the persecution of priests, the destruction of church images including the cross, and (most particularly) the abolition of infant baptism.

They had derived their teachings, they maintained, from Martin Luther's. They had earnestly read the Bible, had reflected on it prayerfully, and had been told by God that infant baptism was meaningless. How could grace be conferred on a recipient not old enough for conscious faith? Infant baptism was found neither in the Old or New Testament, they contended, nor had it been practiced in the apostolic or post-apostolic period.[1] And was it not a basic tenet of Luther's that the faithful should receive instruction from the Bible alone, rejecting all the ecclesiastical and scholastic interpretations that had corrupted the pure Christianity of Christ and the apostles?

"I cannot tell you how deeply I am agitated," wrote Melanchthon. One of the Zwickau Prophets, a weaver named Nicholas Storch, was telling the crowds that an angel had ordained him God's regent on earth. He and his fellow

1. Some scholars maintain that infant baptism was practiced in the first century, inferring from biblical references to individuals "and [their] whole households" being baptized that infants were included. The Didache, an instructional Jewish-Christian manual from the late first century, implies the opposite, in calling for a period of fasting prior to baptism. But by the third century, according to the theologian Origen, infant baptism was customary, and the Catholic Church came to believe that "pedobaptism" conveys God's grace and removes original sin. Among concurring churches today are the Orthodox, Anglican, Methodist, and Lutheran. Most Baptists, Pentecostals, and Mennonites reject infant baptism.

Philipp Melanchthon (above), Martin Luther's chief lieutenant, became so alarmed in early 1522 at the emergence of the Zwickau Prophets—insistent and violent men who claimed their orders came direct from God—that he begged his exiled mentor to return to the Wittenberg headquarters. Luther (whose statue appears below) did so but thought it prudent to travel disguised as a squire.

"prophets"—Marcus Stübner, a student, and Thomas Drechsel, another weaver—were also advocating the abolition of property and law, and proclaiming an imminent apocalypse that would exterminate the ungodly. Some were even rejecting the Bible itself. It was, they said, man-made and thus a corrupted thing, entirely unnecessary, given their direct line to the Spirit, who delivered the word of the scriptures to them unadulterated.

Melanchthon suggested that Luther call on Elector Frederick the Wise of Saxony to stop these "enthusiasts" with force. Luther, protected in the elector's Wartburg Castle (see ch. 3) and determined to complete his translation into German of the Bible, disagreed. "Surely we can restrain these firebrands without such measures," he replied.

Melanchthon thought otherwise. He persuaded Frederick to issue a decree commanding the Prophets to cease their activities forthwith, outraging many of the Wittenberg faithful. The elector Frederick supported Luther, it was true, but he was still a Catholic, and here he was issuing decrees curtailing religious freedom. He was plainly a papist, they charged, and they threatened to take over the town. "The dam has broken and I cannot stem the waters," Melanchthon wrote Luther, "You must come."

So in the guise of a squire—bearded, wearing a red beret, and carrying a sword—Luther secretly returned to Wittenberg. He found to his chagrin that in his name priests had been dragged out of their churches by the hair, sanctuaries defaced, and holy oil set alight—just the sort of chaos, he knew, that his enemies had warned his reformation would cause. Next day, shaved, tonsured, and wearing his old black Augustinian monk's habit, he took to the pulpit and was warmly welcomed by the people.

By directing their energies against unimportant things, he vehemently admonished them, they were abandoning and offending against the faith and charity they so much needed. No one must be compelled against his will to the faith or to the things of the faith, he declared; all must be inspired by faith alone. "I also condemn images," he assured them, "but I would have them assailed by the Word, and not by blows and fire." We must "tarry for the weak," he concluded. Much to the relief of Elector Frederick, the people of Wittenberg obeyed.

Meanwhile, Luther discovered that two once trusty loyalists had been backing the Zwickau Prophets. His former fellow monk Gabriel Zwilling (who was proposing, among other things, that Communion be given in beer mugs) was brought to heel. Not so Luther's thirty-six-year-old university colleague Andreas Karlstadt, however. Stripped of his Wittenberg preacher's license, he departed in outrage. So did the Zwickau Prophets, reviling Luther as "Dr. Slime" and other less than reverential epithets.

But many of their central contentions did not disappear, including the rejection of canon law, the elimination of all sacred music and of visual representation of holy things (even of Jesus himself); the denial of Christ's presence in the Eucharist, the expectation of imminent apocalypse, the communal sharing of property, and the rejection of infant baptism. The violent destruction of church iconography and a fierce rejection of the sacraments—pioneered in Wittenberg prior to Luther's return—became a common theme.

These radical beliefs took root along the Danube from Switzerland through Bavaria and Austria to Moravia, and north along the Rhine through western Germany and into the Netherlands, assuming a variety of permutations. Some of the emerging sects were spiritual and mystical, some doggedly scriptural, some licentious, some pacifist, some militant, some apocalyptic, and some downright bizarre. The common threads of these assorted sects, however, gradually wove themselves into what by the 1530s became an undeniable movement. In the decades and centuries to come, it would significantly shape not only the Mennonites and Hutterites, its direct descendants, but a large segment of Protestantism, along with the political structure of modern democratic states in both Europe and North America. This movement was called Anabaptism.

"There can be no question," wrote the American Mennonite theologian Harold Bender in his landmark 1944 essay *The Anabaptist Vision*, "but that the great principles of freedom of conscience, separation of church and state, and voluntarism in religion, so basic in American Protestantism and so essential to democracy, ultimately are derived from the Anabaptists of the Reformation period, who for the first time clearly enunciated them and challenged the Christian world to follow them in practice."

The beginnings of what, in the sixteenth century, became a sect reviled by Catholic, Calvinist, and Lutheran alike can be traced to Luther's banished colleague Andreas Karlstadt. A Bohemian-born professor who had developed his theology in Luther's shade and thrall at Wittenberg, Karlstadt was described by one contemporary as a short, irascible man with a thick,

A twentieth-century Amish (Mennonite) couple, members of a Pennsylvania colony that makes every effort to live without benefit of twentieth-century technology. Below, Hutterite children at the Forest River Colony near Fordville, North Dakota, pray over the communal evening meal. The generally peaceful lives of such segregated modern Anabaptists presents a radical contrast to those of their forefathers, who lived and died—and sometimes wrought havoc—in the heartland of Europe.

unpleasant accent, a poor memory, and "the complexion of a smoked herring."
Removed from Luther's shadow, however, he came into his own.

Renaming himself "Brother Andreas," he dressed as a peasant and began
through his preaching to establish reform congregations in Switzerland, Denmark,
and the lands along Germany's North Sea coast known as Frisia. Second only to
Luther in exploiting the printing press, he published ninety literary works in more
than two hundred editions on such topics as the Lord's Supper, the banishment of
icons, the errors and inadequacies of Luther's theology, and the iniquity of baptiz-

The Swiss Brethren began baptizing one another, insisting Christians baptized as infants be baptized once more. Hence: 'Anabaptist', from the Greek for 'rebaptized.'

2. Andreas Rudolff-Bodenstein von Karlstadt was aided in publishing his vast output both by Anabaptists in Zurich and by his brother-in-law Gerhard Westerburg, a Cologne nobleman who baptized more than two thousand adults in his private baths. Karlstadt also influenced the English Baptists John Smyth and John Murton, and his insistence upon strict observance of the Sabbath became a key tenet of the Puritans and Calvinists. His final home was in Basel, where he was dean of the university church and taught Hebrew until he died of the plague in 1541, aged fifty-five.

3. According to the manuscript chronicle of the Hutterian Brethren, known as the *Geschicht-Buch*, Conrad Grebel performed the first rebaptism of post-apostolic times on the night of January 21, 1525. Fifteen Brethren had met at Felix Manz's house for prayer following Zurich council's ban on any further propagation of Anabaptism. George Blaurock, an ex-priest, asked Grebel to baptize him on the confession of his faith, recognizing Grebel as the spiritual leader of the community. "Without him," says the *Mennonite Encyclopedia*, "Anabaptism in its historical form would probably never have come into existence and he represents original Anabaptism in the form in which it has been perpetuated to the present day."

ing babies. He greatly influenced the men who would espouse, and commonly die
for, the Anabaptist cause.[2]

Anabaptism became an identifiable movement in Zurich in 1525 when a radical group of followers of Swiss reform leader Huldrych Zwingli broke with him
over his Lutheresque deference to the secular authorities, his refusal to adequately
abandon the Catholic Mass, and his refusal to reject infant baptism. Calling
themselves the Swiss Brethren, they were led by Conrad Grebel, the humanist-
schooled son of a Zurich iron merchant, and Felix Manz, a scholar in biblical
languages and son of a Grossmünster canon. Both were twenty-seven years old,
and both were riveting preachers. The Brethren initially numbered about fifteen
young men, mostly of low estate, who met in private homes, maintained a correspondence with Karlstadt, studied
the Bible, scrupulously sought to
adhere to its revealed word, and
eschewed violence.

They also began baptizing one
another, insisting that Christians
who had been baptized as infants
must be baptized once more—the
practice that earned the movement
its name.[3] The word "Anabaptist"
(*Wiedertäufer* in German) is from
the Greek and means "rebaptized." The term was used disdainfully by Zwingli and for centuries
would remain derogatory.
Moreover, it was considered in a
sense inaccurate by the
Anabaptists themselves, who
believed that infant christening
was not true baptism at all, so the
second was not a "re"-baptism,
but the only one. Zwingli, who

Defaced statues at the Cathedral of Saint Martin in Utrecht bear witness to the determined fury of some sixteenth-century Anabaptists. Luther, by contrast, wanted images combated "by the Word, and not by blows and fire."

particularly deplored rebaptism as damaging to the unity of the reformed faith, induced Zurich's city council to outlaw it (see sidebar, p. 50). Driven from the city, the Swiss Brethren spread out into the countryside, where they preached to a rural population especially receptive to their support of communal property and their rejection of tithing.

Above all else, the Brethren believed that the Bible, interpreted by the inward light possessed by every baptized adult believer, was the only rule of faith, before which all human authority and institutions must bend. "In all disputes concerning faith and religion, the scriptures alone, proceeding from the

An 1880 oil painting on wood by Willem Linnig the Younger shows "Brother Andreas" Karlstadt (in black), a former colleague of Luther, vehemently preaching. During Luther's absence from Wittenberg, Karlstadt orchestrated an attack that despoiled the sanctuary of the town church. The assailants also defaced statuary and paintings, set the holy oil alight, and dragged the priests out bodily. And that was just the beginning.

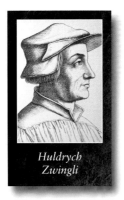

Huldrych Zwingli

Balthasar Hubmaier

mouth of God, ought to be our level and rule," wrote Balthasar Hubmaier, a Bavarian academic, ordained priest, and popular reformist preacher who had been baptized in Waldshut by one of the Brethren. Hubmaier resigned as priest and was immediately elected minister by the congregation, an event that began the democratic "congregationalist" principle of church government.

But in late 1525, when Hubmaier had to flee to Zurich hoping to find refuge there, he encountered instead a changed and hostile Zwingli. He requested a public disputation on their differences, which Zwingli granted. The disputation centered on infant baptism, Hubmaier rejecting it on scriptural grounds and Zwingli countering that it was not a question of baptism but of the introduction of schism and heresy into the church. Christians, said Zwingli, were bound to submit to the majority in ecclesiastical matters, as dictated by the supreme authority of the state. Not surprisingly, the Zurich council ruled in Zwingli's favor and demanded that Hubmaier recant, which he did after torture on the rack.

By the late 1520s, however, Anabaptism was spreading quickly through a common modus operandi developed by Grebel and Manz. They would create an apostolic corps within the group, which then traveled to new areas to spread the word and establish new cells, and these in turn repeated the process. Among those attracted were many survivors of the Peasants' Revolt (see sidebar, p. 44), and as Ernest Belfort Bax writes in *The Rise and Fall of the Anabaptists* (1903), "The purely voluntary communism in imitation of the supposed institutions of the early Christians, which the Zurich Brethren had instituted among themselves, became more and more raised to the position of a cardinal principle, whilst the nonresistance doctrine, in certain quarters, began to fall into the background."

As the movement spread northward along the Rhine, it retained a distinctive core (adult baptism, scriptural primacy, exclusion from the secular world, etc.)

A typical Anabaptist adult baptism, below, in New Bern, North Carolina, in the mid-twentieth century. The Anabaptists insisted from the inception of their movement that only adults are eligible for baptism because no infant is capable of consciously choosing to accept God's grace. Further, baptism must not be administered by a priest nor in a church. It must be conducted by already committed and baptized brethren, preferably with full immersion in a river.

but also acquired a divergence of idiosyncratic practices.
These were described by two contemporary writers: Heinrich
Bullinger, Zwingli's successor as head of the Zurich church
and an enemy of the Anabaptists; and Sebastian Franck, a
reformed priest and freethinker who settled in Strasbourg,
rejected the Lutherans, and came to believe in an invisible
spiritual church. Franck writes sympathetically of "heretics,"
including the Anabaptists, in his account, *Chronica.*

*Heinrich
Bullinger*

Bullinger attached more than a dozen labels to the different varieties of Anabaptism. Those he called the "Apostolic
Baptists" were akin to earlier Franciscan friars, repudiating all personal property
and wandering barefoot, approaching cottages with a greeting of peace, and
entering therein to preach and baptize. Another subgroup, the "Holy and Sinless
Baptists," believed that the elect could not sin and therefore struck the words
"forgive us our trespasses" from the Lord's Prayer. They operated on the assumption that a baptized believer might do as he liked, for if he sinned, it affected the
body alone and not the soul.

There were also the "Silent Brothers," precursors of the Quakers, who held
that preaching was no longer necessary and, if asked about their religion, would
give no answer. Conversely, the so-called "Ecstatic Brothers" dreamed dreams, saw

The Wild Brethren insisted married women committed a sin by having sex with their still-heathen husbands, but not with the Brethren, for theirs was a spiritual bond.

visions, and would fall to the ground in a fit or trance, then come around to
describe what they had seen in the other world. Oftentimes they would declare a
date for the Day of Judgment and sometimes reported having seen Zwingli in hell.

In a more political vein, there were what Bullinger called the "Free Brothers,"
to whom Christian freedom meant not having to pay tithes or debts, nor be bound
by serfdom or villenage. Among them were some whom their coreligionists called
the Wild Brothers, men who liked to persuade credulous women that they could
not be saved without sacrificing their virtue. Had Christ not said that only he who
was willing to lose all he held dear might enter the kingdom of heaven (Luke 14:
26–27)? And was it not written that tax collectors and harlots would be the first
enter the kingdom (Matthew 21: 31–32)? Thus fornication became a source of
sanctification. Moreover, the Wild Brethren insisted, married women did indeed
commit sin by having intercourse with their still-heathen husbands, but not by
having it with the Brethren because between them there was a spiritual bond.

Johannes Kessler, an early chronicler of Anabaptism, describes how one of the
Swiss Brethren, preaching in the Appenzell territory, told his listeners that if they
wished to follow Christ, they must obey his injunction to be as little children
(Matthew 18:3). At this many of the congregation, especially the women, began to
literally act as children—jumping about, clapping their hands, sitting naked on the
ground, and throwing apples at one another. He also relates several cases of religious mania: a woman in Zollikon declaring herself to be God and uttering meaningless sounds; numerous instances of women running about the streets naked;

The eyewitness accounts of Anabaptist permutations recorded by Johannes Kessler, a reformer from St. Gallen, Switzerland, and an alumnus of Wittenberg University, bolster those given both by Heinrich Bullinger and by Sebastian Franck. Kessler's report on religious events between 1523 and 1529, *Sabbata*, is described in the *Mennonite Encyclopedia* as treating the Anabaptist movement with "gratifying objectivity."

In this sketch by the renowned Dutch artist Rembrandt van Rijn, an Anabaptist is being executed by decapitation. Christendom was scandalized not only by their core beliefs but by such other activities as fornication to achieve sanctification and deletion of words from the Lord's Prayer.

imagined possession by demons and deities; and one man who convinced his brother, supposedly on instruction from God, to bind and behead him.[4]

But such were the excesses of an illiterate people instructed by lay preachers often little more literate than themselves, trying to reassert what they supposed to be a primitive and pure Christianity. Anabaptism did not come from the intelligentsia, Bax emphasizes: "It was a movement constituted in the main of the disinherited classes of the time: the peasants, the poorer handicraftsmen, and the journeymen of the towns, to whose oppressed position, economically and politically, it powerfully appealed."

They paid dearly for their convictions, being regarded by some as plainly diabolical because they met in secret, often late at night in the woods, and talked of being an "elect" group. Hans Hut, a southern German Anabaptist leader arrested in 1527, baptized hundreds of converts by making the apocalyptic sign of tau on their foreheads, and spoke of God "leading them into hell and out again." Surely, it was thought, this must indicate demonism.

Hans Hut

From the mid 1520s onward, the violent persecution of the Anabaptists was pursued with vigor by Lutherans and Catholics, and later by Calvinists. The first known martyr, Eberli Bolt of the Swiss Brethren, a man described by Kessler as pious and kindhearted, attracted large crowds with his eloquence. But when he returned to his home region, a Catholic canton, he was seized and sentenced to be burned, alongside a companion who had been a priest. "Both approached the fire cheerfully," reports Kessler, "and died willingly and undismayed." Within two years, executions of Anabaptists in Catholic Austria had become regular public occasions, and a pamphlet of the day describes events in Salzburg in 1527. These included the burning of several renegade priests and monks, the beheading and subsequent burning of a nobleman and a wallet maker, the drowning of a woman and a "beautiful young girl" of sixteen in a horse pond, and the confinement of a number of Anabaptists in the house they used for their meetings, which was presently set alight. "They lived long," writes the pamphleteer, "and pitifully shrieked together, till at last they gave up the ghost."

In the city of Linz on the Austrian Danube seventy-six were executed on heresy charges over a six-week period. Duke Wilhelm of Bavaria issued an order that all those who recanted should be beheaded, while those who refused were to be burned. Between 1525 and 1530, according to one contemporary estimate, a thousand Anabaptists were put to death in the Tirol region of southern Austria. In Catholic territories, burning was the favored method for heretics and witches alike.

Balthasar Hubmaier, convulsed with guilt over his recantation on the rack in Zurich, was arrested again in Moravia and brought to Vienna for execution. This time when tortured, he did not recant. Carted through the streets while being tormented with red-hot tongs, he recited passages from the Bible and, on being bound at the stake, called upon God to give him patience. When the executioner rubbed gunpowder into his long beard—a pyrotechnical flourish adopted as a crowd-pleaser—he reportedly murmured, "Salt me well," and as his hair and beard sparkled into flame, his last words were "Jesus! Jesus!" Onlookers reported that Hubmaier showed more joy than pain, steadfastly encouraged by his wife, who three days later was thrown into the Danube with a stone tied around her neck.

Drowning, considered the more humane execution method, was also used in Zurich to dispatch Swiss Brethren cofounder Felix Manz. Along with Conrad Grebel and a third leader, Georg Blaurock, a converted Catholic priest, Manz had been preaching and converting with great success in the cities and cantons around about, sometimes baptizing crowds as large as five hundred in rivers and lakes.[5] On varying occasions all three had been tried, convicted, and sentenced to imprisonment by Zwinglian municipal authorities, but escaped to preach again. Grebel, never in the best of health, succumbed to a bout of the plague in the summer of 1526 at age twenty-eight, after a ministry of just twenty months.

Manz and Blaurock were arrested in a forest at Grüningen near Zurich later that same year. Blaurock, a tall man with a fiery preaching style, was beaten, tortured, and expelled. He proceeded to carry Anabaptism to other Swiss and then Austrian

An illustration from the The Martyrs' Mirror *shows Ana Ekenden Vlasteran being burned alive for heresy in 1571. This volume, published in 1661 to record their many martyrdoms, is held by Mennonites to be second in importance only to the Bible.*

5. Initially the Anabaptists conducted their adult baptisms in much the same way as the Catholics and Lutherans, by emptying water from a bowl over the candidate's head. On a mission to Schaffhausen in the summer of 1525, however, Conrad Grebel met a citizen of St. Gallen called Wolfgang Wolimann. So enthusiastic was Wolimann about the new doctrines that he insisted on undressing and having his entire body immersed in the Rhine when he was baptized by Grebel. Thus did total immersion baptism become an Anabaptist practice.

The above plaque was installed in 2004 by the Zurich municipal government to honor Felix Manz, co-founder of the radical Zwingli offshoot called the Swiss Brethren, who reputedly baptized as many as five hundred converts at a time. It reads in part: "Here in the middle of the River Limmat from a fishing platform were drowned Felix Manz and five other Anabaptists."

6. Included in the scant written legacy of Felix Manz was a brief testimony of his faith, and a hymn that is contained in the *Ausbund*, a sixteenth-century German hymnal still used by the Hutterites and Amish Mennonites. Its first stanza reads: "With gladness will I sing now; / My heart delights in God, / Who showed me such forbearance, / That I from death was saved / Which never hath an end. / I praise thee, Christ in heaven / Who all my sorrow changed."

Tirol towns before being captured once more and burned in the Tirolean capital of Innsbruck in September 1529. Manz, considered the ringleader, was charged with preaching a doctrine harmful to the unity of Christendom and seditious against the government. He was sentenced to death by drowning and on January 5, 1527, was escorted from the Wellenberg prison to a boat docked by the fish market at the mouth of the Limmat River, and rowed out onto Lake Zurich. As his mother's voice wafted across the cold water urging him to remain true to Christ, Felix Manz, not yet thirty, commended his soul to God and was thrust to his watery death.[6]

But rather than curtail the movement, all these sanctions and executions endowed its leaders with a heroism that spread it farther and faster. "Martyrdom became an Anabaptist hallmark," writes American Baptist historian William R. Estep in *The Anabaptist Story* (1963). (To this day, for many Mennonites *The Martyrs' Mirror*, an account of the lives and deaths of martyred Anabaptists, is second in importance only to the Bible.) One exasperated official in the Tirol, writing to Archduke Ferdinand, complained: "More than seven hundred persons have been either executed, expelled, or fled in misery. They left their property and their children behind . . . These people not only have no horror of punishment but even report themselves; rarely is one converted; nearly all only wish to die for their faith."

Following his execution in Innsbruck, Blaurock's Tirolean congregation was picked up by Jakob Hutter. A hatmaker in the Puster Valley, southeast of Innsbruck, Hutter had been impressed by the Anabaptist movement that was growing in the alpine region—partly as an outgrowth of the Peasants' Revolt, partly from the ministrations of Swiss missionaries like Blaurock. Hutter discovered he had a gift for preaching and began establishing Anabaptist churches in the homes of villagers. Inevitably the authorities began to crack down, seizing and executing members of Hutter's congregation, including his sister Agnes, who was burned in the spring of 1529.

By the autumn of that year when Blaurock was killed, his congregation had joined with Hutter's. With the Tirolean authorities ever more vigilant, the Anabaptists looked for a safe haven elsewhere. Favorable reports had reached Hutter from the Moravian city of Austerlitz. Over the next several years, Hutter oversaw the migration of the Tirolean Brethren to Moravia where one of the most enduring—and radical—of the Anabaptist sects was soon born.

Meanwhile, to the west Anabaptism had moved in the direction of codification, thanks to Michael Sattler. A former Benedictine monk from southwestern Germany, Sattler had turned first to Lutheranism and then broken away. Tall, quiet spoken, and morally upright, Sattler traveled along the Rhine, preaching and baptizing through Switzerland and into Germany until settling in the Austrian-controlled Rottenburg area. On February 24, 1527, he preached at an

Anabaptist conference in Schleitheim, and from this conference he produced the first Anabaptist confession of faith.

The Schleitheim Confession grafted monastic elements into the developing Anabaptist vision, idealizing a literal emulation of Christ's life (including martyrdom) rather than mere obedience to the divine commands, together with uncompromising separation from the secular (fallen) world, refusal of oaths, and pacifism. The Confession also laid down rules regarding membership, and the banishment—or shunning—of those who forsook the faith.

While Sattler was in Schleitheim, the authorities back in Rottenburg began rounding up his coreligionists. On his return he and his wife were arrested, imprisoned, and put on trial with two other leaders for sedition against both church and state. They were considered by the court to be on a level with the feared and hated Turks. It was alleged that Sattler had preached nonresistance to a possible Turkish invasion and had said that if war could be morally justified, he would rather fight Christians than Turks.

Sattler acknowledged preaching nonresistance, quoting the Decalogue: Thou shalt not kill. (More accurately, thou shalt do no murder.) He admitted also a theoretical preference for fighting Christians if those Christians persecuted, captured, and killed the God-fearing. Such as these, he said, were "Turks according to the spirit." The real Turks, knowing nothing of the Christian faith, were merely "Turks according to the flesh." At this, one of the judges drew his sword and almost executed Sattler on the spot.

The final verdict read: "Michael Sattler shall be committed to the executioner. The latter shall take him to the square and there first cut out his tongue, then forge him fast to a wagon, and there with glowing iron tongs twice tear pieces from his body, and then on the way to the site of execution five times more as above, and then burn his body to powder as an arch-heretic."

Stoically Sattler endured it all, presumably retaining enough of his tongue to admonish the onlookers in the market square to convert and repent and to pray for his judges. After being bound to a ladder and pushed into the fire, he prayed:

Michael Sattler, who formulated the first Anabaptist confession of faith, the Schleitheim Confession, was arrested in 1527, tortured (his tongue was cut out), and burned alive, all of which he bore stoically. His wife, Margaretha, was drowned nine days later. The message scrolled on the rock below testifies on their behalf: "Michael and Margaretha Sattler: They died for their faith."

"Almighty eternal God, thou art the way and the truth; because I have not been shown to be in error, I will with thy help on this day testify to the truth and seal it with my blood."[7] The co-accused along with their followers were burned shortly thereafter, while those who recanted were chased from Rottenburg with torches, expelled forever from Austrian territory. Sattler's wife, Margaretha, was drowned in the Neckar River some days later.

Further west, in the city of Strasbourg, the prominent Lutheran reformer Martin Bucer, who had earlier had a friendly debate with Sattler, wrote: "We do not doubt that Michael Sattler, who was burned at Rottenburg, was a dear friend of God, although he was a leader of the Anabaptists, but much more honorable than some."

Hoffmann arrived in Strasbourg in 1531, believing it was the New Jerusalem, and the Apocalypse would occur in two years. The city's more theological reformers were hostile.

By the end of the 1520s, Strasbourg (population about fifteen thousand) was becoming a Protestant city under Bucer's theological activism. Located within the German-French border region of Alsace, it was also a free city (i.e., a republic in itself) and thus a magnet for dispossessed and expelled religionists, including Anabaptists, whose persecution elsewhere was hideously escalating. Following a death decree by the 1529 Diet of Speyer, for example, four hundred extra police were hired in Swabia to hunt them down and hang them on the spot.

In the meantime, northern Germany, Moravia, and the Low Countries had become home to a new generation of generally less-educated leaders. Many of

Melchior Hoffmann

these northern Anabaptists came to believe that the world would end on a certain date, when only the "elect" brethren—the 144,000 specified in Revelation—would be saved. They strongly rejected all oaths and any cooperation with "worldly" governments, and prominent among them was Melchior Hoffmann, a skinner in the fur trade.

Hoffmann, born in Franconia, was a constant reader of the Bible and of assorted mystic writings. At first he had been warmly received by Luther in Wittenberg but later fell into Karlstadt's more radical orbit. Hoffmann developed a pattern of traveling to a new region, landing a prominent preaching job on the strength of his oratory, upsetting the authorities with his condemnation of the nobility and the clergy, and then being summarily ejected from the district.

He arrived in Strasbourg in 1531 in the belief that it was the New Jerusalem, and that the Apocalypse would occur there in 1533. The city's more theologically trained reformers were hostile to this wild-eyed charismatic, and he quietly departed. But he proceeded to issue a series of booklets, including one on the tenets of Anabaptism, *The Ordinance of God*, which to this day is revered by Mennonites. These found a receptive audience, especially in Holland, where Hoffman converted many to the faith. (He has been called the "father of Dutch Anabaptism.")

7. In August 1957 the Sixth Mennonite World Conference dedicated a memorial plaque to Michael Sattler in the Lutheran parish church in Rottenburg. The plaque reads: "The Baptist Michael Sattler was executed by burning after severe torture on the 20th of May, 1527, here on the 'Gallows Hill'. He died as a true witness of Jesus Christ. His wife Margaretha and other members of the congregation were drowned and burned. They acted for the baptism of those who want to follow Christ, for an independent congregation of the faithful, for the peaceful message of the Sermon on the Mount."

In 1533 he returned to Strasbourg, adopting a more conciliatory stance toward secular authority and reversing an earlier position advocating the use of the sword to smite one's enemies. But his millenarian preaching to the town's poorer elements created unrest, and that May the city council had him arrested and jailed on sedition charges. One follower prophesied that Hoffmann would be released in six months, in time to greet the Savior on his return, but he was destined to remain in prison ten years and to die there of illness. Even so, it was he who inspired the notorious takeover by Dutch Anabaptists of the northern German city of Münster—an event that for centuries to come would burden Anabaptists with the additional epithet "Münsterites" (see subchapter, p. 80). For the most part, however, the kind of violence perpetrated there—something that all along had been rejected by the majority—disappeared as the movement strove to rebuild itself in the face of extreme prejudice.

While the Münsterites were conducting their catastrophic experiment in communal living at the point of a sword, the Tirolean exiles in Moravia had developed a pacificist version of Christian communism that would prove more enduring. Jakob Hutter had by 1533 established a communal *Brüderhof* (brotherhood) in the town of Auspitz, based on the idea of brotherly love and drawing its inspiration from the book of Acts. Its central premise, as summed up by Guy F. Hershberger in *The Recovery of the Anabaptist Vision* (1957), was "private property is the greatest enemy of Christian love."

So numerous was the movement becoming, however, that Archduke Ferdinand paid a personal visit to the Moravian Reichstag and an order was issued to expel it from the land. Hutter returned to Austria, where he and his pregnant wife were captured and tried in Innsbruck. When whippings and the rack failed to persuade him to recant, Hutter was burned at the stake in February 1536, at the age of thirty-six. In honor of his heroic conduct the Auspitz Anabaptists, by then dispersed on the estates of sympathetic Moravian nobles, began calling themselves Hutterites.

As such, they would carry the word to every part of German-speaking Europe. Though an estimated eighty percent of their missionaries would be martyred, eventually the Hutterites were able to establish nearly idyllic, self-sufficient, pacifist communal colonies—producing their own goods, educating their own children, training their own doctors, and eschewing immodest dress, dancing, swearing, and drinking—while paying their taxes and obeying the outside authorities in all things that were not contrary to God's word. Even a late-sixteenth-century Catholic antagonist, Christoph Fischer, in a book titled *Of the Cursed Beginnings of the Anabaptists*, wrote: "Among all the heresies and sects which have their origin from Luther . . . not a one has a better appearance than the [Hutterite] Anabaptists."[8]

Around the time of Hutter's death, another enduring figure in the Anabaptist movement was also becoming known. Menno Simons, a Frieslander, had begun

The preaching of Jakob Hutter, a hatmaker born in the Tirol around 1500, soon attracted followers. Leading them into Moravia, he inaugurated a near idyllic rural fellowship based on strict communal ownership of all property. Hutter died at the stake at age thirty-six.

8. Chased from Moravia in the seventeenth century, the Hutterites moved farther east. In the eighteenth century Empress Catherine the Great moved thousands of Mennonite farmers into southern Russia, guaranteeing them freedom of religion and exemption from military service. Their superb farming technology produced great wealth for themselves and for Russia, but later czars began drafting them into the army, causing a major migration into the Americas. As a result of persecution for refusing military service in the United States in the twentieth century, many moved north, and by the beginning of the twenty-first century, three-quarters of North America's sixty thousand Hutterites were living on communal farms on the Canadian prairies.

Menno Simons (above) rejected certain revolutionary and fanatical elements of Anabaptism. He and Jakob Hutter are credited, however, with ensuring that the practices of the faithful survived.

9. Following Menno Simons' death, his followers remained active in Holland and northern Germany, where they continued to be persecuted into the seventeenth century. Some gave up and joined the Swiss state church, some moved to Russia under the protection of Catherine the Great, and others split off as the Amish, named for their leader Jacob Amman. Still other Mennonites came to the New World in the mid-1600s and would later make common cause with the Quakers to oppose slavery there. In time they, too, would divide into varying types, from relatively moderate to extremely conservative "old order" believers like the Amish, who would spurn modern technology. By the early twenty-first century there were 1.5 million Mennonites in sixty-five countries, the largest number in the United States (370,000) and the second largest in the Democratic Republic of Congo (216,000).

his clerical career as a hard-drinking, card-playing priest in the Netherlands in the 1520s. Intrigued first by Luther and then by Zwingli and the Anabaptists of Strasbourg, Menno Simons carefully read the Bible and concluded that he had been particularly deceived by Catholic doctrine concerning the Lord's Supper and infant baptism. In 1536 he withdrew from the Catholic Church, was baptized, and joined the Anabaptists.

Having seen Melchior Hoffmann's prophetic and apocalyptic brand of Anabaptism descend into the chaos of the Münster insurrection, however, Menno Simons rejected all revolutionary and mystical fanaticism. He dedicated himself to shepherding the surviving Anabaptists in the Netherlands on a truer, gentler, and more biblical path. Acutely aware of the personal danger he faced, he conducted a secret and peripatetic ministry, preaching to small groups, producing pamphlets, and debating other Anabaptists on points of doctrine. He made sure that he, his wife, and their small children stayed one step ahead of the authorities, who had put the hefty price of one hundred guilders on his head. For two decades he traveled like this, staying with coreligionists, some of whom were executed when the identity of their recent guest was discovered.

Finally in 1554, near the German city of Oldesloe in Schleswig-Holstein, the fifty-four-year-old Menno Simons made his home with a group of Anabaptists who had found sanctuary on the estate of nobleman Bartholomeus von Ahlefeldt. Here he worked on his books and guided his fellow Mennonites (as they were being called by then) in the creation of a pure apostolic church, disciplined and as far removed as possible from the outside world. In 1557, crippled and on crutches, he traveled to an Anabaptist convention in Strasbourg, where he defended his hard line on shunning apostates and avoiding all those who were not of the faith. He died four years later.

Menno Simons is particularly revered by Mennonites for saving northern Anabaptism following the Münster debacle, and for establishing a disciplined church structure on a strong biblical foundation. Although his voluminous writings are not especially noted for their theological logic or insights, and some twentieth-century scholarship regards the role of Menno Simons as overblown, he along with the Hutterites is widely credited with the survival of a purely Anabaptist movement into the twenty-first century.[9]

Anabaptism would also significantly influence the English Baptists, Quakers, and assorted

other Bible-based evangelical expressions of Christianity. Anabaptist belief in freedom of conscience, in separation of church and state, in pacifism, and in communalism would also leave its mark upon modern western politics and government, and upon founding documents as diverse as the United States Constitution and the Communist Manifesto. "Today the Anabaptist heritage is not the sole possession of some inconspicuous sect in the backwater of civilization," wrote the historian William R. Estep in 1963. "It is the prized possession of every free civilization of the twentieth-century world." ■

Mennonite workers process molasses for the tourist trade in Muddy Pond, Tennessee, in 1985. Through their influence on Baptists, Quakers, and other Bible-based denominations, and through their impassioned defense of freedom of conscience, separation of church and state, pacifism, and communal ownership, the Anabaptists made a unique mark on Western society.

The Anabaptist disaster at Münster

When reformist renegades opted for war instead of peace, they took over a whole town, imposed an iron monarchical rule, and an era of death, horror and depravity ensued

1. Such, anyway, was the general view of the Anabaptist phenomenon commonly held up to the late twentieth century, when some scholars began contending that the Münster endeavor as far more typical of the inclinations of the whole movement, while the pacifist, nonbelligerent Anabaptists were in fact its nonconforming aberration.

The Anabaptists of the 1530s tended to die by the sword but not to live by it. No matter how many were burned in the Tirol or drowned in Zurich or hanged from the trees of Swabia, their response was almost invariably the same: a stoical or even joyful resignation to martyrdom. Their model was the early church, they explained, and persecution was their expectation. Pacifism and nonresistance were the general rule for a people who viewed themselves as living saints. But with a movement so scattered, loosely organized, and necessarily secretive, divergences and aberrations were inevitable, and for the Anabaptists the biggest and most divergent aberration was the nightmare that the citizens of sixteenth-century Christendom came to associate with a single, sinister word: Münster.[1]

Situated in Westphalia, thirty miles southeast of the Dutch border, Münster was then a city of about seven thousand; a center for weaving, metalworking, and agriculture, dominated by the famous spires of thirteenth-century St. Paul's Cathedral and its almost equally venerable St. Lambert's Church. By 1530 its municipal council was a mix of moderate Lutherans and Catholics who handled the city's affairs with a degree of autonomy and had until now largely avoided significant discord with one another or with their prince-bishop. But that was before two radical Dutch reformers, both named Jan, selected Münster as the New Jerusalem.

Jan Matthias was a fifty-five-year-old master baker from Haarlem who renounced pacifism and favored physical combat with or without the heavenly signal that other Anabaptists considered essential. Tall, gaunt, thick-bearded, almost bald, with enormous and piercing black

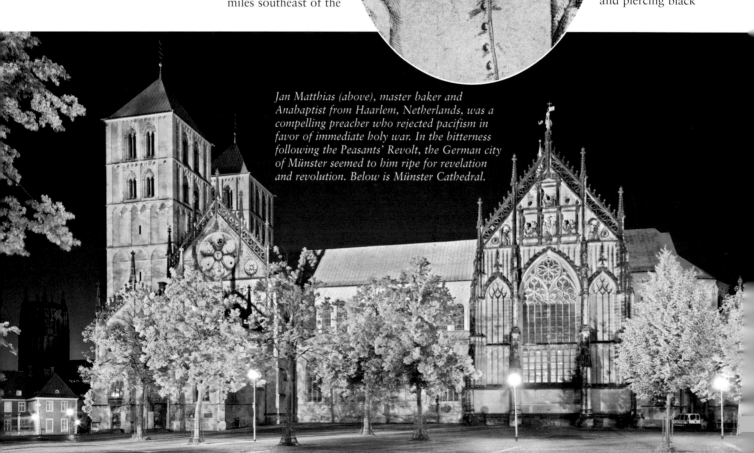

Jan Matthias (above), master baker and Anabaptist from Haarlem, Netherlands, was a compelling preacher who rejected pacifism in favor of immediate holy war. In the bitterness following the Peasants' Revolt, the German city of Münster seemed to him ripe for revelation and revolution. Below is Münster Cathedral.

eyes, he was a compelling preacher, his oratory punctuated with trances and visions. Matthias wanted a holy war, and he wanted it now.

Jan Bockelson was twenty-four, blond, good looking, and with an eye, said his critics, for the ladies. His was the oratory of the theater, picked up from miracle plays, where he often appeared as King David. He was running a seedy dockside bar with his wife in his hometown of Leiden when he attached himself to Matthias to better his lot.

To both Jans, Münster appeared ripe for revelation and revolution. The Peasants' Revolt had left bitterness in its wake. People resented the tax exemptions enjoyed by Catholic churches and the levies of the prince-bishop to bolster his army against the threatening Turk. Then, too, the Lutheran Reformation had reached town in the person of Bernhard Rothmann, an energetic thirty-six-year-old priest who had begun his career as a Catholic chaplain. By 1531 he was preaching the overthrow of what he considered papist trappings and enlivening his services with song, dance, and seemingly pagan feasting in defiance of prescribed fasting days.[2] Public religious ecstasies became common, women throwing themselves on the ground, tearing off their clothes, foaming at the mouth, and stretching their arms into a cross, while scanning the sky for some celestial sign.

Rothmann had a powerful champion in the cloth merchant and city councillor Bernard Knipperdolling, middle-aged, tall, burly, square bearded, and powerful enough to block any civic sanction against Rothmann if his increasingly violent effusions should provoke the wrath of Bishop Franz von Waldeck. But this was unlikely. That great shambling Teuton bishop, with sausage fingers, bushy brows, and sensual wants, cared more for wine, women, and boar hunting than theology, even after Rothmann acolytes began smashing statuary, defacing images, and burning every book save the German Bible. Rothmann's efforts were soon augmented by Bockelson's. He began performing illegal public baptisms in the streets, meanwhile scandalizing the city by bigamously marrying Knipperdolling's daughter.

By 1534, with Anabaptists streaming in from the Netherlands, they comprised about a third of Münster's population. Accumulating weapons, they tried to seize the city hall. Moderate council members, nominally supported by Bishop Franz, mustered enough armed Catholics and Lutherans to stop them. But they did gain control of the schools and set up a special police force to punish drunks, liars, and blasphemers.

In February that year, Jan Matthias

HÆC·FACÍES·HÍC·CVLTVS·ERAT·CV·SEPTRA·TENE·
REX·ανΒατjισωμ·SED·BREVE·TÊPVS·EGO·
HENRÍCVS·ALDEGREVER·SVΣATÍÊ·FACÍEBAT·

made his appearance in Münster, complete with a flowing black robe and carrying two stone tablets upon which the "divine will" had been etched. Obviously a prophet, concluded the faithful. With him came the former Carmelite nun Divara, white clad, beautiful, dark haired, and twenty-nine years Matthias's junior. By then, with most of the councillors fled, Knipperdolling was easily elected mayor, and Rothmann could announce the New Jerusalem: Private property must go, as must buying and selling, working for money, usury, living off "the sweat of the poor," everything that offends against love. "One God, one pot, one egg, and one kitchen," declared Knipperdolling. Four centuries later, "Communist dialecticians would praise Münster as the first dictatorship of the proletariat," writes Anthony Arthur in his *The Tailor-King: The Rise and Fall of the Anabaptist Kingdom of Münster* (New York, 1999).

Matthias enunciated its theology. Münster would be devoted to the worship of God the Father, not his meek and loving Son.

Flamboyant Jan Bockelson (better known as Jan van Leiden), is shown here in an engraving by Lutheran artist Heinrich Aldegrever, c.1502–1555. Bockelson ran a dockside bar in Leiden, the Netherlands, before joining Jan Matthias in establishing an Anabaptist regime in Münster.

2. The theological writings of Bernhard Rothmann were taken seriously in reformist circles. In his treatise *Restitution*, he discerned several prior reformations: one when the Jews fell into bondage in Egypt, another in the second Christian century, and one inaugurated by Luther and Erasmus climaxing in the developments at Münster. Luther was unimpressed, however, and warned Rothmann, "You are drunk and utterly captive to your delusions."

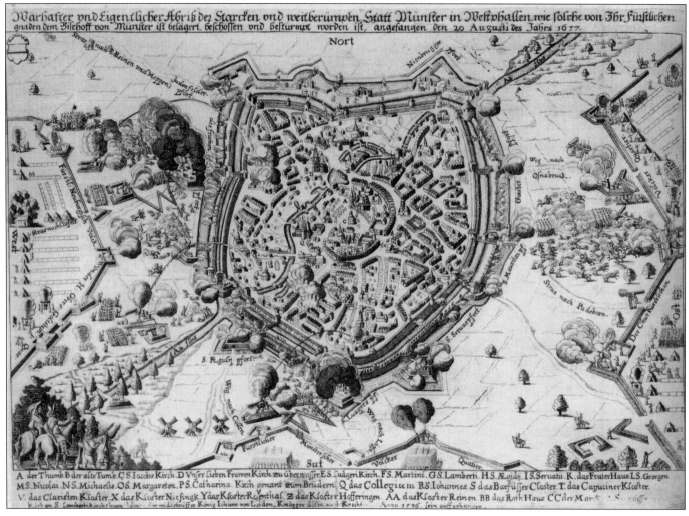

The siege of Münster by Bishop Franz von Waldeck's forces as depicted in a 1535 woodcut, showing the double moat, cannon in the cathedral tower, and the Market Square, where the Mollenbeck rebels were executed. The populace was reduced to frying mice in candle tallow and digging up the dead for sustenance.

Only the rebaptized could expect forgiveness. All others would be executed or banished. He railed against Catholics and Lutherans alike. "Everywhere, we are surrounded by dogs and sorcerers and whores and killers and the godless and all who love lies and commit them!" Many Catholics and Lutherans, unwilling to accept rebaptism, fled with whatever possessions they could smuggle under their clothing.

Matthias meanwhile prepared the city for a siege, stripping the churches of whatever could be sold, demanding that the citizens forfeit all their money, instituting common meals, and assembling some sixteen hundred men whose zeal must outweigh their almost complete ignorance of warfare. Discipline was fierce. When one defender complained that the Dutch were faring better than the Germans, Bockelson paraded the man before the assembled citizenry and told Matthias to execute him. Matthias could not do it, so Bockelson himself ran him through with a halberd.

On Good Friday 1534, Jan Matthias was attending a lavish wedding feast in a tavern when he suddenly fell face downward on the table. Was he dead? No, for he slowly lifted his head, crying, "Dear Father, I

hear and obey." Then, kissing every man and woman present, he left the room. Rothmann explained it. Matthias had been instructed to do battle, he said. Thus, at noon on Easter Sunday with twelve guards he rode out the gate in full armor to meet the bishop's army. They obliged. Some five hundred men on black horses appeared over a hill and cut the thirteen to pieces, planting Matthias's head on a pole and nailing his genitals to the city's gates.

The next day, appropriately white robed and by candlelight, Bockelson again explained. Matthias had been vain, proud, and disobedient. He hadn't first prayed, he hadn't first fasted, and he was supposed to go alone and instead took twelve men to their deaths. So God had now instructed him, Bockelson, to marry the widowed Divara and take Matthias's place. His hearers exploded with joy, tearing off their clothes and dancing naked. Indeed, nudity became a badge of honor in Münster. Were we not all to one day stand naked before a divine judge?

Soon Bockelson himself appeared naked in the market square, racing around town and roaring imprecations, then falling down dumbstruck before awakening to announce

Münster's new constitution: there would be twelve elders; disobeying them would mean death; so too would blasphemy, impurity, and any attempt to flee the city. Mayor Knipperdolling was appointed executioner. He began immediately by beheading six soldiers for stealing wine.

With women outnumbering men three to one, polygamy became compulsory. Doors must be left open so that men could enter and choose females as young as ten for their harems. Bockelson set the pace by increasing his own wife count to sixteen, with all save Divara under the age of twenty. The polygamy ordinance set off a rebellion. Blacksmith Henry Mollenheck and an angry mob locked Knipperdolling and Rothmann in a cellar. But their jailers got drunk, and Knipperdolling's men overcame them. Several dozen of the counter-rebels, having dug their graves in the cathedral square, were then shot and fell into them.

Through 1534 the bishop's forces launched several assaults on Münster, using a great cannon. All were rebuffed. Bockelson celebrated this success by setting up a throne in the marketplace, moving into the bishop's residence, and declaring himself "king of the world." Knipperdolling became prime minister and Rothmann the royal spokesman. In January 1535 Bishop Franz changed his strategy. He built an impenetrable outer wall around the city to starve it into submission. Soon the populace was reduced to frying mice in candle tallow and drinking whitewash as milk. By May the defense force was reduced to eight hundred. People were dying in the street, buried in mass graves, and often disinterred to be devoured by those still living.

King Jan continued to live opulently, but there was an unpleasant incident. When one of his wives objected to this inequity and asked to leave the city, he cut off her head at a royal banquet, then danced the night away with the cadaver, while Rothmann and his other wives intoned, "Glory to God in the highest."

The end came in June. Two men escaped the town and told the bishop's forces of a way to smuggle a small party into the city. These could then open one of the gates and let in a bigger force of some 350, who could then let the main force scale the walls. The plan worked. By midday June 25, Münster again belonged to the bishop, who four days later entered the city in a coach pulled by six white horses. The usual pillage and slaughter

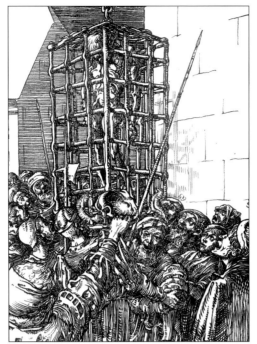

followed, but Knipperdolling and Bockelson were taken alive. Rothmann disappeared, never to be seen again. Divara refused to recant and was executed, as were several hundred other men and women who took the same stance. Most of the three thousand women rounded up were allowed to return to their native villages. A year later, Münster could count only about two hundred former Anabaptists.

The bishop visited King Jan in jail as he awaited execution in chains and rags. "Are you a king?" the bishop asked disdainfully. "Are you a bishop?" Bockelson snarled in reply. Interviewed by a Lutheran theologian, Antonius Corvinus, he recanted nothing. Neither did Knipperdolling. What Bockelson did repent of was his conduct. "He greatly regretted his godlessness, his murders, his looting, his lack of discipline, and his shameful deeds," said Corvinus, "and he renounced all his errors." The night before his death, he was consoled by a priest.[3]

The next day, January 22, 1536, in Münster's market square, Bishop Franz watched from a window as Bockelson, Knipperdolling, and another prisoner were put to a hideous death. Stripped to the waist and fitted with iron collars embedded with spikes to prevent any movement, each was placed inside an iron cage while executioners ripped chunks of flesh from his flanks with red-hot tongs. If he fainted, he was revived, for the new imperial code required that a criminal be kept alive for a full hour of pain before a dagger was thrust into his heart.[4] Jan and the others bore their torture with courage, crying out only a few times. Corvinus attributed their strength to the presence of the devil. ∎

In January 1536 Münster's self-proclaimed king, Jan Bockelson, suffered a horrific execution—reportedly with great courage—along with erstwhile mayor Knipperdolling and a third man whose identity is not recorded. As portrayed in a sixteenth-century Dutch engraving above left, the men were tortured to death in iron cages. The cages were then hoisted up the steeple of St. Lambert's Church to display the corpses. The 2006 photograph above right shows the cages hanging there as a memorial.

3. Bockelson, also known as Jan van Leiden, has achieved immortality another way in the Netherlands in the saying, "Zich met een Jan(tje) van Leiden van iets afmaken" ("to pull a Jan van Leiden"), which means not putting too much effort (or any effort) into something.

4. In 1534 the emperor Charles V had approved the *Constitutio Criminalis Carolina*, the first criminal code applicable to all the German principalities. It defined the maximum punishment allowable for each crime but left the judge free to apply it or mitigate it.

CHAPTER 5

Geneva's John Calvin put reform to work in a model biblical city

Some saw it as a testing ground for faith versus evil, others as a nasty authoritarian theocracy, but it set a form of church government that traveled the world

Martin Luther is widely recognized as the man who started the Protestant Reformation, but his influence over the ensuing centuries is overshadowed by an individual born nearly twenty-six years after him. John Calvin's written works are not nearly so vast as Luther's, and biographies of him far fewer. Much more than Luther, however, Calvin was what a later generation would call a "systems man," and he left behind systems of theology and highly adaptable systems of church government that would be applied across the centuries and across the world.

Calvinism, as it came to be known, would take over the northern Netherlands and have a violent impact on France. It created the Puritan movement in England through which Parliament would execute a king and impose for a time what Winston Churchill would call "the most hated government in English history." However, it would also play a role in creating the parliamentary institution that would gain control of the monarchy and make England a democratic model for much of the world. In Scotland Calvinism formed the Presbyterian Church, in South Africa it created the government that imposed the racist policy of apartheid on the blacks, on the coast of Massachusetts Bay it laid the foundations of what would become the United States of America, and far ahead in the twentieth century it would play the leading role in the amazing Christianization of South Korea.

Yet the man who started it all is described by one sympathetic twenty-first-century biographer, Bruce Gordon (*Calvin*, 2009), as ruthless and bad tempered,

John Calvin, memorialized here in this statue in Geneva's Reformation Wall, has been called ruthless and ill-tempered, but there is little doubt that his impact on history has overshadowed even that of Martin Luther. Besides leaving behind reasoned and adaptable systems of theology and church government, he sought to create the perfect Christian society in the Swiss city of Geneva. The wall, featuring Calvin and other Reformation figures, was completed in 2009 to mark the five hundredth anniversary of Calvin's birth.

John Calvin is shown in this contemporary oil painted in 1555, when he was forty-six years old. It hangs now at the Boymans-van Beuningen Museum in Rotterdam. Calvin was descended from boatmen on the Oise River. His father, however, became a lawyer and sent his son to study law at the University of Paris, where he came under the influence of Reformation teaching, brought to France largely through the writings of Jacques Lefèvre d'Etaples, depicted in this sixteenth-century engraving at the Bibliothèque Nationale in Paris.

1. The house where John Calvin was born was destroyed by shell fire during the First World War, and Noyon was again hit hard in the Second. Of buildings dating back to Calvin's day, there remains standing only a wall of the original cathedral tower, now incorporated into the new cathedral building.

and given to hatred, intimidation, bullying, the humiliation of opponents, and the pursuit of truth at any cost—in short, a man who saw himself as the prophet of God. Like other prophets, he made bitter enemies, chiefly because he was far more interested in being right than in being popular, and more often than not he was the former. Finally, he was no mere theorist. He did not confine himself to advancing formulas for the perfect Christian society. At the Swiss city of Geneva he actually tried to create one, and life in it to some was a crucial battleground between good and evil. To others, it was simply hideous.

Calvin was French, though it was not he who brought the Reformation to France. That distinction belongs to the French humanist and biblical scholar known in France as Jacques Lefèvre d'Etaples (and elsewhere as Jacobus Faber), whose spiritual writings and vernacular Bible translations were circulating throughout the country some time before Luther's. Lefèvre was drawn by a reform-minded bishop to the cathedral city of Meaux, then about twenty-five miles northeast of Paris, where he became the central inspiration for a circle of like-minded preachers who volubly deplored the failings of the church. One of these, a certain Guillaume (i.e., William) Farel, was destined to be John Calvin's principal associate and co-warrior for God. Another, Gerard Roussel, by deciding to remain in the Catholic Church, would earn one of Calvin's more torrid execrations.

Standing foursquare against the "Preachers of Meaux" was the University of Paris in general and its dean of theology, Noel Beda, in particular. Dean Beda denounced even the writings of the judicious Desiderius Erasmus, who advocated change within the existing Catholic structure, but his inquisitional zeal was restrained by Marguerite of Navarre, beloved elder sister of the French king, Francis I. Marguerite sympathized with the preachers, and since the king's distaste for them was exceeded by his distaste for the entire Catholic hierarchy, Francis supported his sister, though not unreservedly. However, when King Francis was held captive after the disastrous Battle of Pavia in 1525, his anti-preacher mother, Louise of Savoy, became regent (see ch. 3, p. 48). This allowed Beda to loose his uninhibited fury upon the Circle of Meaux, and the preachers fled. Most sought the safety of Strasbourg, capital of Alsace, where Catholics and Protestants would somehow manage to coexist fairly peacefully through the whole turbulent sixteenth century.

It was soon after this that the promising young lawyer John Calvin began to take a serious interest in Christian reform. Calvin came from the town of Noyon in Picardy, some sixty miles north of Paris on the Oise River.[1] He descended from a family of riverboat men, but his father had achieved the professional status of notary, changed the family name from Cauvin to Calvin, and acquired Noyon Cathedral as one of his major clients. John, second of his five sons and one of the three who would survive to adulthood, was born July 10, 1509.

At twelve John was tonsured a postulant to the Catholic priesthood. This gained for him a small stipend with almost no ecclesiastical obligations, but by the age of twenty-five he had to take orders or forfeit the income. Just before his twenty-fifth birthday he did the latter. Meanwhile, his father's connections had made him a companion of the sons of Noyon's gentry, giving him speech and manners far above the Cauvin family's riverboat background. In 1523, when plague struck Noyon, John and his titled schoolboy friends were sent to the University of Paris to complete their education, making him at age fourteen the

Studying in Orléans, John set up a work ethic that became part of the Calvinist legacy, beginning his day at 4 a.m., ending it late at night, & marring his health in doing so.

pupil of some of the era's best linguists and classicists.[2] Among other things, they taught him to reason and argue with scholastic proficiency, a skill he honed further after transferring to the study of law at Orléans when he was nineteen. Here, too, he established a work ethic that would find its way into the Calvinist heritage, beginning his day as early as four in the morning and ending it late at night, gravely weakening his health, some said, in the process.

In this cathedral in Noyon, France, whose clergy were major clients of Calvin's father, Calvin was tonsured for the Catholic priesthood at age twelve. With this came the stipend of a postulant priest. Before his twenty-fifth birthday, however, Calvin was required to decide to either take holy orders or forfeit the income. He chose the latter.

In 1531 Calvin's father died,[3] and he transferred to the study of the classics, intent on becoming a humanist writer, a career path that King Francis strongly favored for young men. The king by now had returned to his throne, reversing the fortunes of the reformers. The preachers swarmed back to Paris, and by the spring of 1533 the eloquent Gerard Roussel was addressing crowds of up to five thousand at the Louvre, where Marguerite had won him the job of Lenten preacher. Somewhere in those crowds was John Calvin, who greatly admired Roussel. When Beda and his colleagues at the university formally assailed the Roussel sermons, the king acted swiftly, firing the lot and banishing them from Paris. In Beda's place King Francis appointed his personal physician's son: Nicholas Cop, a professor of philosophy, a known reformer, and a family friend of John Calvin.

2. Calvin arrived at the university in the same year that marked the graduation of a Spanish student named Ignatius of Loyola, who was destined to have as much influence on the Catholic world as Calvin would have on the Protestant one (see ch. 8). There is no evidence that the two ever encountered one another.

3. By the time of his death in 1531, Calvin's father had been excommunicated from the Catholic Church in a dispute over his accounts and thus could not be buried in consecrated ground. Calvin's brother Charles was also excommunicated for assaulting the cathedral mace bearer and beating up a priest. Whether these circumstances influenced John Calvin's attitude toward the church is not recorded. However, writes the historian Williston Walker, "to have a father and brother fall into open conflict with the ecclesiastical authorities . . . must certainly have disposed a boy just passing into manhood toward an attitude of criticism" (*John Calvin* in the *Heroes of the Reformation* series, 1909).

However, Cop's appointment spelled the end of the reformers' brief Parisian heyday. The central message of his inaugural address came straight from Luther, and the university's traditionalists, though subdued by the fate of Beda, were far from vanquished. They presented excerpts from this speech to the Parlement of Paris, which declared them heretical, laid them before the king and indignantly demanded suppression of the Lutherans.[4] Francis, who could ill afford an outright showdown with the Parlement, ordered Cop and his associates arrested.

Cop was soon on his way to Basel in Switzerland with a reward of three hundred crowns on his head, Roussel was arrested, and a search was in progress for the suspected author of the offending Cop speech, namely John Calvin. Warned in time, Calvin by one account lowered himself by rope from a window and escaped the city disguised as a farm laborer. His rooms were searched for proof of heretical teaching, but the ever faithful Marguerite of Navarre managed to quash the charges against him and also to secure Roussel's liberty. Calvin prudently left Paris, however, and for the next year studied in various French centers.

Yet he left behind him an historical puzzle. How was a man largely indifferent to religion in 1531 transformed into a zealous reform activist sought for heresy two years later? Calvin himself leaves two seemingly incompatible accounts of his conversion. In a letter to a Catholic cardinal in 1539 he describes a gradual loss of faith in Catholic worship and theology, followed by a painful despair much like Luther's, and then a dawning reassurance afforded by the reform teachings. However, recounting his conversion twenty years later in a preface to a commentary on the Psalms, he describes a sudden revelation not unlike St. Paul's, the light descending on a divinely designated prophet.

Doubtless reassured by the release of Gerard Roussel, the reformers became more daring. They staged an exhibition that brought a ferocious response from a church and state not nearly as ready to dump the ancient faith as its detractors had supposed. On the night of October 17, 1534, placards denouncing the Catholic Mass as a horrible and unendurable abuse of the Lord's Supper were posted in towns and cities across the country. One was left at the very door of the king's bedchamber, an affront that proved sufficient to terminate any further flirtation Francis may have contemplated with Protestantism. More than two hundred arrests and twenty executions followed, along with property seizures and banishment, effectively obliterating the leadership of the French reform movement. The man destined to assume it made it safely to Marguerite's city of Angoulême, 250 miles south of Paris.

But Calvin didn't stay in Angoulême. For the next two years he lived as a fugitive, often under assumed names, traveling from city to city to rouse support for the Protestant cause. He appears at Nerac to visit the aging Lefèvre, at Poitiers to serve the Lord's Supper under the reform rite, at Orléans to publish a denunciation of the Anabaptists, then back in Angoulême to use the library of his close friend, the Catholic canon Louis du Tillet. This was when he began work on the treatise which would provide the theological and ecclesiastical foundation of Calvinist Christianity for the next four centuries and more. He entitled it the *Institutes of the Christian Religion*, and over the following quarter century would produce successive and extensive revisions of it.

Published in 1536, Calvin's Institutes of the Christian Religion, seen below in its fourth edition, was initially intended to respond to the counterattacking Catholics, who were portraying all Protestants as anarchic Anabaptists. But Calvin's Institutes accomplished much more. Considered by his adherents as second only to the Bible, the work eventually made Calvin the acknowledged leader of Christian reform in all France.

The initial purpose of the *Institutes* (a better translation might be "Fundamentals") was to provide reformers with a response to counterattacking Catholic pamphlets, which were branding them all as Anabaptists—the kind of people who had just presided over the horrors at Münster (see p. 80). The first edition was chiefly confined to this apologetic role, but in its much more elaborate later editions the *Institutes* becomes an instructional catechism, second in importance only to the Bible itself for the emerging reformed faith. In its final form it provides a statement of Christian doctrine: embracing God, the Trinity, man, providence,

the total corruption of human nature, justification, redemption by Christ, faith, repentance and remission of sin, election and predestination, the church, the papacy, the ministry, powers inherent in the church, the sacraments, and civil government. Whatever else it might have accomplished, the *Institutes* soon made Calvin the acknowledged leader of Christian reform in all France.

Its most controversial element, and the one that would occasion greatest discussion and debate among reformers, concerned the doctrine of election and predestination. This inherently suggested that even before men were created, some were destined to be the "elect," bound with certainty for heaven, while others were bound with equal certainty for hell. To many people this seemed to throw the justice of God into serious doubt. Calvin's reply was that no creature can question the path taken by its Creator.

In any case, it soon became evident that the leaders of the French reform movement could not safely live in France. In late 1535 Calvin crossed the Swiss border to Basel, where he embarked on a scholarly career as the central figure in a brotherhood of Protestant thinkers and the printers who published their work. The Reformation had reached Switzerland sixteen years earlier, when Huldrych Zwingli, as pastor of the Grossmünster (cathedral) in Zurich, began attacking such Catholic practices as Lenten fasting, clerical celibacy, and the use of images in worship, and ultimately introduced a new liturgy to replace the Mass (see p. 50). His ideas spread quickly through Zurich and soon to other German-speaking Swiss towns.

Switzerland was a confederacy of independent cantons, city-states, and assorted dependencies. As the reform movement spread, some joined it and others remained Catholic, resulting in 1531 in a localized war in which Zwingli was killed and the Catholic side won. Zurich remained Protestant, however, as did Switzerland's other two major centers, the canton of Bern and the city of Basel. Bern was sufficiently wealthy and powerful to push the forces of the duke of Savoy and bishop of Geneva out of the Genevan hinterland and secure the city from counterattack. As a result, Genevan independence was utterly dependent on Bernese military power, and Geneva was under considerable pressure to comply with Bernese

Forced to flee France in late 1535, Calvin took refuge in Switzerland, where another famous reformer, Huldrych Zwingli, had been killed four years earlier during the Second Battle of Kappel, depicted above by seventeenth-century artist Matthaus Merian. Although the Catholics won the encounter, the three major centers of Switzerland—Zurich, Bern, and Basel—all remained Protestant.

4. The Parlement of Paris was not the equivalent of the English Parliament. It developed through the late Middle Ages as a royal appeal court, eventually asserted a right of approval over royal edicts, and, as in this case, could exercise ecclesiastical authority as well. Though the Parlement of Paris was at first the only such body, fifteen other French cities would later develop such a court. Closer in function to the English Parliament was the Estates-General in France, which gradually asserted some authority over the royal power of taxation.

An Auguste Bachelin portrait of William Farel. His confrontational style of preaching repelled more people than it attracted when he sought to convert the Swiss to the new reformed Christianity. Farel often found himself ejected from one town after another. Even so, he was largely responsible for making the Swiss city of Neuchâtel the first French-speaking center of the Reformation.

desires in matters of both politics and religion.

Since reform expansion from Bern tended westward into the French-speaking districts, it required a French-speaking evangelist,[5] and it found its man in one of the most outrageous of early Calvinist followers. William Farel, a member of the Meaux circle (by then disbanded), had begun his preaching career as a French disciple of Lutheranism, then moved to Zurich as a Zwingli man, and after that to the Lefèvre group at Meaux. There his vitriolic attacks on the Catholic Mass won him the honor of banishment from France long before the Night of the Placards drove out most of his colleagues. Farel's confrontational assault on his listeners offended sensitive people but powerfully drew to his message just as many of the less sensitive.

He may have been warned that his heavy-handed evangelism would not work well on the Swiss. Sent by Bern in 1528 into the area known as the Pays de Vaud around Lausanne on the north side of Lake Geneva, Farel tried sharing his views less exuberantly, but even so found himself ejected from one town after another. Arriving in Neuchâtel, he apparently decided that all this pussyfooting was getting him nowhere and so reasserted some of the invective he had used successfully back in Zurich. Those who celebrate the Mass, he charged, "are villains, murderers, thieves, renouncers of Jesus Christ and seducers of the people." The crowd came alive. Within a few months a wild set of Neuchâtel citizens carried Farel with them into the cathedral, where they broke up the service, destroyed the priestly vestments, and smashed statues and stained glass windows. The town council voted to prohibit the Mass, and Neuchâtel became the first French-speaking city of the Protestant Reformation.

A description of a similar Farel incident at Geneva is preserved in the diary of a Catholic nun:

> On the feast of St. Mary Magdalene, after the bells had solemnly rung for Mass in her church (i.e., of St. Mary), and all the parish and other good Christians of the city had gathered there to hear the holy Mass in great devotion, that miserable preacher Farel led his entire following, wearing just their ordinary clothes, into the church of the blessed Magdalene to destroy the solemnity of her feast. Once inside, they closed the church and barred the doors to force the people to hear his sermons. Everyone was greatly troubled, the women setting up a loud cry and the men making such a ruckus that they (the invaders) had to leave the church in spite of themselves. The divine service had been halted, but after those dogs left, the Christian people returned to the church, and the priests said the Mass even more solemnly than ever and with great devotion. But at vespers those scoundrels did the same thing, taking possession of the holy church. From then on they preached there daily, and later in the Church of Saint-Gervais also. They did the same thing at the Dominican monastery on the Feast of Saint Dominic and did not cease to obstruct the divine service in all the churches.[6]

Churches were also attacked and vandalized by night, priests beaten up, and anti-Catholic placards and pamphlets widely distributed. Nevertheless, Farel's campaign in the Vaud country was far from successful overall. Eight years after he began his mission, only twelve parish churches had turned to reform and the other 142 remained firmly Catholic. Then Bernese troops arrived to coerce conformity with the new order. A kind of "town hall" debate was staged, which the reformers handily won, and altars were ordered removed from all the churches,

5. Switzerland in the sixteenth century, as in the twenty-first, was divided into four language groups. Seventeen of its modern twenty-six cantons speak only German, four speak only French, three speak French and German, and one speaks Italian. The twenty-sixth canton, Graubünden, is trilingual, speaking German, Italian, and Romansh, a language descended directly from Latin, now used by one half of one percent of the total population. The French-speaking segment, where Calvin was most active, composes the western segment of the country.

along with statues, images, and musical instruments. All priests were declared to be ministers and ordered to follow the forms of the new worship, and the Vaud region was formally pronounced Protestant. The result, however, was farcical. After the troops left, Catholic services continued to be held in supposedly Protestant churches by priests who were supposedly ministers, while in Lausanne, the Vaud's largest city, the entire edict was simply ignored.

Calvin, meanwhile, continued his studies at Basel, worked on a new edition of the *Institutes*, and from time to time conferred with Protestant leaders in other cities. One such visit took him to Ferrara in Italy in 1536, traveling under an assumed name. Though Italy, like Spain, was dangerous ground for Protestants, the duchess of Ferrara was known to shelter Protestant refugees from France. As the daughter of the late French king Louis XII she carried some weight of authority. Shortly after Calvin's arrival, however, one of these refugees staged an act of defiance in a Catholic church, was arrested for "Lutheranism," and under torture named all the other refugees. A warrant was issued for Calvin's arrest, but he made it back to Switzerland. Soon after that he visited Geneva, scene of what was to become the major labor of his life, the establishment of what he viewed as a promised land, a miraculously provided gift of God, where truth could directly confront falsehood and goodness confront evil.

There he met the irrepressible Farel, who immediately importuned him to abandon his studies at Basel, move into Geneva, and help further the city's conversion. Calvin demurred. Farel pleaded. Calvin insisted that his mind was made

6. This account of an invasion by reformers into a Geneva church was written by Jeanne de Jussie, a nun born of a noble family with ties to the duke of Savoy. At eighteen she entered a nearby Franciscan convent, the only women's monastery within the city walls. By 1530 she had become its *écrivaine*, handling all written dealings with the outside world. When the nuns perforce left Geneva in 1535, she began writing the history of their experiences, probably completing it by 1547 at Annecy, where she was elected abbess of the exiled community. Described by Abbess Jeanne as a *petite chronique*, it was published after her death with the title *Le levain du calvinisme (The Seeds of Calvinism)*.

Geneva's Reformation Wall honors four great reformers. From the left: John Knox, who brought Calvinism to Scotland; Theodore Beza, a Calvin disciple who became his successor; John Calvin himself; and William Farel, Calvin's longtime colleague in Geneva.

Although he had planned to visit Geneva only briefly before returning to his studies in Basel, an awestruck John Calvin in this Life *magazine illustration is harangued by William Farel, shouting like a man possessed. Farel commands Calvin "in the name of Almighty God" to remain in Geneva and work for the cause of reform. Below right is a pen sketch of Calvin, drawn as he lectured by one of his students.*

up—he was resolved to return to his studies at Basel. Suddenly Farel's visage changed, and he began shouting like a man possessed. "I speak in the name of Almighty God!" he thundered. "You make your studies into an excuse. But if you refuse to give yourself to God's work, he will curse you. For you are pursuing your own interests rather than Christ's!" Calvin later described himself as terrified, with no alternative but to acquiesce.

Farel had arrived in Geneva, a city of about twelve thousand, four years earlier to a less-than-hospitable reception. He had had to be rescued by town officials from a crowd that was threatening to throw him in the river, and when he appeared before the bishop's court, one cleric tried to shoot him dead. (The gun misfired.) One of his assistants, Antoine Froment, later returned to the city, set up as a French teacher, and mixed evangelism with his language lessons. Froment was three times run out of town but eventually managed to create a small congregation, and Bern ordered the Geneva council to permit them to hold services.[7]

7. Antoine Froment was a competent preacher, as was his wife. Though he is commemorated as one of the founders of Protestant Geneva, he left Geneva prior to Calvin's exile and later returned to do secretarial work. After his wife died, he was banished for ten years for committing adultery.

As reform strength grew stronger, a religious riot threatened but was at first prevented by a peacemaker who, armed only with a barrel of wine, induced both sides to drown their differences. Unhappily, however, a party of armed priests arrived on the scene, one of whom was killed in the ensuing brawl, and the

Catholic bishop fled Geneva. After a suspect confessed under torture to the killing and was hanged, the council sought to ease tensions by turning over a Catholic friary to Farel to become a Protestant church. The troops of the still-Catholic duke of Savoy blockaded the city, cutting off food supplies. The Protestants now took charge of its defense and swiftly became its dominant force. The council ruled the Mass illegal, Geneva became Protestant, and Catholic clergy and religious orders either left town or agreed to accept reform.

But Protestant Geneva was soon starving and pleading for help from Protestant Bern. Unwilling to see its subsidiary city actually become independent, Bern refused, so Geneva approached France to send in troops, a prospect which so horrified Bern that it sent a force of six thousand to lift the blockade. The forces of the duke of Savoy withdrew, and in the resulting treaty Geneva gained almost but not quite complete freedom from Bern. In the elections of February 1536 a very pro-Farel council was elected, and it set about making the place truly Protestant. Old rules that prohibited blasphemy, cards, and dice in the taverns were revived and reasserted. No drinks were to be served after nine at night or during the hours when sermons were preached. Absence from church was subject to a fine. All shops must be closed on Sunday. But all this had been legislated before and become disregarded. It was now to be strictly applied. However, writes historian R. N. Carew Hunt (*Calvin*, 1933), "what is generally forgotten is that the basis of the Puritan regime at Geneva was laid before Calvin's day." The reform came in the fact that Calvin more rigorously enforced the rules.

In July 1536, two months after these regulations were formally adopted, Calvin arrived. Though the city was now Protestant, few of its citizens may have fully appreciated what an onerous lifestyle they were facing, nor the icy resolve of the man who would police it. For whatever theological differences Calvin may have had with the Catholic Church, he was in one sense fully in accord with the most authoritarian of popes. In the division of power between the secular authority and the

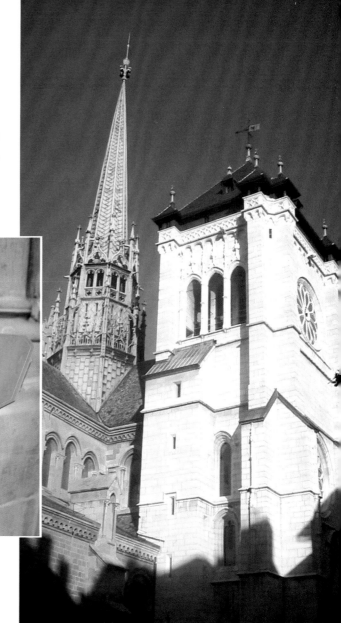

St. Peter's Cathedral (below), once the bastion of Catholicism in Geneva, became Protestant, along with the rest of the city, in 1536 after the reformers took control. They defeated the Catholic duke of Savoy, who had blockaded Geneva, and ruled the Mass illegal. John Calvin arrived in July and took his seat as the supreme authority of the city. He preached in the cathedral between 1536 and 1564, after which it became a guiding center for Protestantism. His followers stripped the building of its altars, statues, paintings, and furniture, leaving only the stained glass windows. They preserved, however, Calvin's chair.

spiritual, the latter must prevail. Pope Gregory VII, the famous "Hildebrand," would have wholeheartedly agreed.

Geneva's government was then headed by four officials called "syndics," elected early in each year by a general assembly of all male citizens. Responsible to the syndics was the twenty-five member "Small Council," the central administrative body that supervised the various municipal departments. (The Small Council was elected by the Council of Two Hundred, which otherwise met rarely and then chiefly to discuss matters of policy.) It is noteworthy that Calvin never became in any official sense part of Geneva's civil government. Always he was referred to as a "preacher" or "teacher." What he did do, as preeminently a systems man, was recommend methods by which Christian purity could be civically enhanced.

First, he devised a catechism to instruct the faithful in Christian beliefs and practices. He also devised a Confession of Faith whereby all citizens would be examined. If their answers revealed them to be Protestant, they became subject to the rules of the new church order. If not, they were deemed to be Catholic and expected to leave town. Second, the Small Council was asked to recommend "persons of upright life and good reputation among the faithful, likewise of firmness and not easily corruptible" who would be "distributed in all the quarters of the city, and shall have an eye to the life and conduct of each person; and if they see any notable fault, to censure in any person they shall communicate this to some one of the ministers." By this was meant the pastor of one of the Protestant churches, who would then counsel the miscreant. If the unsatisfactory conduct persisted, he was to be publicly scorned and excommunicated.

To most of this the Small Council agreed. But it refused to entrust the authority to excommunicate to the clergy. The citizenry proved less submissive, however. Many Genevans, one of them a syndic, refused to take the test and, when bade to leave the city, simply disobeyed. The council was baffled, and the February election of 1537 returned a new council unalterably opposed to the Calvin regime. These opponents grew defiant, then rowdy. Hecklers began interrupting his sermons. Crowds sang lewd songs about him outside his house at night. Guns were fired. This sort of thing may not have unduly disturbed Farel, who had lived with it for years, but Calvin later recalled the sheer terror of these days. "You may imagine," he confided on his deathbed, "how such things astonished a poor, timid scholar such as I am and always have been."

However, the attack that proved fatal to his mission came from without, when Bern announced without warning its adoption of a unified form of worship, a "Bernese rite," for all churches in its jurisdiction, including Geneva's. Henceforth four great festivals were to be observed, namely Christmas, Easter, Pentecost, and Ascension; baptismal fonts must be restored to the churches, and unleavened bread and stone chalices used for Communion. So would Messrs. Calvin and Farel kindly see that these changes were instituted, and come to a synod for further discussion? Farel had dispensed with all these items before Calvin's arrival, but now they found that the new city council had already received and accepted Bern's instructions.

Chaos ensued. Farel and Calvin ignored the Bern rite and the invitation to the synod. Ordered by the council to comply, they refused. Ordered to stop preaching, they preached anyway—but their sermons deploring the utter sinfulness of Geneva were greeted with jeers and boos. The mob threatened them in the streets, and only a bodyguard of volunteers prevented their being thrown into the Rhône River.

In the end the Council of Two Hundred gave them three days to leave the city, which they did. "If we had been serving man," said Calvin, "this would have been a poor recompense for our efforts. But we serve a greater Master who will know how to properly reward us." Why had they failed so disastrously? "They presumed too much on the power of dictatorial oratory to transform human nature," observes historian James MacKinnon (*Calvin and the Reformation*, 1936), "and they sought to dragoon the citizens without taking time to educate them."

Calvin vigorously denied that he had brought back confession. He also denied that he had 'broken' the church—he'd just restored it to what it was, and was always intended to be.

Having neither money nor property, the pair left Geneva with only their lives intact and, while crossing a swollen river in drenching rain, came close to losing those as well. But they made it to Basel and there they parted, Farel for a pastorate in Neuchâtel, Calvin to Strasbourg. Everyone, Protestant or Catholic, was safe in Strasbourg because of the tireless work of the Protestant leader there, Martin Kuhhorn. Better known by his Latinized name, Bucer, his first aim was to unite the increasingly fractured Protestants, and his second was to find reconciliation with Catholicism.

Bucer eventually failed in both but eminently succeeded in something else. Calvin, who greatly admired him, told him his Geneva experience proved he did not belong in the active ministry and should return to scholarly work. No, contended Bucer, that would be running away from the real battle. Rather, he should become pastor to the growing French Protestant community in Strasbourg. Calvin agreed, and there he began to build the church he had failed to build in Geneva.

Here, too, he instituted his membership test, with one important difference. In Geneva failure to qualify assumed exile from the city, but in Strasbourg, only banishment from the congregation. The big stick was gone. There were other differences. Singing of psalms and even some hymns was encouraged, for example. Extemporaneous prayers were allowed during the Communion liturgy, and everyone must present himself before the minister prior to Communion. Aha, said the Catholics, so confession was back! But Calvin vigorously denied this and also denied that he had "broken" the church—he had merely restored it to what it once was and was always intended to be.

In two particular instances, however, Catholicism continued to distress him. When he learned that Gerard Roussel, greatest of the Preachers of Meaux, had become a Catholic bishop, he wrote him in a fury, calling him "a traitor and a murderer" who "daily crucifies the Son of God." As it happens, comments historian Hunt, Roussel spent the rest of his life in a remote Catholic diocese as "the very best type" of Catholic bishop. The other instance was even harder for Calvin to bear. Louis du Tillet, who had sheltered him from arrest at Angoulême, accompanied him on his perilous visit to Italy, and even been with him at Geneva, had disappeared. Fearing he had somehow offended du Tillet, Calvin sought him out and was shocked by the explanation. He, too, had returned to the Catholic Church. What he

Forced from Geneva, Calvin traveled to Strasbourg in Alsace. Due to the influence of Martin Bucer, portrayed below by artist René Boyvin, Strasbourg tolerated both Catholics and Protestants. As a disillusioned Calvin considered returning to his scholarship, Bucer convinced him to become pastor to the growing French Protestant community there.

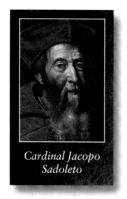

Cardinal Jacopo Sadoleto

saw at Geneva, he explained, made the old faith look much better. Calvin never communicated with him again.

But the reformed faith was working out very well with his people at Strasbourg. Calvin plainly loved his congregation, and they loved him. Though he was living in dire poverty and his household included a dozen or so ministerial students, all going hungry together, his joy was apparent. These young men were destined to carry reformed Christianity across France. Perhaps the sheer size of his domestic establishment persuaded him to marry at age thirty. His bride, Idelette de Bure, a poor but attractive widow with two children, happily took charge of the house. Two years later she gave birth prematurely to a son who died in infancy, and after six years of ill health she herself died. Calvin is said to have never recovered from the loss.

Meanwhile, reports from Geneva were alarming, though perhaps secretly satisfying to Calvin. The city was being depicted as descending into anarchy. Farel's accounts were particularly shocking. He wrote to Calvin that he had heard that brothels were opening, that Anabaptist preaching went undeterred, and that the Mass was again being said in many private homes, although the council had expressly forbidden this. Reformed churches from the abrogated Calvin regime were quarreling with congregations whose ministers had subsequently been appointed. The new clergy seem entirely unable to control their flocks, he said. "In spite of stringent governmental enactments and good advice given by the new preachers, there can be no question that the moral condition of Geneva was decidedly lower," observes the Yale historian Williston Walker (*John Calvin: The Organizer of Reformed Protestantism*, 1903), though later historians regard his view as exaggerated. In any event, relations with Bern were violently strained by conflicting interpretations of an earlier treaty. These conflicts had come to blows; one man had been killed in a riot and a Geneva syndic executed for it. Two men convicted of treason had fled. Another had been fatally injured jumping from a window to escape arrest. Most distressing of all, Cardinal Jacopo Sadoleto had

While John Calvin was exceedingly happy in Strasbourg, things did not go well in Geneva. According to reports sent him by William Farel, brothels were opening, Anabaptists were preaching, and the Mass was being said in many homes. Finally persuaded that Geneva was a cross he must bear, Calvin returned (below) in 1541, devoting the rest of his life to creating a city modeled on biblical authority. The identity of the sketch artist is not recorded.

addressed a letter to the people of Geneva urging their return to the ancient church. The city's reformers needed Calvin to respond to it. They feared a major Catholic initiative to restore Geneva to the faith.

Calvin's written response to the bishop became a classic addition to Protestant polemic, but he had no interest in returning to Geneva. He was now a citizen of Strasbourg and supremely happy. "I would submit to death a hundred times," he wrote to Farel, "rather than submit to that cross on which I had to suffer a hundred deaths daily." But Farel persuaded him that Geneva was indeed a cross—his cross to bear, and he must bear it. Finally Calvin agreed to return, but he wanted constitutional changes to the civic government and, more important, a church independent of secular control. He particularly insisted that a consistory composed of Geneva's reform clergy and twelve elders be appointed, with power to police and discipline the personal behavior of individual citizens. With a few minor changes and one major one, the council agreed. It would not give the consistory power to excommunicate; only the council could do that. Reluctantly acquiescing, Calvin returned to Geneva in 1541 and spent the rest of his life striving to mold the irascible city into a perfect Christian society.

Arrests began almost immediately: 'The old and happy days of fighting and womanizing, or for the respectable, dicing and dancing, were over. Geneva had become a religious town.'

Arrests began almost immediately. Historian T. H. L. Parker describes the sudden change (*Portrait of Calvin*, 1940). "The old and happy days of fighting and womanizing, or for the more respectable, dicing and dancing, were over. Geneva had become a religious town. The councils had always passed laws regulating the lives of the citizens. Nobody minded these rules; they were common to every European city in the sixteenth century. What was so unpleasant was that they should be enforced with any degree of rigor and consistency."

Historian MacKinnon takes a sample list of offenses from the records of the consistory, which met as a court every Thursday: playing cards, expressing Catholic opinions, using charms for healing purposes, criticizing the clergy, absence from sermons or the Lord's Supper, inability to repeat the Lord's Prayer or the Apostles' Creed, family quarrels, frequenting taverns, gambling, defaming John Calvin, drunkenness, promiscuous bathing, prostitution, swearing, praying to the Virgin Mary or the saints, buying and selling crosses or other idolatrous images, marrying a Catholic, expressing hostility to refugees from France, kneeling at the grave of a deceased husband or wife or saying "*requiescat in pace*" (rest in peace), and mocking any part of the Scriptures. MacKinnon omits various other charges, such as falling asleep during sermons, overeating, and telling jokes about clergy.

The list indeed seemed endless, but the consistory's punishment usually consisted of a scolding. It referred the more serious cases—crimes like heresy, sacrilege, and sedition—to the council, where the penalties varied from fines to imprisonment to banishment to execution, and torture was used freely to extract confessions. (The consistory repeatedly demanded the right to excommunicate. Not until 1553 would it finally gain this power.)

The consistory did not shrink, however, from intervening in matters once thought purely familial, such as children's names. The clergy began refusing to bestow in baptism such names as "Jesus" or "Easter" or "Sunday" as being too sacred, but others were refused as being "pagan" and thus not sacred enough. When one minister arbitrarily substituted the name John for a supposedly pagan one, the baby's father assaulted him, and charges were laid. Eventually a list of permitted names was published. Soon all taverns were closed, because besides drunkenness they encouraged singing and dancing. A number of restaurants, called "abbeys," were opened instead, which served only nourishing food and encouraged prayer and Bible reading. They also allowed singing—of psalms only. These attracted so few patrons that eventually they closed and the taverns reopened.

Sex, as always, presented an infinitude of problems. At first the penalty for fornication[8] was three days' imprisonment in the old bishop's palace. However, when those thus confined, far from living on the prescribed bread and water, were discovered to be lavishly supplied with wine and food, probably smuggled

Calvin's estimate of Geneva's spiritual progress was not high. He fired many pastors—one caught bathing nude with two women for example, two others for similar 'immoralities.'

in by sympathetic friends, the sentence was upped to six days, and a fine was added. But it took the consistory four years to close the mixed-gender bathhouses, which, says one record, differed little from brothels, but they were finally separated, with the men's at one end of town and the women's at the other. Calvin's own household was not exempt from vice. The wife of his brother Antoine was repeatedly caught with one of Calvin's servants and finally banished. Antoine, who acted as Calvin's accountant, was granted a divorce.

Like Luther's view of Wittenberg, Calvin's estimate of Geneva's spiritual progress was not high. It was particularly low of his fellow pastors. During an outbreak of plague, for example, only one dedicated minister proved willing to comfort the afflicted and dying in the hospital. After this man was himself stricken and died, the rest refused to go near the place. "They are a hindrance more than a help to me," wrote Calvin in disgust. "They are rude and self-conceited with no zeal and less learning." He fired many—one caught bathing nude with two women, for example, two others for similar "immoralities," and one was suspended and imprisoned for telling his congregation that their pastors, being French, were the divinely designated rulers of Geneva.

But the vigilant search for sin and scandal that made peeping, prying, and gossip into a veritable civic duty was actually not uppermost on Calvin's agenda of concerns. He was far more alert to doctrinal nonconformity, which over a fifteen-year period created a series of celebrated cases. The first developed in 1546 when playing card manufacturer Pierre Ameaux, his business hard hit by Calvin's moral strictures, was overheard while drinking wine to accuse Calvin of "preaching falsehoods." Arrested and charged with "insulting the honor of Christ," Ameaux was steeply fined and ordered to parade through Geneva wearing only a shirt, carrying a torch,

8. Fornication referred to consensual sex between two people not married to one another, adultery to consensual sex where one or both partners were married to someone else. All adultery therefore was fornication, but not all fornication was adultery.

9. When plague struck Geneva and Christian ministers refused to bring comfort to the stricken and dying, Bible school head Sebastian Castellio volunteered to do so. The municipal council refused to allow him to do it, however, on the grounds that he was irreplaceable at the school, and Calvin himself was similarly forbidden to attend plague victims.

and at intervals kneeling in the street to ask God's forgiveness. This was followed a year later by the case of Jacques Gruet, described as a "freethinking atheist." Gruet was accused of pinning a placard to Calvin's pulpit with the warning: "When too much has been endured, revenge is taken." He was charged with treason and beheaded. Later he was discovered to be innocent of the placard offense, though his writings showed him to be an atheist.

A more formidable opponent was Sebastian Castellio, a brilliant scholar and once a member of Calvin's Strasbourg household. When Castellio, who now ran a Geneva Bible school, applied to become a pastor, the council accepted him because he had courageously volunteered to care for the plague-stricken during an epidemic.[9] But Calvin rejected him for maintaining that the biblical Song of Solomon was about sex, not God. If the inerrancy of the Bible is successfully challenged at any point, Calvin maintained, the whole foundation of Protestantism would collapse. Castellio also publicly challenged the exclusive right claimed by the Geneva clergy to interpret Scripture. He wound up as neither pastor nor teacher, forced to beg on the streets to support his wife and seven other dependents. Eventually, however, he gained a senior position at the University of Basel, where he continued to assail Calvin's authority.

Another dangerously disenchanted disciple was Jerome Bolsec, an ex-Carmelite monk who challenged Calvin's teaching at its most controversial point: predestination. How could a good God doom men to be eternally damned, Bolsec demanded, before they were even created? He summed up what he saw as the Calvinist view: The elect were not saved because they had done good, though reprobates were punished because they had done evil. Neither party had any choice in the matter, yet the whole proceeding was to be taken as proof of the goodness of God. Calvin charged Bolsec with heresy, referred the case to other Swiss ministers, and, when their responses were inconclusive, proceeded on his own and banished him. The ex-monk returned to his native France and would die a Catholic.

The pastor Pierre Caroli stirred Calvin's ire when he was discovered to be advocating prayers for the dead. In the resulting clash, Caroli accused both Calvin and Farel of preaching Arianism (see vol. 3, chs. 8 and 9). Challenged by Caroli, Calvin refused to recite the Nicene and Athanasian creeds, a grave abnegation that could have seen him deposed if he had persisted in it. Calvin went home and, according to one record, suffered "hysterics," and later declared that he accepted the creeds. Caroli was banished.

But the case that would continue to assail Calvin throughout subsequent history was that of the Spaniard Michael Servetus, a voluble young man with theological views far closer to Arianism than anything Calvin ever taught. Like Arius, Servetus rejected the doctrine of the Trinity, and when he published his thoughts on this subject in Paris, serious peril was soon evident. So he changed his name, studied medicine, and moved to Vienne, near Lyon, where he established himself as a notable physician[10] and acquired some highly placed patients, one of them the archbishop.

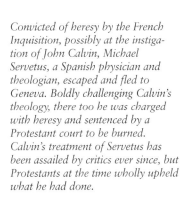

Convicted of heresy by the French Inquisition, possibly at the instigation of John Calvin, Michael Servetus, a Spanish physician and theologian, escaped and fled to Geneva. Boldly challenging Calvin's theology, there too he was charged with heresy and sentenced by a Protestant court to be burned. Calvin's treatment of Servetus has been assailed by critics ever since, but Protestants at the time wholly upheld what he had done.

10. Though Michael Servetus was the first European doctor to describe the function of pulmonary circulation, this achievement was not widely recognized at the time. For one thing, the description appeared in a theological treatise, *Christianismi Restitutio*, not in a book on medicine. Second, most copies of the book were burned shortly after its publication in 1553 because of the persecution of Servetus. Three survived but remained hidden for decades.

Servetus still felt divinely required to seek foundational changes to Christian doctrine, however, and published a plainly heretical book on the nature of Jesus Christ that began circulating, among other places, in Geneva. Someone there—perhaps Calvin himself—sent it to the archbishop of Vienne, and soon the archbishop's doctor was identified as its author. Servetus, charged with heresy, was imprisoned. Unsurprisingly, having friends in high places, he escaped, but then there occurred one of history's more baffling events. Servetus suddenly appeared in Geneva, publicly challenging the Trinitarian views of John Calvin. Why he chose Geneva no historian has adequately explained. Back to prison he went, charged by the Protestants this time. Nor were any high-placed friends available, though he turned out to have some unexpected allies.

The captain-general himself was caught dancing at a wedding and sentenced to prison. His wife was also caught, jailed, but danced again, excoriated the consistory, then escaped the city.

By the 1550s Calvin was vigorously opposed in Geneva by a party of dissidents headed by two of the city's distinguished families. Having welcomed Calvin back to Geneva, they soon ran afoul of his austere theocracy. In the painting below, now at the library of the University of Geneva, Calvin refuses to dispense Communion to his opponents, who, facing increasingly severe retribution, ultimately fled the city.

By the 1550s resentment over Calvin's reforms had created a vigorous opposition party in Geneva that later came to be termed "the Libertines," though they were known at the time as "*Les Enfants de Genève*" (in the sense of "Geneva's Native Sons").[11] It was headed by two of the city's distinguished families, the Favres and Perrins. Earlier in the sixteenth century the Favres had played a key role in defeating the duke of Savoy and establishing the city's independence. Ironically enough, these families had warmly supported Calvin's return in 1540, and the reigning Perrin, Ami by name, had become captain-general of Geneva, the man centrally responsible for the defense of the city.

Things started going wrong when the captain-general himself was caught dancing at a wedding party and summarily sentenced to prison. His wife was also caught, served a sentence, danced again, and loudly excoriated the entire consistory before escaping the city. She was warned that if she returned, she would instantly be imprisoned. Meanwhile, the head of the Favre family had

In this 1861 oil-on-wood piece by Theodor Pixis, Calvin tries one last time to convert the imprisoned Michael Servetus. Unable to speak the language of the court, ill clad and bitterly cold, and denied legal representation, Servetus was burned alive on October 27, 1553. The historian Carew Hunt calls it "the most notorious heresy trial of the sixteenth century . . . a blot on Calvin's reputation and an indictment of his system."

been jailed for living apart from his wife and for having sex with his servant, who was now pregnant.

To these people and hundreds of others, Geneva society as presently constituted had begun to seem neither enjoyable nor particularly Christian, and their fury with Calvin was matched only by his for them. Thus, although they did not in the least sympathize with the theological views of Servetus, the Enfants loudly supported him on the old maxim that their enemy's enemy must be their friend. If Calvin could not defeat Servetus, they reasoned, then his Geneva enterprise would seriously lose credibility.

In the ensuing legal proceeding, some saw the integrity of the whole Protestant Reformation on trial. Was Calvin not proving that any serious attempt to establish a genuinely Christian society, something Rome had ostensibly been trying to do ever since Constantine, must inevitably require harsh enforcement of doctrinal conformity? Making matters much worse was the abject vulnerability of the accused, whose sincerity was nowhere questioned, and the blatant injustice he was suffering. For example, Servetus could not speak the language of the court but was denied the services of a lawyer, and reportedly was so ill clad and ill housed in prison that he was bitterly cold and begging for a swift trial.

The conviction of Servetus, never in doubt, allegedly was followed by an incompetent execution October 27, 1553. He was burned at the stake, and according to

11. As the word "libertine" descends through medieval and modern history, its connotation steadily darkens. Initially it designated a freed man, meaning one who had escaped serfdom, a commendable advance. But later it came to mean a man of independent mind, a freethinker, as doubtful a quality in Calvin's day as it is thought admirable now. Then it slipped farther, to mean sexual licentiousness, nothing more, and now seems to describe an individual undependable in every way. "A man who lives an irresponsible and immoral life," says *Oxford*. "A person who leads a dissolute life," says *Webster*. However recalcitrant, Calvin's foes were far from "libertine" in the modern sense.

Ironically, the University of Geneva, founded by Calvin, would become a major center in the Enlightenment movement of the eighteenth century, whose religious assumptions were much like Michael Servetus's and whose intellectual luminaries Calvin would probably have dispatched to the stake.

one report the wood was so wet that his agony was prolonged for three hours. (Others claimed it was only half an hour.) His reported last words—"Jesus, thou Son of the eternal God, have pity on me"—were seen as affirmation of his heresy. Because in Christian theology all three persons of the Trinity are eternal, he should have said "eternal Son." But Servetus was theologically literate. He would have intended this as an affirmation of his theology, not a recantation of it.

Congratulations for Calvin's triumph came from across the Protestant world, which recognized that if Servetus's views had been sustained, Protestantism itself would be in jeopardy. Christ would have become simply one more great moral teacher offering advice on how to be good, whereas the perennial problem of mankind, recognized long before Christ, is that we have always known fairly well what to do but do not do it. Therefore, if Christ is nothing more than a moral teacher, he really does not matter.

Nevertheless, writes historian Carew Hunt, the trial of Servetus is "the most notorious heresy trial of the sixteenth century . . . a blot on Calvin's reputation and an indictment of his system." MacKinnon calls it "one of the worst scandals of Reformation history." But this, contends historian Gordon, is to judge Calvin by the standards of a much later and more tolerant age. He was a sixteenth-century man, after all, and he did what the sixteenth century required and approved.

The elimination of Servetus left Calvin with one last battle. Since his theocratic state could not countenance an opposition, he must eliminate the Enfants. This took him less than two years, materially aided by Protestant refugees swarming into Geneva to escape persecution by Catholics in France. By 1559 about one in four Genevans was French, enough to produce a pro-Calvin council in February 1555. When drunken Enfants marched in protest that spring, shouting for the ouster of French immigrants, the council declared it a seditious riot. Though there had been no deaths, no property damage, and only one minor injury, and the crowd had dispersed on command, four executions were ordered. One of the condemned was a young man whose father had died a hero in the war that won Geneva's independence from the duchy of Savoy a generation earlier, and his widowed mother pleaded in vain that her son be spared. Other leaders fled the city, and were condemned in absentia to death and forfeiture of their property.

Thus did Calvin's rule in Geneva become absolute. The penalties for sexual immorality or conduct disrespectful of religion were severely increased. "Loose" women, meaning any who plaited their hair or "otherwise sought to adorn themselves," must be paraded through the streets with trumpets sounding. Banquets were forbidden, and parties were limited to four people because "God is mocked" by any ribaldry. In his nine remaining years, Calvin labored hard and efficiently to perfect the ecclesiastical system he was pioneering. He focused particularly on the University of Geneva, founded in 1559 as a seminary and law school, which would turn out many subsequent generations of clergy to staff the churches founded on his teachings.[12]

A nineteenth-century engraving by Ary Scheffer shows an aging John Calvin, his mood content, his rule absolute. Largely triumphant in Geneva, Calvin's final nine years were rewarding—apart from his falling out with William Farel, who at age sixty-nine took a teenaged bride. Calvin never spoke to him again.

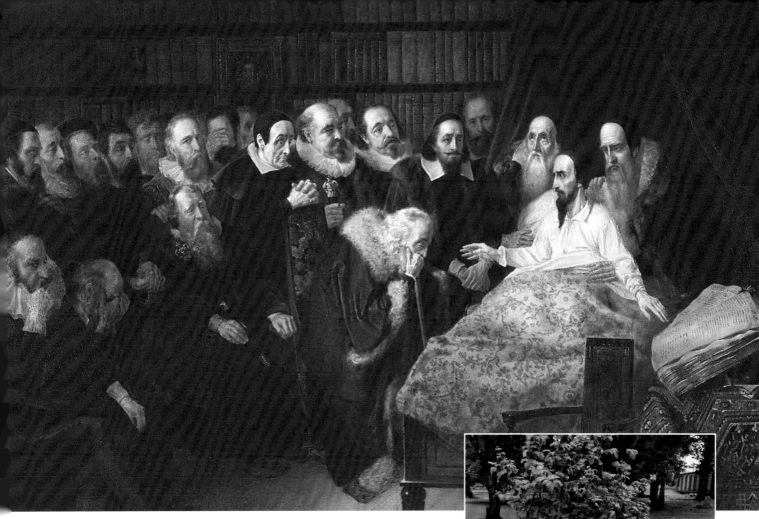

These were triumphant and happy years for Calvin, barring one unsavory incident. William Farel, his companion and unfailing supporter through all those early trials in Geneva, announced at age sixty-nine that he intended to take a teenaged bride. Geneva's Christian community was shocked: Farel was already living in the same house with this girl and her mother. Calvin boycotted the wedding, vowing never again to speak to Farel, though he begged followers to judge gently a man who was now "bereft of his senses" but had served the church so well. Farel would father a child by his young wife and, although he was Calvin's senior by twenty years, would outlive him by a year and a half.

Calvin, aged fifty-four, died on May 24, 1564, working almost to his last day. His reserved nature and chilly manner made him a hard man to know and, at a distance of nearly five hundred years, a harder man to like. Yet he had many lifelong supporters despite a fierce temper when young and a cranky irascibility as he aged. His workday remained at a steady sixteen hours. His writings were prodigious. His preaching style was slow, coolly logical, and, chiefly because of its unmistakable clarity, very convincing. He had no interest in money, and thus was perpetually underpaid and often undernourished.

"All I have done is of no value," he said in his last talk with his ministers. "I am a miserable creature . . . I have meant well, but my faults have always displeased me, and at the root the fear of God has been in my heart." None doubted his sincerity in this, and it curiously resembled the sentiment expressed by the dying Luther, and by many of the great Orthodox and Catholic saints. ∎

As John Calvin lay on his deathbed, depicted above by artist Joseph Hornung, he told his grieving ministers: "I have meant well, but my faults have always displeased me, and at the root the fear of God has been in my heart." He died on May 24, 1564, at the age of fifty-four and is buried in a tomb (inset) in Geneva's "Cemetery of Kings."

The rise and fall of the witchcraft peril

For two centuries, women and some men were tried and burned as malevolent devils, but the toll was about sixty thousand, not the nine million of twentieth-century polemics

The principality of Ellwangen, nestled between the Swabian Alps and the Virngrund Forest, forty miles northeast of Stuttgart, was at the very heart of southwestern Germany's witch country. Through most of the sixteenth century, however, it executed relatively few witches. Records dug up by H.C. Erik Midelfort, who describes these phenomena in his seminal work *Witch Hunting in Southwestern Germany* (1972), record only twelve or thirteen burnings between 1528 and 1589. But this was to change.

By the mid 1500s Ellwangen's monastery had been turned into a secular institution headed by a Fürstpropst (prince-provost), freeing the principality from the episcopal discipline of Augsburg and making it subject only to the distant pope. The Fürstpropst became a virtually independent ruler, and Ellwangen was about to be the panicked locale of one of the most concentrated efforts in the two hundred years of European witch hunting.

That there might be such a problem in Ellwangen occurred to Fürstpropst Johann Christoph von Westerstetten in the early 1600s following some years of bad weather, plague, and mysterious livestock deaths. Through the previous hundred years of witch trials, it had been viewed as well established that such calamities more often than not were conjured up by the local satanic sorceresses. As early as 1487, the book that fueled the anti-witch movement, *Malleus Maleficarum* (*The Witches' Hammer*), had documented how the town of Constance suffered with a plague that subsided only after witchcraft had been expurgated from the region. So Ellwangen officials dusted off their criminal procedures and consulted with neighboring towns on the possible loathsome sources of all the trouble.

The first is believed to have been one Barbara Rufin, aged seventy, from the village of Rindelbach, who was arrested April 7, 1611. She had a reputation as a witch, earned partly because her husband called her that when angry, partly because her son claimed she had tried to poison him with quicksilver (mercury), and partly because she had allegedly desecrated the Sacred Host (a well-known practice of satanically aligned sorceresses). She was also rumored to have sickened cows and horses by rubbing them with evil salves. Under interrogation by a panel of three civic officials, Frau Rufin readily admitted that at the Eucharist the host sometimes almost slipped from her toothless mouth so that she had to grab it but denied the rest. As would become customary in these trials, torture was applied.

On the first day, two fifteen-minute sessions on the rack produced much screaming and entreaties to God but no confession.

No more than a dozen witches were executed in the town of Ellwangen (below) between 1528 and 1589, but things changed in the early seventeenth century following some years of bad weather, plague, and mysterious livestock deaths. As had been established in the book Malleus Maleficarum (inset), such maladies could be combated only by expunging witchcraft. And so the executions began.

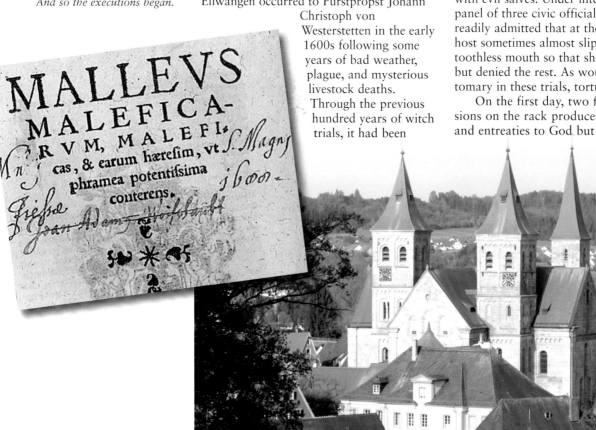

A 1606 *painting by Frans Francken II depicts a witches' Sabbath (sometimes called a black Sabbath), which according to popular information manuals of the era was a regular assembly of witches and their familiars. With scattered skulls, crawling demons, and a background cauldron, this kind of image resonated strongly in seventeenth-century Europe.*

1. The normal method of executing witches in continental Europe and Scotland was to tie them to a stake atop a pile of wood, then garrote them before the flames consumed the body. In Italy and Spain straight burning was generally used. In certain German princedoms, like Ellwangen, the more humane method of beheading with a sword was favored. In England all witches were hanged.

2. The witch trials that occurred between February 1692 and May 1693 in Salem, Massachusetts, and became a celebrated cautionary tale among twentieth-century liberals, jailed and executed relatively few compared to the German trials. But the nineteen jailed and two hundred hanged were proportionally far greater, given that the population of the town of Salem at the time was just six hundred.

3. One prime source of inflated witch fatality estimates was American suffragist Matilda Joslyn Gage, who asserted in her book *Woman, Church and State* (1893): "It is computed from historical records that nine millions of persons were put to death for witchcraft after 1484, or during a period of three hundred years, and this estimate does not include the vast number who were sacrificed in the preceding centuries upon the same accusation." Later feminists, including Mary Daly and Andrea Dworkin, quoted Matilda Gage to bolster their portrayals of patriarchal oppression. Gage's daughter, incidentally, was married to L. Frank Baum, author of the cherished twentieth-century children's classic *The Wizard of Oz*, but Baum consistently denied that the Wicked Witch of the West was inspired by his mother-in-law.

On the second day, after being stretched seven more times, she told her interrogators what they wanted to hear: that she had desecrated the host, made a pact with the devil, also copulated with him, tried to poison her son, ruined crops, sickened livestock, and attended witch dances. She also showed her examiners a "witch mark" on her foot, a patch of insensate skin the size of a coin, ostensibly caused by the devil's claw. On May 16, 1611, several more weeks of torture and interrogation ended in a confession without torture—the legal requirement. Barbara Rufin was then executed with the sword, her corpse was burned, and all her belongings were confiscated by the principality.[1]

Interrogators streamlined their process thereafter to shorten the period from arrest to execution. Torture was used both to extract confessions and to obtain denunciations of other witches, who were then arrested in batches and who, in turn, denounced still others. Most were peasant women, but not all. Three unpopular priests were forced to confess that they had baptized children in the devil's name, which instantly spread the taint of Satan across a number of other Ellwangians. Several highly placed men were convicted.

There were also voluntary confessions, including one from a sixteen-year-old girl who tearfully admitted she was seduced into witchcraft by an aunt (already executed). She then proceeded to denounce thirty-four other women. For her noble-heartedness, she was accorded the mercy of decent burial in a churchyard after her beheading. One hundred witches were executed in Ellwangen in 1611, 160 the next year, and about 60 more the next, as the supply of suspects dwindled.

These Ellwangen prosecutions came at the height of a craze that occurred in varying intensities from the end of the fifteenth century to the late seventeenth both in Europe and in the New World.[2] On the basis of judicial records and educated extrapolations, modern historians estimate that about sixty thousand confessed witches were executed during these two centuries.[3]

The comely suspect here being disrobed for torture may be something of an exception. Many witches, in fact, are thought to have been elderly women, single, reclusive, sometimes senile, often sharp tongued, and disliked by the community—the stereotypical "hag" of popular culture, perhaps not so appealing to artists.

4. Outside the Mediterranean region the power of the Inquisition waned in the sixteenth century as northern European jurisdictions turned to Protestantism and state governments assumed church judicial powers. Where the Inquisition remained powerful—notably in Spain—it showed remarkable leniency toward accused witches. In the largest sweep in Spanish history, for example, nineteen hundred were implicated but only nineteen executed. Inquisitors usually spared them if they confessed and renounced. The secular courts that dominated in the north were not so lenient.

Approximately half occurred in Germany and the adjacent Alpine territories of Austria, Switzerland, and Burgundy. Both Catholic and Protestant jurisdictions were involved. In England and Wales, where the rules of procedure included jury trials, a higher judicial authority, and a ban on torture, fewer than five hundred convicted witches were hanged in these two centuries. (By comparison, an estimated seventy-two thousand citizens were executed for the more than two hundred capital crimes on the books during the thirty-seven-year reign of Henry VIII alone.) Mediterranean Europe was virtually exempt. In Spain, only about a couple of dozen witch executions are estimated to have been ordered by the Inquisition between 1540 and 1700, out of a total of 1,250 heresy executions.[4]

Various theories attempt to explain these disparities. In the first place, Germany and environs were a chaos of political and reli-

gious unrest, where hundreds of separately ruled territories functioned without interference from above. Further, amid the passions of the Protestant Reformation, perhaps witches provided a scapegoat when no other enemy was at hand; prosecutions dropped noticeably during periods of actual religious war. Also, localized trials such as those in Ellwangen were conducted by judges more likely to convict, being more inclined to share the local hysteria and even to fear diabolical reprisal if they failed to measure up.

The overall societal change is well documented. Before the late 1400s healers and seers—men and women who concocted herbal remedies, told fortunes, and cast the occasional spell—were a common and usually benign feature of medieval communities. Even a priest might use their services on occasion, and witch magic was considered for the most part helpful. Indeed, before the late Middle Ages, church doctrine had declared belief in demonically attached witches to be a pagan heresy since God's omnipotence precluded all possibility of malevolent forces being at work in his supernatural realm.

But scholasticism, the theological movement that shaped doctrine in the late Middle Ages, introduced an elaborate demonology. Satan and his demons were fallen angels with supernatural powers, capable of bending God's laws. God had made these creatures too, of course, but only in order to test man, and they could recruit witches for this purpose. Protestantism, influenced by the acutely devil-conscious Martin Luther, later adopted virtually the same demonology. (In a characteristically bawdy metaphor, he called witches the "devil's whores who should be burned.")

In the 1480s Heinrich Kramer, a Dominican inquisitor prosecuting the heretical Waldensians, persuaded Pope Innocent VIII that recent freezing weather, crop failures, rising crime, and mass starvation all were due to Waldensian witchcraft. The pope duly issued a bull condemning those who "have abandoned themselves to devils, incubi, and succubi, and by their incantations, spells, conjurations, and other accursed charms and crafts, enormities, and horrid offenses, have slain infants yet in the mother's womb, as also the offspring of cattle, have demolished the fruits of the earth."

In 1487 Kramer and a University of Cologne theologian named Jakob Sprenger produced the book *Malleus Maleficarum*. On the basis of Exodus 22:18, "You shall not permit a witch to live," it branded disbelief in witchcraft as heresy, detailed their assorted diabolical depravities, and outlined proper trial procedures, including torture. Although *Malleus* noted that men could be witches—and in some areas they would in fact comprise the majority convicted—it claimed that women were more likely to consort with the devil: "All witchcraft comes from carnal lust, which is in women insatiable."[5]

Malleus Maleficarum enjoyed great popularity among both clerics and the educated laity. Benefiting from the recent invention of the printing press, it circulated widely in the sixteenth century, at one point outselling everything but the Bible. This encouraged publication of other works on demonology, and these so-called "devil books" became training manuals and legal texts for an expanding group of legal practitioners— judge and prosecutor rolled into one—who became known as witch hunters.

Prosecutions were scattered and small in scale during the first half of the century, and at this early stage were conducted mostly in ecclesiastical courts. They were usually triggered by one peasant accusing another of using malicious magic to cause a calamity from a disastrous flood to marital impotence. The accused might be a woman under whose care a baby had died or a healer whose remedy had failed.

Occasionally a magistrate might initiate proceedings in reaction to some localized disaster. Sometimes family disputes, over an inheritance perhaps or a marriage, triggered an accusation. A very typical witch was an elderly, single, reclusive woman, sometimes senile, often sharp tongued, and usually disdained or disliked by the community. Thus originated the stereotypical hag of popular culture, from *Macbeth* to Halloween's "trick or treat."

In fact, writes Brian P. Levack in *The Witch-hunt in Early Modern Europe* (1987), there are few if any actual accounts of witches being accused of consorting with devils, participating in black Sabbaths, flying about on a goat, transforming themselves into a black cat, or participating in any of the other diabolical practices that learned judges, versed in the *Malleus Maleficarum* and other pertinent literature, knew to be the case.

'All witchcraft,' said Malleus, comes from 'carnal lust, which is in women insatiable.'

Confessions of satanic activity came from the witches themselves, prompted with leading questions and usually after the application, or threatened application, of racks, thumbscrews, head screws, red-hot tongs, heated and pronged "witches' seats," and other tortures. (Such "judicial torture" had been allowed to court interrogators since the mid-1200s.) These techniques very quickly elicited confessions of satanism from almost any woman. "For this reason," Levack writes, "it is valid to claim that torture in a certain sense 'created' witchcraft, or at least created diabolical witchcraft."

But the accumulation of confessions, embellished by idiosyncratic touches produced by the accused to satisfy their inquisitors, added to the literature and established widespread belief in the witch as Satan's minion. "By the end of the sixteenth century," Levack continues, "most educated Europeans believed that witches, in addition to practicing harmful magic, engaged in a variety of diabolical activities . . . [and] that witches, having made a pact with the devil, gathered periodically with other witches— sometimes numbering in the hundreds or

5. Records of trials and executions show that on average about twenty percent of executed witches were men. Moreover, as University of Alberta scholars Lara Apps and Andrew Gow point out in their book *Male Witches in Modern Europe* (2003), male prosecutions predominated in some regions. For example, in Burgundy males accounted for fifty-two percent between 1580 and 1642, in Russia sixty-eight percent between 1622 and 1700, and in Iceland ninety-two percent between 1645 and 1685. In the Scandinavian countries the split was generally close to even.

Interrogation usually began in a torture chamber, such as the reconstruction at left, and ended with a pyre, as pictured above. The observers seem oddly uninterested, except for the couple at lower right, presumably being berated by the indignant soldier for their grief.

after hail destroyed the vineyards in 1562, and sixty-three individuals were burned. In 1596 thirty-five women were immolated after confessing they were seduced by the devil. In 1602, the aged mayor of Rottenburg, reputed to have himself ordered 108 witches burned, was jailed after admitting to sexual intercourse with the devil disguised as a maiden.

Major sweeps continued well into the seventeenth century, with 199 individuals killed in Baden-Baden between 1627 and 1631, 127 in Mergentheim, and 160 in Würzburg. Parents were denounced by their children, children by their parents. Sometimes as much as a quarter of a town's population might be accused.

Why these phenomena began to diminish in the late 1600s remains a puzzle. Calvinist theologians reasoned that only man's faithlessness could cause God to allow Satan's agents to perform such evil magic.

even thousands—to perform a series of blasphemous, obscene, and heinous rites."

Thus, witch hunts increased in the late 1500s as accumulating tales of diabolism, issuance of anti-witch edicts, and the zeal of the secular courts fueled further panic.[6] At Wiesensteig, near Stuttgart, for example, Count Ulrich von Helfenstein started a hunt

Therefore, faith and virtue would end the problem. Religious skeptics today also credit the moral advance of the Western world since the days of what they sometimes decry as biblical barbarism.

But Brian Levack credits a late-twentieth-century skepticism about the very existence of witchcraft (or at any rate of the malevolent variety). Christian essayist C. S. Lewis agrees. The current lack of witch hunts does not signal any advance in morality, Lewis contends, but rather an advance in human knowledge. We don't burn witches because we no longer believe there are such things. If we did—that is, if we really thought that some human beings were able to cause epidemics, floods, drought, or famine, or strike people blind or insane or dead, and were indeed doing so—

we might not burn them, but we certainly would do everything necessary to rid ourselves of the danger.

Other Christians would not be so quick to concur. They cite biblical authority that witches do, or did, exist. Hence, execution is commanded for witches in the Old Testament (Ex. 22:18, Deuteronomy 18:10-14), and "sorcery" is condemned in the New (Galatians 5:20 and Acts 16:16-19). Though most people no longer believe in witches, they would say, that doesn't necessarily mean they no longer exist. Still others would note that Jesus certainly believed in devil-possession of both men and women. But he didn't execute the possessed. He freed them. ■

6. Author Brian Levack and others have identified a greater tendency for local courts to convict and execute than higher courts. In Scotland, for example, ninety-one percent of those tried in local courts were executed but just sixteen percent in the circuit courts. Levack theorizes that local judges were more likely to be caught up in the witch hysteria of their communities, and also more likely to fear reprisals from witches who were not killed.

The ascension of Henry VIII, England's Catholic prince, depicted here with fur-trimmed hat and speculative gaze by Hans Holbein the Younger, seemed to promise a golden reign—until, that is, his queen, Catherine of Aragon, failed for twenty-four years to produce a male heir. Five royal wives later, the English church would be severed from Rome and the people fiercely divided.

CHAPTER 6

The quest for an heir and the lure of a lady chart England's destiny

Had Catherine of Aragon given Henry VIII a son, the break with Rome might not have happened, nor Henry's luckless brides have lost their heads

Engalnd's lurch into Protestantism during the reign of the Tudors in the sixteenth century was by no means an inevitable thing. It is true that previous centuries saw instances of a breach with Rome. But those disruptions were not enduring, and by the time young Henry VIII ascended the throne in 1509, relations with the papal see were the strongest of any in Europe. Had Henry's Spanish queen, Catherine of Aragon, produced the male heir crucial for the stability of the Tudor realm—and had not a black-eyed young opportunist named Anne Boleyn excited Henry's libidinous instincts and convinced him she could indeed provide that heir—England might never have joined the Protestant Reformation.

Henry's accession came to many in England as the dawn of a golden age. The fair-haired young king stood six-foot-four, weighed an athletic 190 pounds, and was equally adept at tennis and jousting, music and dancing. Destined initially for the clergy, he spoke fluent Latin and French, and passable Italian and Spanish, and seemed a loyal friend to the church.

Beyond this, he also represented a relief from the austerities of his father's reign. The Welshman Henry Tudor had established the family dynasty at the Battle of Bosworth Field in 1485, ending the clash between the royal houses of York and Lancaster known as the Wars of the Roses, and replacing the 331-year reign of the Plantagenet kings with that of the Tudors. As Henry VII he put together a cabinet primarily dedicated to building the royal treasury through high taxes

With his victory at the Battle of Bosworth Field in 1485, the Welshman Henry Tudor defeated King Richard III, ending the three-century rule of England's Plantagenet kings and reigning as King Henry VII, first of the Tudor line (depicted below). His relentless frugality, oppressive taxes, and severe autocracy enabled him to bequeath to his son Henry VIII a bountiful treasury, which his son worked and played hard to spend. The terracotta statue is by Pietro Torrigiano.

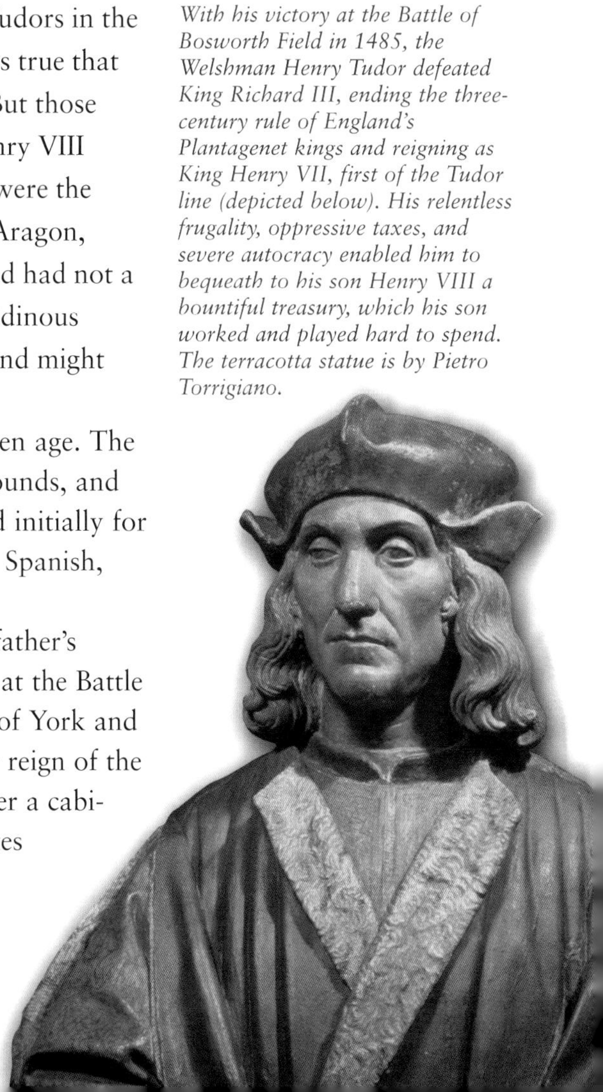

and ferocious debt collection, accumulating a cache of gold bequeathed to his towering young successor.

But the elder Henry's greatest triumph was doubtless the marriage of his eldest son, Arthur, to the Spanish princess Catherine of Aragon, daughter of King Ferdinand and Queen Isabella, cementing a treaty with Habsburg Spain to help hold at bay the perennial enemy, France. Five months after the marriage, however, pale and sickly Arthur had died. Near death himself, Henry Tudor called his seventeen-year-old second son to his bedside in April 1509, made it clear that production of a male heir was to be his chief regal duty, and ordered him to marry Catherine forthwith. Henry VII, age fifty-two, died that night. A church ban on marrying one's brother's widow would be swiftly set aside by Pope Julius II on behalf of the younger brother, now Henry VIII.

Young Henry, quite taken with his golden-haired, blue-eyed sister-in-law, had himself pushed for the marriage, though Catherine was nearly six years older. When the staunchly orthodox archbishop of Canterbury William Warham married them at Westminster Abbey in June of 1509, four days before Henry's eighteenth birthday, England caught its first glimpse of the gorgeous display that would become the Henrician hallmark. The royal procession passed through streets decorated with cloth of gold, Henry on a bejeweled horse leading the way in a crimson coat lined with ermine and encrusted with gold, diamonds, rubies, and emeralds, Catherine behind in a stately litter, followed by her ladies-in-waiting.

Henry soon became the preeminent crowd-pleaser. He jousted furiously, banqueted lavishly, and boar-hunted passionately and almost daily. He rose at eight, rode thirty miles a day, exhausting as many as ten horses, spent an hour or two on official business, then drank and danced until midnight. "This was not only because he preferred pleasure to work," writes Jasper Ridley in his biography *Henry VIII* (1984), "but also because it pleased his subjects." Such sportsmanship and bonhomie, along with his still pretty and pious wife, endeared this magnificent monarchy to the people.

Not that the responsibilities of state were ignored. One of the new king's first acts was to grant amnesty to the many men his father had jailed or fined for real and imagined acts of embezzlement, tax evasion, and debt default. Thomas More, who as young member of Parliament had criticized Henry VII's onerous tax exactions and nearly lost his life for it, was one of the first to declare the new Tudor king the herald of a liberal age. The following year Henry made him a privy councillor.

A young Henry (above), fancying his golden-haired, blue-eyed, and recently widowed sister-in-law, was eager to obey his dying father's command to marry her. All he needed was a papal dispensation. With that easily acquired, pretty Catherine of Aragon (inset) made a popular queen.

Foreign adventures became important to Henry early on. With a population of about three and a half million, England was still a minor player compared to the two warring rivals—France with more than four times that, and the Habsburgs' Holy Roman Empire with untold millions more. But here Henry depended almost wholly on the ingenious Thomas Wolsey, a butcher's son who had risen to become archbishop of York, the second see in England and in 1515 was made a cardinal by Pope Leo X. That same year Henry appointed him lord chancellor of England. From this office, with his great charm, diplomacy, and duplicity, the rotund, triple-chinned cardinal effectively ran the country. He made himself the confidant of foreign kings and prelates and became, it was said, the richest man in England, with his residence, Hampton Court, its grandest palace.

In the near thirty-year confrontation between the Holy Roman Emperor Charles V and King Francis I of France, Henry, guided initially by Wolsey, became the undependable ally first of Charles, then of Francis, then of Charles again, and then of neither. What turned out to matter much more, however, were his relations with the church. These began well but ended in disaster.

For the first twenty years of his reign, the king appeared the devoted Catholic. He attended Mass daily, often more, observed the fast days, and prostrated himself before the cross on Good Fridays. He supported Pope Leo X's bull of excommunication of Martin Luther and permitted a public burning of Luther's books at St. Paul's Cross in London. Most remarkable, the king took time away from his hunting to write a thirty-thousand-word book in Latin called *The Defense of the Seven Sacraments*, which defended Catholic sacramental doctrine and liturgical practices against Luther's attacks.

In addition, the king's treatise supported the issuing of papal indulgences and upheld the supremacy of the pope as self-evident, while also quoting St. Augustine's support of the authority of kings.[1] (In a dispute with the clergy over ecclesiastical jurisdiction in 1515, Henry had ominously declared, "Kings of England had never had superiors but God alone.") Luther was denounced as "this impious fellow" and "this little saint."

Ironically, given what was about to take place, Henry vigorously defended the sacrament of matrimony. Luther had opposed the sacralization of marriage on the grounds that it was not explicitly prescribed by the Bible. Henry argued that since the first man, Adam, was married and Christ's first miracle was performed at a wedding, the sacrament of marriage was implicit. But why, he wrote, "search we for so many proofs in so clear a thing? Especially when that only text is sufficient for all, where Christ says 'Whom God has joined together, let no man put asunder.' O the admirable word! Which none could have spoken, but the Word that was made flesh!"

1. Some scholars have posited that the hedonistic Henry was incapable of producing such an intelligent and forcefully argued work. They suggest that More and other court intellectuals were the true authors. More, however, insisted that although he and others had helped with the research, the king had indeed written the book.

King Henry confers with his astute lord chancellor, Thomas Wolsey. A butcher's son, Wolsey climbed the clerical ranks to become archbishop of York, a cardinal, the confidant of foreign kings and prelates, and the richest man in England (nineteenth-century oil painting by an unidentified artist).

A page from the king's thir-ty-thousand-word treatise, The Defense of the Seven Sacraments, *1521, which testified to Henry's devout catholicity. Ironically, in view of subsequent developments, it includes a vigorous defense of the sacrament of marriage.*

Luther came back characteristically: "If a king of England spits his shameless lies in my face, I have a right to vomit them back down his throat . . . Hal and the pope have exactly the same legitimacy: the pope stole his tiara as the king did his crown, so naturally they are as thick together as two mules in harness." Henry never forgave him.[2]

Henry's opus had a better reception in Rome. After Pope Leo was given a beautifully bound copy by the English ambassador in 1521, he granted Henry and his successors the title Defender of the Faith. Something of a kindred spirit of Henry's in his devotion to feasting and hunting, Leo decreed that if ever any man should try to remove this title, he would suffer the wrath of Almighty God and of the holy apostles Peter and Paul. If Leo had been granted a premonition of imminent events, he would not have been so uninhibited with his encomiums.

Those events began as early as 1520, when Henry had complained that the thirty-five-year-old Catherine was getting "old and deformed." Already Henry was convinced she would never produce the male heir. Of the five children to whom she had given birth, only one survived infancy: a girl, Mary, born in 1516. Nevertheless, Henry delighted in the precocious and tough-minded little dark-haired princess, who at age five entertained the court by playing upon the virginal and of whom the king once boasted, "This girl never cries." With a view to imperial expansion, Henry had betrothed Mary, at age two, to Francis I's son. Four years later, after relations with France soured, she was briefly promised to the twenty-two-year-old Emperor Charles V, her first cousin. Mary had been given the title Princess of Wales, along with a castle and her own court.

Henry FitzRoy

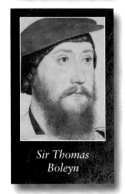

Sir Thomas Boleyn

Henry had also sired an illegitimate son, Henry FitzRoy, made duke of Richmond. But Henry believed bastards made no better heirs than daughters: with either there would always be the risk of a war of succession. There were still nobles about who had stronger blood ties to the Plantagenets than had the Tudors. Like his father before him, Henry was fearful of non-Tudor ambitions and had contrived to execute a number of possible claimants on trumped-up treason charges.[3] Plainly, if the Tudor line was to survive, it must have a male heir.

By the mid-1520s, Henry was growing older but not noticeably wiser. In fact, the grasping nobles of his court were sharing a common fear of the king's wrath, now erupting more frequently and unpredictably. One of them was the ambassador to France, Sir Thomas Boleyn, whose wife was Lady Elizabeth Howard, daughter of the duke of Norfolk. They had two captivating daughters, Mary and Anne, both Paris educated and acculturated in the decadent court of King Francis I. Henry first dallied with

2. Henry's treatise on Luther was considerably more restrained than the *Responsio* written by Thomas More in refutation of Luther's response to Henry. More matches Luther epithet by epithet, calling him a "pimp," a "worm," a "monkey," an "ass," and a "shit-devil." More demands: "Who can endure such a scoundrel who shows himself possessed by a thousand vices and tormented by a legion of demons and yet stupidly boasts thus: 'The holy fathers have all erred. The whole church has often erred. My teaching cannot err'?"

3. Henry had had Edmund de la Pole, a son of the Yorkist King Edward IV's sister, summarily beheaded in 1513. Edmund's brother Richard remained at large in France, protected by King Francis I. Fearing a French-supported challenge to the Tudors, Henry dispatched assassins to France to kill Richard. Before they could, however, he died fighting for Francis at the Battle of Pavia in 1525. Henry ordered church bells rung throughout England. Another dangerous Plantagenet, Reginald Pole, fled to Rome to escape Henry's assassins. Pope Paul III made him a cardinal, but Reginald's mother, Margaret, and brother Henry were beheaded on charges of treason. Reginald would later return to England after the princess Mary became queen and serve as the last Roman Catholic archbishop of Canterbury.

Mary, then, bored with her, turned to the twenty-one-year-old Anne, intelligent, fluent in several languages, an accomplished singer, dancer, and instrumentalist. Henry was instantly smitten.

Anne, however, had no intention of being another royal toy. Being a granddaughter and a kinswoman of successive dukes of Norfolk, she had already been

Henry Percy

promised to Henry Percy, the future earl of Northumberland, the most powerful family in northern England, with strong family connections to the Plantagenets. Anne and Percy were close in age and had been deeply in love. But Wolsey, fearing a threat to the Tudor dynasty from such a powerful marriage, had put an end to the Percy-Boleyn love match and successfully pressured the duke of Northumberland to persuade young Percy to back out of the marriage under pain of disinheritance. Anne, furious, swore revenge on the meddling cardinal.

Now, in the spring of 1526, she discovered the king of England—thirty-four and edging on plump— writing her breathless love letters. "My mistress and friend, I and my heart put ourselves in your hands, begging you to recommend us to your favor. . . . Consider well how greatly your absence grieves me." He would take her as his only mistress, casting off all others, said Henry. Anne ignored his letters, returned the bracelets and other trinkets he had sent. A buck that Henry had killed and sent to her went uneaten.

By the following spring, Henry had made up his mind. He would divorce Queen Catherine and marry Anne. So began the legal, canonical,

Combining two loves, the ardent Henry courts Anne Boleyn while they hunt deer together in Windsor Forest, as here imagined in an early-twentieth-century painting. He also wooed the vivacious Anne with gifts of bracelets and trinkets, and breathless love letters like the sample inset.

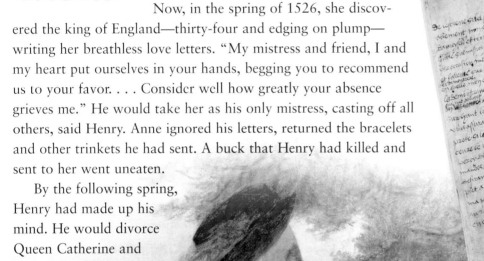

and political crisis known as "The King's Great Matter." Had the pope simply granted Henry an annulment then and there, England might, like France and Spain, have escaped the Reformation and remained Catholic. Popes had been ready enough to grant annulments to kings and nobles in the past. This time, however, there were complications. The case for annulment, devised chiefly by Wolsey, was to be argued on the grounds that Henry's marriage to Catherine had violated the church's prohibition of "affinity." Affinity was based on the book of Leviticus (18:16, 20, and 21), which decreed, "Thou shalt not uncover the nakedness of thy brother's wife, it is an unclean thing: he hath uncovered his brother's nakedness; and they shall be childless." Henry's marriage to brother Arthur's widow thus clearly transgressed biblical decree.

So began 'The King's Great Matter.' If the pope had simply granted Henry an annulment then and there, England might have escaped the Reformation and remained Catholic.

The snag was Julius II's dispensation granting Henry leave to marry his brother's widow. A papal dispensation could be overturned only if it offended "natural law," which, according to scholastic theory, trumped all else. Was the Levitical prohibition natural law? Wolsey turned to the bishop of Rochester, John Fisher, an eminent theologian who had been confessor to Henry's grandmother, had conducted Henry VII's funeral, tutored the young Henry VIII, and vigorously preached against Lutheranism. No, said Fisher, the Leviticus prohibition did not constitute natural law. Furthermore, Deuteronomy 25:5 actually commanded a man to marry his brother's widow if that brother died without children. Thus, Julius II's dispensation stood. From this point on, Fisher was a marked man.

John Fisher

Wolsey next turned to a protégé of Fisher, the Hebrew scholar Robert Wakefield. The Deuteronomic text, said Wakefield, meant that a man was bound to marry his brother's widow only if her marriage had not been consummated. If it had been consummated, the Leviticus prohibition stood as natural law. Thus, the whole Great Matter hinged on whether or not Catherine's marriage to Arthur had been consummated. Catherine would deny until she died that consummation had occurred; other witnesses, recalling boastful jests made by Arthur after his wedding night, were sure it had. Cardinal Wolsey was dispatched to Rome to seek resolution from Pope Clement VII.

Cardinal Lorenzo Campeggio

It was an inopportune time for such a petition. Rome had just been sacked by the Habsburg armies (see vol. 8, ch. 11), and the forty-eight-year-old Pope Clement VII, a less-than-resolute man, was a virtual prisoner of Charles V, Catherine's nephew. Clement, who could afford to offend neither Charles nor Henry, stalled. At length, he agreed to dispatch a legate, Cardinal Lorenzo Campeggio, to London to help decide the issue, and the aging, gout-ridden cleric took three months getting to England and another nine trying to negotiate a settlement without trying the case. He was meanwhile appalled at Henry's seemingly insatiable passion for Anne. "He sees nothing but his Anne," wrote the cardinal. "He cannot be without her for an hour; and it moves one to pity to see how the king's life, the stability and downfall of the whole country, hang upon this one question."

Henry finally convened a legatine court at Blackfriars Church in June of 1529, with him and Wolsey presiding and English bishops watching from the benches. Catherine's performance made the proceedings historically indelible. Instead of taking her place on the allotted golden throne, she walked across the floor and knelt at Henry's feet. In a clear voice, sometimes guttering into sobs, she said, "I beseech you for all the love that hath been between us, let me have justice and right, take for me some pity and compassion, for I am a poor woman and a stranger, born out of your dominion . . . I take God and all the world to witness that I have been to you a true, humble, and obedient wife, ever comfortable to your will and pleasure . . . being always well pleased and contented with all things wherein you had any delight or dalliance, whether it were little or much."

Henry was silent, then made some anodyne remarks about Catherine being a fine queen and how much he would love to stay married to her, were it not for the weight of his guilt over the illegality of the union. But Campeggio was unable to reach a decision, and the matter was postponed indefinitely. That finished Wolsey. He was asked to turn in the Great Seal of England and was shipped off to his archbishopric in York. Evidence against him mounted. He had been extorting money from monasteries to finance his pet projects, colleges at Oxford (later Christchurch) and Ipswich. He had sometimes disregarded the king's direction in clerical appointments. Anne had been bringing these matters to the king's attention. The king then inspected the opulence of Hampton Court, and it was seized by the crown.

Complacent but sly, Henry VIII (caricatured above in a 1548 engraving by Cornelis Massys) presents a notable contrast to the dramatic scene at Blackfriars Church in June of 1529, depicted below in a nineteenth-century painting. At a hearing convened to determine the legitimacy of the king's divorce request, Catherine of Aragon throws herself at her husband's feet, begging for mercy.

But Anne Boleyn and her father, still fearing Wolsey's return, worked up an improbable charge of treason against him, accusing him of hatching, with the king of France, a plot to thwart the divorce and return as chancellor. On his way from York to the Tower, however, Wolsey died, after delivering his famous last words to his escort: "If I had served God as diligently as I have done the king, he would not have given me over in my gray hairs." He was discovered to be wearing a penitential hair shirt next to his skin.

With Wolsey gone, a new guard established itself in Westminster. Thomas More, with some trepidation, agreed to become lord chancellor. Meanwhile, Henry appointed a special ambassador, the Cambridge theologian Thomas Cranmer, to visit the universities of Europe and persuade their theologians to declare the king's marriage to Catherine unlawful. Whether by bribe or genuine conviction, most universities obliged.

Cranmer's career was launched, but the pope still wouldn't budge.

By 1531 Henry had had enough. He used the courts and Parliament to push through a series of bills that hobbled the clergy at home and jettisoned the papacy at Rome. The campaign began by declaring the entire clergy guilty of a *praemunire*—a type of treason—for having supported Wolsey in his supposed usurpation of the king's powers. Henry said he would pardon them if they paid a large fine and recognized him as the supreme head of the church in England. The charge was ridiculous but had wide support among the nobles and merchants. The bishops complied, with the caveat that

Having written a divorce petition to the Vatican (inset), Henry VIII tried to boost the veracity of his claim by sending the Cambridge theologian Thomas Cranmer (top) to persuade leading European academics to pronounce the king's first marriage unlawful. While most of them obliged, the pope was not so forthcoming.

they would accept him as supreme head of the church "as far as the law of God allows." The English Reformation, such as it was, had begun.

In the next two years a series of bills would be rammed through Parliament. One reduced the annates paid to Rome by ninety-five per cent. (Annates were the first year's proceeds of a diocese, paid to Rome following the appointment of a new bishop.) Another transferred to the crown papal powers like excommunication. Still another assigned the appointment of bishops to English archbishops. Finally, one bill made the king master of the church in England without caveat. The bishops, with reluctance, accepted all of this. But Chancellor More and Bishop Fisher would not. Archbishop William Warham, eighty-two, initially acquiesced but just before dying recanted.

Cranmer was appointed archbishop of Canterbury in 1532. He returned from an ambassadorship in Germany, having acquired Lutheran convictions and a German wife, Margarete, whom he brought back in a luggage chest—a surreption that the putatively celibate archbishop maintained through Henry's reign. When consecrated, Cranmer took two oaths, one of allegiance to the pope, the other denouncing the first in favor of allegiance to the king. He became, in effect, Henry's pope.

In January of 1533 Henry and Anne Boleyn were secretly married. Catharine and her daughter, Mary, were banished from court and restricted to separate lodgings. Henry had by now, almost six years after beginning divorce proceedings, convinced himself that his first marriage was null and that marriage to Anne was not therefore bigamous. The lawyers could straighten things out later. Anyway, Anne was pregnant.

Their marriage had the full support of Thomas Cromwell, More's successor as chancellor. A forty-five-year-old solicitor of low birth, Cromwell had been a mercenary soldier, worked as a cloth merchant in Italy and the Netherlands, dabbled in banking, and served as a member of Parliament. He had entered the royal court by helping (and perhaps even inspiring) Wolsey to dissolve twenty-two monasteries, the proceeds of which had built Wolsey's colleges. Cromwell drafted a bill, the Act in Restraint of Appeals, giving the archbishop of Canterbury the power to decide all appeals from ecclesiastical courts—a function formerly held by the pope. Thus Henry, to whom the archbishop was responsible, became the effective pontiff of England; in Henry's own words, "King and Sovereign, recognizing no superior on earth but only God, and not subject to the laws of any earthly creature."[4]

Archbishop Cranmer's new powers enabled him to try Henry and Catherine's divorce case, and in May 1533 he ruled the marriage illegal. On June 1, 1533, Anne Boleyn was crowned queen in a sumptuous ceremony, marred only by the hostility of the public who lined the streets, many in silence. The people had always loved Catherine and felt only contempt for the woman widely referred to as "the great whore." On receiving the news of the divorce in Barcelona, Charles V urged Pope Clement to issue a bull excommunicating Henry and depriving him of his kingdom. But when Clement asked Charles if he and his army were willing to invade England to enforce these measures, Charles backed down.

On September 7 in Greenwich, on a fabulous bed that had been part of a French nobleman's ransom, Anne gave birth to the princess Elizabeth, the red-haired girl destined to become one of England's greatest monarchs. But denied the son Anne had promised him, Henry was enraged. He cursed the nurse who attempted to present the girl to him, then rode away to spend three days at Wolf Hall, home of his old courtier Sir John Seymour. It was at Wolf Hall that Seymour's pretty twenty-five-year-old daughter, Jane, caught the king's eye.

The next year an act was passed vesting succession in Elizabeth. Mary, as the issue of a nullified union, was declared bastardized. (It was a specious declaration, since the children of a nullified union are not viewed as illegitimate.)

Thomas Cromwell, shown above in an undated portrait by Hans Holbein, in 1532 succeeded the beleaguered Thomas More as lord chancellor of England. In that position Cromwell would shepherd through Parliament the Act in Restraint of Appeals, making the king effectively England's pope.

4. The preamble to the Act of Restraint in Appeals begins, "Where by divers sundry old authentic history and chronicles it is manifestly declared that this realm of England is an empire, and so hath been accepted in the world . . ." Befitting his imperial status, Henry now insisted on being addressed as "Your Majesty" rather than by the merely kingly "Your Grace" or "Your Highness."

The succession act also called for everyone in England to swear an oath renouncing allegiance to all foreign authority (like popes), and it decreed that anyone publishing or pronouncing the king to be a tyrant or a heretic was committing high treason, punishable by hanging, drawing, and quartering.

The period of persecution had begun. Cromwell, as well as being chancellor, held the new post of vicar-general, making him, a layman, second only to Henry as head of the church. On Henry's orders, Cromwell pursued the campaign against those now deemed to be "traitors," three hundred of whom would be

With the king's teenaged son in the audience, the six monks were hanged, cut down while still alive, then eviscerated like chickens, their body parts put on spikes around town.

executed in the following seven years. (As Machiavelli had written, every prince needs such a man to deflect the hostility that might otherwise be aimed at him.)

Despite his break with Rome, Henry remained far more traditionally Catholic than Protestant, but he had little interest in theology, leaving all that to Cranmer and Cranmer's growing conclave of Lutherans. For the king, reformation simply meant the suppression of those who opposed his will. Some did—like the priors of three Carthusian monasteries and the prior of the venerable Brigittine house at Syon, founded by Henry V, lavished with royal favor and close to the royal palace

Notwithstanding the best efforts of his monastic supporters, the hapless Pope Clement VII serves as footstool for the triumphant king in this English engraving from 1534. Although his break with Rome was now definite, Henry VIII was still far more Catholic than Protestant. At this point, however, he left the theology to Thomas Cranmer, the archbishop of Canterbury, who had returned from a stint in Germany with Lutheran beliefs—and a closeted wife.

The man that Henry couldn't break

He was the king's gifted confidante, but his refusal to recognize Henry
as head of the church sent More to the block, genially witty to the end

By the time Thomas More was led to his execution on London's Tower Hill on July 6, 1535, most of his friends had deserted him—his genial wit had not. Requesting help to mount the scaffold, he assured onlookers that "I'll fend for myself on the way down." Then he politely requested that the executioner aim carefully with his sword stroke because, he pointed out, "my neck is short." And as he knelt and laid his head on the block, he carefully moved his beard to one side. "It has committed no treason," he quipped.

Many have contended that Sir Thomas More himself had committed no treason either, but he assuredly had thwarted the determined plans and ferocious ambitions of King Henry VIII. Widely recognized as an astute lawyer, dedicated public servant, and arguably the most brilliant English scholar of his time, he had been the king's valued adviser and friend. But nothing must stand in the way of Henry's plans for the succession of the Tudor line. So Thomas More was doomed by his stubbornly principled refusal to accept the king as supreme head of the church in England.

Born in London in 1478, the son of a lawyer, More was a barrister himself at twenty-three and a member of Parliament at twenty-seven. Much influenced in his student days by the Carthusians at their London monastery, he acquired such lifelong habits as rising at 2 a.m. to pray and work, and wearing a penitential hair shirt. He seems to have considered becoming a monk himself, but according to his close friend the great humanist scholar Desiderius Erasmus, he could not "shake off his yearning for a good woman. He preferred being a chaste husband to being a dishonest priest."[1]

So at age twenty-eight the rising bureaucrat wed Jane Colt, seventeen, whose death seven years later ended an apparently blissful marriage. Within six weeks More was married again to Alice Middleton, a widow seven years his senior, who proceeded to take devoted care of his four motherless children. Although of somewhat acerbic nature, Alice also proved to be a redoubtably diligent wife. "She wants to live a long time," More wrote to Erasmus, "so she can lecture me even longer."

Dame Alice also seems to have capably provided a great deal of hospitality. The amiable More, noted for his keen blue-gray glance, his shambling gait, and his gown perpetually askew, was, in Erasmus's words, "a man made for friendship." His friends

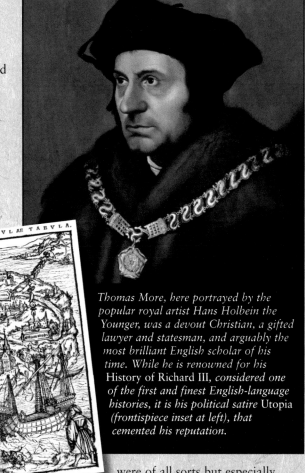

Thomas More, here portrayed by the popular royal artist Hans Holbein the Younger, was a devout Christian, a gifted lawyer and statesman, and arguably the most brilliant English scholar of his time. While he is renowned for his History of Richard III, considered one of the first and finest English-language histories, it is his political satire Utopia (frontispiece inset at left), that cemented his reputation.

were of all sorts but especially included such stars of the English Renaissance as Catholic scholars John Colet (his one-time tutor and later confessor), William Lilye, William Grocyn, and Thomas Linacre. As guests of the More household all enjoyed good talk, good food, and such curiosities as their host's pet monkey, exotic birds, and other oddities.

More's 1516 political satire Utopia firmly cemented his reputation with his contemporaries, and his 1518 History of Richard III is regarded as one of the first and finest English-language histories. Meanwhile, he was also achieving fame as an expert lawyer, skilled negotiator, and notable debater and strategist. In his earliest coup as a member of Parliament in 1504, for example, he had persuaded the Commons to cut back the current financial exactions of the throne by fully three-quarters, so infuriating King Henry VII as to considerably endanger his head at that early stage. (More remained unharmed, however, perhaps because he did not attack the king himself.)

After the accession of Henry VIII, as Cardinal Wolsey drew More into the royal service, appointment followed appointment. Among them were under-sheriff of London in 1510, trade envoy in 1515, diplomatic

Sir Thomas More's family. Back row, left to right: Margaret Clement, adopted daughter; Elizabeth Dauncey, second daughter; Sir John More, father; Anna Cresacre, son's fiancée; Sir Thomas; John More II, son; Henry Patenson, More's jester; and two unidentified men (one reading in an adjacent room). At the front: Cecily Heron, youngest daughter; Margaret Roper, eldest daughter; and Lady Alice Middleton More, Sir Thomas's wife.

ambassador and privy councillor in 1517, knighthood and royal treasurer in 1521, and chancellor of the duchy of Lancaster in 1525. He also became quite wealthy (although seemingly never tinged by graft) and a preferred friend of the new king.

Young Henry admired his scholarship and valued his wit in theological debate—including his facility with scurrilous invective, what Peter Ackroyd in *The Life of Thomas More* (1998) describes as his consummate skill at "calling bad names in good Latin." Thus he provided the king with some advice on his celebrated treatise in defense of the seven sacraments against Martin Luther's two, Further, when the irate German unleashed his invective-laden retort to the king's attack, More replied with a treatise of his own, *Responsio ad Lutherum*, written under a pseudonym. Similarly replete with gutter insults, it too argued the case that the Catholic Church receives its authority from Christ, whose vicar on earth is the pope.

But Henry VIII was moving closer to his shattering conflict with Rome; a divorce he must have, and the pope was still holding out. Thus Wolsey's failure to resolve what was ominously referred to as the king's Great Matter led to his downfall, and in late 1529 Thomas More was appointed his successor as chancellor of England—the first layman ever to hold the office. Describing it as "full of labor and danger," he kept his head down about the Great Matter and spent his time as chancellor clearing a large backlog of legal suits—apparently with immense efficiency.

He also tried to stem the spread of Protestantism and has been vilified ever since as a bloodthirsty heretic hunter, writes biographer Peter Berglar in *Thomas More: Lonely Voice against the Power of the State* (1978). More did indeed hate heresy as a peril to men's souls and described impenitent heretics as loathsome. Moreover, it was his duty as chancellor to administer the civil law,

including the death penalty, with which he undoubtedly agreed in principle.

What he desired above all, however, was the conversion of such men—and not through torture. No suspected heretic in his custody, he declared, "received a single blow, or even a slight tap on his forehead, on orders from me." Berglar also observes that between 1519 and 1531 no one was executed in London for heresy. Only when the bishops of England gave in to the king's demands in early 1531 were "the bonfires relit to provide a show of orthodoxy," and in More's last six months in office, three men, charged by Bishop John Stokesley of London, were burned as heretics.[2]

As Chancellor More pointed out, it was the function of the bishops to prefer heresy charges; nor were they obliged to hand on the matter to the state. "In effect it is the bishop who puts the heretic to death the moment he hands him over to the civil tribunals," he wrote. He claimed that he often returned a man to the bishop, to be jailed rather than executed. "If people only knew what proofs of indulgence and compassion I have given," he complained, "I swear that nobody would contradict me on this score."

More also wrote thousands upon thousands of words in defense of the faith, gradually abandoning Latin for English, and satire for meticulously reasoned arguments (though often couching them, Berglar complains, in a "coarse and vengeful" tone). He directed a massive eight-volume treatise on "what the church is," aimed at Protestant Bible translator William Tyndale. Rome alone must supervise vernacular translation, he argued.

He had been chancellor less than three years when, on May 15, 1532, the English bishops—with the single exception of John Fisher—capitulated to the king by accepting legislation that effectively made him head of the church. More resigned the following day, citing ill health (he suffered chest pains akin to angina). There was more to come. Cromwell soon engineered the royal divorce, and in 1533 Anne Boleyn was crowned queen. Thomas More did not attend the ceremony, greatly angering Henry.

For whatever reason, a year later Sir Thomas was charged with collusion involving one Elizabeth Barton, known as the Mad Maid of Kent, who claimed she saw heavenly visions opposing the royal divorce. He easily countered this accusation, but events came to a head in March 1534 when Cromwell pushed the Act of Succession through Parliament. It declared the marriage to Anne valid and again rejected papal supremacy; any dissenters to the act would be guilty of treason.

"By nature I tend to scare at the slightest flick,

and to complain," More wrote to his favorite daughter, Margaret Roper, and "the horrible fear of death" now oppressed him for anguished hours. But he would not agree to something "which would bring down on me God's deepest disapproval." In April, confronted by Cromwell, he refused to sign an oath assenting to the act. However, because he would not explain why and was willing to accept Anne as queen, he could not be declared guilty of outright treason. Fifteen months of imprisonment in the Tower of London followed, where interrogators harried him and his distraught family begged him to sign. He would not.

Finally, on July 1, 1535, so ill and weak that he could barely stand, Thomas More was brought to trial for treason, based on the dubious testimony of onetime friend Richard Rich, who betrayed More to serve Cromwell, then betrayed Cromwell to serve himself. At trial, More denounced Rich as a perjurer and forcefully maintained that no sovereign could declare himself head of the church. The act of Parliament that claimed so was "in direct contradiction to the laws of God and his holy church." He was sentenced to death.

As he was escorted back to the Tower, daughter Margaret broke through the guards to fling her arms around him. "Do not distress yourself," he told her. "It is God's will." When he was beheaded five days later, his last words were that he died "the king's good servant, and God's first."

More's death stunned and outraged much of Europe. It was, as G. K. Chesterton wrote four centuries later, shocking that "the best friend of the Renaissance was killed as the worst enemy of the Reformation." But More himself, canonized a saint in 1935, was conciliatory, observing to the men who had convicted him that Paul was present at the martyrdom of Stephen and later changed his mind. So might they. "I hope—and will pray with all my heart," he said, "that although you have condemned me here on earth, we may yet hereafter in heaven merrily all meet together." ∎

1. Thomas More likely first met Erasmus at about age twenty, when Erasmus's friend and admirer Lord Mountjoy brought him on extensive visits to England. Later the Dutch scholar would often stay at More's home in Chelsea.

2. Berglar's statistic is specific to London; in 1529 Thomas Hitton was burned at the stake in Maidstone. The *Catholic Encyclopedia* notes that four men perished as heretics during More's tenure as chancellor, while Peter Ackroyd lists five: three in London, Richard Bayfield, John Tewkesbury, James Bainham; one in Norwich, Thomas Bilney; and one in Exeter, Thomas Dugsgate.

His "horrible fear of death" about to be realized, an infirm Thomas More, still steadfastly refusing to recognize King Henry as head of the English church, is escorted toward the chopping block. In a nineteenth-century painting, his daughter Margaret runs forward for a last embrace. "Do not distress yourself," he begs her. "It is God's will."

A synopsis portrayal of three beheadings in 1553. Bishop John Fisher of Rochester, at age eighty, lies dead in the foreground, while the executioner deals with Thomas More on the same platform. At rear right, Margaret Pole, the countess of Salisbury, is executed in place of her son, who had fled England.

at Windsor, all executed for treason because they denied the king could be head of the church. Cranmer had interceded and asked that the Carthusians first be sent to him. Perhaps he could convert them. But Henry had no interest in conversion; he wanted to proclaim the price of defiance. They were partially hanged, cut down while still alive, then eviscerated like chickens, their body parts posted on spikes around London. The king wasn't among the spectators. Many of the court were, including his sixteen-year-old illegitimate son, the duke of Richmond.

Fisher and More, both refusing the oath, were accorded the more humane method of the ax (see sidebar, p. 121). The execution of Fisher, who had just been made a cardinal by Rome, especially outraged the new pope, Paul III, who called Henry "a heretic, schismatic, notorious adulterer, open murderer, sacrilegious despoiler, destroyer, and transgressor against the majesty of God." He issued a bull commencing excommunication proceedings against him, a decree Henry had long expected.

5. Henry's fleet was the precursor of the Royal Navy, and during his reign the number of its ships increased from fifteen to forty-five, a dry dock was built in Portsmouth, and, for the first time, cannon and gunports were installed in the ships, augmenting what had hitherto been merely archers on deck. The pride of Henry's fleet was the carrack-style *Mary Rose* (named for the Virgin and the heraldic Tudor rose). The largest warship in existence at the time, with seven decks on the fore and aft "castles," she had a wartime capacity of 450 men. She capsized in 1545 while approaching the French fleet, probably because, heeling in a high wind, water poured in through the gunports.

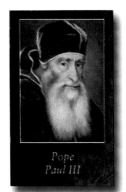

Pope
Paul III

Soon, however, his periodic warring with the French and the Scots, his enlarged navy,[5] his magnificent court, his numerous residences, his jewel-encrusted doublets, his passion for feasts and tournaments, and the high cost of maintaining Anne as the realm's fashion setter had exhausted the gold left him by his father. New revenues were required, and one place to find them lay in the valuable monastic properties of the old church. These could be sold to provide funds, and the revenues they provided their new secular owners could then be taxed to provide even more funds. The expropriation was conducted under the guise of reformation. Inspectors were sent out to the monasteries and returned with horrendous—and often fabricated—tales of clerical immorality and corruption. The first wave of suppression targeted about 220 of the smaller houses. Most of the displaced monks and friars retired, married, or moved to larger monasteries—although it wouldn't be long before Henry grabbed the bigger houses, too.

The landed and mercantile classes applauded the suppression, but the peasantry in the north did not. Many of the poor had found their only succor in the good works of the orders and were now untended. The more traditional northerners also opposed the religious reforms that Cromwell and Cranmer were bringing in, such as the institution of Tyndale's English Bible in the churches and the reduction of saints' days.[6] Hikes in imperial taxation and the taking over of cropland by the sheep-farming mercantile classes were also creating hardship across the countryside.

Rebel forces amassed in Lincolnshire and Yorkshire, swearing to resist the new taxes and maintain the old order of the church. Their leader, the lawyer Robert Aske, called the revolt "the Pilgrimage of Grace." In the fall of 1536 the rebels captured the commissioners of taxes and held them hostage. Caught with no troops, Henry pretended to negotiate with Aske, who naively believed in the king's integrity. Meanwhile, Henry dispatched a force led by the still-Catholic duke of Norfolk, who dispersed the rebels in Lincolnshire. But a new uprising in Yorkshire provided Henry with an excuse to strike. At his insistence 250 were hanged, Aske one of them. Taxes were collected with more vigor than ever, and the suppression of the monasteries continued.[7]

Thereafter, however, Henry came to realize that Protestantism was not nearly as acceptable among the general populace as it was among Cranmer, Cromwell, and their cohort in his court. So now that reform had served its purpose—establishing his supremacy and filling his treasury—he began reining it back. He pushed through Parliament a bill known as the Six Articles, which prescribed the death penalty for anyone transgressing various tenets of Catholicism. These included the presence of the Lord at the Eucharist and the celibacy of priests. (Cranmer quietly had Margarete shipped back to Germany.) Under the Articles a number of Protestants were burned in the latter years of Henry's reign.

At age forty-four, the king suffered a serious injury. During a jousting match, his horse stumbled and fell on him, knocking him unconscious for two hours and injuring his leg. The wound ulcerated and festered for the rest of his life. He could neither ride nor hunt, making him obese (his waist would expand to fifty-seven inches), worsening his rages, and eventually rendering him a cripple. A few days after the accident the ousted Queen Catherine died in exile at fifty, maintaining to the end that she was still queen. She had not seen her beloved daughter, Mary, for seven years. A few days later came a further reversal. Anne Boleyn, blaming the shock of the news of Henry's injury, miscarried. The three-and-a-half-month-old dead fetus was a son. Henry by now had virtually broken off communication with Anne—what with her demanding ways and her occasional insults to his virility. Now, by failing to fulfill his need of an heir, she had signed her own death warrant.

Henry asked Cromwell to investigate ways of disposing of this termagant and of freeing him to marry the pale, blond, and altogether more agreeable Jane Seymour. Cromwell conspired with Anne's uncle Norfolk to concoct charges of adultery with several courtiers and a charge of incest with her brother. (Norfolk had broken with his niece over her haughty alignment with the Protestants, whom he opposed). All but one of the accused denied the charges, and the one who had confessed, a frail court musician, had only done so on threat of torture. All were executed.

Henry, wallowing in self-pity, turned savagely on Anne. On the night of her

6. William Tyndale, a Cambridge theologian exiled to Germany and the Netherlands, produced his English translation of the New Testament in 1526. When a colleague suggested that the pope should be the final word on Scripture, Tyndale famously replied, "I defy the pope and all his laws; and if God spares my life, I will cause the boy that drives the plow to know more of the Scriptures than the pope himself!" Tyndale's book, *The Obedience of the Christian Man*, which had held special appeal to Henry, adapted Lutheran political theory for an English readership, maintaining that Scripture inculcated obedience even to wicked rulers in all things that were not directly contrary to God's law. Thomas More's (see sidebar, p. 121) condemnation of Tyndale as a heretic was used to convict him. He was burned at Antwerp in 1536.

7. The rebellion put the Tudor monarchy in dire danger, writes the historian J. J. Scarisbrick in his biography, *Henry VIII* (1968). It threatened a grand amalgamation of Yorkist sympathizers, Scottish warriors, and an invading army provided by Charles V. Rome had been ready to intervene and had sent Cardinal Reginald Pole to Flanders to muster support for such an effort. It failed because Aske held back his hotheads in the belief that Henry was an honorable man. "Had things been only slightly different, his Reformation might have been wholly or largely undone, Cromwell, Cranmer, and the rest expelled, he himself destroyed, and Mary brought to the throne . . . sixteen years ahead of her time."

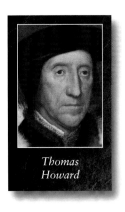
Thomas Howard

arrest, his son, the young duke of Richmond, found Henry in tears. "By God's great mercy," Henry is said to have told the boy, "you and your sister Mary have escaped the hands of that damned poisonous strumpet. She was plotting to poison you both." With Norfolk presiding, the twenty-nine-year-old Anne was convicted of treason and sentenced to death, protesting her innocence to the last. A confession would have made an annulment of their marriage easier, but Cranmer dissolved the union on the ironic grounds of a canonical impediment created by Henry's previous adultery with her sister (an argument earlier employed by Rome when it was attempting to block the marriage with Anne). Henry had demanded the annulment to facilitate the succession of a male heir—either Richmond (who would die seven months later) or a future legitimate son. The annulment was taken to render Princess Elizabeth, until now first in line, as illegitimate, like her half sister Mary. It was the final insult to Anne.

Anne Boleyn, long loved by the king though despised by his subjects, is put to death on a fabricated charge of treason. After praying all night with her attendants and making her last confession, Queen Anne flawlessly fulfilled the role of royal victim, dying with dignity. A French executioner, renowned for his swift accuracy, was brought in from France at her request. The king looks on at left in this German engraving, circa 1640, while at right Henry's next wife, Lady Jane Seymour, turns away.

At Anne's request, Henry agreed to provide a crack swordsman from France who, unlike the English axmen, guaranteed decapitation with a single swipe. To suffer death by execution had become something of an art form in Henrician England, and Anne performed the role flawlessly. Having calmly prayed through the night with her ladies in the Tower and made her final confession, she serenely emerged into the courtyard on the morning of May 19 wearing a beautiful robe

of heavy gray damask trimmed with fur. A crowd of about a thousand watched as the first English queen to be executed mounted the four-foot-high scaffold.

After the customary distribution of alms to some of the spectators and the payment of a purse to the executioner, Anne made her adieu to the world and to history: "I am not here to preach to you, but to die. Pray for the king, for he is a good man and has treated me as well as could be. I do not accuse anyone of causing my death, neither the judges nor anyone else, for I am condemned by the law of the land and die willingly." While one of her ladies applied the blindfold, Anne added, "Pray for me. God have pity on my soul." As promised, the French executioner removed her head with a single hissing stroke.

Ten days later Henry married Jane Seymour. It was his happiest marriage, made happier when she produced a son, the future Edward VI, in October of 1537, before dying from complications of the childbirth. Cromwell's end came two years later. He persuaded the widowed Henry to marry Anne of Cleves, a woman billed by Cromwell as very beautiful. When she arrived in England, Henry found her quite otherwise, dubbing his new Anne "the Flanders mare." Henry did not consummate the marriage. He was thus able to have the union easily annulled the following year.

Already distancing himself from Lutheran reform, the king wished to repair his Catholic credentials to gain a Catholic ally. In this he found Cromwell, heavily attached to the Protestants, a distinct liability. Encouraged by the Catholic faction in court, led by Norfolk, he declared Cromwell guilty of treason. His head went on the block on July 28, 1540; the drunken axman required three strokes to do the job.

Henry took two more wives. The first, another niece of Norfolk's, was seventeen-year-old Catherine Howard, the prettiest but the most foolhardy of Henry's mates. Repulsed by her fifty-year-old husband's obesity and his festering leg, she began a love affair with a young courtier called Culpepper, was discovered, and was beheaded less than two years after the wedding, announcing from the scaffold: "I die a queen but would rather die the wife of Culpepper."

By the time he had married Catherine Parr, wife number six, Henry was in rapid decline. He could no longer walk or stand by himself, and had to be transported up and down stairs with a mechanical device. He weighed more

King Henry looks properly regal in the portrait above, one of many by Hans Holbein the Younger, but he ended his life so obese and crippled by gout that he could not stand or walk unaided. This painting is displayed on one wall of the Prince's Chamber, a small anteroom in the Palace of Westminster, where it is positioned beside matching portraits of five of his six wives (at the top of page, left to right): Anne Boleyn, Jane Seymour, Anne of Cleves, Catherine Howard, and Catherine Parr.

than three hundred pounds, and was in constant pain and ill temper. Catherine, thirty-one, twice widowed, childless, and reputedly less prepossessing even than Anne of Cleves, proved a good wife. She was a Protestant, and the Catholic faction in court came close to having her arrested, but her quick wit and silver tongue won her Henry's support and saved her from the fire.[8] Catherine nursed the king's wound, defused his rages, and reconciled him with his daughter Elizabeth. In his last will he returned both princesses to the line of succession behind Edward.

By the end of 1546 Henry was close to death. Edward, a sickly boy of nine and not old enough to rule alone, would need a pro-

Henry Howard Earl of Surrey

tector. The reformists, led by the earl of Hertford and quietly supported by Cranmer, vied for the position and won it. The Catholic Norfolk and his son Henry Howard, the earl of Surrey, were arrested for treason in December. Surrey, a young and already reputable Renaissance poet, had been heard drunkenly boasting of his descent from Edward III and making optimistic predictions of his family's fortunes once the king was dead.

But the king was still alive. The charge was embellished into a plot to murder the young Edward and place Norfolk on the throne. Henry directed the proceedings, having decided that it would be better that the Catholic faction be eliminated and the Protestants hold the regency when his son came to the throne. Surrey was executed, and his father was condemned to death on the day that Henry went to his deathbed. The sentence was not carried out.

The night of January 27, 1547, was a very cold one, and when Cranmer was summoned to the dying king's bedside to hear his last confession, it took him several hours to travel from Croydon. By the time the archbishop arrived, the king was barely conscious and unable to speak. Cranmer urged him to give some sign with his hand or his eyes that he had put his trust in the mercy

8. Henry, who by now was oscillating between Catholicism and Lutheranism, liked to have theological discussions with his intelligent sixth wife. Sensing the peril posed by the Catholics, however, Catherine gracefully bowed out of the discussions, pleading what she described as the inherent intellectual frailty of females. "What great imperfection and weakness is allotted unto us women, to be ordained and appointed as inferiors and subject unto men as our head," she averred. "How then cometh it now to pass that Your Majesty will seem to require my judgment?"

of Christ. Henry took Cranmer's hand, squeezed as hard as he could; then, at 2 a.m. on January 28, 1547, he died.

Edward VI was king, the Protestants were in control, and the English Reformation appeared assured. But in the era of the Tudors, as events would soon prove, nothing was assured, and the most tumultuous of all their years were immediately ahead. ∎

A nineteenth-century oil painting shows Henry VIII lavishing attention on his toddler son, the future Edward VI, the male heir he had spent so many years and spilled so much blood to produce. He ignores his daughter, Elizabeth, kneeling at right, who in the eyes of many historians became the greatest of the Tudors.

CHAPTER 7

Preacher versus queen: the clash that helped turn Britain Protestant

Fiery, prophetic John Knox, founder of a great church, persuades tens of thousands to see Mary of Scotland as the 'Catholic whore,' setting her forth on a fatal path

The enemies of John Knox—and they included queens, bishops, noblemen, and various others whom he had insulted or otherwise infuriated—took a decidedly dim view of the powerful Scottish preacher and fearless religious reformer. He was, they said, a dwarfish, narrow-minded bigot with a long face, a long beard, and a long tongue who preached sermons that were too long. It was impossible to reason with him because he was obstinate, abrasive, and completely incapable of compromise.

All of which failed to concern either Knox or the rising thousands who believed him. They saw him as he saw himself. He was not in the business of being popular. He was God's trumpet, a prophet divinely commissioned to destroy the Roman Catholic Church in his beloved Scotland. On the ruins of this (as he viewed it) grasping, corrupt, and abusive institution, he must build a new *kirk*—or church—one based on holy scripture and untainted by human greed, vanity, and arrogance. Words were his weapon, and he used them like a sledgehammer to batter and bludgeon the ancient and powerful colossus that was his foe.

A man must love his enemies, Christ had said, but one enemy in particular Knox found it impossible to love. It was, in fact, a woman—tall, slender, and to many instantly attractive, a woman who charmed men as easily as he enraged them. Knox spent much of his turbulent life battling her or her representatives. History knows her as Mary Queen of Scots. Knox knew her as "that Catholic whore."

In a nineteenth-century lithograph (opposite page) the famously determined John Knox (left), who saw it his God-ordained mission to root out Roman Catholicism from Scotland, admonishes an exhausted Mary Queen of Scots on the folly of her intended marriage to Prince Don Carlos of Catholic Spain. But as long as the people accepted her, Knox assured her, he personally would be "as well content to live under Your Grace as St. Paul was to live under Nero." At center is the English reformer Christopher Goodman (1520-1603), who took refuge in Scotland when he was exiled from England during the reign of Catholic queen Mary Tudor.

The queen and the preacher waged their small, intensely personal war in sixteenth-century Scotland—a country that sent shudders up the spines of sophisticated continental Europeans. To them, Scotland was cold, wet, and largely treeless with stony, infertile soil and suspicious, inhospitable people, deeply attached to family and clan and morbidly wary of just about everybody else. Over this chilly habitat there reigned a king—reigned but not ruled. He wielded minimal authority and was beholden to the nobility and the church. The latter controlled

To the extent that Scotland had a national policy at all, it was shaped by one overwhelming fact: notably its larger, wealthier, much more powerful neighbor to the south.

half the national wealth while the former controlled nearly all of the other half. These were mostly violent, lawless men driven almost solely by self-interest rather than anything resembling the national good.

To the extent that Scotland had a national policy at all, it was shaped by one overwhelming geopolitical fact, notably its larger, wealthier, much more powerful neighbor to the south with whom it shared the island the Romans had called Britannia. Scotland's population at mid-sixteenth century has been estimated at eight hundred and fifty thousand, England's at three and a half million. Fearing always an English invasion, the Scots habitually turned for protection to England's perpetual enemy, France. French troops were stationed on Scottish soil. French bureaucrats helped administer the country, and Scottish kings often married the daughters of French monarchs or aristocrats to secure what was known as "the auld alliance."

Always fearful of English invasion, the Scots habitually turned for protection to England's perpetual enemy, France, often cementing their alliance with marriage between Scottish royalty and French nobility. The nineteenth-century oil painting below is of King James V of Scotland (1512–1542) and Mary of Guise (1515–1560), parents of the unfortunate Queen Mary of Scotland.

One such union—the marriage of Scotland's James V and Mary of Guise in 1538—produced a daughter, Mary Queen of Scots, and allowed France's ambitious Guise family to exert what some considered an undue influence on Scotland for nearly three decades. The Guises had risen to prominence in France during the reign of King Francis I. Claude, the first duke of Guise, had thirteen children. Mary, the firstborn and mother of the Mary who became Knox's mortal enemy, lived her life in Scotland after her marriage to James V. Two of her brothers became distinguished in Europe—

Reform preacher George Wishart (below) is led to the stake at St. Andrew's Castle in 1546, to be executed in a manner exceptionally brutal even for the times. This execution had a major impact on John Knox, a Catholic priest for whom Wishart was a mentor.

Francis, the second duke, as a military hero, and Charles as the cardinal of Lorraine who played a pivotal role at the Council of Trent.

All three would come to know the name John Knox and would tangle with him directly or indirectly, which must surely have irked them, given their lofty stations and his humble background. Indeed, almost nothing is known of Knox's early years beyond the fact he was the son of a farmer, born about 1513 near the village of Haddington, eighteen miles east of Edinburgh. Though short, he was ruggedly built with broad shoulders, black hair, and deep-set, gray-blue eyes. Portraits painted later give him a sharp, narrow nose and a long, thick patriarchal beard.

Knox was a Catholic priest who began his career as a church notary and tutor to the children of wealthy families. Two events aroused his hatred of Catholicism. One was the execution in 1528 at St. Andrew's Castle, the seat of ecclesiastical power in Scotland, of the youthful reformer Patrick Hamilton, declared a heretic and burned at the stake so incompetently that it took the man six hours of agony to die. The other was the execution eighteen years later on March 1, 1546, of the gentle reformist preacher George Wishart, burned and blown to bits by bags of gunpowder tied to his sides.

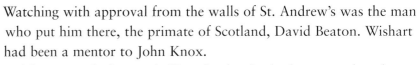

Watching with approval from the walls of St. Andrew's was the man who put him there, the primate of Scotland, David Beaton. Wishart had been a mentor to John Knox.

Three months later, rebellious lords who had converted to the new faith struck their first hard blow against the established order. They slipped into St. Andrew's, drove out the servants, and cornered Beaton in his bedroom. "Fie, fie, ye will not slay me," he said defiantly. "I am a priest." One assassin snarled, "Ye are a vile papist." Another ran a sword through him. They hung his naked body, upside down, from the castle wall, where one onlooker urinated in the gaping mouth. The party, about 150 men, occupied the castle for nearly a year, thwarting all attempts by royal troops to dislodge them. During a brief truce, Knox stole in to join the reformers.[1]

It was a momentous decision. He had tied his fortunes to the reform movement. He began preaching to the Protestant rebels and discovered that he was a powerful and compelling speaker. Soon he was attracting large crowds to the castle to hear him. But in late June, twenty-one French galleys loaded with soldiers arrived at St. Andrew's and quickly took possession. Knox and a dozen others spent the next nineteen months as galley slaves. Their sentence served, they were liberated in an English port in the spring of 1549. Knox had enjoyed nearly five years' preaching to Protestant congregations in England when Catholic Mary Tudor ascended the English throne and began persecuting Protestants.

Knox found a safe haven in John Calvin's Geneva, then moved to Frankfurt to minister to refugee English Protestants there. Finally, he moved to Berwick, on England's Scottish border, where he married Marjorie Bowes, daughter of one of the many women who admired him. He was in his early forties, she much younger, and in the following winter of 1555 to 1556 she happily accompanied him on a triumphant nine-month preaching tour of Scotland. James V had died some thirteen years before, and his widow, Mary of Guise, ruled as regent, but she was protected by French troops while Catholic clerics administered the royal government, a cause of much unrest.

The Scottish nobles wanted the foreign soldiers expelled, the priests fired, and the church estates turned over to themselves. The common people supported them. But what they needed was a firebrand leader. In Knox, many thought they had found one. But Knox turned them down. Neither his contemporaries nor subsequent historians can explain this. Was he chastened by the galleys? Did he prefer a settled family life? For whatever reason, in 1556 he accepted an invitation to become pastor of an English congregation in Geneva. He lived happily there for some six months. Then in May of 1557, two things happened. His wife gave birth to a son, and a delegation arrived from Scotland begging him to return. What should he do? He consulted fellow clergy, even John Calvin himself. Their recommendation was unanimous: he should return to Scotland.

He took their advice, crossed France at considerable personal risk, and arrived in Dieppe in late October. There he received a letter from his Edinburgh friends. Protestantism was not advancing as they had anticipated. Some of the lords had withdrawn their support. Conditions were not right for his return.

David Beaton, primate of Scotland, was among the first victims of the Scottish reform movement. "Ye are a vile papist," snarled one of the vengeful Protestant lords who seized St. Andrew's Castle in 1546. Then they ran Beaton through with a sword and hung his naked body upside down from the castle wall. Shortly thereafter these rebel reformers were joined by John Knox. The portrait is an 1823 lithograph from Lodge's British Portraits.

1. Some historians present a very different picture of Cardinal Beaton, portraying him as a Scottish hero against the aggressive and powerful English. A booklet on Mary Queen of Scots, produced in 1973 by a clergyman, J. A. Carruth, introduces Beaton on its opening page as a "great Scots patriot" and adds that he "was murdered, perhaps at Henry VIII's instigation."

Knox was furious. He had made his first discovery that the Scottish nobility were not dependable. It wouldn't be the last. He spent the winter in Dieppe brooding. "Thoughts of Scotland crowded into his mind," writes his biographer Geddes MacGregor in *The Thundering Scot: A Portrait of John Knox* (1958). His mind "magnified caricatured thoughts of the bishops and friars still smugly sauntering down the High Street at home; still muttering the Mass; still shriving such miserable souls as still cared to be shriven." He fumed at the thought of a French, female, and Catholic regent ruling Scotland until her equally Catholic daughter, heir to its throne, could become its queen. Why was he an exile? Because of the Catholics, that's why, especially Catholic women. That winter, seized by a cataclysmic anger, he took to the pen and produced one of the most extraordinary polemics of all time.

For John Knox (above), the thought of a Scottish monarch who was (a) French, (b) Catholic, and (c) female was intolerable. In the winter of 1557 to 1558, seized by a cataclysmic anger, he put pen to paper and produced one of the most extraordinary polemics of all time, entitled The First Blast of the Trumpet against the Monstrous Regiment of Women, *taking particular aim at England's Catholic queen, Mary Tudor.*

He entitled it *The First Blast of the Trumpet against the Monstrous Regiment of Women.* He took particular aim at England's Queen Mary Tudor. The men of England should stand up against this wicked Jezebel, he declared. Thirty-odd pages later, he concluded with the warning that the word of God would lay waste her wicked rule and, for that matter, all female rulers and all those men who propped them up. "When they are consumed (as shortly they will be, for stubble and dry timber cannot endure the fire), that rotten wall, the usurped and unjust empire of women, shall fall by itself in despite of all men, to the destruction of so many as shall labor to uphold it. And therefore let all men be advertised, for the trumpet has once blown."

Mary I of England

Elizabeth I of England

By mid-March 1558, Knox was back in Geneva, manuscript in hand. Remarkably, he found a publisher brave enough to print it. But that man dared not fix his name to the *First Blast,* and nor did Knox himself. His pamphlet quickly reached England, was immediately deemed seditious, and Queen Mary issued a royal proclamation condemning it. That November there occurred an event that Knox does not appear to have foreseen. Mary died, and her successor was

Mary Stuart, the future Mary Queen of Scots, was born on December 8, 1542, at Linlithgow Palace (left), seventeen miles west of Edinburgh, six days before the death of her father, King James V of Scotland. Princess Mary spent her first five years in Scotland and at age four was anointed queen at Stirling Castle (above). In this same castle, twenty-one years later, her son James would be crowned king of Scotland at the age of thirteen months.

Spending most of her childhood with her mother's family in France, young Mary lived in such scenic palaces as Chambord Castle (below) in the Loire Valley. She was a great favorite of the French king Henry II, who called her "the most perfect child I have ever seen," and would weep bitterly when at age nineteen she had to leave France to claim her Scottish throne. Scotland seemed cold and alien—as did its Protestant religion. Only in her private chapel at Holyrood Castle (inset at right), her principal residence, could she hear Mass.

Elizabeth, a Protestant, a queen, and a woman. She could also read, and she early on read the *First Blast*. She would never forget it. Knox was now ready to return to Scotland. Elizabeth refused him a passport, so he returned by sea.

He landed on May 2, 1559, and immediately allied himself with the Lords of the Congregation, a group of pro-English nobles now in open rebellion against the regent, Mary of Guise, who promptly declared him an out-law. Undeterred, he preached to sizeable crowds in Perth and St. Andrew's in wildly inflammatory language. Furious mobs began ransacking churches in both towns, stripped them bare, smashed stained glass, tore doors from hinges, and barged into friaries and monasteries. They drove out the terrified monks and nuns and carted off gold, silver, meats, wines, and anything else they could carry. On June 30 rebel lords and their followers, now numbering six thousand, marched into Edinburgh. Mary of Guise fled to the coastal town of Dunbar. The following day, Knox preached at St. Giles, Edinburgh's premier church, which stood within sight of the royal palace.

In mid-October, the rebels formally proclaimed the regent deposed and replaced her with a council of twenty-four nobles. By then Mary was seriously ill, but she wasn't finished. She retreated to the port of Leith and mustered an army of three thousand French troops, who marched on Edinburgh and routed the Scottish forces. But she desperately needed reinforcements from France and appealed to her brothers, the duke of Guise and the cardinal of Lorraine. The nobles similarly appealed to the English. In late January an English fleet sailed into the Firth of Forth and blockaded Leith, while two thousand English troops headed north from Berwick. The rule of Mary of Guise was over. Five months later, on June 11, she was dead.

Francis II of France (left) and Mary of Scotland, here depicted in a wedding portrait, were married in 1558 at age fourteen and fifteen respectively. One year later they were crowned king and queen of France, although in reality most of the royal power was wielded by Mary's maternal uncles, the crafty Guise brothers. But when Francis died after only eighteen months on the throne, Mary was quickly brushed aside.

Within a year the old order in Scotland had been destroyed. A new one was emerging, and it was confirmed in the Treaty of Edinburgh, signed July 6, 1560, by representatives of Scotland, England, and France. French troops were to leave Scotland immediately. England was granted the right to intervene in Scottish affairs to defend the Protestant faith against Catholicism or French intervention. Finally, the council of twenty-four would form the government until Mary, daughter of the former regent, would assert her undisputed claim to the Scottish throne.

Mary had been born in 1542 at Linlithgow Palace, seventeen miles west of Edinburgh. Six days later, her father died at age thirty, having sired numerous illegitimate children. Near age four, she was anointed queen of Scots in a solemn ceremony at Stirling Castle on the east coast. In 1548 she was pledged to four-year-old Francis, eldest son of King Henry II of France, as part of an alliance under which

Catherine de' Medici

Charles IX of France

James Stuart Earl of Moray

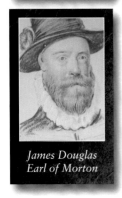

William Maitland

James Douglas Earl of Morton

France would send an army to Scotland and free the country from English control.

That same year Mary of Guise placed her daughter aboard a ship bound for France, where she joined the household of Henry II and his formidable Italian wife, Catherine de' Medici. She was introduced to her future husband, Francis, a short, spindly four-year-old who was physically clumsy and stuttered. Mary, by contrast, was tall, energetic, and vivacious, soon known as "*la petite Reine*," the little queen, to King Henry "the most perfect child I have ever seen."

Mary enjoyed a fairytale childhood. She lived in castles and had an immense wardrobe, servants attending to her needs, and clowns, singers, and dancers entertaining her and the other royal children. Catherine de' Medici and the cardinal of Lorraine supervised her education. But one Sunday in 1558, these idyllic years ended. Thousands of Parisians turned out to watch the spectacular wedding of Francis and Mary at Notre Dame Cathedral. He was fourteen, she a year older, nearly six feet tall and well proportioned, with small, deep-set hazel eyes and ringlets of lustrous auburn hair, all enhanced by a warm, engaging personality and a quick wit.

But she was also far too open and trusting for the murky political waters of sixteenth-century Europe. At the behest of her two conniving Guise uncles, the brothers of her mother, she signed several secret documents stipulating that should she die without producing an heir, the king of France and his heirs would inherit the throne of Scotland and all the revenues of Scotland until France had been paid one million pieces of gold. The uncles also informed Elizabeth that their niece, not Elizabeth, was the rightful queen of England and lobbied other European leaders and the pope to recognize this legitimacy.[2] Their efforts went nowhere, but this dynastic claim was destined to cause Mary untold trouble.

The following year, Henry II died from a jousting accident. Francis and Mary became king and queen of France. This made her two uncles major power brokers in the French court, assiduously advancing Mary's claim to the English throne as part of a bizarre plan to unite the thrones of France, England, and Scotland under the crown of France. But that fantasy met an abrupt end a year later when the sickly Francis died and his ten-year-old brother, Charles, became king with Catherine de' Medici as regent. The Guise brothers, whom Catherine despised, were swiftly banished from the French court and Mary brushed aside. Now eighteen, she pondered her future for several months and reached a conclusion. She would return to Scotland and take up her throne there.

She left France in mid-August 1561, sobbing uncontrollably on the ship's stern as France, the country she had come to cherish, sank beneath the horizon. Scotland was foreign and alien to her. She knew it to be unruly and chaotic. She had no friends there and no counselors. She arrived determined to be a real ruler, respected, obeyed, and perhaps someday loved by her subjects.

So she moved decisively, choosing a privy council of seven Protestant nobles and five Catholic. From these, she selected three as her inner cabinet. Foremost was her half brother, Lord James Stuart, earl of Moray. One of her father's host of illegitimate children, he was big, imposing, ambitious, and twelve years her senior, and would soon prove treacherous. The second was William Maitland, secretary of state, a fervent Protestant and a close friend of William Cecil, Queen Elizabeth's principal minister, who would diligently seek Mary's deposition and death. Yet Maitland would serve Mary longer and more loyally than any other. The third was James Douglas, earl of Morton, whose great strengths as an administrator were offset by a cruel vindictiveness and a sexual attraction to little girls.

Mary soon discovered that prior to her arrival Protestantism had asserted legal control of her country. The nobles had convened a session of parliament and passed legislation making Scotland officially Protestant and prohibiting the celebration of the Mass. Meanwhile, the Catholic Church lay in ruins. Nine of the country's thirteen dioceses were without bishops, and the other four were in the hands of disreputable men. Yet only in Edinburgh and a few other principal towns had the Reformed faith clearly prevailed. Elsewhere Catholicism retained its hold on the people.

Even so, Mary could attend Mass only in the private chapel at Holyrood, her main residence, but not at any other royal palaces. Her personal staff could not attend with her. Some opposed any celebration of the Mass whatever, and on her first Sunday at Edinburgh, zealous reformers broke into the courtyard at Holyrood while Mary was at Mass and tried to barge into the chapel. Lord James held them back with sword drawn, so they resorted to heckling the priest and the queen.

Knox, meanwhile, denounced her and her faith weekly from the pulpit at St. Giles. "One Mass," he declared, "is more fearful than if ten thousand armed enemies were landed in any part of the realm to suppress the whole religion." Mary knew Knox as the author of the *First Blast* and as one of those responsible for her mother's downfall. She concluded that he was now inciting her subjects to rise against her. So she decided to summon him to Holyrood to explain himself.

The interview took place September 4, 1561, and was an extraordinary encounter. The beautiful young queen, who loved music, dance, and extravagant attire, who expected ordinary folk to bow and scurry to meet her every whim and desire, gazed upon a grizzled commoner, a former galley slave no less, who looked far older than his forty-eight years but had the brazen audacity to defy her. He was fomenting political unrest, she said. He was merely preaching the word of God, he replied. "Then you must think I have no just authority." He replied: "Please, Your Majesty, if the realm finds no inconvenience from the rule of a woman, that which they approve I shall not disallow . . . I shall be as well content to live under Your Grace as St. Paul was to live under Nero."

That stung, but Mary pressed the point. "Do you think," she asked, "that

2. Mary could make two claims to the English throne. First, her paternal grandmother (the wife of James IV of Scotland) was the sister of Henry VIII. Second, as a Catholic she had a stronger claim than Elizabeth. Since Elizabeth was born to Anne Boleyn while Henry VIII's legal wife was still alive (see ch. 6), to Catholics Elizabeth was illegitimate, and her claim to the English throne therefore invalid.

The uncompromising John Knox preaches at St. Andrew's Cathedral in Fife, Scotland, as represented (below) by an unknown eighteenth-century artist. Knox's weekly custom was to ferociously denounce Scotland's queen and her Catholic faith from one pulpit or another—a single Mass, in his estimation, being "more fearful than if ten thousand armed enemies were landed in any part of the realm to suppress the whole religion."

Mary Queen of Scots, as portrayed by court artist François Clouet, and her implacable adversary John Knox, in an anonymous nineteenth-century engraving. In a direct confrontation with Knox, the young queen declared that she would defend Rome as the "true Church of God." "Your will, madam, is not an argument," was Knox's uncompromising reply.

subjects have the power to resist their princes?" They did indeed, said Knox. "If princes exceed their bounds and do against that wherefore they should be obeyed, it is no doubt but that they may be resisted, even by power. For there is no greater honor nor greater obedience to be given to kings or princes than God has commended to be given unto father and mother." It was, for the times, an astounding assertion.

But Mary, not yet nineteen years old, held her ground until the conversation shifted to religion. No match for Knox on scriptural matters, she became indignant, struggled to maintain her composure, and resorted, at last, to a flat assertion of her belief in the Church of Rome. "Yours is not the kirk I will support," she said. "I will defend the Church of Rome, for I think it is the true church of God."

"Your will, madam, is not an argument," was his frosty reply. "Neither will it convert the Roman harlot to be the true and immaculate spouse of Jesus Christ. And do not wonder, madam, that I call Rome a harlot; for that church is altogether polluted with all kinds of spiritual fornication, as well in doctrine as in manners."[3]

This chilly encounter was the first of several between the queen and the preacher. Knox could bully her, but he could not bully the Scottish nobles. From the start, they would cause him major problems. He was trying to create a new kirk. Hundreds of ministers needed to be trained, churches maintained, the Reformed faith taught in every corner of the country. He and several other clerics drafted a blueprint for the new kirk. It was called the *Book of Discipline* and they presented it to the Scottish parliament in early 1561.

In it, faith must become the center of Scottish life. Parliament must be subordinate to the kirk. The former properties of the Catholic Church must be used to support ministers, to provide the revenues for relief for the poor, and to fund a system of universal public education under which every child in Scotland would receive at least four years' elementary schooling, while the best students would go beyond. Finally, the new kirk would be democratic. Parishioners would choose their ministers and yearly elect deacons to manage the parish.

Most nobles greeted this with something approaching horror. Only a few were committed Protestants. The rest merely saw the religious uprising as a means of advancing their own interests. They did not subscribe to Knox's notion that all men were equal under God. Moreover, in a thoroughly democratic kirk they might find themselves subjected to the will of commoners. Finally, they were not

3. The source of this astonishing verbatim record is Knox's own account of it. But whether he made the record from memory or took it from another source is not known. Several others were present at the interview.

prepared to turn over the Catholic estates to the new kirk. They had other plans for those estates. Meanwhile, Knox's preachers were becoming ragged, hungry, and impoverished.

The privy council's response was to award two-thirds of the revenues from the Catholic estates to former priests who had lost their positions, one-sixth to ministers of the new faith, and the balance to the state. Now it was Knox's turn to be horrified. "My judgment fails me," he gasped. "I see two parts freely given to the devil, and the third must be divided between God and the devil."

Mary, meanwhile, began contending with the problem that would eventually lead to her downfall. Fomented by Cecil, Elizabeth's fear of Mary was real. What if Mary allied Scotland with France and Spain to create Catholic pincers around Protestant England? What if Mary married and produced a male heir while Elizabeth was childless? Would this not enhance Mary's claim to the English crown? Cecil had slipped a clause into the Treaty of Edinburgh renouncing Mary's claim, and Mary had refused to sign the treaty. To ease such anxieties, Mary tried to promote friendly relations with Elizabeth. She hoped to resolve the succession problem through personal diplomacy and repeat-

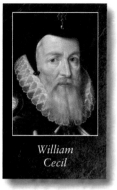

William Cecil

Darnley was extraordinarily handsome and sophisticated, was a Catholic, and had a claim to the English throne. If she wed him, Mary thought, her own claim would be unassailable.

edly sent emissaries to London to arrange a meeting of the two queens. More than once Elizabeth agreed, but the wily Cecil, nervous of Mary's legendary charm, successfully thwarted any meeting.

History offers no evidence that Mary intended Elizabeth's overthrow. Yet she desperately wanted to be recognized as Elizabeth's successor, should the English queen die childless. If nothing else, this would strengthen her authority in Scotland. But Elizabeth saw that to name a successor might hasten her own demise.

In the meantime, Mary was determined to produce an heir and early in 1563 began looking for a husband. She negotiated for the hand of the Spanish prince Don Carlos, which only confirmed Protestant suspicions of her motives. Knox strove to arouse public opposition to a Catholic marriage. Outraged, Mary summoned him again to Holyrood. "What," she demanded, "have you to do with my marriage, and what role do you see yourself playing in this commonwealth?" Knox replied defiantly: "I'm a subject born within the same, madam. And though I'm neither earl, lord, nor baron, and however abject I may be in your eyes, I am nonetheless a profitable member within the same." Their mutual hostility deepened.

Elizabeth and Cecil, meanwhile, decided Mary's marriage was as significant to the English throne as the Scottish, so they should have a voice in it. They insisted she marry an English lord, provided a list of candidates, and offered her Lord Robert Dudley. Mary was understandably insulted. Dudley

Robert Dudley

was said to have been Elizabeth's lover, and strong bonds of affection still existed between them. He would be nothing more than Elizabeth's agent and would keep Mary permanently subordinate to the English queen. So Mary rejected Dudley but kept her marital options open. Elizabeth finally delivered a firm answer in mid-March 1565. "Nothing shall be done," she said, until she (Elizabeth) was either married or had declared an intention not to marry.

Mary was outraged and humiliated. She must not marry until Elizabeth disclosed her marital plans. These efforts at conciliation, she decided, must be abandoned. She would no longer be bullied or dominated. She would marry a man of her own choosing. This led to disaster. In April 1565, when she was twenty-three, she began a courtship with Henry Stuart, Lord Darnley, the seventeen-year-old son of the earl of Lennox, a wealthy and influential noble.

Darnley was extraordinarily handsome. He was urbane and sophisticated, had studied in France, and had spent time at Elizabeth's court. He was Catholic, and he, too, had a claim on the throne of England.[4] By marrying him, Mary reasoned, her claim would be unassailable. But Darnley had serious shortcomings. He was vain, reckless, stupid, and promiscuous and was suspected of bedding both men and women. Mary's uncle the cardinal of Lorraine described him as "a polished trifler," while another contemporary concluded: "No woman of spirit would make a choice of such a man that was more like a woman than a man."

Elizabeth was furious when she learned of Mary's intentions. Cecil regarded the impending union as a threat to England's security and a hostile act. Lord James the earl of Moray, her half brother, was vehemently opposed. He quietly began lining up allies for a revolt against her while she mustered an army to defend her throne. Such was the state of affairs when Mary and Darnley were married on July 29, 1565. By then Mary understood Darnley's character. But to appease his vanity, she proclaimed him king of Scotland, though he must remain uncrowned until the Scottish parliament had ratified the decision.

In anticipation of her looming battle with Moray, she sent for James Hepburn, the earl of Bothwell, a handsome, dashing border lord and one of Scotland's shadiest characters. He had fought a dozen duels. He routinely settled his disputes by violent means. He had fled Scotland in December 1562 before Mary could banish him for a variety of offenses. But now he was useful to her. He was

Resolved upon marriage to a man of her choice, at age twenty-three Queen Mary decided on the dashing and debonair Henry Stuart, Lord Darnley, aged seventeen. Handsome and sophisticated, Darnley even had a claim to the English throne that could bolster Mary's own. Unfortunately, however, he was also vain, reckless, and exceptionally promiscuous as well. Further, their marriage in 1565 (shown below in an early-seventeenth-century engraving by Renold Elstrack) outraged both Mary's English counterpart, Elizabeth I, and influential Scottish lords.

an ardent nationalist, hated the English, had been loyal to Mary's mother. Not least, he was Moray's mortal enemy.

Bothwell had not made it home when Mary rode out of Edinburgh on August 26 to confront Moray and the rebels. She wore a steel cap. She had a pistol tucked into her saddle holster. Darnley was at her side, and more than eight thousand men were behind her. They rode against driving wind and rain. Moray dared not meet such an army head on. He had attracted only a handful of nobles and no more than two thousand men to his cause, and moved his forces from place to place. Mary pursued but was unable to catch and crush them.

By early October the rebel lords had slipped into England. The revolt was over and Mary triumphant. The nobles had never been so united under her. Elizabeth proposed another round of diplomacy. Mary's popularity with the people soared. Even Knox was impressed with her courage. But his role in the conflict would now subside. He continued preaching the same message. He had founded, if not established, a Calvinist church in Scotland, destined to play a central role in the next century. But other figures now moved into Scotland's center stage.

Mary quickly overplayed her hand. She spurned all advice to deal leniently with the rebels. Instead, she accused them of treason and announced that their lands and estates would be confiscated. She called a session of parliament for March 1566 and expected the nobles to confirm the property seizure by a vote. This was too much for many of them. It would set a dangerous precedent. What if they were the next to rebel?

Parliament was also to confirm Darnley as king. But the impetuous and arrogant young man had already begun to exercise monarchal powers. He had never been devout but decided he would become one of Europe's great Catholic kings. So he pursued an alliance with Spain without consulting Mary. He convinced the pope that he had reversed the Protestant Reformation in Scotland and boasted that High Mass would be said again at St. Giles. He was also drinking heavily. By Christmas 1565 there had been several spectacular public rows between husband and wife, and they were no longer living together. In February 1566 the English ambassador, Thomas Randolph, confided to Cecil: "I know now for certain that this queen wishes she hadn't married him, and hates him and his whole family." Mary soon put Darnley in his place. She stripped him of his title and declared that parliament would not be confirming him as king.

This led to a plot that was sinister even by the standards of sixteenth-century Scotland. Darnley and his family, the Lennoxes, betrayed Mary by conspiring with Moray and the other exiled lords. The Lennoxes also brought in a number of other powerful nobles. These conspirators agreed to crown Darnley when parliament met. Darnley would then welcome Moray and the others home. He would overturn the forfeiture of their estates and restore the religious balance that Mary had unsuccessfully sought to preserve. But there was one problem: how to explain Darnley's sudden religious reversal. What happened to the champion of Catholicism? Someone had to be blamed, and the conspirators settled on David Rizzio, an Italian Catholic and

A sixteenth-century Flemish miniature portrays James Hepburn, earl of Bothwell, a handsome, dashing border lord, ardent nationalist, and one of Scotland's shadiest characters. Noted for fighting duels and for settling disputes by violent means, Bothwell had been banished by Queen Mary—but in 1565 she summoned him back to help fight her rebellious half brother.

4. Margaret Tudor, sister of Henry VIII, was married twice. Her first husband was James IV of Scotland, grandfather of Mary Queen of Scots. Her second husband was Archibald earl of Angus, grandfather of Lord Darnley.

Mary's personal secretary. Darnley and his allies falsely accused him of being a papal spy. It was he, they said, who had convinced the king to restore Catholicism. Further, they charged that he had committed adultery with the queen.

Three days before parliament was due to meet, Darnley led several lords and a band of assassins up a secret staircase and into Mary's private chambers at Holyrood. They dragged Rizzio away from a game of cards with the queen and several horrified guests and stabbed him to death in a hallway outside the room. This savage murder derailed the rest of the plot. Mary confronted Darnley, who betrayed his fellow plotters. She pardoned the lesser participants, declared the ringleaders traitors, and stripped them of their estates—sending them into exile in England. Mary forgave Moray and the others who had rebelled against her marriage and welcomed them back. Amazingly, she had taken control of events, although Darnley remained at large—a perpetual and brooding menace.

But he had served his purpose as a husband. Mary was pregnant. Her son, Prince James, was born June 19, 1566. The guns of Edinburgh Castle were fired as a salute. Commoners lit bonfires all over the town and its outskirts. Mary was ecstatic, though her joy was not universal. Elizabeth, it was said, pouted when

Darnley restrains his horrified wife while his co-conspirators stab to death her Italian private secretary, David Rizzio. Supervising the murder, in this 1833 painting by Sir William Allan (now in the National Gallery of Scotland), is James Douglas, the earl of Morton, the man in the black hat at right. Rizzio's assassination was part of a badly bungled plot to confirm Darnley as king. In the ongoing chaos of Scottish affairs, the unfortunate Italian would be amply avenged.

she received word. And fatherhood brought no happiness to Darnley. He was not present for the birth of his son, and his occasional visits invariably ended in heated, acrimonious, and public disputes with Mary. The lords were appalled, and Darnley soon caused them outright alarm. He decided to separate formally from Mary and live abroad where—the nobles imagined—he could plot against them and the queen at will. That autumn a good number of the lords decided that Darnley had to be removed, meaning assassinated.

Around two in the morning of February 10, 1567, the deed was done. The conspirators packed the cellar of his temporary lodging at Edinburgh with gunpowder, and in the dead of night an enormous explosion reduced the building to rubble and shook much of the city. Oddly, however, his body and that of an aide were found in a garden forty feet from the house. Neither man had a mark on him. Historians have never determined exactly what happened but speculate that Darnley was aroused by noises inside the house, glanced out his windows, saw men in the yard and sensed danger. He lowered himself by a rope and made a run for it but was captured, uttered his last words—"O my kinsmen, have mercy on me, for the love of him who had mercy on the world"—and then was smothered.

For all the trouble Lord Darnley caused Queen Mary, he did serve one purpose. He sired a son, James, shown here with the delighted queen. Although the birth of Prince James in June 1566 occasioned jubilant salutes by the guns of Edinburgh Castle and celebratory bonfires by commoners, he would soon lose his feckless father to assassination and would scarcely know his mother. But James was destined nonetheless to rule both Scotland and England.

News of the crime—for this was regicide, and there was no graver offense in sixteenth-century Europe—caused shock in every court of Europe. Mary had to punish those responsible harshly and quickly to save her reputation. But that was plainly impossible. At least half her privy council was involved in the plot or knew of it, and the council was responsible for the administration of justice. She could trust no one, so she resorted to a huge gamble.

She embraced Bothwell as her protector and surrendered her authority to him. Historians have speculated that Mary was exhausted by the endless plotting and obsessive factionalism of the nobles and had lost the will to govern. In any case, the egotistical and wildly ambitious Bothwell was the worst possible choice. He began to wield authority as though he were king. He alienated his fellow nobles, and thirty of them banded together, calling themselves the Confederate Lords.

Then in late April events took a truly bewildering turn. Bothwell's men abducted the queen while she rode from Stirling to Edinburgh and delivered her to his castle at Dunbar, where he raped her. Afterward, she stayed several days, continued to sleep with him, and agreed to marry the already married earl. He obtained a quick divorce from a Protestant court on the grounds of adultery with his wife's maid and on May 15—three months and five days after Darnley's murder—Mary and Bothwell exchanged wedding vows at Holyrood.

At that, Mary became a regal pariah. Her subjects turned decisively against her. Her Guise relatives disowned her, and royal houses throughout Europe were scandalized. The Confederate Lords were assembling their forces, and civil war loomed. The final showdown occurred June 15, a hot Sunday, at an elevated ridge known as Carberry Hill, near the town of Inveresk. Mary and Bothwell and their army of about three thousand occupied the heights of the hill. The Confederate Lords had assembled a force of equal strength. Neither side dared a charge. The French ambassador tried to mediate, but there was no basis for compromise. Finally, the sides decided to settle the matter one on one—Bothwell against anyone the lords put forward.

Mary forbade the fight and agreed to surrender, provided Bothwell was allowed to escape. He rode off, and she returned to Edinburgh—pregnant and a prisoner of her nobles. The lords then decided among themselves that they would rule Scotland until Prince James was old enough to occupy the throne. A few days later, under cover of darkness, they moved Mary to Lochleven, the lonely fortress of the Douglas family that stood on an island in the middle of a lake a safe distance from Edinburgh.

Elizabeth was outraged. She wanted Mary released and restored to the throne, and was prepared to go to war over the issue. But Cecil worked behind the scenes with the Scottish nobles to ensure that Mary stayed where she was, and the nobles made certain that Mary did not get wind of Elizabeth's support. Instead, they sent a delegation to Lochleven on July 24, 1567, with three documents in hand: one stating that she was incapable of governing and was abdicating, a second appointing Moray regent until her son reached adulthood, and a third naming Morton interim regent until Moray returned from voluntary exile in France. Mary had recently miscarried. She was in a weak and depressed state but stood up to the lords and refused to sign until one threatened to deposit her on an island in the sea and another threatened to slit her throat. Only then did she take up the pen and affix her name to the documents. Five days later, the lords crowned thirteen-month-old James at the parish church in Stirling, and on August 22 Moray became regent.

Mary, weak and depressed, stood up to the lords, refusing to sign the abdication documents—until one lord threatened to leave her on an island and another vowed to slit her throat.

But Mary was far from finished. She escaped from Lochleven on May 2, 1568, a Sunday, assisted by a son of the laird and a page. A number of lords rallied to her cause. She established a temporary court and within a week had assembled an army of six thousand. Her nobles advised her to march on Moray and the Confederate forces, and the two sides met May 13 at Langside, just outside Glasgow. Mary commanded about one-third more men, but Moray and his allies triumphed in a battle that lasted just forty-five minutes. Mary dreaded her vengeful half brother and frantically fled south, riding nonstop in stretches of up to sixty miles.

She reached Workington, in the northwest of England on May 15 and hoped Elizabeth would send her back to Scotland with enough troops to recover her throne. But she had not reckoned on Cecil's influence. He wanted her executed and convinced Elizabeth to convene a quasi-judicial tribunal to examine the allegations that Mary

Having become a royal pariah by marrying the egomaniacal earl of Bothwell, Mary surrendered to the Confederate Lords and was locked away in a lonely fortress on the island of Lochleven. But when her hated half brother, the earl of Moray, was made her jailer, she contrived an escape, depicted here in a nineteenth-century lithograph, and managed to fight one more doomed battle against him.

was an adulteress and a participant in Darnley's murder.[5] The Confederate Lords were only too happy to help. Moray formally charged her with murder, and he and his allies supplied incriminating documents, including letters allegedly in Mary's own hand. But Cecil had overreached. The tribunal was so one-sided and unfair that Elizabeth shut it down in early 1569 without awaiting a decision.

For the next eighteen years, Mary remained under house arrest, and for most of that time her life was uneventful. Her guardian for all but the final three years

George Talbot Earl of Shrewsbury

was Earl George Talbot of Shrewsbury. He ensured that she was watched closely, intercepted her mail, and controlled the flow of guests. She was moved from estate to estate. Her health declined to the point where she could not walk unassisted, and she might have withered away and died quietly were it not for Europe's religious wars, which crescendoed violently in the early 1580s.

This changed everything. England was at risk of invasion. Elizabeth was in personal danger, and British Protestants saw Mary as a major threat to national security. Their fears were confirmed when Philip II of Spain conceived a wild scheme in the summer of 1581 to assassinate Elizabeth, liberate Mary, and unleash a Catholic uprising. Cecil could find no evidence that Mary was involved, but he was now more determined than ever to be rid of her.

He sent an emissary to France to arouse support for her execution among enemies of the Guise family. He asked the Scottish lords if they would be willing to take her back, put her on trial, and put her to death. He wanted her watched more closely than ever before, and he had just the man for the job—Elizabeth's principal secretary, Sir Francis Walsingham, a fervid Protestant and a master at gathering intelligence. Walsingham planted spies in Mary's household, read her mail, and

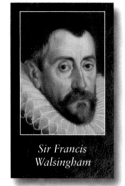

Sir Francis Walsingham

recruited a mole in the French embassy to report any communication between her and the embassy.

Meanwhile, Mary endured a terribly painful personal blow. Her son, James, turned on her. At age sixteen he declared that he had reached the age of majority and would rule Scotland. Elizabeth recognized him as James VI of Scotland and hinted that he might be an appropriate successor following her own death. James, in turn, informed Mary that he would recognize her as queen mother if she wished to return to Scotland, but they would never exercise sovereignty jointly.

At that, the isolated and irrelevant queen of Scots made a final, desperate attempt to reverse her fortunes. A Spanish diplomat who had been expelled from England recruited a zealous young English Catholic, Anthony Babington, to assassinate Elizabeth. They envisioned a revolt by England's Catholics, a Spanish invasion, and the liberation and triumphant coronation of Mary as queen of England. In early July 1586, Babington wrote to Mary and laid out the essentials of the plot. She wrote back consenting to Elizabeth's murder and the Spanish invasion.

Walsingham intercepted and copied the correspondence. Babington was arrested and immediately confessed. On August 11, Mary was arrested and sent to

5. Whether Mary was an accomplice in or even knew of the plot to murder her husband has been examined by historians for centuries, and most have found her innocent. Two clues point to her guilt, both merely circumstantial. For one, prior to his murder she persuaded her husband to return to Edinburgh from his parents' stronghold at Glasgow, where he was being treated for the symptoms of syphilis. This placed him where the assassins could easily get to him. For another, she had exonerated those banished for the Rizzio murder whom Darnley had betrayed, all of whom would be keen on vengeance. These two facts, however, are not considered sufficient to conclude her complicity in his murder.

6. Elizabeth's warrant was signed in a complicated way (torn up, signed again, hidden, etc.) so that she could claim innocence and avoid diplomatic difficulties.

Fotheringhay Castle, seventy-five miles north of London, for her trial. A panel of twenty-four nobles and a number of privy councillors convicted her of treason on October 25 and sentenced her to death. Elizabeth signed a warrant on February 1, 1587, authorizing Mary's execution.[6]

Shortly after 8 a.m. on Wednesday, February 8, when it was bright enough to extinguish the candles at Fotheringhay, Mary descended a grand staircase to the great hall. She was forty-four years old, her shoulders rounded and stooped and her face full. She wore a floor-length black satin gown trimmed with gold embroidery and sable, a thin white linen veil, and a small white cap of the same material. In one hand she carried an ivory crucifix and in the other a Latin prayer book. Before making her entrance, Mary said her farewells to her gently sobbing servants and attendants and told her steward, Andrew Melville: "Tell my friends that I die a true woman to my religion and like a true Scottish woman and a true French woman."

Then she walked, erect and composed, to a raised wooden stage that measured twelve feet square and was beside a blazing fireplace. Three sides of the scaffold were shrouded in black cotton cloth, and the fourth was open, and Mary sat on a low stool facing the open side and the spectators—about one hundred knights, gentlemen, and soldiers. The execution block, also swathed in black, lay in front of her, and the executioners—hooded and wearing black gowns and white aprons—stood to the side.

Two earls, Shrewsbury and Kent, stood to Mary's right and the local sheriff to her left. The clerk of the privy council read the death warrant, and Dr. Richard Fletcher, one of Elizabeth's favorite preachers, attempted to deliver a sermon admonishing Mary for her sins. "I will not hear you," she snapped. "You have nothing to do with me, nor I with you."

Mary of Scotland stands trial in Fotheringhay Castle, Northhamptonshire (lower illustration), on accusations of plotting to assassinate Queen Elizabeth I. Above, in another nineteenth-century engraving, the alleged target of the plot seems to confront with reluctance the necessity of signing her rival's death warrant. Elizabeth's principal adviser, William Cecil, urges her on. Both artists are unknown.

Mary and the preacher became embroiled in a heated exchange, which ended when Shrewsbury told Fletcher to forgo the sermon. The preacher then began to pray, but Mary lifted her crucifix and tried to override Fletcher with prayers of her own. The spectators joined Fletcher, and Mary's servant prayed with her, each side trying to drown out the other.

The prayers concluded, Mary stood. Her weeping gentlewomen removed her outer garments, revealing to the shocked onlookers a petticoat of deep red—the Catholic Church's liturgical color of martyrdom. She knelt, laid her blindfolded face on the block, and cried out three times in Latin: "Into your hands, O Lord, I commend my spirit."

The executioner brought down the ax but missed her neck and sliced into the back of her head. The second blow found its mark but failed to sever the head completely, and the executioner had to slice through the remaining tendon. He then grasped Mary's lustrous hair and raised her head high, but the hair was a wig, and

The execution of the queen of Scots was a sordid affair, as the Protestant minister drowned out her final Catholic prayers and the executioner botched the beheading. But she preserved decency and dignity to the end, and her fateful life continues to draw interest today. Inset, an art auctioneer closely examines her death mask.

her head fell to the floor and rolled toward the stunned spectators. "So perish the queen's enemies," Fletcher bellowed, and this sordid drama was over.

Mary was buried in the yard of a local cathedral, but after her son ascended the throne of England, he had her body exhumed and re-interred in a luxurious marble casket at Westminster Abbey. Cecil, her mortal enemy, died in 1598, a few days before his seventy-eighth birthday. He was wealthy and content. Shakespeare modeled a character after him, and Elizabeth sat at his bedside and fed him with a spoon during his final illness. Elizabeth died in the early morning hours of March 24, 1603, the first English monarch to live until her seventieth birthday.

Mary's Scottish nobles met less pleasant ends. Moray was assassinated in 1570, at age forty, while riding through the streets of Linlithgow. Maitland married Queen Mary's senior lady-in-waiting, took part in a rebellion on Mary's behalf while she was imprisoned in England, was taken prisoner when the rebellion failed, and died or committed suicide in prison. Bothwell fled Scotland after Mary's surrender and sought refuge in Denmark, where he became a state prisoner and died in 1578, likely of cirrhosis of the liver, at Dragsholm Castle, a lonely fortress overlooking the sea. On orders of Mary's son, James VI, when he came of age, Morton was arrested and convicted for his role in the murder of Darnley, the king's father, and was executed in 1581.

Knox was more fortunate. Now a widower, he shocked many of his followers by marrying a sixteen-year-old girl when he was fifty. They had two daughters, and he spent his final years with his wife. He suffered a devastating stroke and died in 1572, at about age fifty-eight. He was buried in the churchyard at St. Giles, Edinburgh.

History has been kinder to Knox than to Mary. Though it's doubtful he fully realized it at the time, he had founded in Scotland a great church, and Presbyterians around the world have named their churches in honor of him. There are no churches named for Mary Queen of Scots, and Rome never proclaimed her a martyr. But her life and career have been studied and debated for four centuries, and though her claim to the throne of England was never recognized in her lifetime, all British monarchs after Elizabeth are descended from her son, James, and therefore also from Mary Queen of Scots. ■

The statue of John Knox by sculptor James P. MacGillivray, which has stood outside St. Giles' Cathedral, Edinburgh, since 1904, is only one of the many remembrances of this remarkable man. Most notable, of course, are the Knox Presbyterian churches scattered the world over. As for his adversary, Queen Mary has no churches named for her—but every British monarch since Elizabeth I is descended from her.

If Ignatius of Loyola, seen here in a commemorative bronze statue on the campus of Boston College, thought his years as a dashing soldier were thrilling, they would pale beside the life into which his commitment to Christ would lead him. Starting with nine fellow pilgrims in what would become the Society of Jesus, he would ultimately attract thousands of disciples—and a great many enemies—and be responsible for launching unique schools and missions around the entire globe.

CHAPTER 8

The shot that changed the man who turned the tide of reformation

Gravely wounded, the born-again Ignatius of Loyola founds an order whose weapons are schools, not guns, and whose conflicts and valor will endure for centuries

I t was "an evil day for newborn Protestantism," writes the nineteenth-century American historian Francis Parkman, "when a French artilleryman fired the shot that struck down Ignatius Loyola in the breach of the walls of Pamplona." In Loyola's long recovery from botched surgery for his smashed leg, says Parkman, "the soldier gave himself to a new warfare. In the forge of his great intellect, heated but not disturbed by the intense fires of his zeal, was wrought the prodigious enginery whose power has been felt to the uttermost confines of the world."

Thus does the man whom many regard as the greatest American writer of history introduce the Jesuits, the Society of Jesus, founded by the ex-soldier, ex-roustabout, and ex-playboy Ignatius of Loyola, a subject Parkman entered upon with undisguised distaste. Skeptical of all religions and particularly Roman Catholicism, he loathed what the Jesuits were trying to do. But he was too deeply swayed by the undeniable heroism of the Jesuit missionaries in North America to suppress his near veneration for how they went about doing it.

Unlike many others, Parkman was of two minds about the Jesuits. Far more have been of one mind. The devout seventeenth-century mathematician and Catholic philosopher Blaise Pascal saw them as "stripped of charity," observing pagan morality, always believing that their lofty goals could justify any means whatever of achieving them (the last a charge the Jesuits vehemently deny). Otto von Bismarck, the nineteenth-century unifier of Germany, said he had indisputable evidence they started the Franco-Prussian War, though he never did produce it.

The American historian David J. Mitchell catalogs criticisms of the Jesuits over the centuries in his *The Jesuits: A History* (1980). In the sixteenth century they were accused of plotting the assassination of William of Orange, Henry III and Henry IV of France, and Elizabeth I of England. In the seventeenth century, they were blamed for authoring a plot to blow up the English parliament. In the eighteenth, the order was dissolved by Pope Clement XIV for conspiring against the papacy. Provided a refuge in Russia, they were back in business in the nineteenth, when the poet Thomas Carlyle described at length their "fanaticism" and the socialist essayist and novelist Charles Kingsley described them as "the Upas-shadow that has blighted the whole Romish church." Could all these crimes and conspiracies be historically well grounded?

Felled by a cannonball that would change the course of history, an infuriated and incapacitated Ignatius of Loyola grips his sword for the last time. Later on, slowly recuperating after botched surgery on his leg, Loyola read spiritual classics, the only books available to him, first among them the New Testament, and vowed to become a soldier of Christ, dedicated not to military glory but to the glory of God.

The answer is no, since all were brought against them by undoubted enemies, jealous and/or fearful of their equally undoubted success. What is not in doubt, however, is the fact they have been embroiled in controversy within and without the church since their formation and they usually appear to thrive on it.

Most instructive, perhaps, is the English adjective derived from their name, "jesuitical." For it, *Roget's International Thesaurus* suggests as synonyms insincere, mealy-mouthed, disingenuous, empty, hollow, and sophistical. A German thesaurus adds two-faced, false, insidious, perfidious, mendacious, dissembling, and sanctimonious.

The order has also attracted some improbable admirers, adds Mitchell, some grudging like the twentieth-century arch-skeptic of religion Aldous Huxley. While deploring them as "mass producers of spirituality," he nonetheless commends their defeating the puritanical Jansenist movement in the Catholic Church. Huxley's co-irreligionist H. G. Wells goes much further. He lauds the society's "attempt to bring the generous and chivalrous traditions of military discipline into the service of religion." The Jesuit order, he writes, "became one of the greatest teaching and missionary societies the world has ever seen. It raised the standard of education throughout the Catholic world and quickened the Catholic conscience everywhere, and it stimulated Protestant Europe to competitive educational efforts."

Whatever their virtues or faults, the Jesuits are either credited or denounced by both Catholics and Protestants for checking and then reversing the whole Protestant Reformation in Europe. "Fifty years after the Lutheran separation," writes the historian Lord Thomas Babington Macaulay, "Catholicism could scarcely maintain itself on the shores of the Mediterranean. A hundred years after the separation, Protestantism could scarcely maintain itself on the shores of the Baltic." Both statements are Macaulay exaggerations, but his tribute to the Jesuit overseas missions is not: "They were to be found in the depths of the Peruvian mines, at the markets of the African slave-caravans, on the shores of the Spice Islands, in the observatories of China. They made converts in regions which neither avarice nor curiosity had tempted any of their countrymen to enter, and preached and disputed in tongues of which no other native of the West understood a word."

All of which was envisioned and made to happen through the mind of the

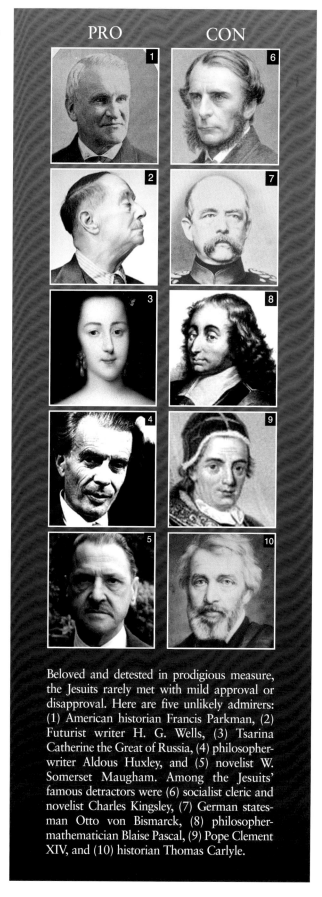

PRO   CON

Beloved and detested in prodigious measure, the Jesuits rarely met with mild approval or disapproval. Here are five unlikely admirers: (1) American historian Francis Parkman, (2) Futurist writer H. G. Wells, (3) Tsarina Catherine the Great of Russia, (4) philosopher-writer Aldous Huxley, and (5) novelist W. Somerset Maugham. Among the Jesuits' famous detractors were (6) socialist cleric and novelist Charles Kingsley, (7) German statesman Otto von Bismarck, (8) philosopher-mathematician Blaise Pascal, (9) Pope Clement XIV, and (10) historian Thomas Carlyle.

man hit by the cannonball at Pamplona. Ignatius of Loyola was a Basque, a people renowned as soldiers, sailors, and good administrators but also as brawlers and ruffians. Ignatius was an adopted name. He was born Iñigo Lopez de Oñaz y Loyola near the town of Azpeitia in the Spanish province of Guipúzcoa, the last of thirteen children of one of the twenty or more families that composed the Basque landed gentry. The probable year was 1491. His mother died when he was about seven and his father when he was sixteen. He was raised by his cousins, latterly by the duke of Nájera, assigned by the Spanish crown to rule in Navarre, where Spaniards were hated. So from his teens, Iñigo went about armed, shaping himself on the model of the Spanish nobility, careful of his dress, his honor, his courtly appeal to women, and his Catholic faith. But he was also given to womanizing and fighting, and in the Mardi Gras of 1515 he was brought up on charges of assault causing bodily harm, statutory rape, and slander. A court record describes him as "treacherous, brutal, and vindictive." He only narrowly escaped a jail term.

Loyola as an armored soldier, in a seventeenth-century French oil on canvas (above). A man of well-publicized vices, he also displayed undeniable courage and a curious sense of honor. It was at the defense of the little Spanish citadel at Pamplona (below) that his life radically changed.

When he joined the duke's army, other qualities appeared. He never blasphemed, he never hated, and when a town was given over to sack, he refused to take part. When the French attacked the little Spanish citadel at Pamplona, the hopelessly outnumbered defenders agreed to surrender. Iñigo would have none of this; he stood steadily in a breach in the walls, awaiting the attack. He was carried from the field bleeding, near death, by his admiring enemies. The initial surgery was botched. He was sent home and spent two years recovering.

In those two years everything began to change. He took to reading, and the only books available in the family castle at Loyola were on the lives of saints, a life of Christ, and the New Testament, probably left by his pious mother. He read them all, but his mind fixed on the Gospels. He underlined the words of Jesus in red and of Mary in blue. He made notes of his own reflections, and eventually these filled three hundred pages. Gradually, he acquired a new aspiration. He must become a soldier of Christ, dedicated not to military glory but to the glory of God. His brother, who wanted him back in the army, was appalled.

Loyola had been given to womanizing and fighting, and in 1515 was brought up on charges of assault, statutory rape and slander, but he hated no one and refused to help sack a town.

There was a great deal to be appalled about. Instead of wanting to serve Christ in the New World, the challenge embraced by many young Spaniards, he felt the four-hundred-year-old calling of the crusaders. He wanted to go to Jerusalem, not to kill but to convert the Muslims to Christ. He also took a vow of chastity, giving up marriage and family to instead help the poor and the wretched. To do this, he became poor and wretched himself, gave away his fine clothing to an astonished tramp, had a tailor make him a full-length garment of sackcloth, and bought a staff, a small gourd, and a pair of sandals. With these and with no money whatever, he set out on foot for Barcelona on the Mediterranean coast en route to Jerusalem.

Years later as he neared death, he saw much of this as a kind of grandstanding for God. He had a great deal to learn, he recalled, about the Christian life, and when he stopped outside the town of Manresa in the Cardener Valley, he began learning it. Beset now with the idea that everything he had so far done was foolish, he gazed down at the river. "There the eyes of my conscience began to open. It was not a vision that was granted me, but rather an understanding of many things—of the mind, of faith, of human knowledge." From these reflections he began composing what came to be called the Spiritual Exercises. They would become the inaugural formula of prayer, meditation, and confession to be undergone by every man aspiring to enter the Jesuit order.

Begging, barefoot, and penniless, he continued on, from Manresa to Barcelona, to Rome, to Venice, to Cyprus, and finally to Jerusalem. There, he walked where Christ had walked, lived where Christ had lived, and decided to remain for the rest of his life. But the Franciscans, official church guardians of the holy places, required him to leave the city, threatening to excommunicate him if he refused. Convinced that God must have some other plan for him, he returned to Barcelona.[1] By that time he had dropped the name Iñigo and adopted the name of the first-century martyr Ignatius of Antioch.

By now also, he had made two discoveries. First, he was academically ignorant. To serve God more effectively, he must acquire learning. Still supporting

1. Jesuit tradition preserves numerous stories of Loyola's journey to and from Jerusalem. At one point, attempting to win a Muslim to the Christian faith, he becomes embroiled in a ferocious argument. The next day, riding a mule someone loaned him, he decides he should seek the man out and kill him. Then he realizes this is hardly what Jesus would have done. So he lets the mule decide. If the animal turns back, he will take this to mean he is to fight. If it continues on its way, he will pray for the man's soul instead. The mule continues on, thereby deciding what would become for all time the Jesuit policy toward Islam. In another story, to cross the Adriatic some wealthy friends find passage for him on a fine, sturdy vessel. But the captain, discovering Loyola can't pay the fare, orders him ashore. He gets free passage on a much smaller, frail vessel that barely survives fierce storms in the crossing. Meanwhile, the bigger ship founders, and all aboard are lost.

2. The Society of Jesus is often portrayed as established to check the Protestant Reformation, something they have consistently denied. This, they say, was the function of the Inquisition, which was steadfastly suspicious of them. Though they in fact did reverse the Protestant Reformation in Germany, Poland, and Austria, they have always maintained that this was a coincidental byproduct of their real work, which was to spread the gospel through education and Christian witness. It's significant that in all the nine thousand letters, treatises, and notes left by Loyola, the name Luther appears only once.

himself by begging, he registered in an elementary school along with children. But he also found that he had an unusual skill in attracting young men and women to the Christian gospel, and when he moved on to audit classes at the University of Alcalá near Madrid, he captured the interest of a circle of young men, who began living in poverty as he did.

They, in turn, captured the interest of the Inquisition, who jailed Ignatius for forty-four days while they exhaustively questioned his theology. They concluded that he was not heretical but forbade him to teach since he was academically unqualified. This was the first of ten encounters he would have with the Inquisition, and in every instance he would be acquitted. Officialdom nonetheless preserved a suspicion that he must be some kind of closet Protestant. To escape such attention, he moved to the University of Salamanca, where he was arrested again, this time while his recorded meditations on the spiritual life were examined. Again the verdict was "favorable, to a degree."[2] Fed up with such harassment, he set out for Paris alone and on foot, his companions of Alcalá having decided to stay behind.

It was at Paris that he found and recruited the men destined to establish the Jesuit order. He registered at Montaigu College, from whose spartan, chilly, dawn-to-late-night regimen John Calvin had recently graduated. Ignatius found it all but impossible to beg enough bread to live on but took up residence with two men who were soon captivated by his person. They were Peter Faber, who would lay the foundations for the astonishing Jesuit mission to Germany, and Francis Xavier, who would lead the Christian mission to Japan, China, and the Far East, in the process circumventing Islam. Seven others would join this core group at Paris.[3]

What undoubtedly swayed them was the conduct of Ignatius himself. He lived in abject poverty. When a fellow student robbed him of money lent him to pay his tuition, he ignored the theft and later walked nearly eighty miles, barefoot and fasting, to minister to the man when he became ill. When he persuaded two wealthy men to meet Christ's challenge to the rich young ruler (Matt. 19:21–22; Mark 10:20; Luke 18:22–23), selling all their belongings and giving the money to the poor, it caused such an uproar in the university that the two were paraded before the university's officialdom and ordered to go back to a conventional life.

An 1881 painting by Konrad Baumeister depicts Ignatius of Loyola (kneeling at front) and his first disciples at a Mass celebrated by Peter Faber (standing), then their only ordained member, at a small Paris chapel. In August 1534 these first Jesuits committed themselves to poverty and chastity, and vowed to make a pilgrimage to Jerusalem—or, if the latter proved impossible, to do whatever the pope commanded.

Finally on a summer day seven men—all but Loyola under twenty-six years old—trekked to Montmartre in Paris and there made three vows that bound them together: they would live a celibate life, they would live in poverty, and they would make a pilgrimage to Jerusalem. But there was a caveat. If they failed to reach Jerusalem within a year, they would place themselves at the disposal of the pope. It was this last proviso that would shape their history and that of much of the world. The date was August 15, 1534. It may be taken to mark the founding of the Jesuit order.

However, they did not yet have the status of an order; they were simply a group. They assembled first in Venice, where they volunteered for the lowest and most repulsive jobs in the hospitals, and Ignatius was once again hauled before the Inquisition, this time on the complaint of Cardinal Giovanni Pietro Carafa, who as Pope Paul IV would become a fierce opponent of the Jesuits. Again the accusations were rejected. They then decided to approach Pope Paul III, seeking permission for their Jerusalem venture and also recognition for their order. Ignatius, fearing his presence would arouse Carafa to opposition, remained at Venice.

Pope Paul obliged them in both their requests, even finding the funding for their passage to Jerusalem. But he was not enthusiastic for it. They were far more needed in Italy than in Palestine, he said, and fate or the hand of God intervened on his behalf. War having broken out anew between Venice and the Turks, all sailings to the Holy Land were canceled.

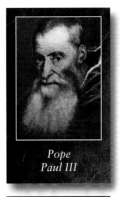

Pope
Paul III

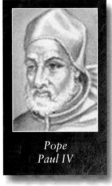

Pope
Paul IV

3. The other founding Jesuits were Diego Lainez, who would succeed Loyola as general of the order, Alfonzo Salmerón, Simon Rodriguez, Nicolàs Bobadilla, Claude Jay, Paschase Broët, and Jean Codure. The latter three were not present for the vows made on August 15, 1534, at Montmartre. Only Xavier would serve outside Europe (see subchapter, p. 172).

On August 15, 1534, in a crypt on Montmartre, the seven young men vowed to live a celibate life, to live in poverty, and to make pilgrimage to Jerusalem. Thus were the Jesuits born.

Moreover, he also approved the constitution for what they proposed to call the Society of Jesus, and that constitution put them at the disposal of himself as pope. It was markedly different from those of the monkish and mendicant orders. They need wear no uniform but could dress as the people to whom they ministered. More shocking still, they had no obligation to say the appointed prayers together "in choir." They could say them alone or apart. They were to be "in the world" as was no other order. But they were not to be "of the world." The stern discipline of the Spiritual Exercises would attend to that. To their earlier vows of poverty and chastity they now added the vow of obedience both to the pope and to the general of their order. They were also limited to sixty members. By now they already numbered twenty, and scores of young men were becoming interested in them.

Their legal birth in September 1540 was attended by controversy. The Dominicans, Franciscans, and Theatines objected to the special status conferred upon them. Many objected to the name. Wasn't the whole church a "society of Jesus"?[4] The society's first order of business was the election of a superior general. That it should be Loyola was obvious to all the members but Loyola. He twice turned it down and was finally persuaded by his confessor that he must accept it.

Thus Loyola set himself up in an office at Rome, and there he worked for the rest of his life, sending his men out to those parts of Europe where their preaching

4. The name Society of Jesus continued to raise ire for years. In 1590, fifty years after the society was founded, Pope Sixtus V decided to change the name to the Ignatine order so that just as the Franciscans were named for their founder Francis and the Dominicans for their founder Dominic, so the Jesuits would be named for their founder Ignatius. The general of the order, who as a Jesuit was under oath to obey the pope, stalled as long as he could, then finally asked that a nine-day cycle of prayer (known as a novena from the Latin word for nine) be held so that the members could receive the grace needed to resignedly accept the change. The novena proceeded, and on the ninth day Pope Sixtus died, with the change not yet legally authorized. Sixtus's successor canceled it.

Ignatius of Loyola (in black) presents himself before Pope Julius III, as portrayed by eighteenth-century artist Giovanni Battista Mariotti. When war prevented their mission to Jerusalem, Loyola set up an office in Rome and spent the rest of his life dispatching his followers throughout Europe and the world, wherever their preaching and teaching would have the best effect. On the occasion depicted above, Pope Julius confirms the Jesuit mandate in 1550.

and teaching would be most effective. Preaching the gospel, he knew, must be a key activity, but the Jesuit approach to it soon became distinguished. They were encouraged to carefully study the concerns and interests of their audience. Among workmen they should become as workmen, among peasants as peasants, among scholars as scholars. From that day to this, they excelled as military chaplains because among soldiers they could become as soldiers.

Their preaching, along with the controversies that seemed constantly to embroil them, brought them wide attention and drew young men into their ranks in a deluge. The sixty-member limit was soon abolished, and when Loyola died sixteen years after the order was founded, there were a thousand Jesuits in one hundred houses throughout Western Europe, Latin America, and Asia. A century after their founding, there were thirty-five Jesuit provinces, five hundred Jesuit colleges, and forty-nine Jesuit seminaries. A century later the membership of the order stood at twenty-two thousand.

The key to this success lay in their novitiate. From the order's beginnings, the training of a Jesuit—in terms of hours of work, disciplined study, and psychological stress demanding intense prayer, meditation, and self-examination—far exceeded that of the toughest military schools or the Christian military orders. Jesuit novices were required to do the most revolting chores in hospitals, to take to the streets as beggars, and of course to submit themselves to Loyola's Spiritual Exercises, the requirement that had drawn all of the order's founders to him.

Drawn from many late medieval spiritual writings, the Exercises were divided by Loyola into four weeklong periods in which the Christian systematically contemplates his own sin, life, mental tendencies, habits, and flaws, redirecting himself under the guidance of a confessor toward the light of Christ and the habit of frequent fasting and perpetual prayer. The Exercises are not, however, some kind of spiritual gymnastic but aim at a genuine personal experience of God and a clear comprehension of heaven and hell, salvation and damnation. The modern reader will find they read nothing like a self-help book. "They are as unemotional as a treatise on geometry," observes one Jesuit.

The Exercises have been savagely attacked and fiercely defended ever since they were made public, something Loyola avoided doing until long after the order was founded. Historian Mitchell estimates that four hundred commentaries have been written on them and recounts how the Dominicans said they presented "a coercive, parade ground attitude to prayer." French intellectuals of the nineteenth century scoffed that they sought "to create ecstatic automata in thirty days," while the American William James, sometimes called the father of modern psychology, described them as intended to create "monoideistic hysteria." But to the twentieth-century English playwright and novelist W. Somerset Maugham they constitute "the most wonderful method that has ever been devised to gain control over that unstable and willful thing, the soul of man."

Curiously Loyola, known for the harsh disciplines he inflicted on himself, followed medieval monastic practice and warned his followers against them. For instance, fasting was essential, but it should never be so dire as to affect health. Scourging[5] was perhaps necessary but not to the point where it caused injury. He should have known. His own health was gravely damaged by his self-inflicted penances. But he was much sterner on the Jesuit pledge of obedience. "The true and genuine sons of this society," he wrote, "should be recognized by this characteristic, that they never regard the individual himself as the one whom they obey, but in him Christ our Lord for whose sake they are offering obedience."

From the start, Pope Paul III exercised his authority over them. In effect, writes historian Mitchell, he reached an understanding with Loyola. "The bargain resembled a 'no prey, no pay' buccaneering commission, and the Jesuits were expected to show quick results." That is, the pope would assign them to the role Loyola envisioned for them, provided they brought about the changes in the church that they themselves considered necessary. In the ensuing years, therefore, he deployed Jesuits to those areas where Catholicism had suffered the greatest reversals and expected them to repair the damage.

At left, an engraving from 1621 by Lucas von Vorsterman shows Loyola at prayer, the cornerstone and foundation of his Spiritual Exercises (cover inset below). First composed before 1541, the Exercises were a required part of daily life for every Jesuit, intended to bring about a genuine personal experience of God.

5. The "mortification of the flesh," or self-scourging with a whip of small cords to bring the body into submission during prayer, was practiced by monks and devout laymen throughout much of the medieval era. It comes to most twenty-first century Christians as incomprehensible. But similarly, forcing oneself to run, jump, bend double, and swing from bars like a monkey, as in any modern "fitness" club, would have been equally incomprehensible to a medieval Christian. Yes, but that's to keep our bodies trim, the modern Christian would explain. Well, scourging was to keep our souls trim, the medieval Christian would reply.

No area had suffered more damage than Germany. By 1540, writes the German historian Manfred Barthel (*The Jesuits: History and Legend of the Society of Jesus*, 1982), "all the states of northwest Germany, and nine-tenths of the entire population had gone over to the reformed religion." The appearance of Luther's complete Bible in 1534 had transformed "a steady stream of Catholic defections into something more like a deluge." Even in ostensibly Catholic southern Germany, says one Jesuit report, bookstores were crowded with Luther's works, and Catholics were reading them. The few supposedly Catholic clergy were "half Lutheran" and "living in open concubinage." For Catholicism, Munich was a disaster area. Lutherans were running the only good schools, and Catholic parents were sending their children to them.

Alms and acts of charity alone would no longer restore the credibility of the church in Germany. Needed were men of boundless, self-sacrificing commitment to their ministry.

Loyola sent into Germany the former shepherd boy who had been one of his first two recruits back in Paris. Peter Faber as a Jesuit was notable for his non-combative approach. To persuade heretics back to the faith, he advised, "one must be solicitous, must bear them much charity and love them truly, excluding from his mind all thoughts which tend to cool his esteem for them. It is necessary to gain their goodwill, so that they may love us and keep a place for us in their hearts." Finally, "we should speak to them of things we have in common and avoid contentious argument."

Faber spent the last five years of his life on what became a Jesuit-commissioned reconnaissance of Germany, and his report on how to return the country to Catholicism faced harsh realities. He set forth three principles. First, stop blaming Luther for the disintegration of Catholicism in Germany. The real cause was the deplorable state of the Catholic clergy. Second, alms and occasional acts of charity were no longer enough to restore the credibility of the church. What was needed were men of boundless, lifelong self-sacrificing commitment to their

Peter
Faber

ministry. Third, due to the development of printing, practically every burgher and peasant family now had their own Bible in German. Anyone who tried to take it away from them would be regarded as an enemy not only of their religion but of Germany as well. Faber's three principles became the basis of the Jesuit campaign to recover the country.

But to achieve this end, he had done one thing more. In 1543 he brought into the Jesuit order its first Dutch member, a twenty-two-year-old theology student from Nijmegen named Peter Kanis, which in Jesuit parlance became Canisius. His rise through the Jesuit order was meteoric—a Jesuit observer at the Council of Trent at twenty-six, rector of the University of Ingolstadt at twenty-nine, and Jesuit provincial over all Germany at thirty-five. In Jesuit history Canisius is recognized as the man almost solely responsible for the

reestablishment of Catholicism in Germany, Austria, Bohemia, and Poland. But his task did not begin easily. Assigned with two other Jesuits to Ingolstadt University in 1549, the other two soon received permission to leave because they found the university hopelessly Lutheran. Canisius stayed on. When he left after nine years, he was given a great fanfare. By what became the usual Jesuit devices—education, almsgiving, preaching, and printing—Catholicism had become dominant at the university.

Canisius's master weapon was the phenomenon known to history as the "Jesuit school." The best way to change a society, Loyola gradually realized, was not by converting adults but by converting their children. The Society of Jesus, writes the Jesuit historian John W. O'Malley (*The First Jesuits*, 1993), was "the first religious order in the Catholic Church to take on formal education as a major ministry." By the end of the sixteenth century, three-quarters of the Jesuit houses were schools and four-fifths of their priests were teachers. (Most of the rest were missionaries in Asia and Latin America.) Unlike the Lutherans and Calvinists, notes Barthel, Loyola laid more emphasis on teaching than on preaching.

The Jesuit school emerged as a new and fascinating phenomenon. It came in four forms—what today would be called elementary schools, along with colleges, seminaries, and eventually whole universities. Its curriculum was a meld of scholasticism and humanism, but it wholly embraced neither, and religion was carefully worked into every subject. The classics were emphasized and taught to "engage the imagination" and thereby to aid in the understanding of scripture.

A nineteenth-century wood relief (above) shows Jesuit Peter Canisius teaching a class of children in Augsburg. Heralded for master-minding and almost singlehandedly reestablishing Catholicism in Germany, Austria, Bohemia, and Poland, Canisius began his mission at the thoroughly Lutheran University of Ingolstadt, where he succeeded in restoring Catholicism as the dominant religion.

The discipline was strict but not brutal.[6] Instruction was in Latin (as it remained in most Lutheran schools), and, most attractive of all, tuition was often free.

Canisius himself made a vital addition to the curriculum. He published what he called "A Summary of Christian Doctrine," in effect a catechism much as Luther had published for Protestantism. Canisius's came in three editions, each adapted to the ability of the reader. Though it was soon used widely throughout Europe, the Jesuits did not adopt it as a master text, but their schools were urged to develop catechisms suited to the people using them. However, the effect over time was to infuse Christian assumptions into the thought processes of Catholics all over Europe.

The success of the Jesuit schools almost worked their undoing. Although men were streaming into the order, sufficient Jesuit teachers could not be found to staff them. Lutheran parents began declaring themselves Catholic to get their children into them, and one Jesuit provincial said that he had requests for Jesuit schools from one hundred and fifty communities that he could not fill. The order soon came down: no more Jesuit schools. Moreover, many existing schools, inadequately staffed and their standards crumbling, had to be closed.

However, with the help of Canisius's longtime friend and onetime mentor, the Jesuit Jerome Nadal, the schools were salvaged and reformed, and by the century's end there were thirty-two Jesuit colleges in Germany, Austria, Christian Hungary, Bohemia, and Flanders, staffed by more than fifteen hundred Jesuit

Peter Canisius (above) achieved phenomenal success as a Catholic missionary in the heart of Lutheran territory due largely to his master weapon—the phenomenon known as the "Jesuit school"—which helped persuade Loyola that the best way to change a society is not through adults but by influencing their children.

Jerome Nadal

teachers, nearly all these institutions funded by Catholic merchants and noblemen. In addition, the Jesuits had gained control of the preexisting universities of Prague, Vienna, and Ingolstadt, while new Jesuit universities were established at Würzburg and Graz. Small wonder, then, that when Spain's Philip II called for a new military base in the Netherlands to oppose the rising Dutch Protestant revolt, his viceroy replied that something else would be more effective: a Jesuit college.

Canisius lived long for a Jesuit, dying in 1597 at age seventy-six. But by then he could consider his work done. Most of southern Germany as well as Austria, and Bohemia, and of Poland had returned to the Catholic fold and Canisius himself was being branded by Protestants as "a dog of a monk" (the Latin for dog, *canis*, being likened to his name), a blasphemer, a gross blockhead, an idolater, a wolf, a swindling trickster, and "the ass of the pope."[7] The Catholics provided another title for him. He was canonized by Pope Pius XI in 1926 as St. Peter Canisius.

The Jesuit performance in France was much less spectacular, chiefly because they early on encountered the determined opposition of the Catholic University of Paris. This clash came to center upon the Jesuit college at Clermont, about thirty miles north of Paris, which the Jesuits wanted declared a part of the university. The university wanted the college closed. Because, replied the Jesuits, their college is drawing too many students from the university. The resulting lawsuit simply validated the status quo.

The Jesuit ventures into both ecclesiastical and national politics came as an inevitable consequence of their work. They were intelligent and firmly dedicated

6. Loyola was adamantly against corporal punishment because he believed it would diminish the status and authority of the teacher who administered it and break the psychological bond between teacher and pupil. But his Jesuits soon discovered it was impossible to teach boys without it. So they began hiring lay teachers, who were not under the Jesuit rule of obedience, to do the spanking. This would constitute, in the eyes of the order's many critics, a typically "jesuitical" solution.

priests and very soon became the confessors first of nobles, then of kings. Indeed, in 1553 the king of Portugal asked two Jesuits to serve as his confessors; both refused. But Loyola himself ordered them to accept the position. A Jesuit became the close confidant of Grand Duke Ferdinand of Austria, and the Jesuits worked through the Polish court to thwart Protestant influence over the Poles. Others were active in the courts of Sweden and Denmark, working diligently, though unsuccessfully, to reverse their commitment to Lutheranism. At the Council of Trent three Jesuits acted as the eyes and ears of the popes, commissioned to thwart every effort of Charles V to compromise Catholic doctrine in order to persuade Lutherans back into the fold. All these functions soon ended the days of barefoot begging and poverty, as the society became an increasing presence in the courts of Catholic Europe.

An allegorical oil on canvas from the sixteenth century shows the ship of faith being propelled forward by the religious orders, headed by the Jesuits. They are represented by their founders: Francis of Assisi for the Franciscans, Bruno for the Carthusians, Dominic for the Dominicans, Basil for Eastern monasticism, Anthony for the monasticism of the desert, and Loyola for the Jesuits.

Typical young men drawn to the society came neither from the nobility nor from poor families. A survey made by the Jesuit administrator Nadal showed them mostly the sons of merchants or professional men. What called them forth were the convincing accounts from the Jesuit missions beyond the seas. These had been pioneered in Asia by Francis Xavier, one of Loyola's first companions in Paris, whose story is told in the following subchapter.

None of these early Jesuit missions was distinguished by immediate success, though they evidenced the raw courage and inexhaustible devotion of the men who conducted them. The Jesuit experience in Africa was a pointed example. It began in Morocco after the Jesuits were able to get two men into the Muslim base of Tétouan, where they discovered what happened to the Christian slaves taken by Muslim raiders in the Mediterranean. Life in Tétouan, says one account, had a "nightmare" quality:

> Gangs of Christian slaves loaded with chains, poor emaciated deformed creatures, half dead with hunger and ill treatment, were always to be seen in the crowded streets. From dawn to dark they sweated, turning millstones, drawing ploughs, or carrying heavy burdens. They seemed to be not men but walking corpses. At night they were herded into foul underground caves, so many to each that they could hardly move hand or foot. Those caves were a living image of hell.

Two Jesuits moved into the caves and for six years lived among the captives, smuggling food and medicine to them, cleaning the caves, preparing their meager dinner, administering the sacraments, hearing their confessions, reading the Gospel to them—"In the world you shall have tribulation, but be of good cheer: I have

7. After the death of Loyola in 1556, the Jesuits abandoned his policy of opposing Luther by never mentioning him, and began giving as good as they got. To Canisius, for instance, Luther was "a hog in heat." Diego Lainez, the order's second general, calls him "perverse." To Jerome Nadal, once the prisoner of the Protestants, Luther was disturbed, diabolical, bestial, enraged, and devilish. Moreover, like so many Germans, he ate and drank too much.

overcome the world." (John 16:33)—and every day attending to the dying, whispering to them Christ's promises of the beautiful country that lay ahead. When their superior called the Jesuits home, they pleaded to be allowed to live and die with these people. One, near death with fever, came back to Portugal and recovered, however, then preached in the churches for money to buy some slaves their freedom. In this way he manumitted some two hundred, then asked permission to return to Tétouan. It was denied.

Meanwhile, the Jesuit Andrew Oviedo was designated to become a bishop in Ethiopia, whose emperor had called for Portuguese troops to stop a Muslim invasion. The Ethiopians, like the Copts of Egypt, were then Monophysite Christians, heretical in the eyes of Rome (see vol. 4, p. 198). Here, then, might lie an opportunity to restore them to the Roman fold. Thirteen Jesuits were dispatched to join the Portuguese troops already sent to Ethiopia.

From the start, things went wrong. Storms beset the expedition, and three Jesuits and about two hundred other passengers were drowned. Once in Ethiopia, they discovered that the "emperor" was a mere figurehead over a number of tribal chiefs who actually ran the country. His "great capital" was in fact a city of mud huts. Worst of all, he was not immediately ready to embrace western Christianity. He would consider it and let them know. His decision took a full year. The answer was no.

Oviedo with five Jesuit companions began preaching directly to the Ethiopian people. Hearing this, the emperor stopped them and called for a public debate between Oviedo and his own clergy. The debate, effectually a rehash of the Monophysite conflict of the fifth century, became like a modern prizefight with the Portuguese soldiers cheering

Two Jesuit novices stand contemplatively in front of a statue of Ignatius at Sacred Heart Novitiate in Los Gatos, California, (above) while a Coptic priest does likewise in front of a mud hut in the holy city of Lalibela, Ethiopia, (below) a country to which the Jesuits sent a mission in the sixteenth century. Many of the missionaries were never seen again.

for Oviedo as he made points and the Ethiopians for their own champions. There was no declared winner, but the Muslim attack settled it by killing the emperor in battle.

When the emperor's brother succeeded him and discovered the numerous Ethiopian converts won by Oviedo, the brother attacked him physically, tore off his robes of office, and sent him to the nearby desert to starve. Ethiopia had erupted into civil war, during which Oviedo, living in the poverty he had always cherished anyway, stayed in the country and along with the remaining Jesuits died ministering to the people there. Meanwhile, another Jesuit, sent to look for the earlier Jesuit party, was captured at sea by the Turks, sold as a slave, and wound up as a laborer in Cairo. Here he was discovered by two fellow Jesuits, who bought his freedom, and another chapter began to unfold.

When the next Ethiopian emperor discovered the numerous converts won by Oviedo, he attacked him, tearing off his robes and sending him to the nearby desert to starve.

The two told this story. Some years earlier an affable Syrian named Abraham had turned up in Rome with a letter he said was from the Coptic patriarch in Alexandria, commissioning Abraham to open negotiations with Rome towards the union of Coptic and Roman churches. The then pope, Paul IV, had asked the Venetian ambassador in Cairo to confirm this. He reported back that indeed the patriarch was aware of Abraham's mission and would be happy to reestablish relations with the Roman pontiff on the friendliest of terms.

By now the pope was Pius IV. Anxious to have the Coptic Church represented at the Council of Trent, he asked the Jesuits to open a mission in Alexandria. But the Jesuits were suspicious of Abraham's legitimacy, so they sent two Jesuits ahead to check the story, the two who found their fellow Jesuit enslaved at Cairo. The Alexandrian Patriarch Gabriel VII seemed flustered by their inquiries. No, he finally told them after several months of procrastination, he was not actually interested in reunion with Rome. His letter had merely been an expression of eastern courtesy. Thus ended the initial Jesuit venture into Africa.

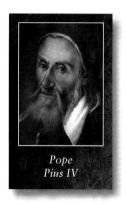

Pope Pius IV

A Jesuit mission to Ireland was even less fruitful. Two Irish lords, rebelling against the Protestant English, sent pleas to Rome for help. Dispatched as papal nuncios by Pope Paul III, two Jesuits reached the Irish coast and discovered the two nobles defeated and now declaring themselves and their people members of the English church, while the loyal Catholics had fled to the forests, where they were feuding among themselves. The two Jesuits, barely escaping with the their lives, returned to France so beaten and bedraggled that they were taken for spies and arrested before the order could rescue them.

Meanwhile, from his office in Rome the tireless Loyola, in grave ill health, tried to micromanage the whole organization, writing the members exhaustive letters of

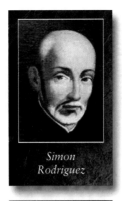

Simon Rodriguez

King John III of Portugal

instruction and advice. When there were ten Jesuits, this was possible. When there were a thousand, it was not. And since the organization was composed of human beings, remarkable though many of them were, it was falling prey to all the foibles and faults of the species. There was, for instance, the Rodriguez problem. Simon Rodriguez, one of the Jesuit originals, had so ingratiated himself with King John III of Portugal that he had become top man at court, attracting 318 men into the Jesuits' Portuguese province. Some of them "hardly understood the meaning of obedience," says the Jesuit historian James Brodrick (*The Origin of the Jesuits*, 1940). When Rodriguez seemed totally out of control, he was ordered back to Rome. But he refused to leave and instead set off a Jesuit rebellion on his behalf at Lisbon, and began a campaign through the whole order to discredit Loyola. The latter never lost patience with him, and after a court trial, banishment, and much sulking, Rodriguez returned to his duties and spent the last twenty years of his life constructively serving in the Jesuit schools.

There was also the continuing necessity to maintain standards. The records are fragmentary, says O'Malley, but in Italy about a third of the men who entered the novitiate quit or were expelled. Of those who joined before they were eighteen, the figure was closer to half. Loyola, he recounts, "dismissed Jesuits from the Roman houses without previous warning and for seemingly minor offenses." Yet he sometimes admitted men against the advice of all others. There was the physically repulsive candidate, for instance, who became a superb teacher. There was the utterly ignorant candidate, so insistent upon joining that Loyola demanded he memorize the entire Bible. Astonishingly, the man did and became one of the foremost biblical scholars of the era.

But Loyola's biggest problem did not develop until the year before his death. On May 23, 1555, when the order was fifteen years old, a man who had been fervidly opposed to Loyola before the order was established was elected pope. This was Giovanni Pietro Carafa, one of the founders of the Theatine order. Years earlier, back in his Vienna days, in a letter to Carafa, Loyola had described the Theatines as so wholly focused on their inner spirituality that they did virtually nothing for the souls of ordinary people "out there" who needed their help. The enraged Carafa never forgot this, and on that fateful day the Jesuits found themselves sworn to obey a man who plainly sought to abolish them. Loyola, says one account, "shook in every bone of his body."

Pope Paul IV did not take long making his views known. He ordered certain changes to the Jesuit constitution, putting them under the same restrictions as the other orders. They must say the daily offices together and in chapel. This, as he was well aware, would destroy the whole concept of the order. But their constitution had the approval of Pope Paul III, said the Jesuits. What one pope does, said Paul, another pope can undo.

This was no doubt much on Loyola's mind on the evening of July 30, 1556, when he fell ill with a stomach ailment. Since this was about the fifteenth time he had suffered the same thing, the doctors were not alarmed. He was found dead

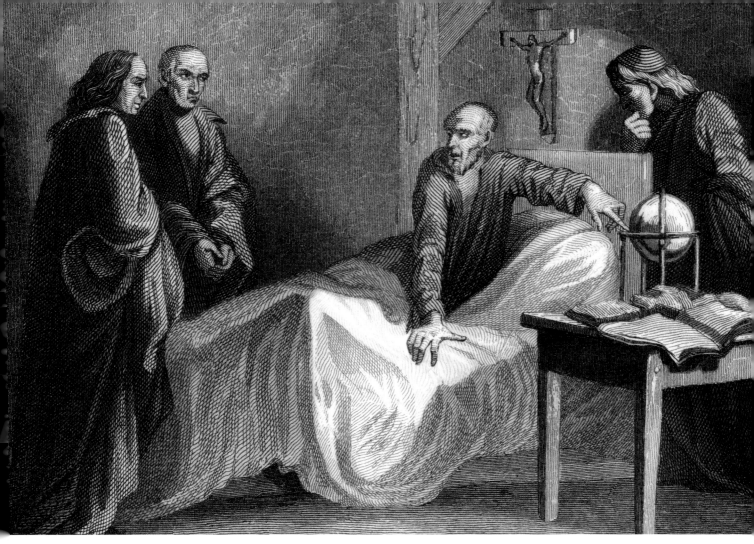

the following morning. His last words, spoken to his secretary the night before, were not about God but about the acquisition of a new Jesuit property in Rome. He died without Viaticum and without Extreme Unction,[8] Brodrick observes. "Death for such as he, to whom God meant everything, was just part of the day's work." A few days later, definite word finally arrived at Rome. His companion from the beginning, Francis Xavier, had died some three years earlier. Both were canonized in 1622.

The question on many minds was, of course: could the Jesuits survive the death of Loyola? History provides the answer. Twenty-nine Jesuit superiors general would succeed Loyola between his death in the sixteenth century and the early twenty-first. Most would preside over serious conflicts with kings, popes, bishops, Protestants, other religious orders, revolutionary governments, counter-revolutionary governments, and theologians of every stripe and persuasion.

Diego Lainez

Loyola's immediate successor was Diego Lainez, one of the originals, with whom, says Brodrick, Loyola had often been uncharacteristically harsh, because he was nominating Lainez as his successor and was plainly testing him. Though Lainez was the society's unanimous choice, it took two years for the succession to occur. There were several reasons: The order's constitution called for a lifetime appointment, and the hostile Pope Paul wanted this cut to three years. Further, the latest Spanish-French war made travel to the Jesuit consistory impossible. Finally, Lainez didn't feel himself adequate for the job, a contention he would himself go on to disprove.

Ignatius of Loyola died alone and quite unexpectedly of natural causes. He had gone to bed, perhaps as pictured above in a nineteenth-century Spanish lithograph, afflicted by the chronic stomach problem that had assailed him so often that little heed was paid to it. Next morning he was found dead. His last words, colleagues recalled, had concerned a Jesuit property in Rome.

8. Viaticum, from a Latin word meaning "provision for a journey," is Communion given to a person believed about to die. Unction means anointing with oil (referred to in Mark 6:13 and James 5:14ff). Extreme Unction was the anointing of a dying Christian. Brodrick was writing in 1940. The Second Vatican Council later renamed the rite the Anointing of the Sick, applicable to any Christian who is seriously ill.

His most formidable task was, of course, thwarting the determination of Pope Paul to effectually suppress the order, a problem solved first by Lainez's stalling for a year and second by Paul's convenient death thirteen months after Lainez took office—so convenient that their enemies said the Jesuits had murdered him. Paul's successor was the much more pro-Jesuit Pius IV.

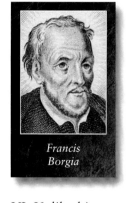

Francis Borgia

The third superior general, viewed widely as the greatest after Loyola, was a man of notorious name but saintly reputation. This was Francis Borgia, fourth duke of Gandia and great grandson of Rodrigo Borgia, the ill-famed Pope Alexander VI. Unlike his ancestor, the duke had been known as a devout Christian all his life, and with the death of his wife, the mother of his eight children, he resigned as lord of Gandia to become a Jesuit novice. He rose quickly in the order, soon becoming Jesuit provincial in Spain, and played a key role in furthering the Jesuit universities. In 1572 he was elected superior general. He was canonized in 1670.

With the next superior, the first non-Spaniard, Everard Mercurian of Luxembourg, the society entered upon a mission to restore the Catholic faith in England. Mercurian, the general, was opposed to it, fearing that some very good men would be sent to a futile death. Though still reluctant, he was finally persuaded by the project's sponsors, two Catholic Englishmen, one a Jesuit and the other a theology professor.

The professor, William Allen, born and raised in Lancashire and a graduate of Oriel College, Oxford, had advanced to become principal and proctor of the affiliated St. Mary's Hall when his refusal to take Queen Elizabeth's Oath of Supremacy cost him his job and forced him to flee to the continent. There, with help from the Benedictines, he created the English College at Douai in France, near the modern Belgian border, where young Catholic men, driven out of England, could be trained as priests and

Fleeing to the continent after refusing to take Queen Elizabeth's Oath of Supremacy, William Allen is portrayed below in an 1823 engraving. With Jesuit help, he established the English College at Douai, France, to train young Englishmen as priests who would secretly return home to restore the old faith. At bottom is St. Cuthbert's College, Ushaw, near Durham, England, founded in 1808 and a direct descendant of the English College. It still primarily educates young men for the Catholic priesthood.

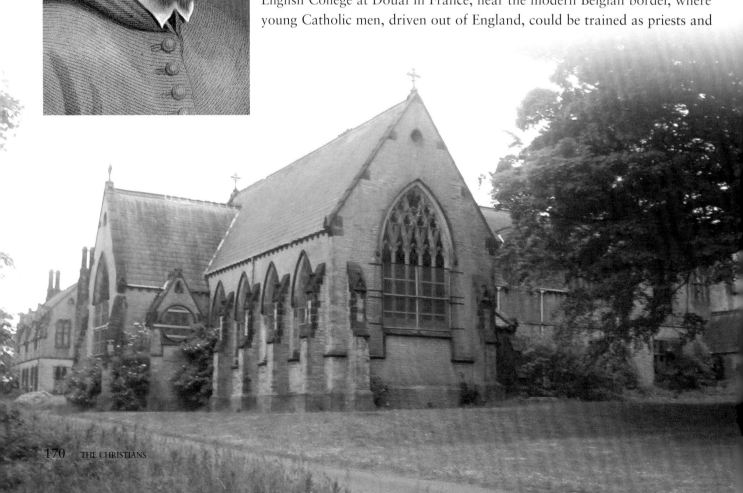

sent back to work in secret for the restoration of the old faith. The college moved temporarily to Reims, and it was there that the Douay-Rheims version of the Bible, the first Catholic Bible in English, was translated from the Latin Vulgate under Allen's direction.

Allen soon became influential at Rome, and it was he who is said to have persuaded Pope Pius V to excommunicate Queen Elizabeth (against the advice of Spain's King Philip II), thereby enabling Elizabeth to force England's Catholics to choose between their faith and their government. He was also said to be the inspiration for the Spanish Armada, because he believed that only with the help of Spanish troops could England be returned to the Catholic fold. Under the plan, he was to become archbishop of Canterbury.

In this Allen began making common cause with the Jesuit Robert Parsons (sometimes spelled Persons), another man ousted from Oxford, though for more clouded reasons. Son of a blacksmith from Somerset, he became a don at Balliol College. By one account, he was dismissed from Oxford for his Catholic leanings; by another, for "dishonorable conduct." In any event, he moved to the continent, joined the Jesuit order, and returned as head of the Jesuit mission, where he and other Jesuits lived under false names. Four were captured within a year; the saintly Edmund Campion and two companions suffered a hideous death for their faith (see sidebar, p. 324). In the end, nine Jesuits would perish in England and Wales.

From Allen's English College, some one hundred and fifty English Catholics were sent back to their native country. Many were arrested and executed; many deserted; some were caught and betrayed others. When the Spanish troops failed to arrive, both the Douai mission and the Jesuit one failed in their purpose. In 1970 Pope Paul VI canonized as martyrs nine Jesuits executed in England and thirty-one others.

Robert
Parsons

But the bloodshed was only beginning. As the seventeenth century unfolded, Protestant-Catholic conflict, by now as political as it was religious, simmered ever more dangerously until 1618, when it exploded. Then the unprecedented violence of the ensuing Thirty Years' War would fulfill the worst fears of such men as the emperor Charles V, who died despairing because he so clearly saw this catastrophe coming. And the real victim would be neither Catholicism nor Protestantism but Christianity itself, whose long European decline it would then inaugurate. ■

The Jesuit who spanned the world

How losing a game of billiards set Francis Xavier on a journey that brought the cross to Malaysia and Japan and Francis to his death at China's door

As some lone pilgrim, with his staff and beads,
Mid forest-brutes whom ignorance makes tame,
He dwelt, and sowed an Eastern Church's seeds;
He reigned, a teacher and a priest of fame:
He died and dying left a murmur and a name.

G. K. Chesterton, *St. Francis Xavier*

Francis Xavier, according to Jesuit history, was one of the tougher cases encountered by the proselytizing Ignatius of Loyola. Arriving at the University of Paris in 1529, Loyola found himself sharing quarters with this proud, handsome, athletic, and eminently affable twenty-three-year-old scion of impoverished nobility in Navarre, seeking what today would be called an arts degree. Like Loyola, he was a Basque. But young Xavier was also part of a clique of loose-living gadabouts who inhabited the taverns of Renaissance Paris, and he was not faintly interested in any message this lame and rumpled thirty-eight-year-old might have to deliver. He openly mocked Loyola for his extravagantly zealous desire to win souls for Christ. Loyola, in fact, would afterward describe Francis Xavier as the "lumpiest dough" he ever had to knead.

But one day a few years later, Xavier, a crack billiards player, challenged Loyola to a game, and Loyola agreed on condition that for one entire month the loser would do whatever the winner demanded. Xavier, unaware that his army veteran opponent was an expert in such

soldierly recreations, accepted the terms. Loyola handily beat the younger man—and for the next thirty days led Xavier through a heavy course of spiritual exercises and fasting.

Xavier consequently had visions that transformed his vainglory into humility. He also had a strange dream: a man from India was standing on his shoulders, a man so heavy he could not lift him. What could it mean? Discovering that answer would take Francis Xavier on a ten-year, sixty-two-thousand-mile odyssey through India, the Malay Peninsula, the Spice Islands, and Japan, and make him his church's most renowned missionary to the Far East.

After university, in a dank crypt in Paris's impoverished Montmartre district, the onetime mocker became one of seven men who pledged themselves to chastity and

Jesuit founder Ignatius Loyola described his early recruit Francis Xavier (above) as the "lumpiest dough" he ever had to knead—but both were Basques from northern Spain, and they understood each other. Once Xavier committed himself to Jesus Christ and the Jesuit endeavor, he became one of its most energetic missionaries. Below, modern pilgrims visit Xavier's birthplace, the Castle of Javier in Navarre.

poverty and to launch within a year a mission to convert the Turks in Jerusalem. But things did not work out as they had expected. Though they obtained the funding and gained papal approval for the Jerusalem mission, a renewed Turkish-Venetian war halted travel in the eastern Mediterranean. So instead, with the pope's approval, they established themselves as the Society of Jesus, the Jesuit order. They renewed their Montmartre pledge of chastity and poverty with an addition. They also swore absolute obedience to the papacy and to their own superior general. To this post they elected Loyola.

All but one of the original group spent the rest of their lives in Europe, and their story is told in the foregoing chapter. The exception was Francis Xavier. He never forgot the big man on his shoulders, and when the pious King John III of Portugal asked Loyola if he could spare any priests for India, Loyola turned to Xavier. "This is your enterprise," he said.[1] Thus in April 1541, at age thirty-five, Xavier set out from Lisbon on a grueling voyage aboard the *Santiago*, a foul vessel that also carried slaves and convicts. Xavier, as always, tended to the sick and poor, limiting the death toll on the thirteen-month voyage to a mere forty-one—a miracle, said the ship's doctor.

This journey ended at Goa, on India's west coast, capital of Portugal's Far Eastern colonies. This "Babylon of Iniquity," as one historian calls it, was a boomtown with all the symptoms of corruption and maladministration that were soon to cost Portugal its eastern empire. Xavier set up his tent among the sick at the hospital and began preaching to the local people—a lost cause, he soon discovered, because he couldn't speak their language. So with the help of two Franciscan friars he opened a school to teach the Christian faith. It soon had sixty pupils ranging from age thirteen to twenty-one, speaking some nine languages. It was to become the Jesuit College of St. Paul, the first in Asia.

The college exemplified what soon became Xavier's most notable quality, an

> Xavier arrived in Goa, capital of Portugal's Far Eastern colonies, a 'Babylon of iniquity.'

The Basilica of Good Jesus, a UNESCO World Heritage Site and guardian of Xavier's remains, is located in Old Goa, capital of Portugal's sixteenth-century colony in the state of Goa, India, a river port which Xavier found afflicted by corrupt administration. Arriving in 1542, Xavier found that his first task was to learn the language (the first of many) so he could preach. The second was to open a school.

1. The early dominance of the Portuguese in southwestern India and other areas rich in spices had been established by the nobleman and military genius Afonso de Albuquerque between 1503 and 1515. His conquests, which included Goa, Malacca, the Spice Islands, and Ormuz in the Persian Gulf, created immense revenues for Portugal at a time when such spices as cloves were literally worth their weight in gold.

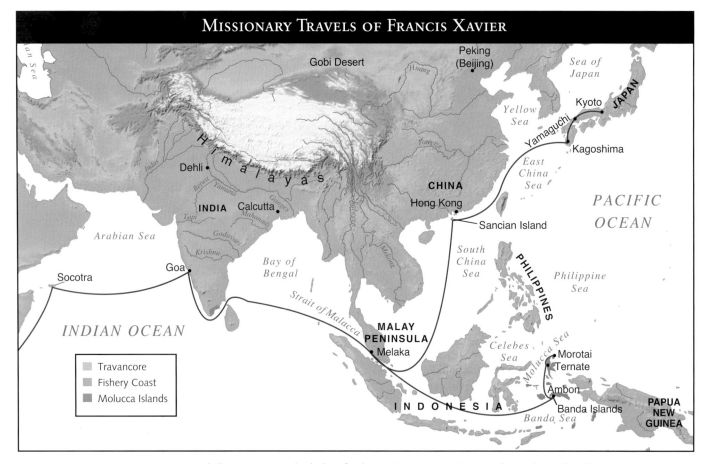

MISSIONARY TRAVELS OF FRANCIS XAVIER

Travancore
Fishery Coast
Molucca Islands

ability to recruit the help of others. Some would call it charm, some diplomacy, some the grace of Christ shining through him. "He would always seem happy," said a man who knew him aboard the *Santiago*, "even when he was overwhelmed with work." Everybody liked him. Xavier was a shabby man in torn gown and bare feet, but he could debate theology with bishops in palaces, crack jokes with sailors in taverns, and inspire Hindu schoolchildren to become his mini-missionaries. (The youngsters, having memorized their Pater Nosters, Ave Marias and Ten Commandments, delighted in reciting them to their families and neighbors.) His acceptance and forgiveness of human frailty greatly eased the seemingly impossible task of converting to Christianity a population at best uninterested and at worst hostile to it.

But as always he must move on. All Asia lay before him, and five months after landing in Goa, he was preaching the gospel to thirty thousand Paravas, a caste of pearl fishers, on the torrid "Fishery Coast" of Malabar, six hundred miles to the southeast. They had been baptized by Franciscans, at their own request, seven years earlier.

Baptism brought with it Portuguese protection from their Muslim enemies, but no priest had ever been permanently stationed there. Xavier now faced the task of instructing this flock—in Tamil. Three native clerics came with him from Goa and helped him translate basic prayers, which he memorized as they tramped from village to village. Their reception was overwhelming. "My arms are often almost paralyzed with baptizing," Xavier wrote to his confreres, "and my voice gives out completely through endlessly repeating in their tongue the creed, the commandments, the prayers, and a sermon on heaven and hell."

The same held true in the kingdom of Travancore, on India's southwest coast. "I went from village to village making Christians," he wrote, reporting that in the fall of 1544 he baptized some ten thousand Mukkuvars, the fishermen caste of Travancore. The following spring he sailed to Melaka, Malaysia, to deal with a new culture, new language, and new set of translations. On the perilous passage through the Strait of Malacca, he recounted, "our ship of four hundred tons ran before a violent wind for more than a league, and during the

> 'My arms are often almost paralyzed from baptizing,' Xavier wrote.

2. Homosexual liaisons were prevalent among the otherwise celibate Buddhist monks in several Japanese sects encountered by Xavier. The practice of sexual relations between monks and novices, reportedly widespread and socially accepted, is thought to have come from China—a sort of ancient Greece to Japan's Rome—in the tenth century.

whole time the rudder was scraping the ocean floor."

In January 1546 he traveled 1,740 nautical miles to the Spice Islands—the Moluccas of Indonesia—where he spent sixteen months evangelizing in Ambon, Ternate, Morotai, and the tiny Banda Islands. Returning to Melaka in the spring of 1547, he found three brother Jesuits priests—the first he had seen in two years—themselves en route to the Moluccas. The Jesuit order was growing, due in no small part to the sensation caused in Europe by Xavier's letters, which Loyola was cannily disseminating.

In Melaka also he met a Japanese man named Anjiro, a disgraced samurai of thirty-five, who had killed a man in a brawl. Haunted by guilt, Anjiro heard about the famous missionary from Portuguese sailors and sought him out. Xavier was delighted. Not only would the Japanese man be baptized; he could also open the door to his country, discovered scarcely five years earlier by Portuguese traders. Anjiro assured him that his people would embrace Christianity, the credulous Xavier wrote to Loyola, for they "are entirely guided by the law of reason."

In June 1549, with Anjiro and three others, Xavier embarked on a Chinese junk on the three thousand-mile voyage from Melaka to Japan. They encountered fierce storms that swept the captain's daughter overboard and caused the terrified crew to beseech aid from the idol on the ship's prow. But on August 15 they reached the southern port of Kagoshima, the native city of Anjiro (who was now named Paul of the Holy Faith).

Xavier was initially enchanted by the Japanese. Their great respect for honor appealed to his Spanish heritage, moving him to call them "the best race yet discovered," but previous hardships were trifling compared to those he now faced. It took nearly a year to translate a rudimentary catechism into Japanese, for example. The Buddhist monks resented his denunciations of their homosexual practices.[2] He and his companions were mocked and stoned as they preached in the streets. "The children ran after us with shouts of derision," he wrote.

A year later, he left with two others to find the emperor in the city of Miako (now Kyoto) four hundred miles north. Stopping for a time to preach in Yamaguchi, roughly midway to their destination, they resumed their arduous trek to the imperial city in early December of 1550. They struggled through often knee-deep snow and waded through icy water. Barefoot after their boots fell apart, they left bloody tracks in the snow, and it was all for nothing. Xavier was unaware that it was the *daimyô* (warlords) who held political power in Japan. The

A sixteenth-century Indian tapestry (above) portrays two black-clad Jesuits, at left, visiting a princely court. Below, Francis Xavier lands at Kagoshima, Japan, as portrayed in a nineteenth-century lithograph. Although initially enchanted by the Japanese and their love of honor, he faced stiff opposition during his two-and-a-half-year stay there.

emperor had no authority, lived in a run-down wooden palace, and sold poetry for extra cash.

Returning to Yamaguchi, Xavier switched tactics. The poverty that endeared him to the people of India obviously repulsed the Japanese. Therefore he changed his persona radically. He dressed in rich robes, assembled thirteen different kinds of gifts (including a cuckoo clock, a harquebus that could fire three times without reloading, and a quantity of Portuguese wine), and approached the local warlord. The daimyô, delighted with these novelties, not only gave the Jesuits permission to preach but set them up in a handsome pagoda.

In the following two months more than five hundred Japanese, many from the ranks of the samurai, asked for baptism. Xavier traveled to Bungo in southwest Japan, where the local warlord, hoping for increased Portuguese trade, also allowed him to evangelize.

In two and a half years, he reported to the order, about two thousand Christians were established in five Japanese towns. Then he returned to Goa to resume his duties as superior of the new Jesuit province for the Indies. Two thousand converts in a population of fifteen million was not the result he had hoped for. But he was consoled that those few were strong in their new faith, and later missionaries would confirm the enduring effect of his work. The moral condition of the city was as deplorable as ever, however, and in his letter to King John he does not mince words, warning him that kings, too, will one day die and face the consequences of what they have and have not done:

Senhor, it is a sort of martyrdom to have patience and watch being destroyed what one has built up with so much labor . . . Experience has taught me that Your Highness has not power in India to spread the faith of Christ, while you do have the power to take away and enjoy all the country's temporal riches . . . It will be a novel thing, unknown in Your Highness's existence, to see yourself at the hour of death dispossessed of your kingdoms . . . and entering into other kingdoms where you may have the new experience, which God avert, of being ordered out of paradise.

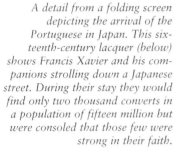

A detail from a folding screen depicting the arrival of the Portuguese in Japan. This six-teenth-century lacquer (below) shows Francis Xavier and his companions strolling down a Japanese street. During their stay they would find only two thousand converts in a population of fifteen million but were consoled that those few were strong in their faith.

For all his efforts, Francis Xavier never did reach mainland China. A nineteenth-century Chinese engraving (left) portrays his death from fever in a makeshift shelter on Sancian, a small island six miles from the coast. Returned to Old Goa in India, his body is preserved there in a silver coffin (below) at the Basilica of Good Jesus.

Next Xavier set his sights on a still greater prize: China. Foreigners were strictly banned from this largest and most influential Asian empire. Therefore, in the spring of 1552 he organized an official delegation that would allow him entry as a papal ambassador. This scheme was blocked, however, by a jealous Portuguese official in Melaka (Álvaro de Ataide da Gama, the youngest son of the famed explorer Vasco da Gama).

Disheartened and uncertain, Xavier decided that September to travel to Sancian. About a hundred miles southwest of Hong Kong and six miles from mainland China, this tiny island was the meeting point for Portuguese smugglers with Cantonese merchants. Xavier persuaded one of the latter to take him to the mainland on his next run. But weeks passed, the merchant did not come, and Xavier fell ill with a fever. He died in a makeshift hut on December 3, 1552. He was forty-six. He and Loyola were both canonized by Pope Gregory XV seventy years later.

Critics of Francis Xavier charge that he left his new Christians without pastoral care, but this is staunchly denied by his defenders. Not only did he train lay catechists and strongly advocate native clergy, writes Jesuit Robert Bireley in the *Encyclopaedia Britannica*, he was the first missionary to adapt to the customs of the people he evangelized. So the man on his shoulders proved heavy indeed, but Francis would not have things otherwise. "There is no better rest in this restless world," he wrote, "than to face imminent peril solely for the love and service of God our Lord." ■

CHAPTER 9

The Council of Trent: 18 years of hot conflict that saved the papacy

It took three popes, two emperors, fierce argument, and a war between the papacy and Catholic Spain to trigger real reform, but finally the curia yielded

Looking back on it today from a distance of over four centuries, the Council of Trent may appear as an inevitable triumph. Devout, determined Catholic Christians joined in common devotion to their church, it seems, to scour corruption from its governance, decree anathema against Protestant heresies, and proclaim the glory of their sacraments and apostolic authority. It reignited a confidence in the Catholic creed that would carry the church through the turbulent age that lay ahead, and to all corners of the earth. Such is the popular view.

The historical reality is much at odds with this. At the time, Trent appeared a council of despair. Catholic clergy came together with purposes so divergent that they seemed incapable of joining in anything. Trent was not a single meeting but three, called sporadically over eighteen years. And only at the third were the resolutions of the earlier two confirmed so that the three could be accurately portrayed as one. Trent was a triumph all right, but far from an inevitable one. It was a triumph fiercely fought and hard won.

Five popes reigned during those eighteen years, one bitterly opposed to the council. Another, the council's most devout advocate, died after only twenty-two days in office. The divisions were so impassioned that at one point the papacy declared war on its most reliably Catholic country, Spain, and made peace only on the brink of a papal defeat. Twice the council was almost scattered by a hostile Lutheran army, a short march away.

Yet the Council of Trent brought harmony from hostility, clarity from confusion,

The Council of Trent, convened by Rome in the wake of the Protestant Reformation, opened on December 13, 1545. Repeatedly stalled by infighting, controversy over its location, agenda, and purposes, by plague, and by war, it concluded eighteen years later, after being twice reconvened. Its inaugural session, as depicted by Niccolo Dorigati in 1703, drew only twenty-six bishops, but over two hundred would attend the final session, vowing unanimously to "always confess" and "always observe" its decisions.

1. Eighteenth-century poet William Cowper (pronounced *Cooper*) would doubtless be amused to see the Council of Trent cited as proof of the truth of his great hymn, since he was a fervent Protestant. God's movements, however, often mystify Christians of every denomination, as Cowper knew. Though celebrated in his day, he was afflicted with bouts of morbid insanity, which his faith survived.

The Catholic Church had in fact been reseeding itself in the generation prior to the Reformation, producing a series of new religious orders. They included the Ursulines, an education mission to young women founded in 1535 by Angela Merici, depicted in a statue outside St. Peter's Basilica (below left); the Barnabites, which ministered to prisons and hospitals and were founded by Anthony Maria Zaccaria (second from left); the strict Theatines, started by St. Cejetan (third from left); and the Capuchins, a Franciscan offshoot recruited among the poor and represented here in by an unidentified member in a portrait that hangs in the São Paulo Museum of Art in Brazil.

and order from chaos, enabling the Catholic Church to survive and prosper right into the twenty-first century. It therefore bears striking witness to the truth of the old hymn:

> *God moves in a mysterious way,*
> *His wonders to perform.*
> *He plants his footstep in the sea*
> *And rides upon the storm.*[1]

There was indeed a storm. The church was being buffeted by ethnic frictions and national ambitions. What good could come of a council bringing those divisions to the table? Yet only Spain, Portugal, and Italy were now loyally Catholic. Protestantism was advancing triumphantly, and Islam, profiting from the discord, was threatening Vienna. Luther's scriptural critiques and inferences had caught Catholic theologians flat-footed, and his rejection of the late medieval church seemed validated by its rampant luxury and office-seeking. So the church must be reformed, and Protestant dissent must be answered, all at the same time—like holding a constitutional convention in time of war.

The different agendas were gusting from all directions. The devout Habsburg emperor Charles V was desperate to battle the Muslim Turks, who were pillaging and about to conquer Catholic Hungary, and he needed a council to reconcile with his Protestant princes—if only that they might tolerate their Catholic subjects. France, fearing Habsburg hegemony in Spain and Germany, would support a council only if the French crown continued to dominate the French church. Pious Spain demanded that the church militantly crusade against all heretics. And across all borders, renewed or new religious orders demanded holier bishops and a revival of religious education.

Ironically, the Catholic Church had been reseeding itself for a generation prior to Luther's challenge. It was the same old pattern: piety had led to service, service to wealth, wealth to corruption, and corruption—eventually—to renewal, percolating from below. In the late 1400s lay fraternities sprang up in Italy, venerating the Eucharist. Then the Spanish crown sponsored the Council of Seville, reforming the universities, renewing their theology, and nurturing that peculiarly Spanish mysticism. By the turn of the century, the Italian Oratory of Divine Love was fostering

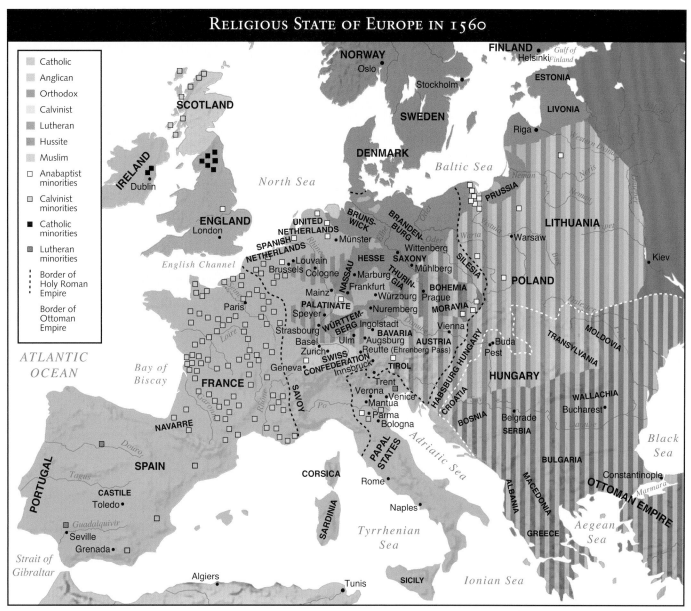

RELIGIOUS STATE OF EUROPE IN 1560

Legend:
- Catholic
- Anglican
- Orthodox
- Calvinist
- Lutheran
- Hussite
- Muslim
- ☐ Anabaptist minorities
- ☐ Calvinist minorities
- ■ Catholic minorities
- ▣ Lutheran minorities
- ⋮ Border of Holy Roman Empire
- Border of Ottoman Empire

Source: The Times Atlas of World History, *edited by Geoffrey Barraclough, London, 1984*

both clerical and lay devotion, and the remarkable Carthusians, encouraged by high nobles and kings who wanted to ensure monasteries of monks who actually prayed.

Then new religious orders began budding, like the strict Theatines, drawing aristocrats into the service of orphanages and hospitals.[2] The hooded Capuchins, a Franciscan offshoot, recruited among the poor. The Somaschi, serving in neighborhoods, were founded by a Venetian soldier after a stint as a prisoner of war. And the Barnabites, organized by a former medical student, were preaching to parish missions in Bohemia, Germany, and France. Their women's branch, the Angelice, was launched in 1535, the same year the Ursulines began their educational mission to young women.

Encouraged by such movements, devout bishops began trimming their bloated households, tightening clerical discipline, and encouraging Bible study. The Theatines held up Padua's Bishop Pietro Barozzi as a model of sanctity. The local reforms of Verona's Bishop Gian Matteo Giberti were eventually codified, and his biography was published under the title *A Good Shepherd*.

But the storm was brewing more swiftly than the moorings could be made fast. As usual, the wealthier orders—Benedictines, Dominicans, and Luther's own

2. Proof that holiness, not numbers, turns the world, the extremely austere Theatines had a huge influence on the diocesan clergy. Founded in 1524 by Gaetano die Conti di Thiene, or St. Cajetan (along with three other men, including Giovanni Pietro Carafa, the future Pope Paul IV), by 1533 they numbered only twenty-one, yet their members included the Benedictine reformer Gregorio Cortese and Cardinal Reginald Pole, grand nephew of Kings Edward IV and Richard III, last of England's renowned Plantagenet line that had preceded the now-reigning Tudors.

Augustinians—were slow to respond. Prelates responded in ones and twos. The curia still ordained absentee bishops, too many parish priests were abysmally ignorant, and only wandering friars preached the gospel, and then only at Advent or Lent.

Then in 1527, Rome was raped and pillaged by a renegade army under Catholic command, which seemed God's judgment on its sins (see vol. 8, pp. 262–268). The church needed institutional renewal, and that meant a willing pope and an ecumenical council. Pope Clement VII, adept at ignoring crises, had stalled for a decade, for good reasons and bad. First, the conciliar movement of the previous century had almost usurped the papacy with a government-by-committee model. Second, the wealthy curia had institutionalized corruption; the sale of church offices, the pocketing of fees, and the stonewalling of reform at the top had become habitual. And yet, after Clement's death in 1534, the cardinals elected a man wily enough and just holy enough to take up the challenge.

Pope Paul III seemed an unlikely reformer. Known as the "Petticoat Cardinal" Alessandro Farnese, he had come to Rome on the hem of the affair between his stunning sister Giulia and Borgia pope Alexander VI. He himself had fathered four bastards and as pope appointed two of his grandsons as cardinals. But late in life he appears to have undergone some kind of spiritual transition, and Titian's portrait shows a man of penetrating eye and steel serenity. He ordered his cardinals to clean up their households, then appointed the nine of them as a commission of reform.

Their *Advice on Reform of the Church* of 1537 spared no one. "Benefices for the cure of souls must not be granted to provide a man with a livelihood, but to secure shepherds for souls," they scolded. The sale of offices generated a quarter of the papal revenue, dispensations were granted for cash, and indulgences might still be hawked without too much thought of their spiritual meaning. Bishops must live in their dioceses and priests in their parishes, said the report. Italians must not be made bishops in foreign countries. Lax religious orders must be chastised and licentious clergy disciplined. The sack of Rome, they warned, was a judgment on their corruption.

Paul willingly suspended the sale of dispensations, but alone his power could go no farther than the city gates, if even that far. Meanwhile, letting no good deed go unpunished, Protestants circulated the *Advice* as proof of Roman iniquity. Still, the commission had publicly pleaded with Paul, "Heal our sickness, unite Christ's sheep again in one fold, and avert the wrath of God." And his initial efforts conferred on him the moral authority to demand more. Twenty years late, the church finally had a pope committed to an ecumenical council.

But where to hold it? With both the French and Turks arrayed against him, the distracted emperor Charles V, now thirty-seven, craved peace with his Protestant princes. That meant a council must be held in Germany, where the mood was harsh on clerical corruption but ready to bend on sacramental theology. However, the pope could not bend on theology, so a council held in theologically rigorous Italy would be better. Besides, France, repeatedly warring with Charles's empire, would not go into Germany at all. Thus Paul summoned the council to meet in 1537 at

Wily Pope Paul III (left) was an improbable church reformer. He was known as the "Petticoat Cardinal" because he had gained ecclesiastical promotion through the influence of his sister and was himself the father of four illegitimate children. Yet he appears to have undergone a spiritual transition and acquired a steel serenity. Coupled with an unshakable resolve, this enabled him to launch the Council of Trent. Something of these new qualities is captured in his portrait by Titian. Trent (below), in the South Tirol, offered the compromise advantage of a German city on the Italian side of the Alps.

Pathfinders of the mystical

How a 52-year-old nun and a 25-year-old friar together explore in prayer God's hidden ways, adding new dimensions to the Christian experience

Among the Catholic reformers of the sixteenth century, it could be argued that the most strikingly unusual were those two redoubtable saints Teresa of Avila and John of the Cross. With Sister Teresa leading, they set about the rejuvenation of the venerable Carmelite order by founding an entirely new version of it—a highly practical endeavor. But meanwhile, through their extraordinary visions and copious writing, these two mystics would also afford to the world deep insight into contemplative prayer—perhaps a still more valuable contribution.

Interestingly enough, both were descended from Jewish *conversos* forced by the Spanish Inquisition two generations earlier to accept Christianity. Teresa Sanchez de Cepeda y Ahumada, born in 1515, came from a large and prosperous family in the province of Avila. Devout and adventurous, at seven she ran off with her little brother Rodrigo to be martyred by the Moors, but they were captured instead by an uncle and returned home. At twenty, as strong willed as ever, she slipped away to join the Carmelite Convent of the Incarnation in the town of Avila—and this time she was allowed to carry through with her intentions.

Her religious life began with three years of painful and debilitating illness, however, and she would suffer lifelong ill health. Then followed, as she recounts in her memoir (*Life Written by Herself*, 1565), a two-decade struggle against earthly distraction and ambition in search of spiritual union with God. At length, one day when she was nearly forty and was contemplating a statue of the much-wounded Christ, her heart broke, and thereafter she gave herself wholly to prayer.

Through her visions, Sister Teresa wrote, she came to understand the awful nature of sin and the impossibility of confronting it alone. She also described visions of great comfort, even from Christ himself, but perhaps the most extraordinary was of a seraph who drove into her heart the fiery tip of a golden lance. "The pain was so great that it made me moan, and yet so surpassing was the sweetness of this excessive pain that I could not wish to be rid of it."

Stories circulated in town that this strange nun actually levitated and that in prayer her face became radiant. Even her spiritual advisers feared she "had a devil," she wrote, and "wanted to exorcize me." One adviser reassured her, however—a Franciscan priest named Peter of Alcantara, himself a mystic whose writing had early influenced her. "Keep on as you are doing," he told her, "we all suffer such trials." He may also have encouraged her in the inspiration that now gripped her, namely the restoration of the Carmelite order to its original ideals.

Sister Teresa resolved to open a second and much stricter contemplative convent in Avila. Its nuns would not confer upon the order the usual dowries, so it must subsist solely on donations. They would live in poverty, simplicity, and complete segregation. They would also go barefoot, giving rise to the name Discalced Carmelites (meaning shoeless).[1]

All this struck many townsfolk as ridiculous, and Teresa was none too popular in ecclesiastical circles either. One typical papal official dismissed her as "a restless gadabout, disobedient and contumacious." Nonetheless, in August 1562 St. Joseph's convent

Teresa of Avila receives the Eucharist in this illustration by Niccolò Bambini from 1710. Giving herself wholly to prayer at the age of thirty-nine, Teresa became known for mystical experiences—including levitation—that some attributed to the devil.

St. John of the Cross (above) and St. Teresa of Avila have given the world deep and valuable insight into contemplative prayer.

opened, with papal approval, with Teresa as prioress and four other nuns. But she never remained still for long.

Five years later, on the road to found more convents, she happened to meet John de Yepes Alvarez. They were an odd match. An intense introvert, John had been raised by his widowed mother in stark poverty. He was twenty-five years old and had been a Carmelite priest for two months. Teresa, at fifty-two, had been a nun for thirty-three years. Also, John was just four feet ten inches tall (causing Teresa to quip on one later occasion that in him she had "half a man").

Seeking greater rigor, John was thinking of joining the ascetic Carthusian order, but Teresa persuaded him to help reform the Carmelites instead. The long-term result was an abiding and productive friendship, though Teresa noted that he sometimes "vexed" her over business matters. The immediate result was that John of the Cross and another friar moved into a dilapidated barn to establish the first monastery for Discalced friars. By 1576 there would be a dozen for women and four for men.

Meanwhile, what Teresa called the "great storm" of persecution had broken out. In 1575 the general chapter of the Carmelite order, convinced Teresa was fomenting rebellion, had ordered her to retire to a monastery of her choice.[2] John, also viewed as a rebel, was abducted from Avila in December 1577 by irate Calced Carmelite friars. Imprisoned in Toledo for nine months in a small, windowless room, he was starved, whipped so mercilessly that his back was scarred for life, and taunted with untrue reports that his reform had failed. Nevertheless, at this time he wrote his most beautiful poetry and began developing his greatly praised theology on "the dark night of the soul."

Finally a sympathetic friar enabled John to escape,

but the bitter Carmelite rift was resolved only with intervention by King Philip II (who admired Teresa's accomplishments). With royal approval the Carmelites petitioned Rome, and in 1580 the Discalced were established as a separate organization. Meanwhile, Teresa, though in failing health, never flagged; in the next two years she brought the total of new foundations to seventeen. In early 1582, relates Jean-Jacques Antier (*Teresa of Avila, God Alone Suffices*, 2007), she stumbled when crossing a swollen stream in heavy rain. Angrily reproaching God, she heard a voice say, "Teresa, this is how I treat my friends," and famously answered, "Oh God of my soul! This is why you have so few!"

Teresa of Avila collapsed and died at her Alba monastery on, October 4, 1582, aged sixty-seven. John of the Cross lived nine years longer, the last marred by bitter dissension among Discalced friars. He had prayed to suffer with Christ, and suffer he did— stripped of authority, stricken with erysipelas (an exceedingly painful skin infection), and mistreated by his fellows—who are said to have repented just before his death at age forty-nine on December 14, 1591.

These two extraordinary individuals, their very active lives notwithstanding, stand as two of the most beloved and approachable among Christian mystics. Teresa's autobiography is, after *Don Quixote*, the most widely read Spanish prose classic. Although she claimed to write reluctantly, chiefly under obedience to her confessors, her prodigious output includes such spiritual classics as *The Way of Perfection* and *The Interior Castle*. As for John, he is regarded as one of the greatest Spanish poets, and his works include *The Ascent of Mount Carmel* and *The Dark Night of the Soul*.

In *Lives of the Saints* (1983), Augustine Kalberer writes that both Teresa and John provide from their own experience invaluable insight on the stages of prayer. Although the more analytical John is perceived by some as too harsh, Kalberer notes that he emphasized charity. "If you do not find love," wrote John of the Cross, "practice love, and you will find love."

As for Teresa of Avila, her practical advice makes prayer "uniquely attractive." "No one who has begun this practice should ever forsake it, no matter how many sins he commits," she advises. Mental prayer is "the means by which we amend our lives again" and is essentially nothing else but "talking, just two alone, with him who we know loves us." ∎

1. The "primitive" rule of the Carmelites had been much eased over time by several popes. The Discalced Carmelites, by contrast, would live in strict enclosure, perpetually abstain from meat, fast from September to Easter, wear coarse habits, and wholly dedicate their lives to prayer and penance for sinners. However, to go about discalced applied more to men than to women, "Teresa's nuns may have gone barefoot at first, but they soon began to wear *alpargatos*, a type of poor sandal made from hemp," observe the Carmelites Kieran Kavanaugh and Otilios Rodriguez in their translation *The Collected Works of St. Teresa of Avila* (1985). "Her friars continued going barefoot and only gradually turned to alpargatos, first allowing them for the sickly."

2. That year the Inquisition investigated Teresa's autobiography, *The Book of Her Life*, approving it in 1580. The Inquisition had caused Teresa grief earlier by placing vernacular religious texts, including Castilian translations of the New Testament, on the Index of Forbidden Books in 1559.

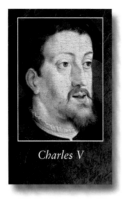
Charles V

Henry VIII

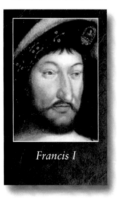
Francis I

Mantua, in Italy's Lombardy. This not only infuriated Charles, but Mantua's duke balked as well. He would need five thousand extra men-at-arms to defend the council, he said. Paul tried again, calling for the meeting in 1538 at Vicenza, about thirty miles west of Venice. For different reasons, Germany's Charles and France's Francis ignored the summons, as did Henry VIII, who had declared himself head of the church in England. So Paul issued a second call for Vicenza in 1539. No bishops came. Finally, still insisting on a council, Charles compromised, suggesting Trent in thc South Tirol, inside the German border but on Italy's side of the Alps.[3]

Acquiescing, Paul called the council for Trent in 1542, only to suffer another reversal. Francis I of France, coveting imperial Milan, declared war on Charles, and refused to consider a German council, on whatever side of the Alps. Angered by the pope's refusal to coerce France and currying support from his own Lutherans, Charles convened an Imperial Reichstag (i.e., parliament) at Speyer. There he granted his Lutheran princes free rein in their own lands, abandoning his Catholic subjects and outraging Pope Paul. Then, with Charles preoccupied with France, the Lutheran princes of Saxony and Hesse invaded still-Catholic Brunswick and Thuringia, pillaging their churches and banning the Mass. Unable to fight both the Lutheran princes and the French, Charles could do little more than sponsor Lutheran-Catholic religious dialogue at Worms and Regensburg. For now.

Paul III doggedly renewed the call for Trent, this time to convene in March 1545. Unexpectedly, Charles's combined Lutheran-Catholic army marched on Paris and forced a peace treaty on Francis, obliging him to support a council. Meanwhile, Charles was also negotiating a secret military alliance with Rome against his Lutheran princes, with the holding of the council as part of the bargain. Paul prayed: "Arm my spirit with strength and constancy."

He needed them. March came and went at Trent. No bishops appeared. So did April, May, June, and July. With the summer over, some slowly dribbled in, only to complain bitterly about their lodgings. Watching from Innsbruck, Charles chided, "Is it asking too much, for such a sacred purpose, that they be content with one room instead of a house?" In his eyes, the council had been delayed eight years by the pope's neutrality in his struggle with France. Meanwhile, Francis was allying with the Turks against the empire to assault Christendom! Still the pope remained neutral. Yet for his part, Paul feared something even worse. The papacy must remain nonaligned, he resolved, lest the perfidious Francis turn France Protestant. Relations between Charles and Paul, both devout men, were poisoned by distrust even as they drafted their alliance against the Lutherans.

The council finally opened in December with only twenty-six archbishops and bishops, and with the winds of internal conflict already buffeting them. From Germany, the emperor insisted that church reform be the only topic of discussion. From Rome, the pope demanded only fidelity to Catholic theology, though two of

3. Charles, meanwhile, despairing of an ecumenical council, repeatedly tried to patch together the German church with synods at Hagenau, Worms, and Regensburg. Catholic historian Warren Carroll, an unwavering admirer, says Charles could never believe the Lutherans "had totally rejected the Catholic faith, to the point where no human effort could bring them back."

his papal legates, English Cardinal Reginald Pole and the Augustinian Girolamo Seripando, favored theological concessions to the Protestants on issues like justification. Against them, stern Cardinal Giovanni Pietro Carafa would allow no doctrinal ambiguity whatever. On the council floor, national antagonisms fueled the tensions. One Spanish bishop, bellowing like a drill sergeant, was silenced by the shout, "Are we at the Council of Toledo?" A Frenchman voicing derogatory opinions of the Roman curia, was mocked with, "How the cock crows!" and shot back a devastating, "At cock-crow, Peter roused himself!" Whenever a vote was expected, Roman bishops flooded back, prompting the bitter quip, "The Holy Spirit arrives in Italian luggage," and Charles V's ambassador incessantly demanded a halt to any theological deliberations.

Yet over the next year, with attendance growing and debate proceeding apace on both doctrine and reform, consensus was somehow "riding upon the storm." First, the Nicene Creed of 325 AD was declared "the common foundation of all Christian faith." Next, scripture and apostolic tradition were declared equal sources of truth, the ancient biblical canon was affirmed against Luther's deletions,[4] and the church was declared the sole authority for the binding interpretation of scripture.

The emperor was unhappy and his ambassadors obstructed. Where was the reform of clerical conduct, particularly at the level of the curia? Even so, Charles

4. By the second century, over two hundred books claiming apostolic authorship were in circulation, most of them plainly spurious. So in 397 the Council of Carthage decided which books would be considered "canonical." Of these, Luther was hesitant to recognize the New Testament books of Hebrews, James, Jude, and the Revelation. Similarly, he rejected the portions of the Greek Septuagint not found in the Hebrew scriptures known as the Deuterocanonical books, or the Apocrypha: Tobit, Judith, Wisdom, Sirach, Baruch, 1 and 2 Maccabees, and a few passages from Esther and Daniel.

Another Sebastiano Ricci rendering shows Pope Paul III invoking angelic aid to prepare the Council of Trent, which opened in December of 1545 with only twenty-six prelates in attendance. Despite the low turnout and the national antagonisms that promptly fueled tensions on the council floor, the assembly grew both in number and in scope of debate.

could find solace in some of the council's pastoral decrees. Bishops were personally obliged to preach the faith and parish priests to give sermons in the local language every Sunday and holy day. The issue of a bishop's residence requirement was most contentious, but after a year of wrangling and failed votes, it was agreed that bishops must live in their dioceses, hold only one see, and be fined for extended absences. The council ignored the issue of the sale of benefices (church incomes) and issued few formal decrees on reform before its anticlimactic recess the next year. Yet a frank discussion of the problems was beneficial, if only to keep alive the grassroots movements for reform.

In mid-1546, citing the unprovoked Lutheran conquest of Brunswick and Thuringia, Charles declared war on rebellious Saxony and Hesse. Having anticipated this move, however, the Lutheran Schmalkaldic League stole a march on him and seized nearby Ehrenberg Pass, within striking distance of Trent. The Lutherans boasted they would scatter the prelates and crucify Charles, only to withdraw when threatened by his ally Bavaria. Shortly after, a papal army corps marched north through Trent to join Charles's imperial army.

When that distraction had passed, the council finally addressed the vexed issue of justification (see sidebar, p. 190), and the sparks flew between dogmatists and pragmatists. When one Italian bishop edged toward Luther's perceived notion of "faith alone," a Greek denounced him as "either a knave or a fool," only to have the Italian grab him by his beard and tear out a handful. (The Italian was sent to his room until the Greek interceded on his assailant's behalf.) Nevertheless, consensus grew. Mankind was not quite as evil as Luther taught, and baptism truly purifies, though an inclination toward sin remains. Men cannot be fully certain of salvation, but grace sanctifies them in this life. Finally, on January 13, 1547, the council agreed that men are saved only by the merits of Christ's suffering but remain free to cooperate or resist. So faith is not enough; there must also be love and hope. The vote was virtually unanimous.

When Emperor Charles learned of the council's dogmatic decrees, he warned that it should "go no further down this road." Yet having affirmed "good works" against the Lutheran "faith alone," the council then defended the seven sacraments, repudiating Luther's common priesthood of believers. The sacraments are not mere signs of faith but real means of grace, regardless of the holiness of a priest, the council ruled. It then prepared decrees on the real presence of Christ in the Eucharist and on confession, matrimony, and ordination, but adjourned debate on them when pope and emperor finally fell out.

The emperor had wanted a council conciliatory towards the Lutherans—an agreement to disagree, perhaps—yet his church insisted on a doctrinal showdown. When Paul had first proposed a council back in 1535, even Luther agreed to attend. But by 1545 Luther's attitude had hardened, and the dying man roared: "Let their tongues be torn from their throats . . . for their idolatry and blasphemy, let them suffer syphilis, epilepsy, scurvy, leprosy." His followers, he knew, were on the march and need no longer consort with idolaters. Charles, too, understood the depth of

When one Italian bishop edged towards Luther's 'faith alone,' a Greek denounced him as 'either a knave or a fool,' only to have the Italian grab him by the beard and tear out a handful.

resentment in parts of Germany. He might subdue Protestants by force of arms, but—remember the Turks! Had the council forgotten the Turks? Stopping them required Christian concord, and that could come only by reuniting Christendom. With the council rejecting Luther's central dogmas, such a hope was vanishing.

France, however, was delighted with what up to this time had been a largely dogmatic council. Its crown had long dominated its church, and its bishops attended because their king told them to attend (driving up the local price of wine). Reform of the curia might lessen their own independence, but a dogmatic rejection of Protestantism was a stick with which to beat their own troublesome Calvinists. Better still, it would widen Germany's religious chasm, weakening the Habsburgs. Conniving Francis likewise promised military subsidies to the Protestant Schmalkaldic League—only to renege on the promise when Charles loosed on the league his counterattack.

As the storm raged, Charles and Paul III's concord on the council lasted only as long as their military alliance. In the autumn of 1546, aided by papal swords and ducats, Charles marched almost unopposed through southern Germany, accepting the surrender of Ulm, Württemberg, Augsburg, and Frankfurt—without, however, demanding their religious submission. The emperor needed political unity, even with heretics. The pope, however, was angered by this leniency. Ever conscious of the empire's threat to the Papal States, he wanted Germany religiously docile but politically disparate. So he suddenly recalled his army corps and cut his subsidies. Betrayed, with victory still uncertain, Charles seethed. He was glad to be rid of the pope's troops, he fumed, because "his name is so hated in Germany." His ambassadors in Rome threatened physical violence, and Pope Paul declared himself ready to die a martyr. However Catholic, they were two strong-minded men.

Major issues of the Reformation

The following statements are intended to summarize some of the central issues that divided Christians during the Protestant and Catholic Reformations. The three positions are given in the chronological order that they occurred, with the two major Protestant movements arising first, followed by the Catholic response to them both. The Lutheran position is taken from the Augsburg Confession, drawn up by Philipp Melanchthon, approved by Martin Luther, and presented to the Emperor Charles V in 1530. Some are from Luther himself. The Calvinist position is drawn from Calvin's own *Institutes of the Christian Religion*. The Catholic position is taken from the canons adopted by the Council of Trent (1545-1563). *Note:* The word "catholic" is not capitalized in the Council of Trent documents. This usage has been preserved in the text here. It should be emphasized that these were the positions taken by the three in the sixteenth and early seventeenth centuries. The terminology they would use to describe them today might somewhat differ.

THE JUSTIFICATION OF MAN BEFORE GOD

Lutheran:

"We cannot obtain forgiveness of sin and righteousness before God by our own merits, works, or satisfactions, but that we receive forgiveness of sin and become righteous before God by grace, for Christ's sake, through faith, when we believe that Christ suffered for us and that for his sake our sin is forgiven and righteousness and eternal life are given to us. For God will regard and reckon this faith as righteousness." [cf. Romans 3:21–26 and 4:5]
—*Augsburg Confession, section 4*

Calvin:

"It is entirely by the intervention of Christ's righteousness that we obtain justification before God. This is equivalent to saying that man is not just in himself, but that the righteousness of Christ is communicated to him by imputation, while he is strictly deserving of punishment. Thus vanishes the absurd dogma that man is justified by faith, inasmuch as it brings him under the influence of the Spirit of God, by whom he is rendered righteous. This is so repugnant to the above doctrine that it never can be reconciled with it."
—*Institutes of the Christian Religion, book 3, chapter 11, section 23*

Catholic:

"When the apostle [i.e. *Paul*] says that a person is justified by faith and as a gift, those words are to be understood in the sense which the perennial consent of the catholic church has maintained and expressed, namely, that we are said to be justified by faith because faith is the first stage of human salvation, the foundation and root of all justification, without which it is impossible to please God [Hebrews 11:6] and come to the fellowship of his children. And we are said to receive justification as a free gift because nothing that precedes justification, neither faith nor works, would merit the grace of justification; for 'if it be by grace, it is no longer on the basis of works; otherwise (as the same apostle says) grace would no longer be grace' [Romans 11:6]."
—*Trent, session 6, chapter 8*

THE NATURE OF ORIGINAL SIN

Lutheran:

"Since the fall of Adam all men who are born according to the course of nature are conceived and born in sin. That is, all men are full of evil lust and inclinations from their mothers' wombs and are unable by nature to have true fear of God and true faith in God. Moreover, this inborn sickness and hereditary sin is truly sin and condemns to the eternal wrath of God all those who are not born again through baptism and the Holy Spirit."
—*Augsburg, section 2*

Calvin:

"As Adam's spiritual life would have consisted in remaining united and bound to his Maker, so estrangement from him was the death of his soul. Nor is it strange that he who perverted the whole order of nature in heaven and earth deteriorated his race by his revolt . . . If the reason is asked, there cannot be a doubt that creation bears part of the punishment deserved by man, for whose use all other creatures were made. Therefore, since through man's fault a curse has extended above and below, over all the regions of the world, there is nothing unreasonable in its extending to all his offspring."
—*Institutes, book 2, chapter 1, section 5*

Catholic:

"If any one does not confess that the first man, Adam, when he had transgressed the commandment of God in paradise, immediately lost the holiness and justice wherein he had been constituted; and that he incurred, through the offense of that prevarication,

the wrath and indignation of God, and consequently death, with which God had previously threatened him, and, together with death, captivity under his power who thenceforth had the empire of death, that is to say, the devil, and that the entire Adam, through that offense of prevarication, was changed, in body and soul, for the worse: let him be anathema."[1]
—*Trent, session 5, chapter 1*

IS SALVATION PREDESTINED?

Lutheran

"You . . . should remember that I have taught that one should not inquire into the predestination of the hidden God but should be satisfied with what is revealed . . . through the ministry of the Word . . . then you can be sure about your faith and salvation."
—*Luther's Genesis Commentary, comment on Genesis 29:9*

"If we look to Christ . . . then predestination will appear lovely . . . For if one forever torments himself with predestination, all one gains is anguish of soul."
—*Martin Luther, 1545, in a letter to a friend, cited in* Historical Introductions to the Book of Concord, *by F. Bente, 1965, p. 223*

Calvin:

"The covenant of life is not preached equally to all, and among those to whom it is preached, does not always meet with the same reception. This diversity displays the unsearchable depth of the divine judgment and is without doubt subordinate to God's purpose of eternal election."
—*Institutes, book 3, chapter 21, section 1*

Catholic:

"No one, so long as he remains in this present life, ought so to presume about the hidden mystery of divine predestination as to hold for certain that he is unquestionably of the number of the predestined, as if it were true that one justified is either no longer capable of sin or, if he sins, may promise himself sure repentance. For, apart from a special revelation, it is impossible to know whom God has chosen for himself."
—*Trent, session 6, chapter 12*

FAITH VERSUS GOOD WORKS

Lutheran:

"Our works cannot reconcile us with God or obtain grace for us, for this happens only through faith . . ."

"Good works should and must be done, not that we are to rely on them to earn grace but that we may do God's will and glorify him."
—*Augsburg, section 20*

---

1. "Anathema," is a Greek word used to translate a Hebrew word, meaning "suspended" or "cut off." As used by the medieval church, it represented a more serious penalty than excommunication which meant exclusion from the sacraments alone. A person who was anathematized was banished entirely from the community.

Calvin:

"The righteousness of works consists in perfect obedience to the law. Hence you cannot be justified by works unless you follow this straight line (if I may so call it) during the whole course of your life. The moment you decline from it, you have fallen into unrighteousness. Hence it appears that righteousness is not obtained by a few works, but by an indefatigable and inflexible observance of the divine will."
—*Institutes, book 3, chapter 18, section 10*

Catholic:

"If anyone says that justice once received is neither preserved nor increased in the sight of God by good works, but that the works themselves are no more than the effects and signs of the justification obtained, and not also a cause of its increase: let him be anathema."
—*Trent, session 6, canon 24*

THE PRESENCE OF CHRIST IN THE HOLY COMMUNION

Lutheran:

"It is taught among us that the true body and blood of Christ are really present in the Supper of our Lord under the form of bread and wine and are there distributed and received."
—*Augsburg, section 10*

Calvin:

"He makes him present with us in three ways in majesty providence, and ineffable grace; under which I comprehend that wondrous communion of his body and blood, provided we understand that it is effected by the power of the Holy Spirit, and not by that fictitious enclosing of his body under the element, since our Lord declared that he had flesh and bones which could be handled and seen."
—*Institutes, book 4, chapter 17, section 26*

Catholic:

"If anyone says that in the venerable sacrament of the Eucharist the substance of the bread and wine remains together with the body and blood of our Lord Jesus Christ, and denies that marvelous and unique change of the whole substance of the bread into the body, and of the whole substance of the wine into the blood, while only the appearance of bread and wine remains, a change which the catholic church most aptly calls transubstantiation: let him be anathema."
—*Trent, session 13, canon 2*

THE NATURE OF THE CHURCH

Lutheran:

"The one holy Christian church will be and remain forever. This is the assembly of all believers among whom the gospel is preached in its purity and the holy sacraments are administered according to the gospel."
—*Augsburg, section 7*

Calvin:

"It is necessary to believe the invisible church, which is manifest to the eye of God only, so we are also enjoined to regard this church which is so called with reference to man, and to cultivate its communion."
—*Institutes, book 4, chapter 1, section 7*

Catholic:

"We believe . . . in One Holy Catholic and Apostolic Church; we acknowledge one baptism for the remission of sins."
—*Nicene Creed, Council of Nicea, A.D. 325*

THE AUTHORITY OF THE CLERGY

Lutheran:

"Nobody should publicly teach or preach or administer the sacraments in the church without a regular call."
—*Augsburg, section 14*

"According to the gospel, the power of keys or the power of bishops is a power and command of God to preach the gospel, to forgive and retain sins, and to administer and distribute the sacraments."
—*Augsburg, section 28*

Calvin:

"A certain rule on this head cannot be obtained from the appointment of the apostles, which was somewhat different from the common call of others. As theirs was an extraordinary ministry, in order to render it conspicuous by some more distinguished mark, those who were to discharge it behaved to be called and appointed by the mouth of the Lord himself. It was not, therefore, by any human election, but at the sole command of God and Christ, that they prepared themselves for the work."
—*Institutes, book 4, chapter 3, section 13*

"But no sober person will deny that the regular mode of lawful calling is that bishops should be designated by men."
—*Institutes, book 4, chapter 3, section 14*

Catholic:

"If anyone denies that there exists in the catholic church a hierarchy consisting of bishops, priests, and ministers, instituted by divine appointment: let him be anathema."
—*Trent, session 23, canon 6*

"If anyone says that in the Roman church (which is the mother and mistress of all the churches) there is not the true teaching on the sacrament of baptism, let him be anathema."
—*Trent, session 7, canon 3*

WHAT SCRIPTURE IS

Lutheran:

Scripture is a collection of sixty-six books (the deuterocanonical books, or Apocrypha, are not considered scriptural since they were missing from the original Jewish scriptures). It is the inspired Word of God and the central means through which humanity becomes privy to the revelation of Jesus Christ. Although there is a close bond between scripture, the Fathers, and the teachings of the church, it is scripture that ultimately judges the church and the Fathers, and not vice versa.
—*cf. Martin Luther, introduction to his translation of the Bible*

Calvin:

"Learned men, and men of the greatest talent . . . if they are not possessed of shameless effrontery, they will be compelled to confess that the Scripture exhibits clear evidence of its being spoken by God and, consequently, of its containing his heavenly doctrine."
—*Institutes, book 1, chapter 7, section 4*

Catholic:

"Moreover, the same sacred and holy synod—considering that no small utility may accrue to the church of God if it be made known which, out of all the Latin editions now in circulation of the [72] sacred books, is to be held as authentic—ordains and declares that the said old and vulgate edition, which, by the lengthened usage of so many years, has been approved of in the church, be, in public lectures, disputations, sermons, and expositions, held as authentic; and that no one is to dare, or presume, to reject it under any pretext whatever."
—*Trent, session 4*

A NOTE ON THE ANABAPTISTS

Though extremely diverse, the various Anabaptist groups were unified in rejecting the very concept of a state church. Similarly, they repudiated the notion that the local church can discipline its members through such measures as excommunication, and denied the right of the magistrate to intervene in church matters. They believed that the Christian life was to be lived by adults who made a life commitment, testified to in baptism by immersion, to follow Christ in a biblical discipleship in separation from the world. Their expectation (supported by history) was that most would earn a martyr's crown for so doing. They were usually determined to live by the Bible's teachings of nonviolence and thus practiced nonparticipation in the army or police force. They viewed Communion as primarily symbolic, as a remembrance, and they likewise held baptism to be primarily an outward declaration of the believer's loyalty to Christ rather than a means of grace. ∎

Then, as Pope Paul's army corps marched back through Trent, they carried south the dreaded "spotted fever," typhus, infecting several bishops and killing one. The doctors advised that the council move, so it voted to adjourn to Bologna, and the pope agreed. Charles again felt betrayed by that "obstinate old man, so intent on destroying the church." Only a quarter of the prelates arrived in papal Bologna; another quarter, the Germans and Spaniards, stayed stubbornly in Trent; and the rest scattered. After one desultory session, the pope prorogued the Council of Trent indefinitely. Four more precious years would be wasted.

Crippled by gout and borne in a litter, Charles won a crushing victory over the Lutheran Schmalkaldic League at Mühlberg in April 1547, proclaiming, "I came, I saw, God conquered." So he was now at least officially in control of Germany's religious destiny. Passing through Wittenberg, he rejected the cry to exhume and scatter the bones of now-dead Luther. "I war only with the living," he replied. The living however, though subdued, remained stubborn. In

Titian is rather generous in his portrayal of Charles V at the Battle of Mühlberg in 1547. Far from riding armed and ready into combat as depicted, Charles was crippled by gout and had to be carried to the battlefield in a litter. Even so, he won a crushing victory over the Lutheran Schmalkaldic League, proclaiming, "I came, I saw, God conquered."

September he convened the imperial Reichstag at Augsburg, only to be confronted by his Lutheran electors, demanding a church council renouncing loyalty to the pope and admitting laymen. Needing them politically and militarily, Charles temporized, then called for a new Council of Trent—without mentioning the pope.

Even with Charles holding sway, an agreement was urgently needed, something German. So in March 1549 he promulgated his "Declaration . . . on the Observance of Religion within the Holy Roman Empire," with the still-hopeful subtitle, "Until a General Council." This "Augsburg Interim" reestablished the Mass, sacraments, and veneration of the saints. But it also permitted clerical marriage and remained silent on justification and the restoration of church property. Despite Charles's ascendancy, when the Mass was said in Marburg, there were "acts of gross indecency." In Strasbourg the bishop was stoned by a mob. A papal legate, traveling secretly through Germany, saw "the Mass everywhere, but in empty churches."

Charles eventually showed the Interim to a legate, announcing coldly that he sought no papal approval. It caused great indignation in Rome, but the pope remained silent. As he lay dying at age eighty-one—having outlived Luther, Henry VIII, and Francis I—Paul III finally saw the depth of German discontent and the emperor's predicament. Had the council stayed in Trent, Charles might have been able to drag the Lutherans there. But never to Bologna. And the Interim was merely a truce.

In an early vote on Paul III's successor, England's by now exiled Cardinal Pole came just one vote shy of election. But then the French arrived, led by young Cardinal Charles Guise of Lorraine, and shifted the conclave. They were under instructions

Henry II

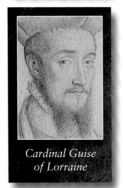

Cardinal Guise of Lorraine

Cardinal Reginald Pole

Duke Maurice of Saxony

from France's new King Henry II to forestall another council. Cherishing an intense hatred of Charles V, they deadlocked the conclave for two full months. Finally, Cardinal Giovanni Maria Ciocchi del Monte emerged as a compromise, a former chairman at Trent known "neither for his prudence nor leadership," in the view of one skeptic. He won the French vote, being thought unfriendly to the emperor. But there the French were wrong. The new Pope Julius III was lukewarm on reform but feared the emperor too much to deny him.

On the first day of 1551, the new pope issued a bull reconvening the Council of Trent and later explained he would "sail in the emperor's ship." Singing his gratitude, Charles liberally distributed safe-conducts to Lutheran theologians. (Even Luther's colleague Philipp Melanchthon took to the road—though the council was again adjourned before his arrival.) Over the summer, while Henry was angrily declaring France free of all heresy, the bishops, mainly Germans and Spaniards, drifted into Trent. Then in September, Henry II invaded central Italy, backing a Farnese rebel in Parma and condemning Julius as "the worst, most ungrateful of men." Henry's embarrassed delegate at Trent read his manifesto declaring that papal aggression made a council impossible and forbidding French attendance. Curiously, however, two Lutheran delegates came from the elector of Brandenburg, promising to abide by the council's decisions. "How many other Protestant princes might have submitted to the council, had it not been so long delayed?" Catholic historian Warren Carroll wonders in print (*The Cleaving of Christendom*, 2000). He has in mind, of course, the frightful price that would be paid by Germany in the next century because the Lutheran-Catholic conflict was not resolved.

In its brief life, Trent's second assembly achieved little except continuity, though that in itself was vital. The Eucharist was confirmed transubstantiated with the continuing presence of the risen Christ, even after Mass. Penance was declared a grace-giving sacrament, not merely a regretful attitude, as was extreme unction (anointing the dying). But little was said about pastoral reform. Then in January 1552 the council was harshly interrupted by another two Lutheran representatives insisting that it annul all past decisions and declare its superiority over the pope. They identified themselves as representing Duke Maurice of Saxony, who hitherto had been an ally of Charles but now treacherously abandoned him, planning an attack both on the council and on Charles.

Meanwhile, France's Henry II raised further trouble. While the ships of his Muslim Turkish allies raided the Italian ports, Henry boycotted Trent and ordered his bishops to prepare a French national council instead. This was clearly a prelude to the separation of the whole French church of which he, the king, would be the head, much as Henry VIII had done in England. Julius's response was to threaten the French king with excommunication. Whatever else he might be, Henry was a believer, and this shook him. So he conceded, bowing to papal authority and abandoning any plan to follow the example of England.

Through the fall of 1552 and the succeeding winter, the council plodded on. In the spring of 1553, when it was deep into a discussion of penance, the turncoat Maurice, now leading the Lutheran forces, struck. His army suddenly seized Augsburg, then the Ehrenberg Pass. It prepared to descend on Trent and nearby

'For twenty years,' said Pope Marcellus, 'people have talked of reform, openly admitting its necessity, and nothing has been done.' Twenty-two days later the new pope was dead of a stroke.

Innsbruck, where Charles, bereft of his customary caution, was resident—by now sick, penniless, and friendless with neither the troops nor gold to fight a new war. Tortured by gout and drenched by rain, he was carried away to safety, leaving Maurice to loot his palace there. Within three months, Charles was forced to accept a treaty completely annulling his victory at Mühlberg, voiding the Augsburg Interim, and permitting his Lutheran princes to enforce their religion on their subjects—with no mention of a council.

Trent had already been deserted by the German bishops who, in the face of the peril, headed for home. The French had never come. So, with only the Italians and Spaniards left, Pope Julius conceded that the council must again be suspended. Three years later he was dead, and the council would not meet again for eleven desperate years.

Even so, an irrepressible hunger for renewal in the church lived on. In less than two weeks, the reformers in the curia—with many of the French absent—elected devout and delicate Marcellus II. He refused to give any customary bonuses to his cardinals and declared an intention to enact a law obliging bishops to reside in their dioceses. "For twenty years, people have talked of reform, openly admitting its necessity," the new pope chided, "and nothing has been done." Great things were expected. Then, after reigning twenty-two days, Marcellus II, aged fifty-three, was dead of a stroke.

Thus the conclave gathered again, with the French now in force. They rejected front-running Cardinal Pole, legate to England's Catholic Queen Mary. In May 1555 the reform-intent Cardinal Giovanni Morone enlisted French support to elect Naples's Cardinal Carafa, the hard-liner at the first Trent meeting. This new pope, Paul IV, was a mass of contradictions. Though seventy-nine, he was lean and taut, with immense energy, a huge head, and "eyes like arrows, ever ready to strike." He was a cofounder of the ascetic Theatines, but of an angry, autocratic character. His iron will was joined to a spectacular absence of judgment and a deep antipathy to Ignatius of Loyola, founder of the Jesuits (see ch. 8). Choosing the motto, "Thou shalt trample underfoot the lion and the dragon," Paul IV said nothing

Elected pope after a two-month stalemate in the conclave, Julius III, portrayed below in a work of unknown origin, promptly reconvened the Council of Trent, declaring his support for the emperor in the process. But opposition from the French and an attack by Duke Maurice of Saxony forced Julius to suspend his council. It would not meet again for eleven years.

Pope Paul IV, seen above, possessed an iron will joined with a spectacular absence of judgment. Seemingly uninterested in reconvening the Council of Trent, the Inquisition remained his first love, along with which he carried on a tireless campaign against seditious preaching, Judaism, usury, hunting, and dancing. In addition, he ordered fig leaves painted over the Sistine Chapel nudes and had tens of thousands of books burned.

about reconvening Trent at his first consistory, though the conclave that elected him had sworn to do so. "The cardinals all looked at one another, and they understood," says historian Henri Daniel-Rops (*Holy History*, 1954). Five days later, Paul appointed his nephew Carlo Carafa cardinal and secretary of state—the first of many nephews to be given appointments. Two weeks later, he launched a series of heresy investigations of his cardinals, who must endure his reign for four long years.

At Carafa's suggestion when a cardinal, his predecessor, Pope Paul III, had earlier revived the Holy Office—the Roman Inquisition—and made Carafa its prefect. And the Inquisition remained the new Pope Paul IV's first love. "In no case employ gentleness," he ordered, and capital punishment became commonplace. "The pope's violence is always great, but with the Inquisition, it is truly indescribable," wrote the Venetian ambassador. "On its meeting days, Thursdays, nothing on earth prevents him attending."

Paul IV's Inquisition cracked down not only on seditious preachers but on prostitutes, usurers, beggars, book peddlers, Moors, and Jews. Wandering "gyrovague" monks, an annoyance in most cities, were rounded up in their hundreds and condemned to the galleys—a slow death. Hunting and dancing were proscribed, and fig leaves were painted over the Sistine Chapel nudes. He also established the Index of Forbidden Books (see sidebar, p. 198). Tens of thousands of books were burned. "Even the best Catholics disapprove of such rigor," lamented the Jesuit Peter Canisius.

Paul IV was a decided reformer. He prohibited simony and offset the lost revenue by slashing his own and his cardinals' pay. But his rigidity crushed his curia. The bishop of Aquilea lost his cardinal's cap for leniency toward a preacher who spoke too lightly about predestination. When Cardinal Pole mildly rebuked the pope's violence (obliquely suggesting he examine his nephews), the pope summoned him from England for a heresy trial. Pole pleaded with the pope, describing himself as "Isaac, about to be sacrificed by his father." Finally, England's Catholic queen Mary forbade Pole to obey. Paul IV eventually turned on the Jesuits, branding them rebellious, and tried to restructure the order. When gentle Cardinal Morone—the man most responsible for his election—mused that religious violence never bore good fruit, the pope imprisoned him as a Lutheran.

Paul IV's most crippling blind spot, however, was the seemingly unbridled rapacity of his nephews, particularly secretary of state Cardinal Carlo. The Neapolitan Carafa family had long chafed under Spanish rule. Now, greedy for spoils, Carlo encouraged Paul's longing to "expel the barbarians" from Italy, and fueled his uncle's hatred of Charles V—"a cripple in body and soul" and "the worst man in a thousand years." The conniving nephew struck an alliance with the French to divide up Spanish Naples and Sicily, the northern imperial cities, and Florence. It was a spectacularly unjust and impractical scheme, hatched with the undeserving French against the pope's only reliably Catholic allies, the devout Habsburgs.

Cardinal Giovanni Morone

Nevertheless, in mid-1556 Paul IV allied with France and declared war on the "heretic and schismatic" Charles V, vowing that Charles and his son Philip would be deprived of all their kingdoms "by virtue of the authority of Christ." The French dallied in their promised invasion of the north, but Paul hurled his papal army against Naples—only to see it repelled contemptuously by Charles's duke of Alva. Again betrayed, Charles first consulted the theologians of Louvain, then resolved, in Alva's words, "to do as any obedient son, attacked by his father: take the weapon from his hand."

As the Spaniards moved north, Cardinal Carlo unsuccessfully invited the Turks to attack their rear in Sicily. But by year's end, Alva's army was approaching the walls of Rome. Blind to the irony, Paul hired hundreds of Lutheran mercenaries to defend the city. But by mid-1557 the war had spread to the Low Countries, and the French defeat at Saint-Quentin forced them to pull out of northern Italy. The abandoned pope first threatened to starve himself in Castel Sant'Angelo, then sued for peace. Embarrassed, the Spaniards insisted only that Paul annul his French alliance. Bishop Seripando called it "a most execrable conflict, setting father against son."

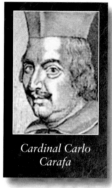

Cardinal Carlo Carafa

Too late wise, Paul IV finally accepted an ambassador's advice to investigate his nephews—their graft, confiscations, and intrigues. He was broken by the findings. In early 1559 he held a secret consistory in which his three closest nephews—Carlo, Paliano, and Montebello—were stripped of their offices and banished.[5] Paul multiplied his own severe fasts and mortifications, and, in vicarious expiation, intensified his war on Roman corruption, instructing his police to spy on private morals and imprisoning violators of the Good Friday fast.

Duke of Alva

Then dropsy set in, and the pope lay bedridden, lamenting, "How bitterly flesh and blood have deceived me!" When he finally died that August, Rome rioted, sacked and burned the offices of the Inquisition, freed the heretics, and dumped his statue in the Tiber. He had to be buried in the dead of night. Ironically, this autocratic pope had enacted reforms much needed by his church but imposed them from the top. Real reform needed the tools adopted by the Calvinists: clarity of doctrine, education, and evangelization.

By then, Holy Roman Emperor Charles V had also reached the end of his race, a man viewed by many historians as a latter-day medievalist whose principled values were alien to his own often amoral times. He could see his reign only as a failure. The council he wanted so badly was twice begun and twice frustrated by an alliance of Catholic France with his own Lutheran princes. A voice of tolerance, he had to accept a repressive partition of Germany. And much of Christian Hungary had by then been lost to the Muslim Turks. Declaring himself broken and exhausted, he began a year-long process of abdicating his crowns to his son Philip and his brother, Ferdinand.

5. Early in the reign of Pope Paul IV's successor, it was discovered that his nephew Giovanni Carafa, suspecting his wife of adultery, had formed a court with two of his cousins, tortured a confession out of a young man, stabbed him twenty-seven times, then strangled Giovanni's seven-months-pregnant wife. With this revelation, all of the Carafas' many enemies rose up, Rome was locked down for their trial, and four, including Cardinal Carlo, were hanged.

Charles had led, from his litter, his last campaign in the Low Countries, but he was then too weak to attend the 1555 imperial Reichstag at Augsburg, leaving that to Ferdinand. There, despite Ferdinand's moving denunciation of German disunity, the delegates would scarcely listen to an appeal for Christian accord. The resulting Religious Peace of Augsburg ratified the Lutheran princes' seizure of church property and the conformity of each territory to its ruler's religion. Those not accepting their prince's faith must either leave or conform. This was not only partition but the divided witness of Christianity. Literally an hour before the Peace was to be proclaimed imperial law, a letter came from Charles in

The peril of the first mass medium

Rome's answer to the 16th-century avalanche of printing was the Index of Forbidden Books that lasted until a liberal 20th century doomed it

In January 1559 the fervidly uncompromising Pope Paul IV sent a further surge of consternation through a Catholic world reeling from the effects of the Protestant Reformation. He promulgated the "Index of Forbidden Books," universally decreeing for the first time precisely what books any Catholic in good standing must not read, possess, sell, or print. But it was not so much the Reformation that brought about the Index as the emergence of the first mass medium, printing.

Censorship of sorts had been considered an essential pastoral care of the church ever since the newly baptized Ephesians, inspired by the apostle Paul, flung their texts on magic into the flames (Acts 19:19-20). After Constantine authorized Christianity as a legal religion in his empire, heretical writings were viewed not only as deadly to the souls of the faithful but also dangerous to civil order, and ecclesial bans were often enforced by the state. When the Council of Nicea condemned Arius as a heretic in 325 and proscribed his treatise *Thalia*, it was Emperor Constantine who ordered it incinerated and the execution of violators of the ban.

Even when books began to replace manuscript copies, reproductions of any particular work remained so scarce that cataloging of prohibited texts was scarcely required; condemnation occurred on a case-by-case basis. With the arrival of the printing press in the mid-fifteenth century, however, this trickle of books soon swelled into a raging river (see p. 14). In 1515 Leo X therefore codified the church's long-standing practice of prior censorship by decreeing that all writings, not only specifically religious ones, be submitted to the local bishop before printing.

This decree proved ineffective. For example, although Pope Leo condemned Martin Luther's numerous works under threat of excommunication, they continued to circulate quite unhindered. Local indexes

Pope Paul IV's Index of Forbidden Books decreed an enormous compendium of books that Catholics were forbidden to read. It was so vast in its proscriptions that enforcing it was patently impossible. Future popes significantly modified the index.

were drawn up and fitfully enforced, the first appearing in the Netherlands in 1529, also with minimal effect.

Concluding that firm and central leadership was clearly needed, the Holy Office took on the job in 1542, and inquisitors in Milan, Naples, and Venice began seizing books and fining booksellers.[1] Venice, which dominated European publishing (it would produce an estimated eight million books between 1450 and 1500), took defensive action and managed to thwart promulgation of a comprehensive index in 1555.

But four years later the fiercely determined Paul IV did not consult the Venetians when he initiated his sweeping index. It included the complete works of more than 550 authors, among them Desiderius Erasmus, Niccolo Machiavelli, popular French writer François Rabelais, and one Pietro Aretino, master of the bawdy sonnet. On the premise that an author's faith would affect all his writing, it prohibited the

Brussels, declaring his imminent abdication and refusal to sign. Ferdinand would likewise refrain from signing, yet the Peace became de facto law.

A month later, at his Brussels palace, Charles conveyed to his son Philip his rule of the Low Countries, the land of Charles's birth fifty-five years earlier. Dressed in black, deathly pale, his beard snow white, his visage pain-wracked, standing only with help, he sorrowed: "I have had to bear the burden of many wars, against my will. Never did I undertake them except regretfully, under compulsion. Even today I grieve that I cannot leave you in peace and quiet . . . but the burden and fatigue . . . the condition to which I am reduced. I have done

Books the Index has banned: John Calvin's Institutes of the Christian Religion; The Prince *by Niccolò Machiavelli;* Gargantua *by François Rabelais; and Galileo's* Dialogue Concerning the Two Chief World Systems.

entire oeuvre of non-Catholic writers in such diverse fields as botany, geography, and medicine, and it blacklisted the total stock of some sixty northern European publishers, regardless of subject matter.

However, efforts to enforce it died with Paul eight months later. Another five years passed before his successor, Pius IV, released a somewhat less restrictive ordinance. Since it was endorsed by the Council of Trent, it was known as the Tridentine Index, and quickly gained general acceptance among Catholics. While it retained ninety-nine percent of the authors and titles condemned by its predecessor, and provided that anyone caught with a heretical text could be excommunicated, it dropped the list of forbidden publishers and did not indiscriminately condemn a man's entire canon. It prohibited, for example, only six of Erasmus's books, and it permitted the circulation of books with what were deemed minor flaws, after these had been corrected. Nevertheless, no vernacular translation of scripture could be disseminated without ecclesial approval, and all Protestant translations were expressly forbidden.

Though the Tridentine Index, with additions and modifications in every age, would survive the next four hundred years, its efficacy over time and across cultures is hard to assess. Venetian booksellers ran a thriving black market well into the sixteenth century, writes Paul Grendler (*Culture and Censorship in Late Renaissance Italy and France*, 1981). During the Catholic Reformation, prohibition of magic and occult literature was generally flouted, but on balance Rome's censorship efforts did restrict Catholic reading. However, writes John Corien ("The End of

the Imprimatur," an article in the canon law journal *Jurist*, 1984), by the turn of the twentieth century many Catholics would ignore the Index as anachronistic. Regular updates would cease in 1948, at which point some four thousand titles were listed.[2]

In 1966 another Pope Paul would abolish the Index of Forbidden Books altogether; a society schooled in Western liberal tradition found the concept alien and repugnant.[3] Nevertheless, Pope Paul VI would observe, this would not obviate a Christian's duty to guard against falsity. Vigilance would be more than ever necessary in a modern world where inherently evil ideas could gain wider acceptance and social approbation more quickly than ever before. Even nineteenth-century atheist philosopher Arthur Schopenhauer, after all, advised that no one under forty read Hegel for fear of intellectual corruption. ■

1. Jewish writings were particularly targeted by inquisitorial censors. In 1553, for example, Rome ordered the destruction of every copy of the Talmud in Italy.

2. Surviving proscribed items included some from philosophers Blaise Pascal, René Descartes, Immanuel Kant, John Stuart Mill, Thomas Hobbes, and Henri Bergson; novelists George Sand, Gustave Flaubert, Anatole France, and Graham Greene; poet John Milton; and satirist Jonathan Swift.

3. The Catholic Church still requires translations of the Bible, liturgical books, prayer books, etc., to be submitted to the appropriate church authorities for approval. As of 2010 the latest update for this process was the new Code of Canon Law, issued in 1983.

what I could, and am sorry I could not do better. I have always known my insufficiency and incapacity."

Tears streamed down the emperor's cheeks as his son Philip fell to his knees and kissed his hand. Philip and the assemblage, too, wept uncontrollably. "We may search the annals of history in vain for such another scene, for such another generation of princes as these of the Habsburg dynasty, who were ready of their own free will to retire from the scene of their sovereignty," writes Charles's German biographer Karl Brandi in *The Emperor Charles* (1939).

In January 1556 Charles abdicated the thrones of Spain, Sicily, and the Indies to Philip, and in September, even while Paul IV was slandering him, he gave up the imperial throne to his brother, Ferdinand. He had resolved to spend his last days in Spain at the monastery of San Jeronimo in Yuste, joined by his widowed sisters Eleanor of France and Mary of Hungary. In August, with his health momentarily improved, he embarked for Spain on his last voyage, borne by a fleet of fifty ships, escorted chivalrously by an English squadron.

His progress home was slow and solemn. In his last twenty-one months of peace, he lived in a small house beside the monastery church, where he joined its daily prayers. He gardened, bird-watched, tended his fishponds, and greeted visitors, surrounded by paintings of his children and his beloved wife, Isabella. He still treasured the crucifix she held when she died, twenty years before. On November 21, 1558, now bedridden, he asked for that crucifix, raised it to his

In this work by the Victorian painter Alfred Elmore, the dying and abdicated emperor Charles V nostalgically views favorite portraits of the people in his past as they are displayed to him by the monks at the monastery of San Jeronimo in Yuste, where he died in 1558. His son, King Philip II, looks on from over the emperor's left shoulder.

lips, and died with the name of Jesus on his tongue. "The greatest man who ever lived," whispered his attendant—a claim Charles would certainly have denied. Yet he was a man of chivalry in an age when religious fervor seemed to endorse lies and treachery.

Forty years had passed since Luther posted his challenge at Wittenberg, and fourteen since the Council of Trent first met. Yet Luther's challenges still went unanswered. The Reformation's first generation never foresaw a permanent rupture of Christendom. Now after two generations—with Britain, Scandinavia, and most of Germany Protestant, and with France and Poland swaying—Rome was still dithering. By September 1559 few thinking men or women in the Catholic Church, whether lay or clergy, did not know what was needed. The question was: who could do it?

The cardinals gathering after Paul IV's death took four despairing months to answer that question, two of them dying there (conclaves being notoriously unhealthy). The conclave split evenly between the French, Spanish, and Carafa partisans, with the Carafas playing off the other two. Four candidates came close to winning but then failed, all the while the Spanish ambassador shouting advice at the cardinals through a breach in the wall of the chamber. By Christmas, so weary were they of Carafa intrigue that "they would have elected a block of wood," in the view of one observer. In that vein of despair, the French and Spanish finally negotiated with each other and agreed on bashful backbencher Gian Angelo Medici of Milan.

With a large red nose, wispy beard, and mincing gait, Pope Pius IV's demeanor drew "laughter rather than respect." He was a commoner, no relation to the powerful Florentine Medicis, so he was soon branded "little Medici"—*il Medichino*. Having no great family ties, he had avoided the church's worst scandals. A man of "astute simplicity," he had only the church's interest at heart. He quickly announced that his first purpose was completing the work of Trent.

Pope Pius IV, whose demeanor reportedly incited "laughter rather than respect," turned out to be exactly what the Catholic Church needed. Immediately reconvening the council at Trent, Pius, portrayed here by an unidentified sixteenth-century artist, was able to assemble a whopping two hundred bishops.

Pius IV first reined in the Roman Inquisition, forbidding its intrusion into morals, then began pruning Paul's detested Index. He freed long-suffering Cardinal Morone, and Rome relaxed. But reconvening the Council of Trent would not be so easy. National jealousy ran deep, and Germany was edgy about anything upsetting the delicate Peace of Augsburg.

France, however, was desperate for a council. By now, their Calvinists numbered perhaps two hundred thousand, a tiny fraction of the population, but this revolutionary gentry, sincere though the religious convictions of many undoubtedly were, was also hungry for church land, was bankrolled by English gold, and was seemingly unstoppable.[6] In March 1560 their plot to seize the royal family was barely forestalled, and they were busily negotiating with Germany's Lutherans. The Catholic nobility waffled vaguely: what did Catholics believe? So Cardinal Guise of Lorraine warned Rome that France could no longer wait for an ecumenical council; only a national council might avert civil war.

Like his predecessors, a horrified Pius IV saw that as a prelude to schism. Thus the pope called for a council to convene at Trent for Easter 1561 under his legates Cardinals Ercole Gonzaga and Girolamo Seripando. By Easter only four

6. The figure two hundred thousand was Cardinal Guise's best guess. Calvinist Admiral de Coligny thought fifty thousand. Yet for French Catholics, a renewed Council of Trent came just in time. Another plot to seize the king was uncovered in September 1560. Then in December young Francis II sickened and died, leaving the crown to ten-year-old Charles IX. England's chancellor, the Protestant William Cecil, wrote to his ambassador Sir Nicholas Throckmorton: "Courage will abash the papists, so well I know their cowardice . . . impugn and suppress the tyranny of the papists."

A cardinal who made Trent work

Even popes feared the reforming zeal of Milan's Charles Borromeo, and one set of monks he called to account attempted his assassination

It was a balmy afternoon in January 1580, and the affable Pope Gregory XIII was determined to enjoy it, lounging in the opulent Vatican gardens with several cardinals, watching his prized horses put through their paces. But this respite was abruptly terminated by an announcement: Cardinal Charles Borromeo, the indefatigable archbishop of Milan, would be dropping by for a visit. Leaping to his feet, the pope hastily mobilized his guests. "It would never do," he exclaimed with a chuckle, "to let Cardinal Borromeo find us here—he'd berate us for wasting our time!"

The formidable reputation of Charles Borromeo, that notably pious and efficient ecclesiastical bureaucrat, had by then been more than three decades in the making. Born in 1538 at Arona, in northern Italy, to an aristocratic Milanese family, Charles had been an unprepossessing child. His small oval face was defined by a dour mouth and an oversized nose and chin. He had a stammer so severe that strangers could scarcely understand him. And he was said to be so serious and withdrawn that he habitually spurned games and playmates to read or pray in solitude.

His father, Count Giberto Borromeo, was very differently inclined, and by 1550 the family finances were in disarray. Something had to be done, and Count Giberto's solution was to have twelve-year-old Charles appointed abbot of a prosperous nearby monastery, thus attaching its revenues. Though this was legal, logical, and satisfactory, the new young abbot kept asking awkward questions. Didn't the monastery's money, he wondered, actually belong to God? Shouldn't it therefore be spent serving the poor?

Charles spent the next nine years completing doctoral degrees in civil and canon law at Milan and Pavia, and putting the family estates in order after his father's death. In 1560 his life underwent a profound change when one of his Medici uncles (a maternal connection) was elected pope. Suddenly Charles Borromeo was summoned to serve as administrator for the new Pope Pius IV and shortly thereafter was appointed cardinal and papal secretary of state. Many a cynical Roman detected obvi-

Charles Borromeo, inexhaustible and fearless, devoted his life to realizing the reformatory decrees of the Council of Trent—disciplining lax clergy, restoring churches, founding colleges, and endowing charities and seminaries.

ous nepotism. Charles perceived a genuine opportunity to serve God.

His inaugural task was to assist Pope Pius in reconvening and concluding the Council of Trent, in which he played a key support role. He would become at least equally integral in upholding and implementing its decisions, especially after being consecrated archbishop of Milan in May 1564. In great excitement he traveled there, intent upon reform and brimming with confidence that he could bring it about.

There was no lack of work—Charles was the first archbishop in eighty years to actually spend any time in the diocese. Quickly selling off the more luxurious appurtenances of the archiepiscopal palace, he augmented the profits with his own salary and benefices and began endowing charities and seminaries, repairing churches, and founding colleges. He journeyed tirelessly from one bishopric to the next, personally ensuring that all was in order and acting decisively when it was not. Lax priests, for example, became his guests until they showed improvement; clerical galas and revelries were canceled; absentee clerics were recalled or removed.

But the archbishop reputedly was toughest on himself, fasting so diligently, for example, that he began to resemble "a body without flesh, a soul without body." His English biographer Margaret Yeo enlarges the portrait: "Borromeo, in tears over ruined chapels, desecrated altars, and broken statues, would often spend the whole night in prayer between four roofless walls and then talk to the people at dawn before they went off to the fields" (*A Prince of Pastors: St. Charles Borromeo*, 1943).

In the midst of all this he would be summoned to Rome, where among much else he supervised production of the catechism incorporating the conclusions of Trent, or he would be dispatched on papal diplomatic negotiations. At one time or another Borromeo held responsibility for implementing Trent's reforms in most of Italy and much of Switzerland. (His own archdiocese, in fact, included three Swiss valleys.)

These activities frequently infuriated both ecclesiastical and secular authorities, but the archbishop was not easily intimidated. In 1569, for instance, he had the governor of Milan, the duke of Alburquerque, excommunicated for defying Rome and shortly thereafter found his residence surrounded by the duke's troops. While his retinue locked themselves away in fear, Charles took firm hold of his episcopal cross and stepped out to meet them, and the hard-boiled soldiers fell to their knees for his blessing.

Two months later came a more dangerous incident concerning the Humiliati, a monastic order he was trying to restore to its original austere ideals. On October 26, while celebrating vespers in his chapel, Charles was struck by a shot in the back. He fell to the floor, seemingly dead, but rose almost immediately and motioned for the service to continue. The musket ball, apparently slowed by his heavy vestments, had inflicted only a bruise. Secular authorities hunted down four Humiliati conspirators, including the attacker, and despite pleas for mercy from Charles (who forgave them), all four were executed.[1]

Truly lethal, however, was the outbreak of bubonic plague that raged in Milan from the summer of 1576 through 1577. The archbishop alone appeared to be impervious to fear or contagion. "God can replace us!" he assured his cowering clergy and led the way in caring for the sick, distributing food, and dispensing Holy Communion to the afflicted. When supplies ran short, he begged for money, pawned his possessions, even tore down the palace drapes to use as fabric. So Milan survived what is still remembered there as the Plague of St. Charles.

Though his demanding and hectic life was gradually wearing him down, for another six years he battled through assorted crises and increasing physical maladies. On November 3, 1584, he died of fever. The Milanese immediately proclaimed him a saint. Rome, always resistant to local enthusiasms, took longer, though not by much. In 1610 the intrepid papal bureaucrat-cum-holy ascetic was proclaimed St. Charles Borromeo (feast day November 4) by Pope Paul V. ∎

1. The Humiliati were an Italian order originating in the twelfth century and distinguished in that they sustained both monastic and later mendicant ways of life. By the sixteenth, however, the order had become quite otherwise and was suppressed by Pope Paul V in 1571. An associated women's order lasted into the twentieth century.

Impervious to the fear of contagion, Borromeo dispenses Holy Communion to the afflicted in plague-ridden Milan, as imagined by the seventeenth-century Baroque painter Sigismondo Caula.

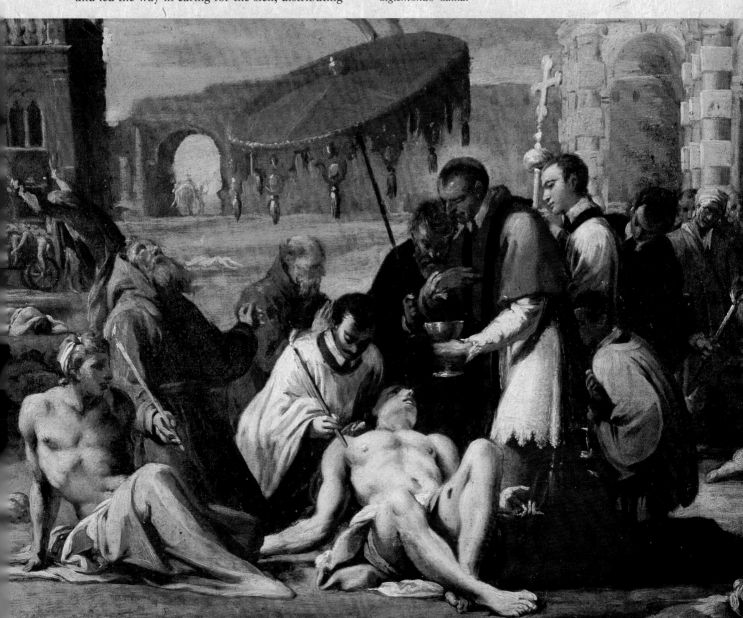

7. The French effort for a national council at Poissy shattered in September 1561; on the first day, Calvinist Theodore Beza threw down an uncompromising denial of the real presence in the Eucharist, scandalizing the Catholics. The cardinal of Lorraine appealed biblically to John 6, "unless you eat my flesh and drink my blood," and the meeting degenerated into a shouting match. For the Calvinists, a sacramental church was idolatry with which there could be no compromise.

Cardinal Ercole Gonzaga

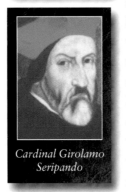

Cardinal Girolamo Seripando

bishops had arrived. Ambassadors were sent to the Protestant princes, but they condemned any council called by a pope. Then in May, Emperor Ferdinand finally endorsed it. Philip of Spain, piously awaiting his uncle, then dispatched his own churchmen, and in July the French bishops gathered to pick their delegates. When the council was finally declared open on January 18, 1562, over a hundred bishops and their retinues crowded tiny Trent. That number soon doubled.[7]

The council almost foundered at its launching over the issue of whether it was resuming the earlier two meetings or beginning a new one. The Germans and French, still seeking wiggle room with Protestantism, wanted the earlier sacramental decrees shelved, while the Spaniards and Italians saw most of those questions as settled. The issue rose again and again, but slowly the difference made no difference. Despite bitter debates on reform, by summer the council was passing overwhelmingly decrees on the Eucharist that would be idolatrous to any Protestant: "the unbloody perpetuation of Christ's sacrifice on the cross," and "the Last Supper as the first Mass," and the John 6 "eat my flesh" passage read not merely as "spiritual" metaphor but literal reality. By autumn the issue of "one council or three?" remained dangling but ignored.

The Castello del Buonconsiglio, a castle on Trent's Pontara Street and seat of the bishopric of Trent from the thirteenth century onward, played host to many sessions of the Council of Trent.

The Spaniards were militant about disciplining absentee bishops and demanded declaration of a *ius divinum*, a divine law, obliging bishops to live in their dioceses. After all, Rome teemed with bishops and their entourages, drones fed by dioceses never seen, flocks straying for want of shepherds. But the curia responded that it could not survive on the tithes of the city, and a divine law barring bishops from Rome would cripple the universal church.

There were now over two hundred prelates at Trent. They all spoke on the issue, month after month, and the council deadlocked. Pius IV wondered nervously whether his own legates, Gonzaga and Seripando, were "plotting to destroy the Roman curia" by encouraging the debate, then peremptorily forbade all discussion of it. The Spaniards, seeing the legates "disgraced for refusing to attack the abuses of the curia," threatened to walk out, only to be bridled eventually by their own King Philip. But by now everyone, except those directly threatened, angrily questioned Rome's commitment to reform.

Cardinal Guise of Lorraine arrived in November with the bulk of the French delegation, pronouncing enthusiastic loyalty to the papacy. A rough formula to answer the demand for a *ius divinum* was being hammered out: bishops are "appointed by Christ, but receive the power of their jurisdictions from the pope." But what statutes could reconcile local bishops with a universal church? Soon, pressured by his own French prelates and frustrated by papal interference,

Despite its obstacles, the Council of Trent completed its twenty-fifth and final session, an occasion memorialized in the German oil-on-canvas piece atop the page. While Pope Pius IV approved its mandates, it would be left to his successor, Pius V (inset), to implement the reforms. He was to prove equal to the challenge.

Ten days that never happened

Pope Gregory XIII wiped them off the calendar, never to be recovered, but the resulting calendrical accuracy looks good for about 20,000 years

On the morning that followed October 4, 1582, Romans awoke to find, so to speak, ten days removed from their lives. The fifth day of October had overnight become the fifteenth—a bewildering change but, as they would discover, an essential one that had in fact been accomplished eight months earlier with the stroke of a pen. For that was when, in his bull *Inter gravissimas*, Pope Gregory XIII had authorized the resetting of time for the Western world.

The Roman calendar had been devised in 46 B.C. by order of Julius Caesar, whose renowned Alexandrian astronomers measured the solar or tropical year—the time from one vernal equinox, or first day of spring, to the next—at 365 days, six hours. To accommodate the extra hours, they instituted the "leap year" by adding one day every fourth year. After Julius was assassinated, a "leap" was mistakenly instituted every third year, but the Emperor Augustus corrected the error by abolishing them from 10 B.C. until A.D. 4, then reverting to the four-year cycle.[1]

The Julian system nevertheless contained a basic inaccuracy. Its year was too long by eleven minutes and fourteen seconds, which over time added up. Thus, in A.D. 325 the Council of Nicea, striving to fix the date of Easter, used the Julian date of March 21 for the vernal equinox. By the sixteenth century, however, the equinox had inched backward to March 11, and church authorities had long been pleading for calendar reform.

After they did so again at the Council of Trent, Pope Gregory took matters in hand. His best astronomers included Christopher Clavius, a German Jesuit. A posthumous contribution from the research of Aloysius Lilius, an Italian doctor, was also crucial. Their correction involved ruling out as leap years all those dates divisible by one hundred, unless they are also divisible by four hundred. (Thus, there would be no leap year in 1700, 1800, and 1900, but there would be a leap year in 1600 and 2000.) The effect was to make the Gregorian calendar accurate within one day in twenty thousand years.

Europe's Catholic countries adopted this papal reform almost immediately, the rest of Europe gradually followed suit, and by the mid-twentieth century so would most of the rest of the world. The Eastern Orthodox and Coptic churches, however, would retain the Julian calendar, holding that only a truly ecumenical council can authorize a calendar reform affecting the date of Easter. They did not attend the Council of Trent because they considered it non-ecumenical.

The Gregorian calendar also initiated the settlement of another irksome issue; it formally made January 1 New Year's Day. Julius Caesar had also done this, but in Christian Europe various days—Christmas or the Annunciation (March 25) or Easter—were chosen to inaugurate the new year. By Gregory's time, many countries, including Germany, Spain, and France, had already adopted January 1. But tardy England did not switch from March 25 to January 1 until 1783, when it finally accepted the Gregorian calendar. Among the Eastern Orthodox, at least eight jurisdictions begin the year on January 1.

1. The term "leap year" likely refers to the fact that the extra day added at the end of February causes subsequent feasts to "leap" forward one day.

The Gregorian calendar was instituted in 1582 by Pope Gregory XIII, seen below discussing the project with assembled astronomers and members of the curia. His reform of the old and inaccurate Julian calendar was only reluctantly accepted by Protestant nations—as evidenced by the dual-natured English calendar above.

the cardinal of Lorraine was balking crossly, momentarily denying even the title of "universal bishop" for the pope. It was a chill wind, and the council looked doomed.

By the turn of 1563, the distrust between the curia party and the Spanish, French, and German reformers had reached a crisis. Riots erupted daily between their retinues, the blood flowing so freely that the sessions for March had to be canceled. Then, exhausted by the tension, Cardinal-legate Gonzaga sickened and died on March 2, whispering the verse, "If it be possible, let this cup pass from me." Two weeks later, even more overwhelmed, assistant legate Seripando repeated on his deathbed, "Lord, make haste to rescue me." Gonzaga was mourned as "a gentleman . . . intelligent and patient," but he may have been too gentlemanly for the Council of Trent.

Then came a stroke of genius: Pope Pius immediately appointed Cardinal Morone, Paul IV's undeserving victim, as his premier legate. A fellow Milanese, Morone was an experienced and gifted diplomat with a rare knowledge of his fel-

Where the Greek recognition of divorce for adultery had caused deadlock, marriage was now embraced as an indissoluble sacrament, with the church empowered to set its conditions.

low men and an untiring ardor for the council. He tackled the core problems head on. First, he faced down a crippling proposal from the late Pope Paul, that curia reform remain exclusively a papal prerogative. Then he eroded the cardinal of Lorraine's leadership of the adamant reformers by deftly inciting him into a two-day tirade against the curia—which wholly alienated the French from the papacy. With that done, Morone politely but unsparingly refuted Lorraine's indictments, point by point and so thoroughly that Lorraine conceded the case.

Within a month Morone had enlisted Lorraine as an ally, drafting the decree on ordination, defending the pope's authority to appoint bishops, yet describing them as "set by the Holy Spirit to rule the church of God" (Acts 20:28)—a sacramental and not merely human institution. Contradicting the Protestant concept of an "invisible church," the Catholic hierarchy was declared divinely ordained. He next addressed the episcopal residency issue, decreeing: "It is a divine command that those entrusted with the care of souls should know their flock." That duty was stated explicitly to include all-too-absent cardinals, yet the source of that duty went undefined, left for theologians to ponder. This decree passed, 231 to six. Equally popular and just as important was a clause requiring bishops to establish seminaries in every diocese to educate their parish clergy.

Other issues soon fell into line. Where the Greek recognition of divorce for adultery had occasioned a deadlock, marriage was now embraced as an indissoluble sacrament, with the church empowered to set its conditions. Coerced marriages (common among nobles) were forbidden on pain of excommunication.

Morone was not finished. In August he unveiled a pastoral renewal decree with twenty-one clauses already vetted by the reformers. Bishops must undertake visitations throughout their dioceses every two years and their metropolitans must enforce this with diligence. Diocesan synods must be annual, provincial synods triennial, and everyone must observe their rulings. Prelates—including cardinals—were forbidden more than one benefice, whether a diocese, monastery, or parish. There were norms for nominating bishops, one of them sweeping: no more could bishops have children.

Though debate sometimes became bitter, consensus grew. Hard-core Spanish Cardinal de Luna remained icily skeptical of the pope's commitment to curia reform. So, hoping to resurrect that debate, he questioned the council's legitimacy, since only papal legates may bring drafts to the floor. Morone replied nonchalantly that the debates, amendments, and votes are all manifestly free. He then pro-

Reform was now defined and approved. But would it happen? Pius IV's successor proved equal to the challenge. Pius V's liturgical revisions would endure into the twentieth century.

posed debate on the "reform of princes," proposing a ban on secular interference in church affairs. De Luna, King Philip's ambassador, quickly backed off. Morone then moved on to a reform of religious orders, leaving them undisturbed in their peculiar callings but enforcing communal life, abolishing private property for members, setting minimum ages for vows, and giving local bishops some oversight. This, too, passed overwhelmingly.

The Council of Trent's twenty-fifth and last session began December 3, 1563. The invocation of the saints, existence of purgatory, veneration of relics and images, and indulgences were affirmed. By way of reform, the rule against the sale of indulgences was affirmed, the pains of purgatory being avoided only through appropriate penances. Then came this final decree: "The authority of the apostolic see must be held inviolate against all the decisions of this council." This passed almost unanimously.

The next day, all the decrees of the earlier assemblies (under Paul III and Julius III) were reconfirmed, and the issue of "one council or three?" was laid to rest. The cardinal of Lorraine moved acclamations for the council's three popes and for emperors Charles V and Ferdinand II. He then cried out, "May we all confess the faith and observe the decrees of the Sacred Ecumenical Council of Trent." The prelates vowed, "We shall always confess . . . always observe." Then many wept, embraced, and kissed those they had so recently vilified. In sum, writes the German Catholic historian Hubert Jedin in his four-volume *History of the Council of Trent* (1951–1976), "it was clearly recognized that new laws and institutions alone would not create new men. But at the same time, it was also known that no renewal was possible without them and that a new spirit in the church required new forms."

Pope Pius IV gave Trent's decrees unconditional assent. But when he died in December 1565, the choice of his replacement was crucial. Reform was now defined and approved. But would it happen? His successor, Cardinal Antonio Ghislieri, who became Pope Pius V, proved equal to the challenge. He sent legates into Germany and France to promulgate Trent's decrees, encouraging

The triumphant church is symbolized by a crowned woman in this depiction of the Council of Trent, created by Pasquale Cati in 1588. Ultimately, it was only after Trent produced wholehearted accord on many pressing theological issues that decisive action could be taken against corruption.

some bishops and deposing others.[8] Lax religious orders were placed under the rule of their stricter brethren. He jailed several bishops who ignored his orders to return to their dioceses. In September 1566 he released the catechism of the Council of Trent, earning the reluctant praise of Protestant leader Tilemann Hesshus: "They might almost pass as Lutherans." His subsequent liturgical revisions endured into the twentieth century. Seminaries and colleges multiplied, many founded by the Jesuits.

Had reform come sooner, would the Luther phenomenon have happened? Like all "what if" questions asked of history, the answer is unknowable. Yet one clue is instructive. Luther protested against both the corruption of the church and also many aspects of its sacramental theology. But it was only after Trent produced wholehearted accord on the theological questions that decisive action could be taken against the corruption. Ultimately, what we genuinely believe will determine what we actually do. Such, perhaps, was the lesson taught to all Christians by the Council of Trent. ∎

8. Six bishops were deposed in France. Five remained defiantly in their dioceses. At Christmas 1566 the sixth, the bishop of Aix, rose in fury from his throne, threw down his staff, denounced the pope, stalked from the cathedral, and rode off to join the Calvinist army as Captain Saint-Roman.

CHAPTER 10

Avarice and cruelty vie with devotion and faith as Spain takes America

The conquistadores are heedless as a people perish, but defiant clergy, championing the victims, found the great Christian society known as Latin America

Columbus had been a cloven man, grievously torn between a passion to spread the gospel of Christ and an equally fervent desire for personal wealth, power, and social recognition (see vol. 8, ch. 9). However, he did not know—in fact, no one knew—how this same schizophrenia was about to afflict and almost mortally poison the whole vast empire he brought into being, an empire so pitilessly cruel that it aided and abetted the virtual extermination of the Carib Indians in the Antilles. Meanwhile, the only champions and determined defenders of those people were Christian missionaries—priests who so thoroughly won the surviving natives' hearts to Jesus Christ that they would create over the ensuing centuries that great bastion of Christianity known to the world as Latin America.

By the time Columbus limped into port for the last time in 1504, Spain was poised for an imperial expansion the likes of which has rarely been witnessed. Within a single generation its *conquistadores* would vanquish two large, sophisticated empires whose existence was not even perceived by Europeans until after Columbus's retirement. Within fifty years they would traverse the breadth of two vast continents, planting settlements in jungles, deserts, and remote mountain valleys. They had no doubt of their right to claim these lands, having been given the pope's blessing to do so—do so, that is, along with the Portuguese, who were provided a clear field in Brazil.

No sooner had the island of Hispaniola been subdued (later to become Haiti and the Dominican Republic) than the restless Spanish adventurers began to cast

The Spanish conquistadores, *here depicted in all their brutality by twentieth-century artist Graham Coton, would vanquish two powerful and sophisticated empires in little more than a generation, engendering an empire whose pitiless cruelty was resisted and denounced first to last by the clergy who championed the native cause. However, the missionaries would so thoroughly win the hearts of the natives that Latin America remains a Christian bastion to this day.*

Diego Velázquez

Christopher Columbus

Cabeza de Vaca

their eyes beyond its shores—moving into Puerto Rico in 1508, for example, and Jamaica in 1509. Cuba, the largest prize in the Greater Antilles, was invaded in 1511 by an army led by Diego Velázquez, who had accompanied Columbus on his second voyage and who turned out to be an unusually able governor once he stamped out native resistance.

Not all went smoothly in the expansion, however. Two expeditions to the mainland in late 1509, one to what would become Colombia and the other to the nearby isthmus of Panama, were nearly wiped out by disease, hunger, and native attacks, with the dead numbering in the hundreds. Fortunately for the Colombian settlement, a relief party included a desperate stowaway by the name of Vasco Núñez de Balboa, whose ruthless decisiveness was so welcomed by most of the survivors that they soon put him in charge. Balboa—in the eyes of historian J. H. Parry (*The Spanish Seaborne Empire*, 1966), "the first of the great conquistadores of the American mainland"—not only founded Darién, the first European settlement in South America, but also, in 1513, led an expedition across the isthmus to the Pacific Ocean.

Called by historian J. H. Perry "the first of the great conquistadores of the American mainland," Vasco Núñez de Balboa, here memorialized by a statue in Madrid, was so ruthlessly decisive that the survivors of the ill-starred Colombian settlement soon put him in charge, and the colony prevailed.

That same year, Juan Ponce de León discovered and named Florida, where he would die a few years later in a battle with natives while returning with a group of colonists. His expedition was the first of several to founder in Florida, usually after attempts to locate a fabled civilization and its "fountain of youth" that existed only in the imagination of native witnesses. Following one such debacle in Tampa Bay in 1528, Cabeza de Vaca and three companions, after death-defying adventures that included long stints in Indian captivity, managed to traverse the continent west through Texas and northern Mexico all the way to the Gulf of California, finally surfacing in Spanish settlements in 1536.

By that time, both the Aztec empire in central Mexico and the

Incan empire in Peru had succumbed to wildly improbable Spanish assaults (about which we shall have more to say shortly). Such was the frenetic pace of the conquistadores' march south from Mexico and north from Darién that by 1524 they were themselves clashing along the southern border of Guatemala and the northern border of Honduras.

Francisco Coronado

Hernando de Soto

Ferdinand Magellan

The next two decades witnessed still more unforgettable expeditions, including Francisco Vásquez de Coronado's astonishing exploration of present-day Arizona, New Mexico, Texas, Oklahoma, and Kansas between 1540 and 1542, and Hernando de Soto's fateful wandering at the same time through what is now the American southeast, as well as Arkansas and Oklahoma. Meanwhile, in an electrifying half dozen years, 1536 to 1542, Spanish rule in South America was extended over territory that includes much of modern Colombia, Ecuador, Peru, Bolivia, Chile, Argentina, and Paraguay, followed by the first European descent of

Such was the frenetic pace of the conquistadores' march south from Mexico and north from Darién that by 1524 they were clashing along the borders of Honduras and Guatemala.

the Amazon River by Francisco de Orellana and a handful of companions.[1] Such was the dynamism of Spanish arms that only two decades later the conquistadores would be using the west coast of Mexico as the staging area for expeditions to the Philippines, where Ferdinand Magellan had perished in 1521 during his historic circumnavigation of the globe.

"The product of centuries of warfare and spare comfort, endurance was bred in their bones, violence was in their blood, and safety was the last of their ambitions," writes historian Kathleen Romoli (*Balboa of Darién: Discoverer of the Pacific*, 1953). Like Columbus, many were devout Christians. But many also shared the great mariner's obsession with wealth, and their craving could be sated only with gold or silver. If they gave a thought to the suffering of the natives from whom they continually demanded tribute and labor, most betrayed no hint of it. Many had come to the New World in part to escape poverty or misfortune, and their own hard lives precluded any empathy with peoples who in many cases seemed to be, after all, pagans of a particularly odious stripe.

Fired by faith, a sense of destiny, a crusading tradition against infidels unparalleled in Europe, and the conviction that great riches were finally within their grasp, they were capable of astonishing ruthlessness against those who stood in their path—as the two great empires in America discovered in especially calamitous fashion.

Hernán Cortés, for instance, was not the sort of candidate who springs to mind to lead a conquering expedition into an unknown empire at the head of a few hundred adventurers. To begin with, he was not a soldier, his military experience being

1. The great river of South America was dubbed the Amazon only after Orellana's expedition recounted an ambush by Indians led by fierce women warriors that recalled the Amazons of Greek mythology. In terms of water volume it is the largest river in the world, with a greater flow than the next ten largest rivers combined, from the world's largest drainage basin. By the year 2010 it had still never been bridged, chiefly because it flows through dense jungles where there are few roads and cities. In terms of length, the Amazon is reputed to be slightly shorter than the Nile, though this fact is disputed by some geographers.

European Conquest of the New World, 1490–1600

KANSAS

OKLAHOMA

ARIZONA

NEW
MEXICO

Acoma
Tigeux

Memphis

Chattanooga

Augusta

ARKANSAS

TEXAS

Mobile

St. Augustine

NEW SPAIN
(MEXICO)

Galveston

Tampa Bay

*Gulf
of Mexico*

FLORIDA

BAHAMAS

Culiacán

NEW GALICIA
(MEXICO)

Compostela

Pátzcuaro

Tenochtitlán
(Mexico City)

Veracruz

MICHOACÁN

Havana

CUBA

GREATER ANTILLES

HISPANIOLA

PUERTO RICO

JAMAICA

St. Germán

Higüey

LESSER
ANTILLES

GUATEMALA

HONDURAS

Caribbean Sea

NICARAGUA

COSTA
RICA

Tuzutlan

PANAMA

Darién

Cumaná

TRINIDAD & TOBAGO

VENEZUELA

*PACIFIC
OCEAN*

*ATLANTIC
OCEAN*

NEW GRANADA
(COLUMBIA)

Quito

Negro

ECUADOR

Amazon

Natal

Cajamarca

VICEROYALTY
OF PERU

Lima

Madre de Dios

BRAZIL

Cuzco

BOLIVIA

PARAGUAY

URUGUAY

ARGENTINA

Buenos Aires

Rio de Janeiro
Sao Paolo

CHILE

The Conquest of Mexico, 1519

Tenochtitlán

Naolinco
Perote

Villa Rica de
Veracruz

Tlaxcala

Jalapa

Cempoala

Cholula

Veracruz

*Lake
Texcoco*

Atoyac

- - - Aztec empire
——— Inca empire
- - - Mayan civilisation
▓ Area of Spanish control
▒ Area of Portuguese control
Route of:
- - - Hernán Cortés, 1519
- - - Vasco Núñez de Balboa, 1510, 1513
——— Ponce de Léon, 1513
——— Alvár Núñez Cabeza de Vaca, 1528–36
Francisco Vásquez de Coronado, 1540–42
——— Hernando de Soto, 1540–42
- - - Francisco de Orellana, 1541–42
——— Francisco Pizarro, 1524–25
——— Francisco Pizarro, 1526–28
——— Francisco Pizarro, 1530–33
✕ Battle

214   THE CHRISTIANS

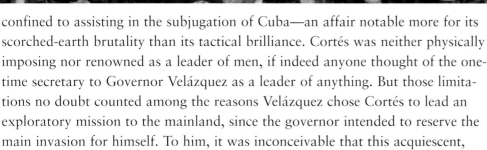

confined to assisting in the subjugation of Cuba—an affair notable more for its scorched-earth brutality than its tactical brilliance. Cortés was neither physically imposing nor renowned as a leader of men, if indeed anyone thought of the one-time secretary to Governor Velázquez as a leader of anything. But those limitations no doubt counted among the reasons Velázquez chose Cortés to lead an exploratory mission to the mainland, since the governor intended to reserve the main invasion for himself. To him, it was inconceivable that this acquiescent, unassertive thirty-four-year-old bureaucrat, who had arrived in America a dozen years before, could possibly emerge as a rival, though he was admittedly resourceful and competent.

Although known as an unassertive if efficient thirty-four-year-old bureaucrat, Hernán Cortés (above right) decisively seized his opportunity for everlasting fame and fortune. Chosen to lead an exploratory force to mainland Mexico, Cortés unleashed his conquistadores (bottom of page) on the seemingly impregnable Aztec capital, Tenochtitlán (above left).

Even Cortés hadn't settled upon his final destination when his eleven ships made a landing at modern-day Veracruz on Good Friday 1519, after several stops in the Yucatán. But he was certain of one thing: this was his opportunity for everlasting fame and fortune, and he was going to seize it. Never once in the months that followed—though he was pitted at times against odds and obstacles that would have made most men wilt—did he seem to consider abandoning his grand project.

The glittering empire Cortés and his men would soon confront was unlike anything the conquistadores had ever seen. Only one city in Europe, Paris, came close to the size of the Aztec capital, Tenochtitlán,

Many features of the Aztec capital, Tenochtitlán, startled and impressed the Spanish: its "floating islands," for example, its enormous population, and its bustling marketplace (bottom of page). What profoundly shocked them, however, were vast rituals in which victims, including children, were dragged to the Great Temple (inset) to have their hearts cut out as a sacrifice to their grim deity Huitzilopochtli.

with its two hundred and fifty thousand inhabitants.[2] But the size of the city that would eventually become Mexico City was hardly the its most startling feature. Built on an island in a large lake one hundred and fifty miles west of the Gulf of Mexico and more than seven thousand feet above sea level, Tenochtitlán was an apparently impregnable base whose causeways to the shore could be raised during a crisis and whose farmers grew crops on "floating islands," or *chinampas*, that were immune to drought. At the center of this daunting complex of palaces, markets, and neighborhoods on stilts rose the Great Temple, the ceremonial focal point of a society in which religion determined everything and whose central deity, the grim Huitzilopochtli, god of sun and war, required human blood for sustenance.

Every year thousands of sacrificial victims, including children, were marched—or sometimes dragged—up the steep steps of the temple and placed on a stone altar, where their still beating hearts would be cut from their chests by a priest and held aloft. Each such occasion was "a messy affair," explains the historian Keith Windschuttle (*The Killing of History: How Literary Critics and Social Theorists are Murdering Our Past*, 1996), "with priests, stone, platform, and steps all drenched by the spurting blood. The head of the victim was usually severed and spitted on a skull rack while

the lifeless body was pushed and rolled down the pyramid steps." There it would be butchered and the limbs distributed for consumption.

No other high civilization has ever embraced human sacrifice and cannibalism on such a scale—not to mention macabre rituals in which, for example, priests would deck themselves out in the skins of flayed victims.[3] The Spaniards were profoundly horrified by such spectacles and repeatedly cited them to justify their own brutality. But in the case at least of Cortés, this rationale was not entirely expedient. Conversion of the natives was not merely an afterthought for Cortés; it was his steadfast goal. True, more than anything he craved gold and glory, and was determined to rule a vast new kingdom. Yet he wanted to rule Christians, not pagans, and he never let up on his attempts to proselytize and to root out the idolatry that he so detested. Even his slogan, "Let us follow the cross and, if we have faith, conquer under this banner," succinctly captured the twin themes of his quest. However, were it not for the repeated warnings of Father Bartolomé de Olmedo, who accompanied the conquest and who insisted that forced conversions were contrary to the Christian spirit and inadvisable on practical grounds, Cortés would have cracked down on native worship even more ruthlessly than he did.

Decisive action was Cortés's trademark in every sphere and an essential reason why his campaign succeeded. To lock in the commitment of his soldiers, for example, he ordered all but one ship scuttled before commencing his army's winding journey up to the Valley of Mexico. But Cortés would require far more than audacity to vanquish Tenochtitlán. He would require horses—so mysterious to the Indians that they first thought they might be dragons. He would need swords and lances forged in Toledo, against which the obsidian blades of the Aztecs were no match. He would need thousands of Indian allies from tribes who resented Aztec ascendancy, allies Cortés succeeded in securing through remarkable political skill and not a little intimidation. Even the powerful Tlaxcalans cast

In a nineteenth-century lithograph the indecisive Aztec emperor, Montezuma II, extends a friendly greeting to Hernán Cortés and his conquistadores. He provided his visitors with a palace near the city's Great Temple—hospitality the Spanish repaid by taking Montezuma prisoner and then massacring the Aztec lords at a friendly fiesta. This set the stage for a death struggle between the Spaniards and Aztecs.

2. A treatise published at Harvard in 1992 by J. Bradford DeLong and Andrei Schleifer (*Princes and Merchants: European City Growth before the Industrial Revolution*) gives the population of Paris in 1500 as 225,000. Naples was second in Europe at 125,000, then Milan at 100,000. The largest city in Spain was Grenada at 70,000. Rome's population was 55,000, London's 50,000.

3. Human sacrifice and cannibalism were by no means rare among Indian tribes in the sixteenth century, and some—such as the fierce Tupi tribes along the Brazilian coast— were partial to both. The Spaniards also encountered human sacrifice within the Mayan civilization but not nearly to the same degree as they observed with the Aztecs.

*Emperor
Montezuma II*

*Pedro de
Alvarado*

their lot with the Castilians, although not until they had experienced firsthand the Spaniards' skill on the battlefield. Not least, Cortés would benefit from the silent ally of smallpox at a critical moment in the fight for the capital.

Perhaps the most unexpected Spanish asset was the Aztec emperor himself, Montezuma II, whose brooding indecision could hardly have contrasted more sharply with Cortés's single-minded confidence. At first Montezuma could not decide whether the pale strangers on his empire's coast were an unusual variety of marauder to be stamped out or some sort of god. After all, Cortés arrived in a "one-reed" year of the Aztec cyclical calendar as predicted for the return of Quetzalcoatl, an exiled priest-king of central Mexico who had in the interim of several centuries attained quasi-divine status. Was Cortés's arrival the long-anticipated return?

Montezuma tried to stall, discourage, or divert the Spaniards, sending emissaries to explain, for example, that the emperor would be too busy to see Cortés should the Spaniards continue on their course. Some Aztec lords urged Montezuma to exterminate the invaders without delay, but still their emperor dallied. Even after Cortés ordered the massacre of the lords of the Aztec city of Cholula and his own city was approaching panic, Montezuma continued to agonize over what to do.

The emperor not only allowed the Spaniards to enter Tenochtitlán in November 1519, he put them up in a palace near the temple—a favor they soon returned by seizing him and taking him prisoner, an astonishingly bold coup on the part of the outnumbered foreigners. But it bought them time—at least until Cortés felt compelled to return to the coast to deal with a fleet sent against him by Velázquez, at which point he split his forces and left Pedro de Alvarado in charge of those left behind. Alvarado did not possess the nerves of Cortés, and to stave off what he believed to be an imminent attack, he ordered the Aztec lords slaughtered at a fiesta, setting the stage for open hostilities that could end only with the utter defeat of one side or the other.

Even the return of Cortés with one thousand conquistadores and additional Indian allies was not enough to restore the balance of power. By now Montezuma had lost his subjects' respect, and he was stoned to death when he tried, at the Spaniards' command, to mollify his people. Sensing the growing peril, Cortés ordered retreat from the city on the night of July 1, 1520—*La Noche Triste*, as it became known—which turned into a deadly rout in which half of the fleeing Spaniards were slaughtered.[4]

The historian Hugh Thomas (*Conquest: Montezuma, Cortés, and the Fall of Old Mexico*, 1993) has written that "Cortés showed himself at his best after this reverse. He never displayed any sign of weakening of his resolve eventually to recapture the Mexican capital" and would return with an even larger army months later to wage war to the death.

The final battle for Tenochtitlán raged for ninety-three days and was, in the opinion of Thomas, one of the most terrible urban clashes in history. Tens of thousands of Aztecs perished in fighting that pitched from street to street and

4. Typically during battle an Aztec warrior would strive to capture his opponent alive in order to hand him over for later sacrifice at the temple. This tactic was yet another Aztec handicap in any engagement with the conquistadores, whose goal during combat was of course to kill. On *La Noche Triste*, however, the Aztecs seemed determined mainly to exterminate their enemy on the spot, and most of the Spaniards who perished did so without being captured first.

dwelling to dwelling, producing mounds of bodies strewn about the rubble. Such was the resistance that Cortés felt he had no choice but to destroy the city he had sought to rule in splendor. By the time the defense dissolved in August 1521, Tenochtitlán resembled not so much an empire's capital as its cemetery.

The conquest of the Aztecs by an invader facing such extraordinary odds was an achievement with few parallels in history, yet such was the audacity of Spanish conquistadores that within a dozen years they would contrive an equally improbable feat of arms, this time in South America.

The Incan empire by the sixteenth century was the largest kingdom in the Americas, stretching from Colombia into Chile and Argentina, or almost three thousand miles. It was also a young empire: only a century earlier, the Quechua-speaking Incan tribe ruled a relatively obscure state centered in Cuzco high in the Andes Mountains. Within a few decades, however, the Incas—and their sovereign, titled "the Inca"—had developed an administrative sophistication more characteristic of an empire centuries old, supported by a military unrivaled on the continent. Consummate engineers and masons, the Incas laid paved roads through perilous mountain passes and quarried blocks of stone so large that they stagger the imagination to this day.

The Inca was said to be a descendant of the sun god, the preeminent deity. And he was treated as befits a god: transported in a litter, shielded from the public by a large retinue of obsequious women who would pluck so much as a single

Hernán Cortés, as depicted in the foreground of a seventeenth-century Spanish oil painting, launches the final terrible battle for Tenochtitlán. Aztecs by the thousands perished in the ensuing clash, reputedly one of the most terrible urban battles in history, with every street and dwelling savagely contested and the city essentially destroyed. In ninety-three blood-drenched days, against extraordinary odds, the Spaniards won the Aztec capital—but they weren't finished yet.

Having defeated the Aztecs in Mexico, the Spanish under the command of Francisco Pizarro (inset) turned their attention to the seemingly boundless Incan empire. The Incas were ruled by a supposed descendent of the sun god named Atahualpa, whose golden statue (above) stands today in Cuzco, Peru. They would become the second major victims of Spanish imperialism. Below, both pages, are pictured the ruins of their famous mountain estate, Machu Picchu.

hair from his garments and eat it, lest its magical qualities bewitch them. Even powerful nobles admitted to his presence were observed sometimes to tremble with anxiety. Meanwhile, tens of thousands of well-trained warriors were poised to do his bidding. Yet the empire was vulnerable to the Europeans rapping at its door, and not only for the usual reasons of inferior technology and lack of horses. With the death of Huayna-Capac Inca, probably to smallpox, in 1525, the brothers Atahualpa and Huascár had set upon each other in a civil war whose concluding chapter had not been written when Francisco Pizarro finalized his plans for an expedition.

Pizarro had accompanied Balboa to the Pacific and settled in Panama, where he formed a partnership with another soldier, Diego de Almagro, and the priest Hernando de Luque with the intention of leading Spaniards farther south. Their explorations began in 1524, when Pizarro was nearly fifty years old, but it wasn't until a voyage near Ecuador two years later that Pizarro and Almagro found evidence of a mysterious civilization unknown to the outside world. Pizarro returned to Spain to seek permission to lead an invasion, which the emperor Charles V—inspired in part by the celebrated success of Cortés—granted in 1529. Pizarro was appointed governor of Peru, while Almagro, to his everlasting ire, was assigned a secondary role as commandant.

No Incan nobleman, least of all Atahualpa, who had by now gained the upper hand against his brother, considered the small contingent of strangers who wished to meet with him in the northern town of Cajamarca in November 1532 to be of ominous significance. Even the conquistadores, sixty-two horsemen and 106 soldiers, were almost unnerved by the discipline they noticed among the Incan troop encampment. But for all of the differences between Pizarro and Cortés—Pizarro seemed to share none of Cortés's interest in converting Indians, for example—they were alike in one crucial respect: whenever

the odds seemed impossible, they would seize the initiative with a daring attack.

Atahualpa and his army, which numbered perhaps forty thousand, were celebrating a victory in the civil war on the plain outside Cajamarca and considered the conquistadores a distraction—although, Atahualpa later admitted, a distraction that would have to be dealt with harshly. The emperor never got his chance. Enticed into the town square with several thousand largely unarmed soldiers under the pretext of a meeting with Pizarro, Atahualpa's litter bearers were hacked apart by sword-wielding Spaniards who had concealed themselves in buildings before launching a headlong charge, breaking the Indians' ranks and slaughtering them like sheep. Thousands died in a shocking rout without the loss of a single Spaniard, while Atahualpa was taken captive.

The Inca's capture changed everything. It checked his massive army, which surrendered the next day at Atahualpa's instructions and mostly dispersed. It provided the Spaniards with valuable time to assess what they were up against should resistance surface elsewhere, as it surely would. And it gave Pizarro and Atahualpa the opportunity to reach agreement on one of history's most infamous ransoms: the

Inca offered to fill a twenty-two-by-seventeen-foot room with gold to a line on the wall eight feet high, and to provide an even greater volume of silver, in return for his freedom. He would fulfill his side of the bargain, he assured Pizarro, within two months. Yet rather than placate the astounded Spaniards, Atahualpa's offer—which Pizarro cynically accepted—only excited their lust for riches. Pizarro took the gold and silver and then, six months after the emperor's capture, condemned the Inca to death, allegedly for ordering one of his generals to rescue him. He was garroted rather than burned alive after an eleventh-hour conversion

The execution of Atahualpa, the Inca ruler, was a watershed moment of Spanish duplicity. First enticing him into the town square of Cajamarca for a peaceful meeting, they routed his guards and took him prisoner. Then they agreed to release him for an enormous ransom in gold and silver, which was paid. Then they killed him.

to Christianity, which an eyewitness account suggests may have been sincere.

Although the Spaniards would suffer only minimal casualties in a series of battles on the road to Cuzco,[5] which they seized in November 1533, the total pacification of the empire took years. As the Indians adjusted to Spanish military superiority and came to terms with the fact that they were fighting for their very existence, they rallied at first behind isolated generals such as Rumiñavi in the north and later behind remaining members of the Incan royal family.

Manco Inca, a brother of Atahualpa whose initial instinct had been to collaborate with the Spaniards, lit the spark for two great rebellions, including a siege of Cuzco in May 1536 in which Juan Pizarro, half brother of Francisco, was killed. But with the capture and execution of Atahualpa's nephew, Tupac Amaru, in 1572, the shattered remnants of Incan defiance vanished.[6]

By now, it was beginning to dawn even on some of the Spanish that the Incan civilizations they had supplanted was in some respects more appealing or humane than their own. Writing in 1589 in "the discharge of my conscience, as I find myself guilty," the last surviving member of Pizarro's band of conquerors, Don Mancio Serra de Leguisamo, lamented the destruction of a society that he remembered as remarkably immune from crime and sin. "They were so free from the committal of crimes or excesses," he wrote, ". . . that the Indian who had one hundred thousand pesos' worth of gold or silver in his house, left it open, merely placing a small stick against the door, as a sign that its master was out. . . . When they saw that we put locks and keys on our doors, they supposed that it was from fear of them . . . So that when they found that we had thieves among us, and men who sought to make their daughters commit sin, they despised us."

The old conquistador obviously exaggerated the blameless nature of Incan citizens, but he nevertheless had reason to be stricken with guilt. The collapse of the Indian population in Latin America is one of history's terrible calamities, and the fact that a Christian nation had a hand in it remains an indelible blot on the story of the faith.

To be sure, Indian numbers would have plummeted under even the best of circumstances, given the diseases—and especially smallpox—against which they had no resistance. "Had it not been for these diseases," argues the historian

It took the Spaniards less than half a century to subdue the Incan empire using firearms and horses against bows and arrows, as shown in this 1904 lithograph. With the capture of Atahualpa's nephew Tupac Amaru in 1572, its subjugation was largely complete, though more than two hundred years later a descendant of Tupac Amaru would lead a rebellion in Peru. But meanwhile disease, especially smallpox, exacerbated by the conditions of slavery, also drastically reduced the Indian population.

Hugh Thomas, "the history of Mexico might have been closer to that of British India than to that of New Spain." Unfortunately, the Indians did not battle for survival against the invading host of microbes under the best of circumstances. In fact, thanks to the Spanish colonists, conditions in some locales could hardly have been worse.

It is not as if Ferdinand and Isabella planned it that way. Isabella in particular admonished Spanish colonists that the Indians "should be free from servitude and be unmolested by anyone, and that they should live as free vassals." She expected the Indians to be evangelized peacefully, not by force. But the queen died in 1504, and even had she lived, she could hardly have slowed the momentum of events or solved the dilemma facing the monarchy. As the historian Paul Vickery (*Bartholemé de Las Casas: Great Prophet of America*, 2006) explains, "On the one hand, Spain's legal and moral justification for being in the Indies was the conversion of the Amerindians and their protection as vassals and members of the church. On the other hand, the conquistadores who had risked their lives and in some cases their fortunes to extend the domain of the monarchs expected to achieve material wealth in the form of land, natives, or valuable goods."

Pope Alexander VI, himself a Spaniard, decreed in 1493 that Spain and Portugal should exercise dominion over the islands and mainland of the New World, with Spain receiving the lion's share of territory. Under threat of excommunication, the Christian monarchs were ordered to "bring to the worship of our Redeemer and the profession of the Catholic faith their residents and inhabitants." In an incredible expression of naïveté—or hope against hope—Alexander also forbade "all other persons of whatsoever rank . . . to go for the purpose of trade or any other reason" except to save souls.

But the papacy and monarchs were hardly blameless in the ensuing tragedy. Although popes would affirm that slavery is evil, with Paul III in 1537 specifically insisting that no Indian should be "given into servitude," they did not consistently oppose coercion in spreading the faith. "You will compel . . . the barbarous nations to come to the knowledge of God," Pope Clement VII (1523–34) ordered, "if necessary by force of arms." Meanwhile, even Isabella authorized the capture of cannibals—a concession easily twisted to cover a multitude of abuses.

5. One of the most daunting obstacles of the journey was the canyon of the Apurímac River, which the Spanish had to cross (fortunately for them, at the driest time of year) without the benefit of a suspension bridge, which the Indians had burned. The successor to the Incan bridge would eventually be featured in Thornton Wilder's *The Bridge of San Luis Rey*.

6. More than two hundred years later, in 1780, a descendant of Tupac Amaru, Tupac Amaru II, led a general Indian rebellion in southern Peru but was captured and executed a year later. Tupac Amaru II, in turn, inspired the Tupac Amaru Revolutionary Movement of the 1980s and '90s, which seized nearly five hundred hostages in the Japanese embassy in Lima in 1996.

An apparition that founded a nation

A poor man's story of the Virgin of Guadalupe triggers a major crisis over its credibility, but it draws Mexicans to Christ in their thousands

When a furious Franciscan publicly accused his rigorous archbishop, Alonso de Montúfar, of promoting idolatry, Mexico's Catholic world shuddered at the charge. Not only was fomenting idolatry a capital offense, but the idol being referred to was not something in stone but the Virgin herself, said to have appeared on a hill outside Mexico City in December of 1531. Where the archbishop saw miracles and authentic conversions resulting from this appearance, the Franciscan saw only a hoax and a reversion to paganism.

The fears of the Franciscan, Francisco de Bustamante, were not unreasonable. Twenty-five years had now passed since that vision of the Virgin had been reported, and for much of that time, writes Eduardo Chávez in *Our Lady of Guadalupe and Saint Juan Diego* (2006), Christian missionaries had battled idolatry. The first bishop of Mexico, in the three years following his 1528 arrival, had overseen the destruction of five hundred Aztec temples and over twenty thousand idols. Yet few conversions to Christianity resulted from these efforts. Nor had Mexico's first missionaries—twelve Franciscans who arrived in 1524—achieved notable success. "The Mexicans," one observed, "remained very cold for five years."

The native antipathy to Christianity is hardly surprising. Apart from the missionaries, Mexicans knew only the Spanish *conquistadores*, Christians who treated them with shocking brutality, enslaving them, taking their women as concubines, and stealing from them with impunity. Moreover, New Spain's government was anarchically corrupt, nepotistic, and incompetent. The rebukes of the Franciscans against the regime were ignored. Their reports to the Spanish monarchy went undelivered. Finally, one bishop, the Franciscan Juan de Zumárraga, hid a letter to Spain in a slab of bacon inside a barrel of oil. "If God does not provide a remedy from his hand," he wrote, "this land is about to be totally lost."

To believers, God did indeed deliver such a remedy, and that was the strange occurrence outside Mexico City. On December 9, 1531, an indigenous man named Juan Diego knocked on the bishop's door.

A prayer card circa 1900 of Our Lady of Guadalupe, whose claimed appearance near Mexico City in December 1531 began the conversion of the country.

He said he'd met a beautiful lady on Tepeyac Hill, about three miles northeast of Mexico City. The lady claimed to be "Our Lady of Guadalupe," referring to a little town in western Spain, about 125 miles southwest of Madrid, where a shrine commemorates a previous appearance of the Virgin there.[1] She wanted a church built on Tepeyac Hill, she said, "where I can show my love, compassion, help, and protection to you." So, said Juan Diego, he was delivering her message. Bishop Zumárraga was not hostile but deeply skeptical; Tepeyac was the site of a former Aztec temple to the goddess Tonantzin. But when Juan Diego returned the next day, quietly insisting his story was true, Bishop Zumárraga asked for a sign.

The account continues: he received one. On December 12 Juan Diego arrived with his *tilma*—a native poncho—filled with roses not native to Mexico, picked, he claimed, at Mary's direction. When Juan let the roses fall to the floor, the bishop was astonished to see on the rough fabric of the tilma the image of a young *mestizo* girl, her blue mantle covered with stars, her hands folded in prayer. The black ribbon encircling her waist signified, in Aztec culture, that she was pregnant.[2] Convinced the apparition was authentic, Zumárraga began construction of the church; people immediately thronged in increasing numbers to see Our Lady of Guadalupe.

But despite Zumárraga's endorsement, his fellow Franciscans, suspicious of syncretism—the retention of pagan beliefs under the guise of Christianity—kept silent about the event. Their circumspection and the scarcity of chronicles—the earliest being the 1556 *Nican Mopohua*, by native Antonio Valeriano—threw doubt on Juan Diego's existence. Critics noted that extant writings of Zumárraga made no mention of the event. However, witnesses aged from 80 to 115, children of Juan Diego's contemporaries, testified at a 1666 inquiry that Juan Diego Cuauhtlatoatzin (in the Aztec dialect, Nahuatl, the "eagle that speaks") was born around 1474 in Cuauhtitlan, in the kingdom of Texcoco. He and his wife, Maria, who had no children, were baptized around 1525. This would make

Juan Diego fifty-seven years old and a widower of two years at the time of the encounter.

Whether these incidents occurred as related or not, the "Guadalupe event" precipitated a cataclysmic change in Mexico. Franciscan Toribio de Benavente Motolinia recounted that from 1531 to 1536 five million indigenous people were baptized. Often they traveled for days and camped near the monasteries to learn the catechism and prayers. "Many received the sacrament with tears in their eyes," he wrote. The *Nican Mopohua* related that Mexicans repudiated idols and "started to believe in and venerate Our Lord Jesus Christ and his precious mother."

"Build me a church," was the lady's request, and the bishop complied—after she sent him the extraordinary roses in Juan Diego's miraculous tilma. Construction of the Basilica of Our Lady of Guadalupe began immediately, on the site where she appeared.

Another radical change was their acceptance of monogamy. Missionary Jeronimo Mendieta observed that many men, in order to be baptized, gave up their several wives for one alone; he recorded as many as five hundred Christian marriages taking place in a day. He also wrote of thousands of natives traveling miles to wait months for confession. According to Warren Carroll (*The Cleaving of Christendom*, 2003) by the time Juan Diego died in 1548, an estimated nine million indigenous people had been baptized.

The message of Guadalupe for the native people, writes Chávez, was that "their world is not finished; it is transformed." The missionary Fidel Gonzales writes in the same volume that the two seemingly irreconcilable worlds of Spain and Mexico were united "in Holy Mary of Guadalupe," under whose influence "the Christian faith totally took root in the Mexican cultural world." The subsequent "intense intermarrying . . . gave birth to the Mexican people in a literal sense, and to the Latin American in the figurative sense."

As for the image itself, it was first scrutinized by scientists and artists during the 1666 inquiry.[3] The former verified that the tilma, woven from agave fibers, should have disintegrated within twenty years. The latter testified that to paint such a vivid portrait on such rough cloth was humanly impossible. Its alleged miraculous character aside, Our Lady of Guadalupe became emblematic of Mexican nationalism, appearing on banners during the 1810 Mexican revolt against the Spanish, the rebellion of 1914, and the civil war in 1926 to 1929. On November 14, 1921, a bomb—allegedly planted by anticlerical government agents—exploded beneath the image, mangling the bronze crucifix and altar candelabra. The tilma was unscathed.

Despite the controversy that has surrounded the Virgin of Guadalupe since the celebrated clash between the Franciscan Bustamante and Archbishop Alonso de Montúfar in 1556, the archbishop's view has prevailed, and the Catholic Church has consistently endorsed the devotion. In 1999 Pope John Paul II declared her the patroness and mother of the Americas, and on July 31, 2002, he canonized Juan Diego. At the beginning of the twenty-first century devotion to her appears undiminished; over a hundred thousand pilgrims annually visit the basilica to venerate her still vivid image. ■

1. A tourist guide to Guadalupe in Spain describes as an "ancient legend" the appearance of the Virgin there to a shepherd around the turn of the fourteenth century. She told him where he would find an image of her buried there at the time of the Muslim invasion about six hundred years before. A statue of a black Virgin was then discovered in the bank of the Guadalupe River. It has been preserved in the monastery at Guadalupe, visited annually by thousands of people. By one theory, the statue predates Christianity and is of pagan origins in ancient Greece.

2. The symbolism of the image of Our Lady of Guadalupe is significant for the native peoples, writes Chávez. She is looking down, which in Aztec culture indicates thinking of those she looks upon. "She is dressed with the stars, steps on the moon." The etymology of the word Mexico is "in the center of the moon." The arabesque flowers on the tunic show in glyphic writing that she appeared on Tepeyac Hill. Significant, too, is the image appearance on a tilma; in the indigenous marriage ceremony, the man knots his tilma to the woman's huipil, or tunic, to symbolize their permanent union.

3. The 1666 scrutiny was far from the last; controversy still rages over the image's genesis. In 1979 biophysicist Philip Callahan of the University of Florida photographed the portrait in infrared light and concluded it was an "inexplicable phenomenon." Other studies show what appear to be three human figures—presumably Juan Diego, his interpreter, and Zumárraga—reflected in the image's right eye. However, in his 2006 book *Our Lady of Guadalupe, the Painting, the Legend, and the Reality,* art historian John Moffitt postulates that the image was painted by indigenous artist Marcos Cípac de Aquino and the story of Juan Diego is apocryphal. Vincentian priest and historian Stafford Poole in *Our Lady of Guadalupe: The Origins and Sources of a Mexican National Symbol, 1531–1797* (1995) likewise argued that the Juan Diego story has no historical basis. However, others question the validity of this "argument from silence," which, they say, ignores or minimizes the oral tradition of the first few decades, which is quite strong.

7. Although some encomenderos were appallingly brutal, it is not fair to characterize them all in this fashion. At the very least, our knowledge is woefully incomplete. As the historian John Hemming explains in *The Conquest of the Incas* (1970), although "an immense volume of official reports and legal documents survives . . . there are no diaries or impartial travelers' accounts, no Indian records, and almost no local administrative sources."

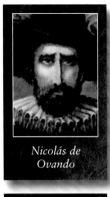

Nicolás de Ovando

Juan Ginés de Sepúlveda

Conquistadores beat their Incan pack-carriers in this sixteenth-century lithograph by a disapproving Flemish artist, Theodore de Bry. Such cruelty reportedly was common, and it was not uncommon for Indians to be worked to death on Spanish enterprises, but Spain tried to justify it all. Who could possibly doubt, reasoned the noted scholar Juan Ginés de Sepúlveda, that the inhabitants of the Americas "have not been justly conquered?"

More ominously, the Spanish crown, which had financed much of the early settlement in Hispaniola, approved allotments of natives or their land (which amounted to much the same thing) to the conquistadores. These *repartimientos*, in which Indians were sometimes worked to death, were critical to maintaining the flow of treasure to Madrid.

In 1503 the monarchs instructed Hispaniola's governor, Nicolás de Ovando, to compel the natives to work for wages, adding the stipulation that they do so "as free persons, for so they are." It was about this time that the term *encomienda* came into common usage to describe this system of forced labor—which, if not always amounting to outright slavery, was at the very least a brutal form of serfdom. As the system evolved under Cortés and Pizarro, the Indians were required to pay tribute to their Spanish *encomenderos*—although theoretically no more than they would have paid to the state as peasants in Spain. In fact, the tribute was set at whatever the encomendero pleased. Some tributes were manageable, but many a hard and greedy colonist squeezed the natives for all they were worth.[7]

Inevitably, such barbarities required a moral justification to set consciences at ease—particularly as some Spaniards protested vociferously against the cruelties, as we shall see. On the other hand, one of the most prominent apologists for the system was actually a Scotsman, the Dominican John Major of the University of Paris, who argued in 1519 that conquest, forcible conversion, and even slavery were justified when infidels rejected the peaceful preaching of the one true faith. Major also drew on Aristotle, portraying the Indians as a race that matched the great philosopher's description of those who are "by nature slaves." His arguments would be adopted and refined most notably by Juan Ginés de Sepúlveda, who, like Major, never visited the New World but who had definite views regarding the Indians' moral character.

"How are we to doubt," Sepúlveda asked in 1547 in his *Concerning the Just Cause of the War against the Indians*, "that these people (the Indians), so uncultivated, so barbarous, and so contaminated with such impiety and lewdness, have not been justly conquered by so excellent, pious, and supremely just a king as Ferdinand the Catholic was and the emperor Charles now is, the kings of a most humane and excellent nation rich in all varieties of virtue?"

The modern mind reels in disbelief

at Sepúlveda's glib portrayal of the Indians as a "cruel" race of "apes . . . in whom you will barely find the vestiges of humanity" and the Spaniards as the "most merciful" and "temperate" of peoples. By the time of Sepúlveda's pronouncements, a majority of the inhabitants of the West Indies had already disappeared, and the number would continue to decline through the rest of the century. The islands' population of perhaps several hundred thousand in 1492 collapsed to a demoralized and overworked remnant who often could not even feed themselves, given the incessant Spanish demands for gold and the resulting neglect of native agriculture.

In Cuba, 'the natives were pursued and torn to pieces by fierce dogs, burned alive, their hands and feet cut off, and the miserable remnant reduced to hopeless slavery.'

Meanwhile, the slightest resistance by the Indians to foreign rule provoked ferocious reprisals. In the campaign to pacify Cuba, the historian Francis MacNutt (*Bartholomew de Las Casas*, 1909) relates, "The natives were pursued and torn to pieces by fierce dogs, burned alive, their hands and feet cut off, and the miserable, terrified remnant speedily reduced to a condition of hopeless slavery." Terrorizing natives by hacking off their hands was not confined to Cuba. Such mutilations began in Hispaniola, where in one campaign hundreds of Indians who suffered such treatment were instructed to return to their chiefs as a warning of what might be in store for the rest. And the practice of amputations as a means of terrorizing a restive population continued on the mainland, too, with both Cortés and Pizarro partial to such demonstrations.

Occasionally the conquistadores' purpose was overtly genocidal, as against the less developed Chichimec Indians in northern Mexico, who were hunted down and slaughtered or brought to town "chained and yoked, for public sale," according to an ecclesiastical protest of the time.

However, this was not a gentle age for anyone. To prevent a wholesale flight of colonists from the Caribbean to Peru during the gold fever that swept the hemisphere after Pizarro's triumphs, for example, Spanish officials resorted to savage measures against their own countrymen. In Puerto Rico, some who tried to leave "were whipped and others had their feet cut off," according to one eyewitness. Such punishment hardly raised an eyebrow in that hard era. Yet the scope of the cruelty against the Indians was so extraordinary in the experience of the Spaniards themselves that it would soon spark one of the great human rights campaigns of all time.

The slightest disobedience or resistance by Amerindians to foreign rule provoked ferocious reprisals. The lithograph below by Theodore de Bry shows conquistadores setting ferocious dogs upon such rebels to tear them apart. The atrocity portrayed here was laid to Vasco Núñez de Balboa (1474–1519), who established the first Spanish settlement in present-day Colombia. Equally awful and more common, however, was the wholesale cutting off of hands or feet of disobedient natives.

In 1502 Bartolomé de Las Casas, aged eighteen, came to New Spain to get rich. But twelve years later, challenged by the Dominican campaign against maltreatment of the natives, he renounced his previous endeavor and launched one of the great human rights campaigns of all time. Below is a painting of de Las Casas by Mexican artist Felix Parra (1845–1919). The frontispiece of one of the reformer's many publications is inset.

The man who would do most to expose to the world such atrocities arrived in New Spain in 1502, along with about twenty-five hundred Spanish colonists, most intent on making a quick fortune and getting out, and nearly half destined to die of disease and hardship long before they could do so. He was Bartolomé de Las Casas, and his motive for being there, he would later confess, was pure avarice. Yet no sooner had the eighteen-year-old Las Casas landed than he noticed an oddity. All Hispaniola, by now sometimes known as Santo Domingo, was in a fever of greed after a native girl had turned up an enormous gold nugget. The Spaniards were using it as a plate on which to serve a magnificent turkey dinner. But the girl received no recompense for it whatever. This, Las Casas reasoned, could not possibly be just. He was to witness far graver injustices in the days and weeks that followed—grave enough, in fact, to redirect his whole life and the whole direction of Latin America as well.

Las Casas's moral formation, although still in its infancy, would get another jolt shortly thereafter when the Spaniards put down a "revolt" in the province of Higüey after the Indians attempted to avenge the murder of a chief. Four hundred Spanish soldiers, accompanied by native allies, slaughtered hundreds of Tainos in an atmosphere of sport, since the victims had no weapons to match Toledo steel. Las Casas apparently accompanied this punitive campaign, as he was at pains later to declare, when he described the expedition in his monumental *Historia de Las Indias*, that "All that I have said is true, because I saw it, and told what I have seen."

It is clear even at this stage that Las Casas did not share the penchant for cruelty that afflicted a disturbing number of his countrymen. He had studied for the priesthood in his native Seville beginning in 1498 and, although not yet ordained, still intended to follow his vocation. But it is equally clear that he saw nothing wrong with slavery and a system of production that enabled indolent men who were distinguished only by their greed to grow rich on the backs of others' labor. Indeed, while still in

Seville, Las Casas had accepted a Taino slave named Juanico as a gift from his father, who had accompanied Columbus on his second voyage—although Juanico and other such "servants" would be released two years later to comply with a royal decree. His next slave was also a gift, this time from Spaniards in Hispaniola who had just massacred a group of native chiefs by trapping them in a building and setting it on fire. On each occasion, Las Casas appears to have been untrou-

It is clear that Las Casas did not share the penchant for cruelty that afflicted many of his countrymen. But it is equally clear that he saw nothing wrong with slavery.

bled by the bloody origins of his new property.

Las Casas returned to Europe after five years, proceeded to Rome, and was ordained a priest in March 1507. After further studies at the university in Salamanca, Spain, he was ready in 1510 for another foray to New Spain, in a voyage with the newly appointed governor, Diego Columbus. Yet even now the earnest young priest had not fully sworn off the crasser aspirations that motivated him at the outset of his adventures.

Every man's journey to the light involves one or more shocks to his system, moments when he confronts the horrifying reality of an evil that he has tolerated or unconsciously assisted—and rebels at the revelation. Las Casas's pivotal moment seems to have occurred in 1513, as chaplain to an expedition to pacify Cuba led by Pánfilo de Narváez. The ferocity of Spanish tactics stunned Las Casas. He protested, but to no avail. Decades later his conscience still burned in shame for what he considered his inadequate response, and particularly for not treating a man whose shoulder had been horribly injured by a Spanish blade. Referring to himself in the third person, Las Casas wrote, "The cleric kept within himself much regret for not treating the man with a kind of turtle-oil paste, which he used to treat so many others. This ointment could have sealed the wound, which may then have healed in about a week."

For his service in the campaign, Las Casas was awarded land and became an encomendero, relying on the labor of Indians for ranching, agricultural, and mining operations. But despite outward signs, something in him had permanently stirred, and it would not be long before it burst to the surface.

Before recounting Las Casas's historic break with his complicity in the Spanish colonial system, we must step back two years, to the fourth Sunday in Advent 1511. That is the date on which a brave and eloquent Dominican friar, Antonio de Montesinos, with the full support of his colleagues in their monastery on Hispaniola, stepped to the pulpit to deliver the first sermon in the Western Hemisphere that decried the treatment of the Indians. The date was carefully chosen to coincide with St. John's Gospel in which John the Baptist declares,

A statue in Santo Domingo, capital of the Dominican Republic, pays tribute to Antonio de Montesinos, the brave and eloquent Dominican friar who, on the fourth Sunday of Advent in 1511, first challenged his countrymen's treatment of the Indians. "You are all in mortal sin," he told his stunned congregation of settlers. "You live in it and you die in it. Why? Because of the cruelty and tyranny you use with these innocent people."

"I am the voice of one crying in the wilderness," and Montesinos's language appears unrestrained in his attempt to be worthy of this prophetic moment.

"You are all in mortal sin," he told the startled settlers in attendance, which included many of the most prominent officials in the colony. "You live in it and you die in it. Why? Because of the cruelty and tyranny you use with these innocent people. Tell me, with what right, with what justice, do you hold these Indians in such cruel and horrible servitude? On whose authority have you waged such detestable wars on these people? . . . And what care do you take that anyone catechize them, so that they may come to know their God and Creator? . . . Are they not human beings? Have they no rational souls? Are you not obligated to love them as you love yourselves?"

'You are in mortal sin,' Montesinos told the startled settlers. 'Why? Because of the cruelty and tyranny you use with these innocent people...Are they not human beings?'

The colonists could no more be saved, Montesinos warned, "than Moors or Turks who have no wish to have the faith of Jesus Christ."

The Dominicans, who had prayed over how to help the natives since their arrival in the colony in 1510, were not naïve. They anticipated angry demands that Montesinos retract his words, and such protests were lodged immediately. But on the following Sunday the priest repeated his warning—only to add that the sacraments would be withheld from those who refused to repent. Henceforth the Dominicans would be locked in struggle with the colonial establishment over the proper treatment of Indians, each side appealing to the monarchy for advantage.

Ferdinand did not appreciate the Dominicans' roiling the water in this fashion and ordered Governor Diego Columbus to deport any priest who persisted. But the king also initiated the first probe into allegations of un-Christian behavior in New Spain, which included testimony from an advocate for the colonists and from Montesinos himself. The result was the promulgation of the Laws of Burgos on December 27, 1512. Writing much later, Las Casas would be scornful of the laws—"wicked, cruel, tyrannical, and contrary to natural law"—claiming they mainly sanctioned the encomienda system that was driving the natives to extinction. But that is not quite fair. While the laws confirmed the system of forced labor, they also included numerous provisions—from bans on pregnant women working in the mines to restrictions on brutal punishments—that would have improved the Indians' lot had they actually been followed. Alas, they were not, but even so, they marked the beginnings of an "intellectual revolution," in the words of historian Thomas, "whose repercussions would help work permanent change in attitudes toward native peoples."

8. Cisneros may have been one of the wealthiest men in Spain, but he was widely admired for his austere and holy life and faithfulness to the crown. When representatives of the nobles protested the authority he was claiming to exercise as regent, he directed them to a window overlooking a large contingent of soldiers, whereupon he explained, "There are the powers I have received from His Catholic Majesty, by which I govern and shall continue to govern Castile, until the king, my master and yours, shall take possession of his kingdom." That was the last time the nobles tried to bully the prelate.

Ferdinand II of Aragon

Las Casas remained a spectator to these events—the last time in his life he would not be in the vanguard of those defending human rights. He was of course aware of the Dominicans' audacious stand and may even have witnessed Montesinos's electrifying sermon of 1511. Regardless, as an encomendero he, too, was a target of the Dominicans' demand for true repentance; indeed, one of the friars denied Las Casas absolution after his confession.

One day, musing over passages in the book of Sirach (sometimes titled Ecclesiasticus) 34:18–22, Las Casas had an epiphany. It was as if all of the lessons of his years in New Spain were compressed into a vivid revelation. How could he reconcile his position as an encomendero with his clerical duty to the most humble? The Bible's words struck him like a divine accusation: "He that sacrificeth of a thing wrongfully gotten, his offering is ridiculous, and the gifts of the unjust are not accepted." Never a man for half measures, Las Casas went to the governor of Cuba and informed the stunned Velázquez that he was about to give up ownership of his Indians, renounce his previous existence, and spend the rest of his life dedicated to justice for the natives. On the feast day of the Assumption 1514, he preached a ser-mon in which he announced his decision to the public—and, like Montesinos before him, minced no words regarding the likelihood of their eternal fate.

The newly minted reformer's first move was to return to Spain to seek to bend the monarchy itself in his direction. Such pleadings would become a pattern in Las Casas's well-traveled life, and on this initial mission of mercy, which began in September 1515, he took with him for support none other than the legendary Montesinos. It is a tribute to Las Casas's force of personality, eloquence, and charm, however, that he would assume the lead in making the case on behalf of the natives and yet managed to finagle a meeting with Ferdinand before the year was out. The king expressed shock at the atrocities recounted by the priest and promised another meeting before Easter, but within weeks he would be dead and Cardinal Ximenes de Cisneros declared regent of the kingdom until young King Charles could arrive in Spain from Flanders.

Despite his advanced age and temporary status, the cardi-nal was no timeserver.[8] He not only took Las Casas seri-ously, he asked him to lead a group to draft possible laws that might protect the natives. Las Casas pro-duced at this time the first of his published works, "A Memorial of Grievances Done to the Indians" and "Memorial of Remedies for the Indians," which included idealistic proposals (such as equal punishments for natives and Spaniards), impractical schemes (recruiting Spanish peasants to settle in Central America), and one odious notion that would haunt Las Casas for many years. "In place of the Indians that are in these communities," he wrote, "Your Majesty could substitute twenty blacks, or other slaves, in the mines . . . they will collect more gold than twice as many Indians."

Las Casas would not only come to repu-diate those words but to oppose all forms of chattel slavery—an advanced position shared by only a handful of clerics of his

Cardinal Ximenes de Cisneros, as portrayed in 1604 by Spanish artist Eugenio Caxés, became regent of Spain following the death of King Ferdinand II of Aragon. Elderly but no timeserver, Cisneros took a lively interest in the reports of New World cruelty brought to him by Bartolomé de Las Casas. Further, he appointed that determined and eloquent campaigner to help draft better laws to protect the Indians.

day and virtually no one else. Yet even at this time he was not, in his mind, simply substituting one set of victims for another. He genuinely believed that slavery was not the death sentence for Africans that he knew it to be for his beloved Indians.

Cardinal Ximenes sent three monks of St. Jerome back to the colonies to investigate Las Casas's claims, armed with the authority to impose reforms. They were, the historian MacNutt writes, "the first of all the men sent by the Spanish government to effect reforms in the colonies, whose intention to discharge their duty was conscientious." But it was for naught. The monks were either persuaded by the settlers' arguments or intimidated by their vehemence, and the tepid recommendations they produced pleased no one—least of all Las Casas, who was back in the colonies as well.

He returned to Europe to press his case again in the royal court, and once again his bold but challenging message drew favorable reviews, this time from the young Charles V. "Our Christian religion is for all," Las Casas told him. "It adapts itself to every people in the world, accepting all equally, removing liberty from no one, sovereignty from no one, and places none under servitude." Charles and his council eventually agreed "that the Indians were free men, should be treated as free and attracted to the faith in the manner Christ established."

To that end, the king agreed to Las Casas's latest colonization scheme, for Cumaná in Venezuela, whose goal was to demonstrate a superior model for populating the New World. To the delight of the priest's enemies, the project ended in utter failure, harassed by nearby pearl fishermen and undermined by the indifference and cupidity of the settlers themselves. Las Casas blamed himself and, after much soul-searching, elected in 1522 to join the Dominican order to discipline his body and spirit for what he still believed was his calling on behalf of the Indians. It was a wise decision. When Las Casas assumed a public role again after several years of study and self-abnegation, he was, as he had hoped, better equipped than ever for his holy mission.

True, he was never able to halt the demographic slide of the Indians or to eliminate their oppression. But his activities maintained ceaseless moral pressure on the crown and colonists, pricking the consciences of some sufficiently to change their ways—demonstrating on the ground, as it were, that force was not necessary to successful evangelization.

For all its brutality, the Spanish empire, due to a Christian heritage, generated a degree of soul-searching and moral dissent unprecedented in the annals of imperial expansion.

Meanwhile, colonial inertia and intransigence could overwhelm even the most powerful directives. In 1532, for example, Las Casas personally delivered a royal edict to the conquistadores in Peru that banned either the slavery or dispossession of the natives. A highly irritated Pizarro accepted the *cedula* with dutiful but insincere assurances that it would be obeyed. Las Casas's influence was also visible in Pope Paul III's bull *Sublimus Deus* of 1537, with its forceful denunciation of violence and slavery. "The Indians we speak of . . . outside the faith though they be, are not to be deprived of their liberty or the right to their property. . . . They must not be enslaved . . . those Indians and other peoples are to be invited into the faith of Christ by the preaching of God's word and the example of a good life."

These sentiments reflected Las Casas's own prescription for converting natives and averting armed conflict. He outlined his theories in his treatise "The Only Way," which he and other friars successfully employed in the late 1530s on a mission to Tuzutlan, in modern Costa Rica, with Indians who were as yet unconquered.

But isolated successes were not enough. The encomienda system must be uprooted, so Las Casas returned to Spain yet again to lobby the monarchy. He released "A Short Account of the Destruction of the Indies" in 1542—by no coincidence, the year that Charles V issued the so-called New Laws, which barred Indian slavery, outlawed encomiendas for such groups as public officials and secular clergy, and, most resented of all, limited all encomiendas to a single generation.

Colonial officials had always been "masters of passive resistance to inconvenient instructions," the historian Romoli has noted, but the New Laws were more than inconvenient—they were a direct threat to a way of life and thus provoked violent resistance. A royal emissary to Peru was murdered, while Las Casas, who agreed to fill the vacant bishopric of Chiapa and who returned to New Spain with forty-four Dominicans, encountered angry defiance at every turn.[9] Such was the clamor, in fact, that Charles V threw up his hands in 1545 and revoked the inheritance provision.

But Las Casas was not finished. His most indelible moment occurred in 1550,

9. By this time Las Casas had concluded that true repentance for the treatment of the Indians required restitution and adopted this theme in his "Twelve Rules for Confessors," written while he was bishop. The idea was so incendiary, however, that the *Confesionario*, as it was known, was initially banned and ordered publicly burned by the viceroy.

when he confronted Juan Ginés de Sepúlveda before a council of theologians at Valladolid summoned by the emperor to debate the morality of Spanish conquest and forcible conversion. After hearing days of exhausting argument, the council never actually rendered a verdict, but it never granted permission for Sepúlveda to publish an inflammatory tract, either, so Las Casas appears to have carried the day. For all of its brutality, the Spanish Empire, thanks to its Christian heritage, generated a degree of soul-searching and moral dissent unprecedented at the time in the annals of imperial expansion. And while Las Casas would die in 1566 with few of his visions even faintly realized, he and his allies had launched a movement destined to work great changes not only in Latin America but in the moral imagination of all of Western civilization as well.

Such great men have a way of dominating not only the conversation of their time but also the history written after them—to the point that it is sometimes easy to forget those whose accomplishments were, in their own way, nearly as impressive. Las Casas may have been the most eloquent, prophetic voice to defend the Indians in the colonial era, but he was neither the first nor the last cleric to do so—and indeed was but one of many during his own lifetime who devoted themselves to the natives' welfare, sometimes giving their lives on the Indians' behalf.

While parish priests in colonial towns who served the European transplants were too often prone to adopt the free and easy morals of their compatriots, becoming complacent or even defensive regarding the rough edges of the colonial enterprise, the mendicant orders—the Franciscans, the Augustinians and the Dominicans—and then, in spectacular fashion, the Jesuits often resisted this temptation. Concluding that the encomienda culture and legal system were intransigently weighted against the natives' material and spiritual interests, they constructed a parallel society of missions. At first tens of thousands of Indians— and, by the mid-seventeenth and eighteenth centuries, hundreds of thousands—

Forcible conversion persisted in New Spain, as portrayed here in a sixteenth-century lithograph of such an event conducted by Jesuits. But in rural missions established throughout Latin America, the Franciscans, Augustinians, and Dominicans, later spectacularly followed by the Jesuits, at length were able to support the natives as human beings, as friars and priests learned their languages, recorded their culture, shared their hardships, and stood between them and predatory colonists. When the Jesuits arrived in Brazil, according to one historian, the natives there described them as "the first Portuguese they could trust . . . who returned Indian hospitality with honest friendship."

would live at these missions, worshiping, working, and entertaining themselves on schedules established by the priest or priests who lived among them.

Critics, then and later, would accuse mission priests of coveting their own fiefdoms and of reveling in the role of paternal autocrat—and there is some truth in the charge, although it varied from mission to mission. It is equally true that many missionaries required that the natives make a disorienting break with a huge swath of their culture, to an extent that offends the modern mind. But however paternalistic, the mission fathers also treated the Indians as human beings, learning their languages and recording their customs, identifying with their poverty and hardships and sharing them fully as well as standing up for the Indians against the predatory encroachments of the foreigners who now ruled their land. Moreover, were it not for the careful observations of the likes of the Franciscan Bernardino de Sahagún, who wrote what historian Robert Ricard (*The Spiritual Conquest of Mexico*, 1966) calls a "kind of encyclopedia of Mexican civilization," our knowledge of Indian cultures would be sadly deficient.

Sometimes the priests held higher aspirations for Indians than for their own race. For example, Vasco de Quiroga, who would become bishop of Michoacán, wrote in 1531 that he hoped to "restore the lost purity of the primitive church" in the missions—his own Patzcuaro mission was a remarkably successful enterprise of thirty thousand souls—and to "raise the life of the Indians to a level of virtue and humanity superior to that of the Europeans."

The spiritual conquest of the mainland, or at least its organized evangelization, commenced in Mexico with the Mission of the Twelve, a group of Franciscans who arrived in 1524. Both the Dominicans (1526) and the Augustinians (1533) were not far behind. With the approval of king and pope, they fanned out across central Mexico and then beyond, concentrating Indians in mission villages, baptizing them in large numbers (although not without rudimentary doctrinal training), building schools and churches, and grappling with such deeply resistant practices as polygamy. By 1559 there were 160 missions among the three orders—an impressive number but not for the magnitude of the task.

Some Indians embraced the new faith from the outset. Many went along with its rituals while maintaining a closet allegiance to the religion of their ancestors. Occasionally, active resistance broke out—as in a 1541 in what was called the New Kingdom of Galicia with its capital, Guadalajara. But open rejection of Christianity was not tolerated, any more than it would have been tolerated in Spain at the time, and the work of evangelization gradually reshaped the religious landscape.

Relations between the missions and secular authorities in the early decades were sometimes bumpy, but the clashes were nothing compared to what transpired once the Jesuits, with their extraordinary energy and single-mindedness, arrived on the scene. In Brazil, for example, "the Indians found in the Jesuits the first Portuguese they could trust, men devoid of material greed, who returned Indian hospitality with honest friendship," the historian John Hemming explains in *Red Gold* (1978).

By the time of the Jesuits' expulsion from Portugal and its possessions in 1759, and from Spain and Spanish possessions in 1767—under the pretext that their priests were fomenting social unrest and rebellion—more than two thousand Jesuits directed at least seven hundred thousand Indians in Latin America, including a vast

Native advocate Bartolomé de Las Casas may have died believing his life a failure, but the legacy of his work still shines today in one of the most steadfastly Christian regions on the globe. Four churches that bear witness to this are, at top left, the Cathedral of Santo Domingo, Cusco, Peru, 1654; top right, the Church of San Francisco in Lima, Peru, 1674; at left, Nuestra Señora de la Luz de Tancoyol (Mission of Our Lady of Light), one of five Franciscan missions in Querataro, Mexico; and below, the Basilica del Voto Nacional (Basilica of the National Vow), the largest neo-Gothic basilica in the Americas, in Quito, Ecuador.

complex of missions in a territory the size of France in what is now Paraguay and Argentina.[10] In this "Jesuit empire" in the heart of South America, the Indians—eventually armed and drilled by the demanding fathers—fought off colonial raiding parties for many years, until the combined forces of the Iberian crowns forced their capitulation in the Guarani War in 1756.

From southern Chile to San Francisco in the north,[11] thousands of missionaries labored decade after decade—indeed, century after century—in an effort to create their vision of a Christian society. A portion of that vision was naïve and impractical, and even when it took root, it was sometimes too fragile to withstand social convulsion or the absence of a charismatic friar. But there is no question what those friars—and the Indians they served, some of whom had their own ideas of what that society should be—managed to achieve over time. They gave birth to a uniquely American Christianity while creating in Latin America one of the most steadfastly Christian regions of the globe. Bartolomé de Las Casas may have died with every reason to have considered his life a failure, but he had built far better than he could possibly have known. ■

10. The greatest figure to emerge from the South American Jesuits was undoubtedly Antonio Vieira, who would rival Las Casas in eloquence, influence and moral clarity. At one point a close adviser to Portugal's King John IV, Vieira returned in 1653 at age forty-five to Brazil, where he had spent his childhood, and from his pulpit in Maranhão he excoriated his countrymen. "What a cheap market," he declared. "An Indian for a soul. That Indian will be your slave for the few days that he lives; but your soul will be enslaved for eternity, as long as God is God."

11. The first of the famous string of twenty-one California missions was established, near San Diego Bay in 1769 by the Franciscan Junípero Serra; the last one was founded at Sonoma in 1823. The missions declined quickly, however, barely a decade later with the onset of the Mexican government's policy of secularization.

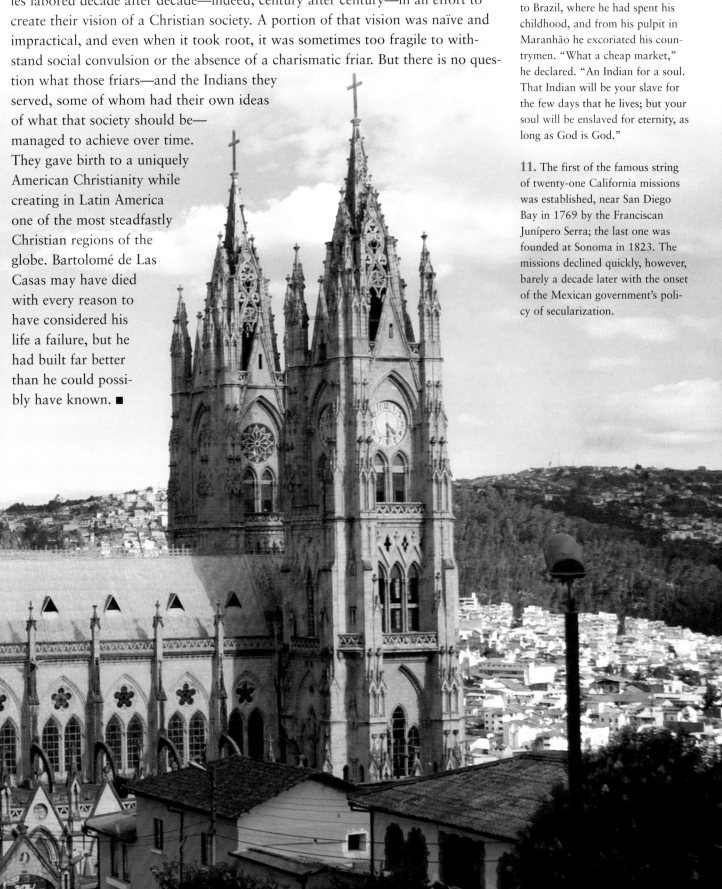

CHAPTER 11

In two great victories the Christians thwart Islam's advance by sea

A crucial showdown at Lepanto breaks Turkish control of the Mediterranean, after Malta's 5,000 defenders stop a massive Muslim assault, saving western Europe

When the Habsburg monarch Philip II arrived in Spain in 1559 to take up his throne after defeating the menace posed by the French, the thirty-one-year-old king found the land of his birth in dire disorder. There were famines, feuds within government, and, thanks to the campaigns of his recently deceased father, the Emperor Charles V, a monstrous debt. But by far the greatest threat facing Habsburg Spain and Italy (in particular) and Christendom (in general) was the Muslim Ottoman Empire.

Although their conquests on land had been checked at Vienna (see ch. 3), Sultan Süleyman's Turks were the biggest, richest, and most technologically advanced force in Europe and the Middle East. Their navy now sought to control the whole twenty-three-hundred-mile length of the Mediterranean Sea. Having aligned with the ferocious Muslim pirates from North Africa's Barbary Coast, the Ottomans embarked on a campaign of terror along the twenty-five-hundred-mile coastline of Italy and Spain. France was allied with the pirates, often providing bases for them, sometimes even facilities for the sale of their enslaved Christian captives.

These coastal raids were not only profitable but also calculated to spread fear and horror. The attackers would descend without warning on a seaside community; kidnap all marketable men, women, and children; steal whatever was moveable, then burn and slay whatever and whoever was left. Such a peril steadily depopulated the coastal towns, making them easily accessible to a major military invasion.

In this allegorical painting The Dream of Philip II *(opposite page), the artist El Greco (1541 1614) highlights the worship of God (the cross, the symbol* IHS, *and the heavenly chorus) while memorializing the Holy League formed by Pope Pius V to safeguard Catholic Europe from the seemingly inexorable Ottoman navy. The League's principal players are portrayed by Spain, represented by Philip II (in black, kneeling); Venice by its doge, Alvise Mocenigo (in yellow robe, kneeling); and the papacy by Pius V (in sacramental vestments). The League's vast fleet was expertly commanded by the relatively obscure Don Juan of Austria (kneeling at left, arms crossed).*

Thus in August 1559 Philip gathered his nobles at the massive Gothic Cathedral of St. Mary in the ancient capital of Toledo and made a declaration.[1] The seaborne Muslim menace had been ignored too long. Spain must confront the Barbary pirates and their Turkish sponsors not on land but at sea. It would be long, hard, dangerous, and costly. But if he achieved nothing else during his reign, Philip solemnly vowed, he would halt the advance of Islam on the Mediterranean.

The question looming on every mind as Spain's nobility filed out of the cathedral was: how? The Spanish navy was small, and the empire owed its bankers the equivalent of two years' worth of gold and silver from its mines in the Americas. Its potential Christian allies were unenthused, undependable, and notoriously unable to work together. Many of them were either too afraid to take on the fearsome Turk or, like France and Venice, beholden to the Ottomans by treaty or trade.[2]

The aging Sultan Süleyman I, ensconced with his five thousand servants and a harem of three hundred at the Grand Seraglio in Constantinople, had amassed an empire that now included Egypt and the Islamic holy cities of Mecca and Medina as well as the Balkan territories gained in the 1520s (see ch. 3). His empire abounded in wealth acquired through trade in gems, spices, and luxury goods, by the thriving commerce in Christian slaves, and by the exorbitant tariffs charged to states such as Venice for the privilege of trading

A sixteenth-century Spanish oil on canvas (inset) portrays the emperor Charles V, at left, with his son Philip II, who succeeded to the throne of Spain in 1556, but, pre-occupied with French wars, did not arrive in that country until 1559. Immediately summoning Spain's nobility to the ancient capital of Toledo (shown below in an El Greco oil painting), King Philip declared to them his determination to terminate Muslim dominance of the Mediterranean.

1. The Toledo cathedral stood upon history. After the city fell in the Reconquest, the Christians had built it on the site of the Great Mosque of Toledo, which the Muslims, after conquering Spain in the eighth century, had built on the site of a Visigoth Christian church. Philip moved his capital to Madrid in 1561.

2. In a treaty between Süleyman and the French king Francis I, renewed by his successor Henry II in 1553, it was stipulated that any Italian towns captured by the Ottoman fleet should be handed over to the French, but only after they had been sacked by the Turks and their inhabitants carried off as slaves.

240   THE CHRISTIANS

in his ports and being spared from his aggression.

The sultan maintained a standing army of fifty thousand. But equally important were the ships that carried his soldiers. The Turkish fleet on the Mediterranean could boast more than three hundred galleys—the low-slung, oared, and square-sailed troop carriers that had been used as maritime fighting platforms since the days of the pharaohs.[3] This tripled the number of ships Catholic Europe could muster.

The Turkish success at sea was largely due to their alliance with the Barbary pirates, scimitar-wielding corsairs who had been raiding Mediterranean towns since the days of the Crusades. However, with the emergence of the notorious "Barbarossa Brothers," the banditry grew more systematic and sinister. The brothers were born on the Ottoman-controlled island of Midilli (also known as Lesbos), just off the Turkish mainland. Their father was a potter, either a Turkish Muslim or an Albanian Christian converted to Islam. He and his Greek wife, Katherine, had six children— two daughters and four sons, the youngest born in 1478.

After one brother was killed and a second captured by the Christian Knights Hospitaller and ransomed, the surviving three sailed west in two small galleys called galliots to the island of Djerba, off the coast of North Africa between Tripoli and Tunis. There they quickly distinguished themselves as dexterous seamen, once capturing two huge Christian galleys because brother Aruj, the oldest, refused their summons to surrender, then boldly attacked and took them. Aruj and his brothers turned themselves into a political force in North Africa, allying with local potentates eager

3. Sixteenth-century war galleys were up to 160 feet long, could attain speeds of ten miles per hour in a burst, and were easy to maneuver. Seamen worked the sails from a gangway down the middle, the slaves chained to benches on either side, usually two abreast, wielding forty-foot oars. They were lashed if they lagged. Most were captured in war or coastal raids. Clad in ragged loincloths, backs exposed to the day sun and the night chill, they were generally fed a piece of hard biscuit and a morsel of fish daily. Few would see their home again. They rowed until they were sick or dying, at which point they were tossed overboard. The European galley oarsmen were mostly convicts.

THE MEDITERRANEAN, C. 1560–1580

Habsburg territories
Venetian territories
Ottoman territories & vassal states
☪ Ottoman victory
✝ Christian victory

to escape the domination of Spain, which maintained a string of forts along the North African coast, and also courting Ottoman Sultan Selim I (Süleyman's father) with lavish gifts and exaggerated accounts of their feats.

In 1516 the brothers made the move that changed Mediterranean history. They drove the remaining Spanish from Algiers, strangled the local Muslim grandee, seized the palace, pillaged homes and shops, raped the women to demonstrate who was now in charge, and appealed to Sultan Selim to authorize them to rule Algiers. The Sultan sent several thousand Janissaries, made Algiers an Ottoman province, and appointed Aruj governor and admiral of his western Mediterranean fleet.

Aruj met his match, however, after driving the Spanish out of the Algerian port of Tlemcen. In May 1518 Charles V counterattacked with a combined force of ten thousand Spaniards and thousands of local Bedouins. Aruj, brother Ishak, and a contingent of Janissaries fled but were cut off and slaughtered en route to Algiers. Aruj was beheaded and his torso nailed to the walls of Tlemcen.

The surviving youngest brother, Khayr al-Din, tinted his hair, bushy eyebrows, and beard red with henna in homage to Aruj. He adopted his brother's chosen name, Barbarossa, and proceeded to outdo him in daring and studied cruelty. From Algiers, which grew in infamy and also in population to seventy thousand, he and other corsairs transported tens of thousands of white captives. Men, women, and children were paraded nearly naked through the streets to the market, where buyers examined them, smacking them with cudgels to separate the healthy, who jumped, from the lame or crippled, who merely cringed and howled. White slaves taken in the Mediterranean in the sixteenth and

Known for their red beards and their thuggish seaborne banditry, the notorious Barbarossa Brothers (inset, in a seventeenth-century Dutch engraving) seized Algiers in 1516 and transformed it into a major slave center. European captives were sold in their thousands in its market, envisioned below in a nineteenth-century English engraving.

seventeenth centuries would number more than a million.[4] Barbarossa helped Süleyman take Rhodes from the Knights Hospitaller in 1522 and roamed the western Mediterranean at will. "The mention of his name," writes William Thomas Walsh in *Philip II* (1937), "was almost enough to depopulate a village."

In 1532, when the future King Philip II was five, Sultan Süleyman called Barbarossa to Constantinople and formally appointed him chief governor of North Africa and admiral of the Ottoman fleet. Two years later Barbarossa took over the city of Tunis, ousting its Muslim potentate, Sultan Mulai Hassan. Then funded by the Ottomans and leading a force of Janissaries, he began to carry out Süleyman's master plan—to move north up the east coast of the Adriatic through the Greek and Ionian islands, capturing each island as a toehold to take the next. These were possessions of Venice, and their loss finally drove Venice to abandon its costly treaties with the Turks and to fight them. Responding to the Venetian appeal, Pope Paul III cobbled together a coalition that also included the Papal States, the Knights Hospitaller, and the dominant western Mediterranean power, Spain.

The enterprise became a disaster. A quarrel over who should command delayed the sailing of its 160 galleys for a year. But then, searching the Adriatic they caught by surprise the storm-battered squadron of Barbarossa at the port of Preveza in Albania and waited for him to come out and fight. He did not. Instead, he let them exhaust their water and supplies, then hit them with

4. The Arabs had been expert slave traders since the days before Islam, initially buying and selling Middle Eastern and North African peoples of various races. The Arab sale of slaves from East Africa predates the European transatlantic slave trade by seven hundred years. It has been estimated that the Arab trade in black slaves numbered between 11 million and 18 million between the years 650 and 1900—compared to between 9.4 and 14 million Africans brought to the Americas by Europeans from the fifteenth to the early nineteenth century.

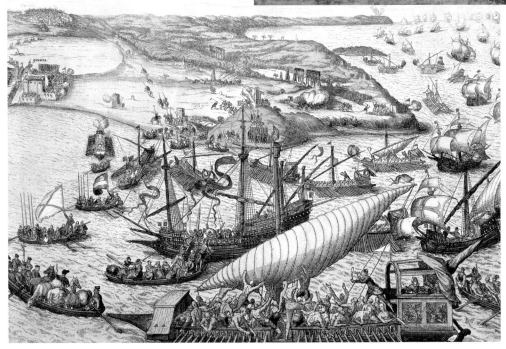

At left, the fleet of Charles V arrives in 1535 to besiege Turkish-controlled Tunis, in an engraving by Netherlander Franz Hogenberg (1540–1590). Above, a Muslim soldier at the forefront of Barbarossa's troops attacks his Christian counterpart outside Tunis, from a tapestry designed by Jan Cornelisz Vermeyen (1500–1559). Relatively easy to capture but difficult to hold, Tunis would again be lost to the Ottomans in 1574.

Portrait in oils of Dragut Reis by twentieth-century artist Feyhaman Duran. Captured as a child by Muslim pirates, Reis became a voluntary convert to Islam, a superb sailor and gunnery expert, and ultimately Barbarossa's chief lieutenant and successor. By 1559 this terror of the Italian coast had left Malta as the sole remaining outpost in Spain's Mediterranean line of defense.

122 galleys as they withdrew. While the Christian commanders quarreled over what to do, he sank about thirty of their ships and escaped triumphant. Venice renewed its treaty with the Turks, paying even higher tributes.

The following year, 1535, Philip's father, the emperor Charles, himself took a direct hand in the Mediterranean. With Tunis now Turkish controlled, Islam was some ninety miles away from Sicily, a two-day sail, offering access to the Italian peninsula and the grand prize of Rome itself. Charles led a major assault on Tunis, easily taking it. Barbarossa escaped to Algiers, some four hundred miles to the west. But Barbarossa was almost as dangerous from Algiers as he was from Tunis, and when Charles attempted to take Algiers nine years later, he failed. In 1574 the Ottomans regained Tunis, and it once again plunged into the slave trade.

Meanwhile, as Philip grew up and went through early manhood, he shuddered to read the accounts of the calamities that followed, as the Turkish scourge made life all but impossible in the coastal towns. One particularly graphic description was written by a French priest sailing in the French vessels accompanying Barbarossa as he spread mayhem down the Italian shore—how at Port Ercole the populace offered thirty men if he would spare the town, and after the thirty were marched off in chains, he burned the place to the ground; how he enslaved 632 people off the island of Giglio after beheading the leading inhabitants; how the people of Lipari, an island off Sicily, offered him fifteen thousand ducats to sail away, how he demanded thirty thousand along with two hundred boys and two hundred girls, and when they refused, he bombarded the island's principal town for ten days, then sacked and burned it. To finish the job, the Janissaries found a group of elderly men and women hiding in the cathedral, stripped them naked, and sliced them open from neck to navel.

Then sailing east to Constantinople, Barbarossa's ships were so packed with slaves and treasure that hundreds of captives had to be thrown overboard in a storm to avoid capsizing. In 1545 he built a luxurious palace, dictated five large volumes of memoirs, and died peacefully in 1546, a hero to his people.

This was thirteen years before Philip II assembled his nobles at Toledo. In that time, Barbarossa's successor was Dragut Reis (sometimes spelled Turgut Reis), a Greek from the Aegean Islands, captured by Muslim pirates as a child, who voluntarily converted to Islam, became a superb sailor skilled in the use of marine cannon, and eventually became Barbarossa's chief lieutenant. By 1559, the year of Philip's Toledo conference, he had become the horror of the Italian coast, overrun Minorca, attacked Nice and Villefranche-sur-Mer, and taken Tripoli from the Knights Hospitaller, leaving Malta the only remaining outpost in Spain's Mediterranean line of defense.

Philip beseeched his Cortes (parliament) in late 1559 to fund a navy. The Cortes took six months but finally granted the king 1.2 million ducats over three years. Philip, cautious to a fault, was determined not to rush hastily into action, though he put his shipbuilders to work immediately.

By now, other Christian forces had already embarked on their own with a preemptive strike against the Turks. On Malta in early 1559, before the Toledo meeting, Jean Parisot de La Valette, the grizzled French aristocrat who was grand master of the Hospitallers, now known as the Knights of Malta, learned that Süleyman had removed his entire fleet to Constantinople for the winter. This was a rare opportunity, La Valette reasoned, to recover Tripoli, lost to the Turks nine years earlier. He enlisted the aid of Don Garcia, the duke of Medinaceli and Philip's viceroy in Sicily. But since the Cortes had not yet acted, Philip himself could offer only troops—no galleys. So Medinaceli and La Valette convinced several Italian states to contribute fifty-four galleys and forty troop transports.

The Italian ships assembled at the Sicilian port of Messina in August. There storms delayed the departure of the low-slung, easily swamped galleys, which did not reach Malta until February 1560. Discovering that the Turkish fleet was again wintering at Constantinople, they headed for Tripoli. Storms hit them again, so they were forced to anchor off the Turkish-held island of Djerba, 120 miles northwest of Tripoli, to take on fresh water. Then typhus struck, killed two thousand men, and left hundreds more seriously ill.

To finish the job, Barbarossa's Janissaries found a group of elderly men and women hiding in the Lipari cathedral, stripped them, and sliced them open from neck to navel.

More grievous events followed. Deciding to take the lesser prize of Djerba instead of Tripoli, they landed their troops, attacked the town, then learned that eighty-five Turkish galleys, headed for Djerba, were only a hundred miles away. The Christian fleet fled for home, abandoning the troops on the shore to their fate. The Turks followed the fleet, sank all but eight of their galleys, then returned to Djerba and slaughtered or enslaved fifteen thousand Christian troops. Equally dismaying—the Christian commander was twenty-one-year-old Giovanni Andrea Doria, grandnephew of the famed Genoese admiral Andrea Doria, naval hero of Charles V's reign. Giovanni personally owned some of the vessels that deserted the troops at Djerba. He survived but fell into wide disfavor.

Four years later Philip scored an initial success. While his shipyards worked tirelessly to build a massive fleet, he launched a fifty-galley attack on Peñón de Vélez de la Gomera, a pirate haven on the African shore opposite Gibraltar. It did not begin well. In landing in heavy surf, a barge carrying their artillery overturned,

Peñón de Vélez de la Gomera, today a Spanish territory off the Moroccan coast, was one of innumerable havens for Muslim pirates in the sixteenth century. Here the navy of King Philip II won its inaugural victory in 1564—the first Christian naval triumph after several disasters. It brought swift retaliation from the Ottoman sultan.

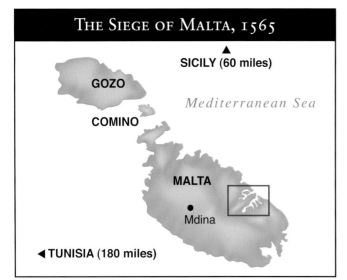

THE SIEGE OF MALTA, 1565

SICILY (60 miles) ▲

Mediterranean Sea

GOZO

COMINO

MALTA

● Mdina

◀ TUNISIA (180 miles)

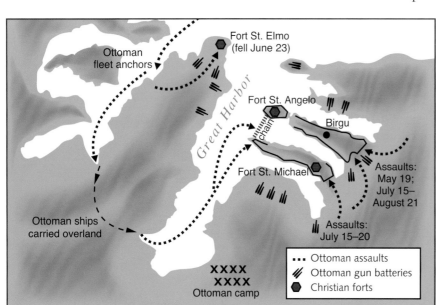

Ottoman fleet anchors ▼

Fort St. Elmo (fell June 23)

Great Harbor

Fort St. Angelo

chain

Birgu

Fort St. Michael

Ottoman ships carried overland

Assaults: May 19; July 15–August 21

Assaults: July 15–20

XXXX
XXXX
Ottoman camp

••• Ottoman assaults
⫽ Ottoman gun batteries
⬡ Christian forts

and the big guns were lost. They then discovered that Morisco spies had warned the Barbary pirates of the expedition and Morisco laborers in the Spanish dock-yard had filled gunpowder sacks with sand.[5] The Spanish fleet was forced to sail home.

But humiliation seemed to stir Philip's resolve. Convincing Pope Pius IV to send reinforcements, he dispatched a big Christian fleet to Peñón the following June and in two months swept the fort and town clean of pirates. It was the first Christian sea victory in most memories, and it pricked the pride of the sultan. All of Europe expected the Turks would retaliate, and rumors abounded. By January of 1565 Christian spies in Constantinople had discerned Süleyman's intent. He was planning a massive amphibious assault on Malta—the rocky 115-square-mile home to the knights. Its strategic location is self-evident. It lies in the midst of the eastern approach to the Sicilian channel, the narrow neck in the Mediterranean. No major seaborne Turkish attack on Spain could be made without their taking Malta.

Süleyman's armada arrived on May 19, 1565. It comprised 193 vessels, a fighting force of some thirty-five thousand men, including sixty-five hundred Janissaries, six thousand cavalry, and sixty big cannon designed to batter and destroy masonry.

For reasons that are still debated but probably because of his having a green fleet less than half the size of the Turks', Philip cautiously—some said cravenly—refused to send immediate naval help. The Italian republics, unhappy because Philip had broken a promise to follow up the Peñón de Vélez victory with an attack on a North African port more threatening to Italy, also stayed home for the time being. Thus the defense of the island was left in the hands of some five thousand Christians: about five hundred knights, four hundred Spanish soldiers, eight hundred Italians, five hundred galley slaves, and three thousand untrained and poorly equipped Maltese farmers.

Grand Master La Valette, now seventy, was of distinguished martial stock, his French forbears having fought in five Crusades. The family name and Christendom itself, as La Valette saw it, were at stake. It looked hopeless, but the white-bearded old warrior with the blazing black eyes was determined to fight to the last man.

La Valette concentrated his meager forces in three fortresses—Fort St. Elmo, Fort St. Angelo, and Fort St. Michael—at the entrance to the Great Harbor on the east end of the island. He laid a huge chain across the entrance to keep the Muslim vessels out. He ordered all crops to be harvested to deny the attackers a local supply of food while stuffing the main town of Birgu's silos and warehouses

5. The Moriscos descended from Muslims who had converted to Catholic Christianity during the Christian Reconquest of Spain. The word literally means "Moor-like," the Moors being the Spanish name for the Muslim inhabitants of northwest Africa (Morocco). However the term Morisco soon came to denote a closet Muslim who still adhered to the Koran while feigning Christianity.

with as much grain as they could hold. Most of the island's wells were poisoned with bitter herbs and dead animals.

For the Turkish admiral Piali Pasha, a renegade Christian, and the military commander General Mustapha Pasha, a thirty-year veteran of Süleyman's land campaigns, instant victory seemed assured. But their artillery bombardment of St. Elmo from land and sea dragged on for more than a month. Fourteen thousand cannonballs were expended. Twice Mustapha's Janissaries had tried to storm the walls but were hurled back.

When they finally took the fort on June 23, the Turks found only nine men alive inside. They immediately decapitated them, tied the headless corpses to crudely constructed crucifixes, tossed them into the harbor, and allowed the currents to carry them to the walls of the other Christian forts. La Valette, no stranger to shock tactics, duly beheaded his Muslim prisoners, stuffed their heads into his cannons, and fired them into the Turkish camp.

The Turks turned to the remaining forts, and the artillery bombardment and infantry assaults continued all through July and August. But the intensity of these attacks gradually diminished as Muslim casualties mounted and their munitions dwindled. Nevertheless, the desperate Christian leader dispatched a number of galleys to Sicily, hoping they could get there with his pleas for reinforcements. When none could run the Turkish naval blockade, La Valette sent his best swimmers to sea—and a few actually managed the sixty-mile crossing by clinging to driftwood and riding the currents.

On the urgings of Sicilian Viceroy Don Garcia, Philip finally agreed to send thirty-five galleys. The Papal States and some of the Italian republics also contributed to a Christian naval force. By early August almost a hundred vessels had

Jean Parisot de La Valette, grand master of the Knights Hospitaller (above), achieved at age seventy a spectacular and totally unexpected military victory, defeating an enormous Ottoman armada at Malta (modern aerial view below) with an army comprised principally of farmers and slaves.

gathered at Messina, Giovanni Andrea Doria had reconnoitered the Maltese situation, but storms and, yet again, inter-nation squabbling delayed the departure for a month.

Now, however, it was the Turks who had become desperate. Their munitions were practically exhausted. Dysentery was striking down the troops. They had suffered, according to some estimates, thirty thousand casualties at the hands of the Christians who had fought with the ferocity of cornered lions. When the Turks had opened breaches in the walls of the town, La Valette had charged them, sword in hand. Even the women fought atop the walls, while the children delivered food and supplies.

A monk reported he had seen Jesus in a vision with several saints and heard a voice say, 'God will save Malta.' The islanders' vigor was renewed and St. Angelo stood strong.

When a monk reported a vision of Jesus and a voice proclaiming, "God will save Malta," the Knights Hospitaller defied terrible odds and succeeded in saving the island— and Christian Europe as well. But the Turkish fleet still remained almost intact. This depiction of the victory is by Antonio Lucini (1610–c. 1661) after Italian artist Mateo Pérez Alesio (1547–1600).

A Capuchin monk, one of the few to escape St. Elmo, reported he had seen Jesus in a vision with John the Baptist, St. Paul, St. Peter, and St. Francis and heard a voice say, "*Salvaria Dios a Malta*" ("God will save Malta"). Hearing this, the vigor of the island's defenders was renewed, and the main fort of St. Angelo stood strong.

With the stormy autumn weather advancing, Süleyman gave up, directing Piali Pasha to bring the fleet home. These orders arrived on September 7, the very day the Christian relief fleet reached Malta. As the Turks were abandoning the island, the Christian forces landed. They discovered just six hundred of the original five

Selim II (1524–1574), by nineteenth-century English artist John Young. Known as Selim the Sot, he inherited the temper of his father, Süleyman the Magnificent, but not his intelligence.

thousand defenders remaining. But these were exultant. They had saved Malta and arguably Spain and Christian Europe against the concerted might of the Ottoman Empire. The failure of the Siege of Malta could be recognized as one of the great triumphs in Christian military history. The eighth of September was also the Feast of the Nativity of the Virgin, something La Valette was not slow to remind his followers.

But the Turkish threat was far from over. Their undefeated fleet had sailed away intact, and until it was destroyed, Christendom could hardly rest easy. The following year, 1566, however, there occurred two events destined to turn the tide in this titanic struggle. The first was the election on January 7 of the sixty-two year old Dominican Pope Pius V. The second was the death of Süleyman the Magnificent, who had ruled for forty-six years.

Pius V had two objectives. One was to heal the wounds to his church caused by the Protestant Reformation, the other to unite the Catholic nations against Islam. Achieving the second, Pius knew, meant winning the support of the Habsburg Empire, the most powerful force in the Christian world, and also the support of the empire's rival Venice, which had the most powerful navy. Initially Pius failed. Then something else arose to help, notably new Turkish aggression. In 1570 the Turks resumed seizing Venetian islands in the Aegean. They also demanded that the Venetians cede to them the island of Cyprus. The Venetians refused, again declared war on the Ottomans, and signaled Pius they were now ready to join his proposed Christian alliance, which had been named the Holy League.

The Ottomans were enraged, but a notable change had afflicted them. Süleyman had been succeeded by his son Selim II, whose prodigious thirst had won him the unaffectionate sobriquet "Selim the Sot."[6] He had inherited his father's tendency to fury but little of his father's intelligence and certainly not his father's handsome bearing. The new sultan, wrote the Venetian ambassador to Constantinople, "is small in size and weak in health. This is due to his intemperance, with women as with wine, drinking great quantities of the latter. He is very ugly indeed, with limbs all out of proportion, according to everyone more a monster than a man . . . He is uncouth in his speech, unversed in state affairs, and lazy, leaving all the great weight of government to the grand vizier."

6. Legend has it that the bibulous Sultan Selim wanted to secure Cyprus because of his taste for the island's fine wine. A more likely reason was strategic; the Turks could not afford to permit an enemy enclave to exist so close to Asia Minor.

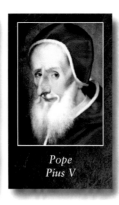

Marc'Antonio Colonna

Giovanni Andrea Doria

Pope Pius V

The galleass, or war galley, depicted below was the battleship of sixteenth-century maritime combat. War galleys had been used as maritime fighting platforms since earliest Roman times but were now becoming both numerous and relatively enormous. By 1571 the combined Christian fleet on the Mediterranean could muster more than three hundred galleys, including six Venetian galleasses, each able to mount seventy cannon.

So angered was he by the Venetians' temerity that he suffered a stroke and lapsed into a weeklong coma. Upon recovering, he ordered three hundred troop-packed ships to the 150-mile-long island. Seventy-year-old General Mustapha Pasha marched inland with ninety thousand men and reached Nicosia, the capital, in late July. The eight thousand defenders behind the city walls held them off until September 9.

Once inside, the Janissaries went on a three-day rampage. They stole everything they could carry, destroyed what they could not, and killed everyone they found alive. Every town on the island surrendered except the fortress of Famagusta, on the eastern peninsula. Mustapha marched to Famagusta with one hundred twenty thousand soldiers and surrounded the town. The seven thousand men inside refused to capitulate, and a siege began that would last until the following July.

Meantime, Pius strained to hold together the Holy League. Spain balked but was talked around. Genoa, mortal enemy of Venice, joined. But the command of the flotilla seemed beyond agreement. Philip favored Giovanni Andrea Doria, still widely loathed for his desertion at Djerba. The Venetian nominee was the old and prickly Girolamo Zanne, utterly unacceptable to Spain. The pope arbitrarily named Marc'Antonio Colonna, head of the small papal fleet, as supreme leader. But neither the Spanish nor the Venetians would heed Colonna's commands.

The combined Christian fleet of 205 galleys and numerous smaller vessels assembled on the Venetian-held island of Crete on August 25, 1570. Bad weather and the delaying tactics by Doria, who deeply feared the Turks and was reluctant to engage them, delayed departure for Cyprus until September 17. The Christian armada was halfway to Cyprus when news of the fall of Nicosia reached

the commanders. At that point Zanne, arguing that Famagusta could take care of itself, suggested they reverse course to attack Turkish possessions in the Adriatic. The fleet quickly disintegrated, each national group heading for home. And while Doria, the most culpable of the captains, again escaped punishment, Zanne was charged with disobeying his orders to relieve Cyprus. He was clapped in irons in Venice and died before a verdict could be delivered. It was an inauspicious beginning. The Holy League was once more a shambles, and all might have ended in complete failure were it not for the determination of Pius V and the appearance of one of history's extraordinary individuals.

The pope led intense negotiations between Spain and Venice through the winter of 1570 to 1571. Though these two Christian powers deeply distrusted one another, necessity forced them to agree. Spain's Mediterranean navy was not big enough to stop the Muslims. Venice needed the financial aid and foodstuffs that Spain could provide since its own supplies had been disrupted by the now hostile Turks.

The great stumbling block, however, remained the command. Venice demanded it because Venice had the best naval officers and best knew the eastern Mediterranean. Spain countered that Christendom's greatest king, carrying the greatest share of the cost, could not allow his armed forces to be led by another nation. Pius broke the deadlock with an astonishing proposal. He nominated as supreme commander a young and little known Habsburg princeling, with the proviso he make no decisive action without the consent of the leaders of the allied contingents. The rivals agreed on him. He is known as Don Juan of Austria.

This handsome and spirited twenty-four-year-old was Philip's half brother—the illegitimate issue of a liaison between Charles V and a mistress, the Bavarian singer Barbara Blomberg, eight years after Charles's wife died. Taken into Charles's care at an early age, Don Juan had originally been intended for the priesthood, but his proclivities were more martial than clerical. After their father's

death, Philip recognized Don Juan as his half brother, provided him with a household, and pointed him to a career in the Spanish military.

The royal recruit gained experience as a naval officer in the relief of Malta and in assorted forays against Barbary pirates. Barely into his twenties, he was appointed head of Philip's land and sea forces. He led the army sent to suppress the revolts by the Moriscos that were erupting in Granada between 1568 and 1570. Like his father, Charles, Don Juan rode with his troops into battle despite the protestations of his ever-cautious half brother. And Don Juan's well-planned, efficient, and sometimes brutal pacification of the Moors earned him a respect among the troops that was never enjoyed by Philip, who diligently remained behind his desk at the Escorial palace in Madrid.

Don Juan bade farewell to his royal half brother on May 25, 1571, took over the Spanish squadron at Barcelona, sailed to Genoa for five days of ceremonials, then moved south to Naples, where a papal representative presented him with the staff of command and the standard of the Holy League—a glorious blue banner, twenty-four feet high, of blue brocade with a huge crucifix and the arms of Spain, the pope, Venice, and Don Juan, all embroidered in gold.

By late August the entire Christian fleet of more than three hundred vessels had arrived. Among them were six big galleasses, the battleships of their day. These newly designed Venetian galleys had three large masts rather than the standard one or two, and were propelled by oars eighty feet long, each requiring nine rowers. Their major advantage, however, was their ability to carry as many as seventy cannon—ten times that of the conventional galleys.

Of the eighty thousand men of the fleet, almost two-thirds were oarsmen and sailors, the rest soldiers. They were a motley multinational group that included mercenaries from as far away as Scandinavia. Before Don Juan's arrival they had

A youthful Don Juan of Austria, illegitimate son of Emperor Charles V, is formally presented to his aging father circa 1560, in an oil painting by Spanish artist Eduardo Rosales (1836–1873). Inset is a portrait by contemporary artist Alonso Sánchez Coello of the increasingly accomplished young warrior, who at age twenty-four would command the Holy League fleet.

spent their time drinking, gambling, and fighting. The officers, as usual, were suspicious of their foreign counterparts. Most being older and more experienced, they initially resented the seeming pup who was now their admiral. In short, this gathering had all the makings of the havoc that came before.

But before, there had been no Don Juan. As he had demonstrated in the Morisco campaign, he had the gift of leadership—and something more. "He seemed to personify," writes Roger B. Merriman in *The Rise of the Spanish Empire in the Old World and the New* (1918), "the crusading ardor of the pope. His inspiring presence swept men off their feet and made them temporarily forget their own selfish aims in an overwhelming enthusiasm for the common cause."

Pope Pius V dispenses his blessing in this sixteenth-century Italian oil on panel portraying the ratification of the Holy League. The League's immense fleet carried the banners of Spain, the pope, Venice, and its relatively obscure leader, Don Juan of Austria. His first challenge was to hold together these disparate components and establish agreement on strategy. The second challenge, no less daunting in fact, was to seek and destroy the Turkish fleet.

Don Juan consulted individually with the commanders of the national fleets on strategy and objectives. Naturally, they disagreed wildly. Then he summoned them to his flagship, the *Real*, and announced that their goal was to seek and destroy the Turkish fleet—something few, if any, of them had yet contemplated. He broke down the national rivalries by forming mixed squadrons with galleys from different countries. This would prevent defections. It would motivate allies from rival nations—fighting side by side—to outdo each other in valor and vigor. And it weakened the authority of the allied commanders and strengthened his own.

Don Juan developed a sound battle plan. The fleet would be divided into four squadrons: three in the forward line of attack, one holding back in reserve. Two galleasses would precede each of the leading squadrons, unleashing an artillery barrage to soften up the enemy. Troop carriers would bring up the rear. Don Juan was to command the central squadron of sixty-two galleys; Doria, with fifty galleys, would be positioned to his right; and Venetian Agostino Barbarigo would be stationed to the left with fifty-three galleys. The reserve of thirty galleys would be commanded by Spanish admiral Don Álvaro de Bazán, the future architect of the Spanish Armada (see ch. 14).

The fleet—the largest in the history of Christendom—left Messina on September 16, 1571. A papal representative and a cluster of lesser clerics blessed the holy warriors as they cleared the breakwater at the mouth of the harbor.

Commander Agostino Barbarigo

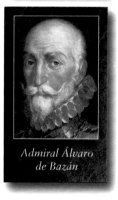

Admiral Álvaro de Bazán

*Ali
Pasha*

*Uluch
Ali*

They sailed past the tip of the Italian peninsula and then proceeded east in single file, a parade of galleys ten miles long searching for the Turkish fleet.

The Turks had embarked from Constantinople in the spring under the command of a new admiral, Ali Pasha, the sultan's brother-in-law. Like Don Juan, he was youthful, courageous, intelligent, and in command of admirals much his senior. He and his chief lieutenant, Uluch Ali, the corsair who was now viceroy of Algiers, had spent the summer raiding Venetian settlements in the Ionian and Adriatic seas. They had scooped up plenty of booty and thousands of captives, had achieved nothing of strategic consequence, but were about to pounce on undefended Venice when urgent word reached them from Constantinople that a massive Christian fleet had been reported in the area east of Sicily. On command of the sultan, Ali Pasha and his ships were ordered south to face the enemy. They headed for the heavily fortified Turkish naval base of Lepanto, on the northwestern shore of the Gulf of Corinth, a long, narrow body of water that extends eastward from the Gulf of Patras, the conjoined gulfs between the Greek mainland and the Peloponnesian peninsula.

Ali Pasha's admirals, fearing a Christian fleet larger than their belated intelligence reported, wished to remain in the shelter of the Lepanto fortifications and await the enemy. But Sultan Selim had ordered the fleet to move west into the Gulf of Patras and seek out the Christians, and he now sent angry word that those orders were not to be disobeyed. Ali Pasha dispatched messenger ships to Cyprus to request all available galleys and sent sixty galleys to southern Greece to pick up thousands of Janissaries stationed at Turkish garrisons.

The Christian fleet was slowed by its mere size, by the galleasses, which had to be towed, and by faulty intelligence obtained from Greek fishermen recruited by the Turks to spread disinformation. Nevertheless, by the end of September Don Juan, through his own agents, had learned that Ali Pasha was in Lepanto. The Christians set sail for the Gulf of Patras. But even as the great battle loomed, dissension nearly destroyed the Holy League.

On October 3 Don Juan was inspecting the fleet. As he passed a Venetian galley, the soldiers fired a salute and two men on his vessel dropped dead. The shots had been an attempt on Don Juan's life, and he had the would-be assassins and the captain of the galley hanged. Then a fight erupted between Spanish and Venetian

*Sebastian
Veniero*

soldiers on a Venetian vessel in Don Juan's squadron. His Venetian lieutenant, Sebastian Veniero, a peppery seventy-seven-year-old, hanged a Spanish officer and three subordinates from the lateen yard without Don Juan's sanction. The young commander was furious and had to be restrained from hanging Veniero. As it was, the Venetian was barred from attending further council meetings.

Two days later, however, national differences were superseded by crusading zeal when the Christians finally heard of events at Famagusta from the captain of a passing brigantine.

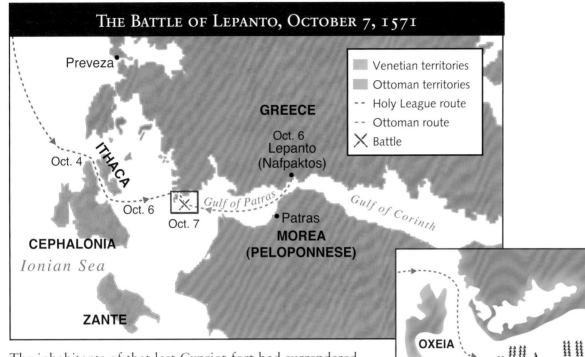

THE BATTLE OF LEPANTO, OCTOBER 7, 1571

Preveza
GREECE
ITHACA
Oct. 4
Oct. 6
Lepanto
(Nafpaktos)
Oct. 6
Gulf of Patras
Oct. 7
Patras
CEPHALONIA
MOREA
(PELOPONNESE)
Ionian Sea
Gulf of Corinth
ZANTE

Venetian territories
Ottoman territories
Holy League route
Ottoman route
Battle

OXEIA
Barbarigo (Left)
Mehmed Sirocco (Right)
Ottoman Fleet
Galleasses
Don Juan (Center)
Ali Pasha (Center)
Bazán (Reserve)
Doria (Right)
Uluch Ali (Left)
Gulf of Patras
Holy League Fleet

The inhabitants of that last Cypriot fort had surrendered two months earlier after a siege of nearly a year. General Mustapha Pasha had had the Venetian leaders cut to pieces, the officers beheaded, and the soldiers made galley slaves. The general had then ordered the civic governor's nose and ears cut off, before having him flayed alive, and finally having his skin stuffed with straw and hung from the yardarm of Mustapha's ship, whence it was transported home to Sultan Selim. These details aroused in the Christian soldiers an understandable thirst for vengeance.

Their opportunity came on October 7, 1571. As the sun rose over the ruffled waters of the Gulf of Patras, the chaplains were saying Mass aboard the galleys. Sentinels high in the masts spotted the enemy fleet fifteen miles away. Don Juan, his lean frame elegantly encased in silver-embossed armor, ordered the firing of a cannon—the signal to take up battle positions. The blue standard of the Holy League was unfurled from the main mast of his vessel to the cheers of every Christian man, each holding his cross aloft.

There was a final moment of hesitation. Doria, seeing that the Turkish fleet, at more than three hundred vessels, was much larger than anticipated, pleaded with Don Juan to turn back. "Gentlemen," Don Juan replied, "the time for counsel is past. The time for battle has come." Any officer who dared desert, he warned, eyeing the thirty-two-year-old Genoese, would meet a traitor's death.

Ali Pasha had had an almost identical conversation with his admirals, who continued to urge retreat into the anchorage of Lepanto. But the sultan's orders to attack brooked no deviation. Shortly after noon the Turkish side fired a single cannon shot acknowledging their willingness to do battle. The Christians fired two shots in return, indicating their readiness. Ali Pasha, on his flagship, the *Sultana*, raised the green, crescent-emblazoned Islamic standard as his men called out their many names for God and recited verses from the Koran.

His three squadrons—significantly lacking a fourth, reserve grouping—

Chesterton's epic tribute to the victor of Lepanto

In what is among his best known and some would say greatest work in verse, the twentieth-century Christian poet and essayist G. K. Chesterton pens this memorable account of the naval battle that ended the Turkish advance in the Mediterranean. Titled simply "Lepanto," the poem's militant drumbeat meter captivates schoolchildren and adults alike by demonstrating how the tempo of language can convey meaning. The illustration shows the San Lorenzo, a Venetian galleass, attacking the Turkish fleet at Lepanto with cannon blazing. This masterful work of digital art is by Rado Javor.

White founts falling in the courts of the sun,
And the Soldan of Byzantium is smiling as they run;
There is laughter like the fountains in that face of all men feared,
It stirs the forest darkness, the darkness of his beard,
It curls the blood-red crescent, the crescent of his lips,
For the inmost sea of all the earth is shaken with his ships.
They have dared the white republics up the capes of Italy,
They have dashed the Adriatic round the Lion of the Sea,
And the Pope has cast his arms abroad for agony and loss,
And called the kings of Christendom for swords about the Cross,
The cold queen of England is looking in the glass;
The shadow of the Valois is yawning at the Mass;
From evening isles fantastical rings faint the Spanish gun,
And the Lord upon the Golden Horn is laughing in the sun.

Dim drums throbbing, in the hills half heard,
Where only on a nameless throne a crownless prince has stirred,
Where, risen from a doubtful seat and half-attainted stall,

The last knight of Europe takes weapons from the wall,
The last and lingering troubadour to whom the bird has sung,
That once went singing southward when all the world was young,
In that enormous silence, tiny and unafraid,
Comes up along a winding road the noise of the Crusade.
Strong gongs groaning as the guns boom far,
Don John of Austria is going to the war,
Stiff flags straining in the night-blasts cold
In the gloom black-purple, in the glint old-gold,
Torchlight crimson on the copper kettle-drums,
Then the tuckets, then the trumpets, then the cannon, and he comes.
Don John laughing in the brave beard curled,
Spurning of his stirrups like the thrones of all the world,
Holding his head up for a flag of all the free.
Love-light of Spain—hurrah!
Death-light of Africa!
Don John of Austria
Is riding to the sea.

Mahound is in his paradise above the evening star,
(Don John of Austria is going to the war.)
He moves a mighty turban on the timeless houri's knees,
His turban that is woven of the sunset and the seas.
He shakes the peacock gardens as he rises from his ease,
And he strides among the tree-tops and is taller than the trees,
And his voice through all the garden is a thunder sent to bring
Black Azrael and Ariel and Ammon on the wing.
Giants and the Genii,
Multiplex of wing and eye,
Whose strong obedience broke the sky
When Solomon was king.

They rush in red and purple from the red clouds of the morn,
From temples where the yellow gods shut up their eyes in scorn;
They rise in green robes roaring from the green hells of the sea
Where fallen skies and evil hues and eyeless creatures be;
On them the sea-valves cluster and the grey sea-forests curl,
Splashed with a splendid sickness, the sickness of the pearl;
They swell in sapphire smoke out of the blue cracks of the ground,—
They gather and they wonder and give worship to Mahound.
And he saith, "Break up the mountains where the hermit-folk may hide,
And sift the red and silver sands lest bone of saint abide,
And chase the Giaours flying night and day, not giving rest,
For that which was our trouble comes again out of the west.
We have set the seal of Solomon on all things under sun,
Of knowledge and of sorrow and endurance of things done,
But a noise is in the mountains, in the mountains, and I know
The voice that shook our palaces—four hundred years ago:
It is he that saith not 'Kismet'; it is he that knows not Fate;
It is Richard, it is Raymond, it is Godfrey in the gate!
It is he whose loss is laughter when he counts the wager worth,
Put down your feet upon him, that our peace be on the earth."
For he heard drums groaning and he heard guns jar,
(Don John of Austria is going to the war.)
Sudden and still—hurrah!
Bolt from Iberia!
Don John of Austria
Is gone by Alcalar.

St. Michael's on his Mountain in the sea-roads of the north
(Don John of Austria is girt and going forth.)
Where the grey seas glitter and the sharp tides shift
And the sea-folk labor and the red sails lift.
He shakes his lance of iron and he claps his wings of stone;
The noise is gone through Normandy; the noise is gone alone;
The North is full of tangled things and texts and aching eyes
And dead is all the innocence of anger and surprise,
And Christian killeth Christian in a narrow dusty room,
And Christian dreadeth Christ that hath a newer face of doom,
And Christian hateth Mary that God kissed in Galilee,
But Don John of Austria is riding to the sea.
Don John calling through the blast and the eclipse
Crying with the trumpet, with the trumpet of his lips,
Trumpet that sayeth ha!
Domino gloria!
Don John of Austria
Is shouting to the ships.

King Philip's in his closet with the Fleece about his neck
(Don John of Austria is armed upon the deck.)
The walls are hung with velvet that is black and soft as sin,
And little dwarfs creep out of it and little dwarfs creep in.
He holds a crystal phial that has colors like the moon,
He touches, and it tingles, and he trembles very soon,
And his face is as a fungus of a leprous white and grey
Like plants in the high houses that are shuttered from the day,
And death is in the phial, and the end of noble work,
But Don John of Austria has fired upon the Turk.
Don John's hunting, and his hounds have bayed—
Booms away past Italy the rumor of his raid.
Gun upon gun, ha! ha!
Gun upon gun, hurrah!
Don John of Austria
Has loosed the cannonade.

The Pope was in his chapel before day or battle broke,
(Don John of Austria is hidden in the smoke.)
The hidden room in a man's house where God sits all the year,
The secret window whence the world looks small and very dear.
He sees as in a mirror on the monstrous twilight sea
The crescent of his cruel ships whose name is mystery;
They fling great shadows foe-wards, making Cross and Castle dark,
They veil the plumèd lions on the galleys of St. Mark;
And above the ships are palaces of brown, black-bearded chiefs,
And below the ships are prisons, where with multitudinous griefs,
Christian captives sick and sunless, all a laboring race repines
Like a race in sunken cities, like a nation in the mines.
They are lost like slaves that swat, and in the skies of morning hung
The stair-ways of the tallest gods when tyranny was young.
They are countless, voiceless, hopeless as those fallen or fleeing on
Before the high Kings' horses in the granite of Babylon.
And many a one grows witless in his quiet room in hell
Where a yellow face looks inward through the lattice of his cell,
And he finds his God forgotten, and he seeks no more a sign—
(But Don John of Austria has burst the battle-line!)
Don John pounding from the slaughter-painted poop,
Purpling all the ocean like a bloody pirate's sloop,
Scarlet running over on the silvers and the golds,
Breaking of the hatches up and bursting of the holds,
Thronging of the thousands up that labor under sea
White for bliss and blind for sun and stunned for liberty.
Vivat Hispania!
Domino Gloria!
Don John of Austria
Has set his people free!

Cervantes on his galley sets the sword back in the sheath
(Don John of Austria rides homeward with a wreath.)
And he sees across a weary land a straggling road in Spain,
Up which a lean and foolish knight forever rides in vain,
And he smiles, but not as Sultans smile, and settles back the blade....
(But Don John of Austria rides home from the Crusade.)

More than six hundred ships and a hundred and forty thousand men fought at Lepanto, here portrayed by Spanish artist Juan Luna y Novicio (1857–1900). Twice Don Juan led charges on Ali Pasha's flagship Sultana *and twice was beaten back, but the third charge succeeded when the Muslim commander was felled by a ball from a harquebus, and Don Juan ordered the Holy League banner raised aloft on* Sultana. *But that was not the end. The battle continued for hours of the bloodiest maritime fighting on record before the League emerged victorious. Some forty thousand men died in it, twelve thousand Christian slaves were liberated, some hundred vessels were sunk, and one hundred and thirty-seven Muslim vessels, including their treasury ship, were captured. Not least, Lepanto conclusively dismantled the Western illusion of Ottoman invincibility.*

assumed a mirror formation to the Christians'. The pasha's squadron faced Don Juan's, Uluch Ali's faced Doria's, and the third, led by Mehmed Sirocco Pasha, governor of Alexandria, faced Barbarigo's.

On Don Juan's ships the artillery pieces were charged, sand was placed on the decks to afford better footing, portable platforms were placed over the rowing benches to provide more fighting space, and triple portions of wine—a customary pre-battle inducement—were served to all hands. Priests handed out rosaries, and Don Juan knelt at the prow of the *Real* and prayed to God for victory as thousands of his armed men fell to their knees. As an insouciant afterthought, the Christian commander danced a galliard on the gun platform to the music of fifes.

As the warm autumn sun shone vertically down on the Mediterranean and the two great fleets—more than six hundred ships carrying a hundred and forty thousand men—came within two miles of each other along a four-mile front, the wind evaporated and the sea became as glass. With no breeze to favor either side's sails, it was as though God had leveled the playing field.

The Turks fired the first cannon shots. Don Juan's galleasses responded with a thunderous artillery barrage that shattered masts and sent bodies flying. Two Turkish galleys quickly sank, and twenty others were crippled. Turkish archers responded with a deadly deluge of arrows and for a time got the better of the battle thanks to a far quicker reload time than that of the Christians with their harquebuses.[7]

Sirocco's right wing then sneaked twelve Turkish galleys past the galleasses and came around, close in to the shore and behind Barbarigo's squadron. The Christian galleys were caught in a dreadful crossfire, and Barbarigo's own vessel, which he had interposed to block any further Turkish flank movement, was engulfed in a storm of arrows. He lost ten officers to Muslim arrows in a moment and, raising the visor of his helmet to be heard, took an arrow to the left eye and was carried below and died.

After an hour of ferocious fighting, the Turks seemed ready to break through the Christians' left flank. But then galleys from Admiral Bazán's reserve moved in from behind, a galleass crept toward shore and began to pulverize Ottoman ships, Christian slaves broke free on one of the galleys and launched a furious attack on their Turkish masters, and Uluch's flagship was rammed and began to sink. Venetians fished the mortally wounded governor from the water and decapitated him. The Christian left began to move forward and envelop the Turkish right wing. Many of the Turkish men gave up the fight and fled to the shore, pursued by Venetians who with shouts of "Famagusta!" summarily executed all they could catch.

The Christians fought with astonishing fury, and the hottest action took place at the very center. Don Juan and Ali Pasha steered their flagships together, and the two vessels became one nightmarish battlefield. War-hardened Muslim Janissaries and equally tough Spanish infantrymen wielded swords, scimitars, battle-axes, and clubs. The decks of the two ships were a jumble of hundreds of men fighting back and forth at close quarters in the slippery blood that drenched the deck and turned the surrounding waters red.

As the warm autumn sun shone vertically down, the wind died and the sea became as glass. With no breeze to favor either side, it was as if God had leveled the playing field.

Christians twice boarded the *Sultana* and twice were beaten back. Don Juan led the third charge armed with a huge broadsword and a battle-ax, and Ali Pasha dashed forward to meet him. But the young Muslim commander suddenly fell onto a rowing bench, dropped by a harquebus ball. A Christian galley slave severed his head, and the triumphant Spaniards stuck it on a pike and hoisted it high. Don Juan ordered the Muslim standard cut down and a Holy League banner raised in its place.

The Christians had carried the day on their left and center flanks, but the right—Doria's squadron—was another matter. Uluch Ali on the Turkish left wing had, by veering further left, drawn Doria's ships away from the main front. That opened to attack a more than mile-wide gap to the right side of Don Juan's squadron. The Christian commander and his men suddenly saw a sub-squadron of Uluch Ali's galleys coming through this gap. Meanwhile, the rest of Ali's ships pounced on the disarrayed portions of Doria's right, including the three vessels of the Knights of Malta—long-time nemeses of the corsair—which were lost after a valiant fight.

It looked for a time as though Ali's thrust might turn the tide back toward the Turks. But Doria, confounding many expectations, regrouped and attacked Ali from the south. And Don Juan, Veniero, and others from the Christian center, left, and reserve attacked from the north. Uluch Ali ditched the Maltese ship he'd been towing as a trophy for the sultan and slipped away with fourteen of his vessels.

By four o'clock in the afternoon, after four hours of the bloodiest fighting the sea had yet seen, the Battle of Lepanto was over. Forty thousand men—twenty-five thousand of them Ottoman—were dead. Nearly a hundred ships had been destroyed and

7. The harquebus (or arquebus), a precursor to the musket, was a shoulder-held, smoothbore metal long gun from which an iron ball was shot by gunpowder ignited by a match. Originally used by the Ming dynasty Chinese to ward off Mongols in the late fourteenth century, the gun was in common use by European armies by the mid-sixteenth century. The harquebus's advantages over the bow included the portability and easy manufacture of its ammunition, and its effectiveness against cavalry. Its disadvantages included its uselessness in wet weather, the slowness of reloading, the great amount of smoke created, and the tendency of both the gun and its gunpowder-laden harquebusier to explode unexpectedly.

one hundred thirty-seven Muslim ships, including the treasury ship, had been captured by the Holy League. Twelve thousand Christian slaves were liberated, and thirty-five hundred Muslim captives were taken.

News of this tremendous and unexpected victory triggered joyous celebrations in Venice, Messina, the Papal States, Genoa, and all over Spain. Don Juan returned a hero. The Venetians proclaimed October 7 a national holiday in perpetuity. Attributing the victory of Lepanto to the intercession of the Virgin Mary, Pope Pius V declared October 7 the Feast of Our Lady of Victory, later to be changed by Pope Gregory XIII to the Feast of

Below, an oil-on-canvas panorama of the Battle of Lepanto by sixteenth-century artist Andrea Vicentino, stretches across both pages. Above, soldier Miguel Cervantes, not yet a famous novelist, directs fire from a lifeboat slung from his galleon (lithograph by Fortunino Matania, 1881–1963).

the Rosary. Today it is called Our Lady of the Rosary. Spain came to regard Lepanto as its great naval triumph. The battle was celebrated in painting, sculpture, and poetry, and was mentioned in one of the greatest novels of all time, *Don Quixote*, written by Miguel de Cervantes, who was wounded at Lepanto.[8]

The Battle of Lepanto changed some things forever and left others completely unaltered. The old jealousies, rivalries, and squabbling quickly resurfaced among the European nations, which had briefly put aside petty differences and united to

such great effect. Pius V died in 1572, and the Holy League expired with him. The Venetians ceded Cyprus to the Turks and agreed to pay a protective tariff even greater than before.

The future of Don Juan was similarly bleak. He had long cherished a plan to rescue Mary Queen of Scots from English captivity, and four years after Lepanto, when Philip appointed him governor of the Netherlands, he thought the opportunity to do so had arrived. But when Philip withdrew the Spanish army from the Low Countries, any hope of rescuing Mary evaporated. Left without an army to negotiate with the tough-minded Protestants who controlled the seven northern provinces, Don Juan inaugurated the policies that would one day see the remaining ten in the south—today's Belgium, Luxembourg, and most of the French Netherlands—still within the Catholic fold. He died of typhus in a military camp at what is now the Belgian city of Namur. He was thirty-one years old. Spain remembers him as a great military leader. However, it was his genius as a diplomat that truly distinguished him.

Muslim terrorism by piracy was not beaten, and the Barbary corsairs continued to plague shipping and towns in the western Mediterranean area for some two hundred and fifty years. However, though the Turks rebuilt their navy and remained a dominant power, any serious threat of a massive Turkish invasion by sea of southern Europe ended with Lepanto, where the Ottoman Empire had been beaten soundly. As Cervantes put it, "All the world learned how mistaken it had been in believing that the Turks were invincible." Philip, that is, had proved as good as his word. ∎

8. Cervantes, an impoverished and bookish twenty-four-year old from Alcalá de Henares, near Madrid, had joined the Spanish Navy as a volunteer. On the day of Lepanto he had been sick with fever but left his bed to command a detachment of soldiers. He was struck in the chest by two harquebus balls and permanently maimed in the left hand. His military career continued until his capture by Algerian pirates in 1575. Ransomed, he returned to Spain and held various civil service jobs, writing on the side, until the success of the first part of his *Don Quixote* in 1605.

The massacre of French Protestants that began in Paris on August 24, 1572—the Feast of St. Bartholomew—in a contemporary painting by François Dubois (1529–1584). Huguenot victims are shown being cut down as they try to flee the Louvre, while the queen mother, Catherine de' Medici, seems to gloat over a pile of naked corpses. Such killing went on for a week and spread to other French cities.

CHAPTER 12

The Reformation fury rages across France in a 36-year bloodbath

Murder, riot, street slaughter, mayhem, and horror, capped by the massacre of St. Bartholomew, leave the country bitterly divided and blacken its history

King Henry III of France—frivolous, ostentatious, and delusional—knew himself to be a veritable royal disaster. He had lost the south of his country to the Protestants and the rest of it to a league of powerful Catholic nobles. He had failed to sire an heir. He had been forced to flee his capital after ordering the killing of a prominent and popular nobleman. He was about to be excommunicated by the pope. What he did not know in that spring of 1589 was that he had roughly three months left to live.

King Henry's chief foes had always by necessity been the Protestants, but necessities come and go, especially when one is hard pressed—and it now seemed to him a necessity to parley with his namesake Henry, the Calvinist ruler of Navarre. Bold, magnetic, and adroit, Henry of Navarre appeared to be everything that Henry of France was not, but he had long been a thorn in the Catholic side. Would he now actually stand alongside the French monarch?

Indeed he would. As Henry III must have suspected, Navarre was not the man to pass up an opportunity. Their combined armies were soon besieging Paris. The city's enraged Catholic citizens, however, became convinced that their monarch was acting tantamount to an agent of Satan, and one of them, a young friar, resolved to take action. On August 1 he ventured into the royalists' camp, claiming to have a message from their allies. Admitted to the king's presence, he attacked and fatally stabbed his monarch.

The dashing Henry of Navarre, who reigned as Henry IV of France from 1589 to 1610, is portrayed in an oil painting circa 1600 as the classical Greek hero Hercules, victorious over the Hydra, a monstrous nine-headed water snake.

An enraged Dominican friar, having gained entrance as a friend to the royalist camp, fatally stabs King Henry III on August 1, 1589. Last of the Valois line but considered by powerful Catholic lords to be far too conciliatory toward Huguenots, the king had decided that his best ally was his brother-in-law the Calvinist Henry of Navarre. Now both Henrys were besieging Paris, which was held by the Catholic League, and Catholic Parisians feared the worst. (Seventeenth-century work in copper by the German engraver Ludwig Friedrich Kaiser.)

The dying king called Henry of Navarre to his side and made two predictions: first, that Navarre would be proclaimed heir to the French throne; second, that only a Catholic could ever rule France. Navarre would have needed no explanation for this caveat. Steeped in Gallic history, he would be fully aware of the close historical association between Paris and the papacy. Rightly or wrongly, the king of France was known across Christendom as the Sword of God and the Most Christian King, and how far some Catholics would go to preserve that reputation had just been brutally demonstrated.

But Henry of Navarre would also have known that France was not immune to the reforming spirit. Early on, the papacy had faced a serious challenge there on the score of clerical corruption, and for the first third of the sixteenth century the crown had tolerated moderate dissent. During the seventeen-year reign of Louis XII (1498–1515), some of the Roman Church's harshest critics were employed at court, and in 1515 came twenty-year-old Francis I, the first French king to receive a humanist education. The amorous, poetry-loving Francis, much admired as an up-to-date Renaissance monarch, showed no interest whatsoever in repressing free thought so long as his kingdom remained stable.

When Lutheran ideas began infiltrating Paris in 1520, King Francis protected key reform activists, to the intense chagrin of the Sorbonne (the University of

*Francis I
King of France*

Paris) and the Parlement of Paris (France's highest court), the two institutions chiefly responsible for safeguarding religious orthodoxy. To these recognized arbiters, the matter was clear: the so-called reformers were heretics who ought to be stamped out. A sinister pattern developed. Whenever the king was absent, Sorbonne and Parlement would strike, imprisoning, torturing, and even executing reformers.[1]

But this deadly standoff between king and councillors came to a crashing halt in 1534, on a single October night. Throughout France devoted reformers secretly posted leaflets

1. While King Francis I was a prisoner in Italy in 1525, the Sorbonne and the Parlement moved swiftly against French reformers. Although most of these men considered themselves Catholic, they were imprisoned, driven into exile, had their tongues cut out, were strangled, or were burned alive. Freed in 1526, the king had difficulty halting these activities. Similarly, while he was on holiday three years later, the two institutions had the reformer Louis de Berquin, a doctor of theology and royal councillor, hastily tried, convicted, and executed—all before noon on April 16.

entitled "True Articles on the Horrible, Gross, and Insufferable Abuses of the Papal Mass"—one of them on the very door of the king's bedchamber. Catholics, including King Francis, were outraged, and royal reaction to the Night of the Placards was swift. Solemn and angry Catholic processions were followed by arrests and executions. Many reformers fled the country, including one John Calvin (see ch. 5). The more the movement was persecuted, however, the more it grew, although it seemingly lacked cohesion until Calvin began directing it from Geneva. Under his influence most reformers in France would become full-fledged Protestants and Calvinists. Later in France they would become popularly known as Huguenots.[2]

King Francis abruptly switched from protecting reform to supporting its Catholic adversaries. In 1545, with his agreement, the Parlement sent an army into Provence to deal with the persistent Waldensian sect. Established in the late twelfth century and declared heretical in the early thirteenth, the Waldensians had survived several earlier crusades, but the effect of this one was truly horrific. Two out of three Provençal villages were burned to the ground, thousands died or were displaced, and the Waldensians were effectively wiped out in France.[3] The aging Francis, it was said, was sickened by the reports.

Francis I died in 1547 and was succeeded by his son, a man as barbarous as his father had been cultured, whose ascension to the throne as Henry II spelled very bad news for Calvinists. Within six months he had instituted what became known as the "burning court" to deal exclusively with heresy. In 1557 his judiciary persuaded the king not to bring the Inquisition into France, but that September 135 reformers were nevertheless arrested in one swoop, and many were tortured and executed.

2. The name "Huguenot," first applied to French Calvinists in 1560, was originally a term of contempt. It may have been a corruption of the German word *Eidgenossen* (meaning "confederate") or, more probably, a reference to Besançon Hugues, who as head of the Calvinist Confederate Party encouraged an alliance between the city-state of Geneva and the larger Swiss Federation. Others suggest it may allude to the Gate of King Hugo, a popular meeting point for Calvinists in Tours, regarded by many Catholics as haunted by malevolent ghosts.

3. Founded by Peter Waldo, a twelfth-century Lyon merchant who forsook his wealth for a vow of poverty, the Waldensians were noted for their abstemious lifestyle, their opposition to warfare and to all temporality, and for denying purgatory, indulgences, and prayers for the dead. After the slaughter by French troops in 1545, Waldensian survivors prudently disappeared from sight. They would emerge again in France after the Reformation as members of the Calvinist Church.

A page from a contemporary pamphlet entitled "The Horrible Cruelties of the Huguenots in France." A priest is being garroted at left, while at right a Catholic's feet are held to the fire. This pamphlet is held at the Bibliothèque Nationale, Paris.

When a "prince of the blood" was needed in 1559 to represent and guide young Francis II, the normal genealogical choice lay between King Anthony of Navarre (above, center) and his brother, Prince Louis (far right)—both certified Bourbons. As Calvinists however, they were unacceptable to the Catholic Guise brothers (pictured below), who controlled the royal council. King Anthony and Prince Louis had to retreat to their royal palace in Olite, Navarre, pictured above left.

French Protestants petitioning God for relief must have thought on June 30, 1559, that their prayers had indeed been answered. While celebrating both a truce with Spain and his daughter's wedding, King Henry was accidentally struck down during a jousting tournament and died ten days later.[4] His son Francis, though at fifteen was eligible to rule, was considered too immature to do so, and a regent could be appointed only for an heir who was in fact underage. Therefore, a "prince of the blood," a direct male relative of the monarch, was temporarily required—in this case a member of the historic Bourbon family.

The proper choice lay between King Anthony of Navarre and his brother, Prince Louis of Condé, certified Bourbons but both Calvinists—and a Calvinist king was something that Francis duc de Guise (Francis duke of Guise, pronounced geez) and his brother, Charles de Guise, cardinal of Lorraine, could not and would not countenance. Though their family had been undistinguished in the French court until King Francis I had appointed their father the first duke de Guise, they were staunch Catholics who could credibly trace their lineage back to Charlemagne. The two brothers managed to secure effective control of the royal council before Navarre and Condé could reach Paris. Finding the Guises solidly entrenched and Duke Francis signing documents with royal pomp, the Bourbon brothers had no choice but to leave for home, and Huguenot hopes appeared to go with them.

Charles de Guise

Francis de Guise

4. Henry II was killed when an opponent's lance pierced his headgear and splintered in two, one piece penetrating his eye, the other his temple. The court astrologer, Nostradamus (see sidebar, p. 268), reportedly had warned him not to fight and had predicted his death in this verse: "The Lion shall overcome the old / On the field of war in a single combat. / He will pierce his eyes in a cage of gold. / This is the first of two lappings, / Then he dies a cruel death."

The Guises seem to have been everywhere either reviled or revered, one or the other, with no middle ground. Duke Francis achieved celebrity status for affability at court and bravado in war. Famous for remembering the name of the commonest soldier and for going into battle with visor raised, he earned the nickname Scarface and the title grand chamberlain of France. Brother Charles became a bishop at age thirteen and was created cardinal of Lorraine nine years later. He crowned three successive kings and was believed to be the wealthiest man in the country. But he was also said to lead an abstemious life, attracted huge crowds with his eloquent preaching, and was credited on one occasion with the seemingly impossible feat of distributing Communion to twelve thousand people.

Other historians, however, depict the brothers de Guise as so repressive and so violent that they plunged France into decades of civil war. Many contemporaries appear to have viewed Cardinal Charles in particular as vain and vindictive, a Machiavellian figure using religion to mask naked self-interest. A Venetian ambassador, for example, wrote home that "everybody so detests the cardinal of Lorraine that if the matter depended upon universal suffrage, not only would he have no part in the government, but perhaps not in this world."

The Guises' 1559 power play engendered a predictable backlash, inspiring an attempt by a group of impoverished Protestant noblemen to overthrow them and apprehend the young king. Perhaps with the blessing of Louis of Condé, perhaps funded by Queen Elizabeth of England, and certainly with the foreknowledge of John Calvin (although not his approval), they gathered an army and set a date. On March 10, 1560, their troops set out for the royal residence at Amboise, seventeen miles east of Tours—and walked straight into an ambush. They had been betrayed. Some thousand men perished, many of them drowned in the Loire River, or seized and hanged.

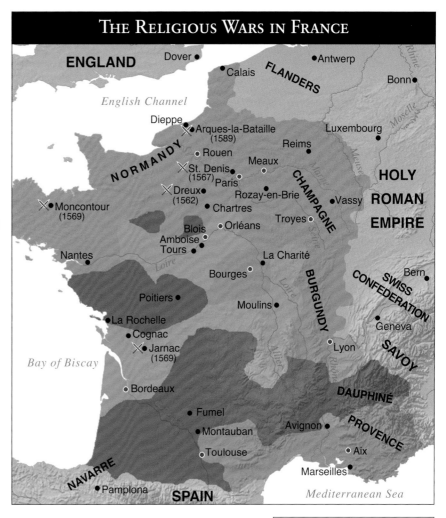

THE RELIGIOUS WARS IN FRANCE

ENGLAND
Dover
Calais
FLANDERS
Antwerp
Bonn
English Channel
Dieppe
Arques-la-Bataille (1589)
Luxembourg
Reims
Rouen
Meaux
NORMANDY
St. Denis (1567)
Paris
Dreux (1562)
Rozay-en-Brie
CHAMPAGNE
Vassy
HOLY ROMAN EMPIRE
Moncontour (1569)
Chartres
Troyes
Blois
Orléans
Amboise
Tours
La Charité
Nantes
Bourges
BURGUNDY
SWISS CONFEDERATION
Bern
Poitiers
Moulins
Geneva
La Rochelle
Cognac
Jarnac (1569)
Lyon
SAVOY
Bay of Biscay
Bordeaux
DAUPHINÉ
Fumel
Montauban
Avignon
PROVENCE
Toulouse
Aix
Marseilles
NAVARRE
Pamplona
SPAIN
Mediterranean Sea

Greatest reach of Catholic League 1590

Territories under Huguenot control 1598

Territories disputed by Catholics and Huguenots

● Towns involved in the St. Bartholomew Day Massacre 1572

✕ Battles

The Tumult of Amboise occurred when a small Protestant army marched on the royal residence at Amboise, near Tours, to extract young Francis II from (as they saw it) the clutches of the Guise brothers. Betrayed and ambushed, some thousand of them perished—many by hanging, as shown at left.

Most Reformed churches, following Calvin's lead, had largely declined participation in what was known as the Tumult of Amboise, and there was no concrete evidence against Condé. The Guises nevertheless tried to besmirch them all, and a brutal crackdown looked inevitable. But it never happened. Instead, religious prisoners were released and accused reformers encouraged to petition the king.

This seems to have been due to the queen mother, Catherine de' Medici. Described as possessing "a mouth too large and eyes too prominent and colorless for beauty," she was destined to see three of her four sons become successive kings of France. But she was resented for her Italian heritage, was long neglected by Henry II in favor of his mistress, and after his death was presumed by many to be simply a Guise pawn. But now Queen Catherine suddenly began flexing her political muscles. Her natural allegiance to Rome was probably inborn and firm, but it paled in

A prophet who denied he was one

In the baffling works of Nostradamus, the French court seer of the 16th century, some see previsions of momentous events, but only after they actually happen

The destruction by terrorists on September 11, 2001, of the Twin Towers in New York City once again piqued public interest in a man who had lived fully four hundred years earlier. Internet sites devoted to him were deluged; sales of hitherto obscure books soared. Seekers for certainty, inspired by rumors that this sixteenth-century pundit had actually foreseen the twenty-first-century calamity, turned again to the enigmatic writings of an astrologer named Nostradamus.

Among other things, this French apothecary (1503–1566) has been credited with predicting the French Revolution of 1789, the rise of Adolf Hitler in the 1930s, and the 2009 election of Barack Obama as U.S. president—not to mention the end of the world in 1999. With the exception of the last, however, his supporters generally have made these assertions after the event, not before it, and Nostradamus himself is on record as disavowing the title of prophet.

To claim powers of prognostication, after all, carried danger of condemnation by the church if seen as veering over into magic, but even so, he entitled his major work *The Prophecies of Michel de Nostradamus.* Published circa 1555, this consists of

Noted prognosticator and apothecary Nostradamus (1503–1556) prepares a medicinal "potion" for a pensive Queen Catherine de' Medici, mother of the French kings Francis II, Charles IX, and Henry III, as depicted in a nineteenth-century woodcut.

some thousand abstruse four-line quatrains grouped in hundreds, most of them rhymed, written in French interspersed with Latin, Greek, and Nostradamus's native Provençal dialect. His style was deliberately cryptic, he explained, "to avoid any actual human eventualities scandalizing the fragility of what has been sensed by oracle."

He began as a traveling apothecary and healer, and at the age of about fifty began publishing almanacs that typically included a calendar, astronomical information, and several thousands of astrological predictions. By tapping into the thriving market of astrology, these almanacs brought him fame and caught the attention of Catherine de' Medici, wife of Henry II of France, who invited him to her court to cast horoscopes for her children.

Astrology was then seen as presenting two very different aspects. "Natural" astrology (or astronomy) gauged the influence of heavenly spheres on the physical world, while "judicial" astrology was thought to determine the effect of these same stars on human actions and affairs. The Christian church had early denounced judicial astrology for its fatalism and implicit denial of free will, and even more for its involvement with the occult. Under the Christian emperor Constantine, astrologers were comparison to the allegiance she would bestow upon her sons. To safeguard their throne from the connivances of the nobility, she would tirelessly play off the ambitious families against each other, favoring Catholic and Huguenot in turn.

She may also have concluded that persecuting the Calvinists would not lead to peace and that a new approach was needed. In any case, a spirit of moderation took hold at court. Even Cardinal Charles de Guise began to argue against continued repression of Protestantism and in favor of church reform. Queen Mother Catherine promoted legislation permitting private Protestant worship. May 1560 saw the proclamation of the Edict of Romorantin, which aimed to separate prosecution of religious dissent from the more serious matter of political sedition.

subject to capital punishment. In the fifth century St. Augustine categorically condemned judicial astrology, warning that such divination enabled demons to ensnare unwary men.

Eleven centuries later, however, Nostradamus could sell his almanacs quite freely, most European courts had an official astrologer, and state decisions often turned on the position of the stars. How had Augustine's fifth-century rationality turned into this sixteenth-century credulity? One theory hinges on the increasing exposure of Christian countries to the Muslim cultures of the Middle East, where astronomy and astrology had continued to flourish. Another influence was the Renaissance rediscovery of Greek learning in general and Aristotle in particular.

Aristotle taught that a "prime mover" regulated the cycles of the heavenly spheres around the earth, and the earth, in turn, was affected by their movement—a cosmology considered compatible with Christianity and a plausible scientific basis for astrology.[1] Thus, astrology had achieved wide acceptance as a putative science, although divination was at least theoretically forbidden as mere magic. It may have been especially appealing during the uncertainties of the Avignon papacy and the Great Western Schism (see vol. 8, ch. 3). Emperors Charles IV and Charles V, along with popes Sixtus IV, Julius II, Leo X, and Paul III, all consulted astrologers, and Luther's colleague Philipp Melanchthon was an avid believer.

So Nostradamus did well with astrology, although scorned by some of his peers as a quack, a charge still leveled today. When he died from edema July 2, 1566—an event he allegedly had foretold the previous evening—he was physician to the French court and famous for his prognostications. He had also predicted more fame to come:

Michel de Nostradamus, shown above in a detail from a Provençal mural, has been credited with predicting events from the rise of Adolf Hitler to the election of Barack Obama. Such fame could have doomed him in some centuries—but not the sixteenth. Below left is depicted a 1668 edition of his Prophesies, *first published a century earlier.*

"After my death my name will live on throughout the world." This one has proven fairly correct; his *Prophecies* has seldom been out of print.

But astrology's credibility had already begun to decline with the publication in 1543 of Copernicus's heliocentric theory (to be covered in Volume 10). As Copernican cosmology gradually gained credence, Aristotle's erroneous theories would be discarded along with their astrological complement. Nevertheless, it would take more than a century to thoroughly discredit judicial astrology, even among the educated elite. To supplement his income, the brilliant German astronomer Johannes Kepler (1571–1630) found a ready market for horoscopes. ∎

1. The thirteenth-century theologian Thomas Aquinas unambiguously ruled out divination by judicial astrology, writes Theodore Wedel (*The Medieval Attitude Toward Astrology*, 1968). Aquinas also asserted (as had Augustine) that human bodies, being corporeal, could be affected by the movement of the stars—but not man's intellect and will since they are incorporeal. Only indirectly and accidentally, insofar as they are intimately connected with the body, might will and intellect be influenced by the stars. The will's freedom is preeminent: "Nothing prevents a man from resisting the dictates of his lower faculties," Aquinas wrote.

LES VRAYES CENTVRIES ET
PROPHETIES
DE MAISTRE
MICHEL NOSTRADAMVS,
Où se void reprefenté tout ce qui s'eft passé,
tant en France, Efpagne, Italie, Allemagne, Angleterre, qu'autres parties du monde.
Reveües & corrigées fuivant les premieres Editions imprimées en Avignon en l'an 1558. & à Lyon en l'an 1558. & autres.

Avec la vie de l'Autheur.

A PARIS
Chez JEAN RIBOU, vis à vis la Sainte Chapelle à l'Image S. Louys.
M. D C. LXVIII.

5. Knowing that the death of young Francis II would allow his mother, Catherine de' Medici, to become regent for his little brother, Charles IX, and fearing an increase in Huguenot influence at the expense of the Guise faction, Cardinal Charles de Guise tearfully declared that he and his family were now "lost." His assessment—if not his sentiment—was shared by John Calvin. "Did you ever read or hear of anything more timely," Calvin wrote, "than the death of the little king?"

But dissent and sedition proved difficult to distinguish as Guise properties in and around Paris were set aflame, along with effigies of Cardinal Charles. In rural areas Huguenots not only worshiped openly, they seized churches and ran priests out of town. Unrest assumed alarming proportions in the Dauphiné and in Provence. In order to question the prince of Condé, the Guises had to mobilize an army to arrest him. In response to all these alarming developments, the crown scheduled an assembly of the Estates General to begin on December 10, 1560. But this plan, too, was derailed when Francis II died of a brain abscess on December 5, at age sixteen.[5]

Since his brother and heir, Charles IX, was just ten, Catherine de' Medici was immediately named regent. With her hold on power now secure, she no longer needed to rely on the brothers Guise and sought to check the influence of the Catholic nobles by promoting Huguenots. As Easter approached, the doors of court and royal council opened wide to Protestants, and on one occasion the queen mother even took her children to a Calvinist sermon.

But during this period, called the Huguenot Lent, Protestant passions continued to run wild and riots broke out countrywide. In vain the queen tried to calm the Huguenot population with further concessions, but still they kept demanding more. By this time, writes historian R. J. Knecht (*The French Wars of Religion*, 1996), many were "envisaging a Protestant France."

The Catholics were by no means vanquished, and on Easter Sunday 1561, three powerful nobles forged a coalition vowed to the protection of the faith: Francis de Guise; Duke Anne de Montmorency, constable of France; and Jacques d'Albon. Each of these men could muster a formidable army, and they had the support of the king of Spain. This Triumvirate presented a major challenge to Queen Catherine's policy of leniency.

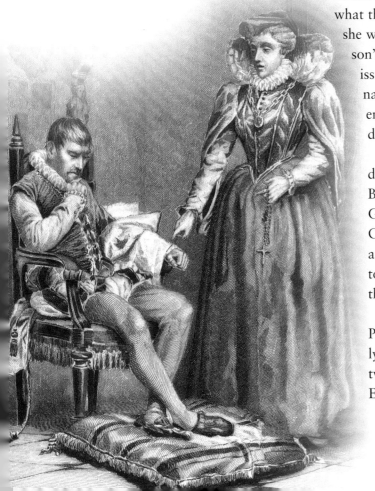

Catherine de' Medici (below) seems to be admonishing her son Charles IX, who reigned from age ten to twenty-four with his mother as a major influence. Charles died in 1574 of tuberculosis, probably exacerbated by his horror of the religious wars and mutual massacres that disfigured his reign.

She responded by inviting both Catholics and Protestants to a national council. It was said of the queen that she did not understand what the word *dogma* meant, but clearly she understood what she wanted—namely, peace for France and stability for her son's throne. Was she naive in believing that the foundational issues of the Reformation could be solved at a French national assembly? Perhaps, but she was seemingly being encouraged by none other than Charles de Guise, the cardinal of Lorraine and Catholic champion.

Some days before the council opened, in fact, the cardinal met with Calvin's second-in-command, Theodore de Beza, who had traveled from Geneva to attend it. When Guise icily questioned Beza about the real presence of Christ in the Eucharist, the Calvinist appeared to him to answer like any good Catholic. Elated, the cardinal is said to have warmly embraced him, declaring, "You will find that I am not as black as they make me out to be."

But the council itself, convening at Poissy (now a Parisian suburb) on September 9, 1561, did not go so tidily. Beza spoke first, outlining the similarities between the two faiths and confirming Christ's actual presence in the Eucharist. So far, so good—but the devil, as they say, is in the details. Beza kept getting more and more specific and soon was describing Christ's presence as spiritual, not bodily. "His body is as far removed from the bread and wine as is heaven from earth." That did it. One cardinal, shedding tears, wondered aloud how Queen Catherine could permit "these horrible blasphemies in the presence of the king."

Anne de Montmorency

Jacques d'Albon

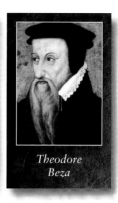

Theodore Beza

The next day, Cardinal de Guise was elected spokesman for Rome, and everyone expected him to expound on the Eucharist. They assuredly did not expect him to maintain, however, that Luther's stance on the real presence was for the most part analogous to the position of both the Eastern Orthodox and Western Catholic churches. This tactic, so seemingly ecumenical, actually would undermine the Calvinist position, leaving them isolated. While many of the Huguenots in attendance are said to have approved Guise's message, Theodore Beza was furious.

Fascination with Lutheranism was indeed in the air. Duke Francis de Guise and Prince Louis of Condé became publicly reconciled. A suggestion from King Anthony of Navarre that the Lutheran princes of Germany should also be invited to Poissy was enthusiastically endorsed. And when a document was slid across the bargaining table for Beza to sign as a symbol of good faith, he saw to his horror that it was none other than the Augsburg Confession, the Lutheran creed.

Had the world indeed turned upside down? Was Charles de Guise, a cardinal of the Catholic Church, really insisting that his Calvinist counterpart endorse this Lutheran manifesto as a prerequisite for reconciliation? Many scholars have regarded Guise's approach as a cynical attempt to put the two major Protestant movements at odds with each other. Catholic historian Stuart Carroll (*Martyrs and Murderers*, 2009) sees "nothing conspiratorial," however, in Guise's willingness to accept a "variant of Catholicism," if only the Huguenots would endorse Luther's position on the Eucharist.[6]

With Beza's refusal to do so, the council adjourned, and the implications of its failure were extensive. Cardinal Charles, having angered both Rome and Geneva, lost all influence. The queen continued her policy of toleration. The members of the Catholic Triumvirate also dug in their heels, however, and moderates were soon forced to take sides as violence reached new heights. Paris was perpetually on the brink of erupting into an orgy of street fighting. Two thousand Huguenots stormed the home of the baron of Fumel and murdered him. There were similar attacks on the nobility throughout France.

6. Even if the Council of Poissy had accepted Cardinal de Guise's reconciliation formula, it would not likely have met popular approval. Many Catholics and Huguenots were fully as serious about their respective faiths as was council participant Theodore Beza, and would surely have spurned this compromise. Most Huguenots attending the council, however, belonged to the party of *Politiques* and regarded Protestantism as a way to satisfy their political ambitions first and their religious consciences second.

Unable to satisfy either the rampaging Huguenots or the furious Catholic nobles, Catherine de' Medici invited theologians from both sides to a national council at Poissy, near Paris, in September 1561. This oil painting, circa 1840, shows her presiding with the young king Charles at her side.

The Massacre of Vassy occurred in March 1562 when troops of the Catholic Triumvirate allegedly found Huguenots worshiping in a country barn and slaughtered them. Above, a contemporary engraving by Jacques Tortorel and Jean-Jacques Perrissin shows Duke Francis de Guise commanding the operation. At its far left, Cardinal Charles looks on approvingly. Center, a painting by Antoine Caron (1521–1599), Massacre under the Triumvirate, allegorically compares the situation in France to the civil wars of ancient Rome. And at far right a Catholic pamphlet, "The Horrible Cruelties of the Huguenots in France," similarly compares the activities of "the cursed race of Huguenots" to the "horror-filled tales of Diomedes in Thrace."

The spark that turned civil strife into civil war came on March 1, 1562. As Francis de Guise led his army through Vassy, about 120 miles southeast of Paris, they discovered several hundred Huguenots worshiping in a barn. What happened next has been much disputed. Guise claimed that the congregation pelted his men with rocks; the Huguenots claimed that the troops tried to roughly disperse them. In any event, whatever the provocation, some thirty Protestants were killed and about one hundred wounded.

French Catholics celebrated the Massacre of Vassy as a victory, while the Huguenots demanded justice. The queen regent summoned Duke Francis to explain himself, but his Triumvirate partners persuaded him to march on Paris instead. Its citizens met him with a hero's welcome, and the city council promised him troops and money to become the defender of the faith. The Huguenots, responding in kind, took to arms under the leadership of Condé.

Prince Louis was an unlikely leader. The twelfth born in his family, he never managed to accumulate great power or wealth. Reportedly stoop backed, sexually ravenous, and bad tempered, he was described by a Venetian ambassador as "very different from his brother, who was of a most amiable and easy character." But he did possess one crucial attribute. He kept faith with the Huguenot cause, while brother Anthony sold his allegiance to the triumvirs, who promised to help him recapture southern Navarre from Spain.

With both Francis de Guise and Louis of Condé in Paris, tensions were at a maximum and gunfire so common that one contemporary described the city as resembling a frontline outpost. Finally the rivals were induced to distance their armies from the city, and if Condé had approached Queen Catherine right then, he might have won her over. Instead, he quietly retired to Meaux (now a suburb of Paris). The triumvirs reached her first and threatened to place her under house arrest unless she agreed to respect their wishes. She capitulated.

Condé did manage to use the spring of 1562 to seize several key cities to southward, including Lyon, the country's second-largest metropolis. This dumbfounded

the Triumvirate, but the Huguenots had long been anticipating a war and were fully prepared. "It is a miracle that this country has survived," commented one Catholic lieutenant, "given the secret intelligence which the Huguenots had in all the towns."

Even now, riots and massacres were more common than battles. The Protestants reputedly murdered priests and monks and defiled churches and graves, while the Catholics allegedly butchered combatants and civilians alike. On July 13 the Parlement sanctioned wholesale slaughter of Huguenots and destruction of Protestant meetinghouses in Paris. Now came the entry of foreign powers—Spain for the Triumvirate and England for the Huguenots. The Catholics reclaimed several cities, including Rouen, Normandy's wealthy capital, after a five-month siege. The Huguenots exacted some satisfaction by killing turncoat Anthony of Navarre, the first of many prominent casualties.

In December 1562 the Huguenots marched on Paris. As Francis de Guise reinforced its defenses and Catherine de' Medici negotiated with Louis of Condé, rival nobles spent the respite amiably socializing with one another. This procedure astonished the German mercenaries involved. "Who are these madmen," they wondered, "who fraternize one day and kill each other the next?"

The Huguenots, who were seeking only to force the crown's hand, tried to withdraw as soon as battle threatened, but on their march back to Normandy they encountered the royal army near Dreux, fifty miles southwest of Paris. Condé, outnumbered overall though he possessed more cavalry, was not keen on a battle. But it was open country. There was nowhere to run. The triumvirs, also hesitant, sought counsel from the crown. Queen Catherine replied expressing her surprise that hardened warriors, having taken France to the brink of civil war, would now seek "the advice of a woman and child who are full of regret to see things in such an extreme state." Finally, on December 19 the Catholic leaders commanded their men to advance.

Even so, for two long hours there was no action. The two armies stood facing one another in silence. "Each one braced himself for battle," wrote the Huguenot captain, Francis de La Noue, "contemplating that the men he saw coming were neither Spanish, English, nor Italian, but French, indeed the bravest of them all, among whom could be found his own comrades, relatives, and friends, and that within the hour it would be necessary to start killing each other."

The Calvinists struck first, their cavalry storming the left wing of the royal army, routing Montmorency's infantry and taking him prisoner. When news of the constable's capture reached Paris, the queen is said to have remarked resignedly, "Then we shall have to learn to say our prayers in French" (as opposed to Latin). The Huguenots had not yet won the battle, however, for the troops of Francis de Guise remained intact. In a ferocious charge they captured Condé, forcing his men into a panicked retreat. A thousand surviving Huguenots held out until nightfall, then withdrew.

Among the bloodiest engagements of the 16th century, the Dreux battlefield was strewn with some 6,000 corpses. And the high death count among the nobility transformed the political scene.

Gaspard de Coligny, shown here in a contemporary oil painting, became a Huguenot convert in the 1550s, yet continued to serve the French crown and to strive for peace. In 1562 however, he became the main leader of the Huguenot army and was also accused of ordering the assassination of Francis de Guise—an accusation he denied.

That this engagement was a Catholic victory was not immediately obvious. Among the bloodiest of the sixteenth century, it strewed the battlefield with, at a conservative estimate, some six thousand corpses—perhaps one for every five combatants. Even more disconcerting, from the crown's perspective, were the casualties among the nobility. "The political scene was transformed as the leaders on both sides were killed, maimed, or captured," writes R. J. Knecht in *The French Civil Wars* (2000). But even this carnage, he adds, apparently succeeded only in "hardening sensibilities."

With Condé imprisoned in Paris, leadership of the Huguenot army passed to Gaspard de Coligny, who in some respects typified the French Reformation. Coligny had converted to Calvinism in 1557 despite the fact that as admiral of France he had much to lose. Furthermore, Anne de Montmorency, one of the Triumvirate and now the Huguenots' most valued prisoner, was his beloved uncle. As a Calvinist Coligny had continued to diligently serve the crown and to work toward a peaceful resolution, but once war began, he fought resolutely for the Protestant cause. Even now, notwithstanding the debacle at Dreux, he shepherded his army to Orléans, vowing to struggle on.

Such a vow rarely falls on deaf ears and especially not with Francis de Guise in the vicinity. With the other members of the Triumvirate dead or imprisoned, and the Huguenots now official enemies of the state, Duke Francis had a vested interest in maintaining the war. By striking immediately, he might topple the Protestants and cleanse France of heresy. Then, having fulfilled his vow as a triumvir, what could prevent him from becoming king?

So while everyone else called for a truce, Guise marched on Orléans, arrived on February 5, 1563, and immediately besieged the city. By the 18th, deeming the inhabitants sufficiently desperate, he ordered an assault for the next day. It was his last command. That night, while strolling from the siege trenches toward his quarters, he was shot in the back by a hidden assassin. He died eight days later. "Even by the admission of his enemies, the duke of Guise was the greatest man of his century," wrote the chronicler Jacques-Auguste de Thou.

Not everyone mourned him, however. Coligny described his death as the "greatest good that could have happened to this kingdom and to God's church," a remark that put him in further danger. Under torture Guise's killer had implicated Coligny, who then admitted that he had hired the man—but only as a spy, not an assassin. The house of Guise, bent upon revenge, demanded that all its supporters work to "avenge the death of the duke up to the fourth generation of those who committed the homicide or connived at it, and of those who are yet defending the culprits."

The duke's death left Catherine de' Medici free to pursue peace, but in negotiating the subsequent treaty, the Huguenots made two crucial errors. First, they surrendered their most valuable asset by releasing Montmorency when the queen chose him to make the Catholic case. Second, they accepted as their own representative Louis of Condé without insisting that he, too, be freed. Still a prisoner of war, he was primarily intent on securing his own release. Although Coligny pleaded with Condé to exploit the Huguenot military gains, he allowed Montmorency to dictate the terms.

The Peace of Amboise, issued March 19, 1563, which allowed Protestant worship but only in the private households of the nobility, severely disappointed Protestants. Calvin condemned Condé as a "wretch who had betrayed God out of vanity." Coligny declared that the Protestant churches were "ruined more by this stroke of the pen than by all the enemy forces could do in ten years." Many Catholics were equally disappointed, however, because Protestant worship had not been outright abolished. The Estates and Parlement of Burgundy issued a statement that may well have summarized the prevailing Catholic view: "In religion there is neither mediation nor neutrality; the line is straight with Jesus

The sketch at left shows the distribution of cavalry, harquebusiers, and pikemen at the Battle of Dreux in 1562, the first major engagement between the Catholic Triumvirate and the Huguenot army led by Prince Louis of Condé. The battle was in fact accidental. Condé had marched on Paris as a bargaining ploy and was heading back to Normandy when he unexpectedly encountered the royal army near Dreux, fifty miles southwest of Paris. With neither side eager to kill their friends and relatives in the enemy camp, they delayed for two hours. The outcome—six thousand men killed, including many nobles—confirmed their reservations.

Above, the future king Henry III of France in a contemporary portrait attributed to François Clouet or Jean Decourt. Third son of Catherine de' Medici and her favorite, in his late teens Henry fought in the Catholic army at Jarnac and Moncontour. As a child, however, he reputedly had shown Huguenot sympathies.

Christ, and he who is not with him is against him."

So the crown's edicts were ignored, and violence continued endemic. The young king, crowned Charles IX that August, undertook a nationwide tour. Visiting both Catholic and Protestant regions, he called upon their various courts and parlements to uphold his law or face the consequences. The point was reinforced in February 1566 by the Ordinance of Moulins, amplifying royal authority at the expense of the judiciary.

These tactics preserved order but did not build trust. Hence when the crown sent troops north in May 1567 in response to an altercation between the Spanish and the Dutch (see ch. 13), the Huguenots feared the army would soon come after them. Suspicion grew when the danger to France abated and still the soldiers remained. Was this some diabolical scheme on the part of a French-Spanish alliance? In a frenzy of fear, they resolved to launch a preemptive strike by attempting to seize the king and his mother, then residing at Meaux. To that end, Coligny and Condé gathered troops at Rozay-en-Brie, not far from the royal residence. They were foiled, however, by the regal and maternal intuition of Catherine de' Medici, who insisted upon a prompt retreat into Paris and summoned the royal army to escort them. Although the Huguenot plan was now hopeless, they nevertheless pursued it. Bringing the Huguenot army to a halt, Condé sought an audience with the king, apparently still hoping to abduct him. King Charles, suspicious, refused to see him and marched on into Paris.

Two weeks later, on November 10, 1567, Constable de Montmorency attacked the Huguenot force at Saint-Denis, but his troops, consisting largely of inexperienced Parisian volunteers, were quickly overrun. When ordered by a bold Huguenot soldier to surrender, Montmorency nevertheless responded by breaking the man's jaw. Shortly thereafter, however, he was fatally wounded by a pistol shot, and the royal force retreated under the command of the king's sixteen-year-old brother, Henry of Anjou. Despite its defeat at Saint-Denis, the royal army continued to gather troops and soon numbered around forty thousand, but the memory of the death toll at Dreux lingered long. How many more nobles could the crown consign to death? "In risking a single battle," fretted Charles IX, "not enough of them would remain to fight a second." And so it was decided that the Catholic army, though larger than many French cities at the time, would not fight.

The Huguenots had won that battle, but one battle was all they could afford. After a failed siege of Chartres during which most of their unpaid soldiers deserted, they were ready to talk. On March 23, 1568, the Peace of Longjumeau was signed, restoring the terms of Amboise but different in one crucial aspect—from the very first the Catholics had no intention of keeping it.

This policy shift coincided with the reemergence at court of Charles de Guise, the cardinal. Embittered by the assassination of his brother, he had abandoned theological compromise and embraced the primacy of Rome. With the pope's blessing, he offered to place the church's wealth at the disposal of the crown, on one condition. The money must be spent solely to suppress "the uprisings of heretical and rebellious Huguenots." King Charles, who despite the truce had not disbanded his army, readily agreed, although several moderates in the royal council resigned.

The Peace of Longjumeau thus became a farce. Violence against Huguenots, no longer inciting royal disapproval, broke out again. Coligny and Condé were warned of imminent arrest and fled to La Rochelle on the Atlantic coast, reaching it on September 18. Knowing that it would provide easy access to their English and Dutch allies, Condé made the city a primary base of operations. He was shortly joined there by twenty-five thousand troops.

After some skirmishing and a winter reprieve, the combatants reengaged on March 13, 1569, at Jarnac, about sixty miles southwest of Bordeaux. Condé, thrown from his horse, felt his leg snap beneath him and immediately surrendered to the nearest enemy soldier. The enemy was in no mood to take captives, however. The man shot him square in the face. Other Protestant prisoners had their throats slit. Coligny, with most of his army still intact, took revenge by slaughtering Catholic peasants and besieging Poitiers. On October 3 he moved against the royal forces at nearby Moncontour, although by then his army was both tired and outnumbered. The result was total defeat, with the royal army losing a few hundred men and the Huguenots a staggering ten thousand.

But while Catherine de' Medici thanked God for this victory, Coligny performed a military miracle. Slipping away to the south, he consolidated all the Huguenot forces, divided them into small, agile units, and marched them toward Paris. This rally is considered by Coligny's biographer, Junko Shimizu (*Conflict of Loyalties*, 1970), to be "one of the greatest achievements in his military career." To the royal court, he now

The assassination of Duke Francis de Guise in 1563 so embittered his brother, Cardinal Charles de Guise, that he abandoned all efforts at conciliation with the Huguenots. Shown in a contemporary oil painting by El Greco (above), the cardinal pledged the entire wealth of the French church to suppress "the uprisings of heretical and rebellious Huguenots." An engraving by Jean-Jacques Perrissin (left) shows the battle of Moncontour, near Poitiers, where in October 1569 Coligny's army lost a staggering ten thousand men.

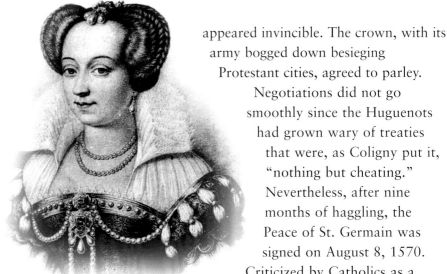

appeared invincible. The crown, with its army bogged down besieging Protestant cities, agreed to parley. Negotiations did not go smoothly since the Huguenots had grown wary of treaties that were, as Coligny put it, "nothing but cheating." Nevertheless, after nine months of haggling, the Peace of St. Germain was signed on August 8, 1570. Criticized by Catholics as a "Calvinist charter," it guaranteed freedom of conscience throughout the kingdom, allowed for restricted freedom of worship, and, most significantly, recognized four "secure" Protestant towns: La Rochelle, Cognac, Montauban, and La Charité.

The betrothal of Marguerite of Valois (above right) and King Henry of Navarre (above left) was arranged by Marguerite's mother, Catherine de' Medici. She saw it as a diplomatic coup, but French Catholics saw it as further royal flirtation with Protestantism. The spectacular wedding in Notre Dame Cathedral is shown below in a nineteenth-century engraving.

Moreover, on this occasion peace was given a chance. Charles de Guise was dismissed from the court,[7] and Catherine de' Medici began to negotiate a diplomatic marriage between her daughter Marguerite of Valois and King Henry of Navarre. Although only sixteen, Navarre was of royal blood and had succeeded his uncle Louis of Condé as the recognized leader of the Huguenots. The queen mother saw this marriage as a major diplomatic coup.

But many Catholics saw it as one more crown flirtation with Protestantism, and one too many. The Treaty of St. Germain was bad enough, and Admiral de Coligny was again back in the royal council, exerting Huguenot influence on the king. There were rumors about a possible war against Spain (a country where they were serious about suppressing heresy), and now a French royal princess was to be married to the enemy!

The royal wedding, held at Notre Dame Cathedral without untoward incident, was perceived by the crown as a confirmation of national peace.[8] This perception lasted barely four days. On August 22, 1572, as Gaspard de Coligny strolled home from a meeting at the Louvre, a bullet fired from the window of a Guise palace broke his arm, though it did not kill him. The Guises were and are the chief suspects,

7. Charles de Guise, the great cardinal of Lorraine, lived out his remaining years a political nonentity. On December 8, 1574, after walking barefoot alongside flagellants in a penitential procession, he came down with a chill. He died the day after Christmas and was buried in Reims Cathedral.

On August 24, 1572, soldiers led by Henry de Guise, son of Duke Francis, killed Huguenot leader Gaspard de Coligny and his entire household, triggering the St. Bartholomew's Day Massacre. The woodcut at left, based on a nineteenth-century painting by Nathanael Sichel, shows Coligny's head being presented to Cardinal Charles de Guise in Rome.

of course, although which one remains a matter of debate. Other historians have suggested that Catherine de' Medici may have become alarmed about Coligny's influence on the king. Still others suggest a lone assailant.[9]

Nor has there been any satisfactory explanation for what came next. Early on August 24, St. Bartholomew's Day, soldiers led by Francis de Guise's son Henry burst into Coligny's home and overwhelmed his bodyguard. The admiral, only then warned of the attack, is said to have responded: "I have long been ready to die." In this assault not one member of his retinue was left alive. Coligny's corpse was beheaded and tossed out the window to be paraded and mutilated by a gathering mob.

There then ensued a terrible massacre of Huguenots, a weeklong orgy that spared neither man, woman, nor child. Charles IX ordered that the killing stop and was ignored. In the capital alone some four thousand Protestants were butchered, and the violence spread from Paris to a dozen other cities. In some places the local authorities reportedly tried to impose a systematized sequence of killings, while in others there apparently was little or no attempt to control the mobs.

One notable survivor was Henry of Navarre, who at dawn on the 24th was summoned to the king's apartment, still unaware of Coligny's fate. Even so, he would later recall that he bade farewell to his retinue with "hair standing on end" and the words, "God knows if I will ever see you again." He was locked in the royal suite until King Charles entered and claimed to have uncovered evidence of a Huguenot plot against him. He offered Navarre his life in return for an immediate conversion to Catholicism. Navarre, hearing screams of Huguenot victims outside, agreed to do so. He had probably been made exempt only by his marriage to the king's sister.

The St. Bartholomew's Day Massacre sent shockwaves throughout Europe. The new pope, Gregory XIII, was jubilant. He had frescoes painted in the Vatican

8. The marriage of Henry of Navarre and Marguerite of Valois would soon provide some of the era's greater scandals. Marguerite was said to have taught her husband that "a cavalier without love was without soul." Taking the lesson to heart, he began courting her attendants, and she responded in kind. Following a series of well-publicized affairs and squabbles, the childless couple had their marriage annulled in 1599. One reconciliation attempt became the subject of William Shakespeare's comedy *Love's Labour's Lost*, and Marguerite is the protagonist in Alexandre Dumas's famous novel *La Reine Margot*.

9. The man long held responsible for wounding Admiral de Coligny was Charles de Louviers, lord of Maurevert, who in 1569 was serving under a Protestant captain who had a bounty on his head. When the admiral wandered away from his troops to urinate, Louviers reputedly pursued him, shot him in the back, and collected the money. Five years later he murdered his cousin and later still lost an arm in a fight with his nephew. Convicted in 1583 when the son of the Protestant captain managed to track him down, he was said to have died "regretted by none, hated by all."

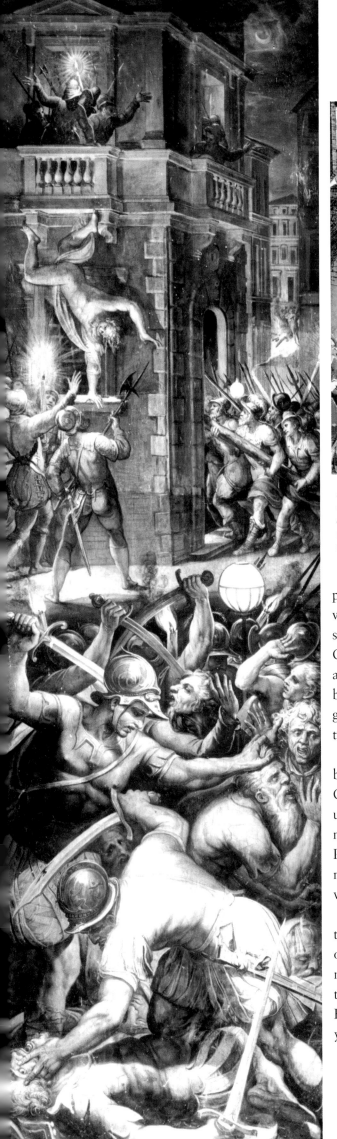

At left, a fresco by Giorgio Vasari in the Vatican Museums in Rome, dated 1573, depicts the killing by Guise soldiers of the Huguenot leader Gaspard de Coligny and his family and servants. Above, in a copper engraving by Gaspard Bouttats (1640–1695), the St. Bartholomew's Day violence has spread like wildfire into the Paris streets.

palace to memorialize the event. Many Protestants believed it was instigated by a French-Spanish-Italian coalition as a first step in the annihilation of their faith. A number of French Catholics were equally appalled at the extent of the violence; not a few had hidden Huguenots in their homes. It was a deadly blow for the French Reformation. Thousands of Huguenots emigrated or, reasoning that God would have protected them if they truly were his children, returned to the Catholic Church.[10]

There is no historical consensus as to what set off this horror, but one plausible theory emerges. It may be that after Admiral de Coligny was shot, the crown greatly feared a massive Huguenot uprising. Charles IX, remembering his close call five years earlier, may have believed that swift preventive action was needed. Perhaps he intended to eliminate the Huguenot leadership but had not counted on his subjects responding with mass murder. If so, it was a miscalculation with particularly gruesome consequences.

King Charles, it was said, was never again the same man. For the next two years he would succumb to fits of anguish, crying out, "What evil counsel I have followed! Oh, my God, forgive me. I am lost!" So violent were his moods that his mother came to believe him a lunatic. On May 30, 1574, he summoned Henry of Navarre to his bedroom and embraced him. "Brother, you are losing a good friend," the king whispered. "Had I

believed all that I was told, you would not be alive. But I always loved you. Pray to God for me." Charles IX died that day of tuberculosis, just shy of his twenty-fourth birthday.

Battles were again raging across France, but the new king, Henry of Anjou, now Henry III, seemed more concerned with his coronation, his wedding ceremony, and the etiquette of his court. Even in the court of France, Henry was an oddity. Always Queen Catherine's favored child, he seemed as a youth to possess clearly regal qualities: charm, intelligence, faithfulness, and courage. Succeeding Montmorency as commander of the royal army, he had won a series of victories, culminating in the rout of the Huguenots at Moncontour. Yet as monarch he would often emerge as ineffectual, and his lavish court entertainments were outdone only by dramatic displays of piety, when he reportedly would indulge in extreme mortifications.

His failure to immediately confront his nation's religious discord paid dividends for the Huguenots. In September 1575 his younger brother and heir,

10. Although the massacre had reduced their ranks and shaken their faith, the Huguenots quickly demonstrated the endurance of their collective spirit. Mere weeks after St. Bartholomew's Day, the citizens of La Rochelle refused to permit the royal governor to enter the city. Besieged by crown troops, the Huguenots repelled eight major assaults between November 1572 and July 1573. Only half the royal army survived. This fourth civil war ended with a Catholic withdrawal and the signing of yet another unworkable treaty.

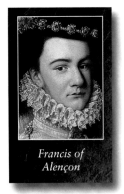

Francis of Alençon

Francis of Alençon, left the court and declared for the enemy. Six months later Henry of Navarre did likewise, renouncing his enforced Catholicity. With the Huguenots again on the ascent and the royal treasury emptied by the previous wars, the king capitulated. In the Edict of Beaulieu he at last extended to the Huguenots the "free, public, and general exercise" of their religion.

But the Triumvirate had been succeeded by the Catholic League, led by Duke Henry de Guise, which won much popular approval by vehemently opposing this edict. With the prestige of the crown diminishing, the king summoned the Estates General in November 1576. There he reiterated that his kingdom would assert solely the Catholic faith, although it would tolerate peaceful Huguenots. The League, however, remained determined to eradicate Protestantism.[11]

Not for eight years did matters again reach a head, with the death from tuberculosis of Francis of Alençon in 1584. Alençon had flirted with Calvinism but

Henry of Navarre, though not considered handsome, enthralled many women; though not a renowned military tactician, rarely lost a battle; and, while not pious, could mollify the zealous.

strictly for political gain, not from conviction, and had been easily persuaded to recant. He died a Catholic and likely would have ruled as one. Hence the crisis, for the same was by no means true of Henry of Navarre, the next in line.

Born in 1553 to the infamous Huguenot defector Anthony of Navarre and his devout Calvinist wife Jeanne, Henry combined his father's genial faith and attractive personality with his mother's resolve. Though not considered handsome, he enthralled many women, and though not renowned as a military tactician, he rarely lost a battle. Never noted for piety, he still could mollify the zealous. Such magnetism defies easy explanation. Perhaps it is sufficient to note that he appears to have been gracious to all regardless of status or religion and therefore loved by most.

The chief concern in 1585, however, was that Navarre, heir to the throne, was again a Huguenot. As they had after the death of Henry II, the Guises responded vigorously to this succession crisis. First, they concluded a secret alliance with the Spanish crown; second, they recognized as heir Navarre's aging but Catholic uncle; and third, they mobilized an army. By March they had begun capturing cities. In control of much of northern and central France, often by popular acclaim, the League released a manifesto denouncing Protestantism and urging Catholics to prepare for full-scale war.

This was actually as threatening to King Henry III as to the Huguenots. By July 1585 he had been forced to concede control of significant territory to the League, to ban Calvinist worship and exile their preachers, and to repudiate Navarre as his successor. But still Guise troops continued to seize royal cities, and two separate abduction plots forced the king to take refuge in the Louvre. By early 1586 France was his by the thinnest of margins.

11. The Huguenots quickly rearmed after the November 1576 edict of Henry III, fearing that the Catholic League might instigate another Bartholomew's Day. An inconclusive war did eventuate, resulting in curtailment of the previous concessions made to them. Two years later came the so-called Lovers' War, caused according to popular gossip by Marguerite of Valois. Angry with her brother, she reportedly persuaded Navarre to attack him. This relatively halfhearted affair was the only lapse in peace between 1577 and 1584.

In an engagement with the Huguenots in August 1587, however, he thought he saw an opportunity to reclaim his kingdom. Taking personal command of the Catholic army, he assigned his best troops to a trusted comrade who was to attack Navarre. He ordered Henry de Guise, now left with a relatively inadequate force, to attack a legion of German mercenaries. It was a clever ploy, but in this so-called War of the Three Henrys the king was the only loser. Navarre overcame the crack royal troops. Guise routed the Germans.

Desperation now chiefly informed the king's policies and decisions. Next spring, to deny the triumphant Henry de Guise a hero's welcome in Paris, he ordered him to remain in Champagne. Guise headed for the capital regardless. The king dispatched soldiers throughout the city, hoping to frighten him away by a show of strength, but the citizens of Paris, jealous of their customary autonomy, thwarted this plan, too.

Pouring into the streets, the Parisians built blockades around the royal soldiers. A tense standoff ensued until Guise, defying a royal order to depart forthwith, strolled among the throng instead, chatted with supporters, and escorted the beleaguered royal troops to safety. When a mob formed and marched on the Louvre, it was Henry III who had to quietly slip away. Curiously enough, during this Day of the Barricades the only casualty was the credibility of the French monarchy.

With Henry de Guise now de facto ruler of the capital, enacting legislation and appointing a new governor and mayor, the harried king seemed to lose heart entirely. "I wish to be king," he lamented, "not a prisoner and slave as I have been." Increasingly desperate, he played his last ill-fated card. On December 23, 1588, he summoned Guise to his bedchamber, where the royal bodyguard was waiting. The king's men, crying, "Traitor! You will die for it!" rushed forward

With the Guise-inspired Catholic League in control of much of France and the popular Duke Henry de Guise acting as de facto monarch, in December 1588 King Henry III took a desperate and disastrous measure. He summoned Guise to his bedchamber, where the duke was stabbed to death by the royal guard and his body burned. Other Guises were arrested, and Louis de Guise, Henry's brother, was hacked to death on Christmas Eve. But the king had gone too far. Public indignation forced him to flee his capital.

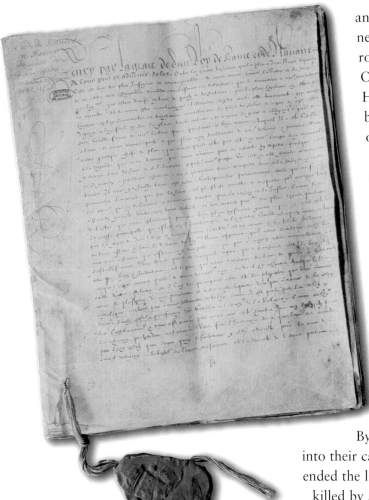

In 1598, four years after his coronation, Henry of Navarre was able to proclaim the Edict of Nantes (facsimile of first page shown above), giving significant rights and general toleration to the Calvinist Church. Putting this fully into practice, however, would be even more difficult.

12. The accession of Henry IV formally ended the reign of the Valois kings, who had been on the throne since 1328. The Bourbons would reign until King Louis XVI was deposed in 1792 by the French Revolution and executed the following year. His son Louis XVII never ruled and died in prison. The Bourbon Louis XVIII resumed the throne in 1814. The last Bourbon king, Louis Philippe, was forced to abdicate in the Revolution of 1848.

and thrust daggers into de Guise's breast, back, kidney, and finally throat. He collapsed at the foot of the royal bed, and his body was taken away and burned. Other members of the Guise family were arrested. Henry's brother, Louis de Guise, a cardinal and archbishop as his uncle had been, was hacked to death on Christmas Eve.

But this time the king had gone too far. He had alienated himself from Paris by murdering its popular duke, and from Rome by murdering the cardinal. Two weeks later, on behalf of all Frenchmen, the University of Paris repudiated the oath of loyalty to King Henry III. The pope demanded he appear at the Vatican to explain himself. Soon most major Catholic cities in the kingdom had sworn obedience to the League, but the final stroke for the unhappy king probably came on January 5, 1589, when the queen mother, the venerable Catherine de' Medici, died. Bereft of his last support, he secretly departed his capital and sought out Navarre.

By April they had concluded a treaty. They were well into their campaign when an indignant young Dominican friar ended the life of Henry III—making him the first French king killed by a Frenchman. The kingdom, what was left of it, was pledged to Navarre, but his prospects were extremely poor. Much of the royal army quickly melted away, and Henry of Navarre was soon retreating toward Normandy.

In pursuit was the chief remaining Guise, Duke Charles of Mayenne, vowing to either toss this Huguenot claimant into the sea or escort him to Paris in chains.

Establishing his base at Arques, Navarre fortified the city and prepared its artillery. Mayenne attacked in September 1589. Although menaced by a force four times his own and deserted for lack of payment by his Swiss troops, Navarre emerged victorious. Fighting persisted for three more years, and even by the end of 1592 Navarre seemed nowhere near fulfilling his main objective: the capture of Paris. But everyone had grown desperately tired of this protracted and destructive conflict. In addition, the Catholic League had become increasingly dependent on foreign (namely Spanish) support and was therefore losing popularity. In May 1593 the Estates General made a crucial decision, and a message was relayed to Henry of Navarre. The crown was his—on one condition. He must become Catholic. Henry III had been right.

His assessment of his Huguenot ally was also correct. Navarre accepted the required condition. "Paris is worth a Mass," he famously remarked, and his return to the Catholic faith was announced on May 17. It took some time to iron out the details, but Navarre was crowned Henry IV of France in February 1594.[12] He spent the following month smashing the final remnants of resistance in Paris.

Henry of Navarre, invited by a war-weary country to become king of France, fulfills the necessary condition by renouncing his Huguenot faith, as shown here in a seventeenth-century Italian painting. He was crowned in February 1594 and would reign for sixteen productive if troubled years before falling victim to an assassin.

Then, having attended Mass at Notre Dame Cathedral, he watched the departure of the Spanish garrison, cheerfully calling to them, "My compliments to your master, but do not come back."

Not until April 1598 was King Henry IV able to proclaim the Edict of Nantes, which did not give the Calvinist Church equal standing with the Catholic but did accord it significant rights and general toleration. The freedoms the Edict outlined would be fully implemented only after years of hard and sometimes deadly bargaining, and maintained only by means of the strictest vigilance. Such was the tradeoff for a reign free at last from civil war.[13]

Even so, this troubled decade would underline two vital truths: that peace is more than the absence of war and that mere toleration of one's neighbor is a long way short of loving him. Otherwise, the reign of Henry of Navarre as king of France would not have featured both Catholics and Huguenots swamping the courts with lawsuits or the long-lasting chill of a kind of cold war. And it would certainly not have included nineteen attempts on Navarre's life—or his eventual assassination in 1610. ∎

13. Called "a king without favorites" and "companion and friend of everyone," Henry of Navarre arguably was one of the most popular monarchs in French history. His common touch and concern for all his subjects, evidenced, for example, in one typical promise of a chicken in every pot on Sundays, were particularly celebrated. The lyrics to the very popular *Marche Henri IV* may be indicative: "Long live Henry IV. / Long live this valiant king, / This fourfold devil / With the three talents / Of drinking, fighting, / And womanizing. / To hell with wars / And enmity, and spouses. / Let us all together, / Sing as true friends, / Clink the glasses, / The roses and the lilies."

In the great hall of the ancient Brabant line in Brussels the aging emperor Charles V confers lordship of the Netherlands, his own birthplace, on his son, Philip. The emperor regarded Prince William of Orange (standing beside him) as almost another son, destined to help Philip govern this inheritance. Both young men would try to do so—but things would go wrong, and the outcome would be a horror of death and destruction. The oil painting is by Louis Gallait (1810–1887).

CHAPTER 13

Out of sectarian strife, carnage, and insurrection, a Dutch nation is born

Failing to heed his father's advice, Spain's Philip imposes a harsh Catholicism, triggering a revolt and making Calvinism the republic's state religion

I t was a time and a place and a scene that the Holy Roman Emperor Charles V wanted long and fondly remembered. The day was October 25, 1555. The place was the great hall of the ancient dukes of Brabant in Brussels. The occasion was the formal abdication of the weary and worn Charles, patriarch of the Habsburgs, Europe's most powerful ruler since Charlemagne, come home to say goodbye, for he had been born and raised in the Netherlands. Others saw the occasion as foreshadowing the death of the old and birth of the new. Charles, they said, was the last exemplar of Christian chivalry.

Sobbing softly from nostalgia, gasping from gout, the exhausted old warrior was supported by his dark and brooding son, the future Philip II of Spain, and his household favorite, a tall young general named William of Orange. From the gowned and bejeweled lords, bishops, marshals, and ladies of the Netherlands, he begged forgiveness for his shortcomings, swore that he had always longed for peace, and prayed that his people would be as loyal to his son Philip as they had been to him. The assembled nobility wept unashamedly. But they would have wept more copiously still had they known that the two men who supported the emperor—the royal Philip and the stalwart William—would soon be locked in a merciless civil war that would deeply rend his beloved homeland.

Over the next century, the history of the Netherlands would be written in blood. The seventeen provinces would split down sectarian religious lines, seven of its seventeen dismissing with disgust the old religion, liberating the new merchant class, and creating a sovereign Protestant nation, one of whose first acts would be to execute as treasonous the Protestant leader primarily responsible for bringing it about.

Netherlandish Proverbs *by Pieter Bruegel the Elder, a 1559 oil-on-oak-panel painting, presents the acting out of scores of pithy Flemish proverbs. Some have been forgotten or never made it into English. But many are still remembered—such as "hitting one's head against a brick wall" and "some sheer sheep and some sheer pigs," meaning that some people have all the advantages (both at lower left) and "big fish eat little fish" (middle right).*

1. In 1560 Antwerp had three hundred artists (as against only seventy-eight butchers), who organized the first art market in northern Europe. Its printers produced over two hundred new titles yearly, and the city employed five musicians, who promoted the popular custom of singing in the street.

But by then thousands would have been slain on its battlefields, city walls, and streets. Europe's greatest port, Antwerp, would have been reduced to ruins, much of its population fled or dead. Yet out of this chaos the Dutch Republic was destined to emerge as one of Europe's most powerful, affluent, and culturally civilized peoples.

Philip as crown prince had already made a state tour of his father's northern dominions, his first departure from Spain. He found the Netherlanders both appalling and intriguing—the vast beer consumption, unbridled gluttony, and rollicking slovenly banquets of the males, much at odds with their large, cold, gossipy, and spotlessly fastidious wives, the fascination of the men with all things mechanical, and the size and number of their families that gave them much the same population as England but in only two-thirds the area. They were mainly town dwellers and surprisingly literate. It seemed nearly everyone, even women, could read. Antwerp alone had 150 schools.[1]

Philip also found not one Netherlands but two. The ten southern provinces, centered on Flanders and Brabant, formed northern Europe's first manufacturing society, with mills, foundries, and warehouses. Antwerp's harbor could accommodate five hundred ships. Fifteen hundred carts came and went daily. The seven northern provinces—dominated by Holland, Zeeland, Friesland, and Utrecht—were isolated by rivers, dikes, and lakes, a terrain sometimes impassable even to horses. But the northerners, too, were wealthy, and even farmers lived in well-diked towns. Yet to southerners, Paris seemed closer than Amsterdam.[2]

Producing only three-quarters of its food, the Netherlands flourished on trade at a volume twice England's. But despite their wealth, economic slumps hit the urban poor very hard, particularly in Flanders and Brabant. Bread prices might triple in a week, and one in five wage laborers fell on public relief. Yet wealth generated by trade drew bankers, musicians, artists, and printers to Amsterdam. "No other town in the world offers me more facilities," boasted immigrant French printer Christopher Platin—particularly financial services. Its new exchange pioneered innovations like bill-brokering, and its brokers would make book on anything, whether the next pope or the next war.

The Netherlanders were also politically explosive, having set off some thirty-five revolts in the last two centuries. Each province had its assembly, or Estate, of burghers and gentry, jealously watchdogging local privileges against intrusions by the imperial governors, the *stadtholders*. They were most jealous of each other until they were united by Brabant-born Charles. Mainly by carefully calculated marriages, the Habsburgs of Burgundy had acquired Flanders and Brabant in 1484, then Holland and Zeeland forty years later.

When named emperor in 1530 and realizing the surly self-reliance of the Netherlanders, Charles wrangled their independence from the Imperial Reichstag (parliament) and united them instead under Brussels. His government there comprised his regent (first his aunt, then his sister) and the noble Council of State and the Estates General, with representatives from each provincial Estate. This centralization had the unintended effect of magnifying Holland's domination over the north. Yet while Charles reigned, he was always known not as their emperor but as the duke of Burgundy. He shared their *patria*, their fatherland, and they were very fond of him. His hope had been that the tour taken by his dour Spanish-raised son would similarly endear him to these people. It didn't.

Meanwhile, the once-vigorous Catholic Church of the Netherlands had largely ignored this prosperous people. Though they numbered more than three million, they had only four bishops, mostly absentees. The great monasteries, always spiritual bellwethers, were no longer attracting talent and intelligence, and the number of novices was plunging. At least one in five clerics kept a mistress; the feasts and festivities of the church were desolate. Netherlanders instead attended their "chambers of rhetoric," town debating clubs, and their new unofficial patron saint was the celebrity philosopher Desiderius Erasmus, whose liberal humanist premises they eagerly embraced (see sidebar, p. 20).

Even so, many Netherlanders hungered for devotion, and this appetite gnawed at nobles, burghers, craftsmen, and farmers alike. Yet in their innate pragmatism they at first produced few visible sectarian movements. They dissented in a manner described by historian Jonathan Israel (*The Dutch Republic,* 1995) as "Nicodemism"—after the Jewish

2. The Netherlands was linguistically diverse, with Frisian to the north, "Ooster" Dutch to the northeast, Low German in the eastern fringe, and French in the south. But events would be dominated by the educated West Dutch speakers of Flanders, Brabant, Holland, Utrecht, and Zeeland. Amsterdam's printers worked in Latin and the major vernaculars but particularly in the local Dutch market.

A Leiden wool shop, the city visible through the open window, in a painting by Isaac Claesz van Swanenburgh (1537–1614). The ten southern provinces of the Netherlands constituted northern Europe's first industrialized society and by the sixteenth century were thriving mightily. Meanwhile, the seven water-bound northern provinces, centered on Amsterdam and such cities as Leiden, were energetically reclaiming land from the sea and prospering in agriculture and allied enterprises like the wool trade.

The Netherlands at the Time of the Twelve Years' Truce, 1609

Legend:
- United Netherlands
- Spanish Netherlands
- Common Lands
- Conquered by Spain 1584–89; regained by Dutch 1590–1607
- ✕ Significant battles

North Sea

ENGLAND

English Channel

Jemmigen (1568) ✕

GRONINGEN
• Groningen

FRIESLAND

DRENTHE
Steenwijk •

HOLLAND

Alkmaar (1573) ✕
Egmond •
Edam •

Zuider Zee

OVERYSSEL

Haarlem (1572–73) ✕
Amsterdam •
Naarden •

Zutphen (1586) ✕

• Münster

Leiden (1574) ✕
The Hague •
Delft •
Gouda •
Schiedam •
Rotterdam •
Brill •

UTRECHT
Utrecht •

GELDERLAND

Culemborg •

Mooker Heath •
• Cleves

Geertruidenberg •

ZEELAND
Middelburg •

Breda •

BRABANT

UPPER GELDERLAND

Flushing (Vlissingen) (1573) ✕

Rhine

Ostende •
Brugge •

Antwerp (1585) ✕

• Dover

Ghent (1584) ✕

• Mechelen

BISHOPRIC OF LIÈGE

• Cologne

Dunkirk •
Gravelines •

Aalst •

Louvain •

• Maastricht

LIMBURG

Calais •

FLANDERS

Scheldt

Brussels •

• Bonn

Ypres •

Lille •
Lannoy •

Gembloux (1578) ✕

Liège •

Tournai •

Namur •
NAMUR

ARTOIS

Mons (1572) ✕

Valenciennes •

Arras •

HAINAULT

Cambrai •

CAMBRÉSIS

LUXEMBOURG

• Saint-Quentin

FRANCE

Luxembourg •

Meuse

Moselle

Seine

Marne

• Verdun
• Metz

Paris •

Pharisee who visited Jesus only by night. Anabaptism early on made its appearance. In fact, during the bloody Anabaptist insurrection at Münster, sword-wielding supporters ran naked through Amsterdam, menacing the godless, and in the 1540s armed Anabaptists seized and fortified a half dozen "New Jerusalems." But all were crushed by the local stadtholders, until the Anabaptist movement was saved in the mid-century by Menno Simons (see ch. 4).[3]

Whatever their affection for him, Charles's insistence on religious conformity strained his subjects' loyalty. In 1521 he banned Luther's books, and in 1523 introduced an Inquisition. That July the Reformation's first martyrs, two Augustinian monks, were burned as heretics at Brussels, and Luther's praise for these "pearls of Christ" echoed across the empire. The executions that followed—perhaps two thousand over the next thirty years—aroused increasing popular protest, as did the public confiscation of heretics' estates, which stirred great sympathy for their families. Yet by the time of Charles's abdication, most Protestant agitators in the Netherlands were dead or had been driven into exile.

What was not suppressed, however, was a rising consciousness of national identity, something almost unknown to the Middle Ages but now fostered by trade, printing, and literacy. In the northern Netherlands this came to center on William the Silent, the young general who was Charles's favorite. William was born not a Netherlander but a German, first son of the count of Nassau-Dillenburg, whose young second wife, a devout Lutheran, had produced for her husband seventeen children. The historian C. V. Wedgwood in her award-winning biography, *William the Silent* (1944), describes their "noisy, happy" childhood in the ancient rush-strewn castle above the prosperous village of Dillenburg, where the mother taught the girls spinning, sewing, and mending while the boys learned to wrestle and ride.

At age eleven, in 1544, William suddenly became very wealthy. With the untimely death of a cousin, he inherited the title prince of Orange—an inheritance that included much of Brabant, Flanders, and Luxembourg; twenty-seven grand titles in Italy, France, and Germany; fifty baronies; and three hundred smaller estates. The homespun boy was yanked from cozy, cheerful Dillenburg and dropped into the gilt and marble imperial palace at Brussels, under Emperor Charles's guardianship, with handpicked playmates and three Flemish noblemen teaching him the silken life of a courtier, diplomat, soldier—and Catholic.[4] William, though rustic, was robust, outgoing, intelligent, affectionate, and a good listener. He soon became the weary, paternal emperor's constant companion and aide, at eighteen commanding a troop of horse, at nineteen a regiment of foot, and at twenty the army of the Netherlands.

William of Orange, hero of the Dutch republic, began life as a Lutheran, eldest in the seventeen-child family of the count of Nassau in Germany. But in 1544 eleven-year-old William inherited the vast holdings of his childless cousin René, prince of Orange in France and holder of vast territories in the Netherlands—on condition that he be raised Catholic. Emperor Charles V then became his guardian and supervised his education.

3. From 1522 to 1565 there were 161 executions for heresy in Antwerp, of which 139 were Anabaptists. Of fifty-six executed at Ghent, fifty were Anabaptists. In Friesland, almost persecution-free, Anabaptism eventually drew twenty percent of the people, but in the south whole families (like Jan de Zwarte's) died, and Anabaptism was never significant in numbers.

4. The Nassaus had ancient lineage, with an emperor among their forebears, but the Dillenburg branch was younger and poorer. William's uncle Henry, his father's brother, had married into the Châlons family, princes of tiny Orange in the middle of France. Then in 1544, his heir René, aged twenty-six, went to war. That prince had only illegitimate children, so Emperor Charles insisted he bequeath his great titles and wealth to his young cousin William to prevent his Lutheran uncle from inheriting. "Should disaster befall René, the religion of a child heir could easily be altered," writes historian Wedgwood; and disaster did befall René at Saint-Dizier, in the shape of a French bullet.

*Anna
of Egmond*

With a lavish palace at Breda and the *palais de Nassau* in Brussels, William managed Brussels' diplomatic entertainment, and he married the emperor's selection, the delicate Anna of Egmond, heiress of the wealthy count of Buren. They seemed to love one another, writes biographer Wedgwood, though she once confided that she hardly knew him. She died of a fever a month before his twenty-fifth birthday, leaving him "the unhappiest man in the world." By then, Charles's abdication was three years past, and William had become the stadtholder of Holland, Zeeland, Utrecht, and Burgundy. But his liege lord now was the pious Philip of Spain. Philip ignored his father's advice to trust William, who began earning his nickname *schluew*, or "sly," in Dutch, *taciturnus*, or "silent," in Latin. However, William could only watch as Philip provoked his Netherlanders, increasingly resentful of Spanish taxes, troops, overseers, and inquisitors.

Brussels' Spanish administrators grew tougher. They added 14 bishops to the existing four—each served by two inquisitors. This united nobles, burghers, and clerics against the crown.

Charles's taxes had been onerous enough. In fact, three generations of Habsburg rulers would increase the tax burden on the Netherlands twelvefold, and Charles had been forced to repeatedly call the Estates General to wheedle funds for the defense of Spanish Italy. But now under Philip, Spain's debt was

*Anna of
Saxony*

seven times its revenues, and when he presented a new nine-year tax schedule, the Estates General demanded the right to supervise the expenditure. Philip resentfully agreed. Finally, in 1557, when Spanish and Netherlands troops together decisively defeated a French invasion force at Saint-Quentin, thereby ending for the moment the French menace, the Estates General demanded the immediate withdrawal of Spanish troops from their provinces. Philip balked, the Estates withheld the funding, the troops went unpaid and mutinied, Philip was forced to yield, and in 1561 the Spanish occupation force was dispatched south to Italy.

Charles had warned Philip to employ only Netherlanders—and surely no Spaniards—in their government. Ignoring this, Philip made his half sister Margaret of Parma his regent, surrounding her with Spanish advisers under the haughty Cardinal Antoine de Granvelle, who froze out Charles's old counselors, among them William of Orange. Contrary to his sovereign's wishes, William in 1564 married the wealthy Lutheran heiress Anna of Saxony,[5] while he and others formally withdrew from Margaret's Council of State, instantly making themselves the champions of Dutch rights and Philip's foes.

But Dutch rights were only one element of the resistance. At least as significant was the religious element. Charles in his time had launched his crackdown on Protestantism, but it did not really work. He had declared heresy a form of

5. William's father died in 1559, leaving the Nassau-Dillenburgs deeply in debt. A family conclave decided that William had to marry a rich heiress. Anna of Saxony's dowry was huge, and her grandfather the family's major creditor, the bigamous landgrave Philip of Hesse. Anna, "a lumpish blonde of fifteen with a slight curvature of the spine . . . would do," writes Wedgwood. But she was the daughter of Maurice of Saxony, who betrayed Emperor Charles to the Lutherans in 1551. Philip hated the marriage and the entanglement with German Lutherans.

treason, leaving the local magistrates to enforce it. To the burghers, this was a usurpation of local justice; the Antwerp Exchange had always welcomed foreign Protestants. People were appalled by the tortures and incinerations. That's why relatively few were charged and only the violent executed. The inquisitors were evicted from Brabant, and Brugge arrested two of them. Holland after 1553 refused to execute any heretics at all.

So Brussels's Spanish administrators grew tougher. They added fourteen bishops to the existing four—each served by two inquisitors. This united nobles, burghers, and clerics against the crown. Granvelle was openly lampooned at banquets; Brabant withheld

Hoping to strengthen the Catholic Church in the Netherlands, King Philip named his half sister Margaret of Parma as regent (above, in a contemporary painting). This might have been successful had he not surrounded her with Spanish advisers and in 1559 appointed the rigid Cardinal Antoine de Granvelle as her prime minister (right, in a portrait by Scipione Pulzone, 1550–1598). Granvelle imported fourteen new bishops, with two inquisitors each, and William of Orange left the regent's council in despair.

its taxes. So in early 1564 Philip recalled Granvelle. The rebellious stadtholders, though now thoroughly detested by the king, rejoined Margaret's Council of State and sent an emissary to Philip urging him to rescind or relax the heresy laws. Instead he ordered them far more vigorously enforced.

Philip was gambling that such resolve on his part would stir the Netherlands' apathetic Catholic majority to rise and defend their faith. They didn't. Instead they were turning in astonishing numbers not to Lutheranism but to another, more structured version of Protestantism that appealed to the structured Netherlands mentality, particularly in the north. It was the teaching of Geneva's John Calvin. There were five Calvinist communities in the Netherlands in 1560, three hundred in 1565, all gripped by Calvin's *Institutes* and a vision of a Commonwealth of the Elect that had wide appeal—to Bible-reading merchants and dockworkers alike. Calvinism also drew the beau monde, "sweeping the lesser nobility like a fashionable new doublet," writes historian Wedgwood. "It was smart, it was advanced, it was popular with the people—and young nobles like to be popular."

They also like to make trouble. Thus in April 1566 Louis of Nassau, William's young brother, and Count Henry van Brederode rode into Brussels with hundreds of armed retainers and spent three days of "unsuitable hilarity and free-flowing drink," drawing up a petition to Regent Margaret, demanding repeal of the heresy laws. Two hundred raucous young nobles then invaded the regent's palace to present their petition, with the Brussels mob thundering outside. Margaret, already panicking from the reports of her spies, burst into tears. A loyal councillor calmed her, mocking the petitioners as "beggars." The revelers caught the slur and instantly made it their own. Within hours, "Long live the Beggars" was echoing down Brussels streets, with the rebellious drinking their wine from wooden beggars' bowls.

Within weeks, knickknack makers were doing brisk trade in beggars' bowls of all sorts, including small replicas as earrings and clasps for dandies' capes. Folk

Louis of Nassau

Henry van Brederode

When Louis of Nassau and Henry van Brederode (at right) led two hundred riotous and well-armed young Calvinist nobles to the court of Regent Margaret in Brussels, demanding repeal of the heresy laws, one of the royal councillors dismissed them as "beggars." They responded by adopting the slogan "Long live the Beggars!" and popularized a begging bowl as their symbol (below). The Beggars next invaded the busy seaport of Antwerp, whose famous stock exchange is shown above, and defiant Calvinists were soon preaching openly throughout the northern Netherlands.

songs boasted new "beggars" lyrics. Then Brederode, a born propagandist, rode out of Brussels with his crowd, wearing friars' robes and begging bowls, firing pistols into the air, and heading for huge, cosmopolitan Antwerp, where they settled in. The port's Calvinists preachers publicly demanded the right to preach openly. When the city council refused, they went outside the walls to preach in the fields. Their flock grew to thirty thousand, most fully armed. Exiled preachers began returning from England and Germany. By summer open-air preaching spread to Amsterdam and Haarlem. At Tournai the militia would not intervene since "our families and friends will be there." In July twenty thousand met outside Ghent.

Margaret's spies had warned her that three of her councillors—Admiral Philip de Montmorency, count of Horne and stadtholder of Guelders, along with General Lamoraal, count of Egmond and victor at Saint-Quentin, and William of Orange had all publicly toasted the Beggars. William was particularly suspect because his Lutheran wife repeatedly insulted the matronly regent.[6] Margaret's government depended entirely on the Netherlands' four thousand aristocrats and gentry to oversee the militias, courts, and taxes. Panicking lest they become ungovernable, she wrote Philip that he must either relax his religious policy or use force.

Philip always suspected Netherlanders of heresy, and "ungovernable" was no more acceptable to him than his father. Like Charles V, Philip embraced his divine duty to Holy Mother Church. But the son was not the father. Charles had been all Burgundy, chivalrous and urbane, and preferring a rule of affection and persuasion. The son was all Castile, militant, humorless, speaking only Spanish, and resentful of informality and contradiction. Yet a Venetian observer described Philip as "a gentleman . . . slight of stature, round-faced, with pale blue eyes, prominent lip and pink skin, but his overall appearance very attractive . . . in everything, courteous and gracious." Even his most bitter Dutch and English enemies never accused him of self-interest or greed, and he was likely no crueler than the age in general.[7]

Like him or not, the Netherlands belonged to the Spanish crown, and in accordance with ancient usage, that included its faith. "Never have I thought of introducing the Inquisition of Spain, prosecuting private beliefs," he repeatedly insisted. But preaching heresy publicly was a breach of the king's peace, and as their king he was within his right—a right acknowledged by Protestants—to insist on obedience in worship. However, it was a bad time to insist on anything. The worst winter in a century had been followed by failing crops, and a Baltic war and an English embargo had left the wharves deserted, bread prices soaring, and the unemployed dangerously idle.

Thus on August 19, 1566, hatmaker-preacher Sebastian Matte sent out his rural congregation near Brussels to smash the idols, and what became known as the *beeldenstorm* erupted. This "image-cleansing fury" spread to Antwerp the next day, with small, methodical mobs smashing all the statues and stained glass in forty-two churches. Eucharist hosts were trampled and monastery libraries burned. Two days later the fury spread to

Philip II by the Venetian artist Titian. For this determined defender of the Catholic faith, public proclamation of heresy was simply too much.

Ghent, Breda, and Middelburg, then three dozen other cities. There were "no assaults on government officials, town halls, or tax-farmers, no plundering of shops and food stores," writes historian Israel. "The beeldenstorm was purely and simply an attack on the church." Four hundred churches were sacked in western Flanders alone, by surprisingly small groups. Often "there were not above ten or twelve who spoiled," wrote an English eyewitness, "but there were many lookers-on." In the north the havoc was spontaneous and amateur, but in the south a hard core of a hundred former exiles, paid laborers' wages, passed from town to town.

6. William's second wife, Anna, proved an unbearably spoiled scold and a huge political liability, publicly insulting Regent Margaret, berating her own husband for his amatory inadequacies, and carousing drunkenly with a bad set. Margaret tried to break up Egmond and Orange's friendship by preferring the countess of Egmond to Anna. Ironically, however, Anna would bear William's heroic son, Maurice of Orange-Nassau, who would take leadership of the revolt in the 1590s.

7. In 1900 Spanish historians and others began repudiating the Black Legend propounded by English, Dutch, and other historians who indicted Spain for its oppression of the Dutch, its assault against England, its American conquests, and other barbarities. By typical feudal marriages and conquests, the Spanish Habsburgs became Europe's dominant dynasty just when Catholicism was shattered by national uprisings. Spain emerged as the universal enemy and first victim of popular propaganda. Spain's defenders argued that Spaniards were no more vicious than anyone else, but Spain lost the military, cultural, and economic conflicts of the seventeenth and eighteenth centuries, and it was the victorious, they note, who wrote the histories.

In the summer of 1566 the preaching of Sebastian Matte launched the orgy of ecclesiastical destruction the Dutch called the beeldenstorm, *when Matte's hearers smashed statues and stained glass in forty-two Antwerp churches. Outbursts spread quickly throughout the country, as depicted here in an etching by Frans Hogenberg (1540–1592).*

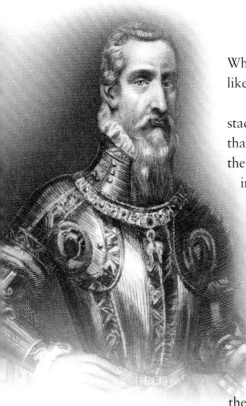

Where the city guard stood firm (as in Brugge), churches were spared. Most often, like the people, the guard only watched the vandalism.[8]

Professing themselves powerless to stop it, William, Egmond, and other stadtholders quickly granted blanket toleration for Calvinist services, an "accord" that Margaret first impotently disavowed, then resignedly endorsed. When word of the desecrations reached Spain, however, Philip became physically ill. He had failed in his duty to defend the church. By September he resolved to send an army with the duke of Alva, Europe's toughest general leading its finest troops. Alva's march to the Low Countries would take a year, but with news of his coming, Calvinists began arming and recruiting abroad. Despite her deep suspicions, Margaret begged William the Silent to keep the peace in all-important Antwerp, and he tried, promoting the accord there and throughout the north.

Then suddenly the southern Catholic gentry came alive, eagerly answering Margaret's call for subsidies and troop levies. Some towns had closed their gates, defying the regent, so she had one of them, Valenciennes, besieged. In December royalists ambushed a Calvinist relief force of three thousand at Lannoy, killing six hundred. Southern towns began expelling their preachers, opening their gates to royalist forces, and prohibiting open preaching. The south, in short, had rejected revolution.

Rashly, however, young Brederode insisted on raising his flag in unruly Antwerp, while John Marnix, baron of Toulouse, gathered four thousand militiamen in a camp outside its walls. On March 13 Egmond, with eight hundred picked royalist troops, attacked the camp, killing Marnix and half of his rebels. When the battle was heard in the city, two thousand Calvinists stormed out with only knives and pistols, intent on rescue. Galloping up, William threw himself before them, begging them to return. "You run to your deaths!" he implored. "Their cavalry will murder you!" At first the frenzied crowd almost murdered him, but slowly he herded them inside the gate and spent a long night pacifying the mob.[9]

Forestalling the slaughter of Antwerp's Calvinists was William's last act as Philip's vassal. He had quietly shifted his wealth to Germany for reasons his Antwerp bankers understood. In April, on the pretext of visiting relatives, the

The fearsome duke of Alva (above), appointed by King Philip to subdue the rebellious Dutch, as portrayed in a nineteenth-century English lithograph. Subdue them he did, disbanding the army of the regent Margaret of Parma while billeting his ten thousand often abusive Spanish troops even in loyalist cities. The painting below, by Louis Eugene Gabriel Isabey (1803–1886), is of the detested Alva arriving with his army in Rotterdam.

prince rode across the border with his family and entourage. The Calvinist spasm had been suppressed by loyal, if tolerant, Catholic Netherlanders like Egmond. Under their own king, there might now have been reconciliation. But Alva and ten thousand Spaniards were en route, intent on punishing sacrilege and treason. "Alas, Egmond," William warned, "you and your kind build the bridge for the Spaniard to cross into our country." And Egmond would indeed pay for it.

Fernando Álvarez de Toledo, third duke of Alva, the wiry, steely-gazed warrior, left for his army at Milan in April 1567—the very day Philip received a letter from Margaret declaring the rebellion crushed. No need for an army, she assured him. An army could do only harm. Yet Calvinists were still reported mustering in France and Germany, so Alva's army crossed the Alps and marched into Brussels in August. Twenty years earlier, he had led Charles V's victory over the Lutherans at Mühlberg, only to see it later squandered by a Lutheran betrayal. This time, aged sixty and wracked by gout, he intended a military occupation. "There is a new world to be created here," he wrote his king.

Alva billeted his Spaniards even in loyal cities like Brussels, and despising all as treacherous heretics, they cursed the gentry and thrashed the local merchants. He next disbanded Margaret's loyal regiments. Then he had her invite Horne, Egmond, and Orange to a council banquet where Horne and Egmond were arrested—William remaining prudently in Germany. The loyal Egmond handed over his sword, dazed and speechless, unaware that Alva had already organized his Council of Troubles to punish the beeldenstorm treason. Within days, the humiliated Margaret of Parma resigned the regency, leaving the government totally in the duke's hands.

The first eighty-four hangings took place on January 4, 1568. Two months later, in one sweep, fifteen hundred prominent citizens were arrested. The next month, sixty more died in Brussels. Orange's eldest son, Philip William, a student at Louvain and Philip's godson, was shipped to Spain, a hostage for life. At midsummer Horne and Egmond were both beheaded, still loyally bewildered. There were no trials and no appeals. There were only tortures and interrogations by Alva and two Spanish lawyers. The secrecy, omniscience, and ruthlessness of this Council of Blood (as people renamed it) terrified the innocent, one blameless tax collector preferring suicide to arrest. "Now the very papists perceive that the duke of Alva makes them all slaves," an Englishman wrote from Antwerp.

The surprise arrest of the counts of Egmond and Horne by the duke of Alva at a royal council banquet in September 1567. Devoutly Catholic but opposed to Inquisition tactics, they backed William of Orange in subduing the Calvinist uprising of the Dutch beeldenstorm on behalf of regent Margaret of Parma, and had come willingly to the council at her invitation. The nineteenth-century oil on canvas above is by Julius Hamel.

8. Just before the iconoclastic fury hit Ghent, 1,767 well-to-do citizens were polled whether they would physically defend their churches from attack, records historian Parker. Only 332 said they would, and when the vandals came, none did. For the moment, clerics and churches were denied the protection of law. But a lone Spanish soldier, armed only with a pike, saved one church in Brussels.

9. Historian Wedgwood argues that William kept his distance from the "confederate" rebellion and allowed them to meet at his palaces only because of his easygoing congeniality toward brother Louis of Nassau's friends. Historian Geoffrey Parker (*The Dutch Revolt*, 1977) reveals, however, that William provided Brederode with three cannon for the defense of his castle, suggesting Orange was only preserving a facade of neutrality.

Dutch historians would date their Eighty Years' War from the execution of Horne and Egmond. The other victims included Horne's brother Baron Montmorency, representing the Netherlands at Segovia, who was secretly strangled in a Spanish prison in October 1570. Montmorency may have been plotting with Philip's insane son, Don Carlos, to come to the Low Countries and proclaim himself his father's successor.

11. At this time, with French help, William sought Ottoman support and received Süleyman the Magnificent's offer of troops. Süleyman claimed to feel religiously close to Protestants "since they do not worship idols, believe in one God, and fight the pope and emperor." Sea Beggars began flying banners with a red crescent and the slogan "Better Turkish than Papist." The best Ottoman forces, however, were engaging Philip in the Mediterranean.

Over the next eight years, twelve thousand Netherlanders would be secretly tried, almost nine thousand found guilty and impoverished, and a thousand executed—though Dutch accounts would number the executions at twelve or eighteen thousand. "Such totals were far from excessive in that day for a major revolt," argues Catholic historian Warren H. Carroll (*The Cleaving of Christendom*, 2000), yet Carroll concedes that Alva did "lack charity." This was not restoration of order; it was a foreign occupation. Some sixty thousand fled to England or Germany. Exiles found guilty in absentia—like William—lost their patrimonies, leaving them no recourse for recovery but revolution.[10]

Meanwhile, in Germany William pondered. He had tried to confine the issue to the diplomatic level, but he nevertheless needed allies. Emperor Maximilian and the German princes ignored him. His only supporters were the French Huguenots, and they would seem mere rowdies creating yet another Calvinist riot, anathema to the Catholic majority. So at Dillenburg William penned and printed his manifesto, "The Justification," protesting loyalty to the king but defiance of his evil minister Alva—casting the conflict in the mold of feudal loyalties, the defense of ancient charters. Even as the Justification flooded the

A contemporary engraving at right depicts a mass execution in 1568. When the duke of Alva "cleansed" the southern provinces of Calvinism, there were no real trials or appeals—only what Netherlanders called the duke's "Council of Blood"—and the first eighty-four hangings took place within months of his arrival. In the following eight years, some twelve thousand accused Protestants would be arrested, nine thousand found guilty, and at least a thousand executed. An estimated sixty thousand fled to Germany and England and were convicted in absentia, thus losing their property.

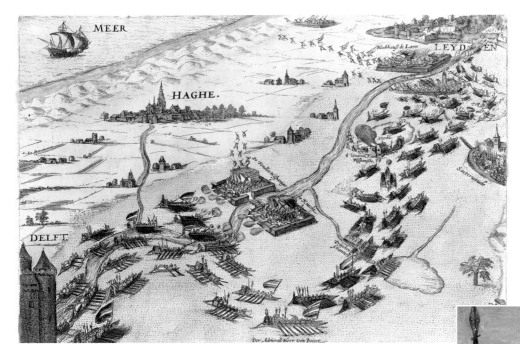

MEER · HAGHE. · DELFT · LEYDEN ·

At left, a contemporary engraving by Frans Hogenberg diagrams a naval engagement off the coast of The Hague between the Sea Beggars, the fleet of freebooters hired by Louis of Nassau, brother of William of Orange, and the Spanish fleet. The Beggars brought supplies to Louis' rebel army and, by seizing merchant ships, provided William with war funds as well. Twenty-five of their ships under the exuberant William de La Marck (below) seized the small Zeeland port of Brill in April 1572.

Netherlands, William was investing all of his personal wealth, and as much again in debt, assembling his army.[11]

William's return to the Netherlands in 1568 with what he intended as an army of liberation became instead a disorganized fiasco. While he trained the main body, three subsidiary forces opened the campaign. Spanish troops slaughtered the first three-thousand-man contingent in Limburg after the towns refused to open their gates. Another three thousand, these French Huguenots, invaded the south, met closed gates, and in retreating were butchered by French royalist forces. Louis of Nassau, invading Groningen from the north, routed the first Spanish army sent against him, but again the town gates remained closed. Alva penned Louis against the Ems River at Jemmigen, and a bloodbath followed: Spanish losses: eighty dead; rebel losses: seven thousand dead, most drowned. Louis escaped only by swimming naked to the German shore.

By October William's main army of twenty-five thousand mercenaries attacked Brussels. Alva simply parried him blow for blow until William's money ran out, his army dissolved, and he retreated into France, hungry, humiliated, and surrounded by mutinous mercenaries. Too weak to even ride, he had lost everything: men, money, credit, and reputation.[12] "We regard the prince of Orange as a dead man," Alva declared and ordered erected a huge bronze statue of himself as the hero who "reduced rebellion, restored religion, secured justice, and established peace."

But Alva had his own problems. The ships carrying the gold to pay his army were driven into Plymouth by Huguenot pirates and seized by the English. To raise more funds, he levied a ten percent sales tax on all Netherlands transactions. Known as the "tenth penny," it became a rallying cry for rebellion. The Estates General refused to ratify it, and he levied it anyway. The Antwerp Exchange closed in protest. Bakers, butchers, and brewers shut their shops. Mills and foundries in Flanders and Brabant went silent. People bartered for food; the unemployed crowded hungry and angry in the streets. The sales tax failed because nothing was being sold.

12. At this time, William's personal life was also in total disarray. His dissolute Saxon wife Anna escaped boring Dillenburg for the wild parties of Cologne, where she became pregnant by exiled Flemish lawyer John Rubens. When William's brother John arrested them both, her lover pleaded that many others could be her child's father. Anna begged that they both be executed, but William simply divorced her and returned Rubens to his wife—with whom, six years later, he would father the artist Peter Paul.

13. The province of Holland reneged on the 1572 declaration of toleration, outlawing Catholic worship in February 1573. As Calvinist magistrates expropriated church property, Calvinism became the established church, says historian Geoffrey Parker. Though certainly the most militant faction in the revolt, Calvinists were in fact a tiny elite, even in the north. Of Dordrecht's thirteen thousand people, three hundred and sixty-eight were Calvinist; of Delft's fourteen thousand, two hundred; of Alkmaar's five thousand, seventy-six. Even by 1587 Calvinist preachers assumed their communicants comprised no more than ten percent of the northern Dutch.

14. Alva retired to Spain in 1573 in some disgrace when it was discovered he had thwarted Philip's marital plans for Alva's son. This did not prevent Philip from calling the old general out of retirement to salvage his war over the succession to the Portuguese crown. Alva won a decisive victory for Philip, enabling him to become king of Portugal as well as Spain, then retired again. Alva died two years later on December 11, 1582, at the age of seventy-five.

Meanwhile Louis had hired local pirates to supply him. Proclaiming themselves the Sea Beggars, they flew the Orange colors, sheltered in English ports, and seized merchantmen, feeding William's war chest with the proceeds. Eventually, England's Elizabeth nervously banned them. So in April 1572 twenty-five ships under the jovial freebooter William de La Marck sailed into the tiny Zeeland port of Brill, landed six hundred men, ran up the Orange flag, tortured thirteen priests to death, and drafted the townsfolk to repair Brill's defenses against the inevitable Spanish attack. The rest of the Beggar fleet, sheltering at the Huguenot port of La Rochelle in France, sailed north and seized Flushing. Then the Dutch garrisons of Rotterdam, Schiedam, Gouda, and Edam declared for Orange. In May Louis of Nassau and a small Huguenot force were welcomed into the southern fortress of Mons. Alva now faced enemies north and south. The revolt was on again.

By June nine northern cities and some southern towns flew the Orange flag. Holland, Zeeland, Utrecht, and Friesland declared William commander in chief and voted a one-hundred-thousand-crown subsidy. William insisted they accept the politic declaration: "Free exercise of religion should be allowed as well to Papists as Protestants." On July 8, 1572, with an army of twenty thousand, William crossed again into the Netherlands. "I have come to make this land my grave," he said. He was never to leave it again.[13]

William first marched against Alva, but soon realizing he had no hope of holding the southern provinces against him, he headed north for Holland. Alva followed, leaving behind him a trail of horror and destruction. Though Mechelen surrendered at his approach, the duke turned it over to his long-unpaid Spaniards "to refresh them a little." The sack lasted three bloody days—a memory that still made his hair stand on end, one witness recounted. Zutphen was next, where he butchered its garrison and burghers—their screams heard far beyond their walls. Then he besieged Naarden on the Zuider Zee. Legend says the town first resisted, then repented and banqueted its besiegers, only to have the latter to turn berserk

Spanish soldiers of the duke of Alva conduct executions in Haarlem around 1568. Dutch accounts claim a death toll of eighteen thousand overall, though the surviving records place the number of dead at slightly over one thousand.

NAERDEN.

after dinner. "Not a mother's son escaped," Alva reported.

In December 1572 it was Haarlem's turn. After a siege of seven months, the starving city yielded on Alva's promise of clemency. The Spaniards marched in and confined the slaughter to the twenty-three hundred men in the garrison. However, Alva paid dearly for Haarlem, for by then there were ten thousand Spanish corpses moldering under its walls. When the now-dispirited Spaniards next turned against Alkmaar, the unpaid troops twice refused to attack. Then the town cut its dikes, and the rising sea inundated their siege works, forcing their retreat. Days later on the Zuider Zee, the Beggars trounced the Spanish fleet, capturing three battleships and the Spanish admiral. So the tide was turning, and Philip saw that Alva's strategy of atrocity was failing. In November of 1573 he recalled the bewildered old warrior.[14]

Alva's replacement, Don Luis de Requesens, was horrified at the posting, and he had good reason. His unpaid troops constantly verged on mutiny, and he took over from Alva the battle that would prove crucial in the outcome of the war. Before Alva had departed, he had split Holland north from south at Haarlem, then turned south and laid siege to the rebel-held city of Leiden, with The Hague, Delft, and Rotterdam just beyond. William's initial attempt to relieve Leiden from the landward side was blocked by the Spanish army, but Leiden lay only twenty-two

When William of Orange attacked the Spanish occupation forces, his army was quickly driven from Flanders, as shown above left in a contemporary engraving by Frans Hogenberg. The rebels retreated northward, with Alva pressing them mercilessly and seizing town after town. Above right, in an engraving by Mathias Merian (1593–1650), Holland's old capital of Naarden resisted, then capitulated and was subjected to general massacre. Below, Antwerp citizens joyfully tear down the bronze statue that Alva had erected to himself as the man who "secured justice and established peace." (The nineteenth-century painting is by Charles Raoul Verlet.)

15. At this time, William's private life was both bitter and sweet. Cheerful brother Louis of Nassau was ambushed by Spanish veterans at Mooker Heath on April 14, 1574. His body and that of their brother Henry were never recovered. Then in early 1575 William married Charlotte de Bourbon, a young daughter of French royalty. She had been forced into a convent young, slated to become its abbess. Instead, she fled penniless to Lutheran Germany, where she first met William. As Anna of Saxony was still alive, though divorced, this marriage angered William's in-laws, and as Charlotte was penniless, the marriage apparently had no motive but love.

miles from the sea across reclaimed land protected by dikes. The account of William's effort to supply the besieged city by opening the dikes and sailing relief barges across the gradually rising waters is arguably the most thrilling story in the history of the Dutch Republic.

As the water gradually crept forward, the barges repeatedly ran aground as they crept forward behind it. Communicating with the soon starving defenders by carrier pigeon, William pleaded with them to hold fast, but what finally persuaded them was not William but the Spanish. So merciless had they been to the people of those cities that had capitulated, Leiden's defenders concluded, that surrender meant certain death, where continued defiance offered a slim chance of survival. With the city's walls about to collapse and let the enemy in to slaughter the town, a sudden storm drove the waters forward, forcing the Spaniards to abandon the siege and run, just as the relief vessels arrived at the walls. Thousands had starved to death, but Leiden was saved. The date was October 3, 1574, commemorated to this day with a major civic festivity marking Leiden's day of deliverance. To mark the occasion himself, William early in 1575 founded a school of higher learning there. It was destined to become one of the greatest universities in the world.

Momentarily William of Orange ruled all the Low Countries —but too late. In 1576, Spanish troops sacked Antwerp and spared 'neither age nor sex, young nor old, rich nor poor.'

In November the eighty-five-thousand-man unpaid Spanish army again mutinied, abandoning all Holland to the rebels and terrorizing the southern cities, still Catholic and even loyal to Philip but as keen as the north to be rid of the Spanish army. The following April Requesens died in despair, and the now leaderless southern provinces called on William to send troops to protect them from the marauding Spanish freebooters. William had already been made protector of the Netherlands by the northern Estates with supreme command by land and sea, the right to make all appointments, and even the right to confer allegiance upon a foreign prince.[15] He now rode south to cheering crowds showering him with flower petals. In October all seventeen provinces signed the Pacification of Ghent, acknowledging Calvinist regimes in Holland and Zeeland, Catholic rule elsewhere, a moratorium on persecution, and a military alliance against the Spaniards. Momentarily, William of Orange was de facto ruler of all the Low Countries.

But he was too late. On November 4, 1576, five thousand Spanish troops sacked the entire city of Antwerp, sparing "neither age nor sex, young nor old, rich nor poor," wrote English soldier-poet William Gascoigne. "They slew great numbers of young children . . . As great a respect they had to the churchyard as a butcher hath to his shambles." Seven thousand died in the "Spanish Rage," and flames consumed a thousand buildings, a third of Antwerp. There the Spanish stayed, holding the whole city hostage.

In response, Philip appointed his half brother, Don Juan of Austria, hero of Lepanto (see ch. 11), as regent of the Netherlands. By skillful negotiation Don Juan persuaded a majority of the Estates General to acknowledge his regency and

Don Juan of Austria

preserve Catholicism outside Holland and Zeeland, provided he remove the Spaniards. Then in early 1577, he persuaded the smirking, booty-laden mutineers in Antwerp to leave for Spain, and his prestige soared. But this time the utterly unforeseen occurred: the northern Calvinist troops, whom William had brought south, ran wild. They began staging local coups throughout the Netherlands. Over the next two years at Brugge, Ypres, Arras, Amsterdam, and a dozen other cities, they drove out the Catholic magistrates, trashed the churches, murdered the clergy, and thoroughly soured Catholics on their Calvinist allies. Don Juan had no choice. He recalled his Spanish regiments.

Philip, solvent again with a huge infusion of gold from Peru, sent twenty thousand Spaniards to the Netherlands under Alessandro Farnese, the prince of Parma and son of the former regent Margaret. With an army lethally effective, highly disciplined, and plainly safer than the radical Calvinists, Parma methodically trounced the Netherlanders at Gembloux, chased Orange and the Estates General from Brussels to Antwerp, then moved through the south. At summer's end, Don Juan, dying of typhus in an army camp at Namur, handed over his command to the

The Spanish Fury in Antwerp on 4th November 1576, *by a contemporary artist (name unknown) memorializes the day when occupying troops put seven thousand citizens to the sword and burned a third of the city. At left is Alessandro Farnese, who replaced Don Juan in the Netherlands, in a portrait by Frans Pourbus the Younger, and (below) Farnese's battle helmet.*

After King Philip offered a twenty-five-thousand-crown reward for the assassination of William of Orange, the Dutch leader survived several attempts, but in 1584 he was gunned down by an ostensible ally on the steps of his palace in Delft (today's Prinsenhof). His last words: "My God, have pity on my soul—my God, have pity on this poor people." This nineteenth-century engraving is by Wilhelm von Lindenschmit.

16. Fathering a son and daughter by Anna of Buren, then a son Maurice by Anna of Saxony, William found domestic bliss in Charlotte of Bourbon, who bore him six daughters in seven years. Following the first assassination attempt in 1582, William hovered on the edge of death for over a month, and Charlotte exhausted herself nursing him, dying of pneumonia two weeks after his recovery. Following Charlotte's death, William married a fourth time—to Louisa de Coligny in April 1583.

gifted Parma, who then drafted the Treaty of Arras, wooing any city still Catholic, loyal to the crown, or desperate for peace into an alliance. William countered with a similar treaty in the north, known as the Union of Utrecht.

But William desperately needed a foreign ally, one with the credibility of royal credentials equal to Philip's. He found one, or thought he did, in France. He easily convinced the Estates General to pass the Act of Abjuration in June 1581, repudiating their loyalty to Philip, but only with great difficulty did he persuade them to confer it instead on the French king's younger brother, Francis of Anjou and Alençon, as their new prince. A vain, pockmarked gnome of a man with a painted, foppish retinue, he was soon hated in the north as Catholic and in the south as French. Even so, early in 1582 William made Anjou the duke of Brabant and lord of the seven northern provinces. It is regarded as William's greatest mistake. Meanwhile, Philip placed a bounty on William's head, a rich reward for whoever assassinated him.

Arriving with ten thousand French soldiers under his command, Anjou took exactly twelve months to demonstrate both his ineptitude and his instability. Exasperated by negotiations with the stodgy Flemish, he resolved in January 1583 to seize Antwerp. His escort murdered the Dutch sentries, and his waiting battalions stormed through the gates. But then came a shock. The burghers, hardened by years of contending with the Spanish, had their barricades up, snipers on rooftops, and cannon sweeping the street. Over two thousand Frenchmen died, mostly in the moat, trying to flee. With them died Anjou's hope for a crown and William's esteem among southerners.

Parma was now taking Dunkirk, then Ypres, and then Brugge. William, utterly discredited in Antwerp, could only retire to his old headquarters at Delft to shore up his support in the north. Anjou, meanwhile, terminated the French venture by dying of tuberculosis on June 19, 1584. Precisely three weeks later, Philip's reward plan worked: William was assassinated. Several would-be assassins had already tried to claim Philip's bounty; earlier in Antwerp, he almost died, shot through the mouth. Yet he still forbade his guards to hinder any well-wishers or petitioners. On July 10 he met with a poor courier to whom he'd earlier given twelve gold pieces. Balthasar Gerards instead used the money to buy two pistols, returned, and shot William through the stomach. The prince of Orange was dead within minutes. He was mourned as Father of the Fatherland—a fatherland still in infancy.[16]

Within months of William's assassination, Parma conquered troubled Ghent. Starving Brussels surrendered in March 1585, bitter that three dozen towns had fallen without Holland offering help. By then Parma was besieging Antwerp and blockading the Scheldt estuary with a twenty-four-hundred-foot bridge on seventy-five-foot piles. Finally, given the deadly threat to the Protestant Netherlands (and with Spanish America ripe for plunder), England's Queen Elizabeth risked supporting the Dutch revolt, ascribing to the Treaty of Nonsuch, so named for the palace in Surrey, England, where it was signed. It provided eight thousand English troops, a hefty subsidy, and a governor to build a unified administration. Antwerp had fallen three days earlier, on August 10, 1585, and the Catholic country that would one day be called Belgium made its debut in history.

But the English intervention fared no better than the French. Elizabeth's governor, the politically inept Robert Dudley, earl of Leicester, took two years to alienate the Netherlanders with a clumsy effort to centralize the government of all the Low Countries under the English crown. In 1587 he returned to England defeated and virtually bankrupt. But his queen's decision to back the Dutch rebels amounted to a declaration of war on Philip. His response was the Spanish Armada, a master plan by which the Spanish fleet was to be reinforced by Parma's army and invade England. But the armada was too damaged to land, and the plan failed (see ch. 14). Facing now the dire possibility of a Protestant France, Philip changed his priorities and ordered Parma to withdraw his army from the Netherlands and intervene in the French civil war (see ch. 12). Parma twice marched south, relieving Paris from siege by the Protestant Huguenots in 1590 and Rouen in 1591, thereby thwarting the phenomenon of a Protestant France. But a minor hand wound failed to heal, and he returned to Madrid, where rivals in the Spanish court forced his retirement, and he died at Arras in 1592.

Meanwhile, his departure made possible in the north the birth of the Dutch Republic. Calling themselves the United Provinces, they were initially governed by a "regent class" of religiously tolerant, "states-rights" burghers, who presided over a booming economy and what was at first a religiously unobservant population. This rapidly changed, however, with the arrival of about thirty-eight thousand militant Calvinists fleeing the now Catholic Antwerp. But the success of the northern provinces was primarily due to the leadership of two men.

Johan van Oldenbarnevelt was a lawyer at The Hague and a Calvinist, who served under William through much of the war with Spain. He strongly supported William's Union of Utrecht in 1579, fiercely opposed the centralizing efforts of England's Leicester, and played such a powerful role in uniting the northern provinces under Holland's leadership that he became effectively the first president of the Dutch Republic. Probably his greatest achievement, however, was to advance the promotion of Maurice of Nassau, William's son who with the death of an older half brother would inherit the title prince of Orange, to become

Johan van Oldenbarnevelt (below left) served effectively under William of Orange and after William's death played a major role in uniting the northern provinces. He also effectively advanced the promotion of Maurice of Nassau, William's son, as leader of the northern army. (The eighteenth-century engraving is by Jacobus Houbraaken.) Maurice, portrayed below right in an oil on wood attributed to Michiel van Mierevelt (1567–1641), reorganized the army and completed the assembly of the Netherlands' northern republic.

A cenotaph for Philip II in the Escorial palace in Madrid shows the king armored and at prayer, with his three queens behind him: Maria of Portugal, Mary of England, and Isabella Valois of France. Objective assessments of King Philip's life and reign are rare—in the English-speaking and Protestant world he is generally seen as a fanatic and cruel tyrant, while most Spanish-speakers and Catholics see him as God's devout and faithful servant. But his many practical accomplishments in governance are undeniable, and his devotion to his faith without question. He died a painful death in September, 1598, clutching his father's crucifix, after listening to a reading of the Passion of Christ.

supreme commander of the northern armed forces. Maurice reorganized the army and developed a technique in siege warfare that brought Breda, Steenwijk, Geertruidenberg, and even Catholic Groningen into the republic, completing its unification of the north. Only when Maurice took his army into Flanders in 1600, challenging the Spaniards on the open plain, did the republic lurch close to disaster.

By then, Philip II of Spain was gone. In his last days, sores formed all over his wasted body, so painful he had to be left lying in his own excrement. He called his son to his bedside to show him the end of all the world's pomp. Then on September 13, 1598, having heard read Christ's Passion from John and clutching his father's crucifix, he died. Soon after, under Philip III, Genoese financier Ambrogio Spinola took charge in the Spanish Netherlands, consolidating the south with an epic three-year siege of Ostend while Maurice strengthened the United Provinces' grip on the north. Stalemated—and with Dutch energy now absorbed overseas—the Twelve Years' Truce was signed in April 1609.

Ambrogio Spinola

The truce held until 1621. By then Dutch ships were trading not only into the Baltic, where they had long traded, but also into the Mediterranean and Caribbean, to Brazil, Africa, and the East Indies. With Holland's population soaring, agricultural demand required a square mile of land to be wrested yearly from the sea. Its regime was business, epitomized when the Estates General founded its East India Company in 1602.

But within the republic itself these, ironically, were years not of peace but of fierce conflict, not with Spain but within Dutch Protestantism. During the early tolerant years of the republic, the Amsterdam theologian Jacob Hermans (in Latin, Arminius) publicly challenged Calvinist orthodoxy, insisting that a sovereign God could nevertheless permit human free will, that Christ died for all men and not only for an "elect," and that the Calvinist view of predestination was unbiblical.

He also insisted that pastors be subject to the laws of the state. His principal opponent and defender of Calvinism was the Flemish exile Francis Gomarus.

In wartime magistrates suppressed the quarrel, and Arminius died peacefully in 1609. But with the truce signed that year, the controversy erupted in pamphlets and riots, everyone declaring himself either Arminian or Gomarist.[17] Oldenbarnevelt and the Arminian regents had favored peace with Spain. Maurice of Orange-Nassau, opposing the truce, had allies in the Calvinist army, among militant exiles, and in the small provinces. Attacks on Arminian churches and preachers mounted, and the army refused to protect them. So in 1617 Oldenbarnevelt passed a law allowing local towns to raise their own militias and placing the army under each provincial Estate. Civil war loomed.

Maurice, confessing he made neither head nor tail of the theology, still had the army. He first purged the inland provinces of Arminian magistrates, then forced the Estates General to declare provincial militias disbanded. Finally, he arrested his patron Oldenbarnevelt for treason against the United Provinces. In a show trial lasting months, twenty-four judges lectured the defiant old man that individual provinces could not settle their own churches or raise their own troops. In May 1619, to Oldenbarnevelt's amazement, he was sentenced to death and the next day publicly beheaded. The regents still tended the nation's accounts, but Orange-Nassau was now its ruling house.

Four days before Oldenbarnevelt was executed, a national synod rejected Arminianism and affirmed traditional Calvinist doctrines as the religion of the Dutch Republic. So now the republic knew not only who ruled it but what it believed. But this was not to endure: Arminians were tolerated within two generations. Much of their theology would be adopted by Mennonites, Hutterites, and Amish, and soon the Dutch would be recognized as the people most tolerant and committed to free speech. All the energy ensnared by schism and faction was now turned to trade, colonization, and war—with Sweden, France, Portugal, England, and archenemy Spain. The Thirty Years' War would engulf the next generation, Europe's last and bloodiest religious war. But when that ended with the Peace of Westphalia in 1648, the Dutch were a nation among nations, energetic, prosperous, and uncontested, almost as envied in their century as the Spanish had been in theirs. ■

17. In 1610 Arminians presented what they called their "Remonstrance" to Holland's Estate, asserting political authority over the church, eschewing confessional rigidity, and restating Arminian objections to predestination. Their Gomarist foes became known as Counter-Remonstrants. Celebrity humanist de Groot, heir to Desiderius Erasmus, sided with the Remonstrants for liberty of conscience. He was tried with Oldenbarnevelt and sentenced to prison, where he penned "The Truth of the Christian Religion." He later escaped in an empty book chest and eventually settled in Paris.

In a painting by Ludolf Backhuyzen (1631–1708) a Dutch East India Company fleet heads for the Far East. Netherlanders were previously only middlemen in the spice trade, but when King Philip made Portugal part of Spain, it too became the enemy of the new Dutch Republic. By 1600 Dutch ships had tracked the "secret" Portuguese routes to the Spice Islands. Many were lost and the market extremely volatile, but profits in pepper ranged up to four hundred percent.

Elizabeth

Marye

Edward

CHAPTER 14

Elizabeth I of England, who stilled the storm without a civil war

With compromise, caution, craft, and equivocation the Virgin Queen steers the Christian middle course, defeats Spain's Armada, and ushers in Anglicanism

As Henry VIII was laid to rest beside his singularly beloved wife, Jane Seymour, in Westminster Abbey in January of 1547, his three children contemplated their futures. The immediate fate of Henry's sole male heir—the boy Jane Seymour had given her life to deliver—was clear enough: he was now King Edward VI. The lot of Henry's two daughters was not nearly so obvious. The elder, Edward's half sister Mary, offered the best hope for Catholics at home and abroad. The younger seemed to have the least chance of succeeding to the throne. This was Elizabeth, the red-haired, black-eyed, ivory-skinned daughter of the disgraced and beheaded Anne Boleyn, destined to become Elizabeth of England, last and greatest of the Tudors and to some the greatest monarch in English history.

Being only nine, Edward had to reign under a regency, a Protestant-dominated council led by his uncle Edward Seymour, the late Queen Jane's forty-one-year-old brother. Upon becoming the king's chief protector, Seymour, a balding, ginger-bearded man of military accomplishment and high aspirations, persuaded the council to award him a twenty-five-thousand-pound annual stipend and the title duke of Somerset.

The Seymours and their supporters were among the nobles who had fared well through Henry's dissolution and expropriation of the Catholic monasteries. They were now prepared to fare better still. They had all but eradicated the big Catholic power in court, the Howard family, just prior to Henry's death. Thomas Howard, the seventy-four-year-old duke of Norfolk, narrowly escaping the block

Opposite page, the three successive heirs of Henry VIII at the time of his death in 1547, with their signatures. At center is King Edward, nine, who would reign for just six years; at the right Princess Mary, thirty-one, who would be queen of England from 1553 to 1558; and at left Princess Elizabeth, fourteen, England's ruler for the following nearly half century. The oil painting of Elizabeth is of the sixteenth-century Anglo-Italian school, Mary's is by Jan Ewoutsz of Flanders, and Edward's is by an unknown Flemish artist. The pen-and-ink signatures were collected by Bridgeman Art Library.

A contemporary allegorical painting shows Henry VIII enthroned. On his left are young Prince Edward receiving the sword of justice and the future queen Elizabeth attended by "Peace" and "Plenty." On his right are Mary and her husband, Philip of Spain, attended by the god of war.

1. Though it claimed ancient credentials, the doctrine known as the divine right of kings was a Renaissance innovation. Drawing on late Roman theories about the emperor, the medieval concept of the king as the fount of virtue, and biblical precursors like David and Solomon, sixteenth-century advocates of national monarchy posited the king as second only to God and therefore inherently superior to both parliaments and popes. It was not universally embraced. Some critics, both Catholic and Protestant, disdained it. Thomas More, in his *Utopia*, portrays his imaginary pagan world as more "Christian" for its lack of kingly supremacy. More understood how this new absolutist divine right differed from medieval divine right. Kings ruled by divine right in the Middle Ages but as only one of two powers, spiritual and temporal. By contrast, the new Renaissance theory made absolute the right of the monarchy alone. Meanwhile, the Scottish Calvinist John Knox (see ch. 7) argued that the authority of the ruler rested on the consent of the people.

that had claimed his son the earl of Surrey (see ch. 6), remained imprisoned in the Tower of London, his property forfeited to the crown. Stephen Gardiner, the fifty-year-old bishop of Winchester who had been another powerful proponent of the old religion in Henry's court, would soon join him there.

Archbishop of Canterbury Thomas Cranmer, his beard white but his head still in place, had weathered Henry's later Catholic period by suppressing his Protestant inclinations. Now those ambitions could be given free rein. As for the young king, according to Henry's will his assent was required on all matters despite his years. In any event, he seemed to acquiesce in everything. Tutored by Cranmer appointees, the fair, bright-eyed, though frail boy was already writing precocious tracts in which he declaimed against the the pope as the Antichrist. The all-out conversion of England to the Reformation faith therefore appeared assured.

Meanwhile, Catholic Mary, daughter of Henry's first wife, Catherine of Aragon, and declared illegitimate when Henry, over powerful papal objections, disavowed her mother, had been permitted back in court during Henry's final years. She had been placed second in the line of succession behind Edward by her father's will. Now a sickly and rather nervous woman of thirty-one, she still commanded the affectionate sympathies of ordinary people everywhere and particularly the persisting Catholic nobility in the north of England. Next after Mary in line of succession, Elizabeth too had been declared illegitimate following the posthumous annulment of Henry's marriage to her mother. Pretty and almost fourteen, Elizabeth was Protestant, though not nearly so zealously as her young half brother, whom she nonetheless watched and adored.

There was a great deal to watch. In Edward's name, Somerset and Cranmer were proceeding with their transformation of England into one of the first Protestant nation-states. Edward was accorded the realm's first Protestant coronation. The lavish ceremony was distinguished by Archbishop Cranmer's inaugural declaration of the divine right of kings—which added ecclesiastical gravitas to Henry's 1534 Act of Supremacy, making the monarch accountable only to God.[1]

In 1549 the Act of Uniformity was passed by Parliament. It established the first version of Cranmer's seminal Book of Common Prayer as the governing document for the Church of England liturgy.[2] Its majestic English prose style was pure Cranmer; its doctrine was a synthesis of the Lutheran theologies the archbishop had developed with the help of Protestant friends in Germany and exiles who had returned to England after Henry's death.

The first book, and its more comprehensive but shorter lived 1552 successor, notably omitted the word "transubstantiation" relating to Christ's real presence in the Holy Communion. It prescribed the taking of both bread and wine for all communicants, replaced the altars formerly used in Mass with Communion tables, and prohibited the elevation of the Host during Communion as it betokened "popish superstition."

Archbishop Thomas Cranmer (above left) and Edward Seymour (right), uncle of the young king and first controller of his council of regency, began the transformation of England into one of Christendom's first Protestant nations. Inset is the title page of the Anglican Book of Common Prayer, adopted in 1549. Clergy failing to use its prescribed liturgy were subject to life imprisonment on the third offense.

Henry VIII's Six Articles—the legislation that had returned a mostly Catholic liturgy to the churches in 1539—were repealed and, in 1552, briefly replaced with Cranmer's Forty-two Articles (later to be amended to thirty-nine). Clergy failing to use the prayer book or follow its dictates faced confiscation of their benefices and, on the third offense, life imprisonment. All "idols," statuary and unnecessary ornamentation, were to be removed from English churches.

Of more interest to the ruling plutocracy was the dissolution of the chantries, the numerous church foundations for religious, charitable, educational, and funereal purposes. The proceeds were funneled into the royal treasury, and then passed by sale and grant to the nobility. Somerset built his grand new palace from the stones dug up at St. Paul's, the bones from the demolished crypts having been heedlessly scattered in the process.

Though such lucrative reforms made enthusiastic Protestants out of many otherwise religiously apathetic grandees, they met with violent opposition in the hinterlands. The rural unrest was exacerbated by the "enclosures," whereby nobles in the wool trade converted croplands, previously owned by the church and shared by peasant farmers, into sheep pastures owned by the nobility. Somerset, although he had made his own fortune from such expropriations, now played the fair-minded Renaissance ruler and appointed a commissioner to investigate.

2. Cranmer's Book of Common Prayer sets out a regimen for the services, Bible readings, psalms, and prayers to be used for the various holy days and sacramental occasions, specifying "that all things shall be read and sung in the church in the English tongue, to the end that the congregation may be thereby edified." It recognizes only two sacraments, baptism and Holy Communion. (Catholicism observes five more: confession, confirmation, matrimony, holy orders, and the anointing of the sick.) Cranmer's more comprehensive 1552 version was never used because of the death of Edward VI and the accession of the Catholic Mary. But under Elizabeth in 1559 a compromise version was adopted. It was revised in 1662 under Charles II and would remain the official prayer book of the Anglican Church into the twentieth century.

The commissioner blamed the peasants' plight on the ruthless greed of the nobles, setting off a peasant rebellion in Norfolk and Cornwall. Giving up on Somerset, the nobles turned instead to his chief critic, John Dudley earl of Warwick, who tried negotiating with the peasants and, when that failed, killed thirty-five hundred of them with a small force of German mercenaries.

Somerset had another problem, notably his lascivious brother Thomas Seymour, who had opportunely married Henry VIII's widow, the dowager queen Catherine Parr, official guardian of the young princess Elizabeth. Seymour had been made grand admiral of England, but he had much higher ambitions. With his wife's initial approval, he took to entering Princess Elizabeth's room in the

Catherine Parr

Thomas Seymour

An engraving of Somerset House, palace of the newly enriched regent, Edward Seymour, duke of Somerset, on London's Strand. Inset above are Catherine Parr, widow of Henry VIII, and Edward Seymour's lascivious and avaricious brother Thomas, who married her. Still not content, Thomas also made advances upon the young princess Elizabeth and would finally be charged with treason for allegedly plotting the abduction of the young king Edward.

morning, playfully smacking her bottom, and tickling her under the covers. Elizabeth was said to have rather liked the attentions of the dashing older man, but Catherine, by now pregnant, soon tired of her husband's growing ardor for her ward and sent Elizabeth to live with another family.

Catherine died after giving birth to a daughter in September 1548, becoming the recipient of England's first Protestant royal funeral. Having now set his sights on eventual marriage to Elizabeth, Thomas began ingratiating himself to the king by giving Edward the extra pocket money denied by the parsimonious Somerset. Soon Thomas was suspected of plotting the capture of Edward to force a change in government in his favor. The suspicion was borne out in 1549 when he entered the king's bedchamber, used his sword to kill the boy's yapping pet spaniel, and was promptly arrested by guards and charged with treason.

Elizabeth was summoned as a possible accomplice, her alleged intention being to marry Thomas without the permission of king and council—a treasonable act. It was rumored she was pregnant. But when interrogated, she displayed a

sangfroid that would serve her well throughout her life, disdainfully dismissing any connubial or carnal involvement with Seymour. "She has a good wit," her examiner told Somerset, "and nothing is to be gotten from her but by great policy." Seymour, meanwhile, was condemned and beheaded.

Elizabeth's encounter with ambitious matrimonial endeavor was a practical lesson in the hazards she would face. It reinforced what would become her characteristic traits: to watch her step, hold her peace, avoid overt committal, and play whatever role might best facilitate survival. For several years she dressed plainly and eschewed makeup, "playing the Quaker maid," as the twentieth-century Tudor specialist David Starkey puts it (*Elizabeth: The Struggle for the Throne*, 2000). Living on her estate at Hatfield, twenty miles north of London, she devoted herself to studies of the ancient classics, daily readings of the Greek New Testament, and the works of Protestant theologians such as Philipp Melanchthon.

Ironically, young King Edward, often described as priggish, took to calling Elizabeth "sweet sister Temperance" while denouncing their elder sister Mary for indulging in "foreign dances and merriments which do not become a most Christian princess." Despite such Protestant distaste for Catholic practice, Mary had been allowed to continue in her religion, receiving Communion at her own estate at Beaulieu in Essex, retaining her chapel, and occasionally leading processions through London. This was in part to allay the enmity of Mary's first cousin the emperor Charles V, whose support was needed against their common foe, France.

Meanwhile, Warwick was on the move against Somerset in Westminster. He was a man of vulpine countenance and prestigious pedigree. His father, Edmund Dudley, had been executed early in Henry VIII's reign for treason. But son John had served Henry so well against the Scots and French that Henry made him earl of Warwick and in his will appointed him to Edward's regency council. Gradually Warwick won the respect of the young king, turning him against uncle-protector Somerset and convincing both king and council that Somerset had actually been in league with the Norfolk rebels against the king. Somerset was dismissed from his offices but spared immediate execution. Warwick was made in fact, if not title, the king's protector and gained the title duke of Northumberland. Now confident of his authority, he ordered Somerset executed in January of 1552.

Late in that year, however, there came a reversal of dire import to all Protestant England. Edward, now fifteen, became suddenly and seriously ill, probably with tuberculosis. By the spring of 1553, his condition was much worse. As the Catholic faction, encouraged by

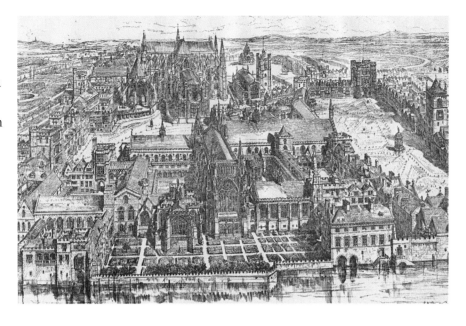

The Palace of Westminster as it may have looked in 1550, in an 1884 engraving by H. J. Brewer. Situated on the Thames, it had intermittently been a royal residence since the tenth-century reign of King Canute, and the meeting place for royal councils. After Henry VIII moved his court to Whitehall Palace (acquired from his ill-fated chancellor, Cardinal Thomas Wolsey), Westminster was increasingly devoted to Parliament. Depicted below in a nineteenth-century engraving is John Dudley, earl of Warwick and later duke of Northumberland, who soon achieved effective control of Edward VI.

The woodcut right shows the execution of Edward Seymour, duke of Somerset, eldest uncle of Edward VI, after his precipitous fall from favor. Edward laconically noted in his diary for January 22, 1552, "the duke of Somerset had his head cut off upon Tower Hill between eight and nine o'clock in the morning." The charge: felony. The actual cause: Somerset's failure to thwart his rival, the duke of Northumberland. A nineteenth-century engraving (below) depicts the death of the young monarch little more than a year later, in July 1553.

Charles V, began preparing for Mary Tudor's succession, Warwick, now Northumberland, acted swiftly. He knew that Catholic Mary could soon reverse the whole process of the English Reformation. He persuaded the dying Edward to strike Mary from the succession because of her illegitimacy—a legal maneuver that also required the illegitimate Elizabeth to be removed. Elizabeth, having no desire to usurp her half sister's crown, did not protest.

But would the young king's dying gesture prevent Mary's accession? How could Northumberland be sure? He resorted to one last expedient, one he had already prepared for but whose failure would cost him his life and create a notably tragic page in Christian history. If both Mary and Elizabeth were deemed illegitimate, the succession fell next on the auburn-haired, bookish, and primly Protestant young woman known as Lady Jane Grey.[3] Northumberland had married his son Guildford to her, doubtless in anticipation of just such an eventuality as now obtained. Before Edward died on July 6, 1553, he signed the order proclaiming Jane queen. Four days after the king's death, Northumberland set out with an army of three thousand to arrest Mary. But he was too late and had too little. Mary evaded capture and moved to Norfolk, where Catholic nobles proclaimed her queen the same day as Jane. An army of twenty thousand gathered to accompany Henry VIII's firstborn child to London to claim her throne.

Northumberland, meanwhile, encountered massive popular support for the Catholic queen.

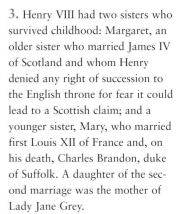

3. Henry VIII had two sisters who survived childhood: Margaret, an older sister who married James IV of Scotland and whom Henry denied any right of succession to the English throne for fear it could lead to a Scottish claim; and a younger sister, Mary, who married first Louis XII of France and, on his death, Charles Brandon, duke of Suffolk. A daughter of the second marriage was the mother of Lady Jane Grey.

4. Most lists of the English monarchy show Lady Jane Grey as reigning for nine days in 1553 between the reigns of Edward VI and Mary. Though some mark her reign as "disputed," she is usually known as the Nine-day Queen. Some lists, dating her accession from the death of Edward VI, call her the Thirteen-day Queen.

Lady Jane Grey, named heir to the throne by her dying cousin Edward VI, and backed by her father-in-law the duke of Northumberland, was queen for nine days and a prisoner for six months. The portrait is by F. R. Pickersgill (1820–1900).

Soon his troops began abandoning him to join Mary. Queen Jane's council in Westminster, discerning a shift in the wind, crumpled. Her father, the earl of Suffolk, told his daughter she was finished. Northumberland was hauled off to the Tower, pelted with stones as he went. Lady Jane Grey, having reigned just nine days,[4] joined him there, along with her husband and Northumberland's eldest son, Robert Dudley, a lifelong friend of Elizabeth's. On August 3, 1553, Mary, dressed in royal purple, rode into London to rousing acclaim. Hearing the news in Rome, Pope Julius III wept for joy. The thirty-seven-year-old woman Winston Churchill called "probably the most unhappy and unsuccessful of England's monarchs" had begun her perilous reign.

Though she is often dubbed Bloody Mary, the fact is that she began with a conciliatory policy. She executed Northumberland and his closest confreres but spared Lady Jane Grey and others who had sought to block her succession. Elizabeth joined her sister in court. Mary added some Catholic nobles to the Privy Council, including the newly freed duke of Norfolk, and made Bishop Stephen Gardiner her chancellor. For the purposes of a smooth transition and peace, many of those who had served during the Protestant period retained their positions or were reassigned.

Among the reassignments was the already seasoned mandarin William Cecil. This little man with a long, gray, sphinx-like face was to flourish throughout the second half of the century. The son of one of Henry VIII's trusted aides, he was a Protestant product of Cambridge, where he'd studied law and shared two tutors with Elizabeth. He became the loyal personal secretary to Somerset but readily transferred that

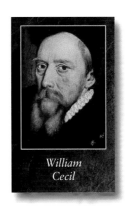

William Cecil

loyalty to Northumberland. He was now confronted by the queen he had helped Northumberland to thwart. His sharp gray eyes softened into something that resembled remorse. He had supported Lady Jane, he said, only because he feared Northumberland. He was, her majesty must understand, a coward.

Mary not only spared Cecil's life but employed him as a minor functionary in her court. His knowledge of the law and the methods of the previous regime were invaluable. During the Catholic queen's reign, he could be spotted about court fingering his brand-new rosary beads and biding his time.

Reversing the Reformation in England was Mary's first task, and she tackled it with the encouragement of cousin Charles V and the compliance of the two houses of Parliament, which had been assured that the monastic and chantry properties would not have to be returned. The Act of Uniformity was repealed, the English Bibles and Book of Common Prayer were thrown out, and the Mass and imagery reinstalled in the churches. Oxford and

Queen Mary Tudor enters London in 1553, followed by her half sister, Princess Elizabeth, in a lithograph by John Liston Shaw (1872–1919). Although she would be known as "Bloody Mary," she began as a conciliator, and the English people largely welcomed the measures she took to ease Protestant austerities and restore the country to the Catholic fold. But when plans were announced in 1554 for their new queen to marry the future Philip II of Spain, England's archenemy, that was quite another matter.

Cambridge were repopulated with Catholic theologians, new monasteries were commissioned, crucifixes re-erected in the front of churches, saints' days restored, and Thomas Cranmer, his luck having run out, sent to the Tower. Reginald de la Pole, who as a young Catholic noble of Plantagenet lineage had been chased by his cousin Henry VIII from the country for not supporting the king's supremacy, had been made a cardinal in Rome. He now returned as Mary's chief counselor, eventually replacing Cranmer as archbishop of Canterbury.

Mary's returning the English realm to the Roman see was popular with a people who had never really taken to Protestantism. The return of high holidays and the mysteries, entrenched over a millennium, was a comfort. Not nearly so well received, however, was Mary's next move. She agreed to marry Philip, Charles V's son, slated in two years to become king of Spain. It would be a coup for Spain, providing a platform for attacks on France and opening ports of refuge for Spanish supply ships bound for the Spanish forces in the Netherlands. For Mary, it might meet an even greater need, namely that of a male heir. There wasn't much time. She was thirty-seven years old. In the words of the Spanish ambassador, "Philip was the chosen of heaven for her." However, he was ten years younger and not overly taken with the short, squat, red-haired woman with the croaky voice. He went along with the marriage only in deference to his father, it was said.

The English were even less enthused. In fact, soon after the betrothal was announced in January of 1554, four Protestant nobles planned to converge with their armies on London, block the Spanish marriage, overthrow Mary, and install Elizabeth. The French ambassador had assured the rebels of French aid. The leading rebel, Sir Thomas Wyatt, had forewarned Elizabeth of his intention. Wisely, she did not respond.

As it was, Gardiner got word of the plot before the armies moved, and only one of the four was even assembled. Norfolk, now eighty-one, was dispatched to suppress the revolt, but more than half of his soldiers joyfully joined Wyatt. Mary herself, however, was equal to the challenge. She rode to London and addressed the city government with words as rousing as any of her sister's future famous orations; she would never marry outside the realm without her council's consent or the people's approval, she declared. The Londoners rallied; Wyatt's forces were blocked from entering the city. The rebels were rounded up, and the executions began. The guiltless Lady Jane Grey and her young husband were beheaded along with fifty Wyatt conspirators, including Jane's father, the duke of Suffolk.

Philip of Spain, above left in an exceedingly unflattering portrait by the contemporary Flemish painter Jan Ewoutsz, allegedly was no keener about marriage to thirty-seven-year-old Mary Tudor (above right) than the English people were about him. The silver medal (inset), inscribed "England, thou shalt rise again," was issued by Pope Julius III to celebrate the restoration of the Catholic Church in England.

Elizabeth, in whose name the rebels had acted, feared the worst. She was escorted to London, held in the same rooms of the Tower that once held her mother, Anne Boleyn, and could well have gone to the block had not her eloquent protests in a letter to her sister forestalled matters. She was moved to Woodstock Castle in Oxfordshire (later the site of Blenheim Palace, the Churchill family seat). There she remained under house arrest.

The ill-starred Lady Jane Grey faced execution at age seventeen with courage and grace. Mounting the scaffold, she recited Psalm 51 and politely requested of the axman, "I pray you, dispatch me quickly."

Mary and Philip were married by Bishop Gardiner in a Catholic ceremony at the cathedral in the ancient English capital of Winchester on July 25, 1554. But Mary's beloved Catholic king would depart from England a year later, receiving his Spanish kingship from Charles and attending to affairs in the unsettled Netherlands. Mary sobbed inconsolably from the window of her apartments in Greenwich as Philip's barges disappeared down the Thames.

By early 1555 England was once more aligned with Rome, Henry's Act of Supremacy was repealed, and Parliament had reinstated the old heresy statutes. Almost three hundred Protestants would be burned for heresy under Mary. Most of the leading Edwardian churchmen had fled to the continent, and the majority of those executed were of the lower orders—but not all. Several Protestant bishops, celebrated in John Foxe's famous *Book of Martyrs*, were burned.[5] Reformers Hugh Latimer, bishop of Worcester, and Nicholas Ridley, bishop of London, were ignited side by side in Oxford in October of 1555. As the flames rose, Foxe quotes Latimer: "Be of good comfort, Master Ridley, and play the man; we shall this day light such a candle, by God's grace, in England as I trust shall never be put out."

Thomas Cranmer watched these executions from the roof of his nearby prison. Horrified by the excruciating slowness of the burnings—a result of poor faggot placement—the sixty-five-year-old churchman fearfully recanted his Protestantism. Later, however, when it seemed the recantation would have no bearing on his fate, Cranmer turned what was supposed to be his public recantation at Oxford University Church into a resounding denunciation of his earlier reversal. It concluded: "And as for the pope, I refuse him, as Christ's enemy, and Antichrist with all his false doctrine." When the fire was lit beneath him that same day, Cranmer thrust his right hand which had signed the recantation into the flames.

Charles V had warned Mary against heresy prosecutions, convinced they would turn the country against the queen and her religion. But Mary and Pole ardently believed that heresy was a disease of the soul that could be cured only by fire. Unlike Elizabeth and their father, Henry VIII, whose enemies were executed for treason, politics was a secondary consideration for Mary. Heresy mattered more. Moreover, "Mary burned few as compared with continental practice," writes Geoffrey Elton in *England Under the Tudors* (1955), "but for English conditions and traditions her activities were unprecedented and left an ineradicable memory . . . The fires of Smithfield and the like places all over southern England created an undying hatred of the pope and Roman Catholicism which became one of the most marked characteristics of the English for some 350 years."

Mary's hopes for restoring England to the faith soon faded. Philip's quarrel with radically conservative Pope Paul IV over the territorial division of Italy led

5. The Protestant scholar John Foxe completed his famous book while in exile in Germany and Switzerland during the Marian reign. More fully entitled *Actes and Monuments of these Latter and Perillous Days, Touching Matters of the Church*, it was first published during Elizabeth's reign in the 1560s, became a bestseller, and would remain a staple of Protestant English education into the nineteenth century. The gruesomely illustrated book, whose editions sometimes ran to four thousand pages, details the sufferings of English Protestant martyrs dating back to the fourteenth century. It was vilified by Catholics for bias and embellishment—charges increasingly supported by secular historians and implicit in some of Foxe's phraseology. (Sample phrase: "Mark the apish pageants of these popelings.")

to his excommunication (see ch. 9). Even Archbishop Pole was accused by the pope of heresy because of his proposed Catholic reforms. After Chancellor Gardiner died in late 1555, Pole as archbishop of Canterbury became Mary's chief adviser. This alienated Parliament because Gardiner had consistently opposed the burnings, while Pole advocated them.

When Philip drew England into his war with France in 1557 and taxed England's resources, he created concern that England, like the Netherlands, was becoming another Spanish province. The loss to the French of English-held Calais in January 1558 was a final blow to the unhappy queen's reputation. (Calais, a key port in the English wool trade, was the last English possession on the continent.) "The failure," writes historian Elton, "broke her spirit and destroyed the last vestige of loyalty to her." An old tradition quotes her sad comment: "When they open my tomb, they will find I have Philip and Calais on my heart."

Clinging to a fantasy that she might yet provide her kingdom with a male heir, Mary had twice imagined herself pregnant, but the symptoms were really those of cancer, which appeared terminal. Philip, mostly absent from England for the last three years of Mary's reign, now set his connubial sights on Mary's younger and prettier half sister. But to preserve his hold on the English crown, Elizabeth's succession would first have to be assured. At Philip's urging, Mary signed the necessary letters patent. Then, on November 17, 1558, she partook of a final Communion in her bedroom and died peacefully in the early hours. Archbishop Pole followed eight hours later. With their deaths, so died Catholic England.

Informed of her imminent succession, Elizabeth promised the dying Mary she hoped "this earth might swallow her alive" if she abandoned Catholicism, quips the acerbic Catholic historian Hilaire Belloc, "but this the earth never did" (*Shorter History of England*, 1934). Though Philip's ambassador to England was impressed by the prospective queen's "intelligence and resolve," he warned Philip that "she seems inclined to favor men who are supposed to be heretics." He added pointedly: "She is determined to be governed by no one." That may be why, to the end, she would refuse to marry.

Following her triumphal ride into London, she dismissed the most Catholic of Mary's thirty privy councillors and reduced the council to nineteen members. "A multitude makes for disorder and confusion rather than a good council," she said. They included no clergy. But Robert Dudley, son of the beheaded Northumberland, was among them and would become a lifelong royal favorite.

Reform bishops Latimer and Ridley, above in an engraving from Foxe's Book of Martyrs, were executed in October 1555. Watching horrified from his prison tower is Archbishop Thomas Cranmer, who consequently recanted his Protestant views. But six months later, Cranmer is condemned nonetheless to the flames, as depicted in a nineteenth-century illustration, below. The dying Cranmer resoundingly repudiated his recantation, denouncing the pope as the enemy of Jesus Christ.

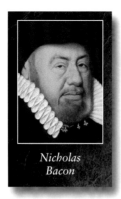

Nicholas Bacon

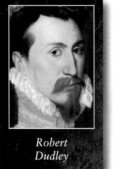

Robert Dudley

Elizabeth I in her coronation robes is seen below in a contemporary oil painting. The strong-minded queen, aged twenty-five, cut her Privy Council almost in half by dismissing most of its Catholic members. For the next half century she would conduct her country's religio-politics with intelligence and great caution. And for forty of those years her closest adviser was her extraordinarily durable principal secretary William Cecil (latterly 1st Baron Burghley). Below right, an unattributed sixteenth-century painting has Cecil riding a mule—a symbol of humility.

Nicholas Bacon, a hard-line Protestant lawyer and William Cecil's brother-in-law, became her chancellor. (His philosopher son, Francis, was destined for fame in the next century.) But it was Cecil himself, thirty-eight, who would hold the key post of principal secretary until his death forty years later. Churchill calls him "undoubtedly the greatest statesman of the century." He must not "be corrupted by any manner of gifts," said Elizabeth, "and without respect to any private will, you will give me that counsel you think best." Cecil would rarely disappoint her, though it has been argued that it was Cecil who ran Parliament and the queen, and not the reverse.

Though most of Elizabeth's appointees were Protestants who had profited from the dissolution of the Catholic properties, her personal faith has been long debated. Belloc describes her as "indifferent to religion" and twentieth-century secularists embrace her as an early-day forerunner. But her impatience with clerics and both Catholic and Protestant extremism may have been rooted more in belief than in unbelief.

"There is only one Christ Jesus, one faith," she once declared. "All else is a dispute over trifles."

She plainly cherished the ceremonial trappings of the old church, its priestly vestments and music, and prayed daily in royal chapels with the candles and crucifixes that would presently be removed from all other churches in the realm.

She must, of course, satisfy the Protestants that she was one with them. Thus, soon after her accession, she displayed her disdain for the Catholic sacraments by walking out of a Christmas Mass being conducted by Marian bishops. And at her lavish coronation—which cost an astounding £16,000—she grandiloquently kissed the papally condemned English Bible. But she carried with her a book of Latin prayers that she herself had composed, and in English she prayed, "Suffused all over with shame, I scarcely dare to lift up mine eyes to thee." Her speech of accession to the throne was a moving appeal for the help of Christ.

Her topmost religious goal, however, was encapsulated in a word she frequently used: "concord." She knew that Protestantism was far from wholeheartedly embraced by the population when she took power, and England's formidable ally, Spain, could be alienated if a program of religious reform were too vigorously enforced. The goal was to make England Protestant—but not too Protestant and not too quickly. This would require the gradual neutralization of her prede-

The Act of Uniformity made Elizabeth supreme governor of the church and required all clerics accept her supremacy. Thus the Elizabethan Settlement created a Church of England.

cessor's Catholic bishops and the northern nobles, but also the suppression of the more radical Protestants, the austere men who were now flowing back into England from exile in Switzerland and Germany, greatly influenced by John Calvin and coming to be known as Puritans.

Such a man was Richard Cox, former chancellor of the University of Oxford, remembered for his rigorous cleansing of all "popish" images, icons, and books from the university during the era of Edward VI. Yet Cox was far from an unswerving Calvinist, and though he was too close to the Puritans for Elizabeth's tastes, it was from men like Cox that the new bishops would be drawn. Cox himself became bishop of Ely, and it was the Coxians and their allies in the queen's court and government who drove the great parliamentary compromise of 1559 known as the Elizabethan Settlement. The Settlement represented a Protestant victory but neither a total nor an easy one. The House of Commons was dominated by Coxians, who wanted the kind of church envisioned by Edward VI. The House of Lords, although presided over by Chancellor Nicholas Bacon, still had a majority of Marian bishops bound to preserve Catholicism.

The legislation introduced by Cecil in February 1559 sought to restore Cranmer's liturgy and declare the monarch's supremacy. Predictably, it sailed through the Commons, then sank in the Lords. So the government presented a slightly softened bill but demanded it be debated in English, not Latin, and that the questions be confined to what could be justified by Scripture. The Catholics walked out, and the bill passed both houses unanimously. Known as the Act of Uniformity, it made Elizabeth "supreme governor" of the church and required all clerics to accept her supremacy on oath.[6] The Elizabethan Settlement had, with some compromises, established as Protestant the Church of England. The Marian bishops, of course, refused to take the Oath of Supremacy. They were quickly replaced by Protestants.

6. The title of "governor" instead of "head" (as it had been under Henry) was in part a sop to those ecclesiastics on both sides of the religious divide who had objections to the idea of a woman as head of the church on the grounds that St. Paul had forbidden women to even speak in church, much less control it. But the title also bespoke a reduction in the power of the monarch over the church. Henry had made himself an ecclesiastical ruler—the virtual pope in England; Elizabeth had agreed to a lay role outside of the clergy as the queen-governor in Parliament. While the strong Elizabethan regime ruled, this reduction made little difference. In the next century, it would cause major difficulties.

Queen Elizabeth I addresses her Parliament, in a contemporary engraving. Her avowed goal was peace and prosperity for England, and she displayed a remarkable ability to keep her head, in every sense. On the vexed question of the Eucharist, for example, she composed a reply in verse form:
" *'Twas God the Word that spake it,*
He took the bread and brake it;
And what the Word did make it,
That I believe, and take it."
(From The Marrow of Ecclesiastical History, *1675, by S. Clarke)*

The Thirty-nine Articles of Religion—an adaptation of Cranmer's Forty-two Articles—spelled out the theology of the Settlement, or at least affected to do so. They were later approved by the convocation of, by then, mostly Protestant bishops. Critics both Catholic and Protestant complained that they actually skirted most key issues rather than resolved them. But this was in fact their intention. This founding document of Anglicanism (destined to become known in the United States as Episcopalianism) reflected Elizabeth's best-of-both-worlds desires—the *via media*, or middle path, between Catholicism and Puritanism. It recognized the apostolic tradition (bishops as the spiritual descendants of the apostles) and retained the three-tier hierarchy of clergy: bishops, priests, and deacons.

While recognizing the Lutheran doctrine of justification by faith alone, the Articles gave some recognition to the authority of the church and its sacraments, retained priestly vestments, and allowed the practice of kneeling before the Communion table (not the Catholic altar). They acknowledged the real presence of Christ in Holy Communion but did not adopt the Catholic formula of transubstantiation as the means by which the real presence came about.[7] Heavy fines and jail were specified for noncompliance, but these punishments were not at first rigorously enforced. Elizabeth believed that if things were simply made inconvenient for Catholics, Catholicism would gradually die out. The queen said she had "no desire to make windows into men's souls." And while the Puritans complained, they were not yet ready to challenge the queen's authority.

Soon, however, it became plain that Elizabeth's greatest religious problem lay not in her theology but in her marital status. If she died childless, the next in line of succession was Mary Stuart, Queen of Scots, a Catholic and a militant one, who would undoubtedly return the country to Catholicism and possibly into the bosom of France as well. The anxiety among Elizabeth's council for a successor approached panic in 1562 after the queen contracted smallpox and nearly died.[8]

The queen had repeatedly put off her early suitor, the politically poisonous Philip II. The council persistently urged her to consider some Protestant foreign prince, but she dismissed all the possible candidates as beneath her. Growing desperate, they began to look locally. What about Robert Dudley, whom they had

7. The words spoken at the delivery of the consecrated bread were, "The body of our Lord Jesus Christ which was given for thee, preserve thy body and soul into everlasting life: take and eat this, in remembrance that Christ died for thee, and *feed on him in thy heart* by faith, with thanksgiving" (italics added). The cup is given with the same words but for last sentence: "Drink this in remembrance that Christ's blood was shed for thee and be thankful."

8. The disease disfigured Elizabeth's skin and took much of her hair—a great blow to the queen's vanity. From this point on she took to caking her face in the white, lead-based makeup known as the "mask of youth" and wearing the elaborate red wigs that appear in her later portraits.

hitherto loathed because he had always been her favorite? At this she flew into a rage, much like her father, and cursed them.

Then in June of 1566 came more alarming news. Mary Stuart had married a Scottish noble with a claim almost equal to Mary's on the English throne, and Mary had given birth to a son. If Elizabeth did not produce an heir, Catholic Mary or her son would rule England (see ch. 7). Hearing of this, Elizabeth lamented to one of her ladies that she feared she (Elizabeth) was of "barren stock." Meanwhile, the Scots, for the moment, anyway, solved the Mary problem by chasing their Catholic queen into England, where Elizabeth imprisoned her. In the end Elizabeth married no one and remained until her death the Virgin Queen.[9]

In 1570 Rome finally reacted to the Elizabethan Settlement. Pope Pius V, reflecting the renewed vigor infused into Catholicism by the Council of Trent, issued a bull of excommunication and deposition against Elizabeth. But since neither Spain nor France was ready to invade England, the bull could not be enforced. The papal edict, however, had the effect of foiling Elizabeth's strategy. She had hoped to lull Catholics gradually into Anglicanism. Now they must choose between Christ and queen. If they obeyed the queen in matters of faith, the pope would excommunicate them. Elizabeth then completed their dilemma. She made it a capital offense to hear or say Mass. So if they (as they saw it) obeyed Christ, the government would execute them. The author of this dire edict was Cecil, now made Lord Burghley (pronounced *Burly*). It was a common foreign view that the English people would always put their king before their faith. But Burghley knew them better, and

9. Despite her renowned virginity, Elizabeth was certainly not without an interest in men. In her mid-forties she became infatuated with and then betrothed to the French king's brother, Francis duke of Anjou, a Catholic twenty years her junior. The affair, which some historians claim was merely a strategy to unsettle King Philip, lasted a decade and had every appearance of love. The queen wrote tender letters to the humpbacked and pockmarked Francis, calling him her "little frog." When someone published a tract denouncing the proposed marriage, she had his and his printer's right hands severed. The dominant Protestant faction in Parliament resisted the match, and it eventually died after Francis's disastrous (and English-financed) campaign in the Netherlands in 1583 (see ch. 13). Francis died of tuberculosis the following year.

Elizabethan moderation abruptly ended after Pope Pius V excommunicated and deposed the queen in 1570, thus releasing her Catholic subjects from obedience to their sovereign. The Forty Martyrs of England and Wales, *at left, depicts a consequently illegal Mass. A color lithograph by Daphne Pollen, it celebrated the canonizing in 1970 of forty named individuals, including Edmund Campion, representing all the Elizabethan martyrdoms. Meanwhile, the claim of the Scottish boy-king James VI to the English crown posed the childless Elizabeth another major problem. A contemporary oil portrait (above) by Arnold Bronckorst shows him at about age eight, holding a sparrow hawk.*

Shining forth in both life and death

In the hideous torture-execution of Christians like the Jesuit Edmund Campion the Catholic light is dimmed in England, but it is not by any means extinguished

Edmund Campion returned to his native England at the age of forty, slipping quietly ashore at Dover well before sunrise on June 24, 1580. He was traveling as Mr. Edmunds, dealer in jewelry, for Europe abounded with Queen Elizabeth's spies, and royal authorities were undoubtedly aware that Campion, after an absence of nine years, was coming home. He was no longer the dazzling scholar who once had so impressed the queen, and even inspired her astute and scheming principal secretary, William Cecil, to describe him as "one of the diamonds of England." To the contrary, he was now being hunted by the English crown as the basest of traitors—namely, a Jesuit priest.

Born in London in 1540, the year the Society of Jesus received papal approval, Campion was of modest pedigree. His brilliant scholarship, however, drew this mere son of a bookseller to the attention of the highest circles at court. At fifteen he won a scholarship to Oxford and at seventeen was an admired and much-imitated junior fellow there.

When the queen visited the university in 1566, she offered to this impressive young man any post he fancied in the English church. She had need of such men. In the first year of her reign seven years earlier, when Elizabeth in effect outlawed Catholicism, nearly half its priests and all but one bishop, appointed under the prior Catholic reign of Queen Mary, chose deprivation or imprisonment rather than conform to the royal order.[1]

Campion was sufficiently interested in the royal offer to seek ordination as an Anglican deacon at age twenty-eight, thus severing himself from Rome, but doubts tormented him. He left Oxford for

Edmund Campion—scholar, martyr, and saint. In 1566 Queen Elizabeth I offered him any post he fancied in the English church. Rejecting them all, he became a Jesuit priest, returned in disguise to England, was caught, and in 1581 was hanged, drawn, and quartered.

Dublin as a known papist sympathizer (ostensibly to help found a university there) and later came under further suspicion after the 1569 Catholic uprising in northern England.

After hiding for a time in Ireland and among English Catholics, he fled to the seminary founded a year earlier in Douai, France, by an exiled Englishman, William Allen. Here he resolved at last to become a priest. Journeying on foot to Rome, he was accepted by the Jesuits, sent to Prague as a teacher, and ordained at age thirty-eight.

Meanwhile, the relative leniency of Elizabeth's early reign had hardened into severe repression after Pope Pius V published a bull in 1570 declaring Queen Elizabeth excommunicated, and in effect forbidding her Catholic subjects to obey her in all matters touching on her claimed headship of the Church of England. The queen responded by declaring it high treason to reconcile anyone to the Catholic Church or to be so reconciled. Nor was Queen Elizabeth at all mollified when the next pope, Gregory XIII, explained that in nonreligious matters English Catholics could in good conscience obey their queen after all.[2]

Thus it was that in 1580 Edmund Campion, with two Jesuit companions, Ralph Emerson and Robert Parsons, was dispatched to England. When Campion left Prague, some prescient impulse is said to have inspired a colleague to write above his door, "Edmund Campion, Martyr." It was only too real a possibility. Already one priest, Cuthbert Mayne, had been executed in 1577. They took great care. Describing his efforts at disguise, Campion wrote: "The enemy has so many eyes, so many tongues, so many scouts and crafts, that I am in apparel to myself very ridiculous. I often change it, and my name also." His statement of purpose, written in case of arrest but prematurely disseminated by supporters, was derisively dubbed "Campion's Brag" by adversaries.

The Brag made Campion so notorious that he had to work mainly among the many Catholic families of northern England, hearing confessions, saying Mass, and preaching. London-based Robert Parsons meanwhile established a clandestine press and in mid-June 1581 Campion's apologia, *Decem rationes* ("Ten reasons"), created a sensation at Oxford. "There will come, Elizabeth, the day that will show thee clearly which have loved thee," it warned, "the Society of Jesus or the brood of Luther."

Scarcely three weeks later one George Eliot, a convicted felon turned priest hunter, appeared at Lyford Grange, a known Catholic household ten miles southwest of Oxford. Posing as a Catholic, Eliot attended a clandestine Mass there, sped off as soon as the last altar candle was extinguished, and returned with a search party. For two days he and some sixty men ransacked the rambling manor and had called off the search when someone spotted a shaft of light above a stairwell. Smashing the wall with a crowbar, Eliot discovered three priests in a hidden room.[3] Edmund Campion had been captured.

He was paraded through the streets of London bound to his horse, with "Campion the Seditious Jesuit" pinned to his hat. After four days in a windowless Tower of London cell known as the Little Ease, where one could neither stand upright nor lie fully, he was brought to Queen Elizabeth and offered freedom.

Refusing to renounce his faith, over the next four months he was subjected to three rackings, and his fingernails were torn out. There then followed a fourth racking so brutal that he thought it would kill him. Asked later how he felt, he replied, "Not ill, because not at all."[4] Finally, together with twelve other priests and one layman, he was formally accused that November of plotting to murder the queen.

By the time he appeared in court, Campion could not raise his wrenched arm to take the oath; a companion kissed his hand and raised it for him. Based on testimony by Eliot and three other professional informers (improbably surnamed Caddy, Munday, and Sledd), the jury found them all guilty. By doing so, Campion told them, "you condemn all your own ancestors . . . all that was the glory of England, for what have we taught, however you may qualify it with the odious name of treason, that they did not uniformly teach?"

In December of 1581 Edmund Campion and two other priests—Ralph Sherwin, thirty-one, and Alexander Briant, twenty-five—were hanged, drawn, and quartered at Tyburn, causing drops of blood to spatter the white doublet of one of the spectators, a young nobleman named Henry Walpole. The experience would inspire Walpole to become a Catholic and to join the Jesuits in 1584. Sent back to England, he, too, would be executed at Tyburn in 1592. Like Campion, Sherwin, and Briant, Walpole, too, was canonized.

Persecution intensified after Campion's death. Debilitating fines were levied on anyone absent from services of the state church. Hearing Mass was punishable by imprisonment, repeat offenders faced execution, and informers were rewarded with one-third of any fines or forfeiture assessed against the convicted recusant. As John Coffey relates in *Persecution and Toleration in Protestant England* (2000), torture became habitual. In 1585 it was declared treason for any Catholic priest to be in the country, and it was a felony to harbor one. According to the *Catholic Encyclopedia*, of the 189 Catholics executed under Queen Elizabeth, 128 were priests, and of these, at least six were Jesuits, including the poet Robert Southwell. Yet when the queen died in 1603, recounts the encyclopedia, there were still some 365 Catholic priests in England.

Edmund Campion had predicted it would be so. Some months into his harrowing mission he wrote: "There will never want in England men that will have care of their own salvation, nor such as shall advance other men's, neither shall this church here ever fail so long as priests and pastors shall be found for their sheep, rage man or devil never so much." ∎

1. The Act of Supremacy of 1559 required all of England's clerics to acknowledge the queen as supreme, repudiating any foreign spiritual authority. The Act of Uniformity of the same year made attendance at Protestant services compulsory and prohibited any Catholic worship.

2. In reaction to the papal deposition of Queen Elizabeth, her government promulgated legislation whereby Catholics could be forced to answer: "If a Catholic army invaded England, would you support the queen or the pope?" Edmund Campion during his trial would condemn this as "the bloody question." (During the attack of the Spanish Armada, English Catholics reportedly declared almost unanimous allegiance to their queen.)

3. Hidden rooms and secret tunnels became a major feature in recusant homes. Many were constructed by Nicholas Owen, a Jesuit lay brother and a skilled craftsman, working alone and at dead of night. He is also thought to have aided in the escape of Jesuit John Gerard from the Tower of London in 1597. Captured in 1606, Nicholas Owen died under mutilating torture. He and Campion are among the Forty Martyrs of England and Wales canonized by Pope Paul VI in 1970.

4. Novelist Evelyn Waugh recounts, in his biography of Edmund Campion, that the priest hunter George Eliot, fearing for his own life, visited Campion in the Tower. Campion reassured him that Catholics would not take revenge on him and offered to try to find him a post in Germany. Eliot refused, continued as an informant, and reputedly went mad with paranoia.

Vice admirals of the English fleet that met the armada in 1588 were ex-slaver John Hawkins (above left in a portrait c. 1581) and global circumnavigator Francis Drake (at right c. 1591). Both were highly effective privateers against Spanish treasure ships. The queen herself had secretly invested in Drake's maritime syndicate and had received a handsome five-hundred-percent return).

10. Cardinal Giovanni Michele Saraceni, ambassador during Mary's reign, had a typically dismal view of English religious loyalties. "With the English the example and authority of the sovereign is everything," he wrote, "and religion is only so far valued as it inculcates the duty due from the subject to the prince. They live as he lives, they believe as he believes . . . They would be full as zealous followers of the Muhammadan or Jewish religions did the king profess either of them . . . In short, they will accommodate themselves to any religious persuasion, but most readily to one that promises to minister to licentiousness and profit." The events of the next century would, however, prove how catastrophically wrong he was, when religion was a major factor in the execution of their king.

events of the next century would prove him right.[10]

He also knew that the Catholic Reformation had already arrested the spread of Protestantism in northern Europe and that the chief instrument of this reversal was the Society of Jesus, the Jesuit order. Finally, he knew that the Jesuits were beginning to send missionaries into England despite the virtual certitude they would be caught and cruelly executed (see ch. 8). True, they were under orders not to meddle in politics or speak against the queen, but Cecil considered their very presence in England on behalf of a hostile pope to be seditious. Thus Elizabeth's policy of toleration came to an end. All told, about two hundred and fifty would die during the Elizabethan persecutions, only about fifty fewer than the toll exacted in the era of "Bloody Mary" Tudor.

But it was neither the Jesuits nor Mary Stuart who posed the greatest threat to English Protestantism. The final and most ominous peril was posed by Elizabeth's rejected suitor, Philip II. Her policy toward Spain had been growing increasingly hostile since Mary Stuart's imprisonment. England had supported the rebellion of the Dutch Protestants against the Spanish crown (see ch. 13). More provocatively still, English privateers like John Hawkins, a pioneering African slave trader, and Francis Drake, the first Englishman to circumnavigate the globe, were attacking and looting Spanish treasure ships in the New World.[11] Drake, a national celebrity, had even been knighted for his exploits against Spain, partly as thanks for Elizabeth's five hundred percent return on her secret investment in his piratical syndicate, a profit equal to the annual government budget.

As war with England became more likely, Spanish agents lured the imprisoned Mary Stuart into a plot to overthrow Elizabeth. When Burghley discovered this and proved it conclusively to Elizabeth, she signed the order to execute Mary Stuart. News of Mary's death reduced King Philip to tears. He ordered a Requiem Mass be held for her at his palace near Madrid. Then in the summer of 1588 he and Pope Sixtus V launched what Philip called the "Enterprise of England." History calls it the Spanish Armada.

Philip himself, now sixty and grievously afflicted with gout, took personal charge, a costly mistake. Álvaro de Bazán, marquis of Santa Cruz and distinguished veteran of the great Christian victory at Lepanto (see ch. 11), who planned the armada, died before it sailed. Philip replaced him with the thirty-eight-year-old Alonso Pérez de Guzmán, the duke of Medina Sidonia, a competent administrator but without military or naval experience. He didn't want the job but was made to take it anyway.

The plan was elementary. The huge fleet was to sail north from Lisbon, then east up the English Channel, rendezvous with additional troops being supplied from the Spanish forces in the Netherlands, then with a combined force of fifty-five thousand attack up the Thames, take London, oust Elizabeth and her council, then unite with massive support from English Catholics and restore the country to the ancient faith.

England's defeat of the armada launched it on a naval career that would one day see it become mistress of the seas, its flag flying over about one quarter of the earth's lands.

It did not start well. Drake, now raiding Spanish coastal towns, struck and burned the key port of Cádiz, then sank some twenty supply vessels for the armada. The Spanish navy wanted the supplies replaced, but Philip would brook no delay. The armada—about 150 warships, armed merchantmen, troop transports, and freighters—appeared off England's southwestern corner, the point known as the Lizard, on July 30, 1588. Along the south shores of England, a series of hilltop beacons were lit, signaling that the war with Spain had begun.

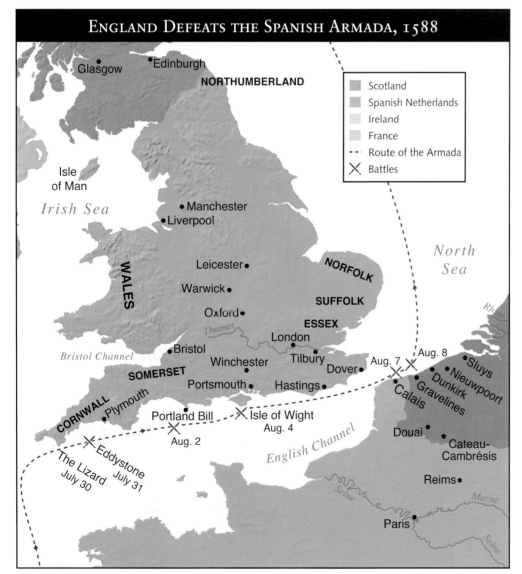

ENGLAND DEFEATS THE SPANISH ARMADA, 1588

Scotland
Spanish Netherlands
Ireland
France
- - - Route of the Armada
✗ Battles

11. The Spanish government, which held a monopoly of trade between its ports in the New World, forbade the importation of African slaves. But there was a thriving illicit traffic in blacks to meet the demand for labor, often conducted by the same Dutch, French, and English pirates (or privateers) who preyed on the outgoing Spanish treasure ships. Hawkins commanded a small squadron of these armed pirate and slaving ships. But he cared neither for religion nor nationality and at one point offered his services to the king of Spain—something Cecil, through his spies, had discovered. Henceforth Hawkins, knowing he could be hanged for treason at any moment, became Cecil's agent against Spain and a most useful addition in imminent hostilities.

Lying await in Plymouth was the English fleet, some 190 vessels, commanded by fifty-two-year-old Admiral Lord Howard of Effingham, one of the many Boleyn family descendants in Elizabeth's court. Drake and Hawkins served as vice admirals. Dudley was dispatched with twenty thousand troops to Tilbury on the Thames, to await the Spanish landing.

It never happened. Where Medina Sidonia could have pounced on the English at Plymouth, Philip's strict orders were to proceed directly to the rendezvous with the Netherlands troops. Thus, as the armada made its stately progress eastward in crescent formation along the channel, the English departed Plymouth and nipped at them like hounds from behind. Shots were exchanged with regularity but with little effect.

Then on August 2 there came a ferocious exchange of cannon fire off Portland Bill. The only significant result was the severe depletion of English and Spanish gunpowder and cannonballs. The English were able to replenish from shore—an option unavailable to the Spanish. Two more battles failed to stop the armada's march up the channel. But when Medina Sidonia anchored his fleet off Calais, at the cusp of the North Sea, the supplies denied him by Philip's haste told critically. Moreover, the Netherlands troops that were supposed to emerge from the Flemish ports were stymied by inclement tides and marauding Dutch rebel gunships.

Now the pursuing English fleet moved in on the stalled, ammunition-starved Spaniards. Shortly after midnight on August 7, the English sailed eight blazing, pitch-laden fireships into the midst of the anchored armada. Faced with this hellish approach, the Spanish panicked, broke anchor, and fell into disarray—some ships colliding with others, some running aground. But by daylight on August 8, Medina Sidonia had reassembled his fleet in time to face the full might of the English. All day, off the sands of Gravelines, the Spanish, without ammunition for their cannon, desperately fought the English with only small arms: muskets and harquebuses. It was hopeless. The English ships were coming closer and raking the Spanish decks, which soon ran with blood. Many Spanish ships were lost, many grounded, and it looked like the English would force the entire fleet onto the Gravelines sandbars. But a sudden squall allowed the Spanish to regain deep water and re-form. They appeared ready to fight again, but the English, out

The Spanish Armada—the fleet designated to carry out what King Philip II and Pope Sixtus V called the "Enterprise of England"—squares off against the English at Calais, in a painting by Hendrik Cornelius Vroom (1566–1640). Numbering some 150 vessels, from warships to troop transports, the armada was to pick up reinforcements there, cross the Channel, sail up the Thames, capture London, seize the queen, and take over the country. The intended result was to reverse the Protestant Reformation in both England and the Netherlands.

of ammunition, dropped back to await further supplies.

In the end, however, it was the weather that defeated the armada. Driven by powerful southwest winds, the Spanish were forced northward up the English east coast, circumnavigated the British Isles, and finally regained Spain, fighting tempests, disease, and near-starvation all the way. Two-thirds of the original fleet limped home, but half the men were lost and half the returning vessels too crippled to sail again. The English had lost not a single ship. England's defeat of the armada launched it on a naval career that would one day see it become mistress of the seas, with its flag flying over about one-quarter of the earth's land surface and a quarter of the world speaking its language.[12] But as in all pivotal victories, plain good fortune and/or God's grace played a major role in the armada's failure, as did Spanish mismanagement, ill fortune, or grace denied.

Eleven days after Gravelines, the fifty-four-year-old Elizabeth, mounted on a gray gelding and wearing a silver breastplate as if to engage in battle herself, made to the troops at Tilbury her most famous speech.

"I know I have the body but of a weak and feeble woman," she said, "but I have the heart and stomach of a king, and of a king of England, too, and think foul scorn that any prince of Europe should dare to invade the borders of my realm; to which rather than any dishonor shall grow by me, I myself will take up arms, I myself will be your general, judge, and rewarder of every one of your virtues in the field."

She was at the apex of her reign. When news of the armada's fate finally reached London, the bells rang, coins were struck, and the mythologizing of the Virgin Queen— "Gloriana"—began in earnest. Philip, shocked to the core, remained outwardly stoical, raised taxes, and set about rebuilding the Spanish navy.

The late Elizabethan period saw playwrights Shakespeare and Marlowe add new glory to the English theater, Drake and Sir Walter Raleigh open new paths into North America, and a group of London financiers found the East India Company and so plant the seeds of empire.[13] Catholicism, now associated in

Sir Walter Raleigh

After midnight on August 7, 1588, the English filled eight warships with pitch, gunpowder, and tar, set them ablaze, and sent them downwind into the Spanish fleet. Scattering, the Spaniards avoided the fireships, but their formation was broken and the English closed in. Thus began the Battle of Gravelines off the sands of Flanders, which along with adverse weather finished the armada as a threat to England. The color lithograph is by Jean-Leon Huens (1921–1982).

12. English is an official language in seventy-five countries. According to one early twenty-first century study, 375 million speak English as a first language and 375 million more as a second. One in four human beings speaks it "with some level of competence." A study of Internet usage showed 495 million English users, 407 million Chinese, and 139 million Spanish.

13. In 1600 Elizabeth granted a royal charter to a group of London merchants and financiers who had raised a capital of seventy-two thousand pounds with which to trade in tea, silks, dyes, salt, and opium in south Asia and China (known as the East Indies). In time the East India Company established a dominance on the Indian subcontinent that became company rule in 1757. The British government took over the administration of India (the raj) in 1858 and held it until independence in 1947.

the public mind with the thwarted Spanish invaders, was no longer a threat to an English church whose liturgy and practices were becoming more widely acceptable to many people, though certainly not to all. The Puritan movement, ever gaining in numbers, wealth, and confidence, was not ready to challenge the Elizabethan Settlement, but that would change when there was no longer an Elizabeth.

The war with Spain was to last for fifteen years, outliving Philip—who died in 1598—and being taken over by Philip III, the pious but feckless son by his father's fourth and favorite wife, Anna of Austria. In the end, the war cost England more money than it did Spain. Philip II's improved navy meant the English privateers were unable to capture as many gold ships in the West Indies as they once had, resulting in more revenue for Spain and less for England. Then, too, the Spanish sponsorship of a Catholic rebellion under the earl of Tyrone in English-held Ireland—the most serious insurrection of Elizabeth's reign—cost England more in military expenditures than the whole Spanish war.[14]

By the century's end, Elizabeth's old friends and colleagues were either dead or dying, replaced by an ambitious new generation that expected to be ruled by Mary Tudor's son, James, who had reigned as James VI of Scotland since 1581. Elizabeth's beloved Dudley had died shortly after the defeat of the armada, to be replaced at court by his stepson Robert Devereux earl of Essex. He was another dashing young man who had become a national hero after leading a successful raid on Cádiz.

Elizabeth was smitten by the flatteries of the tall, athletic, and elegant noble. She still imagined herself irresistibly attractive, though her teeth were so rotten she held a perfumed handkerchief over her mouth to spare others and took two hours every morning to have herself tricked out, so she fancied, as a young maid.

Philip II (above) after learning the fate of his armada—one-third of its ships lost and half the men. The lithograph is by John S. Lucas (1884–1918). In a contemporary engraving (below) Queen Elizabeth assures her defense troops that although she may be "a weak and feeble woman," she possesses "the heart and stomach of a king, and of a king of England, too."

But the infatuation turned sour when Essex failed to follow her instructions as commander in charge of suppressing the Irish rebellion. She punished him by revoking his royal charter to import sweet wines. Facing ruin, he attempted a coup and failed. He went to the block on February 25, 1601, at age thirty-three.

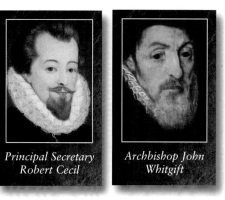

Principal Secretary Robert Cecil

Archbishop John Whitgift

The courtier instrumental in Essex's fall was William Cecil's son Robert. In 1598, despite the ministrations of Elizabeth, who fed him soup in his deathbed, the seventy-eight-year-old William had died. Robert Cecil, a dwarfish, slightly deformed young man but with an intellect as quick as his father's, became principal secretary.

The queen's health gradually worsened. By February 1603 she was losing her appetite, unable to sleep, and feverish, yet denying to the last that she was dying. She spent many days standing silently with a finger in her mouth, sometimes plagued by fearful visions. Urged by Cecil to take to her bed, she replied grimly, "If you were in the habit of seeing such things in your bed as I do when in mine, you would not persuade me to go there."

Cecil, meanwhile, had opened a secret correspondence with James Stuart, smoothing the anticipated transition of the monarchy. Unable to the end to extract from Elizabeth an assertion of James's right to the succession, Cecil put together a board of fifteen nobles ready to declare for the monarch who was next in line under the terms of Henry VIII's will.

Finally, after lapsing into a stupor, Elizabeth was carried to bed. John Whitgift, the archbishop of Canterbury during the last decades of her reign, came to her bedside, took her hand, and elicited, some said, a squeeze of acknowledgement. She died at 3 a.m. in her bedchamber at the Palace of Whitehall on March 24, 1603. She was sixty-nine. The age of the Tudors was over; the age of the Stuarts had begun.

Nearly four years later, three vessels carrying 144 men and boys in the service of something called the London Company sailed down the Thames to the sea. Their destination was Chesapeake Bay. Their destiny was to found what would become the United States of America. To honor the great queen who never married, they called their colony Virginia. ■

14. English control over Ireland went back to the 1100s, had lapsed in the ensuing centuries, but had been reestablished by Henry VIII. In 1598, however, Hugh O'Neill earl of Tyrone, financed by Spain, raised a big rebel force that reclaimed half of Ireland for the Gaelic-Catholic chieftains. Elizabeth sent Essex over with a huge army to drive back the rebels, but, unable to receive the support he requested, he was forced to accept a truce with Tyrone and then, disobeying Elizabeth's instructions, returned to England. The war resumed, with Philip III of Spain sending troops to aid the rebels. But the English, under Charles Blount, finally defeated the Irish-Spanish force in 1603 and regained control of the island.

The great queen Elizabeth Belphoebe Virginia Gloriana in old age, as depicted in a seventeenth-century oil on panel. Hers was a remarkable reign, almost half a century of triumphs, and she hated to admit that she and it were both reaching their end.

PREVIOUS VOLUMES IN THIS SERIES

VOLUME ONE:

The Veil is Torn
A.D. 30 to A.D. 70
Pentecost to the
Destruction of
Jerusalem

VOLUME TWO:

A Pinch of Incense
A.D. 70 to 250
From the Fall of Jerusalem
to the Decian Persecution

VOLUME THREE:

By This Sign
A.D. 250 to 350
From the Decian
Persecution to the
Constantine era

VOLUME FOUR:

Darkness Descends
A.D. 350 to 565
The Fall of the
Western Roman Empire

VOLUME FIVE:

The Sword of Islam
A.D. 565 to 740
The Muslim Onslaught
all but Destroys
Christendom

VOLUME SIX:

The Quest for the City
A.D. 740 to 1100
Pursuing the Next World,
They Founded this One

VOLUME SEVEN:

A Glorious Disaster
A.D. 1100 to 1300
The Crusades: blood,
valor, iniquity, reason,
faith

VOLUME EIGHT:

**The Renaissance:
God in Man**
A.D. 1300 to 1500
But amid its splendors,
night falls on medieval
Christianity

BIBLIOGRAPHY

Ackroyd, Peter. *The Life of Thomas More*. New York: Nan A. Talese, Bantam Doubleday Dell Publishing Group, 1998.

Aglialoro, Todd M. Edmund Campion—1540–1581. *This Rock Magazine*, September 1994.

Anderson, Charles S. *Augsburg Historical Atlas of Christianity in the Middle Ages and Reformation*. Minneapolis, MN: Augsburg Publishing House, 1967.

Antier, Jean-Jacques. *Teresa of Avila, God Alone Suffices*. Translated by Claire Quintal. Boston: Pauline Books and Media, 2007.

Arthur, Anthony. *The Tailor-King: The Rise and Fall of the Anabaptist Kingdom of Münster*. New York. St. Martin's Press, 1999.

Bainton, Roland Hebert. *Here I Stand: A Life of Martin Luther*. New York: Meridian, 1977.

Balbi di Corregio, Francisco. *The Siege of Malta, 1565*. Translated by Ernle Bradford. London: The Folio Society, 1965.

Barber, Noel. *The Lords of the Golden Horn; from Suleiman the Magnificent to Kamal Ataturk*. London. Macmillan, 1973.

Barraclough, Geoffrey, editor. *The Times Atlas of World History, Revised Edition*. London, UK: Times Books, 1984.

Barthell, Manfred. *The Jesuits: History and Legend of the Society of Jesus*. Translated by Mark Howson. New York: Quill, 1987.

Bax, Ernest Belfort. *Rise and Fall of the Anabaptists*. New York: A. M. Kelley, 1903.

—. *The Peasant War (Germany)*. London: Swan Sonnenschein, 1899.

Belloc, Hilaire. *A Shorter History of England*. London. Harrap, 1934.

Berglar, Peter. *Thomas More: A Lonely Voice Against the Power of the State*. Translated by Hector de Cavilla. New York: Scepter, 1999.

Black, Jeremy. *Cambridge Illustrated Atlas: Warfare—Renaissance to Revolution 1492–1792*. Cambridge, UK: Cambridge University Press, 1996.

Bradford, Ernle. *The Sultan's Admiral: The Life of Barbarossa*. London: Hodder and Stoughton, 1968.

Braght, Thielman J. van. *Martyrs Mirror: The Story of Seventeen Centuries of Christian Martyrdom from the Time of Christ to A.D. 1660*. 5th ed. Translated by Joseph F. Sohm. Scottsdale, PA: Mennonite Publishing House, 1951.

Braudel, Fernand. *The Mediterranean and the Mediterranean World in the Age of Philip II*. New York: Harper & Row, 1966.

Broderick, James, S. J. *The Origin of the Jesuits*. New York: Longmans, Green, 1940.

—. *The Progress of the Jesuits*. New York: Longmans, Green, 1949.

—. *Saint Francis Xavier, 1506–1552*. Garden City: Image Books, 1957.

Burke-Gaffney, M. W. *Kepler and the Jesuits*. Milwaukee, WI: Bruce, 1944.

Calvin, John. *Institutes of the Christian Religion*. Translated by Henry Beveridge (1599). Reprint, Center for Reformed Theology and Apologetics. http://www.reformed.org/master/index.html?main-frame=/books/institutes

Capponi, Niccolo. *Victory of the West: The Story of the Battle of Lepanto*. Oxford, UK: Macmillan, 2006.

Carroll, Stuart. *Martyrs and Murderers: The Guise Family and the Making of Europe*. Oxford, UK: Oxford University Press, 2009.

Carroll, Warren H. *The Cleaving of Christendom*. A History of Christendom, vol. 4. Front Royal, VA: Christendom Press, 2000.

Cartledge, Bryan. *A Will to Survive: The History of Hungary*. London: Timewell, 2006.

Chasteen, John Charles. *Born in Blood and Fire*. New York: Norton, 2001.

Chavez, Eduardo. *Our Lady of Guadalupe and Saint Juan Diego, the Historical Evidence*. Translated by Carmen Trevino and Veronica Montano. Lanham, MD: Rowman and Littlefield Publishers, 2006.

Chudoba, Bohdan. *Spain and the Empire, 1519–1643*. Chicago: University of Chicago Press, 1952.

Church of England. *The Book of Common Prayer: 1662 version*. London: Everyman's Library, 1999.

Churchill, Winston. *A History of the English-Speaking Peoples*, vols. 2 and 3. New York: Dodd, Mead, 1956.

Coffey, John. *Persecution and Toleration in Protestant England 1558–1689*. Harlow, UK: Longman Publishing Group, 2000.

Coleman, Christopher, and David Starkey, editors. *Revolution Reassessed: Revisions in the History of Tudor Government and Administration*. Oxford, UK: Clarendon, 1986.

Coriden, James A. "The End of the Imprimatur." *The Jurist* 44 (1984): 339–356.

Crowley, Roger. *Empires of the Sea: The Final Battle of the Mediterranean 1521–1580*. London: Faber and Faber, 2008.

Daniel-Rops, Henri. *The Catholic Reformation*. Translated by John Warrington. London: Dent, 1962.

Davis, Robert C. *Christian Slaves, Muslim Masters*. New York: Palgrave Macmillan, 2003.

Diefendorf, Barbara B. *Beneath the Cross: Catholics and Huguenots in Sixteenth-Century Paris*. New York: Oxford University Press, 1991.

Donnelly, John Patrick. *Reform and Renewal*. Faith of Our Fathers, vol. 2. Wilmington, NC: Consortium, 1977.

Dubay, Thomas, S. M. *The Fire Within: St. Teresa of Avila, St. John of the Cross, and the Gospel—On Prayer*. San Francisco: Ignatius Press, 1989.

Dunn, Richard S. *The Age of Religious Wars, 1559–1715*. 2nd ed. New York: W. W. Norton, 1970.

Dyck, Cornelius J., and Dennis D. Martin. editors. *The Mennonite Encyclopedia*. Hillsboro, KS: Mennonite Brethren Publishing House, 1955.

Edwards, Francis, S. J. *The Jesuits in England from 1580 to the Present Day*. Kent, UK: Burns and Oates, 1985.

Elton, Geoffrey Rudolph. *England under the Tudors*. New York: Methuen, 1955.

Encyclopaedia Britannica. http://www.britannica.com

Estep, William R. *The Anabaptist Story*. Nashville, TN: Broadman, 1963.

Evennett, H. Outram. *The Cardinal of Lorraine and the Council of Trent*. Cambridge, UK: Cambridge University Press, 1930.

Franck, Sebastian. *Chronica*. Darmstadt, Germany: Wissenschaftliche Buchges, 1531.

Froude, James Anthony. *The Reign of Henry the Eighth*. London: Dent, 1909.

Fuller, J. F. C. *The Decisive Battles of the Western World*, vol. 1. London: Eyre & Spottiswoode, 1954.

Füssel, Stephen. *Gutenberg and the Impact of Printing*. Translated by Martin Douglas. Burlington, VT: Ashgate, 2005.

Goff, Frederick R. *The Permanence of Johann Gutenberg*. Austin: University of Texas Press, 1970.

Gonzalez de Camera, Luis. *St. Ignatius' Own Story*. Translated by William J. Young. Chicago: Loyola University Press, 1956.

Goodier, Alban, S. J. *Saints for Sinners*. New York: Image Books Edition (Doubleday), 1959.

Gordon, Bruce. *Calvin*. New Haven, CT: Yale University Press, 2009.

Grendler, Paul. *Culture and Censorship in Late Renaissance Italy and France*. London: Variorum Reprints, 1981.

Grierson, Edward. *The Fatal Inheritance: Philip II and the Spanish Netherlands*. Garden City, NY: Doubleday, 1969.

Grimm Harold J. *The Reformation Era*. London: Macmillan, 1954.

Guy, John. *Queen of Scots: The True Life of Mary Stuart*. New York: Houghton Mifflin. 2004.

Guy, John. *Tudor England*. Oxford, UK: Oxford University Press, 1988.

Hale, John. *The Civilization of Europe in the Renaissance*. New York: Simon & Schuster, 1995.

Hall, S. C. "Pilgrimage to the Home of Sir Thomas More." *Harper's New Monthly Magazine*, August 1850.

Hanke, Lewis. *The Spanish Struggle for Justice in the Conquest of America*. Boston: Little, Brown, 1965.

Hansard, T. C., et al., editors. *The Parliamentary History of England from the Earliest Period to the Year 1803*, vol. 1. London: T. C. Hansard, 1806.

Hardy, Richard P. *John of the Cross Man and Mystic*. Boston: Pauline Books and Media, 2004.

Hare, Christopher. *A Great Emperor: Charles V*. London: Stanley, Paul, 1917.

Heers, Jacques. *The Barbary Corsairs: Warfare in the Mediterranean, 1480–1580*. Translated by Jonathan North. London: Greenhill, 2003.

Hemming, John. *The Conquest of the Incas*. London: Macmillan, 1993.

Holder, R. Ward. *Crisis and Renewal: The Era of the Reformations*. The Westminster History of Christian Thought. Louisville, KY: John Knox Press, 2009.

Holt, Mack P. *The French Wars of Religion, 1562–1629*. Cambridge, :UK Cambridge University Press, 1995.

Hsia, R. Po-Chia, ed. *Reform and Expansion 1500–1660*. Cambridge History of Christianity 6. Cambridge, UK: Cambridge University Press, 2007.

Hughes, Philip. *A Popular History of the Reformation*. Garden City, NY: Image Books, 1957.

Hunt, R. N. Carew. *Calvin*. London: Centenary Press, 1933.

Hupchick, Dennis P., and Harold E. Cox. *The Palgrave Concise Historical Atlas of Eastern Europe*. New York: Palgrave, 2001.

Ignatius of Loyola, St. *St. Ignatius' Own Story, As Told to Luis González de Cámera*. Translated by William J. Young, Chicago: Loyola University Press, 1956.

Idigoras, J. Ignacio Tellechea. *Ignatius of Loyola: The Pilgrim Saint*. Translated by Cornelius Buckley. Chicago: Loyola University Press, 1994.

Israel, Jonathan. *The Dutch Republic: Its Rise, Greatness, and Fall*. Oxford, UK: Clarendon, 1995.

Iserloh, Erwin, Joseph Glazik, and Hubert Jedin *Reformation and Counter Reformation*. Translated by Anselm Biggs, and Peter W. Becker. New York: Seabury Press, 1980.

Jackson, Samuel Macauley. *Huldriech Zwingli, the Reformer of German Switzerland*. New York: G. P. Putnam's Sons, The Knickerbocker Press, 1903.

Jedin, Hubert. *Crisis and Closure of the Council of Trent*. Translated by N. D. Smith. London: Smith, Sheed, & Ward, 1967.

Jones, Tom B., and W. Donald Beatty. *An Introduction to Spanish American History*. New York: Harper's Press, 1939.

Kalberer, Augustine. *Lives of the Saints: Daily Readings*. Quincy, IL: Franciscan Press, 1983.

Kamen, Henry. *Philip of Spain*. New Haven, CT: Yale University Press, 1997.

Kimball, Roger. *The Long March: How the Cultural Revolution of the 1960s Changed America*. San Francisco: Encounter Books, 2000.

Knecht, R. J. *The French Wars of Religion, 1559–1598*. New York: Longman, 1996.

———. *The French Civil Wars, 1562–1598*. Essex, UK: Pearson Education, 2000.

Knox, Ronald, Hilaire Belloc, G.K. Chesterton. *The Fame of Blessed Thomas More: Being Addresses Delivered in his Honor in Chelsea, July 1929*. London: Sheed and Ward, 1929.

Konstam Angus. *Historical Atlas of Exploration: 1492–1600*. New York: Checkmark Books, 2000.

L'Osservatore Romano. *Our Lady of Guadalupe: Historical Sources*. English edition, January 23, 2002, p. 8.

Larkin, Ernest E., O. Carm. "Teresa of Avila Speaks on Mental Prayer," *St. Mary, National Catholic Quarterly*, 26, no. 1 (Winter 1965): 42–46.

Lee, Stephen J. *The Mid Tudors: Edward VI and Mary,*

1547–1558. New York: Routledge, 2007.

Levack, Brian P. *The Witch Hunt in Early Modern Europe*. New York: Longman, 1996.

Loades, D. M. *Henry VIII: Court, Church and Conflict*. London: National Archives, 2007.

——— *Mary Tudor: The Tragical History of the First Queen of England*. London: National Archives, 2006.

MacCaffrey, Wallace. *Elizabeth I, London*. New York: Macmillan, 1993.

MacKinnon, James. *Calvin and the Reformation*. New York: Russell & Russell, 1962

MacNutt, Francis. *Bartholomew de Las Casas*. New York: Putnam, 1909.

Maltby, William. *The Reign of Charles V*. Basingstoke, UK: Palgrave, 2002.

Marius, Richard. *Martin Luther: The Christian between God and Death*. Cambridge, MA: Belknap Press of Harvard University Press, 1999.

Marx, Robert F. *The Battle of Lepanto 1571*. Cleveland, OH: World Publishing Company, 1966.

Mattingly, Garrett. *The "Invincible" Armada and Elizabethan England*. Washington, DC: Folger Shakespeare Library, 1963.

McHugh, John. *The Mother of Jesus in the New Testament*. London: Dartmon, Longman & Todd, 1975.

Melanchthon, Philipp. *The Augsburg Confession*. Translated by F. Bente. Book of Concord, http://www.bookofconcord.org/augsburgconfession.php

Merriman, Roger Bigelow. *The Rise of the Spanish Empire in the Old World and in the New*. New York: Cooper Square, 1962.

Meyer, G. J. *The Tudors: The Complete Story of England's Most Notorious Dynasty*. New York: Delacorte Press, 2010.

Midelfort, H. C. Erik. *Witch Hunting in Southwestern Germany, 1562–1684; the Social and Intellectual Foundations*. Stanford, CA: Stanford University Press, 1972.

Mitchell, David. *The Jesuits: A History*. London: McDonnalt Futura, 1980.

Moczar, Diane. *Islam at the Gates: How Christendom Defeated the Ottoman Turks*. Manchester, NH: Sophia Institute Press, 2008.

Moffitt, John F. *Our Lady of Guadalupe: The Painting, the Legend and the Reality*. Jefferson, NC: McFarland & Company, 2006.

Morrill, John, editor. *The Oxford Illustrated History of Tudor and Stuart Britain*. New York: Oxford University Press, 1996.

Nogueres, Henri. *The Massacre of Saint Bartholomew*. Translated by Claire Eliane Engel. London: Allen & Unwin, 1962.

Oberman, Heiko A. *Luther: Man between God and Devil*. Translated by Eileen Walliser-Schwarzbart. New Haven, CT: Yale University Press, 1982.

O'Malley, John W. *The First Jesuits*. Cambridge, MA: Harvard University Press, 1993.

O'Shea, Stephen. *Sea of Faith*. New York: Walker, 2006.

Packull, Werner O. *Hutterite Beginnings: Communitarian Experiments during the Reformation*. Baltimore, MD: Johns Hopkins University Press, 1995.

Parker, Geoffrey. *The Dutch Revolt*. Middlesex, UK: Penguin, 1977.

Parker, T. H. L. *John Calvin: A Bibliography*. London: Dent & Sons, 1975.

———. *Portrait of Calvin*. London: SCM Press, 1956.

Petrie, Charles. *Philip II of Spain*. London: Eyre & Spottiswoode, 1963.

Pitts, Vincent J. *Henri IV of France: His Reign and Age*. Baltimore, MD: Johns Hopkins University Press, 2009.

Prescott, William Hickling. *History of the Reign of Philip the Second, King of Spain*. 3 vols. Boston: Phillips, Sampson, 1855–58.

Prior, John H. *Geography, Technology, and War*. Cambridge, UK: Cambridge University Press, 1988.

Rady, Martyn. *The Emperor Charles V*. New York: Longman, 1988.

Repcheck, Jack. *Copernicus's Secret*. New York: Simon & Schuster, 2007.

Reston, James, Jr. *Defenders of the Faith: Charles V, Suleyman the Magnificent, and the Battle for Europe, 1520–1536*. New York: Penguin, 2009.

Reynolds, E. E. *Campion and Parsons The Jesuit Mission of 1580–1*. London: Sheed and Ward, 1980.

Ricard, Robert. *The Spiritual Conquest of Mexico*. Berkeley: University of California Press, 1966.

Ridley, Jasper. *Statesman and Saint: Cardinal Wolsey, Sir Thomas More, and the Politics of Henry VIII*. New York: Viking Press, 1982.

Romoli, Kathleen. *Balboa of Darién, Discoverer of the Pacific*. Garden City, NY: Doubleday, 1953.

Rothrock, G. A. *The Huguenots: A Biography of a Minority*. Chicago: Nelson-Hall, 1979.

Rowland, Wade. *Galileo's Mistake: The Archaeology of a Myth*. Toronto, Canada: Thomas Allen, 2001.

Scarisbrick, J. J. *Henry VIII*. Berkeley: University of California Press, 1968.

Schmitt, Charles B., editor. *The Cambridge History of Renaissance Philosophy*. Cambridge, :UK Cambridge University Press, 1988.

Scholderer, Victor. *Johann Gutenberg: The Inventor of Printing*. Oxford, UK: The Trustees of the British Museum University Press, 1963.

Sessions, Kyle C. *Reformation and Authority: The Meaning of the Peasants' Revolt*. Lexington, MA: D. C. Heath, 1968.

Setton, Kenneth Meyer. *The Papacy and the Levant (1204–1571)*, vol. 4. Philadelphia: American Philosophical Society, 1984.

Shennan, J. H. *The Bourbons: The History of a Dynasty*. New York: Continuum Books, 2007.

Shimizu, Junko. *Conflict of Loyalties: Politics and Religion in the Career of Gaspard de Coligny*. Geneva, Switzerland: Librairie Droz, 1970.

Simon, Edith. *Luther Alive: Martin Luther and the Making of the Reformation*. London: Hodder & Stoughton, 1968.

Stark, Rodney. *For the Glory of God: How Monotheism Led to Reformations, Science, Witch-Hunts, and the End of Slavery*. Princeton, NJ: Princeton University Press, 2003.

Starkey, David. *Elizabeth: Apprenticeship*. London: Chatto & Windus, 2000.

———. *Six Wives: The Queens of Henry VIII*. New York: HarperCollins, 2003.

Steggink, O. *St Teresa of Avila*. http://www.karmel.at/eng.teresa.htm

Thomas, Hugh. *The Conquest of Mexico*. London: Hutchinson, 1993.

Todd, William B. *The Gutenberg Bible, New Evidence of the Original Printing*. Third Hanes Lecture. Chapel Hill: University of North Carolina at Chapel Hill, 1982.

Vann, Joseph. *Lives of the Saints*. New York: John J. Crawley and Company, 1954.

Vickery, Paul S. *Bartolomé de Las Casas: Great Prophet of the Americas*. New York: Paulist Press, 2006.

Walker, Wiliston. *Heroes of the Reformation*. New York: Schoken Books, 1906.

Walsh, William Thomas. *Philip II*. New York: McMullen Books, 1937.

Waugh, Evelyn. *Edmund Campion*. Harmondsworth, UK: Penguin Books, 1935.

Waterworth, J., editor. *The Council of Trent*. Translated by J. Waterworth. Hanover, Germany: University of Hanover, 1848. http://history.hanover.edu/texts/trent.html

Wedel, Theodore Otto. *The Medieval Attitude Toward Astrology Particularly in England*. Hamden, CT: Archon Books, 1968.

Wedgwood, C. V. *William the Silent*. New Haven, CT: Yale University Press, 1944.

Wegemer, Gerard B. and Stephen W. Smith, editors. *A Thomas More Source Book*. Washington, DC: The Catholic University of America Press. 2004.

Wikipedia. http://en.wikipedia.org/wiki

Wilson, Ian. *Nostradamus: The Man behind the Prophecies*. New York: St. Martin's Press, 2002.

Windschuttle, Keith. *The Killing of History: How Literary Critics and Social Theorists are Murdering Our Past*. San Francisco: Encounter, 2000.

Wolfe, Michael. *The Conversion of Henri IV: Politics, Power, and Religious Belief in Early Modern France*. Cambridge, MA: Harvard University Press, 1993.

Yeo, Margaret. *A Prince of Pastors: St. Charles Borromeo*. London: Catholic Book Club, 1943.

Photographic Credits

75 Mark R. Hattlie, http://sites-of-memory.de/main/index.html; 229 Gianni Sabato; 256 Rado Javor

AKG Images
14 © akg-images; 15 inset © akg-images; 23 © akg-images; 46 top left © akg-images/ Erich Lessing; 64 © akg-images; 67 top © akg-images; 69 © akg-images; 73 © IAM/ akg/NA; 78 top © akg-images; 86 top © akg-images; 89 © akg-images; 99 © IAM/ akg/World History Archive; 101 © akg-images; 104 bottom © akg-images/Bildarchiv Monheim; 126 bottom © akg-images; 136 bottom © akg-images/ Schütze/ Rodemann; 160 © akg-images; 161 top © akg-images; 163 top © akg-images; 164 top © akg-images; 180 third from left © akg-images/ Cameraphoto; 182 © akg-images; 195 © Sotheby's/ akg-images; 196 top © akg-images; 247 top © akg-images, bottom © akg-images/ Rainer Hackenberg; 248 © akg-images; 262 © akg-images/ André Held; 264 top © akg-images; 266 top left © akg-images Schütze Rodemann; 268 © akg-images; 272 left © IAM/ akg/ World History Archive; 277 top © akg-images/ André Held; 278 top right © akg-images; 279 © akg-images; 280 right © akg-images; 285 © akg-images/ Rabatti–Domingie; 286 © akg-images / Paul M.R. Maeyaert; 294 top © akg-images; 297 © akg-images; 298 © akg-images; 301 top right © akg-images; 303 top © akg-images; 304 © akg-images; 305 left © akg-images; 324 © akg-images/ British Library

Art Resource
4 top © Erich Lessing/ Art Resource, NY, bottom © Réunion des Musées Nationaux/ Art Resources, NY; 6 top © Erich Lessing/ Art Resource, NY; 278 top left © Réunion des Musées Nationaux/ Art Resource, NY; 281 right © Erich Lessing/ Art Resource, NY; 283 © Trustees of the Wallace Collection, London/ Art Resource, NY; 289 © Erich Lessing/ Art Resource, NY; 295 bottom © Bildarchiv Preussischer Kulturbestiz/ Art Resource, NY; 303 center © Scala/ Art Resource, NY, bottom right, © Erich Lessing/ Art Resource, NY; 305 right © Réunion des Musées Nationaux; 306 © Erich Lessing/ Art Resource, NY; 307 © Erich Lessing/ Art Resource, NY; 311 bottom inset © DeA Picture Library/ Art Resource, NY; 320 bottom right © HIP/Art Resource, NY; 328 © Scala/ White Images /Art Resource, NY

Bridgeman
vi © Bridgeman Art Library; 0 © Bridgeman Art Library; 2 © Christie's Images/ Bridgeman Art Library; 3 © Bridgeman Art Library; 5 © Bridgeman Art Library; 9 © Bridgeman Art Library; 17 © DHM/ Bridgeman Art Library; 19 bottom © DHM / Bridgeman Art Library; 30 top © DHM/ Bridgeman Art Library; 34 © The Stapleton Collection/ Bridgeman Art Library; 36 inset © The Stapleton Collection/ Bridgeman Art Library; 39 bottom right © Museumslandschaft Hessen Kassel Ute Brunzel/ Bridgeman Art Library; 45 © DHM/ Bridgeman Art Library; 49 top © Bridgeman Art Library, inset © Wallace Collection, London, UK/ Bridgeman Art Library; 52 © Rafael Valls Gallery, London, UK/ Bridgeman Art Library; 53 inset © DHM/ Bridgeman Art Library; 56 © Bridgeman Art Library; 58 © Rafael Valls Gallery, London, UK/ Bridgeman Art Library; 59 © Bridgeman Art Library; 60 © Bridgeman Art Library; 61 © Bridgeman Art Library; 63 © Bridgeman Art Library; 81 © Bridgeman Art Library; 83 right © Bridgeman Art Library; 95 © Peter Nahum at The Leicester Galleries, London/ Bridgeman Art Library; 117 top © The National Portait Gallery, London/ Bridgeman Art Library, bottom © Birmingham Museums and Art Gallery/ Bridgeman Art Library; 118 top © The National Portrait Gallery, London/ Bridgeman Art Library; 119 © Bridgeman Art Library; 121 top Photo © Philip Mould Ltd., London/ Bridgeman Art Library; inset © Bridgeman Art Library; 122 © Bridgeman Art Library; 123 © Bridgeman Art Library; 125 © The Stapleton Collection/ Bridgeman Art Library; 128-129 © Bridgeman Art Library; 130 © Bridgeman Art Library; 132 © Mark Fienne/ Bridgeman Art Library; 133 © Bridgeman Art Library; 142 © Bridgeman Art Library; 143 © Bridgeman Art Library; 144–145 © National Gallery of Scotland, Edinburgh, Scotland/ Bridgeman Art Library; 147 © Bridgeman Art Library; 149 inset © Bridgeman Art Library, bottom © Bridgeman Art Library; 150 top © Bridgeman Art Library; 156 top © Bridgeman Art Library; 165 © Bridgeman Art Library; 169 top © Ken Welsh/ Bridgeman Art Library; 170 inset © Bridgeman Art Library; 172 top © Index/ Bridgeman Art Library; 175 top © Otus/ Index Bridgeman Art Library; 175 bottom © Peter Newark Pictures/ Bridgeman Art Library; 176 © Bridgeman Art Library; 177 top © Bridgeman Art Library; 178 © Bridgeman Art Library; 183 top © AISA/ Bridgeman Art Library; 185 © Index/ Bridgeman Art Library; 193 © Bridgeman Art Library; 200 © Royal Holloway and Bedford New College, Surrey, UK/ Bridgeman Art Library; 205 top © DHM/ Bridgeman Art Library, bottom © Bridgeman Art Library; 206 bottom © Bridgeman Art Library; 210 © Look and Learn/ Bridgeman Art Library; 215 left © Bildarchiv Steffens/ Bridgeman Art Library, bottom © Look and Learn/ Bridgeman Art Library; 219 © Bridgeman Art Library; 220 inset © Index/ Bridgeman Art Library; 222 © Ken Welsh/ Bridgeman Art Library; 224 © Archives Charmet/ Bridgeman Art Library; 225 © Bridgeman Art Library; 226 © Peter Newark American Pictures/ Bridgeman Art Library; 227 © Giraudon/ Bridgeman Art Library; 228 bottom © Bridgeman Art Library, inset © Giraudon/ Bridgeman Art Library; 231 © Index/ Bridgeman Art Library; 232 © Index/ Bridgeman Art Library; 234 © Peter Newark American Pictures/ Bridgeman Art Library; 240 top © Bridgeman Art Library; 242 top © Bridgeman Art Library, bottom © Bridgeman Art Library; 243 bottom © Bridgeman Art Library; 249 © Bridgeman Art Library; 252 top © Bridgeman Art Library, bottom © Bridgeman Art Library; 253 © Alinari/ Bridgeman Art Library; 258 © Index/ Bridgeman Art Library; 260 top © Look and Learn/ Bridgeman Art Library, bottom © Cameraphoto Arte Venezia/ Bridgeman Art Library; 265 © Bridgeman Art Library; 267 © Bridgeman Art Library; 273 right © Bridgeman Art Library; 274 © Giraudon/ Bridgeman Art Library; 276 © Bridgeman Art Library; 277 bottom © Bridgeman Art Library; 278 bottom © Giraudon/ Bridgeman Art Library; 280 left © Alinari/ Bridgeman Art Library; 284 © Giraudon/ Bridgeman Art Library; 293 left © Bridgeman Art Library, left © Giraudon/ Bridgeman Art Library; 294 center right © Giraudon/ Bridgeman Art Library; 295 top © Giraudon/ Bridgeman Art Library; 296 top © Ken Walsh/ Bridgeman Art Library, bottom © Peter Willi/ Bridgeman Art Library; 299 top © Giraudon/ Bridgeman Art Library; 300 bottom © Bridgeman Art Library; 301 top left © Giraudon/ Bridgeman Art Library, bottom © The Stapleton Collection/ Bridgeman Art Library; 308 top left (Elizabeth) photo © Philip Mould Ltd., London/ Bridgeman Art Library, top right (Mary) © Bridgeman Art Library; signatures © Bridgeman Art Library; 310 © Bridgeman Art Library; 311 left © Bridgeman Art Library, right © The Trustees of the Weston Park Foundation/ Bridgeman Art Library; 313 bottom © Ken Welsh/ Bridgeman Art Library; 314 top © Bridgeman Art Library, bottom © Bridgeman Art Library; 315 top photo © The Fine Art Society, London, UK/ Bridgeman Art Library; 316 © The Stapleton Collection/ Bridgeman Art Library; 317 top & inset © Bridgeman Art Library; 318 © Bridgeman Art Library; 319 top © Bridgeman Art Library, inset © Ken Welsh/ Bridgeman Art Library; 320 bottom left © Bridgeman Art Library; 322 © Bridgeman Art Library; 323 bottom © Bridgeman Art Library; 329 top © National Geographic Image Collection/ Bridgeman Art Library; 330 top © The Stapleton Collection/ Bridgeman Art Library; 331 © Bridgeman Art Library

Corbis
6 bottom © Luca da Ros/Grand Tour/Corbis; 31 © Ho/Reuters/Corbis; 15 bottom © Bettmann/Corbis; 46 bottom © Adam Woolfitt/ Corbis; 67 bottom © Kevin Fleming/Corbis; 78 bottom © Richard Hamilton Smith/ Corbis; 79 © Karen Kasmauski/Corbis; 91 © Salvatore di Nolfi/epa/Corbis; 93 left © Martal TREZZINI/epa/Corbis; 96 © Bettmann/Corbis; 103 inset © Martial TREZZINI/epa/Corbis; 106 © Christel Gerstenberg/Corbis; 108 © Bettmann/Corbis; 109 © Bettmann/Corbis; 115 inset right © Ho/Reuters/Corbis; 127 top © Richard Bryant/ Arcald/ Corbis; 135 © Bettmann/Corbis; 150 bottom © David Moir/ Reuters/ Corbis; 151 © Adam Woolfit/ Robert Harding World Imagery/Corbis; 166 bottom © Frank Guizou/Hemis/Corbis; 172 bottom © Pablo Sanchez/Reuters/Corbis; 183 bottom © Grand Tour/ Corbis; 196 inset © Mike Kemp/Rudderball/Corbis; 204 bottom © Nicola Angeli/Grand Tour/Corbis; 215 right © PoodlesRock/Corbis; 217 © Bettmannn/Corbis; 236 top right © Paolo Aguilar/epa/Corbis; 221 top © Bettmann /Corbis; 251 top © John Springer Collection/Corbis; 269 top © Chris Hellier/Corbis, bottom © Ruet Stephane/Corbis sygma; 270 © Bettmann/Corbis; 312 bottom © Historical Picture Archive/CORBIS

Dreamstime
136 third from top © Lindamore/ Dreamstime.com; 152 © Vera Handojo/ Dreamstime; 156 bottom © Quintanilla/ Dreamstime.com

Getty
10 © Emma Lee/Life File; 26 bottom © 3LH-Fine Art; 55 © National Geographic/ Getty Images; 80 inset © Getty Images; 84 © AFP/Getty Images; 92 top © Time & Life Pictures/ Getty Images; 94 right © Time & Life Pictures/Getty Images; 124 top © Getty Images; 139 © Getty Images; 166 top © Time & Life Pictures/Getty Images; 177 bottom © Time & Life Pictures/Getty Images; 206 top © SSPL via Getty Images; 250 bottom © Dea picture library; 330 bottom © Getty Images

iStock
66 bottom © iStockphoto LP; 80 bottom © iStockphoto LP; 220 top © iStockphoto LP; 236 top left © iStockphoto LP

National Geographic
37 © James L. Amos/National Geographic Stock; 47 top © James L. Stanfield/ National Geographic Stock; 173 © James L. Stanfield/National Geographic Stock; 216 © H. Tom Hall/National Geographic Stock; 223 top © National Geographic Stock; 223 inset © Maria Stenzel/National Geographic Stock

INDEX

A

Abraham (Syrian negotiator), 167
Ackroyd, Peter, 122
Act in Restraint of Appeals (1533), 119
Act of Abjuration (1581), 304
Act of Succession (1534), 122–123
Act of Supremacy (1534), 311, 318
Act of Supremacy (1559), 325
Act of Uniformity (1549), 311, 316
Act of Uniformity (1559), 321, 325
Adagia (Luther), 20
Address to the Christian Nobility of the German Nation (Luther), 27
Adolph of Mainz, Archbishop, 15
Adrian of Utrecht, 4, 35–36. *See also* Adrian VI, Pope
Adrian VI, Pope, 39–40, 41. *See also* Adrian of Utrecht
Advice on Reform of the Church, 182
affinity, 116
Africa, 58, 165–167, 242, 244
Against the Heavenly Prophets (Luther), 38
Ahlefeldt, Bartholomeus von, 78
al-Khattab, Umar ibn, 59
Albon, Jacques d', 270
Albrecht, Archbishop, 22
Albuquerque, Afonso de, 173
Aldegrever, Heinrich, 82
Aleandro, Girolamo, 28–29, 30
Alexander VI, Pope, 223
Algiers (Algeria), 242, 244
Ali Pasha, 254, 255, 258, 259
Alkmaar (Netherlands), 301
Allan, William, 144
Allen, William, 170–171, 324
Almagro, Diego de, 220
Alva, Duke of, 197, 296–301
Alvarado, Pedro de, 218
Amazon River, 213
Ameaux, Pierre, 98–99
Amish, 78
Amsterdam (Netherlands), 289, 291, 294
Anabaptists
    beliefs of, 50, 69–71, 192
    effect of Peasants' Revolt on, 45
    in Geneva, 96
    in Münster, 77, 80–83
    in Netherlands, 291
    persecution of, 64, 72–74, 75, 77, 78, 80, 83
    spread of movement, 65–68, 74–79
    and Swiss Brethren, 68–69
    varieties of, 71–72
Angelice, 181
Anglicanism, 322
Anjiro (Japanese samurai), 175
Anna of Austria, 330

Anna of Buren, 304
Anna of Egmond, 292
Anna of Saxony, 292, 295, 299, 302
annates, 118
Anne of Cleves, 127
Anthony of Navarre, King, 266, 271, 272, 273
Antier, Jean-Jacques, 185
Antwerp (Belgium)
    Anabaptists in, 291
    Calvinists in, 294, 301, 303
    site of religious conflict, 295–296, 302, 304, 305
    as thriving port, 288
apocalypse, 67
Apollos, 38
Apostolic Baptists, 71
apostolic tradition, 322
Apps, Lara, 107
Aquinas, Thomas, 13, 269
Aquino, Marcos Cipac de, 225
Aretino, Pietro, 198
Arianism, 99
Aristotle, 13, 269
Arius, 198
Arminians, 307
Arminius, 306–307
Arthur, Anthony, 81
Arthur, Prince (son of Henry VII), 112, 116
The Ascent of Mount Carmel (John of the Cross), 185
Aske, Robert, 125
astrology, 268–269
Atahualpa, 220, 221–222
Augsburg Confession, 271
Augsburg Interim, 193, 195
Augsburg Reichstag, 193, 198
Augustine, Bishop of Hippo, 16
Augustine, St., 269
Augustinians, order of, 22
Augustus, Emperor, 206
Ausbund, 74
Aztec empire, 213–219

B

Babington, Anthony, 148
Babylonian Captivity of the Church (Luther), 21, 27
Bacchiacca, Francesco, 39
Bach, J. S., 55
Bachelin, Auguste, 90
Backhuyzen, Ludolf, 307
Bacon, Francis, 320
Bacon, Nicholas, 320, 321
Baden-Baden (Germany), 108
Bainham, James, 123
Bainton, Roland H., 24, 28, 29
Balboa, Vasco Núñez de, 212, 227
Balbus, Hieronymus, 33
Balzac, Honoré de, 48

Bambini, Niccolò, 184
baptism, 50, 55, 65, 68–69, 70, 73
Barbarigo, Agostino, 253, 258–259
Barbarossa Brothers, 241–246
Barbary Coast pirates, 41, 239, 241–246, 261
Barnabites, 181
Barozzi, Pietro, 181
Barthel, Manfred, 162, 163
Barton, Elizabeth, 122
Basilica del Voto Nacional, 236
Basilica of Good Jesus, 173, 177
Basilicus the Heraclid, James, 62–63
Bat Ye'or (Giséle Littman), 58, 60, 62
Baum, L. Frank, 105
Baumeister, Konrad, 158
Bax, Ernest Belfort, 44, 70, 72
Bayezid II, Ottoman sultan, 1–2
Bayfield, Richard, 123
Bazán, Álvaro de, 253, 259, 326
Beaton, David, 134
Beda, Noel, 86
beeldenstorm, 295–296
Beggars protest, 293–294
Belgrade, 37
Belloc, Hilaire, 319, 320
Bender, Harold, 67
benefices, 182, 188
Berglar, Peter, 122, 123
Bern (Switzerland), 89–95
Berquin, Louis de, 264
Beza, Theodore, 91, 204, 270–271
Bible
    Douay-Rheims version, 171
    and Erasmus, 20
    Gutenberg, 14–15
    Luther-Zwingli differences over, 50, 51
    and Luther's New Testament, 32, 33, 162
    Luther's view of, 13, 16, 37–38, 162
    Tyndale translation, 124
Bilney, Thomas, 123
Bireley, Robert, 177
Bismarck, Otto von, 153–154
Blaurock, George, 68, 73–74
Blomberg, Barbara, 251
Blount, Charles, 331
Blount, William, 20
Bobadilla, Nicolàs, 159
Bockelson, Jan, 81, 82
Boleyn, Anne, 114–115, 117, 118, 119, 122, 125–127
Boleyn, Mary, 114–115
Boleyn, Thomas, 114, 118
Bologna (Italy), 193
Bolsec, Jerome, 99
Bolt, Eberli, 72
book burning, 26, 28, 57, 81, 99, 196
Book of Common Prayer, 311

Book of Discipline, 140
The Book of Her Life (Teresa of Avila), 185
Book of Martyrs (Foxe), 318
Bora, Katherine von, 42–43
Borgia, Francis, 170
Borromeo, Charles, 202–203
Borromeo, Giberto, 202
Bothwell, Earl of (James Hepburn), 142–143, 146, 151
Bouttats, Gaspard, 280
Bowes, Majorie, 134
boy tribute, 60, 63
Boyvin, René, 95
Brabant (Netherlands), 293
Brandi, Karl, 5, 57, 200
Brandon, Charles (Earl of Suffolk), 315, 317
Brazil, 235
Brederode, Henry van, 293, 294, 296, 297
Brewer, H. J., 313
Briant, Alexander, 325
Brill (Netherlands), 300
Brodrick, James, 168, 169
Broët, Paschase, 159
Bronckorst, Arnold, 323
Bruegel the Elder, Pieter, 288
Brugge (Netherlands), 293
Brussels (Belgium), 289, 293–294, 295, 299, 304
Bry, Theodore de, 226, 227
Bucer, Martin, 76, 95
Buddhism, 174, 175
Bulgaria, 49
Bullinger, Heinrich, 51, 71
Buonconsiglio, Castello del, 204
Bure, Idelette de, 96
Burghley, Lord. *See* Cecil, William
Bustamante, Francisco de, 224
Byzantium, 62

C

Caesar, Julius, 206
Caffi, Ippolito, 60
Cajetan, Cardinal (Tommaso de Vio Gaetanus), 24, 25
Cajetan, St. (Gaetano die Conti di Thiene), 180, 181
calendar reform, 206
Callahan, Philip, 225
Callinicus III, 62
Calvin, Antoine, 98
Calvin, Charles, 87
Calvin, John
    background, 86–87
    character, 84, 85–86, 95–96, 103
    death, 103
    early years, 87, 88
    and J. Knox, 134
    opponents of, 98–102

and religious unrest in France,
265, 267, 270, 275
in Strasbourg, 95–96
in Switzerland, 89, 91–92,
93–95, 96–, 102
and Zwingli, 51
Calvinism
in Antwerp, 294, 301, 303
and excommunication, 94, 97
in France, 85–88, 201, 269,
270–271
and the *Institutes,* 88–89
legacy of, 85
in Netherlands, 293, 294, 296,
300, 305
opponents of, 98–102, 306–307
and Orthodox church, 63
in Scotland, 143
in Switzerland, 89–95, 96–97,
100, 102
views on points of doctrine,
190–192, 204
Cameron, Euan, 45
Campeggio, Lorenzo, 117
Campion, Edmund, 171, 323,
324–325
Canisius (Peter Kanis), 162–163,
164, 196
cannibalism, 217, 223
canon law, 66
canonical texts, 187
Capuchins, 180
Carafa, Carlo, 196–197
Carafa, Giovanni (nephew of Pope
Paul IV), 197
Carafa, Giovanni P., 159, 168, 181,
187, 195. *See also* Paul IV, Pope
Carberry Hill, 146
Carew Hunt, R. N., 93, 95, 102
Carlyle, Thomas, 154
Carmelite order, 184–185
Caroli, Pierre, 99
Caron, Antoine, 272
Carroll, Stuart, 271
Carroll, Warren H., 41, 186, 194,
225, 298
Carruth, J. A., 134
Carthusians, 120, 121, 124, 181
Cartledge, Brian, 46
Casas, Bartolomé de las, 228–229,
230–234, 236
Castellio, Sebastian, 98, 99
catechism, 164
Cathedral of Santo Domingo, 236
Catherine of Aragon, 112, 116–118,
119, 125
Catherine of Portugal, 5
Catherine the Great, 155
Catholic League, 282, 283–284
Catholic Triumvirate, 270, 271,
272–273, 274–275
Cati, Pasquale, 209
Caula, Sigismondo, 203
Cecil, Robert, 331
Cecil, William (Lord Burghley)

as anti-papist, 201
death, 151, 331
as Elizabeth's counselor, 149,
320, 321, 323, 326
during Mary I's reign, 315–316
and Mary Queen of Scots'
marriage, 142, 143
plots against Mary Queen of
Scots, 138, 141, 146–148, 326
celibacy, clerical, 38, 50, 61, 208
censorship, 198–199
Cervantes, Miguel de, 260, 261
Chambord Castle, 136
Charles IX, King of France
becomes king, 138, 276
and Peace of Longjumeau,
276–277
and St. Bartholomew's Day
Massacre, 279, 280–281
youth, 270, 271
Charles V, Holy Roman Emperor
abdication of, 286–287
and America, 220, 232, 233
attempts to stop Luther, 21, 28,
35, 43
and Council of Trent, 180, 183,
186, 187–188, 189, 208
depiction of, 240
and England, 313, 314, 316
fights in North Africa, 242, 244
foreign policy problems, 35–37
and Francis I, 35, 37, 47–48,
57, 186, 187
and Henry VIII, 8, 36, 47, 48,
113, 119, 125
and Jesuits, 165
later years, 197–201
and Lutherans, 53, 57
and Luther's grave, 193
in Netherlands, 289, 291,
292–293
and Ottoman empire, 41, 53, 54
personal life, 43, 294
and Pope Clement VII, 9, 41, 48
and Pope Paul III, 57, 188, 189
and popes, 188, 189, 194, 197
religion of, 32, 57
and Religious Peace at
Augsburg, 198–199
rule of, x, 3, 4–9, 27–28, 83
and Spain, 35–36
tries Luther, 29, 30, 31, 33
war with Lutheran princes, 186,
188, 189, 193, 195
Charlotte of Bourbon, 302, 304
Chávez, Eduardo, 224, 225
Chesterton, G. K., 123, 256–257
Chichimec, 227
China, 177
Christian subjects, 58–61
Christianismi Restitutio, 99
Chronica (Franck), 71
church, nature of, 191–192, 205,
207–208
Church of San Francisco, 236

church property, 193, 311–312
Cisneros, Ximenes de, 230, 231, 232
Claude, duchess of Brittany, 8, 9
Clavius, Christopher, 206
Clement, Margaret, 122
Clement VII, Pope
and Charles V, 9, 41, 48
and church troubles, 182
and Henry VIII, 116, 118, 119,
120
and slavery, 223
Clement XIV, Pope, 154
clergy
appointment of, 39, 44, 55,
207–208
celibacy of, 38, 50, 61, 208
Henry VIII's bills against, 118
and living in diocese, 207–208
marriage of, 193
reaction to Lutheranism, 42
views on authority of, 192
Clouet, François, 140, 276
Codure, Jean, 159
Coello, Alonso Sánchez, 252
Coffey, John, 325
Colet, John, 20, 121
Coligny, Gaspard de, 201, 274, 275,
276, 277–279
Coligny, Louisa de, 304
Colonna, Marc'Antonio, 250
Colt, Jane, 121
Columbus, Christopher, 211
Columbus, Diego, 229, 230
communism, 81
The Complaint of Peace (Erasmus),
21
*Concerning the Just Cause of the
War against the Indians*
(Sepúlveda), 226
Condé, Prince Louis of
as leader of Huguenots,
272–273, 274, 275, 276, 277
and religious unrest, 266, 267,
268, 270, 271
Confederate Lords, 146–147, 148
Confesionario, 233
conquistadors
extent of expansion in America,
210–213
in Mexico, 213–219
in Peru, 220–223
and slavery, 223, 226, 227
Consensus Tigurinus, 51
Constantine, Emperor, 268–269
Constantinople, 1, 61–62, 63
Constitutio Criminalis Carolina, 83
consubstantiation, doctrine of, 17
conversion
of American natives, 233–237
of Aztecs, 217
of Christians to Islam, 58, 60
forced on Amerindians, 223
of Incas, 221–222
to Islam, 36
of Mexicans, 224–225, 235

of Slavs to Christianity, 63
Cop, Nicholas, 87–88
Copernicus, 269
Coptic church, 166–167
Coronado, Francisco Vásquez de,
213
Cortés, Hernán, 213, 215–216,
217–219
Cortese, Gregorio, 181
Corvinus, Antonius, 83
Coton, Graham, 211
Council of Nicea, 198, 206
Council of Trent
agenda for, 182–183, 186
background to, 180–182
and calendar reform, 206
depictions of, 178, 188, 205, 209
first assembly (1545-1547),
186–189, 193
Jesuits at, 165
legacy of, 179–180
and Pope Paul IV, 196
putting decrees into effect, 202,
208–209
second assembly (1551-1553),
194–195
third assembly (1561-1562),
201, 204–205, 207–208
and Tridentine Index, 199
Counter-Remonstrants, 307
Cowper, William, 180
Cox, Richard, 321
Cranach the Elder, Lucas, 12, 18
Cranmer, Margarete, 119, 125
Cranmer, Thomas
as Archbishop of Canterbury,
118–119, 124, 125, 126
death, 318
and Edward VI, 128, 310–311
and Henry VIII's death, 128–129
sent to tower, 316, 319
Cresacre, Anna, 122
Crete, 250
Cromwell, Thomas, 119, 120,
122–123, 125, 127
crusades, 24
Cuauhtlatoatzin, Juan Diego,
224–225
Cuba, 212, 227, 229
Culpepper (Catherine Howard's
lover), 127
Cumaná (Venezuela), 232–233
Cuzco (Peru), 222
Cyprus, 249–251, 254–255

D

Daniel-Rops, Henri, 196
Darién (Panama), 212
The Dark Night of the Soul (John of
the Cross), 185
Darnley, Lord (Henry Stuart), 142,
143–144, 145, 148
Dauncey, Elizabeth, 122
Day of the Barricades, 283

pfaffensturm (priest-storm), 38
Philip I 'the Handsome,' 3, 4–5
Philip II, King of Spain
    birth, 43
    and Charles V, 199, 200, 286, 287
    and Council of Trent, 204, 205
    death, 306, 330
    and Elizabeth I, 305, 319, 326
    and Jesuits, 164
    and Low Countries, 261, 288
    and Mary I, 310, 316–317, 318,
      319
    and Ottoman Empire, 239, 240,
      244, 245
    personality, 185, 294–295
    plot against England, 148
    rule of Netherlands, 292, 293,
      295–296, 301–303, 304
    and siege of Malta, 246, 247
    and Spanish Armada, 326, 329,
      330
    succession plans of, 300
Philip III, King of Spain, 306, 330,
   331
Philip of Hesse, 39, 49, 53, 57, 292
Philip William (William the Silent's
   son), 297
Piali Pasha, 247
Pickersgill, F. R., 315
Pius IV, Pope, 167, 199, 201, 205, 208,
   246. See also Medici, Gian Angelo
Pius V, Pope
    and Battle of Lepanto, 260
    and Council of Trent, 205,
      208–209
    death, 261
    election of, 249
    and Elizabethan Settlement, 323
    and Holy League, 239, 251, 253
    and Jesuits, 171
Pixis, Theodor, 101
Pizarro, Francisco, 220–221, 233
Pizarro, Juan, 222
plague
    in France, 87
    in Italy, 39, 48, 203
    in Switzerland, 68, 73, 98
    and witchcraft, 104
Platin, Christopher, 289
Poissy (France), 204, 270–271
Poland, 165
Pole, Edmund de la, 114
Pole, Henry de la, 114
Pole, Margaret de la, 114, 124
Pole, Reginald de la
    as church envoy, 125
    as contender for papacy, 193, 195
    at Council of Trent, 187
    flees England, 114
    heresy trial of, 196
    as Mary I's counselor, 316, 319
    as Theatine, 181
Pole, Richard de la, 114
Pollen, Daphne, 323
polygamy, 57, 82, 235

Ponce de León, 212
Poole, Stafford, 225
Port Ercole (Italy), 244
Portugal, 166–167, 168
Pourbus the Younger, Frans, 303
predestination, doctrine of, 89, 99,
   306
Presbyterian church, 151
Preveza (Albania), 243
Prierias (Silvestro Mazzolini da
   Prierio), 22
primacy of Rome, 16
printing press, 14–15, 198–199
Protestant Reformation
    Catholic response to, 49, 201
    and Confession of Augsburg, 53
    effect of Peasants' Revolt on, 45
    in England, 118, 310–311
    and Jesuits, 155, 158
    Luther's role in, 54–55
    reversing in England, 316,
      318–319
Protestantism (See also Calvinism;
   Huguenots; Lutheranism)
    and Canisius, 164
    and Council of Trent, 180, 183
    in England, 122, 125, 320–323
    and Luther's theology, 13, 16–17
    and Ninety-five Theses, 15, 22, 23
    and witchcraft, 107
Puerto Rico, 212, 227
Pulzone, Scipione, 293
purgatory, 208
Puritan movement, 85, 321, 322, 330

Q

Quevedo, Juan de, 232
Quiroga, Vasco de, 235

R

Rabelais, François, 198
Radierung, William Wilke von, 14
Raleigh, Walter, 329
Randolph, Thomas, 143
Regensburg Reichstag, 57
Reinhard, Anna, 50
relics, 22, 24
Religious Peace of Augsburg,
   198–199
Rembrandt van Rijn, 72
Renée (Louis XII's daughter), 8
repartimientos, 226
Requesens, Luis de, 301, 302
Restitution (Rothmann), 81
Rhodes, 8–9, 39–41, 243
Ricard, Robert, 235
Ricci, Sebastiano, 187, 188
Rich, Richard, 123
Richmond, Duke of (Henry Fitzroy),
   114, 124, 126
Ridley, Jasper, 112
Ridley, Nicholas, 318, 319

Rizzio, David, 143–144
Rodriguez, Simon, 159, 168
Rohrbach, Jäcklein, 44, 45
Roman Catholic church (See also
   Jesuits; papacy and specfic names
   of popes)
    and Catholic Reformation, 326
    confronts Lutherans, 49, 53
    and Coptic church, 166–167
    and corruption, 182
    in Elizabeth's England, 324–325,
      329–330
    in Germany after Luther,
      162–163
    and Henry's divorce, 116–118
    and Jesuits, 155
    in Mary I's England, 316, 318–319
    in Netherlands, 289, 296
    relations with Orthodox church,
      61
    in Scotland, 131, 139
    and taxation, 29
    views on points of doctrine,
      190–192
Rome, 182
Romoli, Kathleen, 213, 233
Roper, Margaret, 122, 123
Ros, Luca de, 6
Rosales, Eduardo, 252
Rothmann, Bernhard, 81, 82, 83
Rottenburg (Austria), 74–76, 108
Roussel, Gerard, 86, 87, 88, 95
Rubens, John, 299
Rubens, Peter Paul, 299
Rufin, Barbara, 104–105
Rumiñavi, 222
Runciman, Steven, 61, 62
Russia, 63, 77
Rycaut, Paul, 62

S

Saal, Margarethe von der, 57
Sabbata (Kessler), 72
sacramentarian movement, 50
sacraments
    and Augsburg interim, 193
    and Book of Common Prayer, 311
    and Council of Trent, 189, 194,
      204
    and Elizabethan Settlement, 322
    of matrimony, 113, 116–117
Sadoleto, Jacopo, 96–97
Sahagún, Bernardino de, 235
Saint Martin, Cathedral of, 68
Salmerón, Alfonzo, 159
salvation, 21, 191
Salzburg (Austria), 64, 72
Sancian (China), 177
Saraceni, Giovanni Michele, 326
Sattler, Margaretha, 75, 76
Sattler, Michael, 74–76
Scarisbrick, J. J., 125
Schaff, Philip, 33

Scheffer, Ary, 102
Schleitheim Confession, 75
Schmalkaldic League, 188, 189, 193
Schoeffer, Peter, 14
Scholarius, George (Gennadius II), 61
Schopenhauer, Arthur, 199
Scotland, 85, 109, 132–133,
   140–141, 145–147, 151
scourging, 161
scripture, 192
Sea Beggars, 298, 300, 301
Selim I, the Grim, Ottoman sultan, 1,
   2, 8–9, 62, 242
Selim II, the Sot, Ottoman sultan, 54,
   249–251, 254
Seljuk Turks, 59
September Testament (Luther), 37
Sepúlveda, Juan Ginés de, 226–227,
   234
Seripando, Girolamo, 187, 197, 201,
   207
Serra, Junipero, 237
Servetus, Michael, 99–100, 101–102
sex, 98, 102
Seymour, Edward (Duke of
   Somerset), 309, 311–312, 313,
   314
Seymour, Jane, 119, 125, 126, 127
Seymour, John, 119
Seymour, Thomas, 312
Shakespeare, William, 151, 279, 329
Shaw, John Liston, 316
Sherwin, Ralph, 325
Shi'ites, 2
Shimizu, Junko, 277
Shrewsbury, Earl of, 149, 150
Sichel, Nathanael, 279
Sicily, 197
Sigismund, Holy Roman Emperor, 22
Silent Brothers, 71
Simon, Edith, 19
Simons, Menno, 77–78, 291
simony, 196
Sirocco Pasha, Mehmed, 258
Sixtus V, Pope, 21, 159, 328
slavery
    Arab, 242–243, 244
    and Jesuit missions, 165
    in New World, 223, 226–229,
      231–232
    in Ottoman empire, 60, 61
smallpox, 218, 220, 222–223, 322
Smyth, John, 68
Snayers, Pieter, 52
Somaschi, 181
Somerset, Duke of (Edward
   Seymour), 309, 311–312, 313, 314
Soto, Hernando de, 213
South Africa, 85
Southwell, Robert, 325
Spain (See also Ferdinand II of
   Aragon; Philip II; Philip III)
    alliance with Scotland, 143
    and Black Legend, 295
    under Charles V, 35–36

Do you have Volumes One through Eight?

Subsequent volumes will bring the Christian story to the end of the twentieth century

Volume 1
A.D. 30 to A.D. 70

Volume 2
A.D. 70 to A.D. 250

Volume 3
A.D. 250 to A.D. 350

Volume 4
A.D. 350 to A.D. 565

Volume 5
A.D. 565 to A.D. 740

Volume 6
A.D. 740 to A.D. 1100

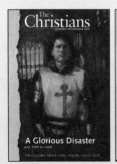

Volume 7
A.D. 1100 to A.D. 1300

Volume 8
A.D. 1300 to A.D. 1500

Volume 9
A.D. 1500 to A.D. 1600

Volume 10
A.D. 1600 to A.D. 1789

Volume 11
A.D. 1789 to A.D. 1918

Volume 12
A.D. 1918 to A.D. 2001